Introduction to Data Mining for the Life Sciences

Rob Sullivan

Introduction to Data Mining
for the Life Sciences

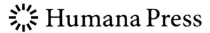

::: Humana Press

Rob Sullivan
Cincinnati, OH, USA

ISBN 978-1-58829-942-0   e-ISBN 978-1-59745-290-8
DOI 10.1007/978-1-59745-290-8
Springer New York Dordrecht Heidelberg London

Library of Congress Control Number: 2011941596

Printed on acid-free paper

Humana Press is part of Springer Science+Business Media (www.springer.com)

To my wife, without whose support, encouragement, love, and caffeine, none of this would have been possible.

Preface

A search for the word "zettabyte" will return a page that predicts that we will enter the zettabyte age around 2015. To store this amount of data on DVDs would require over 215 billion disks. The search itself (on September 20, 2011) returned 775,000 results, many relevant, many irrelevant, and many duplicates. The challenge is to elicit knowledge from all this data.

Scientific endeavors are constantly generating more and more data. As new generations of instruments are created, one of the characteristics is typically more sensitive results. In turn, this typically means more data is generated. New techniques made available by new instrumentation, techniques, and understanding allows us to consider approaches such as genome-wide association studies (GWAS) that were outside of our ability to consider just a few years ago. Again, the challenge is to elicit knowledge from all this data.

But as we continue to generate this ever-increasing amount of data, we would also like to know what relationships and patterns exist between the data. This, in essence, is the goal of data mining: find the patterns within the data. This is what this book is about. Is there some quantity X that is related to some other quantity Y that isn't obvious to us? If so, what could those relationships tell us? Is there something novel, something new, that these patterns tell us? Can it advance our knowledge?

There is no obvious end in sight to the increasing generation of data. To the contrary, as tools, techniques, and instrumentation continue to become smaller, cheaper, and thus, more available, it is likely that the opposite will be the case and data will continue to be generated in ever-increasing volumes. It is for this reason that automated approaches to processing data, understanding data, and finding these patterns will be even more important.

This leads to the major challenge of a book like this: what to include and what to leave out. We felt it important to cover as much of the theory of data mining as possible, including statistical, analytical, visualization, and machine learning techniques. Much exciting work is being done under the umbrella of machine learning, and much of it is seeing fruition within the data mining discipline itself. To say that this covers a wide area – and a multitude of sins – is an understatement. To those readers who question why we included a particular topic, and to those who question why we omitted some other topic, we can only apologize for this. In writing a book aimed at introducing data mining techniques to the life sciences, describing a broad range of techniques is a necessity to allow the researcher to select the most appropriate tools for his/her investigation. Many of the techniques we discuss are not necessarily in widespread use, but we believe can be valuable to the researcher.

Many people over many years triggered our enthusiasm for developing this text and thanks to them that we have created this book. Particular thanks goes to Bruce Lucarelli and Viswanath Balasubramanian for their contributions and insights on various parts of the text.

Cincinnati, OH, USA   Rob Sullivan

Contents

1	**Introduction**	1
	1.1 Context	1
	1.2 New Scientific Techniques, New Data Challenges in Life Sciences	8
	1.3 The Ethics of Data Mining	10
	1.4 Data Mining: Problems and Issues	12
	1.5 From Data to Information: The Process	17
	1.5.1 CRISP-DM	19
	1.6 What Can Be Mined?	24
	1.7 Standards and Terminologies	25
	1.8 Interestingness	26
	1.9 How Good Is Good Enough?	27
	1.10 The Datasets Used in This Book	28
	1.11 The Rest of the Story	28
	1.12 What Have We Missed in the Introduction?	31
	References	31
2	**Fundamental Concepts**	33
	2.1 Introduction	33
	2.2 Data Mining Activities	37
	2.3 Models	38
	2.4 Input Representation	39
	2.5 Missing Data	40
	2.6 Does Data Expire?	41
	2.7 Frequent Patterns	42
	2.8 Bias	43
	2.9 Generalization	45
	2.10 Data Characterization and Discrimination	45
	2.11 Association Analysis	46
	2.12 Classification and Prediction	46
	2.12.1 Relevance Analysis	47

2.13   Cluster Analysis..   47
2.14   Outlier Analysis...   48
2.15   Normalization..   49
2.16   Dimensionality...   49
2.17   Model Overfitting..   51
2.18   Concept Hierarchies   52
2.19   Bias-Variance Decomposition...................................   55
2.20   Advanced Techniques...   55
        2.20.1   Principal Component Analysis   56
        2.20.2   Monte Carlo Strategies   56
2.21   Some Introductory Methods.....................................   60
        2.21.1   The 1R Method   60
        2.21.2   Decision Trees   63
        2.21.3   Classification Rules....................................   66
        2.21.4   Association Rules.......................................   69
        2.21.5   Relational Rules   72
        2.21.6   Clustering   73
        2.21.7   Simple Statistical Measures   74
        2.21.8   Linear Models   74
        2.21.9   Neighbors and Distance   76
2.22   Feature Selection..   79
        2.22.1   Global Feature Selection   80
        2.22.2   Local Feature Selection...............................   81
2.23   Conclusion   82
References..   82

3   Data Architecture and Data Modeling.............................   85
3.1   Introduction   85
3.2   Data Modeling, a Whirlwind Tour   86
3.3   Qualitative and Quantitative Data.............................   90
3.4   Interpretive Data..   93
3.5   Sequence Data   93
3.6   Gene Ontology..   95
3.7   Image Data..   96
3.8   Text Data...   97
3.9   Protein and Compound 3D Structural Data   97
3.10   Data Integration...   102
        3.10.1   Same Entity, Different Identifiers   102
        3.10.2   Data in Different Formats   103
        3.10.3   Default Values   103
        3.10.4   Multiscale Data Integration...........................   104
3.11   The Test Subject Area   106
3.12   The Transactional Data Model, Operational Data Store,
        Data Warehouse, and Data Mart................................   110

3.13 Modeling Data with a Time Dimension........................ 112
3.14 Historical Data and Archiving: Another Temporal Issue?....... 113
3.15 Data Management.. 114
3.16 Agile Modeling, Adaptive Data Warehouses,
     and Hybrid Models... 115
3.17 Gene Ontology Database 116
3.18 Broadening Our Concept of Data: Images, Structures,
     and so on... 119
3.19 Conclusion 122
References.. 122

4 Representing Data Mining Results.................................. 125
4.1 Introduction 125
4.2 Tabular Representations 126
4.3 Decision Tables, Decision Trees,
    and Classification Rules 127
4.4 Classification and Regression Trees (CARTs) 129
    4.4.1 Process 133
    4.4.2 Cross-validation.. 143
    4.4.3 Summary 144
4.5 Association Rules.. 145
    4.5.1 Context 145
    4.5.2 The Apriori Algorithm................................... 148
    4.5.3 Rules, Rules, and More Rules 150
4.6 Some Basic Graphical Representations........................... 152
    4.6.1 Representing the Instances Themselves 152
    4.6.2 Histograms 153
    4.6.3 Frequency Polygrams 154
    4.6.4 Data Plots 154
4.7 Representing the Output from Statistical Models................ 158
    4.7.1 Boxplots.. 159
    4.7.2 Scatterplots.. 161
    4.7.3 Q-Q Plots... 162
4.8 Heat Maps.. 166
4.9 Position Maps.. 170
    4.9.1 Microbial Genome Viewer 170
    4.9.2 GenomePlot 171
    4.9.3 GenoMap... 171
    4.9.4 Circular Genome Viewer 171
4.10 Genotype Visualization.. 171
4.11 Network Visualizations.. 172
4.12 Some Tools.. 175
    4.12.1 Cytoscape 176
    4.12.2 TreeView: Phylogenetic Tree Visualization 177

	4.12.3	Systems Biology Markup Language	178
	4.12.4	R and RStudio	181
	4.12.5	Weka	183
	4.12.6	Systems Biology Graphical Notation..................	183
4.13	Conclusion		185
References			189

5	**The Input Side of the Equation**		191
	5.1	Data Preparation	194
	5.2	Internal Consistency	195
	5.3	External Consistency	197
	5.4	Standardization	198
	5.5	Transformation	198
		5.5.1 Transforming Categorical Attributes	199
	5.6	Normalization	200
		5.6.1 Averaging	200
		5.6.2 Min-Max Normalization	200
	5.7	Denormalization	201
		5.7.1 Prejoining Tables	201
		5.7.2 Report Tables	202
		5.7.3 Mirroring Tables	202
		5.7.4 Splitting Tables	203
		5.7.5 Combining Tables	203
		5.7.6 Copying Data Across Entities	203
		5.7.7 Repeating Groups	204
		5.7.8 Derived Data	205
		5.7.9 Hierarchies of Data	205
	5.8	Extract, Transform, and Load (ETL)	206
		5.8.1 Integrating External Data	207
		5.8.2 Gene/Protein Identifier Cross-Referencing	208
	5.9	Aggregation and Calculation	209
		5.9.1 Aggregation	209
		5.9.2 Calculation	211
	5.10	Noisy Data	211
		5.10.1 Regression	212
		5.10.2 Binning	212
		5.10.3 Clustering	215
	5.11	Metadata	215
		5.11.1 Attribute Type	215
		5.11.2 Attribute Role	216
		5.11.3 Attribute Description	217
	5.12	Missing Values	217
		5.12.1 Other Issues with Missing Data	223
	5.13	Data Reduction	224

		5.13.1	Attribute Subsets	224
		5.13.2	Data Aggregation	225
		5.13.3	Dimensional Reduction	225
		5.13.4	Alternate Representations	225
		5.13.5	Generalization	226
		5.13.6	Discretization	227
	5.14	Refreshing the Dataset		228
		5.14.1	Adding Data to Our Dataset	229
		5.14.2	Removing Data from Our Dataset	229
		5.14.3	Correcting the Data in Our Dataset	230
		5.14.4	Data Changes that Significantly Affect Our Dataset	232
	5.15	Conclusion		233
	References			233
6	**Statistical Methods**			235
	6.1	Introduction		235
		6.1.1	Basic Statistical Methods	237
	6.2	Statistical Inference and Hypothesis Testing		239
		6.2.1	What Constitutes a "Good" Hypothesis?	241
		6.2.2	The Null Hypothesis	242
		6.2.3	p Value	243
		6.2.4	Type I and Type II Errors	245
		6.2.5	An Example: Comparing Two Groups, the t Test	246
		6.2.6	Back to Square One?	252
		6.2.7	Some Other Hypothesis Testing Methods	254
		6.2.8	Multiple Comparisons and Multiple-Testing Correlation	259
	6.3	Measures of Central Tendency, Variability, and Other Descriptive Statistics		266
		6.3.1	Location	266
		6.3.2	Variability	268
		6.3.3	Heterogeneity	269
		6.3.4	Concentration	270
		6.3.5	Asymmetry	272
		6.3.6	Kurtosis	273
		6.3.7	Same Means, Different Variances – Different Variances, Same Means	274
	6.4	Frequency Distributions		276
	6.5	Confidence Intervals		278
		6.5.1	Continuous Data Confidence Levels	278
	6.6	Regression Analysis		282
		6.6.1	Linear Regression	283
		6.6.2	Correlation Coefficient	289
		6.6.3	Multiple Linear Regression	289

6.7	Maximum Likelihood Estimation Method	290
	6.7.1 Illustration of the MLE Method	291
	6.7.2 Use in Data Mining	292
6.8	Maximum A Posteriori (MAP) Estimation	293
6.9	Enrichment Analysis	294
6.10	False Discover Rate (FDR)	297
6.11	Statistical Significance and Clinical Relevance	300
6.12	Conclusion	300
References		301

7 Bayesian Statistics — 303

7.1	Introduction	303
7.2	Bayesian Formulations	304
	7.2.1 Bayes' Theorem	309
7.3	Assigning Probabilities, Odds Ratios, and Bayes Factor	312
	7.3.1 Probability Assignment	312
	7.3.2 Odds Ratios	314
	7.3.3 Bayes Factor	314
7.4	Putting It All Together	315
7.5	Bayesian Reasoning	322
	7.5.1 A Simple Illustration	324
7.6	Bayesian Classification	327
7.7	Bayesian Belief Networks	337
7.8	Parameter Estimation Methods	340
7.9	Multiple Datasets	342
7.10	Hidden Markov Models (HMM)	342
7.11	Conditional Random Field (CRF)	351
7.12	Array Comparative Genomic Hybridization	355
7.13	Conclusion	360
References		360

8 Machine-Learning Techniques — 363

8.1	Introduction	363
	8.1.1 Missing and Erroneous Data	366
8.2	Measure of Similarity	368
8.3	Supervised Learning	370
	8.3.1 Classification Learning	371
8.4	Unsupervised Learning	372
	8.4.1 Association Learning	372
	8.4.2 Clustering	372
8.5	Semisupervised Learning	373
	8.5.1 Expectation Maximization	374
	8.5.2 Cotraining	377
	8.5.3 Graph-Based SSL Methods	381
	8.5.4 Is This Type of Approach Always Helpful?	383

8.6   Kernel Learning Methods.. 383
8.7   Let's Break for Some Examples................................. 385
        8.7.1   String and Tree Matching.............................. 386
        8.7.2   Protein Structure Classification and Prediction 386
8.8   Support Vector Machines... 389
        8.8.1   Gene Expression Analysis 394
8.9   Artificial Neural Networks....................................... 399
        8.9.1   Introduction 399
        8.9.2   Neurons 399
        8.9.3   Neuronal Functions 401
        8.9.4   Encoding the Input..................................... 406
        8.9.5   Training Methods 406
        8.9.6   ANN Architectures 424
        8.9.7   Application to Data Mining............................. 424
8.10   Reinforcement Learning.. 425
8.11   Some Other Techniques 425
        8.11.1 Random Walk, Diffusion Map,
                and Spectral Clustering................................. 426
        8.11.2 Network (Graph)-Based Analysis 431
        8.11.3 Network Motif Discovery 431
        8.11.4 Binary Tree Algorithm in Drug Target
                Discovery Studies....................................... 436
        8.11.5 Petri Nets 437
        8.11.6 Boolean and Fuzzy Logic 440
8.12   Conclusion 448
References... 449

9 Classification and Prediction... 455
9.1   Introduction 455
9.2   Data Preparation 459
9.3   Linear Regression.. 460
9.4   Decision Trees 463
9.5   1R 466
9.6   Nearest Neighbor 469
9.7   Bayesian Modeling 471
9.8   Neural Networks... 477
9.9   k-Means... 481
9.10   Distance Measures... 486
9.11   Measuring Accuracy... 489
        9.11.1 Classifiers 489
        9.11.2 Predictors 492
        9.11.3 Evaluating Accuracy................................... 493
        9.11.4 Improving Classifier/Predictor Accuracy............... 496
9.12   Conclusion 497
References... 498

10   Informatics 501
   10.1   Introduction 501
      10.1.1   Sources of Genomic and Proteomic Data 503
   10.2   Data Integration.. 504
      10.2.1   Integrating Annotations for a Common Sequence 505
      10.2.2   Data in Different Formats 505
   10.3   Tools and Databases 508
      10.3.1   Programming Languages and Environments............ 511
   10.4   Standardization.. 512
   10.5   Microarrays 513
      10.5.1   Challenges and Opportunities 514
      10.5.2   Classification... 515
      10.5.3   Gene Selection 515
   10.6   Finding Motifs 516
      10.6.1   Regular Expressions 516
   10.7   Analyzing DNA.. 521
      10.7.1   Pairwise Sequence Alignment.......................... 521
      10.7.2   Multiple Alignment..................................... 527
      10.7.3   Trees 531
   10.8   Conclusion 538
   References... 541

11   Systems Biology 543
   11.1   What Is This Systems Biology of Which You Speak?.......... 543
   11.2   Biological Networks 547
   11.3   How Much Biology Do We Need?.............................. 553
      11.3.1   Biological Processes As Ordered
              Sequences of Events 553
   11.4   But, We Do Need Some Graph Theory 554
      11.4.1   Data Mining by Navigation 561
      11.4.2   So...How Are We Going to Cram
              All This into a Single Chapter? 562
   11.5   Gene Ontology and Microarray Databases...................... 563
      11.5.1   Gene Ontology (GO) 564
      11.5.2   Microarray Databases................................... 565
   11.6   Text Mining... 565
   11.7   Some Core Problems and Techniques........................... 571
      11.7.1   Shotgun Fragment Assembly 572
      11.7.2   The BioCreAtIvE Initiative.............................. 575
   11.8   Data Mining in Systems Biology................................ 576
      11.8.1   Network Analysis....................................... 577
   11.9   Novel Initiatives 577
      11.9.1   Data Mining Promises to Dig Up New Drugs 577
      11.9.2   Temporal Interactions Among Genes 578

11.10	The Cloud	579
11.11	Where to Next?	580
11.12	Have We Left Anything Out? Boy, Have We Ever	580
	References	581
12	**Let's Call It a Day**	**585**
12.1	We've Covered a Lot, But Not Really	585
12.2	When Two Models Are Better Than One	586
12.3	The Most Widely Used Algorithms?	587
12.4	Documenting Your Process	588
12.5	Where To From Here?	589
	References	590
Appendix A		**593**
Appendix B		**603**
Appendix C		**623**
Appendix D		**627**
References		**629**
Index		**631**

Chapter 1
Introduction

Abstract What is this "data mining" thing that has been gradually percolating through our scientific consciousness and why would I want to use its techniques? In fact, what are those techniques and how can the results returned from using them help me? What are some of the problems we encounter within the data mining domain and how can we use these different techniques to not only overcome them, but to provide us with new insight into the data we have at hand? These are some of the questions we're going to try and answer, to put into context, and set the foundation for more detailed discussion in the remainder of this text. Our objective in this chapter is not to provide the depth and the breadth of the issues and opportunities we face, but to provide an introduction – the overall context – for everything else. In a nutshell, we want to try and begin to answer the question "why do we need data mining?"

1.1 Context

As any discipline matures, the amount of data collected grows. We only need to look at the plethora of business systems to see that the amount of data generated and manipulated in any organization today is vast.

In fact, a research project by Peter Lyman and Hal Varian at UC Berkeley estimated that "Print, film, magnetic, and optical storage media produced about 5 exabytes of new information in 2002."[1] To put this in perspective, they give the analogy that "If digitized with full formatting, the seventeen million books in the Library of Congress contain about 136 terabytes of information; five exabytes of information is equivalent in size to the information contained in 37,000 new libraries the size of the Library of Congress book collections." Their analysis

---

[1] Lyman, Peter and Hal R. Varian, "How Much Information," 2003. Retrieved from http://www.sims.berkeley.edu/how-much-info-2003 on August 4, 2006.

R. Sullivan, *Introduction to Data Mining for the Life Sciences*,
DOI 10.1007/978-1-59745-290-8_1, © Springer Science+Business Media, LLC 2012

goes on to state that the amount of information generated in 2002 is double that generated in 1999. An interesting infographic was created by Cisco in 2011[2] that predicts that we'll move beyond exabytes and petabytes and enter the realm of the zettabyte by 2015. For a point of reference, a zettabyte is roughly equivalent to the amount of data that can be stored on 250,000,000 DVDs! That might take some time to analyze.

Obviously, most domains of study won't come anywhere near to needing to deal with data of that size, but almost any domain is dealing with gigabytes and terabytes. Some are already skirting the petabyte range, so our techniques definitely need to be scalable.

In this text, we consider the data asset to be important in and of itself since it is a cornerstone of almost every process and discipline, allowing people to leverage its contents, make conclusions, and support the decision-making process. However, in order to do so, various techniques, approaches, and tools are necessary to get the most out of this asset. We begin with discussing general infrastructure and fundamental concepts and then move on to discussing a variety of techniques.

The focus of this book is data mining, but data mining with application to the life sciences. The first question, therefore, is *what constitutes data mining?* A (very) brief search on the Internet brought up the following definitions, among others:

The process of analyzing data to identify patterns or relationships.

The ability to query very large databases in order to satisfy a hypothesis ("top down" data mining); or to interrogate a database in order to generate new hypotheses based on rigorous statistical correlations ("bottom-up" data mining).

Searching large volumes of data looking for patterns that accurately predict behavior in customers and prospects.

Nontrivial extraction of implicit, previously unknown and potentially useful information from data, or the search for relationships and global patterns that exist in databases.

The process of autonomously extracting useful information or knowledge ("actionable assets") from large data stores or sets. Data mining can be performed on a variety of data stores, including the World Wide Web, relational databases, transactional databases, internal legacy systems, pdf documents, and data warehouses.

The process of using statistical techniques to discover subtle relationships between data items, and the construction of predictive models based on them. The process is not the same as just using an OLAP tool to find exceptional items. Generally, data mining is a very different and more specialist application than OLAP, and uses different tools from different vendors.

Data mining serves to find information that is hidden within the available data.

---

[2] http://blogs.cisco.com/news/the-dawn-of-the-zettabyte-era-infographic/

The comparison and study of large databases in order to discover new data relationships. Mining a clinical database may produce new insights on outcomes, alternate treatments or effects of treatment on different races and genders.

The unguided (or minimally guided) application of a collection of mathematical procedures to a company's data warehouse in an effort to find "nuggets" in the form of statistical relationships.

The automated or semi-automated search for relationships and global patterning within data. Data mining techniques include data visualization, neural network analysis, and genetic algorithms.

Using advanced statistical tools to identify commercially useful patterns in databases.

Analyzing data to discover patterns and relationships that are important to decision making.

A process of analyzing business data (often stored in a data warehouse) to uncover hidden trends and patterns and establish relationships. Data mining is normally performed by expert analysts who use specialist software tools.

A means of extracting previously unknown, actionable information from the growing base of accessible data in data warehouses using sophisticated, automated algorithms to discover hidden patterns, correlations and relationships.

The collection and mathematical analysis of vast amounts of computerized data to discover previously hidden patterns or unknown relationships.

Data mining uses complex algorithms to search large amounts of data and find patterns, correlation's, and trends in that data.

Data mining, also known as knowledge-discovery in databases (KDD), is the practice of automatically searching large stores of data for patterns. To do this, data mining uses computational techniques from statistics and pattern recognition.

These definitions highlight many of the common themes we will encounter throughout this book, including:

- Identifying patterns and/or relationships that are previously unknown
- Satisfying and/or generating hypotheses
- Building models for prediction
- Statistical techniques, neural networks, and genetic algorithms
- Proposing new insights
- Automated (unguided) or semiautomated (minimally guided) search

Finding new phenomena within the vast data reserves being generated by organizations potentially offers tremendous value both in the short term and the long term. We may, for example, be able to highlight side effects of a treatment for subsets of the target population before they become significant. We may be able to identify new indications for an existing product. We may even be able to identify previously unknown, and unsuspected, patterns within the genomic and proteomic data that have been one of the causes of the data explosion at the end of the twentieth century and into the twenty-first century.

Data mining, or *knowledge discovery*, therefore has become an important topic in many areas of science and technology since one of its predicates is the (semi) autonomous trolling of data. With many databases growing exponentially, this capability has moved from the nice-to-have category into the must-have category. For most data-mining activities, data from multiple sources are often combined into a single environment – most often called a *data warehouse*. However, integrating different sources is often a source (sic) of challenge since the source domains may differ, key fields or other designators may be incompatible with each other, or, even after data attributes from different sources are matched, their coverage may still be a source of problems. We consider these and other issues concerned with building the data architecture to provide a robust platform for data-mining efforts.

Within this book, we consider the objective of data mining to provide a framework for making predictions and discoveries using large amounts of data. Within this context, we will consider many different perspectives, identifying tools and techniques from each, along with a focus on their use in a number of scientific disciplines to provide a comprehensive handbook for data mining in the life sciences. Such perspectives[3] include:

- Statistics
- Pattern recognition
- Database management systems
- Artificial intelligence

The next question we ask is what constitutes data mining? This is actually a more difficult question to answer than one might initially think since data mining and knowledge discovery from databases mean different things to different people, such as:

• Generalization	• Deviation analysis
• Classification	• Stream data mining
• Association	• Biological data mining
• Clustering	• Time-series analysis
• Frequent pattern analysis	• Text mining
• Structured pattern analysis	• Intrusion detection
• Outlier analysis	• Web mining
• Trend analysis	• Privacy-preserving mining

Note that although the above list includes a number of items, it is by no means exhaustive. Further, many of these areas have been grouped together to provide value, such as with frequent pattern and structured pattern analysis, of trend and deviation analysis.

---

[3] This list contains entries which overlap, some of which are contained in other entries, and some of which have vastly different scopes. Our purpose is to highlight some of the more commonly recognized subject areas.

Information technology has revolutionized many areas of science and industry. Today, hardly any step of the pharmaceutical development process, for example, is untouched by the information technology revolution of the latter part of the twentieth century. However, we have an overabundance of data which we are struggling to extract information from. This "information rich but data poor" condition is causing a challenge for our industry, as Fayyad (1996) succinctly stated in the Preface:

> Our capabilities for collecting and storing data of all kinds have far outpaced our abilities to analyze, summarize, and extract "knowledge" from this data.

Without powerful tools and techniques, we will find it increasingly difficult, if not impossible, to analyze and comprehend this ever-increasing, distributed base of data. We believe that the key word here is knowledge: in many disciplines, scientific or otherwise, certain data is valued over other data since it has been shown to have more significance and thus, higher value. Eliciting knowledge from this data is often the domain of specialists who have built up their knowledge and expertise over time. Being able to provide tools and techniques to elicit this knowledge as quickly as possible is obviously a major goal of data mining which has tremendous potential for those specialists and lay person alike. Understanding how data elements relate to each other is not always intuitive. As the accuracy of tests improves and the breadth of tests improves, the amount of data increases, often exponentially. Our existing heuristics and knowledge serves us well, but the interrelationships are often nonintuitive. Stepping outside of the scientific discipline for a moment, a business school professor posed the following question: why would a (barbeque) grill manufacturer buy a company that makes fire-starter logs? The answer was because the grill manufacturer's revenue model dipped in the winter season whereas the fire-starter log's revenue model increased in that same season (and dipped in the summer season), thus smoothing out the revenue model for the combined company. Not necessarily an intuitive relationship.

Consider an example: what do the following drugs have in common? (Fig. 1.1)

They are all drugs which have been withdrawn from the market since 1990.[4] The reasons for withdrawal range from toxicity to elevated risks (stroke, myocardial infarction, cardiac arrhythmias, etc.). Are there any common factors between some[5] or all of the problems with these drugs? Can we see any relationships between the toxicity issues seen in a drug class, for example?

Much of the work performed throughout the drug discovery and development process to mitigate issues which may be seen later, but it is a significant challenge for any organization. Data mining has the potential to help in several areas:

- Aggregate and synthesize data using *intelligent* techniques to allow us to get a higher level view of our data and drill down into the details thus allowing a manageable stepping down into the data

---

[4] http://en.wikipedia.org/w/index.php?title=List_of_withdrawn_drugs

[5] As we shall discuss throughout, any sufficiently complex area of study will not allow us to see global patterns of any complexity and value.

Triazolam	Cerivastatin
Fen-phen	Rapacuronium
Terfenadine	Rofecoxib
Mibefradil	Palladone
Troglitazone	Vioxx
Alosetron	Pemoline
Cisapride	Tysabri

Fig. 1.1 Drugs withdrawn from US market since 1990

- Identify (hidden) relationships, patterns, associations, and correlations that exist in the very large amounts of data captured through the discovery and development process so that we can uncover potential issues before they occur
- Compare data from one clinical program with another program in the same therapeutic class, introducing normalization and standardization across programs to make the comparisons meaningful
- Help understand where/if there are dependencies and interactions with factors completely outside of our area of focus[6]

The various subjects discussed in this book leverage the gamut of breakthroughs which comprise this discipline. While we attempt to avoid acronyms and techno-babble wherever possible, it is sometimes unavoidable. The level of knowledge that is projected for the typical reader would assume a reasonable level of information technology knowledge, along with a basic understanding of the various life sciences disciplines. Thus, topics such as domain names, IP addresses, the Internet, the world-wide-web file transfer protocol, and the like are assumed to be familiar to the reader from the usage perspective. Also, molecular biology, the pharmaceutical discovery and development process, and the data aspects of the genomics and proteomics disciplines are assumed. This book does not cover probability theory as it is assumed the reader will have a command of this subject in both its single variable and multivariate forms.

---

[6] Viagra might be one of the best known products, in recent times, that started off as a drug for hypertension and angina pectoris and ended up as an erectile dysfunction (ED) drug: "... a telephone conversation with the clinician who was running the trials: 'He mentioned that at 50 mg taken every 8 h for 10 days, there were episodes of indigestion [and of] aches in patients' backs and legs. And he said, "Oh, there are also some reports of penile erections."'" (Kling 1998 #134).

To provide a holistic context to these areas, we consider where the various data-mining algorithms and models may be useful within the pharmaceutical discovery and development process. The information asset is very important within the pharmaceutical development effort: it is something which is gathered from the very inception of the idea and, as we are finding from press releases in the years after 2003, which never goes away. This valuable piece of the puzzle adds a significant amount to our overall understanding of the data at hand but also allows us to predict, extrapolate, and view the future through a somewhat clear lens. Thus, we included a significant second section that dealt with leveraging that asset. Once you have a comprehensive data environment, how can you use it? What are some of the new, and classic, techniques which can provide significant value to your processes? We hope to provide some answers to these questions and also spur on other questions.

Much data is gathered through clinical trials. Since the different clinical trial design types impact the type of data captured, we will often refer to them as *phases I, II, III*, and *IV*. We use the definitions as described in Piantadosi (1997):

Phase I: pharmacologically oriented (best dose of drug to employ)
Phase II: preliminary evidence of efficacy (and side effects at a fixed dose)
Phase III: new treatments compared (with standard therapy, no therapy, or placebo)
Phase IV: postmarketing surveillance

Throughout this book, we have avoided a few terms currently in common usage. Terms such as bioinformatics, chemoinformatics, immunological bioinformatics, and their like are robust disciplines and worthy approaches in their own rights. The reason for our avoiding any specific term is that much of what we describe – from the data, methodology, algorithm, and subject are perspectives – are applicable in any of these disciplines. We will, however, consider models and approaches and use subjects within these areas. Bioinformatics as a term, for example, covers a multitude of areas, and a book on data mining in the life sciences would not be complete without considering such things.

We are seeing a confluence of subjects within the concept of *systems biology*, and data mining is providing significant value within this discipline. It does not take too much to predict that the amount of data that will be generated into the future will be significantly more than has already been seen.

A valid question to ask at this point is whether all patterns uncovered by a data-mining effort are interesting? A corollary is how do we avoid the work and processing associated with such "uninteresting" discoveries? As we shall see, the individual does not become ancillary to the process but continues to drive the process, investing effort in different steps. Further, we can keep some considerations in mind and ask ourselves whether:

? The results are easily understood.
? They are valid on new data or on the remaining test data, with some degree of certainty.
? They are potentially useful.
? They are novel, or they validate some hypothesis.

These and other questions should be the ad hoc criteria we use whenever undertaking a data-mining exercise. But we must also ask whether the association we find really does define a trend or causality. Does drinking diet soda *really* lead to obesity? Is there a correlation between barbecue sauce, hot dogs, and hamburgers (Heckerman 1999)? Were those results valid, or were they entered incorrectly by humans?

1.2   New Scientific Techniques, New Data Challenges in Life Sciences

Europe's Very Long Baseline Interferometry (VLBI) comprises a set of 16 telescopes that capture data over a 25-day observation period. What is interesting about this project is that it generates a massive 1 Gigabit of data from each telescope **each second**. The latter part of the twentieth century saw the advent of a plethora of new scientific techniques. The early years of the twenty-first century look to continue this explosion of new approaches with startling discoveries being made at an ever-increasing pace. With data being generated as such high volumes, how do we manage this volume of data and make sense of it? Some companies are now generating such vast amounts of data that they cannot store everything and so have to manipulate it as it arrives, extracting knowledge and throwing the raw data away.

We have become used to seeing technologies radically improve our lives; for example, we only need consider that today, many organ transplants warrant no mention on the news, but underlying each of these breakthroughs has been significant research and development. Techniques are available that only a few years ago were the realm of science fiction. With them come an ever-increasing need to consider the safety and efficacy of the technique or product. Medical devices, pharmaceutical products, innovative medical techniques, and natural remedies, to name a few all come with significant data being collected as part of the scientific process. As genomic and proteomic data, medical images, collaborative research from around the world, and more sophistication on the part of the general public, as well as scientists, all increase the importance of capturing, synthesizing, understanding, and making conclusions on the data: to create information.

Many techniques which are now being used in the laboratory may soon see their way into our daily lives. For example, Mark Schena (Schena 2002 #1) says "It is tempting to speculate a significant role of microarray technology and genomics in the physical examination of the future, and their gradual and expanded role over time." He illustrates this with Fig. 1.2 (Fig. 16.1, (Schena 2002 #1)).

In Tramontano (2005), the problems she listed all deal with massive amounts of data that need to be processed in an efficient, repeatable, and deterministic way. Developing further methods of dealing with such large amounts of data will be of paramount importance. As the lab-on-a-chip concept moves into a daily reality, at a reasonable (a.k.a. low) cost, the data generated will continue to be a challenge.

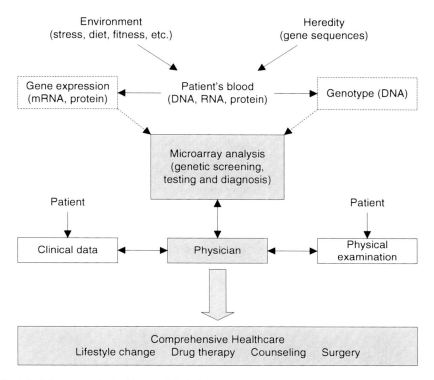

Fig. 1.2   Microarrays in health care (Mark Schena)

A perfect example of the growth, and value, in this area is the new M2A (mouth-to-anus) "pill cam." The leading exponent of this, as of 2006, is the pill cam from Given Imaging.[7] This vitamin tablet–sized camera takes two images every second for (approximately) 8 h as it traverses through the body, taking an average of 57,000 images, each of 256-by-256 resolution. A single image is 55,158 bytes in size. The average (2006) cost for this procedure is $1,000, making it a very attractive procedure for doctors, insurance companies, and patients. Consider the alternative endoscopy or colonoscopy, its cost and discomfort, and the value of this procedure is self-evident. This is a good example of the new types of techniques which are becoming the norm in medicine.

Storing substantial amounts of data has become less of a problem as servers have increased in capability, with reduced cost, and as storage has seen a similar capacity growth-cost reduction profile. However, too often, these large data repositories become black boxes where the data goes in and never comes out. Thus, often, decisions are made based upon an individual's intuition as opposed to being based upon data since the knowledge is often not easily extracted from the data. Further,

---

[7] Given Imaging, www.givenimaging.com

in certain instances, *bias* or *errors* can be extremely expensive and time-consuming to avoid.

But there are challenges. We are often dealing with several, not one, sources for data. In any one of these sources, different kinds of knowledge exist. Interactive mining of the data occurs at multiple levels of abstraction, and we need to ensure that they dovetail together *correctly*. How do we also introduce the *world knowledge* or background knowledge that is necessary to effectively understand the knowledge we create from the data? No knowledge or information stands alone, but in context. What about noise in the data? What do we do in the event that missing or incomplete data exists within our data set? How can we tell that a pattern or relationship uncovered by our model actually tells us something of interest? What is the best way of visualizing the data and subsequently communicating it to others? Does our model scale? Is it efficient enough to use as the data volumes increase? Each of these nontrivial issues needs to be considered as we develop our understanding of the data we collect, and each is a significant issue in its own right.

Even with these challenges, data mining or knowledge discovery has tremendous upside in offering the opportunity to uncover patterns of data, contribute to business strategies and scientific research, and contribute to our use and meaning of the data we are collecting.

1.3   The Ethics of Data Mining

As we have said above, the ever-increasing amounts of data provide us with many new opportunities to understand the data under study and also to *discover* much about the data. In fact, *knowledge discovery* is a widely used term in this arena and concisely defines one of the goals we hope to achieve.

But there is also a danger; a concern we must keep in mind.

Statistically speaking, the more data we have on a particular subject, the larger a sample can be taken. Care must be taken, however, as is well known to ensure that the same underlying population constitutes the basis for the sample. If not, the statistical inference taken will not be pertinent to the hypothesis being considered.

In data mining, we often *deduce* a hypothesis based upon the activities we perform on the data rather than *inducing* the accuracy of the model from the data at hand. This is an important difference we shall return to later. We must be careful that the patterns we discern from the data we are mining are accurate and *appropriate*. Data mining poses as many ethical challenges as it does scientific and technical hurdles to overcome.

Consider a hypothetical condition:

During a data mining analysis of 1,000,000 patient histories, a pattern is identified that patients who have elevated iron are also 30% more likely to suffer a stroke by the age of 50.

Consider another hypothetical example:

Infants whose genome has a base pair corruption at position 100,290 on chromosome 11 are four times more likely to suffer the onset of Alzheimer's disease before the age of 55 than is the average person.

We reiterate that each of the above is a *fictional* example, so far as we know. But consider the type of issues which each of these questions raise. What would be the health insurance ramifications for the individual and his/her family? How about employment? What other factors would come into play here?

In 2006, we have seen a major public discourse into the appropriateness and ethics of a program reported by USA Today about a government agency collecting information about the calls made by US citizens.[8] This information purportedly includes the phone numbers of both of the parties to the call, but little is actually known about other information. The question of whether the program is legal or not is being played out at the time of writing. Our concern here is in what **could** be happening as much as it is in the ethics of what is happening. That is, what could an organization, any organization – government or otherwise – uncover and what **should** be communicated. Also, what is the *specificity* of information uncovered through mining efforts? *Causality* is also an important issue, as Piero Bonissone discovered when he concluded via correlation that "drinking diet drinks leads to obesity."

Results concluded from mining need to take all of these issues into account. We can easily initiate a thread of hypotheses that lead us into uncharted and inconvenient territory. Erroneous correlations, incorrect classifications, and invalid associations are just a few of the things which could occur. Even when correct correlations occur, we need to treat them conservatively and consider their impact. This is especially true when dealing with sensitive data such as patient or research data: is there really a causal relationship between a patient contracting X when they exhibit Y? How would/could this impact the individual **and** the organization?

Questions surrounding how medical data could be used, and misused, are fast entering the public consciousness in the USA as discussions about security, privacy, and use of electronic medical records (EMRs) mature. If widespread adoption of EMRs occurs, issues will first surround privacy and accessibility. But as time goes on, a natural adjunct is to consider what could be accomplished by using this data for investigational purposes. Could we begin to uncover important information – information that might be very valuable in researching new therapies – by mining this data? Could we uncover important information – information that might be useful to health insurance providers or other commercial entities – by mining this data? Could such findings be misused or misapplied? Should we even be concerned?

As is the case with any technological advance, the propensity for its use for common benefit, and misuse to adversely impact some (sub)population, is a fine balance, and we need to be diligent in considering all of the potential applications of

---

[8] USA Today, May 10, 2006: "NSA has massive database of Americans' phone calls."

said technologies. However, it is often impossible to discern all of the possible uses to which any specific technology may be put. But we can be careful. And we can ask whether we should. Data captured about individuals does provide a *model* of a population, but we are not yet good enough to say that this model is a *good model* of that population. Mining activities we perform, and the conclusions we reach, should be put through the filters of "should we do this?" but also through the filter of "do our conclusions effectively model reality?"

1.4 Data Mining: Problems and Issues

Data mining is a very valuable discipline that can be used in a variety of domains and uncover significant value and knowledge. However, it is not a panacea. As we have discussed above, the ethical issues remain challenging and are unlikely to diminish in importance or complexity. But this is not the only issue we encounter.

Data-mining activities will often generate vast numbers of patterns; being able to differentiate between those of interest to us and those which are not of interest require some (deterministic) method(s) to support the differentiation. This is a particular problem since the value of any given set of patterns to a specific user community is a very subjective measure.

Historically, incomplete data and noisy data within the data repository have been a problem in the data management discipline as a whole. This issue is exacerbated for data mining since these issues may cause problems with the model overfitting the data, for example, which affects the overall accuracy of the results generated by the model.

Consider the separation between the underlying data repository and the data-mining interests that each user has; the data was most likely generated without specific analysis efforts in mind, being either captured directly from end users or was incorporated from other systems or devices. Once the data is available, different people will be interested in exploring the data for different purposes. Some might be interested in simply summarizing the data using descriptive data analysis techniques, while others may apply advanced techniques to uncover those hidden patterns that fundamentally comprise data mining. But whoever is using the data, and whatever their intent, it will be very unlikely that the data itself was captured with that *specific* intent in mind; it will be a more general repository of data, usable by a wide range of people, for a wide range of purposes.

The majority of businesses today use relational database management systems as its platform of choice. However, there is still a vast amount of data that is stored outside of this architecture that we often need to incorporate into our data-mining efforts. This *distributed* data platform[9] introduces a level of complexity in and of its own right that should not be underestimated. This data platform may also be a

---

[9] This type of highly distributed data platform is also often described as a *federated* data architecture.

heterogeneous data platform in that the different data repositories which comprise the overall data repository may be very different from each other. As a simple example, your own internal (i.e., within your own network/organization) data warehouse may be an Oracle-based data architecture but integrating GenBank will immediately require your systems to be able to support a very different data architecture, at least from the data access perspective.

Let us add another dimension to this issue; that of different data types. As we have stated above, much data is available in traditional data repositories and so can be accessed with some degree of confidence and determinism using (potentially custom) query engines, but it is also true that significant information is available in other, more complex data formats such as multimedia format, documents, temporal data, spatial data, or a myriad other forms. To gain access to the knowledge inherent in these different formats requires several systems to be integrated together. To expect a single system to be able to access such a disparate set of data sources is currently beyond the state of the art.[10]

The third dimension to this problem can be most visibly seen in the efforts around the semantic web. Knowledge is often encoded as relationships or networks which are not necessarily instantiated as individual data elements within a given repository. This extends the challenge of dealing with complexity in the underlying data since these relationships are definitely temporal in nature and, in many respects, ephemeral, which only increases the issue of repeatability.[11]

How confident are we that the data within our data repository is accurate, certain, or valid? The question of uncertainty regarding our data is a large one. The majority of data that we will be mining was entered either by a human, or extracted from another data repository. If we ignore the contextual issue for the moment – something we will come back to below – we can safely limit our current question to one of "was the data accurately entered/loaded into our data repository?" Anyone involved with clinical trials will immediately see the concern: data entered by the person generating it (such as a nurse, investigator, or the like) may not have been entered correctly. If, instead, it was transcribed by a third party, the issue may be even greater since that person would need to have interpreted the original notes, to use but one example. We have to therefore introduce the concept of uncertainty into the equation, and not only when considering the data entry aspect of the challenge. Uncertainty can also be a very valuable tool when looking at noisy and/or incomplete data also.

---

[10] This is quite rightly up for discussion. There is a very large community actively pursuing various aspects of this and other data-mining problems. It is not inconceivable for a single system to be developed to support mining against all of the possible complex data types and sources that are mentioned above. However, this is not currently commercially available, and such is the issue today.

[11] We should clarify that the concept of networks and relationships we talk about here is very different to the concept of biochemical networks and the like. Here we raise the issue of relationships which manifest themselves not because of explicit data elements captured within the individual data repositories but the fact that relationships *exist* which are *not* explicitly stored. We shall return to this issue and the modeling of biochemical networks later.

We mentioned the context of data in the above paragraph, and this raises a cornucopia of issues within this context (sic). Contextual knowledge, or background knowledge, is a very important facet of data mining. The knowledge of the user comes into play in guiding the data-mining effort and in determining whether a pattern is material or immaterial to provide just two examples. This necessarily subjective aspect to the whole also shows its value in many of the Bayesian techniques that we shall discuss later.

We have avoided describing the data repository so far, other than through oblique references to certain aspects of its architecture. One aspect of it that provides a challenge is that the same data elements, entities, relationships, etc., will be used in different ways by different people who are all interested in mining the data. For example, similarity patterns are vitally important from the perspective of phylogenetic analysis, thus clustering will be a major data-mining technique they will employ. However, some of the same data may be used by another individual investigating association relationships within the data. Can we afford to consider these as discrete and disjoint efforts, or do we need to understand the interaction, or lack thereof, at the underlying data level?

A tried and trusted methodology for many analytical activities has traditionally been to first validate the model using a manageable amount of data – even to the level of being able to manually or otherwise independently validate the model's performance. However, the size of the "production" data repository may be orders of magnitude greater than the test data we used for validation purposes. Ensuring the scalability and efficiency of the model as data volumes grow is a very real issue as we continue to see rapid increases in the sizes of many standard data repositories. For example, consider Fig. 1.3 which shows the growth of the GenBank database (http://www.ncbi.nlm.nih.gov/genbank/).

As we can see from this graph, the pace of growth has substantially increased every year, with that growth being particularly significant in the last 10 years. This is a widely used repository for genomic analysis in particular, and this is not the exception. One of the challenges that many organizations are facing is that their own internal repositories of data are growing at a similar rate as well. The volume of data is thus a very real problem, as we keep indicating, but integrating repositories together in a meaningful and useful way is also a major challenge as well as a major opportunity for data mining.

When dealing with such large repositories of data, efficiency and scalability become particular challenges. This issue, along with the complexity inherent in many data-mining algorithms, has been a prime motivation for developing data-mining algorithms that can partition the data, run the algorithm against each partition, and merge the results together. This is an exciting area of research and development but is outside the scope of this book.[12]

---

[12] We made the conscious decision to omit any consideration of parallel processing and distributed processing from this book as our intent is to provide an introduction to the various disciplines which constitute data mining in the life sciences.

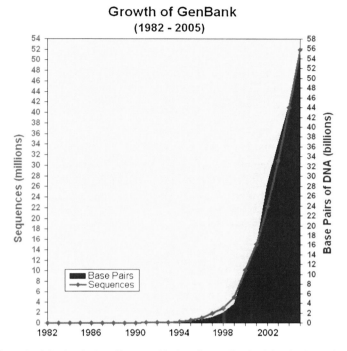

Fig. 1.3 Growth of Genbank (http://www.ncbi.nlm.nih.gov/Genbank/genbankstats.html)

The second issue of integration manifests itself in many ways. The first issue we often face is how to identify what a single entry in one repository maps to in the second...or third...or fourth.[13] However, we often have to deal with the fact that there is not a one-to-one mapping between two repositories; sometimes there will not be a direct mapping at all. Integrating the data from several repositories and making it manageable for our purposes is often the biggest challenge of all during the preparation phases. In fact, up to 80% of the data-mining effort could be in preparing the data (Refaat 2007 #135).

Once our model has executed how the results are presented needs consideration. Graphical results, representation in a high-level language, or other methods for communicating the results to the user in a form that can be easily understood as well as directly usable offer their own challenges. As we shall see, this requires comprehensive knowledge representation methods to be employed and to ensure that the system is interactive. This last point is just as important. We will often need to pursue an iterative approach to the data-mining process (see below) in order to get the most out of our efforts.

---

[13] We will use the term *instance* (Witten and Frank 2005 #11) to define a single entry in a repository.

Just as we avoided discussing any concrete attributes of the data model above, we have also avoided any mention of the *language* used for data mining. Many readers will be familiar with the *structured query language* (SQL) which is ubiquitous when it comes to data retrieval, especially for data stored in relational databases. We need similar methods for data mining, allowing users to specify the subset of data to be considered, contextual (or domain) knowledge, what knowledge should be mined, the conditions and constraints to be used, and for the languages to allow optimization of the query.

This list is by no means exhaustive, and readers may well be left with the impression that effective data mining is an intractable task. On the contrary, data mining can be very effective using some very simple techniques as we shall see when discussing the 1R method later. However, it is fair to state that these issues are real and we need to consider each of them carefully as we build our data-mining systems. Some will be more important than others in any given domain of study, and this gives us an opportunity to focus on the issues which are of most concern to us within that domain.

So, in a nutshell, what *are* the problems of data mining? They include:

• Huge amounts of data are being generated, faster than we can keep pace with, and we need to look at new techniques to understand that data.
• Data is generated for myriad purposes and not (necessarily) for analytical reasons; this typically means a lot of preprocessing work, preparatory activities that must be completed before we can even get to the core of our work.
• We'll often need data from disparate sources. If you think the bullet point above is a challenge, add to it that the different sources typically introduce an additional layer of complexity: can we map your definition of data (e.g., bacteria identification) to my definition of the same data element?
• Analyzing data in these large repositories can be overwhelming, and the physical processes themselves can take minutes, hours, or even days to execute. We will not necessarily get the instant feedback that we are used to from our computational infrastructure. This leads to our needing to think through our hypotheses very carefully... but also to be prepared to change our thinking once we get that feedback.
• The most interesting stuff we want to elicit is not usually obvious: finding hidden patterns, the basis of data mining, isn't a trivial activity, but when we find some patterns, we have to be sure that they are real. When we are dealing with such large amounts of data, noise becomes a real problem. As our repositories get larger, the likelihood of finding a relationship between any two data elements, or even data values, increases. We must be sure that such relationships are real, which can be as challenging.

We can go on and on, but we won't, but hopefully this gives the reader a sense of the magnitude of the problems we face, and in the rest of this text, we'll be exploring these and many other problems faced by data miners today. As with any discipline, data mining is not a simple activity, although we can make significant progress with simple techniques, but it has the potential to provide tremendous rewards.

1.5   From Data to Information: The Process

The process of which data-mining forms a significant part is a naturally iterative one, with feedback loops at various points in the process, as depicted in Fig. 1.4.

1. *Extract, clean, and integrate* to eliminate any noise that has found its way into the data, "eliminate" inconsistent data, standardize and normalize across the data sources, and integrate them into a single, coherent source for our data warehouse.[14]
2. *Select, transform, and load* to subset the data to include only those data elements pertinent to the analysis being targeted, transform it to correspond with the vagaries of the physical data model into which it will then be loaded.
3. *Aggregate* to provide an a priori grouping, summation, or other aggregate data for use during analysis execution. This is performed prior to use in order to provide a performance improvement during normal processing.
4. *Model hypothesis* to implement the analysis or mining hypothesis into the model language used by the data-mining environment. This model language may range from the completely graphical to a traditional *third-generation language*.
5. *Execute model* to physically interact with the data, perform any model analysis, and generate the output (candidate) knowledge.
6. *Evaluate* to identify the patterns which are of interest to us and which truly represent knowledge.
7. *Visualize and publish* to present the results in a form useful to the user.

In order to support this process, we define a conceptual data-mining architecture as shown in Fig. 1.5. We consider only a conceptual architecture since the physical implementation may be accomplished using any number of different components. However, each such system requires these major components.

The *data warehouse server* is the component which provides all of the infrastructure responsible for actually interacting with the data; all data access is performed by this layer of the architecture. This layer of the architecture will typically be encapsulated within a third-party product such as the RDBMS or the RDBMS along with a specialized engine.

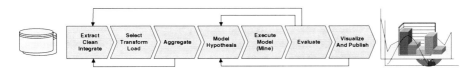

Fig. 1.4   Data to information process

---

[14] We consider that the data repository being used for data mining is in the form of a data warehouse. As we shall see later, the exact structure of our data environment does play a major role in the efficiency, scalability, and usefulness of the models. However, there is nothing to prevent the structure being of any applicable form at this point in the text.

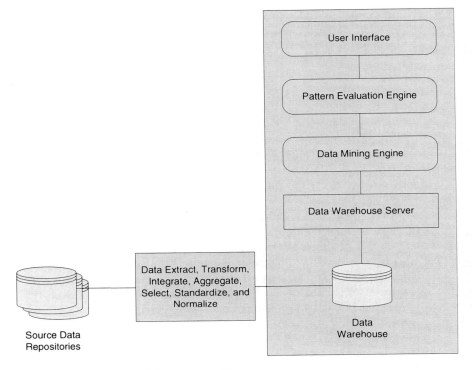

Fig. 1.5 Conceptual data-mining system architecture

The *data-mining engine* usually comprises a set of interrelated modules that perform classification, prediction, association, correlation, cluster analysis, or any of the other mining-specific functions.

The *pattern evaluation engine* performs a vitally important role: it is responsible for eliminating, if possible, all patterns returned by the data-mining engine that do not add to the repository of knowledge we are building. That is, it would typically comprise functions that apply thresholds of various forms to the patterns returned by the data-mining engine and filter out those patterns that do not meet the threshold criteria. As we shall see, the earlier we can apply this test (or set of tests) and determine whether the pattern is of interest or not, the better: if we could integrate this within the data-mining engine, for example, this may provide us with a means of determining the value of the pattern early in the process, thus improving the performance of the analysis.

The *user interface* is intuitively responsible for all interactions between the user and the system. This layer provides the mechanisms for defining the models and queries which will be used, providing information to help the system target the search, and provides means for analyzing intermediary data sets, which may in turn repeat steps in the process based upon the new intelligence provided.

1.5.1   CRISP-DM

A widely used methodology for data mining is the CRoss-Industry Standard Process for Data Mining (CRISP-DM)[15] which was initiated in 1996 by Daimler Chrysler (Daimler-Benz, at that time), SPSS (ISL at that time), and NCR with the intent of providing a process that is reliable and repeatable by people with little data-mining background, with a framework within which experience can be recorded, to support the replication of projects, to support planning and management, as well as to demonstrate data mining as a mature discipline.

In order to enable adoption and utilization, the project aimed to be nonproprietary by being application/industry neutral as well as product/tool neutral, and to include a business issue focus in addition to the technical focus prevalent in many methodologies. In this way, a framework for guidance could be developed and, by use of templates for analysis, an experience base could be built.

The methodology comprises six phases that cover defining the business requirements and formulating the data-mining problem (business understanding), through collecting and familiarizing oneself with the data and identifying data quality problems (data understanding), selecting, transforming, and cleaning the data (data preparation), and then selecting and applying the relevant modeling techniques, calibrating the models as necessary (modeling), evaluating the model against the business objectives (evaluation), and finally deploying the model and implementing a repeatable data-mining process (deployment) (Fig. 1.6).

We provide a cursory introduction to the CRISP-DM methodology in this section but refer the reader to the CRISP-DM web site (www.crisp-dm.org) for more details.[16]

1.5.1.1   Business Understanding

The intent of this phase of the methodology is to understand the project from the business perspective, to take this knowledge about the problem and convert it into a problem definition appropriate for data mining, and subsequently to create a plan to achieve these business objectives. Four primary tasks comprise this phase:

1. Determine the business objectives
   We need to thoroughly understand what we are trying to achieve and uncover **any** fact that can influence the outcome of the project.
2. Assess the situation
   Identify constraints, assumption, and restrictions which may impact the project along with any resources (required or constrained) which will affect the success of the project.

---

[15] www.crisp-dm.org

[16] At the time of writing, the CRISP-DM methodology was to be updated.

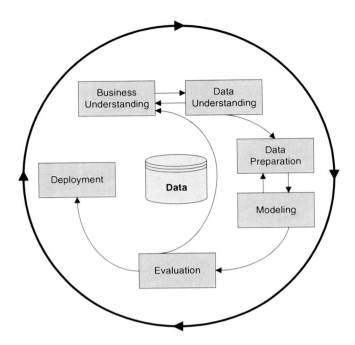

Fig. 1.6 CRISP-DM methodology

3. Determine the data-mining goals
   We need to convert the business requirements into technical terms that a data-mining project can support. As is the case with almost every IT project, this is one area where a misinterpretation, or mistranslation, can significantly impact the value of the conclusions we draw. For example, a business/scientific goal such as
   Increase the efficacy of XYZ-1987 by 10% over its current efficacy profile
   would not typically be used directly as a data-mining goal but may be converted to goals such as
   Identify the interrelationships between the therapy given to patients across the 6 Phase I projects previously conducted that appear to be the most significant 'drivers' that may increase salt and water elimination through urine
   or
   Predict the factors which affect the efficacy of XYZ-1987 positively, given the efficacy and safety data generated by the 6 Phase I projects previously conducted[17]

---

[17] It is important to note that the data-mining goal may be only indirectly associated with the business objective. After all, the data-mining goal may not be able to answer the business objective on its own but may instead offer sufficient supporting data for the (larger) business project.

to identify information and patterns that can be used to support the overarching business objective.

4. Develop the project plan

Bringing together the items we've discussed above into a formal approach that can be communicated and appropriately defended is a valuable task to perform at the beginning of a data-mining effort. It not only lays out the primary activities, but also allows us to see whether or not we have the right balance between those activities and between those activities and the intended end results. For example, as we shall see later, data preparation is typically one of the largest activities in a data-mining effort: do we have enough time allocated in our plan for this activity? A further value of the plan is that it allows us to bound our activity – often knowing when enough is enough is a challenge – or when to change our tack – incorporating checkpoints into our process so that we can track our efforts and ensure that we are producing the required value is a good test to determine when/if we should revisit our objectives.

1.5.1.2   Data Understanding

In this phase, we are interested in gaining a better understanding of the structure and nature of the data itself to be able to identify any data quality problems which may exist within the data, gain any insights we can, and attempt to detect any interesting subsets through which we may be able to form hypotheses about the hidden patterns within the data. Four primary tasks comprise this phase:

1. Collect the initial data

This may involve integrating the data from multiple sources.

2. Describe the data

Here, we examine the gross properties of the data.

3. Explore the data

This stage is the first time in which we begin to address the data-mining questions we defined in the earlier phase by querying, visualizing, and reporting on the data. We may look at the distributions of key attributes, what happens in the face of aggregation, how the properties of pairs of attributes (or triples or other tuples) affect the data, perform statistical analyses, look at significant subpopulations, or perform outlier analysis.

4. Verify the data quality

Data completeness and missing data are the most important aspects of data quality we must determine and address at this point.

Outlier analysis is a useful technique at this stage, a topic we return to later.

1.5.1.3   Data Preparation

This phase is typically the most time-consuming and accounts for the most significant amount of time for any data-mining project,[18] comprises all of the activities we need to perform in order to construct the data set we will actually use for the mining activities from the raw data we first considered above. Unfortunately, this often iterative phase leverages several sets of techniques which may be performed in any one of many orders – there is no nice sequence of tasks here!

- Select data
  What data will we use for our analysis? To answer this question, we not only look at the business goals we have previously defined but also at what technical constraints come into play. By investigating all of these issues we will be able to select both the set of attributes we want to use as well as the records (instances, rows) we will include in our data set.
- Clean data
  It is very rare that our data can be directly used by all of the techniques we wish to consider, and in this task we need to increase the quality of the data we will input to our selected mining techniques. This may be as simple as selecting a subset of our data; it may involve our deciding upon reasonable default values; and it may require a significant modeling effort so that we can estimate missing values.
- Construct data
  Here, we may produce derived attributes (such as the BMI from height/weight measurements), transformed values (possibly by normalizing or standardizing), and possibly generating complete new instances in our data set.
- Integrate data
  Combining information from multiple sources into our single, holistic dataset, often involving our created new instances as we go.
- Format data
  This activity is primarily oriented toward transformations which affect the data *syntactically* as opposed to *semantically* and is typically required because of the modeling tool(s) we are using. This being said, we can often simplify our modeling process by leveraging this type of transformation also.

We like to consider how, and if, this set of activities can be performed so that the data is reusable for future efforts or whether the activity can be partitioned into some generalized tasks and some mining effort-specific tasks. For example, some of the data cleaning activities that attempt to eliminate errors, missing values, and manage outliers may actually be performed once and used for all efforts subsequently. However, this must be considered very carefully since this approach will

---

[18] Refaat (2007 #135) suggested that data extraction and preparation could account for as much as 80% of the overall data-mining effort. We concur that this is a very time-consuming activity that has probably the most significant impact on your mining efforts: if we don't extract the correct data, if it is not put together in the correct way, all our subsequent efforts are built on a fragile foundation.

affect *every* subsequent data-mining project, not just the current project. We must therefore be very confident in the preparation steps we take and be able to state the appropriateness of any such actions to a very high degree of certainty.

1.5.1.4 Modeling

The phases above have all been oriented toward reaching this phase. We now want to select the technique(s) we are interested in, although we will often identify these before now, returning to previous steps as necessary and revisit activities that can be affected by our modeling techniques. We then build our model(s), calibrating and tweaking as we go, and then assess the models to determine which is/are the best.

- Select modeling technique
  We select the specific technique(s) we are interested in, for example, building a decision tree, and then move to the next task. If we are interested in multiple techniques, we will typically perform this task for each technique separately.
- Generate test design
  How do we determine the model's quality and validity? This is the purpose of this task: to generate a procedure to test the quality/validity of the model before we actually build the model. For example, if we are interested in classification, we commonly use error rates as quality measures. We would typically separate the dataset into two – the training dataset and a validation dataset. We then build the model using only the test dataset and determine its quality using the (separate) validation dataset.
- Build model
  Now we build the model(s) using our modeling tools.
- Assess model
  In this task, we are left to determine which model is the "best" according to the success criteria we earlier defined, the test design, and also our domain knowledge. As we consider the success of the model and discovery techniques and also look at the results in a business context, we restrict our consideration only to the model(s) themselves – we consider other factors later in the evaluation phase.

1.5.1.5 Evaluation Phase

In this phase, we review not only the model but also the steps taken to construct the model. Our objective is to ensure that it meets the business/scientific objectives as well as to consider whether there is some business/scientific issue that has not been sufficiently considered. By the end of this phase, we need to make the decision as to whether or not we should use the data-mining results.

- Evaluate results
  Did the model meet the business/scientific needs? Is there some reason why the model is deficient? Can we test the model using a completely independent,

"real-world" dataset?[19] What other data-mining results were generated, and what, if anything, did these tell us? Do we see anything (challenges, information, hints) which may help us in the future?

- Review process
  Did we somehow overlook any factors or tasks during the process which may be important? Did we review the process and uncover all quality assurance issues? Did we correctly build the model?
- Determine next steps
  Now, we need to determine how we are going to proceed. Do we feel confident enough to deploy the model? Or do we need to perform further iterations on the model? Was the test/validation data sufficient, or do we need to run our models against other datasets? There will be many factors which come into play at this stage – scientific, technical, and resource/budgetary.

1.5.1.6 Deployment

In finalizing the data-mining effort, we now need to determine how the results will be used, by whom, and how often. Do we need to deploy the results in the form of business rules for the business/scientific users? Will they be used in terms of database scoring? The knowledge we have gained from the data-mining process will need to be organized and presented so that the user community can make use of it. The deployment may be as simple as deploying a report, or as complex as implementing a repeatable data-mining process for the whole company. A further complication in many scientific disciplines relates to the evaluation by outside third parties and/or regulatory agencies: how do we deploy with this in mind?

1.6   What Can Be Mined?

One of the strengths, and complexities, of data mining is directly related to the question *what can be mined?* The obvious answer is that it depends upon the type(s) of data under consideration, the nature of the discipline targeted by the user, and the overall goal. Are we trying to classify data into nonintuitive classes? Are we trying to predict what we will see in the future based upon what we have seen in the past? Are we simply looking for **any** correlations which might exist in the data?

For example, we may have a time series of clinical test results that have been measured according to some repeated measurements of time. We could use data mining to allow us to elicit trends of change for the items under study. Conversely, we might be interested in finding the characteristics of the evolution of the items under study.

---

[19] The ability/opportunity to perform the tasks highlighted by this question may rest solely on time/budget constraints.

If the data is spatial, we can uncover patterns between climate and height above sea level, proximities between locations, or demographic information.

If the data is textual in nature, we can uncover references between content, clustering of concepts, or associations between concepts (based upon inclusion in text-based material).

If the data comprises image-based data, we can uncover nuances which may not be visible to the naked eye, look at how images of the same object have changed over time, or uncover differences between images in a sequence (or "movie").

It should be stated up front that not all problems are amenable to data mining. We can, however, begin to define the characteristics of problems and applications which are likely to result in successful data-mining efforts:

- Require nondeterministic decisions where subject matter expertise is involved; knowledge-based decisions.
- Data and the environment surrounding the data are not invariant.
- Current methods do not offer the accuracy, breadth, completeness, or ease-of-use necessary.
- Data is available, relevant to the problem at hand, and sufficient.
- Correct decision-making processes have a high return on investment.

Many of the characteristics listed above apply to data we are capturing in many walks of life, and especially in the life sciences: data about people. Privacy and ethical concerns, discussed elsewhere, are likely to be a major issue over the coming years as the breadth and depth of data captured continue to grow. With classification and clustering, two common data-mining approaches, our ability to categorize to smaller and smaller groupings raise further questions. These are only some of the reasons why the question of suitability of the problem should be considered carefully.

1.7 Standards and Terminologies

Throughout this book, we will use a controlled vocabulary of terms to convey meaning and to provide a standard language for data mining as defined within this volume. We have attempted to use terms consistent within the discipline. However, where we use a different term, we will include the term and its reference for completeness.

While mathematical notation, theorems, proofs, and the like are used throughout this book both to exemplify application and support the theory, the intent is not to develop a book for theoreticians, but to provide approaches which can be applied to help the search for solutions to today's and tomorrow's problems. The reader is recommended to reference (Bronshtein 2003) or other mathematical texts for fundamental topics such as dot products.

Pattern value is a measure of the appropriateness of that pattern within the context of the hypothesis or model under consideration.

1.8 Interestingness

As a last topic for this chapter, we ask the question "is every pattern interesting?" This innocuous question is actually very important. Any data-mining system has the potential, and maybe the propensity, to generate hundreds, thousands, and even millions of patterns or rules, which can quickly replace one very large database – the dataset we are analyzing – with another very large database – the patterns and rules generated by the mining activity. So what's the answer? Typically, only a small percentage of the patterns that are identified by a mining activity will be of interest to us.

The natural corollary to the above question is now to ask "how do we determine whether or not a pattern is interesting?" Although we advocate some characteristics which at first glance seem objective, there is a significant amount of subjectivity in the answer to this question:

- Is it easily understood?
  If we can easily understand the pattern offered up by the system, this is a good measure to use. There isn't much value to the system returning a set of patterns that don't allow us to build on what we already know and understand: patterns which have such a convoluted basis that we cannot understand them easily and intuitively are only trading one unknown for another.[20]
- Can we confirm its validity (to some objective measure of certainty) on some data not used to generate the pattern?
  We shall see in the next chapter that model overfitting is a real problem we have to deal with. Succinctly, this is where our model works very well for the data we used to test/train on, but does poorly on as yet unseen data. If we can take a pattern generated by our system and confirm its value on some other dataset, this is a good measure of its value to us. Note that we require some *objective measure* of *certainty*. This will often be some statistical measure such as a confidence factor.
- Is it useful?
  If anyone is saying "well, duh!" at this point, bear with us. Remember that one of the major value points for a data-mining system is that it will uncover unexpected or hidden patterns. These patterns are ones we would not necessarily uncover on our own. As such patterns are uncovered, we need to ask whether or not we can use the pattern in our daily work. If we uncover a pattern that says there is a relationship between breast cancer and osteoporosis, this would immediately highlight itself as a useful pattern. But what about a pattern which says that "a large percentage of people who eat more than 3,000 cal a

---

[20] This is not to say that such patterns won't *become* interesting at a later phase, when and if our understanding of the data, or context, improves. This is a good example of where the importance of the iterative nature of data mining becomes apparent.

day are obese"? This type of pattern is too common and would result in too much noise to be useful.

• Is it novel?

The unexpected nature of a pattern highlighted by the data-mining system is probably its biggest value. If we could easily identify it ourselves, we wouldn't need or want to go through the effort of performing the mining effort in the first place.

With these questions in mind, we can turn our attention to measuring interestingness. The measures traditionally used are based on the structure of the patterns discovered and basic statistical methods. We discuss these in the chapter on Statistical Methods later in this book.

The third question in this thread is to ask "can we restrict our data-mining system so that it only generates the interesting patterns?" In short, the answer is no!

Before we are lynched by data-mining specialists everywhere, we caveat this emphatic answer. The concept of an interesting pattern, as we discuss above, has a healthy dose of subjectivity associated with it: what I may find interesting may not be of interest to you. Further, what is interesting tomorrow may be uninteresting today. Trying to restrict our system to generate only those patterns which are interesting is therefore not an activity we think worthwhile. The more we try and restrict, the more we run the risk of overfitting our model to the data – after all interesting patterns are generated from the data – and also of excluding patterns which may be interesting in the future.

1.9   How Good Is Good Enough?

One last question we pose that will resonate throughout this book is "how good is good enough?" We touched on this earlier when we talked about the data-mining goals and project plan. Data-mining techniques cover the gamut of models and theories. If we consider just the activity of classification, we have a large number of techniques to choose from. For one form of classification, numeric prediction, the most common form of model is generated by using regression analysis techniques from statistics. In and of itself, regression comes in various forms – simple linear regression, logistic regression, multiple regression, nonlinear regression (in general), and Poisson regression, to name a few. While each of these has its own limitations, they also have differing levels of complexity.

This is something we see throughout: developing more complex models or using more complex techniques may not improve our results sufficiently and/or give us sufficient granularity to warrant the additional effort. Pareto's[21] 80/20 principle

---

[21] Vilfredo Pareto, an Italian economist, originally proposed the 80/20 principle in 1897.

certainly needs to be considered, if only to ensure that we do actually need to mine our data further.

We encourage the reader to consider their objectives at each step of the way. If the intent is to initially corroborate an hypothesis, a simple technique may allow us to get an initial idea that we are on the right track; it is often very beneficial to implement a simple model and then a more complex model on a subsequent iteration rather than spend a huge amount of time building a very complex model without the initial corroboration. Occam's razor definitely comes into play here.

What all of this implies is that when defining the problem we are addressing, it is valuable to also define the level of "goodness." Aligning this with the interestingness of the problem provides us with a good (sic) set of metrics from the very beginning.

1.10 The Datasets Used in This Book

The wide range of data collected in the life sciences today covers the gamut of data types which have been used in traditional transactional systems as well as in niche areas. Today, it is not unusual to collect test result data, images, survey publications, and incorporate gene and protein sequence data.

Throughout this book, we will use several different datasets when considering specific techniques and domains. However, for much of the book, we will be using a single dataset to illustrate the majority of approaches we can take. The structure of the dataset is described in Appendix B and can be downloaded from the companion web site (www.lsdm.org).

This dataset contains over 60 different attributes and several thousand instances so that the dataset itself is sufficiently large to be valuable, but not so large as to be completely unwieldy. We note, however, that the content itself has actually been generated using the DataGen utility that is also available from the companion web site. This utility allows data attributes to be defined in terms of their overall nature, allowing large-scale test datasets to be developed for training and illustration purposes. For the purposes of this book, this utility provided an additional value in that the data does not reflect any real persons' data!

1.11 The Rest of the Story

As we have already stated, data mining involves uncovering the patterns inherent within the data. But as we shall see, we can classify these patterns within two gross categories: *descriptive* and *predictive*. With the former, we are interested in understanding the general properties of the data we have in our data repository. For the latter, we want to perform inference on the data so that we can make predictions about data that we haven't yet encountered. We can use a plethora of different techniques to accomplish this; such techniques are the primary content of the remainder of this book.

Chapter 2 of this book concentrates on describing and developing the fundamental concepts underlying data-mining functions. Its' purpose is to provide as complete a definition of the models, concepts, and algorithms which may be encountered in data mining. However, we wish to stress that data mining is the focus of significant active research, and it is impossible to include a complete inventory in a volume such as this.

Chapter 3 of this book includes a complete description of the data architecture. We define the various forms of data architectures in widespread use, such as relational databases, transactional databases, data warehouses, data marts, data cubes, object-relational databases, temporal databases, sequence databases,[22] time-series databases, and spatial databases. We also consider standard terminologies and functions such as drill down and roll up, dimensional modeling and processing of specialized types of data such as text, multimedia, heterogeneous data, images, and sequence (e.g., gene, protein) data.

With each set of techniques, we have attempted to ensure that we provide tangible examples to support them. We would not expect every technique to be used in every area where they can provide value. In fact, it is fair to say that many techniques from different subdisciplines, such as Bayesian statistics or machine learning, to indicate just two, can be used to accomplish the same overall objective; that of identifying patterns within the data.

We will continue to stress the detection of patterns. With large amounts of data, this is a very important subject. But this raises the question of whether **every** pattern that is identified is actually interesting or not. The simple and honest answer is that every pattern uncovered is typically **not** interesting, and certainly not important. As we shall see with even the most simple technique, it is easy to generate thousands of patterns or rules to "describe" the data (current or yet to be encountered), and this can have a significantly negative impact on the effort itself. The rules generated can often be so large as to be unwieldy, if not unusable, in their own right.

This in turn begs the following question: what makes a pattern interesting? This is of fundamental importance for any data-mining effort. Firstly, the pattern must be easily understood by those of us involved in the mining effort. It may only be a subset – such as the scientific subject matter expert – but if it is not understandable, even somewhat intuitive – then it does not provide value to us. Secondly, we must be able to validate the results with some degree of certainty. This validation may be against an existing set of data, often a *training set*, or against some new data. The degree of certainty is usually measured as a probability. Thirdly, the pattern must be useful in some sense. The measure of usefulness, however, is a lot like beauty, it is in the eye of the beholder. How can we quantify such a subjective measure? What I find useful may be completely irrelevant to someone else. This is

---

[22] In this context, a sequence is a set of ordered events rather than a genetic or protein sequence.

an important point in its own right: patterns and rules are unlikely to be universal since we are each mining the data from different, sometimes overlapping, subjectivities. Fourthly, a pattern identified through a mining effort must be novel. If it is not, it would be visible (not hidden) and intuitive and thus not require the use of techniques from multiple disciplines. We would be able to identify such patterns a priori.

All in all, interesting patterns contain and represent knowledge. We learn something new through their identification. If the patterns or rules we identify support a hypothesis we made, or refute a hypothesis we made, this provides us with insight. During the time we were writing this book, several high-profile drugs encountered problems and in certain cases withdrawn from the market. Subsequent information suggested that hidden in the data was additional information that was not uncovered through the normal analytical process. Could any such case be considered an error of omission or an error of commission? We believe not. Even using the most advanced mining techniques is no guarantee of uncovering everything of significance. In fact, it begs the question of what **is** significant. Certainly, with the benefit of hindsight, we can differentiate between significant patterns and insignificant patterns and, as the use of data mining in the life sciences increases, our knowledge and expertise with the techniques themselves will allow us to more easily deal with these issues when we are in the middle of the process.

Data mining can alternatively be described as the confluence of tools, techniques, and concepts from the disciplines of machine learning, statistics, computer science, visualization, data management, genomics, and many other scientific disciplines, whose aim is to convert the vast amount of data we generate through our endeavors into information we can use to progress toward our goals. In more and more disciplines, techniques result in increasing amounts of data being generated. As we can see from the discussion above, and from subjects we consider elsewhere, the end result can be a tsunami of data that is not effectively used.

We purposely avoid programming (toolkits and libraries) wherever possible in the remainder of this book. We do this for two reasons. First, many readers will not necessarily be IT professionals and may not have any interest in developing these skills. The exceptions we make to this premise relate to the R environment and to Perl. The former because the breadth and depth of R packages that have been developed for that environment provide a very rich set of tools for any scientific discipline and are very relevant to today's scientific data-mining efforts. The latter is an interpretive language that is very widely used in the bioinformatics area: we therefore use some of these routines in our bioinformatics discussions. The second reason why we avoid programming is that there are many tools available today that can support data mining – or at least an initial effort – that can be used without needing a significant amount of programming knowledge. Instead of focusing on programming, therefore, we have made the decision to discuss techniques and approaches that can be used through existing tools or by engaging specialists in the event that custom programs are needed. For more information on software and databases used in this book, see Appendix B.

We hope to provide a set of techniques, in context, that can help the life scientist leverage the valuable data asset, continuously generated, that is housed within his/her organization and available through third-party sources and use this to identify opportunities as well as challenges through the discovery and development process. The vast majority of techniques we discuss are general in nature and pertinent to a wide variety of activities since the majority of techniques originate elsewhere. This is strength of both the techniques themselves and the activity of data mining.

1.12   What Have We Missed in the Introduction?

A question that we'll keep coming back to throughout this text is "what did we omit?" The life sciences is a vast, multidisciplinary area, and data mining is growing rapidly by the day. But even within this text, knowing the right place to include a particular topic is challenging. For example, including gene expression, SNP array, next generation sequencing, fluorescent microscopy imaging et al. data, which are being widely used in current life science studies are all important topics, and we will address them throughout the text. Stay tuned.

References

Bronshtein IN (2003) Handbook of mathematics. Springer, Berlin/New York

Fayyad UM (1996) Advances in knowledge discovery and data mining. AAAI Press/MIT Press, Menlo Park

Heckerman D (1999) Learning Bayes nets from data. IJCAI

Kling J (1998) From hypertention to angina to Viagra. Mod Drug Discov 1:31, 33–34, 36, 38

Lyman P, Varian HR (2003) How much information. Universirty of California, Berkeley, p 100

Piantadosi S (1997) Clinical trials: a methodologic perspective. Wiley, New York

Refaat M (2007) Data preparation for data mining using SAS. Morgan Kaufmann Publishers, San Francisco

Schena M (2002) Microarray analysis. Wiley, Hoboken

Tramontano A (2005) The ten most wanted solutions in protein bioinformatics, Chapman & Hall/CRC mathematical biology and medicine series. Chapman & Hall/CRC, Boca Raton

Witten IH, Frank E (2005) Data mining : practical machine learning tools and techniques. Morgan Kaufman, Amsterdam, Boston

Chapter 2
Fundamental Concepts

Abstract Data mining aims to go beyond the mere describing of a set of data to identify those relationships – patterns – that exist between seemingly unrelated items. In this chapter, we pose some of the types of questions we might need to answer, basic concepts such as that of overfitting, bias, normalization, and dimensionality. We also introduce a broad, but certainly not exhaustive, range of techniques to illustrate how widely we can cast our net when looking for techniques to help us. For example, principal component analysis (PCA) can help us with the curse of dimensionality. We also list a number of statistical measures that we use consistently in data mining. In fact, statistical analysis is still one of, if not the, major sets of techniques used in analysis. We also include some important topics such as distance; distance is used in many techniques as a measure of similarity.

2.1 Introduction

Consider the following questions:

?. Is there a correlation between drug X and condition Y?
?. An increase in Z is seen when conditions A and B occur. Do the occurrences of these two conditions cause the increase in Z or is it the other way around?
?. Is there a correlation between highly expressed genes and highly expressed proteins?
?. Given a set of microarray sample results, can we accurately diagnose the disease? Can we predict what the outcome will be for a given therapeutic treatment? Can we recommend the best therapeutic treatment?
?. Why are we seeing that as X changes, Y changes also?

Questions like this need to be considered more and more often as we extend our knowledge, expertise, and the data we capture through our business and scientific efforts. As we better understand the genome, proteome, and transcriptome, the nature of these questions becomes more complex and may not always be able to be

R. Sullivan, *Introduction to Data Mining for the Life Sciences*,
DOI 10.1007/978-1-59745-290-8_2, © Springer Science+Business Media, LLC 2012

predetermined. Or the nature of the question may be able to be predetermined, but may arise from patterns within the data.

As databases grow in size, the amount of data describing any given facet of data stored in the database becomes a more accurate reflection of the distribution of the data itself. For example, the more individuals for whom a salary is recorded will typically give a more accurate reflection of the statistics associated with that data point. What can be as interesting as the statistical analysis on individual pieces of data is how data interrelates to other data and how we can elicit new information from the data we are capturing.

As we analyze and model processes which occur around us, we find a surprisingly complex set of interactions between data characteristics. The process of human in vitro fertilization, for example, uses over 60 different characteristics to determine which embryos should be implanted (Witten and Frank 2005).

In 1985, a personal computer with a 10-Mb hard disk was uncommon. In 2005, a laptop can be purchased with 160 GB of hard disk storage. Inexpensive storage, complex analysis software, and automation have enabled us to capture data more broadly and deeply than ever before. Each year, organizations significantly increase their data storage volumes – not decrease. In an informal straw poll of IT professionals, the authors could not find a single person that confirmed their company had reduced its data storage volumes over the previous year! To put this in perspective, the average novel contains 60,000 words. If each word is assumed to be 10 characters in length, this is 600,000 characters. If a character can be stored in a single byte of storage, this equates to 600,000 bytes, or 586 Kb (or 0.00056 GB). Thus a 106 GB disk can store over 286,000 novels! Large databases run into the upper gigabyte range, and many are now entering the terabyte range.

In the life sciences, we are typically not dealing with novels, but instead with large amounts of numeric and string data. It is not unusual for us to deal with sequence data consisting of thousands of base pairs. We also encounter circumstances where the data is contained in several disparate databases, disparate in location and content. These individual sources, usually containing complex and heterogeneous data, must then be brought together and managed as a coherent whole. This process is easier said than done, as we shall describe later.

But there are many processes for which deterministic, algorithmic approaches are not yet available. Weather prediction, fraud detection, and protein conformation are three widely studied. Yet for each of these subject areas, significant amounts of data are captured daily.

Today, it is fair to say that data overwhelms us. A 30-s Google session returned 105,000,000 hits for the keywords "data mining," 7,580,000 for the keywords "data mining machine learning," and 37,500 for the keywords "data mining machine learning-protein conformation"! While informal, this illustrates that we are generating data at a much faster rate than we understand the data.

In data mining, we are interested in discovering patterns that are hidden in data. In order to do this, we use techniques from machine learning, statistics and inference, and data analysis, to name a few. In order to accomplish this, we use these techniques with automated searching techniques to identify patterns which can then be validated and then used for prediction.

We can, therefore, also consider data mining as being about problem solving through analyzing existing data by finding patterns within the data. Patterns can be expressed in any number of different ways. On one end of the spectrum, we have a completely opaque pattern – the black box – while on the other end of the spectrum is the completely transparent pattern that allows us to see and understand its structure. Witten and Frank (2005) call patterns which are represented in terms of structures that can be examined, reasoned about, and used for future decision-making *structural* since they capture the decision structure in an explicit way; that is, they help to explain the data in some respect. We will use the same definition since the objective is to uncover and describe such structural patterns in data.

We often find that certain patterns occur frequently enough in our data for us to consider them specifically. Inferring that these patterns will occur with a similar frequency in data yet unseen offers valuable insight into the larger dataset and to other patterns we can uncover. One correlation of this is that we may be able to identify not only patterns but sequences and other structures within the data. Using a consumer-based example, buying a camera could lead to buying additional memory cards, an intuitive sequence, but how often does this also lead to buying photo editing software and even a new PC?

Data mining techniques are often compartmentalized into statistical and machine-learning categories. However, many techniques use a combination of techniques from both categories, either sequentially or in parallel. Further, many problems can be solved through either type of approach. An example of this can be seen in the area of classification and regression trees.

In order to identify patterns in data and to use the results for decision-making in the future, we have to have methods which *learn*. On one level, learning can be thought of as searching through some space of possible definitions to determine (the) one that best fits the data we have. Theoretically, we can consider this as a problem whereby we enumerate each definition in our space and eliminate those which do not fit the *training data* (examples) we are given.[1] With each example in our training set, the set of definitions remaining will reduce or remain the same until we have exhausted our training set.

We can then be left with a set of definitions, or in the extreme, a single definition. In the latter case, it is the target we are looking for. In the former case, the set of definitions left may still be used to classify previously unseen definitions. If a previously unseen object matched every definition in our set, we can definitely consider it to have matched the target. If it does not match any definition in our set, we can definitely consider it to be outside of our target. However, the ambiguity and complexity comes in when some subsets of our definitions are matched. We have to be careful since if we classify the object into some classification, the definitions in our set for which the match failed will be eliminated, which may not be acceptable.

---

[1] Note that we can elect to exclude those that *do* match our examples, or those which *do not* match our examples.

This overclassification would make the system fragile and error-prone as it can overfits the training data when incremented with the previously unseen object.

Continuing with our conceptualization of learning as search, the first question that needs to be addressed is how the search space is defined or enumerated.

Consider that each *characteristic* or attribute in each concept definition can have a range of values. As an example, consider the following set of characteristics that we might define as our *patient* object:

- Age (0–99)
- Gender (male, female)
- Race (Caucasian, Asian, African, Hispanic)
- Pregnant (true, false)

If we were to only consider the following attribute set, we would have a total of $100 \times 2 \times 4 = 800$ combinations we would have to consider *for each rule*. In reality, we will have vastly more than this – both in terms of the domain of values for each characteristic and the number of characteristics themselves. Each of these combinations could be implemented as a *rule* such as

```
if age > 16 and gender = female

      and pregnant = true then inclusion = false
```

This results in a huge number of possible rules.

We could decide to create a rule set with a limited set of rules. For example, if we have 20 training examples, we might elect to generate a rule set containing an equivalent number of rules. In this case, we have a total of 800^{20} or 1.15×10^{58} possible rule sets! As we stated, the type and number of attributes we used to come up with this number are patently naïve and would not provide a rich enough environment for real-world problems.

This *enumeration* issue is definitely a challenge, although various techniques are available which can help. But it is not the only issue. A related issue involves the fact that in the majority of cases, a unique object is rarely returned: the process will not typically converge on a unique result.

There are only three possible outcomes for processing a search space: either a unique result is returned, as discussed above, or no result is returned, or more than one result is returned.

When no result is returned, it means that the language we are using to describe the problem under study is not rich enough to capture the concept, or that there is too much noise in the set of training examples. An example may be incorrectly classified because the values provided contain some level of noise. If we were to consider a classical problem in artificial intelligence, that of handwriting recognition, for example, then the scanned character images may contain noise due to dust on the scanner platen. This could result in a "c" character being mistakenly classified as an "o" character if the dust was in the right position.

When more than one result is returned, it is typically because the example set we have used to train our system is not sufficiently rich to allow us to obtain just the single result we are ultimately striving to obtain. In such cases, the goal may be to return the "best" result from the set of results, and we may use some additional criteria for this purpose.

We can consider this *generalization as search* problem from another perspective also: as hill climbing in the problem space to find the result which best matches the example set we use for training our system, according to some specification of matching criteria. This is how most practical machine-learning methods work. It should be noted, however, that for any real-world problem, it is infeasible to exhaustively search the problem space; most algorithms use heuristic search methods. These, obviously, cannot guarantee to find the optimal solution.

In this chapter, we introduce a large number of different techniques which can be used within the data mining effort. Prior to this, we make note that data mining and knowledge discovery use different definitions to mean the same thing. We particularly like the terms used in Witten and Frank (2005):

- *Concept description* refers to the thing to be learned.
- The input takes the form of *concepts, instances,* and *attributes*, where an instance is an independent example of the concept and comprises a set of attributes.

We also pause to introduce the concept of *supervised* learning and its complement *unsupervised* learning. We will define these more precisely and formally later, but at this stage it suffices to say that with supervised learning methods we are provided with output *labels* for each training set instance; with unsupervised learning, the method needs to identify such labels from the training data itself. Both of these areas of machine learning provide significant value in their respective domains.

2.2   Data Mining Activities

Every person initiating a data mining activity will do so with a particular form of analysis that he/she would like to perform. This objective will typically be described as a *data mining query* that will be used as the primary input to the system.[2] We do, however, need to decompose this query a little further in order to direct the mining effort itself to optimize the overall process as much as possible. While this decomposition typically occurs intuitively, we dissect it here in order to provide context for some of the discussions later.

- Mining data subset
  In any given mining activity, only a subset of the overall data repository will be relevant and of interest to the user. This will include all the dimensions of the data warehouse, subset of attributes, and subset of the data domain itself.

---

[2] Note that we consider the data repository to be an integral part of the data mining system, thus the data itself – training data or otherwise – is not designated as an input.

- Mining functions
  This defines the type of function that is to be performed within the mining activity. Examples include classification, outlier analysis, association, or any combination of such functions.
- Contextual knowledge
  This is the knowledge and information available to the user or subject matter expert that relates to the domain under study and provides significant value in guiding the overall discovery process as well as for pattern evaluation once such patterns have been uncovered. We shall consider several techniques, such as concept hierarchies that provide support in this area.
- Value measures
  These are the measures, thresholds, and probabilities which we will primarily use to evaluate the patterns uncovered by the mining effort. However, they may also be valuable in helping to direct the mining process as well as postdiscovery.
- Visualization representation
  How are we going to visualize the output from our efforts? Tables, charts, cubes, graphs, rules, decision trees, and many other representations may be used.[3]

As we shall see, these concepts and components come together in the models and query languages we use to physically perform the mining activity.

2.3   Models

In much of our discussions on data mining, the concept of a *model* is used. A model is a representation of reality, but usually in a constrained domain. While it encapsulates the essential characteristics of the part of reality it is representing, any aspect of its real-world counterpart which is extraneous to what is being studied is usually omitted. An example of this is the primary structure of a protein, a string of amino-acid representations that provides us with significant scientific value, but which does not encapsulate all of the characteristics of a protein and is clearly not the protein itself. Thus, a model is a theory or hypothesis about some aspect of reality.

We often need to consider multiple hypotheses rather than any single one since the data we are dealing with may be effectively explained by more than one model. We can then use the multiple models to direct our efforts and seek additional data to distinguish between the models under consideration. Using this additional data, we can iteratively evaluate the plausibility of each model in light of the new data we are using, with the goal being to identify the model which most effectively satisfies the data. We shall return to this concept throughout our discussions.

Developing models, therefore, provides a mechanism for us to define a facet of reality that we are interested in and to overlay this with our data repository. Once

---

[3] The authors particularly like the creative approaches to displaying information stimulated by Tufte (1990 #531, 1997 #538, 2001 #535).

we develop a model, we will often go through an iterative process of training the model to perform efficiently and effectively against our data, but use a smaller set – the *training data* – that will allow us to tune the model's architecture and parameters. Since the overall purpose of our model is to generalize to finding patterns in data as yet unseen, it is important to ensure that the model we have developed is not so specific to our training data that its performance is severely impacted as the data volume, and distribution, grows.

2.4 Input Representation

Since every data mining effort works on a set of input records, rows, or *instances*, and this set of inputs is what we will classify, cluster, associate, or otherwise process, representing the data effectively is an important part of the overall architecture.

The most common, and arguably pragmatic, way of representing the input data instances is for each such input to be comprised of a predetermined set of attributes. While this is undeniably valuable, when relationships between instances or attributes are our objective, this representation may not be the most effective.

Consider the example where we are interested in drugs which are *agonists*, a compound which binds to a receptor and produces a biological response. If we have 20 compounds in our input, along with 20 receptors, say, then this would result in $20 \times 20 = 400$ pairs, with the likelihood that most of the pairs do not have an agonistic relationship. Further, if we are interested in whether any of our compounds are *coagonists*, we would similarly have 400 pairs where most of the pairs of compounds are not coagonists. Specifying a "yes" or "no" value for each combination of compounds will result in a large number of rows in which the value is "no," as shown below:

Compound 1	Compound 2	Coagonist?
C1	C2	Yes
C1	C3	No
C1	C4	No
. . .	. . .	
C2	C1	Yes
C2	C3	Yes
C2	C4	No
. . .	. . .	
C3	C1	No
C3	C2	Yes
C3	C4	No
. . .	. . .	
C4	C1	No
C4	C2	No
C4	C3	No
. . .	. . .	

An alternative approach is called the *closed world assumption* which is based on the presumption that what is not currently known to be true is false. Here, we can just specify the true ("yes") values and assume that any "missing" values are false ("no"). In our example, the table would be

Compound 1	Compound 2	Coagonist?
C1	C2	Yes
C2	C1	Yes
C2	C3	Yes
C3	C2	Yes

In the above table, any combination not included (e.g., C4 and any of C1, C2, and C3) is assumed to have a value of "no."

As we shall see later, this example of converting a relationship into an appropriate form for data mining is vital and often as challenging as the mining effort itself. We shall consider concepts such as *denormalization* to allow us to flatten tables for more effective analysis.

The above examples informally introduce the concept of qualitative attributes, which are usually expressed as categories (e.g., sex, zip/postal code), and quantitative data which are intrinsically numerical quantities (e.g., age, temperature, cholesterol level). Qualitative data is *nominal* if it is categorized, but has no implicit or explicit order. For this type of data, the equality or inequality relation is the only operation we can establish. If the data is *ordinal*, there is an ordering of the values, and this allows us to establish an ordering ($>. <. =$), but not to make any statements on the differences between the categories. For example, we may be interested in academic achievement and assign values for non-high school graduation (0), high school graduation (1), college education (2), bachelor's degree (3), master's degree (4), and Ph.D. (5). Here we can clearly see that there is an ordering, but to ask whether "college education – high school graduation" (2–1) is the same as "bachelor's degree – college education" (3–2) is nonsensical. However, we can intuitively say that "bachelor's degree > college education" in this scheme.

2.5 Missing Data

Any analytical activity is only as good as the data being analyzed. If the data contains erroneous data, the results will at least be skewed, if not totally worthless. This pretty obvious statement does contain some not so obvious issues that we will discuss in more depth later. One of the most visible aspects to this issue, however, is where data is simply not available to us.

In some respects, missing data can be even more problematic in that we do not know what the missing data should be – the old "would everyone not in the room please raise their hands" syndrome. This problem takes on an additional complexion as we deal with larger and larger numbers of attributes since missing data is not as easily dealt with and it can also cause problems with our models that are not readily apparent.

Our first question should be to ask why the data is missing. Is it because the instruments capturing the data malfunctioned? Is it because the people who are the sources of the data declined to provide the data? Did our experiment change midway through? Did (any) aggregation task eliminate the data? Was it never collected in the first place?

The reason *why* the data is missing is as important as how we will deal with the fact that it does not appear in our dataset. To be able to answer some of the questions we raise in this section, we will need access to people who are subject matter experts on the data itself. While this knowledge may be readily available to you – you may even have that knowledge yourself – it may also reside outside the team. It is important not to minimize this issue because only such subject matter experts can tell us if there is additional significance to the missing data other than the fact that it is missing.

Many of the techniques we cover will allow us to handle missing values, even very simple methods such as the 1R method that we discuss below. However, a conscious decision must be made as to how we wish the various methods to handle missing values.

One method is to explicitly include a value of "missing" for those attributes where a value is unknown. In categorical data, we can include an additional class, say called "missing," for any value which is not provided. For numeric data, we could use values such as 0 or 1, depending upon what has the least impact.

The question of impact is an important one. If we are going to apply mathematical operators to the data, a value of 1 may have a minimal impact, whereas a value of 0 could result in the dreaded "divide by zero" error. Of course, simple arithmetic activities may require a value of 0 to avoid inflating our counts.

We shall return to this issue as we discuss various methods throughout this book since the approach we take will often be driven as much by the method as by the data itself.

2.6   Does Data Expire?

Food, medicines, and many other items we interact with on a daily basis have a "sell-by" or "use-by" data. Can the same be said for data? Does it expire? Is there a point after which using the data would, or could introduce errors into our model? As is always the case, the answer is "it depends."

If we are using information to draw conclusions of a transient nature, such as recommending a therapy, the answer is typically yes, the data expires. A patient's condition will change over time and may change very quickly. We would not want to use results from a blood panel taken 3 months ago, for example.

The above example, however, is probably not going to be where our issues lie. We may need to be very careful if we are using geographical data for individuals, since addresses will often change. In such cases, we need to determine whether or not such changes can affect our model: does it matter if the addresses of patients in our dataset have changed? The answer will depend on what conclusions we are trying to draw from our models and also what the underlying meaning is for both our input data and our models. Once again, we need to have a good understanding of our data, or at least, access to someone with a good understanding of our data.

2.7 Frequent Patterns

We have already alluded to the fact that frequent patterns, patterns that occur again and again in our data, provide a natural starting point for data mining. After all, we would definitely want to be cognizant of these quotidian patterns before analyzing the more esoteric patterns inherent in our data.

Such patterns provide additional understanding of our data in that sequences and other structures will often be inherent within the frequent patterns themselves. For example, the use of stimulants will obviously show increased heart rates and other heightened metabolic factors. Can we also elicit other subsequent physiological relationships from our data?

Association analysis, described below, provides a good first step in this process. We are interested in the association (or implication) between two or more facets of the data. For example, an MIC[4] of 4 for a *Streptococcus pneumoniae* isolate taken from a patient when tested against vancomycin and ampicillin would be a good indicator of multidrug resistance for that isolate, a determination we can make without testing against other compounds. We may describe this rule as follows:

> Vancomyin MIC > 2 and ampicillin MIC > 2 → multiDrugResistance
>   Confidence = 75%
>   DataSupport = 4%

Our measure of confidence, also called accuracy, means that 75% of the time that a vancomycin MIC > 2 occurred and that an ampicillin MIC > 2 occurred, multidrug resistance also occurred. Similarly, our measure of data support, also called coverage, means that 4% of the instances in our dataset showed that isolates that had an MIC value greater than 2 for vancomycin and an MIC value of greater than 2 for ampicillin **and** a designation of multidrug resistance occurred together. There is a subtle nuance to the above values: in one, we are looking at how often these characteristics physically occurred in the data (data support), whereas in the other, we are looking at how often the characteristics to the left of the arrow inferred the characteristics to the right of the arrow (confidence).

---

[4] MIC stands for minimum inhibitory concentration and is the minimum concentration of a drug that inhibits the growth of a microorganism after overnight incubation. It is an important value for antimicrobial agents as it is used as an indicator for antimicrobial resistance and antimicrobial agent activity.

2.8 Bias

Our intuitive concept of bias will serve us well as a launching point for considering how and where this issue rears its ugly head in our data mining processes, models, data, and objectivity. In statistics, a *biased sample* is a sample in which the members of the statistical population are not likely to be equally likely chosen. A *biased estimator* is one which consistently overestimates, or underestimates the quantity it is intended to estimate. Either of these conditions could lead to our concluding invalid results. In data mining and machine learning, these and other forms of bias can leak into the system.

As we have defined elsewhere, our data mining models will typically be tested and validated against a subset of the data on which it will operate when fully implemented. *Generalizing* the model is therefore fundamentally important. In one respect, therefore, we can consider generalization as a search through some state space of possible descriptions, in order to identify the one which best fits our data. For example, we may have a set of results from our data mining model expressed as a set of rules. Suppose that we list every possible combination, or set, of rules and we then iterate through them to find the subset which best fits a particular set of data we have. This is certainly a large job, but not impossible.[5] What we need to be concerned about when viewing generalization in this way is that the order in which the state space is searched, and the way in which the model may be overfitted to the training data must be considered throughout. Even the language we use to define the problem may introduce a level of bias.

We will return to this concept at several points through this book, but introduce several generic forms which must be carefully considered and which are relevant.

The language we use to describe the concepts that we are targeting can, in and of themselves, impose constraints on what we are trying to learn. We need to ensure that the language we use in defining what we are trying to learn and, by extension, what our models tell us does not prevent us from representing every possible subset of examples. While this is not always a practical issue due to the fact that the set of possible examples is usually very large, it can come into play if the language cannot allow for disjunctions ("or") to be represented[6]: in such a case, our model may not be able to achieve good performance. A more usual form of language bias that we see comes from domain knowledge. A subject matter expert will often know if certain combinations of attribute values can never occur. For example, a microbiologist would know that microorganism A can never be resistant to antimicrobial B and also that microorganism C is not a β-lactamase producer. More generally, this type of situation occurs when one attribute implies another. In such cases, knowing

---

[5] For more details on generalization as search, the reader is referred to Witten (2005 #11, pp. 30–32).
[6] We purposely exclude discussion of this issue herein as most languages we would encounter in practice will allow conjunctions and disjunctions.

these facts and eliminating such data can significantly reduce the state space our model has to search.

We will typically encounter data mining problems where there are many alternative "solutions" to the problem; we must then determine how we find the "best" one. The definition of "best" will often be specific to the problem at hand, although we often use a criterion such as simplicity. However, under any circumstance, the question of which solution has the best fit to the data will be considered. By fit, we want a solution that represents the data as close as possible. However, one of the challenges in computer science is to determine whether we have the best solution possible: it is usually computationally infeasible to search the complete state space and ensure that we return the best solution possible. Thus, our search will by necessity be a heuristic process. In turn, this introduces bias as different search algorithms implement search in different ways. For example, when we build a decision tree, we make decisions on when to branch on a given attribute: doing this at an early stage may turn out to be ill-conceived based upon the subtree below that node.[7] But probably the most common form of search bias that we encounter depends on whether we begin with a general description of our goal and refine it or start with a specific description and try to generalize it. The former is referred to as a *general-to-specific* bias, the latter as a *specific-to-general* bias. We shall see examples of both forms of model in this book and consider this type of bias within each context.

In our above discussion, we mentioned that our goal is to get the best fit we can to our data. In order to accomplish this, we can use many techniques, including domain knowledge and other heuristics. We might, for example, begin by focusing on the simplest data/solutions and build up to including more and more complex solutions in our model. We can stop when we reach a sufficiently complex solution and then review our data to determine how we move forward, introducing an iterative approach to the problem. However, we can go overboard and quickly find that our solution is, in fact, the best solution – but the best solution only for our current dataset. Generalization of our model may not be possible. Although this issue is an example of bias, it is sufficiently general and common that we consider it separately in Sect. 2.16 below. We further examine the *bias-variance decomposition* concept in Sect. 2.19 below.

One of the strengths of data mining is that we can test a large number of hypotheses about a particular dataset in a very short time. Exhaustively searching the dataset using combinations of variables in the hope that they might show a correlation is a factor of the processing power and size of the dataset; our ability to perform such an exhaustive search increases almost daily. But this is also a weakness. Statistical significance testing, based on the probability that an observation arose by chance, would indicate that it is reasonable to assume that 10% of randomly chosen hypotheses will be significant at the 10% level, 5% will turn out to

---

[7] This particular problem has been well studied in the automated reasoning realm. See, for example, Gallier (1986 #86).

be significant at the 5% level, 1% at the 1% significance level, 0.1% at the 0.1% significance level, and so on by chance alone. We can, therefore, safely assume that if we test enough hypotheses, some of them will appear to be highly significant – even if the dataset contains no real correlations!

   This last concept might be best referred to as *miner bias* since we want to find patterns in the data and will often do so. However, there are many cases of published correlation results which subsequently turn out not to be correlations at all. Not every pattern has real meaning. One case, from the financial sector, has become infamous: David Leinweber "sifted through a United Nations CD-ROM and discovered that historically, the single best predictor of the Standard & Poor's 500-stock index was butter production in Bangladesh" (Peter Coy[8]). We must be careful to validate that our mining results really **do** have merit.

2.9   Generalization

Generalization, the ability to leverage our models outside of the initial domain for which they were defined, is an important topic. We have already raised this concept in our discussions so far, for example, when considering generalization as search, and will return to it at various points throughout this book.

   Leveraging a model to other datasets and, potentially, even to other domains provides a significant value for any organization. But while we have an intuitive understanding of what we mean by generalization that will serve us well, we also have to consider *how general* is general enough?

   We shall see that one outcome of considering generalization when mining data is that complex models are often penalized; the more complex a model, the more likely it is that the complex model could not be effectively leveraged to other datasets and domains. Thus, we consider the predictive power and performance of any model we build. This is a primary factor in penalizing complex models.

2.10   Data Characterization and Discrimination

Data characterization is summarizing data of the class under study. Specifically, we are interested in the general characteristics or features of the data. These summaries may be based on simple statistical measures, or cube-based roll-up along a specified dimension.

   Data discrimination is comparison of the target class with one of a set of comparative classes.

---

[8] Peter Coy's BusinessWeek article "He Who Mines Data May Strike Fool's Gold," BusinessWeek June 16, 1997.

2.11   Association Analysis

One area of significant interest is to understand the relationships (affinities) between entities and variables in our dataset. Association analysis provides us with a set of techniques to model and analyze what these relationships may be. By what means these relationships occur is of secondary consequence to us: it is primarily *if* they are related on which we focus.

One area in which this set of techniques has been used to great advantage is in the area of disease-marker association.[9] These efforts have shown, for example, a close association between the E4 allele in APOE and Alzheimer's disease: this allele is three times more frequent in Alzheimer's patients than in healthy control patients.

As we shall see when we consider association analysis in more detail later, we are interested in identifying direct, *causal* effects between entities/variables, indirect *correlated* effects, where an intermediary entity/variable may provide the link, but also to identify where associations may *appear* to exist, but which in fact may be false positives in our dataset. This is as valuable as identifying real associations since we can safely eliminate these associations from our dataset and ensure that our conclusions are as valid as possible.

2.12   Classification and Prediction

The processes of *classification* and *prediction* form a significant base for many data mining operations and constitute an important, fundamental technique. Note the singular form: classification is normally associated with categorical data, whereas prediction is the equivalent for dealing with continuous valued data.

The central idea of classification is to define a *model* that adequately describes the data provided in a *training set*. The data will partition into several classes,[10] and the training set will include the concept labels along with the input data. We use the *trained model* to predict the concept associated with inputs that we have not previously seen and for which concept labels are unknown.

As stated above, prediction refers to continuous data as opposed to categorical data, and, instead of labels, we are aiming to predict missing or unavailable *numerical* data. *Regression analysis* (see later) is often used for numeric data prediction, but as we shall see, this is only one of many techniques we can use. In fact, a wide range of different techniques are used by researchers to predict data, including support vector machines, Gaussian processes, Bayes' nets, and neural networks.

---

[9] http://bioinformatics.well.ox.ac.uk/lectures/Association_260404.ppt

[10] Alternative terms include categories or concepts as used in Witten and Frank (2005).

As indicated above, classification is often used with categorical data and prediction is used for continuous valued functions and data, we use the term classification to cover both cases within this book when describing general principles and underlying theory.

2.12.1   Relevance Analysis

As a precursor to performing classification or prediction, it is often useful to try and identify any attributes that do not contribute to the process being performed through *relevance analysis*. In such cases, the attributes can be excluded from the process. This is a very powerful technique we can use at the beginning of our mining effort; if we can simplify our dataset by excluding irrelevant data attributes, our algorithms will be more efficient since they do not have to process as much data, they will not be adversely affected by considering irrelevant data to be relevant, which could then bias our results, and enhance our ability to intuitively understand the results generated.

However, the problem of excluding attributes which are, in fact, relevant can lead to erroneous inferences being made. Care must be taken when performing relevance analysis to ensure that we **really** understand an attributes' relevance.

2.13   Cluster Analysis

On many occasions, target labels for the input data are not known. In such cases, we may not be able to generate a training set for our model. However, this may not be of particular issue: we can use the method of maximizing similarities between inputs in the same class and minimizing the similarities between inputs in different classes. As stated in Han and Kamber (2006),

> ...the principle of maximizing the intraclass similarity and minimizing the interclass similarity.

What we need to do is generate clusters of objects where the members of that cluster have high similarity[11] in comparison to one another, but which are dissimilar to objects in other clusters. As indicated by the vagueness of *similarity*, this can cover a wide range. In fact, multiple similarity measures may be applied to a single dataset depending upon the perspective of the user and the mining intent.

---

[11] The concept of similarity will be a common theme through much of this book. If there is a fundamental concept for data mining, it is to identify things which are similar and things which are dissimilar. The concept of similarity, however, as we shall see later, can be defined in a wide range of terms.

Fig. 2.1 Two-dimensional
cluster plot

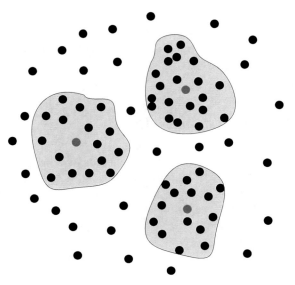

We could have a similarity measure that identifies different groups of patients who have exhibited a particular reaction to a therapy. The "patient" data in Fig. 2.1 depicts how these different clusters may arise. The red spot indicates the cluster's center measure.

2.14   Outlier Analysis

We introduce another premining technique that is often a necessary part of the mining effort. In the real world, we will often encounter datasets that contain data that does not conform to the model we define, or to the general behavior of the data. For example, our blood pressure measurements may include a value or two that cannot be valid if the patient is, in fact, alive. In such cases, we will discard such *outliers* as exceptions, or consider them to be noise in our dataset. However, in certain cases, we may be more interested in these exceptions than in the data which conforms to our model.[12] We often identify such outliers by using statistical methods that assume the dataset as a whole conforms to a probability distribution or model, or by using distance measures to highlight data points which are a substantial distance away from any of the clusters identified in our model. Another method is to look at the most interesting and important characteristics of the data in our dataset and identify any which deviates from these characteristics, by some substantial amount, as outliers.

---

[12] A good example of this is in the area of fraud detection, which is completely outside the scope of this book.

Outliers can therefore be a nuisance, or a value, depending on our perspective, but in either case, they constitute a factor that we need to consider: even some of our basic measures, such as the mean of a data set, can be affected by outliers.

2.15 Normalization

Normalization transforms continuous or discrete values or ranges to numbers, converting individual attribute values in such a way that all attribute values lie in the same range. Normally, values are converted to be in the range 0.0 to 1.0 or the range -1 to $+1$ to ease in further processing, ensuring that attributes do not receive artificial weighting caused by differences in the ranges that they span.

This technique is of particular value when using any statistical technique since a fundamental assumption is that a probability ranges between 0 and 1. But it also helps in many other mathematical algorithms since they will typically be well defined in this range. Further, we can be more comfortable with our analysis since all of our scales will be the same. This avoids any problems that might occur as we try and compare or associate variables that have different scales of values.

2.16 Dimensionality

All data mining algorithms work on a set of *data points*. These data points may have associated output labels, in which case we can take advantage of supervised learning algorithms such as hidden Markov models, neural networks, and the like, or they may not, in which case we use unsupervised learning algorithms such as k-means, SOM, etc. In either case, we typically represent each data point as a vector in a space (continuous or discrete as appropriate). We define the *dimensionality of a dataset* as the length of the vectors in the dataset. One *feature* per dimension of the dataset is another common term, where we define feature as being a data attribute of interest.

For example, consider the type of information we may feel it necessary to capture for a patient during each encounter (visit) for a study. This data could include:

- Age
- Height
- Weight
- Blood pressure
- Heart rate
- 30-panel clinical test results

Even here we have a total of 35 attributes; each vector within the dataset would have 35 attributes, giving us a 35-dimension dataset.

But a question we need to ask is whether or not every attribute is actually needed for the algorithm we are using. The algorithm will try and identify some of the parameters to model the distribution of the data points. Thus, the dimensionality of the parameter's space will necessarily be proportional to the dimensionality of the dataset. But this in turn means that the number of independent data points must be at least equal to, or greater than, the number of parameters needed for the model.

It is therefore important to carefully consider how the data points will be converted to vectors. This will have significant impact on the algorithm's success. Let's consider this issue in more detail. In many cases, converting the input data points, vectors in their own right, to vectors in some other form may increase the probability of an algorithm successfully processing the data. Thus, as well as leaving the data points as is, we can look to converting them to improve the chances of success. In kernel learning terms, this is where the input space is converted to a *feature space*, which we discuss later.

One method we can employ is to ask the question: do we have any attributes (dimensions) which are incidental to our goal? If we can identify such attributes, we can afford to reduce the dimensionality by excluding those attributes.

However, we must be careful with whatever approach we take. If we have too many dimensions, our model will require too many parameters, and therefore, more data points than we have in our data set. There is a danger that we may *overtrain* the algorithm and, when we try and generalize outside of our training set, that the model performs badly. Conversely, if we are able to reduce the dimensionality, we may end up with too few dimensions, in which case we may lose information that may be essential to identify the pattern, class, or other feature we are interested in. Bellman (1961) first coined the term "curse of dimensionality" which refers to the exponential growth of hypervolume as a function of dimensionality.

Another question we need to carefully consider is whether any of the attributes essentially duplicate other information. For example, if we have the date of birth of a patient, we need not capture the age (or vice versa).

As we consider mappings from our input space to an output space, our model needs to be able to cover or represent every part of the input space in order to know how that part of the space should be mapped (to its representative output space). The amount of resources necessary to accomplish this is proportional to the hypervolume of the input space.

Thus, the curse of dimensionality comes from the fact that models with lots of irrelevant inputs behave relatively badly. For models where the dimension of the input space is high, the model implementation uses an inordinate amount of its resources to represent irrelevant portions of the space. Many unsupervised learning algorithms are particularly susceptible to this problem.[13] One way to alleviate this is to preprocess the input by normalization, scaling the input attributes according to some level of importance (so that some of the irrelevancies are eliminated), or other techniques which we

---

[13] As radial basis functions (RBFs) that we consider later under Gaussian methods in learning.

will explore later. However, the higher the dimensionality of the input space, the more data which may be needed to find out what is important and what is not.

A priori information can be very helpful in managing the dimensionality issue. Careful feature selection and scaling of the input attributes fundamentally affect the severity of the problem as well as selection of the model.

Although we can use *guesswork* when considering what dimensions are necessary, there are several formal methods which can be valuable. *Principal component analysis* (PCA) rotates the dataset in such a way as to maximize the dispersion across major axes. *Singular value decomposition* (SVD) reduces a dataset containing a large number of values to a dataset containing significantly fewer values, while still maintaining a large fraction of the variability present in the original data. Both techniques are closely related to each other and offer significant value in managing the dimensionality issue, as we shall see later.

2.17 Model Overfitting

In any dataset sufficiently complex to be valuable for analysis, we will typically begin, and maybe end, with some form of simplification, or *modeling*, as we've already discussed. In building our model, we will encounter many points at which we have to make decisions that could dramatically affect the results of our analysis. Consider a set of data points, as depicted in Fig. 2.2.

Although both the curve and the straight line might be valid models of the data, most of us would agree that the straight line would be the better model due to its

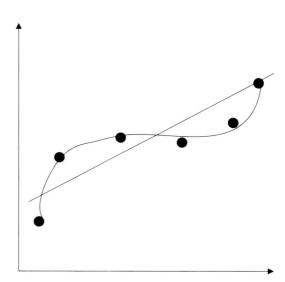

Fig. 2.2 Overfitting

simplicity and applicability.[14] Further, as new data comes in, rerunning our model to recreate the straight line will be much simpler than to recreate the polynomial (hopefully!?) associated with the more complex curve. This being said, the curve would give a more accurate estimate/value for any point in our dataset.

This is a good example of the concern we expressed above: we can easily fall into the trap of developing a model where the architecture and parameters have been so tuned to the data we have used for training that its performance against a more generalized base of data is severely and negatively impacted. This situation can occur because of a number of factors:

- The features (characteristics) used may not be specific enough – or may be too specific.
- The model architecture may not be too sensitive, and not specific enough, or vice versa.

Overfitting occurs, therefore, when anomalies in the data presented to the model are incorporated into the model. That is, any *training data* that is used will naturally contain characteristics which are not necessarily in the general universe of data we will encounter once our model is used beyond its training stage, and we must ensure that when we validate our model, we do so using a dataset that is *independent* of the training data.

An overfitted model will obviously not make accurate predictions on unseen data. How can we ensure that the model is not overfitted? One approach we can take to determine whether a model M_1 is overfitting a training set is to identify an alternative model M_2 where this second model exhibits higher training prediction and lower test prediction errors with respect to M_1.

Another approach is to consider a separate *validation dataset* that is independently selected and used once the model's training period has been completed. This can be used to determine initial overfitting, but is also a valuable technique which can be applied to the model periodically to see if the model needs to be tuned and/or trained to improve its generalization.

2.18 Concept Hierarchies

A *concept hierarchy* is any hierarchically organized collection of domain concepts, where the organizing relationship is the "part-of" relationship. One such example that we each deal with on a daily basis relates to the geographical location concept hierarchy where we have cities as a part of counties, which are parts of states or provinces, which are parts of countries. The Linnean binomial scientific classification

---

[14] Would most of us agree with this contention? Certainly, a straight line provides a simplicity of representation, and it also provides a wealth of techniques based on relatively simple mathematical concepts that we began to learn in high school, but a pertinent question to ask at this point would be whether the straight line is the *most appropriate* model. Note that we avoided the use of the word "best"!

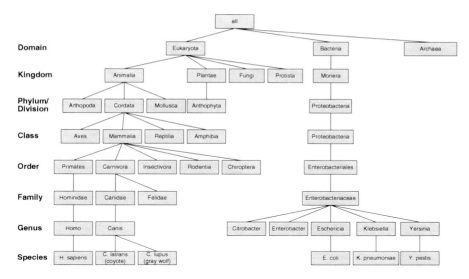

Fig. 2.3   Concept hierarchy fragment for Linnean binomial classification system

system also provides an example of a concept hierarchy, a fragment of which is illustrated in Fig. 2.3.

As we shall see in Chap. 3, our database schema will often implicitly contain many concept hierarchies through parent-child relationships.

Implementations of concept hierarchies will usually have a *total ordering*, or a *partial ordering* (also referred to as a lattice). A total ordering is probably most clearly seen by using the geographic location example referred to above. We may be interested in capturing information about the specific address (street and city), the state or province, postal code or zip code, and the country. We can easily see that there is an ordering where "street is within city, city is within state/province, state/province is within country." Using the standard relational operators, this is often written as "street < city < state/province < country." Here, we can see that each element on the left of the greater than symbol is completely contained within the element on the right of the greater than symbol. Our geographic location ordering is often physically implemented as a data *dimension*, which we discuss in more detail in Chap. 3.

Another dimension, ubiquitous to data warehouse environments, is the time dimension. This is a good example of a partial ordering. Consider that we typically think of time from some fragment of a second – say the millisecond – up to some larger interval – say the year. Our ordering would then be "millisecond < second < minute < hour < day < week < month < quarter < year."[15] However, if we look carefully, we can see that this is not a totally accurate ordering, since a week may well start in 1 month and end in the next. For this reason, we typically begin to break this

---

[15] This ordering covers almost all of the time intervals that *any* data environment would be looking for! Decades, centuries, millennia, and beyond are outside the scope of this book?!

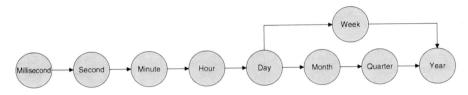

Fig. 2.4 Time concept hierarchy

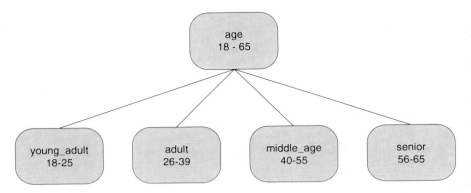

Fig. 2.5 Age concept hierarchy

ordering into several *partial* orders. The "millisecond < second < minute < hour < day" ordering does meet our definition of a total ordering. It is when we look at the "week < month < quarter" ordering that things change. A week may span months, but it may also span quarters. So we really have three options to link the day to the year: "day < year," "day < week < year," and "day < month < quarter < year." Diagrammatically, we can represent this set of hierarchies as shown in Fig. 2.4. Hierarchies such as this will often be embedded in the data environment.

We can create concept hierarchies for any given dimension or attribute (variable) by grouping values or discretizing the values. An example we use elsewhere in this book is that of age. For a large-scale, international, phase III clinical trial, we may have patients of every age between 18 and 65. We may not really be interested in discretely separating all 48 ages; we may instead be interested in patients who are *young adult* (18–25), *adult* (26–39), *middle age* (40–55), *senior* (56–65) (Fig. 2.5).

This is a particularly simple example of a concept hierarchy. We may want to define multiple hierarchies for a single attribute. For example, we may be interested in segmenting the age by decade (18–19, 20–29, 30–39, 40–49, 50–59, 60–65).

The key point is that concept hierarchies allow us to analyze data at multiple levels of abstraction. While we typically want to consider data at the lowest level of granularity, being able to abstract some elements of the data can be very valuable, if for no other reason than our being able to get a sense of where the data and model are leading us.

That being said, we also have to be careful and ensure that our abstractions make sense. While there are obviously similarities between all members of the *Enterobacteriaceae* family, for example, we must ask ourselves whether our model and results will make sense, or whether we should really be looking at the *Escherichia* genus or *E. coli* species.

2.19 Bias-Variance Decomposition

Any model we develop will have an inherently built-in error component inherently due to noise, missing data, assumptions, and other considerations we have discussed elsewhere. We therefore want to try and calculate the expected error of our model for a given target result (concept, pattern, correlation, etc.) and a given training dataset size. This expected error can be broken out into two parts: a bias component and a variance component.

One of the important factors of this decomposition is that it is valid for finite training sets and not just in the asymptotic, or limiting case. Thus, we can measure each of the terms experimentally.

The bias component measures how closely our model's results match the target. Specifically, we measure the average guess over all possible training sets of a given size and correlate these with the target. The variance component measures the variation of the model's output for different training sets of the specified size.

Unfortunately, trying to improve one of these components on its own often leads to frustration. One approach often used is to increase the state space for the model in order to reduce the bias component. This will often reduce the bias term but increase the variance term. For example, Kohavi (2000) shows a subset of data that has a reasonable fit using a quadratic and a perfect fit using a 9th order equation. Since every training set will inevitably generate a different 9th degree polynomial, the result will be a high variance component.

Models that fit a linear model will typically be biased for quadratic and higher-order models, but for several algorithms, regularization techniques can balance this trade-off.[16]

2.20 Advanced Techniques

We are going to take a short sidebar and introduce two concepts that some readers may be familiar with, but which we'll return to later in the text. For this reason, it is safe to skip this section.

---

[16] We will touch upon this subject a little further in later chapters, but a full consideration is outside the scope of this book. The interested reader may find Kohavi (2000) or Duda (2001) valuable starting points for a further understanding.

However, *principal component analysis* (PCA) and *Monte Carlo* strategies provide good illustration into how we can incorporate tools, techniques, and concepts from other disciplines to help us in our analysis efforts.

These two techniques are only illustrations. There are myriad other techniques, some of which we explore in this text, that provide novel solutions using novel approaches. This is one of the exciting things about data mining, and the reader is strongly encouraged to keep abreast of research endeavors of this dynamic field. You never know when a technique used in a novel way might be just what you are looking for.

2.20.1 *Principal Component Analysis*

Principal component analysis (PCA) is a valuable statistical technique which is used in a wide variety of fields and is a common technique for finding patterns in high-dimensional data and to express the data so as to highlight their similarities and differences.

High-dimensional data can be a challenging analytical problem since we do not have the luxury of a visual representation to help us. But using PCA to find patterns subsequently helps with this problem since once patterns have been identified, we can reduce the number of dimensions (compress the data) without losing information.[17]

Given a set of data, we can use the following process to perform PCA:

1. Subtract the mean from each data dimension.
2. Calculate the covariance matrix for each pair of dimensions.
3. Calculate the eigenvectors and eigenvalues for the covariance matrix.
4. Order the eigenvectors by eigenvalue (largest to smallest) to give the principal components.
5. (Elect to) ignore components with small eigenvalues (loss of information **should** be minimal).
6. Derive the new data set.

2.20.2 *Monte Carlo Strategies*

Any reader familiar with Monte Carlo strategies will probably be wondering why we would describe an advanced technique at this point in the text. We will be considering Monte Carlo strategies in significant depth later in this book, but introduce and illustrate the concept here for completeness and because it provides a good example of how some of these more advanced stochastic techniques are providing tremendous value in the analysis of life science data through their ability to provide a modeling framework, allowing simulation of physical systems.

---

[17] This is particularly useful in image management.

The nondeterministic nature is typically apparent through the use of random numbers[18] as input to the methods. In addition to this, these methods are characterized by repetition of the algorithm – often a large number of repetitions – and a (very) large number of calculations. These characteristics make them well suited to the computer environment. One factor that has made such algorithms very attractive in many areas of scientific research has to do with their relative efficiency, when compared to other methods, as the number of dimensions increases.

For readers interested in a little more detail, please see the box below. Those readers not interested in further explanation of the theory at this time may skip the box without a loss of understanding.

In data mining, and in scientific disciplines in general, our region of interest will often be a high-dimensional space, along with some target function within that space. Mathematically, we often model this as the computation of an integral, I:

$$I = \int_{S_d} f(x)\mathrm{d}x,$$

where S_d is our space with dimension d, and f is the function we are interested in.

However, such integrals may not always be easy to solve, and so we undertake to use some computational techniques to compute an estimate for I, denoted by $\hat{I}$. A prerequisite for this is being able to select independent and identically distributed random samples from our dataset. Using the *law of large numbers*, which states that the average of a large number of such random variables with common mean (and finite variances) will tend to their common mean, we can obtain an estimate as close to the real value as we like by increasing the number of iterations we perform.

Where problems exist that involve large degrees of freedom, or where there is significant uncertainty in the inputs, this class of method has shown itself to be particularly valuable. For example, the *cellular Potts model* is a model that simulates the collective behavior of cellular structures (Graner and Glazier 1992 #142).

Monte Carlo methods have been successfully applied to many areas both within the scientific discipline and without. Areas include molecular simulation, inference in population genetics, finding motif patterns in DNA, risk in business – especially in the insurance industry – as well as being very important in disciplines such as computational physics and physical chemistry. Other areas include graphics, modeling light transport in multilayered tissues (MCML), finance, reliability engineering, protein structure prediction, modeling transport of current carriers in

---

[18] Really, pseudorandom numbers.

semiconductor research, contaminant behavior in environmental science, molecular modeling, counter-pollution models, simulation of atomic clusters, computer science, movement of impurity atoms and ions in plasmas, and particle physics. Their use in computational mathematics has been varied, such as in primality testing (Rabin's algorithm (Rabin 1980 #143)). In addition, Monte Carlo methods have been used to help with the missing data problem.

We include a brief description of a very widely known experiment – "Buffon's needle" – that illustrates the basic ideas of Monte Carlo strategies.[19] In this experiment, a needle of some predetermined length l is dropped onto a flat surface that contained a square grid with spacing D, where $D > l$. Under ideal conditions, the probability of the needle intersecting one of the lines is $\frac{2l}{\pi D}$. If we let the proportion of times that the needle has intersected a line in n throws to be denoted by $p(n)$, we can compute an estimated value forπ, denoted by $\hat{\pi}$ to be

$$\hat{\pi} = \lim_{n\to\infty} \frac{2l}{p(n)D}.$$

As the above equation illustrates, and the previous discussion highlights, generating random samples from our probability distribution is a fundamental step in using Monte Carlo methods.

As an illustration, let us generate an estimate for the value of π. This is a very widely used, simple example of a Monte Carlo method and can be found in many places in the Internet. If we wish to calculate a value for π, we can use a circumscribed unit circle within a square and model the algorithm below using the whole circle. However, we can simplify our model a little by considering only a single quadrant, with radius r, inside a square of radius r.

If we were to throw darts at the figure, we can see that

$$\frac{\#\text{darts in quadrant}}{\#\text{darts in sqaure}} = \frac{\text{area of quadrant}}{\text{area of square}}$$

Or, from geometry,

$$\frac{\#\text{darts in quadrant}}{\#\text{darts in sqaure}} = \frac{\frac{1}{4}\pi r^2}{r^2} = \frac{\pi}{4}$$

which gives us

$$\pi = 4\frac{\#\text{darts in quadrant}}{\#\text{darts in sqaure}}$$

We can implement this algorithm very simply and effectively, as the following R function shows.

---

[19] Louis Leclerc Comte be Buffon, 1777.

```
piHat <- function(N) {
# N <- 1000
x <- runif(N)
y <- runif(N)
idx <- x^2 + y^2 <= 1.00000000000000000
piHat <- length(which(idx))/N*4 # estimate of pi
plot(x,y,main=piHat)
points(x[idx], y[idx], col='red')
sprintf("Estimate of pi = %.9f after %d iterations", piHat, N)
}
```

The parameter N is the number of observations which should be used for generating random values from the uniform distribution (`runif`). Running this function for four values provides the following output:

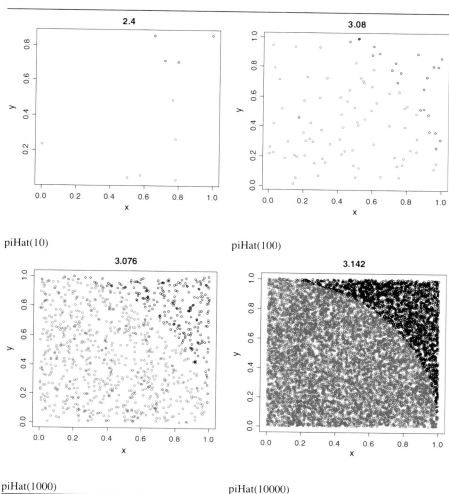

piHat(10)   piHat(100)

piHat(1000)   piHat(10000)

The above examples also illustrate one of the key attributes of Monte Carlo methods: a large number of repetitions are often necessary to generate good estimates. Commenting out the plot and points functions in piHat provides the following estimates for a number of different values of N:

```
> piHat(10)
[1] "Estimate of pi = 3.600000000 after 10 iterations"
> piHat(100)
[1] "Estimate of pi = 3.320000000 after 100 iterations"
> piHat(1000)
[1] "Estimate of pi = 3.024000000 after 1000 iterations"
> piHat(10000)
[1] "Estimate of pi = 3.162400000 after 10000 iterations"
> piHat(100000)
[1] "Estimate of pi = 3.140360000 after 100000 iterations"
> piHat(1000000)
[1] "Estimate of pi = 3.141168000 after 1000000 iterations"
> piHat(10000000)
[1] "Estimate of pi = 3.141554800 after 10000000 iterations"
```

2.21   Some Introductory Methods

Now...back to our program already in progress....

To conclude this chapter, we highlight some simple methods that provide surprisingly good results even though the methods are very simple. In this section, just as was the case above, we'll introduce them, but go into more detail later in the text.

These techniques provide a good heuristic for any analysis effort: using as simple a technique as possible has many benefits. Often the simplest approaches provide not only the valuable outputs in their own right but also a mechanism for targeting subsequent mining activities. This is not to be exhaustive by any means, but simply an attempt to introduce techniques that are widely used and which are typically some of the first to be encountered.

2.21.1   The 1R Method

The 1R (for 1-rule) method outlined in (Witten and Frank 2005) considers a single attribute in each instance of our dataset and develops rules based upon this categorization.

The way in which this method works is to look at a single attribute and count the number of times that each value, or class of values, occurs. Assign the most frequent (class) value to this attribute (as the default) and then calculate the error as being the number of times the attribute has a value other than the most frequent value. Repeat this for each attribute and then select the rules with the smallest error rates.

For each attribute in our dataset
    For each value of the attribute
        Count the number of times each value (class) occurs
        Assign the most frequent value (class) to the attribute
        Calculate the error rate as the count of all other values
    Select the rule(s) with the smallest error rates

Consider the following table of (made-up) data:

Organism	Compound	MIC	Interpretation[20]	Safety	Efficacy
SP001001	C00100101	2.0	I	Medium	Yes
SP001001	C00100102	1.0	S	High	Yes
SP001001	C00100103	4.0	R	Low	No
SP001002	C00100101	1.0	S	High	Yes
SP001002	C00100104	0.5	I	Medium	No
SP001003	C00100101	2.0	I	Medium	Yes
SP001003	C00100102	2.0	I	Medium	Yes
SP001003	C00100103	0.125	S	High	Yes
Sp001003	C00100104	0.25	S	High	Yes

When there are equal numbers of values that can be selected as the assignment (i.e., where there are an equal number of errors), we randomly make a choice. For the above example dataset, we will classify on "efficacy," and the rules we define, with the smallest error rates, are as follows:

Attribute	Rules	Errors	Total errors
Safety	High → yes	0/4	1/9
	Medium → yes	1/4	
	Low → no	0/1	

The "rules" column shows the default (majority) value. In the first case, a "safety" value of "high" maps to an efficacy value of "yes" more often than any other value. The same is said for the other two rules. The "errors" column then displays the number of times that the rule **does not** occur; for the "medium → yes" rule, this is once (row 5).

---

[20] This table contains example microbiological data where the interpretation is determined according to the breakpoints issued by the FDA and/or CLSI for a particular organism-compound combination in a given issuance period (typically a year).

2.21.1.1   Missing Values

For missing values, we can often look to the class of values and add a value which corresponds to missing data, thus explicitly incorporating it into our dataset, while similarly partitioning the attribute's value domain. This can be immensely valuable as we can immediately see what impact, if any missing values have.

Consider a dataset where the cholesterol level is not provided for several patients, and for the rest, we have nominal values of critical, very high, high, normal, and low. Adding the nominal value "missing" now gives six different values for the attribute.

Using the 1R method, we may find that "missing" forms a significant number of errors in our algorithm. What should we do? In the extreme, what do we do in the event that this is the most frequent value?

We can also consider our dataset *excluding* any instances with missing values. Oftentimes, performing the analysis by including and then excluding such instances will provide us with significant insight into the dataset itself since we may find that the missing data as little to no impact on our analytical results. However, the converse could also be true.

An alternative would be to look at the attribute's domain of values and assign missing values to one of the existing values rather than create an additional one. Using our cholesterol value domain above as an example, we could assign the value "normal" to our missing data. Obviously, this is dangerous since assigning such a value must be done with a complete understanding of its impact. Would we arbitrarily inflate the number of people with "normal" values? The answer is a definite yes if we are counting. However, for identifying patterns, we may find this a valuable technique.[21]

2.21.1.2   Numeric Data

Although not explicitly identified above, the 1R method provides most of its value when dealing with discrete data values which can be categorized rather than dealing with (raw) numeric data. However, numeric data can be converted to nominal data to maximize the value of this method.

One way of doing this is to use the concept of discretization. Consider a dataset where we have captured the patient's age. We may have a dataset as follows, where the yes/no values indicate whether therapy was considered successful at the test of cure encounter.

22	24	27	29	31	34	37	41	42	49	55
yes	no	yes	yes	yes	no	no	yes	no	no	no

---

[21] We introduce this idea here but will return to it at different times in this book as its value waxes and wanes with the different techniques we consider.

We now place a breakpoint in the data. The most intuitive way is to place a breakpoint in wherever the class changes, as follows:

22	24	27	29	31	34	37	41	42	49	55
yes	no	yes	yes	yes	no	no	yes	no	no	no

which produces a total of six categories in this example. We can then place a breakpoint midway between each pair delimiting a category change. However, this would cause a problem if we had two patients, each aged 34, one of whose therapy was successful, whereas the other was unsuccessful. In such cases, we can move the breakpoint up to the next partition (between ages 34 and 37) and consider a single partition with a mixture of outcomes.

However, this is not the only approach we can take. For many of these issues, we must consider the dataset in question and the objective of our analysis; a different approach may be more appropriate.

2.21.2   Decision Trees

Decision trees are arguably one of the most widely used techniques in data mining. In many disciplines, we are familiar with the technique of "dividing and conquering" as a means of decomposing a problem into increasingly simple subcomponents until we reach a point at which each component can now be (easily) solved. A natural way to represent such decomposition is a tree structure.

Each *node* in our tree structure represents the testing of an attribute and is usually a test of the attribute with a constant value. For example, we may have a node in our tree that tests a patient's cholesterol level against the upper recommended value of 200 mg/dL (Tietz 1995) and branch based upon whether the patient's value is above this value or not.[22] We can continue to build our tree by introducing further subnodes to continually refine our tree until we reach a level containing *leaf nodes*, each of which gives a classification to all instances which reach this node. In the simplest case, this classification is a single classification, but as we shall see later, this can also be a set of classifications or a probability distribution over all the possible classifications which reach this node. Consider our naïve example of comparing a patient's cholesterol against the upper normal range value (Fig. 2.6).

We see here that we classify a patient as either "normal" or "at risk." Any new patient data that we receive, previously unknown, would be processed through the successive nodes of the tree, being tested at each level, until it reaches the leaf node which classifies it according to the classification of the leaf node itself.

---

[22] As we shall see later, more complex trees can test two attributes against each other, or even use functions to effect these tests.

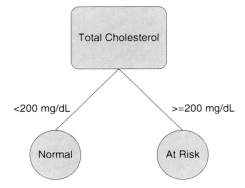

Fig. 2.6 Simple decision tree

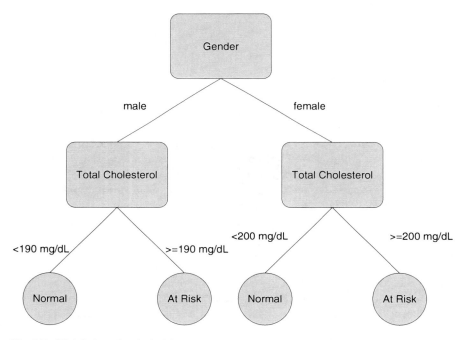

Fig. 2.7 Slightly less simple decision tree

The decision tree shown in Fig. 2.6 provides very little classification, and in real life, we would need to consider (many) more patient demographics to more closely model reality. The next step might be to consider that test result reference ranges are known to be different by gender, ethnicity, and age, for example. We might, therefore, expand our decision tree by introducing gender, to give us the tree shown in Fig. 2.7.

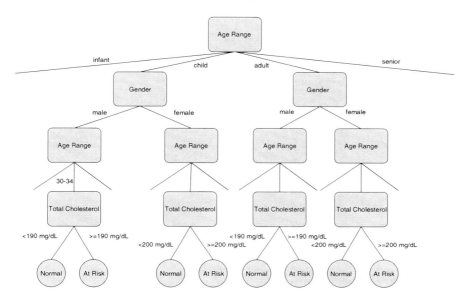

Fig. 2.8 Still simple decision tree

Here, we have decided that gender is the first decision point we need. Based upon the gender, we then test the total cholesterol value to classify the individual.[23] We see that our tree now contains a copy of the "total cholesterol" subtree. This often occurs, and we shall see how to better deal with this situation when we return to decision trees in more detail later.

In each node in our example trees above, we have had binary decision points. Trees can be generated with more than two branches. However, complexity also increases. If the attribute being tested is a numeric attribute, the test is usually a "greater than value"[24] type of test, giving a binary split as we have seen in our example. We may also use a three-way split, which has a number of additional valuable characteristics. We shall return to this later. Testing using the "greater than value" may not be valuable, especially at the initial levels of the tree, and we will often subset the attribute's values. For example, we may not be interested, initially, in looking at a very granular breakdown of a person's age, but may instead be interested to know if they are an infant (<2 years), child (2–16 years), adult(17–65 years), or senior (>65 years), where the parenthetical values represent our model of these age groups. In this case, a 34-year-old would be classified in the upper levels of the tree as being "adult." However, when we look at that patient's cholesterol level, we may use the partitioning in (Tietz 1995) (page 130) which has separate reference ranges for each 5-year increment in age. In such a case, the age would be tested once to partition into infant, child, adult, and senior and once again to put the patient into the 30–34 age range for our test. Thus, numeric attributes are often tested multiple times in a decision tree (Fig. 2.8).

---

[23] Note that we have changed the upper limit value for males. This is for illustration purposes only and should not be construed as of any medical significance.

[24] This is meant to stand for the group of binary tests which include $<$, $>$, $<=$, $>=$.

If the attribute being tested is a nominal attribute, the number of branches is typically the same as the possible values of the attribute. This may not be valuable, especially at the initial levels of the tree, and we will often subset the attribute's values.

Figure 2.8 illustrates another factor of decision trees which must be considered when designing the tree itself. We can see that subtrees are cloned in various places in the tree. These arise from two particular cases. The first relates to the *order* in which we decide to test attributes. In the above example, we elected to begin by testing the patient's age. Since we decided to partition the age into gross ranges first, we had to test it a second time further down the tree (as we described above). By choosing a different ordering, we may either change/reduce the cloned subtrees or even eliminate them together, although in real-world cases, this latter case is exceptional. The second case arises as a result of the *granularity* we are trying to achieve. Using the age test once again, is it really important to obtain the level of granularity greater than the infant/child/adult/senior partitioning?

An obvious problem with decision trees relates to missing values. If the dataset being studied is missing gender, for example, how do we handle the gender test in Fig. 2.7? If we cannot consider the missing value as a separate attribute value in its own right, we should process it in a special way rather than treating it as just another possible value for that attribute. Consider the age we decided to include in our decision tree of Fig. 2.8. What could we do if the age is missing for a number of patients? If we know something about the patients as a whole, we can use this information. For example, in a phase I clinical trial, we know that the patients will typically be healthy volunteers. We can make some assumptions about this type of demographic, especially if we are primarily looking for healthy adults – the 18–45 age range seems to be particular popular at the time of writing, according to radio advertisements for clinical trials. Using this information, we could use a Gaussian probability function to "replace" the missing information. Alternatively, we could use another branch at the decision point. We shall return to both of these in more detail later.

Before we leave our discussion on decision trees, there is one limitation that needs to be highlighted that relates to using classification rules (see below) to generate a decision tree. Modeling the disjunction that is implicit in classification rules in a rule set is not a straightforward activity. We will discuss this further in the next section.

2.21.3 Classification Rules

In many respects, classification rules can be considered a direct alternative to decision trees. They are certainly, justifiably popular, and it is possible to move between these two techniques.

Classification rules can most easily be thought of as "if…then…" rules where we have an *antecedent* that specifies the preconditions for the rule to *fire*, and the *consequent* (or conclusion) which specifies the conclusion of the rule – the results of it firing. Using the same model used to create the decision tree in Fig. 2.8, we might first begin with a classification rule as follows:

```
if total_cholesterol > 200 then risk_factor = high
```

In the above, we conclude that the variable `risk_factor` should be given the value of "high" if this rule fires. Instead, we can also define a probability distribution over the classes covered by this rule, as we shall see later.

The precondition section of a classification rule will often include several clauses that are logically ANDed together or may even be more complex logical expressions. For example, we might change our classification rule above to include gender as follows:

```
if gender = male and total_cholesterol > 200

    then risk_factor = high

if gender = female and total_cholesterol > 190

    then risk_factor = high
```

We have now developed two classification rules, one for each gender. For a rule to fire successfully, all of the clauses in the precondition must be true. The two rules illustrate another facet of classification rules: the *rule base* containing the set of rules (in our current example, the two rules) considers the rules to be ORed together. That is if any one of the rules applies, the class (or probability distribution) in the consequent is applied to the instance of our dataset we are currently considering. As the rule base grows in its number of rules, problems of conflict between the rules and circular dependencies become apparent.

We indicated earlier that we can easily move between decision trees and classification rules; this is true. In fact, we can usually create a classification rule for each leaf of the tree. The antecedent for each such rule will include a condition for every node on the path from the root of the tree to that leaf node. While the rules thus defined are unambiguous in our rule base, the rules tend to be more complex than necessary. However, we can easily prune the rules to remove redundant tests. One advantage of developing classification rules from decision trees is that execution of the rules can occur in any order.

Reversing the process – creating a decision tree from a set of classification rules – is not quite as straightforward as going from decision trees to classification rules. The primary reason for this has to do with our statement that the rules are considered to be ORed together (disjunction). This requires us to do make some decisions and perform some extra work to ensure that the resulting tree operates correctly. Let us consider a simple abstract example to illustrate this. Let us assume our rule set contains the following rules:

if a and b then X
if c and d then X

Logically, the above rules are equivalent to

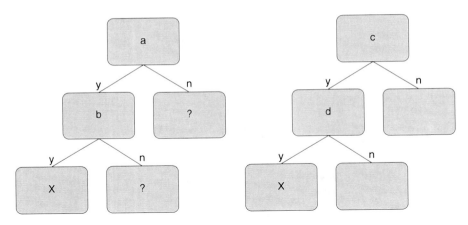

Fig. 2.9 Two subtrees in a disjunction relationship

if (a and b) or (c and d) then X

That is, if *a* and *b* are both true, *or* if *c* and *d* are both true, then we can validly make the conclusion that X is true.

But in order to accommodate this disjunction, we need to select a test for the root node of this tree fragment, and, as we shall see, we end up having to replicate part of the tree represented by these rules. This is known as the *replicated subtree problem*. Let us begin by visualizing the two rules we defined above in terms of individual subtrees (Fig. 2.9).

Since our intent is to combine these two subtrees into a single subtree, our first issue is to select the test for the root of the subtree. Intuitively, selecting to test "a" or "c" would seem to be a good starting point. Without loss of generality, we'll choose to test "a" first. In doing so, our subtree looks exactly like the left-hand tree in Fig. 2.9. Where does the right-hand subtree fit in? It needs to be replicated in two places – shown in Fig. 2.9 by "?" – to provide a complete definition of our disjunction. The complete tree is shown in Fig. 2.10.

This problem can quickly cause it to become impractical to convert rules into decision trees. Imagine, for a moment that instead of two sets of binary conditions leading to a single conclusion, we have 3, or 4, or .... Now envision our rules having 3, 4, or even more conditions on the left-hand side!

Rules, themselves, have a long history in knowledge elicitation, artificial intelligence, and mathematical logic. We can envision each rule has holding some piece of valuable knowledge, and adding new rules will not necessarily perturbate the existing knowledge base. However, there is an issue that can arise from here that we need to consider: does adding new rules cause cycles or inconsistencies to occur? When our rule bases are small, we can visually inspect them to ensure that such cycles do not occur, but as our rule bases grow, such cycles may not be obvious.

A second problem that arises is due to the order in which rules are executed. Some environments will execute the rules in the order in which they are entered in the rule base. This leaves the problem of ordering to us. Other environments consider the ordering of the rules to be immaterial. Both cases highlight challenges that we need to be careful of when we develop our rule bases. In the former case, if

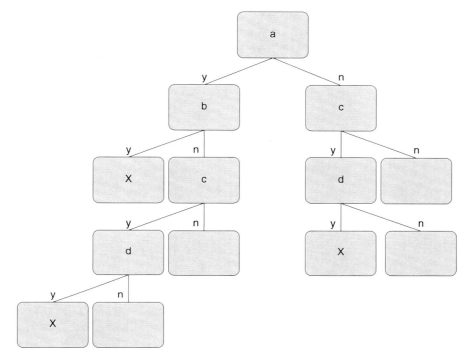

Fig. 2.10   Replicated subtree problem for two instances

we do not have the optimal order,[25] then we need to consider very carefully how we handle this issue at the validation stage or by reordering our rules to see how the ordering affects the conclusions. In the latter case, the engine itself can cause very different conclusions to be drawn based upon how it executes the rules. Again, we need to ask how we can determine the optimal results. One approach might be to execute the rules multiple times and average them in some way.

2.21.4   Association Rules

The only significant differences between an association rule and a classification rule are that an association rule can actually predict an attribute rather than just the class and that association rules are not intended to be used as a group (our rule base) in the way that classification rules are. This ability to predict an attribute by extension also means that we can predict combinations of attributes also.

---

[25] Here, optimal is not simply from a performance standpoint but also relates to our needing to draw the optimal conclusions from our model.

Association rules define or express the regularities underlying the dataset. For this reason, each rule predicts a different thing. Since we are *associating* two or more facets of our dataset together – the regularity – the number of association rules that can be elicited from even a small dataset can quickly become huge.

Let us consider our patient dataset.[26] From our first example dataset, we can identify the following association rules:

```
if (weight/(height²) > 39 then weight_category = extreme_obesity

if (weight/(height²) > 29 and (weight/(height²) < 40  then

    weight_category = obese

if (weight/(height²) > 24 and (weight/(height²) < 30  then

    weight_category = overweight

if (weight/(height²) > 18 and (weight/(height²) < 25  then

    weight_category = normal

if (weight/(height²) < 19 then weight_category = underweight
```

Let's pause to illustrate a challenge with association rules. As we can see from the above sets of rules, we have defined rules for a very small part of our dataset. In fact, the above five rules really identify a single conclusion, the body mass index. This situation or generating a large number of rules from a very small set of attributes (not the data itself) is common and can lead to an unwieldy set of rules if we are not very careful. We can use several techniques to help us to manage association rule, and we now consider some of the more common.

In order to keep the rules we elicit manageable, we define two characteristics:

- The *coverage* (a.k.a. *support*) of a rule is the number of instances from our dataset that the rule predicts correctly.
- The *accuracy* (a.k.a. *confidence*) of the rule is the number of instances from our dataset that the rule predicts correctly as a proportion of the number of instances to which it applies.

Suppose we have a rule in our set that can be applied to 50 instances in our dataset (its coverage or support) and would predict 10 of those instances correctly. We can calculate its accuracy to be 20%. The question we next need to ask is whether this is valuable or not. As we shall see later, we can set minimum values for these two characteristics and eliminate association rules which do not meet these criteria. For example, if our dataset contains 1,000,000 instances and a particular set of rules only applies to 50 instances and only correctly predicts 10 of those

---

[26] We will have cause to consider a dataset that needs to be more complex than some of our other datasets in order to provide some meaningful output; we will use our patient dataset for this purpose. See Appendix C for a full description of the dataset and for example data.

instances, we may eliminate this rule from our association set on the grounds that its
applicability is too limited for our current purposes.

Association rules, as shown above, do provide a lot of value, but they need to be
identified, and even crafted, carefully. For example, our set of association rules for
body mass index would probably be eliminated on the grounds that they are really
calculations that we might elect to implement as an additional attribute in our
dataset instead. This would then allow us to use them across a wider range of
applications. We could then use that attribute, together with other information to
form a different set of rules, such as those shown below.

```
if weight_category = extreme_obesity then risk_factor = 8.0

if  weight_category = obese           then risk_factor = 4.0

if weight_category = overweight       then risk_factor = 2.0

if weight_category = normal           then risk_factor = 1.0

if weight_category = underweight      then risk_factor = 2.0
```

Here, we have assigned a factor that can be used elsewhere in our rule set.

So far, we haven't discussed conjunctions ("and") and disjunctions ("or") in our
rule set, but these natural extensions, along with negation ("not"), can expand the
value of association rules. For example, National Football League players are more
often than not in a higher than normal weight category, but it is questionable
whether they would have a higher risk factor because of their BMI value. We
might change the above rules as follows:

```
if weight_category = extreme_obesity and activity_factor < 8

    then risk_factor = 8.0

if  weight_category = obese and activity_factor < 7

    then risk_factor = 4.0

if weight_category = overweight and activity_factor < 6

    then risk_factor = 2.0

if weight_category = normal and activity_factor > 2

    then risk_factor = 1.0

if weight_category = underweight and activity_factor > 2

    then risk_factor = 2.0
```

This is one of the reasons why our rule sets can become much larger, very quickly. We now need to ask ourselves whether or not the conditions not included in the above rule set are important or not. For example, just using the first rule:

```
if weight_category = extreme_obesity and activity_factor < 8

      then risk_factor = 8.0
```

The condition not covered is

```
if weight_category = extreme_obesity and activity_factor >= 8

      then risk_factor = ???
```

(Note that the other condition, where `weight_category != extreme_obesity`, is covered by other rules.) Is it important for us to include this additional rule? Unfortunately, the answer is "that depends."

We can extend classification rules or association rules in some intuitively natural ways to increase their flexibility. One such way is to introduce the concept of *exceptions* to the rules. We may, for example, discover that there is a relationship between a patient's total cholesterol and their LDL cholesterol such that if their LDL cholesterol is below a certain threshold, it reduces their risk.

```
if total_cholesterol > 200 then risk_factor = high

      except if ldl_cholesterol < ?? then risk_factor = moderate
```

Without this exception category, we would either misclassify the instance or would require additional rules, with the potential for causing other problems.

2.21.5 Relational Rules

The rules we have considered so far are called *propositional rules*,[27] but these are oftentimes insufficient for our needs. Such situations typically require us to be able to express the *relationships* between the instances in our dataset. For example, we may be interested in the relationship between weight and height. For these types of situations, we need more expressive rules.

Consider relating weight and height through the body mass index that we introduced in our discussion on association rules above. The formal definition of the BMI is

$$bmi = \frac{weight(kg)}{height^2(m^2)} \times 100$$
$$= \frac{weight(pounds)}{height^2(in^2)} \times 703.1$$

---

[27] The language in which we express such rules has the same expressive power as the propositional logic.

BMI tables exist all over the Internet.[28] From the above equation, or the tables, we can easily see a relationship between height and weight. We may be interested in expressing this type of relationship within our association rules. For example, we can say that

```
if height < 65 and weight > 150 then risk_factor = high
```

to represent a baseline, since it appears that a $5'$ $5''$ person is more likely to weigh more than 150 lb in today's society than not. Similarly, we might elect to include a rule as follows:

```
if height > 74 then risk_factor = undetermined
```

since there is some debate as to how effective the BMI measure is at the tails of the population and for athletes, etc., as we mentioned earlier. For the same reasons we discussed for association rules, we might therefore want to introduce rules that cover such cases. We can use activity factor attribute in our patient dataset for this purpose, in which case the relational rules will look very similar to our association rules.

2.21.6   Clustering

The intuitive concept of clustering is to group similar instances together. This allows us to simplify our dataset – especially since we will typically be dealing with vast amounts of data – for further processing. However, the challenge here relates to the fact that as soon as we start grouping similar instances together, we lose the fine granular details that make each instance distinct and unique. Further, we need to be careful about our definition of similarity since we can easily end up with too few clusters – meaning that we have too gross a definition of similarity – and lose too much detail. The conclusions we then draw will essentially be naïve, or too simplistic, on the one hand, or of little value on the other.

As we shall see later, clustering is a widely used technique and has a rich history in the machine-learning community where *unsupervised learning* algorithms have been successfully implemented to uncover *hidden patterns* in data. This fundamental capability of clustering, and other techniques, of being able to elicit hidden patterns from data makes it a very important data mining technique and is an area of active research in machine learning, pattern recognition, and statistics, to name a few.

In data mining, the large amounts of data, and the typically large number of attributes for each instance of data, introduce some further complications in many techniques, and this is certainly the case with clustering techniques.

---

[28] For example, http://www.nhlbi.nih.gov/guidelines/obesity/bmi_tbl.htm

The computational constraints on how to deal with eliciting hidden patterns within large sets of data have resulted in many efficient algorithms being developed through such research, especially in the machine-learning discipline.

Clustering algorithms come in many flavors including:

- Hierarchical methods (agglomerative, divisive)
- Partitioning methods (relocation, probabilistic, k-means, density-based)
- Grid-based methods
- Constraint-based methods
- Machine learning (gradient descent, evolutionary)
- Scalable clustering
- High-dimensionality data

2.21.7   Simple Statistical Measures

We introduce a number of basic statistical measures that are widely used in data mining in the table below without significant explanation since statistical analysis is the subject of a chapter of this book (Table 2.1).

These and other statistical measures provide a generalized toolkit for data mining. In fact, statistical analysis typically plays a primary role in any data-mining effort.

2.21.8   Linear Models

In many cases, accurate models can be developed where the relationship between the response and explanatory variables can be assumed to be a linear function of the parameters,

$$Y = X\beta + \varepsilon, \tag{2.1}$$

where β is a set of unobservable parameters and ε is a vector of "error" values with expected value of 0 and variance σ^2. Our objective is to then infer the values of β and ε, typically using *maximum likelihood* or *least squares*.

In cases of simple linear regression, where we have one explanatory variable and two parameters, the above equation reduces to

$$y = a + bx + \varepsilon.$$

Table 2.1 Simple statistical measures

Location (central tendency)	Mode: most common value Median: middle value Mean: $\bar{x} = \frac{\sum_{i=1}^{n} x_i}{n}$
Variation	Range: high–low Quartiles: Q1 (25%), Q2 (50%), Q3 (75%) Variance: $s^2 = \frac{\sum_{i=1}^{n}(x_i-\bar{x})^2}{n-1}$ / $\sqrt{\sum_{i=1}^{n}(x_i-\bar{x})^2}$ Standard deviation: $s = \sqrt{\frac{\sum_{i=1}^{n}(x_i-\bar{x})^2}{n-1}}$ z-score: $z = \frac{x_i-\bar{x}}{s}$
Confidence levels	Mean (>30 observations): $\bar{x} \pm z_C \frac{s}{\sqrt{n}}$ Mean (<30 observations): $\bar{x} \pm t_C \frac{s}{\sqrt{n}}$ Proportion: $p \pm z_C \sqrt{\frac{p(1-p)}{n}}$
Heterogeneity	Gini index: $G = 1 - \sum_{i=1}^{n} p_i^2$; normalized: $G' = \frac{G}{(k-1)/k}$ Entropy: $E = -\sum_{i=1}^{n} p_i \log p_i$; normalized: $E' = \frac{E}{\log k}$
Asymmetry or skewness	Skew: $\gamma_1 = \frac{m_3}{\sigma^3} = \frac{\frac{\sum (y-\bar{y})^3}{n}}{\sigma^3} = \frac{1}{n}\frac{\sum (y-\bar{y})^3}{\sigma^3}$ Measure of how long the tail of the distribution on one side or the other. $\gamma_1 < 0$ means the distribution skews to the left; $\gamma_1 > 0$ means a skew to the right
Kurtosis	Kurtosis: $\gamma_2 = \frac{m_4}{\sigma^4} - 3 = \frac{\frac{\sum (y-\bar{y})^4}{n}}{\sigma^4} - 3 = \frac{1}{n}\frac{\sum (y-\bar{y})^4}{\sigma^4} - 3$ Measure of "peakyness" (leptokurtotic) or "flat-toppedness" (platykurtotic) of the distribution. Normal distribution has $\gamma_2 = \frac{m_4}{\sigma^4} = 3$, hence the "−3" value
Hypothesis test	1. Specify the null hypothesis (e.g., $H_0 : \mu = \mu_0$) and the alternate hypothesis (e.g., $H_a : \mu > \mu_0$) 2. Select significance level (e.g., $\alpha = 0.05$) 3. Compute the test statistic (t or z) 4. Determine the critical value for t or z using $\frac{\alpha}{2}$ for two-sided tests 5. Reject the null hypothesis if the test statistic falls into the "reject H_0" region
Comparing (more than 2) groups	Categorical data: chi-square test Continuous data: one-way ANOVA
Comparing variables	Correlation coefficient (r): $r = \frac{\sum_{i=1}^{n}(x_i-\bar{x})(y_i-\bar{y})}{(n-1)s_x s_y}$

Maximum-likelihood estimation (MLE) is used to make inferences about the parameters of the underlying probability distribution for a given dataset and is very widely used across a multitude of scientific disciplines. We typically assume that the data is independent and identically distributed (iid) within a particular distribution, where the parameters are unknown. We then use MLE to create estimators for the unknown parameters.

For example, we may be interested in the weights of patients. We have a sample of our patient population, but not the complete population. We shall also assume that the weights are normally distributed,[29] but with a mean and variance currently unknown. We would now use MLE to determine the mean and variance for the specific $N(\mu, \sigma^2)$ by "fixing" the data and picking the distribution parameters that are "most likely" given the data.

We have already mentioned the fact that all data contains noise: even if we manage to keep all of our independent variables constant, the dependent variables (our outcomes) will still vary, and so, as we have already indicated, we need to estimate the distribution underlying the dependent variable(s). The method of *least squares* is another method for allowing us to estimate the parameters of the distribution.

Essentially, we want to find the best fit curve for our data, we can look at the "errors" of a given set of data, given a particular curve. That is, we can look at how large the offsets (or residuals) of our data values are given a particular curve.

Given a dataset $(x_1, y_1), ..., (x_n, y_n)$, we are interested in determining a function $f(x)$ that will be the best fit for our data. However, we assume that each point has an associated error value, $e_i = y_i - f(x_i)$, which we wish to minimize – ideally to 0. As we shall see later, we are actually looking for $f(x, a)$, where a is the set of parameters for the underlying distribution.

The Gauss-Markov theorem[30] proved that for a linear model where the errors have a mean of zero, with equal variances and which are uncorrelated to each other, the least squares method provides the best estimators for the underlying model.

2.21.9 Neighbors and Distance

Our intuitive definition of a *neighbor* is someone, or something, that is located near another. This simple concept is important in many areas of data mining, but especially so to the concept of *clustering*. Our concept of *neighbor* can be used to offer a measure of *similarity* between two instances or variables. During our high school education, we encountered the concept of Euclidean distance between two points. We can use this for illustration here also.[31] Consider the example where we are capturing patient age and weight, $(a_1, w_1), ...(a_n, w_n)$, for our patient population, and we have the resulting data (18, 110), (25, 121), (37, 145), (49, 178), (55, 187), (63, 176), (72, 169). We can plot this data to provide Fig. 2.11.

By simple visual inspection, we can see that the second data point (25, 121) is nearer to the first (18, 110) than to the third (37, 145). (Our ordering of the data points simply flows from left to right.) But it's not quite as obvious whether the sixth data

---

[29] As we have indicated, we are interested in making inferences about parameters of the *underlying* probability distribution. We thus need to be able to define which family of probability distributions the data is a part of. We will discuss this and other issues more fully in Chap. 6.

[30] Proven by Carl Friedrich Gauss in 1829.

[31] In fact, as we shall see later, the Euclidean concept of distance is used in many algorithms.

Fig. 2.11 Distance and
neighborhood

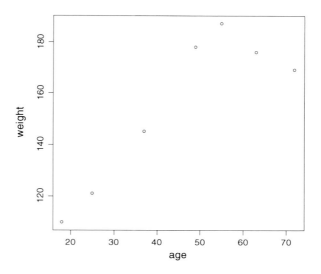

point (63, 176) is closer to the fifth (55, 187), or the seventh (72, 169), but we can use a very simple equation, found widely on the Internet, to compute a distance value.[32]

We italicized the words similarity and neighbor above. Intuitively, neighbor and distance have an important relationship, but the term neighbor needs a little more explanation and is, in many techniques, tied to the concept of clustering data points together, although not always. We'll treat these concepts much more formally, and in more detail, later in the books. For now, we'll provide a more informal discussion, illustrating with our two-dimensional data from above.

As in the real world, a neighbor is simply something that is close. Our distance measure allows us a means for determining how close two of our data points are, but it doesn't necessarily provide us with a means of determining how distant is "too distant." If the distance measure between two points A and B is 3, and the distance between A and C is 4, is the difference in distance significant? Obviously, without some context, we don't know. More often than not, the context will be relevant to the data we are studying, the models we use, the methods we are following, and the conclusions we are drawing. However, we can intuit some characteristics:

- Data points with smaller distance measures will likely be more similar to each other than those with larger distance measures (because the underlying data will have been used as input to our distance measure algorithm).
- Data points with smaller distance measures will likely be in the same neighborhood, whereas those with larger distances will more likely be in different neighborhoods (assuming our definition of a neighborhood).

---

[32] http://mathworld.wolfram.com/Distance.html, for example.

Fig. 2.12 Neighborhoods

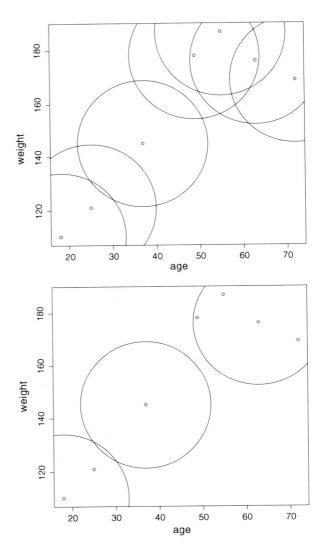

So in addition to our distance measure, the definition of the neighborhood is an integral part of our ability to accurately and effectively analyze our data. So how do we define our neighborhoods?

Simply, these will be dependent on our analysis and on your data; we will discuss this concept in detail later in the text. For now, we consider a neighborhood to be a localized area sized according to specific distance value. That is, we will consider anything with a distance value less than some limiting value d_{max}. This will give us circular neighborhoods for 2D data, spherical for 3D, and so forth.

Figure 2.12a shows our data overlaid by circles with an arbitrary radius of 15, from which we can see that there is a way in which we can separate the data points into three neighborhoods. Figure 2.12b depicts the same data, but with only the three neighborhoods highlighted.

We should make some observations about our separation of data into neighborhoods. The first is that we used a single parameter for our neighborhoods so that each one is the same size. This certainly simplifies some aspects of the model, but may not be pertinent. Second, we took an arbitrary size – really – which is obviously not appropriate in *any* analysis. It just worked for our illustration. But there is an important point this illustrates: what would happen if we received additional data elements that filled in some of the gaps in our data? How would, or should, our neighborhoods change? This brings us to a third point: we partitioned our data into three neighborhoods, or would have if we'd taken a slightly smaller radius and avoided the overlap between the first and second neighborhood: but how many is appropriate? The larger the number of neighborhoods, the more specific each is, and vice versa. These will also affect where new data is positioned, or how new data affects the regions previously defined.

2.22 Feature Selection

We now turn our attention to the topic of feature selection. Features and attributes are often used synonymously in the literature. We make the distinction so that features are those subsets of attributes that we, or our models, have selected and will use to make decisions. With this definition, we can see that our feature set will often be a subset of our attribute set. If we consider a specific data mining technique, this will almost always be the case, except in the most trivial of situations, since it is unlikely that we would want every attribute in our dataset to be used in any given situation. The question that we, therefore, need to ask is how do we select the appropriate attributes for the techniques and/or models we are considering? A corollary is how do we determine the *best* attribute(s) to use?

Later in this book, we discuss machine-learning techniques in detail. We will use these to illustrate an example. We will not define what a machine-learning system is, but leave the intuitive definition of a system where the learning is done by the model itself. Consider a simple machine-learning system that includes a decision tree component, such as the C4.5 system (see Appendix B). Since decision trees will select the most appropriate attribute to use to split the tree at any given point, it would seem intuitive that we should allow the system to select from as many attributes as possible. If we supply every attribute contained in our dataset, for example, then the decision tree learner *should* select the most appropriate at each point – correct?

Unfortunately, this isn't always the case. Witten (2005 #11) used an example for the C4.5 system and the effect of introducing a random binary attribute (populated by tossing an unbiased coin) into a dataset used by the system and suggested that the performance deterioration may be as much as 5–10% in the experiments performed. But why is this?

In the case of a decision tree, we are bifurcating based upon an attribute. As we drill down the tree, less and less data is available to us, and a random attribute could look better than any other attribute, and this problem increases the deeper we go down the tree.

The problem occurs with rule learning systems also, and for similar reasons: less and less data is used for the basis of decision-making, and so irrelevant attributes can have an overwhelming effect on the learning process. In general, the class of learning systems referred to as instance-based learning systems, which we describe later, typically works with what are called "local neighborhoods," and so irrelevant attributes can have a significant impact on their accuracy and effectiveness.

We mention in passing that there are models for which this issue does not arise: the naïve Bayes model does not suffer from this problem due to its assumption (and design) that all attributes are independent. It, however, suffers in other ways, which we describe later.

In our discussion so far we have concentrated on those attributes which can be classified as irrelevant. This is not the whole story, however: relevant attributes may have a similar impact. An example from Witten (2005 #11) again suggests that relevant attributes selected at the wrong point can lead to sparse datasets being used subsequently, thus affecting the capability of the model.

To overcome these issues, we typically include an attribute selection step in our process. By weeding out those attributes that are irrelevant, and to focus on only those attributes which are most relevant, we hope to be able to optimize our model. This activity of *reducing the dimensionality* of our data can have a tremendous positive impact on our model. It can also, however, be a challenge if we eliminate the wrong attribute. Later in this book, we describe the method of *principal component analysis* (PCA) that iteratively identifies the most important components of a dataset and allows us to reduce the dimensionality in a deterministic way. Reducing the dimensionality also allows us to have a more easily understandable and interpretable definition of our problem and conclusions since we have eliminated as many of the attributes as possible and can thus focus on only the most important attributes.

We can intuitively take two approaches to selecting the features of interest, which are described in the following sections.

2.22.1 *Global Feature Selection*

We define *global feature selection* as selecting the attributes we are interested in solely on the basis of the dataset under study and without any consideration of the approach(es) we will use to mine the data. This is sometimes referred to as *filtering* the data prior to feeding it into our models.

One of the first challenges we encounter with this method is to determine the relevance of any attribute we are considering for exclusion. This is fundamentally difficult because we have to understand the *relevance* of the attribute to the overall problem at hand. If we exclude consideration of how a particular method may define relevance in its learning phase, how can we be sure that we understand that attributes' relevance in the great scheme of things?

A second challenge is the one we have discussed at several points already – generalization. Since we are looking to exclude attributes, any system that separates the data out into different classifications will not be able to use those attributes. If we exclude no attribute, the system may end up separating every instance, or close to every instance, into its own partition in the solution space. If we exclude every attribute except one, the system will partition the instances into; however, many partitions map to the number of different values for that one attribute.[33] Whatever the model does during the learning (training) phase may lead to the overfitting issue we have already discussed. This global selection is, therefore, not as simple as might at first be thought. When we consider the issue of noise, the problem takes on a further nuance in that inconsistencies due to noise may result in the system overcompensating.

2.22.2 Local Feature Selection

We define *local feature selection* as selecting the attributes we are interested in with a focus on the methods we will be using to mine the data as well as the dataset itself. This is sometimes referred to as the *wrapper* method: the model(s) for mining is wrapped into the selection process. We should also mention at this stage that we might use methods that will *not* be used directly in our mining efforts to select features for methods which *will* be used. An example where this is very valuable to us is when we intend to use *nearest neighbor* methods. We will discuss these in more detail later in the book but introduce one characteristic of these models that makes them challenging to use. They are very susceptible to being biased by irrelevant attributes. To overcome this, other models, such as decision trees, can be used to remove irrelevant attributes and thus improve the performance of the nearest neighbor algorithm. Another approach we can use is to build a linear model and rank the attribute coefficients.

For the interested reader, Puuronen and Tsymbal (2001 #1035) has an interesting discussion on local feature selection in the context of classification, a topic we will return to later in this text. Ribeiro et al. (2010 #1037) considered this topic with specific emphasis on text clustering. Yijun (2010 #1038) described this challenge in the context of high-dimensional data analysis.

---

[33] We recognize that this is somewhat of a simplification because the classification method may still classify unique instances into the same class or may result in a smaller number of classifications than the number of discrete values for the single attribute.

2.23 Conclusion

We intentionally covered a wide range of topics in this chapter, many of which we shall return to in later chapters so that we can cover them in more detail. Our purpose in this chapter was to broadly introduce the wide range of challenges and opportunities which have to be considered in a data mining effort and to discuss various approaches we can take to mine our data. We can very quickly, and simply, begin to get a sense of our dataset by using a simple method such as 1R, or to begin looking for simple association rules, for example. In so doing, we can often see an effective path to pursue in order to uncover more and more value; an iterative approach that will serve us well.

How our dataset is represented can severely compromise which approaches we can use and how effective they are. Missing data and noise are two significant issues and need to be "eliminated" before we move forward. We have to be careful that our overt and subconscious decisions don't result in a model that is overfitted to the data we use for the learning stage and thus has reduced generalization. Selecting the attributes (features) which are most relevant, and defining relevance itself, is not a trivial exercise, but can be relieved by using some models to help.

A significant part of the effort involved in data mining actually occurs *before* we even get to the analytics phase: preparing our data for analysis by getting it in the correct format, cleaning up the noise and errors, and providing data that the techniques we choose to leverage can actually use should not be minimized. Effort we put in at this stage will save us pain and heartache later on.

We will build upon the concepts we have introduced in this chapter as we explore the various issues that arise from the underlying data architecture and how we might need to restructure it in order to more effectively elicit the hidden patterns we are striving to understand; the input and the transformations necessary to convert it from generated data to analyzable data; how we wish to represent the output for our users, customers, and downstream systems; and what are the most appropriate techniques for us to use as we leverage statistical and machine-learning methods, among others, to support our data mining goals.

References

Bellman RE (1961) Adaptive control processes: a guided tour. Princeton University Press, Princeton

Duda RO, Hart PE, Stork DG (2001) Pattern classification. Wiley, New York

Gallier JH (1986) Logic for computer science: foundations of automatic theorem proving, Harper & Row computer science and technology series. Harper & Row, New York

Graner F, Glazier JA (1992) Simulation of biological cell sorting using a two-dimensional extended Potts model. Phys Rev Lett 69:2014–2016

Han J, Kamber M (2006) Data mining: concepts and techniques. Morgan Kaufmann, San Francisco

Kohavi R (2000) Data mining and visualization. US Frontiers of Engineering

Puuronen S, Tsymbal A (2001) Local feature selection with dynamic integration of classifiers. Fundam Inform 47:91–117

Rabin MO (1980) Probabilistic algorithm for testing primality. J Number Theory 12:128–138

Ribeiro MN et al (2010) Local feature selection for generation of ensembles in text clustering. Neural Networks (SBRN), 2010 Eleventh Brazilian Symposium on. pp 67–72

Tietz NW (1995) Clinical guide to laboratory tests. W.B. Saunders Co., Philadelphia, pp xxxix, 1096

Tufte ER (1990) Envisioning information. Graphics Press, Cheshire

Tufte ER (1997) Visual explanations: images and quantities, evidence and narrative. Graphics Press, Cheshire

Tufte ER (2001) The visual display of quantitative information. Graphics Press, Cheshire

Witten IH, Frank E (2005) Data mining: practical machine learning tools and techniques. Morgan Kaufman, Amsterdam/Boston

Yijun S (2010) Local-learning-based feature selection for high-dimensional data analysis. IEEE Trans Pattern Anal Mach Intell 32:1610–1626

Chapter 3
Data Architecture and Data Modeling

Abstract Unless we have a good solid data repository, all the techniques in the world are of limited use. In this chapter, we focus on the data layer: what the primary repository types are that you can expect to encounter, specifically the relational database environment – an example model – and some of the issues you will have to deal with, such as with time and historical data. The primary purpose of this chapter is to set the scene for how we deal with the data issues that inevitably occur.

3.1 Introduction

Over the last 30 years, the *relational data model* as originally proposed by Edgar F. (Ted) Codd (1923–2003) (Codd 1970) has become the standard model for implementing physical data storage systems. While other models remain, the relational model is, by far and away, the most predominant model. Oracle™, IBM's DB2™, Microsoft Corporation's SQL Server™, and the open-source MySQL™ comprise a few of the most well-known products implementing this architecture. As of today, over 95% of the Fortune Magazine Fortune 1000™ companies use relational database management systems to implement their data architecture. For this reason, throughout this text, we assume that the relational model comprises a fundamental source for much of the data that will be used and therefore constitutes the foundation of the data architecture that we will describe.

Further, any individual analyzing data in corporate or research settings is highly likely to encounter the relational model in all its glory, and so we provide this short chapter in order to introduce some of the fundamental concepts underlying this ubiquitous technical infrastructure.

A full treatise on data modeling is beyond the scope of this book, and the reader is referred to a resource such as (Date 2004) for a complete treatise on the relational model and its implementation. This being said, we describe some of the fundamental concepts in this chapter to provide the reader with an entry point for further reading.

R. Sullivan, *Introduction to Data Mining for the Life Sciences*,
DOI 10.1007/978-1-59745-290-8_3, © Springer Science+Business Media, LLC 2012

We have also needed to consider a "standard" data architecture for our discussions and have selected a relational database-based, star schema data warehouse architecture as being a likely candidate for the data architecture implemented at your organization. This being said, organization-specific issues will have driven the physical implementation, and so there may be differences that you need to consider carefully.

Our primary test dataset, containing patient test result data, will be used throughout this chapter to build the model and support its inclusion into a relational database environment. Versions for Oracle and MySQL are available on the companion website with the relevant load scripts. We have elected to include both a widely used commercial implementation, using Oracle, along with an open-source version, using MySQL, in the belief that these two versions alone will provide a broad base of our readers with an implementation that they can use without a significant amount of configuration effort. Versions are also available for the R environment as an R package and for the Weka environment as an ARFF file.

To provide some context as to the importance of the underlying data architecture, consider the following quote:

> We now have unprecedented ability to collect data about nature...but there is now a crisis developing in biology, in that completely unstructured information does not enhance understanding – Sydney Brenner, 2003, BISTI conference

Heterogeneity of data models, conceptual schemata, and semantics pose a difficult, yet tractable problem for all data analysis efforts and require that we consider our architecture from the foundation up: how we structure our data repositories and ensure holistic semantics for our data will impact our ability to analyze and mine the data for the foreseeable future. At the very least, having to change this layer of our architecture will lead to complications and expense, but also to the possibility of error being introduced as we transition to one architectural model to another.

3.2   Data Modeling, a Whirlwind Tour

For most people, data modeling involves analyzing the data context of the subject under study, eliciting the persistent aspects, and developing a data model. The data model is usually represented as an entity-relationship diagram (ERD). Within this context, therefore, the data model is the conceptual representation of the data structures required by the application and which will be instantiated within a relational database management system (RDBMS). The data structures include the data objects (entities), associations between entities, and the rules which govern the operations on the objects. It is often useful to think of the data model as the analogous to an architect's blueprint for a building.

The ERD was first introduced by Peter Chen (1976) 30 years ago and is widely used as it correlates well to the relational model, allowing constructs from the ERD to be easily implemented in the relational model; it is simple and easy to understand, facilitating communication between specialists and nonspecialists, and can be used to implement the model in a particular RDBMS, even though it is system independent.

The ERD uses a number of concepts and diagrammatic conventions which are now described.

An *entity* is the principal data object about which information is to be collected within the system. These will typically be intuitive concrete or abstract concepts such as patient, study, test, test result, or investigator. To further classify an entity, an *independent* entity does not rely on another entity for identification, while a *dependent* entity does. An *associative entity* is a special type of entity that is used to reconcile a *many-to-many* relationship (see below). A *subtype entity* is used to define a *generalization hierarchy* where specialized types of an entity occur. For example, patient entity is a subtype of person entity.

Entities are described by *attributes* that contain the individual pieces of information we desire to collect. A patient entity may, for example, contain the patient's last name, first name, date of birth, subject number, randomization number, and gender. Values, such as 12/1/1976 for a date of birth are the values while the set of all possible values is referred to as its domain of values. Certain attributes provide a mechanism for (uniquely) identifying an entity instance and are called identifiers or keys. Each entity has one such key, the primary key, which is designated as the primary mechanism for uniquely identifying that entity instance. This key value may actually be propagated to other entities as a means for associating entities with each other through relationships.

Very few entities exist without associations to other entities. For example, a patient is enrolled on a study. In this example, there is an association between the patient entity and the study entity. Such associations are modeled using *relationships* between entities. A relationship can be classified by its degree, cardinality, direction, type, or instance, and different modeling methodologies will use different classification approaches.

The number of entities associated with a relationship is referred to as its *degree*. In general, a relationship can be an n-ary relationship (where *n* entities are involved), and the 2-ary and 3-ary cases are typically referred to as binary and ternary relationships. By far, the most common type of relationship is the binary relationship. Ternary relationships are usually decomposed into multiple binary relationships. A special case of the binary relationship is the recursive binary relationship. This is where there is a relationship from the entity to itself. For example, some laboratory tests are groups of other laboratory tests.

The cardinality of a relationship defines the number of occurrences of one entity in relation to the other. This is usually modeled using a generic *connectivity* measure – one or many – and a *cardinality* that identifies the actual number of instances of each of the entities involved in the relationship. When communicating relationships, we typically use the connectivity definitions of one-to-one, one-to-many, and many-to-many to describe the relationships with the definitions in Table 3.1.

Table 3.1 Relational entity types

One-to-one (1:1)	Relationship where at most one instance of entity A is associated with one instance of entity B	A person may only be enrolled in a single clinical trial at any point in time
One-to-many (1:M)	Relationship where at most one instance of entity A is associated with zero, one, or many instances of entity B	A patient may have 0, 1, or many specimens collected during a hospital stay
Many-to-many (M:M)	Relationship where zero, one, or many instances of entity A are associated with zero, one, or many instances of entity B	A specific specimen may contain more than one organism, and a specific organism may be found in more than one specimen

The connectivity of the relationship provides us with a mechanism for identifying its direction. The direction of a relationship goes from an originating entity (called the *parent entity*) to the terminating, *child entity*. For the 1:1 relationship, the parent is the independent entity; for 1:M relationship, the parent is the entity on the "1" end of the relationship; and for the M:M relationship, the parent is an arbitrary selection.

If the child entity in a relationship is also a dependent entity, the relationship is defined as an *identifying relationship*. If both entities are independent, then the relationship is defined as a *nonidentifying relationship*.

We further refine our relationships by designating whether or not the existence of one of the entities relies on the existence of the other. If an entity instance is necessary for it to be included in a relationship, then the relationship is defined as being a *mandatory* relationship. If this is not a necessary condition, then the relationship is said to be *optional*. For example, the relationship "every project has an individual designated as the project manager" would designate a mandatory relationship between the PERSON entity and the PROJECT entity. The relationship "each person may be assigned to a project" would designate an optional relationship.

The concept of a generalization hierarchy was identified earlier. This is a hierarchy of entities which share some attributes in common, but which also have some number of attributes which differ from each other. In this case, the common attributes can be *generalized* into a more abstract entity that is a *supertype* entity. An example of this is often seen when information about people is modeled. If we consider a study INVESTIGATOR and a study PATIENT, they will have a number of attributes in common that we can generalize to the PERSON supertype. INVESTIGATOR and PATIENT then become *subtypes*. Whenever we have a generalization hierarchy, subtypes are dependent entities.

Subtypes can either be mutually exclusive or overlapping. Other terms used for this categorization are disjoint or inclusive, respectively. In the former case, an instance of one subtype cannot be an instance of another; in the latter case, an instance of one subtype may also be an instance of another. In our above example hierarchy, INVESTIGATOR and PATIENT are mutually exclusive since an investigator instance would not also be allowed to simultaneously be a patient on that

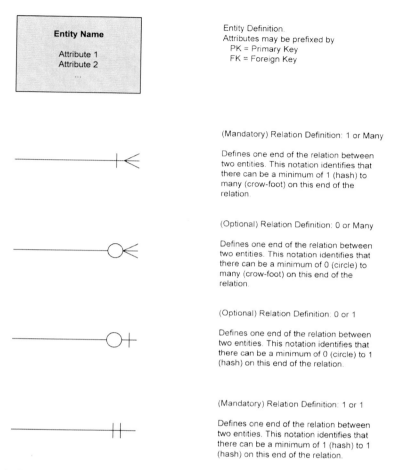

Entity Definition.
Attributes may be prefixed by
  PK = Primary Key
  FK = Foreign Key

(Mandatory) Relation Definition: 1 or Many

Defines one end of the relation between
two entities. This notation identifies that
there can be a minimum of 1 (hash) to
many (crow-foot) on this end of the
relation.

(Optional) Relation Definition: 0 or Many

Defines one end of the relation between
two entities. This notation identifies that
there can be a minimum of 0 (circle) to
many (crow-foot) on this end of the
relation.

(Optional) Relation Definition: 0 or 1

Defines one end of the relation between
two entities. This notation identifies that
there can be a minimum of 0 (circle) to 1
(hash) on this end of the relation.

(Mandatory) Relation Definition: 1 or 1

Defines one end of the relation between
two entities. This notation identifies that
there can be a minimum of 1 (hash) to 1
(hash) on this end of the relation.

Fig. 3.1 ERD notation

same study; thus the subtypes would be mutually exclusive. However, if we were modeling a university environment, we might have UNIVERSITY_EMPLOYEE and UNIVERSITY_STUDENT as subtypes of PERSON. In this case, an employee could also be a student at that university.

Generalization hierarchies may be nested: a subtype in one hierarchy may be a supertype in another. Note that the definition requires that all instances of the subtype must exist in the supertype. Also note that a subtype may be the parent in a relationship but not a child.

Entity-relationship diagram notation differs widely, with no single universally adopted notation. In this book, we use the notation informally known as the "crow's foot" notation, which is summarized in Fig. 3.1.

Let us look at a simple example to illustrate these concepts. Our model fragment for the specimens collected for patients during a clinical trial might be modeled as

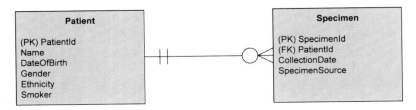

Fig. 3.2 Patient-specimen ERD fragment. This fragment includes only a subset of the attributes we would have in our complete model

the relationship where a PATIENT has many SPECIMEN instances. Pictorially, we would model the entities in Fig. 3.2.

The two entities, patient and specimen, are denoted by the rectangular boxes, and in our notation, the entity name is in boldface. The list of attributes is listed below. The relation between the two entities indicates that the patient entity **must exist** (the two hash marks on the relation) for a particular specimen instance. That is, each specimen instance must have an associated patient. However, the existence of a specimen is **optional** for any given patient (the circle), but if they exist, there can be many specimens for a patient. So we can see that we read the relation by taking one entity and the *opposite* end of the relation.

We should mention that the above notation is a mixture of both the logical and physical models that a data architect would use. Further, we have eliminated the additional information such as the data types and statistical data that is also available. We have found this approach to be a good communication vehicle for non-IT people.

An important concept in data modeling is that of data *normalization*. In normalization, we try to use guidelines to ensure that our model will not include data inconsistencies or update transaction anomalies. To accomplish this, we use a set of rules, each of which results in a specific *normal form* (NF), as shown in Table 3.2.

As we apply each rule, we move from one normal form to another, thus a model in 3NF is also in 2NF and 1NF. There are more specialized normal forms, such as domain-key normal form, but 5NF is usually more than sufficient for robust data models, and in many real-world implementations, 3NF models will often be encountered.

3.3   Qualitative and Quantitative Data

The majority of data we encounter in data mining is quantitative in nature. That is, it *measures* some quantity or amount. However, we sometimes come across data that does not offer a direct measurement, but instead *describes* something. To illustrate, the statement "Mary is 8 cm taller than Joe" offers a quantitative statement; "Mary is taller than Joe" is qualitative. We encounter this issue a lot in daily life. Words such as taller, shorter, darker, lighter, broken, and so forth are

Table 3.2 Normalization rules

1NF	**Eliminate repeating groups**
	Repeating groups of data abound in the real world. For example, consider the set of skills you have. In first normal form (1NF), we extract all such groups, creating a separate entity for each. Each table also receives a primary key. Using our person with a set of skills, for example, we would create a PERSON entity, containing information about the individual, and a SKILL entity, containing information about the subject of the skill. We would include the primary key from the PERSON entity in the SKILL entity as a foreign key so that the tables can be related to each other through a *join*
2NF	**Eliminate redundant data**
	Redundant data can occur in a couple of different ways: we can have the situation where an entity has a primary key made up of more than one attribute, but have some of the other data in that entity only be dependent upon one of the key attributes. We can also have non-key data replicated in the table; that is, data included in a column that is replicated for different key values. An example from our SKILL entity might be that we have the skill name replicated for each person that claims that skill. If we decide to reclassify the data, or if there is a skill claimed by only one person and they leave the company, we lose that information: a delete anomaly. To avoid such issues, we separate attributes that rely on all parts of the key from those which rely on a subset of the parts (and so on until we separate those attributes which only depend on single parts of the key). Each such subset is placed in a new entity with its own primary key
3NF	**Eliminate columns not dependent on the (primary) key**
	On occasion, we find that data contained in an entity which complies with 2NF which does not rely on the key identified for that entity. For example, our PERSON entity may also include company information (name, SIC, etc.) which does not depend on the primary key of the PERSON entity. In 3NF, we remove such data to a separate entity. In this way, we can avoid update and delete anomalies within our system
BCNF	**Boyce-Codd normal form**
	Under certain very specific circumstances, 3NF can miss interdependencies between non-key attributes. (Note that although we refer to them as non-key attributes, they are certainly candidate keys.) Mathematically, BCNF says that
	A relation R is in BCNF if whenever $X \rightarrow A$ holds in R, and A is not in X, then X is a candidate key for R
	Typically, any entity that is in 3NF is also in BCNF except where (a) there are multiple candidate keys, (b) keys are composed of multiple attributes, and (c) there are common attributes between the keys. A mantra that can be found in many places on the Internet sums the process up:
	The key, the whole key, and nothing but the key, so help me Codd
4NF	**Isolate independent multiple relationships**
	This form typically only arises when we are dealing with key-only associative entities and, further, where we have a ternary relationship that has been incorrectly modeled by merging two distinct, independent binary relationships. Consider the situation where we need to track the education and training records of individuals within the organization. There are M:M relationships from the PERSON entity to the COURSE entity and from the PERSON entity to the CERTIFICATION entity. We may be tempted to resolve the M:M relationships by creating a PERSON_COURSE_CERTIFICATION entity: an associative entity with a ternary relationship with PERSON, COURSE, and CERTIFICATION. However, it is quite conceivable that a given person instance did not attend a given course and that another person instance does not

(continued)

Table 3.2 (continued)

	have a specific certification. Although this solution is correct in 3NF, it violates 4NF and requires us to create dummy records in cases such as the two examples above
	The correct solution in 4NF is to resolve each M:M relationship independently, if they are indeed independent
	This being said, there are valid cases where a ternary relationship should be modeled. If, for example, we have a specific certification that is taken as a test following the participation in a particular course, the ternary relationship would be valid and resolving the M:M relationships independently would actually lose valuable information about the ternary relationship between PERSON, COURSE, and CERTIFICATION
5NF	**Isolate semantically related multiple relationships**
	In complex models, we often find sets of relationships that provide multiple relationship sets to get from one place to another. Consider the example we described in 4NF above and add an explicit M:M relationship between COURSE and CERTIFICATION. Now we have M:M relationships between each pair of entities. As in the 4NF case, resolving to a single associative entity in a ternary relationship would continue to require our creating dummy records. Instead, as in the 4NF case, we resolve each relationship independently. We now store information about people and courses, courses and certifications, and certifications and people independently, even though there is an obvious semantic relationship between them all

often used in a qualitative context. For data we receive in the sciences, such qualitative data is also a fact of life.

Qualitative data, often provided in answer to questions such as "describe your level of pain," will often have domains of values such as "uncomfortable," "very painful," "painful," and the like. Attempts to convert such qualitative data into quantitative data are often attempted through changing the questions asked at data collection time to "on a scale of 1 to 10, what is your level of pain," or even by offering a set of values, in an explicit ordering, from which a selection can be made. This is obviously the preferred approach since it eliminates the qualitative data issue for us; however, this is not always feasible. In the latter case, how do we handle qualitative data?

The first question we should ask is how relevant the qualitative attribute is to our problem and the conclusions we wish to draw. If we continue with our "pain threshold" example, what would be the overall effect if we simply eliminated it from our dataset?

If we cannot eliminate the attribute, the second approach we may consider is to look at the domain of values and see if there is an intuitive ordering we can make for the values. If our pain threshold answers turned out to be "not very," "painful," "very painful," and "excruciating," we can see that ordering them in this way takes us from the "lowest" to the "highest." We can at least say that "very painful" < "excruciating," giving us ordinal data.

Can we go one step further and generate a rational equivalent where we can say that "excruciating" is three times "very painful?" Typically not, or at least, not in a way that is meaningful. But do we even need to?

The answer lies in what we want to conclude from our model. If we are undertaking a classification effort, it really does not matter: the different values may, or may not, be relevant to the model's operation, but if they are, they will help drive different classifications anyway.

So what can we conclude? We definitely need to look at qualitative data, but what we need to do with it during our data preparation stage will be dependent upon a number of different factors. Is it necessary or relevant? Can we order it? Do we need to? These questions need to be considered, but need to be correlated to the techniques we are intending to use.

3.4   Interpretive Data

We differentiate data that is generated by an individual's subjective evaluation as being *interpretive*. The salient point of this type of data is that it has a decidedly human perspective to it. This is not to say that this type of data is not valuable – it is. For example, both the FDA and CLSI issue interpretive breakpoints for organism-compound combinations, typically annually, which are used to categorize minimum inhibitory concentrations (MICs) into susceptible, intermediate, and resistant categories. These interpretive values are just as valuable from a clinical perspective as the actual MIC value, especially on antibiograms.

3.5   Sequence Data

Genomic and proteomic sequences comprise strings over controlled alphabets. For gene sequences, the alphabet is A, C, G, T, N[1]; for protein sequences, the alphabet is A, C, D, E, F, G, H, I, K, L, M, N, P, Q, R, S, T, V, W, Y.[2] The structure of the genome, the double helix, has been known for over 50 years, but the structures of proteins are still being uncovered. Gene expression, protein synthesis, is defined by the central dogma of molecular biology and can be mapped from the gene sequence to its appropriate protein sequence where triads of gene sequence base pairs (codons) are mapped to 1 of the 20 amino acids comprising the protein, using an open reading frame (ORF). However, this only gives the primary structure of the protein, using the 20 amino acids mentioned above. The secondary, tertiary, and quaternary structures are the subject of significant research.

---

[1] For adenine, cytosine, guanine, and thymine, and unknown, where the nucleotide could be any of the four.

[2] For alanine (A), cysteine (C), aspartic acid (D), glutamic acid (E), phenylalanine (F), glycine (G), histidine (H), isoleucine (I), lysine (K), leucine (L), methionine (M), asparagine (N), proline (P), glutamine (Q), arginine (R), serine (S), threonine (T), valine (V), tryptophan (W), tyrosine (Y).

Storing and manipulating such sequence data introduces its own challenges, and while effective, the relational data model is not necessarily the most effective data storage mechanism for this type of data.[3] This is particularly true when mining this type of data. We are often interested in questions such as:

- How similar[4] are the two (or more) sequences to each other?
- What "missing data" in one (or more) sequence will improve the similarity between the sequences we are looking at? What substitutions (insertions and deletions[5]) should we be considering?
- What motifs (short segments of DNA or protein) of interest are in our dataset? Do particular motifs occur, and how frequently, and where?

These, and many other questions, only begin to touch the surface of *bioinformatics*, and we introduce this important subject later in the book. These types of questions do, however, allow us to consider some of the data architecture issues associated with sequence data.

The first question, which we have already mentioned above, relates to the physical data architecture within which sequences are stored. Your organization will probably already have standard in place to answer this question, but we will consider some of the issues that need to be addressed in the event that such standards do not already exist. These issues, while being discussed in the context of sequence data, apply to any type of data.

?. How volatile is the data?
   Is the data going through substantial change? Is it likely to change in the future?
?. Where is the source for this data?
   Does the source exist outside of your organization? Does the data exist outside of your control?
?. How big is the data attribute?
   Is the size of the data (in our example, the sequence data) likely to have any performance or physical impact on the proposed storage mechanism? (For example, physical page sizes within the relational database environment.[6])
?. What do we want to do with the data?
   What types of processing are we likely to perform on the data?

---

[3] This is more an issue of efficiency than capability. Today's relational database management systems allow for string of effectively unlimited lengths. However, more traditional file-based storage offers advantages for this type of data. We discuss this a little later.

[4] We will purposely gloss over the concept of similarity in this chapter as this is a broader topic that we address later. For now, our intuitive sense of similarity will be sufficient.

[5] Insertions and deletions are generally referred to as *gaps*.

[6] For those readers familiar with database management systems, we do not recommend storing sequence data as binary large objects (BLOBs) due to both performance and the type of processing performed on sequence data.

These questions, and other like them, will help determine the most appropriate storage approach for the data. We have generally elected to store sequence data, for example, outside of the relational data environment due to:

(a) The typical length of sequence data being hundreds, thousands, or even more characters in length
(b) The performance impact imposed by the combination of sequence length, RDBMS physical characteristics (see footnote)
(c) The type of processing performed on sequence data

3.6 Gene Ontology

The Gene Ontology (GO) is a bioinformatics initiative aimed at standardizing the representation of gene and gene product attributes (RNA or proteins resulting from the expression of a gene) across all species by developing a controlled vocabulary, annotating genes and gene products, assimilating and disseminating the annotations, and providing tools to access the data, such as the AmiGO browser.

GO covers three domains:

- Cellular components – parts of the cell or its extracellular environment
- Molecular function – elemental activities of a gene product at the molecular level
- Biological process – operations or sets of molecular events, with a defined beginning and end, pertinent to the functioning of integrated living units: cells, tissues, organs, and organisms

Let's look at an example entry. From the Gene Ontology website,[7] search for "GO:0040012," identifying this as a GO term or id, and then select the "downloads" tab on the returned page. From here, select the OBO format. The resulting page provides the GO hierarchy, and finding our search term on the page, we have the following definition for our term:

```
id: GO:0040012
name: regulation of locomotion
namespace: biological_process
def: "Any process that modulates the frequency, rate or extent of
locomotion of a cell or organism." [GOC:ems]
is_a: GO:0050789
relationship: regulates GO:0040011
```

The GO ontology is a living entity with additions, corrections, or other alterations being made continuously under a rigorous review process.

It is important to understand what the GO does and does not cover. For example, oncogenesis is not included in the ontology since it is not a normal function of

---

[7] See Appendix B.

genes, and neither are attributes specific to mutants or diseases. Further, sequence attributes are not a core part of the GO since they are not considered attributes of gene products.[8]

So how and where is the GO important?

Typically, any individual researcher's area of interest is in a relatively small area and to exhaustively search all of the different repositories of information can be expensive. When we consider that different repositories often use different terms for similar concepts and that terminology in common usage at any given time may vary widely also, manual and automated searches can unintentionally exclude important information. Consider an example: you may be interested in uncovering new drug targets for a class of antibiotics, which means that you would be interested in finding all RNA or proteins that are involved in bacterial protein synthesis, but limited to these where the genetic sequence is different to that in humans, so that we distinct targets to aim for (sic). Different databases may use different terms for describing the molecules we are interested in. Terms such as "translation" or "protein synthesis" may be used, which means that we need to spend time on building queries that handle the differences, and then merge our results together, or manually construct our result set. But above and beyond this problem, we also have to ensure that the terms we map to each other really are functionally equivalent for our purposes; otherwise, we have introduced noise into our data.

The GO initiative, whose aim is to attempt to produce consistent descriptions of gene products across different databases, allowing us to easily analyze data from multiple different sources, confident that the meaning of a description has the same semantic across them all.

3.7 Image Data

Images are being generated from more and more sources in today's scientific world. As many medical devices now deliver output as digital image files, the storage, management, and interpretation of the data thus generated becomes a larger challenge.

The image itself needs to be considered as an immutable object as it is the physical manifestation of the subject, at a particular point in time, according to a specific instrument calibration: the baseline for processing.

Complete consideration of mining image data is outside the scope of this book.

---

[8] As explicitly identified at the GO website, these are part of the Open Biological and Biomedical Ontologies (OBO).

3.8   Text Data

In the bibliography for this text, we have included several hundred entries. Each entry contains a plethora of information within the domain of the publication. In life sciences, the vast majority of publications will include information about biological entities such as genes and proteins, descriptions of experiments, results, conclusions, and other contextual information that might be very helpful.

Automated analysis of text data and text mining has seen a significant increase in attention over recent years, particularly in the area of Systems Biology, a discipline we will return to later in this text.

3.9   Protein and Compound 3D Structural Data

As mentioned elsewhere in this text, how the protein folds in three-dimensional space is a vital input to many of the (currently) most intractable problems in protein bioinformatics (Tramontano 2005). Broadening this, we can see that how other compounds interact with cellular components is an important factor in many areas of life sciences research. For these reasons, consideration of the 3D structure of compounds has seen an increasing interest from researchers in many disciplines.

Structure-based drug design, or direct drug design, for example, relies on knowledge of the 3D structure of the biological target, which can be obtained through methods such as X-ray crystallography, NMR, spectroscopy, or other methods.[9] Using the structure of the biological target, candidate drugs predicted to bind with high affinity and be selective to the target may be designed. Computational procedures are increasingly being used to suggest new drug candidates.

Consider the partial grouping of drugs shown in Table 3.3 which shows some of the structural similarities between related drugs. While certain similarities can be described from simple structural definitions, interesting interactions that may only be apparent, or more apparent, when considering the three-dimensional structure and the interactions that arise by the shape(s) of interacting molecules and the changes that are caused by the forces on such molecules. The common component of steroids (Fig. 3.3) has attachments for three separate residues, which may be duplicates of each other, or different. The different residues that may be attached to the common elements are why we recognize hundreds of different steroids.

The forces that exist on molecules cause the molecule to have a different shape in three dimensions, obviously causing its overall size to be different. These configurations have biological impacts, for example, as shown by the *receptor theory*.

---

[9] If an experimental structure of the target is not available, a *homology structure* may be developed based on the structures of related proteins.

Table 3.3 Antibiotic structure (From http://www.microbiologyprocedure.com/
bacterial-cheomotherapy/structure-of-antibiotics.htm)

Class	Molecular structure
Penicillins and cephalosporins	B-lactam ring
Aminoglycosides	Amino sugars in a glycosidic linkage
Macrolides	Macrocyclic lactone
Tetracyclines	Polycyclic napthone carboxide
Chloramphenicol	Nitrobenzene derivative of dichloroacetic acid
Peptide antibiotics	Peptide-linked D and L amino acids
Antifungal antibiotics	Polyens and nonpolyens
Ansamacrolides	Naphto and benzoquinone nuclei derivatives
Anthracycline antibiotics	Anthracycline

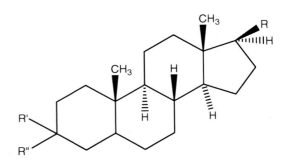

Fig. 3.3 Steroids

Being able to analyze molecules in 3D and understand their conformations as well as the forces on them can provide significant insight into their effect.

As indicated at the beginning of this section, how proteins fold is of particular interest because misfolding of proteins is associated with prion-related conditions (e.g., Creutzfeldt-Jakob disease and bovine spongiform encephalopathy ["mad cow disease"]), amyloid-related illnesses (e.g., Alzheimer's disease and familial amyloid cardiomyopathy), as well as Huntingdon's and Parkinson's diseases. In such cases, the misfolded proteins are multimerized into insoluble extracellular aggregates or intracellular inclusions.

Sources of 3D structural data come from:

- Experimental data
- Computational chemistry (quantum mechanics, molecular mechanics, molecular dynamics)
- Structure-generation methods for databases of molecules

Probably the best-known repository of experimental 3D data is the *Cambridge Structure Database* (CSD) that, as of the time of writing, includes bibliographic, chemical, and crystallographic information for over 400,000 organic and metalorganic compounds, where the 3D structures have been determined using X-ray diffraction and neutron diffraction. Single crystal and powder diffraction studies provide 3D atomic coordinates for (at least) all nonhydrogen atoms, where possible, although some incomplete entries do exist. Open literature publications and private deposits to the CSD provide crystal structure data as well.

Several other repositories containing structural data are available for searching.

In *Entrez*, for example, protein structure neighbors are determined by comparing their 3D structures with the *VAST* algorithm. Each of the more than 87,804 domains in the molecular modeling database (*MMDB*) is compared to every other one. The Conserved Domain Database (*CDD*) comprises a protein annotation resource, hosting a collection of well-annotated multiple sequence alignment models for ancient domains and full-length proteins which are available as position-specific score matrices (PSSMs) for fast identification of conserved domains in protein sequences via the RPS-BLAST tool. In addition to NCBI-curated domains, domain models from external sources such as Pfam, SMART, COG, PRK, and TIGRFAM are included. *PubChem* provides information on the biological activities of small molecules, organized as three linked databases within Entrez.[10] PubChem also provides a fast chemical structure similarity search tool.

The NCBI Inferred Biomolecular Interaction Server (*IBIS*) organizes, analyzes, and predicts interaction partners as well as locations of binding sites in proteins *from experimentally determined structures*. IBIS annotations cover several different types of binding partners: protein, chemical, nucleic acid, peptides, and ions. Interactions observed in experimentally determined structural complexes of a given protein are presented, along with inferences for binding sites/interacting partners, modeled by inspecting the protein complexes formed by homologous proteins.

NCBI also provides a set of analysis tools and services to help navigate 3D data:

- *Cn3D*, which allows us to view molecular structures and create structural and sequence alignments
- *CD-Search*, Conserved Domain Search, or RPS-BLAST, to hunt for multiple alignments of conserved, functional domains that match a specified protein
- *CDART*, Conserved Domain Architecture Retrieval Tool, to identify proteins with similar domain architectures to a specified protein
- *VAST*, Vector Alignment Search Tool, for creating structural alignments
- *SA LTO*, Structure-based Alignment Tool, to assemble structure-linked sequence alignments
- *NCBI Threader*, for aligning a protein sequence to a 3D structure using associated multiple sequence alignments and chemical potentials[11]
- *Related Structures*, a service for creating sequence-structure alignments

These are only a very small set of the tools available for analyzing 3D structures. There is a vast array of software available to today's researcher. Several of these are included in an appendix, with more on the associated website.

An interesting use of 3D data is in substructure searching. Suppose we are aware of an antihistamine pharmacophore[12] such as that shown in Fig. 3.4.

---

[10] PubChem Substance, PubChem Compound, and PubChem BioAssay.

[11] This capability has very recently been incorporated into Cn3D.

[12] The group of atoms in the molecule of a drug responsible for the drug's action.

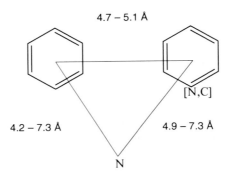

Fig. 3.4 Structure of interest for substructure searching (Leach and Gillet 2003)

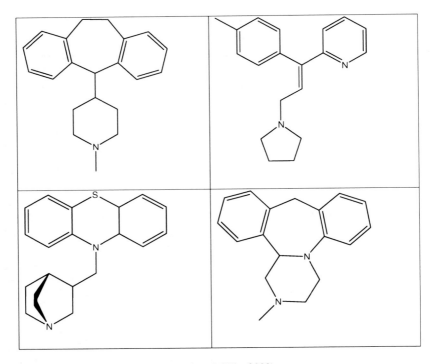

Fig. 3.5 3D substructure searching (Leach and Gillet 2003)

We can use this information to search for compounds containing this structure, such as those shown in Fig. 3.5.

We may be able to extract the salient information from our structure of interest such that we can determine that structures we may be interested in are effectively modeled by a simpler structure, such as shown in Fig. 3.6.

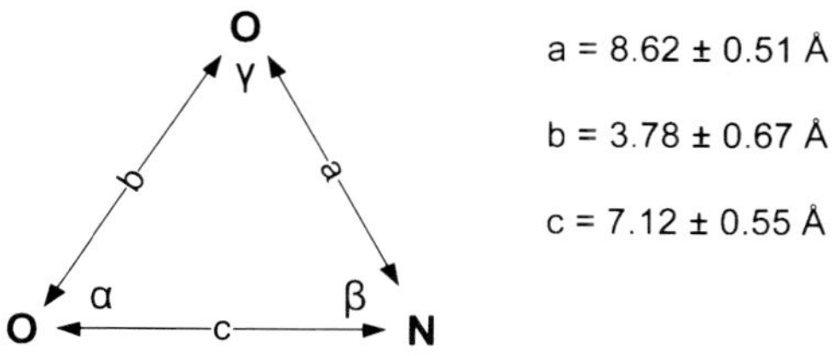
O
γ
b
a
α
β
O
c
N
a = 8.62 ± 0.51 Å
b = 3.78 ± 0.67 Å
c = 7.12 ± 0.55 Å

Fig. 3.6 Substructure model

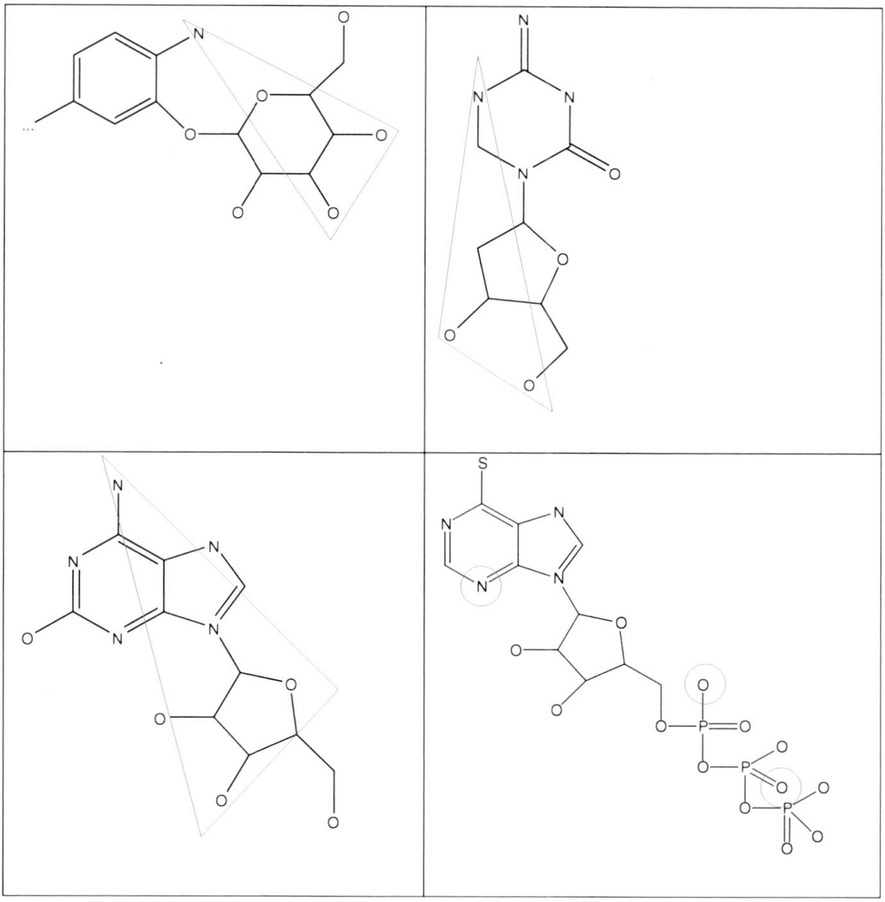

Fig. 3.7 Discovered substructures

Since each side of our substructure "triangle" can vary, we can search our molecular structure data to obtain all molecules that contain acceptable substructures, using basic trigonometric mathematics and molecular modeling to aid us, giving results similar to those shown in Fig. 3.7.

Real-world mining initiatives can use this type of pattern elicitation to identify many other structures in our repository that might be valuable options for drug research and development. If we identify the salient characteristics of the pharmacophore and troll through all of the structures available within our private repositories as well as the public repositories, we may be able to identify candidates much more quickly, and less expensively, than traditional methods.

We've tried to provide some context to the value of 3D data, to some of the types of data, and to some sources of the data. But many readers will rightfully state that we've not even touched on the gamut of structural data available for proteins and compounds, nor on its growing use and value. Since such data was so important to one of the most important discoveries of the twentieth century – crystallography's important role in determining the structure of DNA – there is no doubt of its importance. In addition to the CSD, the Protein Data Bank (PDB) also has tens of thousands of X-ray and NMR structures for protein and protein-ligand complexes, with the number growing daily. In recent years, this type of data has becoming much more important in many areas of analysis. For example, an important advance has been to use 3D structural data that has been used in QSAR analyses to facilitate a structure-based approach to drug discovery. However, a full treatise is beyond the scope of this introductory text.

3.10   Data Integration

Integrating data from disparate sources is a major challenge in the Data Management discipline and, as we shall see later, is of specific importance in the life sciences. In this section, we discuss some of the general issues and resolutions that arise from developing a data mining platform that comprises a set of discrete, distributed data repositories that contain complex and heterogeneous data.

3.10.1   Same Entity, Different Identifiers

Very often, we will have data for the same type of entity coming from different sources, and being identified differently. Consider, as an example, patient information coming from two investigator sites for a single clinical trial. If the investigators use some form of electronic method for storing the information, there is a good possibility that the identifiers used by the two applications are different. For example, one might uniquely identify a patient using (say) a combination of patient initials and date of birth; the other might use a sequential number as its identifier. They both contain patient information, so how can we combine them together?

Further, we may need to be able to track back to the original data, as provided by the sources, the investigator sites in our example, and so we need to maintain the original identifier data also. So we need to think about how to best manage this problem. Do we generate a separate identifier and add the two (or more) source identifiers as simple attributes of the entity? This is a simple, yet effective approach that also allows us to easily determine where the patient information came from.

The above scenario has the implicit assumption that the data from various sources is *partitioned* rather than overlapping. In this latter case, the problem becomes more severe since we now have to merge two instances together into a single instance. Techniques for managing such instances are the topic of Chap. 5. Within the data architecture, we often support these through ancillary model fragments that contain the original data and an integrated version that forms a core part of the model (and datasets generated from that model) used for our mining efforts.

3.10.2 Data in Different Formats

How do we handle data in different formats? This simple question actually contains several facets of complexity. At the most basic level, we have the situation where attributes from separate data sources constitute a single domain, but have been stored in physically distinct forms: one might be stored as a numeric value, the other in a string variable. The second form of this is where the attribute values have used different domains of values: for example, "positive/negative" in one source and "yes/no" in another source. Data transformation, as we shall see, will often account for the vast majority of the effort involved in data mining. One way in which the data architecture can help is to include *synonymous* data in the data architecture. The particularly simple example above illustrates this with allowing a mapping of "positive" to "yes" and "negative" to "no." However, care must be taken to ensure that this mapping is consistent throughout, or that we carefully control how and where the synonyms are used. We return to this issue in detail later.

3.10.3 Default Values

Many relational database management systems allow us to define default value clauses for cases where the data is not available. We could, for example, introduce a default value clause for a specimen collection date as being the current date. In this example, we have to be sure that this default value clause is actually a valid condition: how many times will it provide a value that is incorrect because, for example, the specimen was collected a few minutes before midnight, but the data was not received into the data environment until just after midnight. Worse, what about cases where the load occurs nightly – just after midnight – for all the specimens collected the previous day?

Many readers will be rolling their eyes at this naïve example. But we have seen this happen. Further, although we began by talking about the facility *within* the database management system to specify a default value, this same challenge occurs if we elect to handle the issue either at the time of the data load (actually, at the time of the transformation) or at the time of the analysis itself.

Why would we even worry about default values? Typically, it is because of missing data. If we do not have a value for (say) a patient's gender, how do we handle it? As we shall discuss in Chap. 5, the whole question of missing data is a very large and challenging issue. Default values are only one solution to this problem. Wherever possible, we recommend making sure that any database management capabilities for generating default values are turned off by default (sic) and instead should be evident as missing data so that explicit techniques can be applied as necessary. For example, we may find out by applying some of our techniques that the gender attribute does not affect our model to any significant degree. In such cases, we may be able to exclude it from our dataset without affecting the quality of our conclusions.

3.10.4 Multiscale Data Integration

Throughout this text, we discuss some of the different types of data we encounter in data mining initiatives and, as we hope we have communicated, how the disparate forms of data will continue to grow, but also need to be holistically brought together. While we have already explored the issues of data coming from different sources, and this will continue to be a challenge we explore throughout the text, we have not yet discussed one of the greatest challenges: the scale of the data being captured.

A good way to illustrate this is to consider a patient being diagnosed and subsequently treated for a tumor. We would expect to have data captured from the typical blood chemistry, hematology, and urinalysis tests, along with the battery of normal clinician events (visits) such as weight, blood pressure, and the like. We may also get biopsy data for the tumor such as a histology report, including microscopic image data, such as fluorescence microscopy image data, which we consider elsewhere, along with possible molecular results from spectroscopy, NMR, X-ray crystallography, and the like. Thus, the *scale* of our data runs the gamut from microscopic (or even atomic), through large scale. Thus, in addition to the challenges of integrating this data, we also have *semantic* questions: what is the meaning of each data element in the multiscale environment?

Putting this another way, the dataset resulting from integrating data at these different scales is going to be used for some analytical effort – not just data mining, but obviously that's the focus of this text – so when we have all this data combined together, and we build our models, how do we ensure that comparing and contrasting data at different scales is handled in a consistent and valid way so that our results are similarly consistent, valid, and reproducible? Thus, we have heterogeneity of data models, conceptual schema, and semantic to deal with.

Different interpretations of data, encoded in different datasets, in conjunction with the complexity of the data are the main cause of *semantic heterogeneity*, caused by differences in the meaning, interpretation, or use of the same or related data. Semantic heterogeneity is caused by differences in the meaning, interpretation, or use of the same or related data, which can arise due to difference scientific fields, application contexts, levels of detail, or temporal (time-related) issues.

For example, consider a scenario where we have image data for a tumor, taken (say) at monthly intervals, along with biopsies taken at 3-month intervals, and blood test data taken weekly. We have three different scales of data, but also the temporal dimension to contend with, complicating our analysis significantly.

What are the scales we use in biological contexts? They include atomic, molecular, molecular complexes, sub-cellular, cellular, multicell systems, tissue, organ, multi-organ systems, organism, population, and behavior. As data is gathered at each of these levels, integrating them together will obviously be the challenge. Bridging across the different levels so that the inferences can be made using molecular, tissue, and organism-level data, for example, will be necessary in order of us to continue to expand the value we can accrue from our analytical efforts.

Ontologies and graphs are valuable tools in bridging scales. We can, for example, use ontologies to link anatomy (data and geometry) at multiple scales (of space and time) to enable intuitive exploration of the relationships (structural, functional, connectivity, etc.) between elements to derive insight and knowledge for future endeavors. But often, we need to analyze locally and use our ontologies, say a gross anatomy ontology and molecular entity ontology, to infer across the different scales. For example, the Subcellular Anatomy Ontology (SAO) for the nervous system provides a formal ontology to describe structures from the dimensional range known as the "mesoscale," encompassing cellular and subcellular structure, supracellular domains, and macromolecules.[13]

One approach for multiscale data mediation (Martone 2007) suggests:

1. Create multimodal databases that leverage a standard set of metadata
2. Create conceptual links to a shared ontology
3. Situate the data in a common (spatial) framework
4. Use mediation software[14] to navigate and query across data sources

Just from the simple introduction above, we can see the importance of standard nomenclatures. Even projects with overlapping interests will tend to categorize their data according to their specific needs, a fact that impacts and hinders data interchange, and association of elements and semantics across those projects.

---

[13] http://ccdb.ucsd.edu/CCDBWebSite/sao.html

[14] See, for example, the Biomedical Informatics Research Network (BIRN) Mediator architecture as an example.

This issue not only occurs with initiatives driven by different organizations but often occurs within an organization itself, making it difficult to convince different bodies of the need for harmonization standards when different initiatives within a single body often suffer from this same issue.

Empirical approaches have often been used to resolve individual heterogeneities across data for specific information interchange and reuse, but this type of approach which deals only with a specific problem does not provide an overall, uniform solution, . Hence the importance and need for semantic, ontological approaches.

Multiscale data integration is a complex challenge for any organization wanting to integrate disparate data elements.

3.11 The Test Subject Area

Let us consider an abstract model fragment – a *subject area* – that we might include in our model. The *test subject area* allows us to capture the information about the tests performed on patients' specimens. The transactional fragment is shown in Fig. 3.8.

To keep things readable, we excluded listing the attributes in Fig. 3.8. Partial entity definitions are included below.

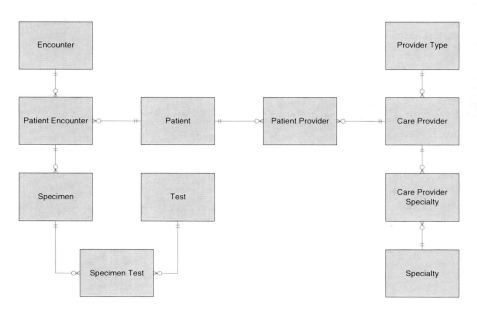

Fig. 3.8 Test subject area – transactional model fragment

Patient Entity

Key	Attribute	Format	Domain	Description
Entity Description	Patient			
Key	**Attribute**	**Format**	**Domain**	**Description**
PK	Id	Integer		
	First Name	String		
	Last Name	String		
	Initials	String		
	Dob	Date		
	Gender	Character	F, M, ' '	
	Ethnicity	Character		
FK	Address Id	Integer		
FK	Primary Care Provider Id	Integer		
	Phone Number	String		
	Email Address	String		

Care Provider Entity

Key	Attribute	Format	Domain	Description
Entity Description	Care Provider			
Key	**Attribute**	**Format**	**Domain**	**Description**
PK	Id	Integer		
	First Name	String		
	Last Name	String		
	Specialty	String		
	Address Line 1	String		
	Address Line 2	String		
FK	Provider Type Id	Integer		Hospital, clinic, office

Encounter Entity

Key	Attribute	Format	Domain	Description
Entity Description	Encounter			
Key	**Attribute**	**Format**	**Domain**	**Description**
PK	Id	Integer		
	Encounter Start Date	Date		
	Encounter End Date	Date		
FK	Location Id	Integer		
	Encounter Title	String		
	Encounter Description	String		Reason and description of objective

Patient Encounter

Key	Attribute	Format	Domain	Description
Entity Description	Patient Encounter			
Key	**Attribute**	**Format**	**Domain**	**Description**
PK	Id	Integer		
FK	Patient Id	Integer		
FK	Encounter Id	Integer		

Specimen Entity

Entity Description	Specimen			
Key	**Attribute**	**Format**	**Domain**	**Description**
PK	Id	Integer		
FK	Collected By Id	Integer		
	Collection Date	Datetime		
FK	Specimen Source Id	Integer		
	Accession	String		
	Special Handling Required	Boolean		
FK	Patient Encounter Id	Integer		

Test Entity

Entity Description	Test			
Key	**Attribute**	**Format**	**Domain**	**Description**
PK	Id	Integer		
	Name	String		

Specimen Test

Entity Description	Specimen Test			
Key	**Attribute**	**Format**	**Domain**	**Description**
PK	Id	Integer		
FK	Specimen Id	Integer		
FK	Test Id	Integer		
	Contract Identifier	String		Contract number/identifier used within the organization
FK	External Customer Id	String		The customer identifier used within the organization

Patient Provider

Entity Description	Patient Provider			
Key	**Attribute**	**Format**	**Domain**	**Description**
PK	Id	Integer		
FK	Patient Id	Integer		
FK	Care Provider Id	Integer		

Specialty

Entity Description	Specialty			
Key	**Attribute**	**Format**	**Domain**	**Description**
PK	Id	Integer		
	Specialty Name	String		

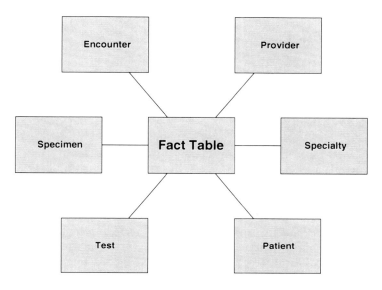

Fig. 3.9 Star schema for the test subject area

Care Provider Specialty

Entity Description	Specimen Test			
Key	**Attribute**	**Format**	**Domain**	**Description**
PK	Id	Integer		
FK	Care Provider Id	Integer		
FK	Specialty Id	Integer		

Provider Type

Entity Description	Provider Type			
Key	**Attribute**	**Format**	**Domain**	**Description**
PK	Id	Integer		
	Provider Type Name	String		

Our star schema may be defined, as shown in Fig. 3.9.

Each entity represented in the outer ring denotes a *dimension* of interest in our model. We have indicated that we are interested in performing analysis driven by the encounter,[15] health-care provider, provider specialty, patient, test (definition), and specimen. The *fact table* primarily comprises identifier fields for the dimensions along with core data elements that constitute *facts* in our model.

---

[15] An encounter is defined as any intersection between a patient and a health-care professional.

3.12 The Transactional Data Model, Operational Data Store, Data Warehouse, and Data Mart

We now turn our attention to the physical aspects of the data architecture and infrastructure. Broadly speaking, three major models are utilized in business: the online transactional processing (OLTP) model, the operational data store (ODS), and the data warehouse (DW).

Typically, data mining systems are built on top of a robust data infrastructure that may comprise a homogeneous relational database platform, a heterogeneous data environment comprising different types of technology **and** different data repositories, or anything in between. We will consider some of the differences between these models in sections below. Herein, we intend to provide a brief introduction to these three important model types.

The OLTP model, as its name suggests, is optimized for transactional process, which typically comprises inserting new information into the database, or updating information already in the database. Figure 3.8 depicts a fragment of an OLTP model. The data is as "fresh" as it can be and allows for an up-to-the-minute view of the organizations' data.

The DW model, as its name suggests, is typically an enterprise-level repository of data, "warehoused" through transformation processes to support the analytical processes of the organization. The data in a data warehouse is typically loaded only once it has stabilized and not susceptible to change. Thus, the "freshness" of the data is a real question.

The ODS model tries to balance the transactional model strengths and the warehouse strengths into a single environment and can support analytics along with a pseudo-real-time need.

Table 3.4 shows a side-by-side comparison of these common data architectures.

While data warehouses can comprise several subject areas spanning the entire enterprise, data marts tend to focus on either a single subject area or a few subject areas. Whereas data warehouses traditionally tend to bog down the end user because of the abundance of information. Data marts tend to work around this issue by focusing on a single subject. Typically, data marts are populated from data warehouses; however independent data marts built directly from transactional systems are becoming common. The drawback of having independent data marts is that, as the organization grows, different departments tend to build marts of their own, leading to overlapping data which quickly becomes a synchronization problem.

Just as in a data warehouse, data marts are modeled on a *star* or *snowflake* dimensional model, performance tuned for aggregations and complex queries. The size of the mart can be kept to a manageable level as it contains data pertaining only to one subject area, or a very few subject areas.

Figure 3.10 depicts an abstract illustration for how data marts fit into the overall enterprise data architecture.

Table 3.4 Comparison of common data architectures

Criterion	OLTP	ODS	DW
Intent	OLTP systems are designed to get the data in (capture data) on a real-time basis. Data captured is usually limited to individual systems	While providing a "data hub," ODS provides an enterprise view of data. While not transactional, ODS does provide a more up-to-date snapshot of data	Data from transactional systems (OLTP) and ODS is put through a more rigorous curation process and intended for analysis and mining purposes
Frequency of operations	Insert and update operations occur in real time	Usually ODSs do not hold real-time data. However, data is kept up-to-date more frequently than a DW	Data is loaded less frequently usually using a ETL process
Freshness of data	Data is maintained in real time	Though not real time, data from ODS usually can be used for reporting and other pseudo-real-time operations	Data from DW is usually not used in real-time operations but for analysis
Validity of data	By definition, not all data can be considered valid as it is in real time. Systems operating on top of OLTP databases can apply business rules, validation, etc. in stages	Although validity cannot be guaranteed, usually only data passing validity/business rule checks are loaded	Since no real-time validation is required, all data is considered to have passed through business rules and other validation
Optimization	Optimized for inserts and updates. The number of rows retrieved is usually limited to single digits (1 row)	Depending on usage, ODS can be optimized for bulk selects	Optimized for bulk loads, aggregations, and complex queries
Concurrent users	Maximum	Compared to OLTP, the number of concurrent users is limited	The number of concurrent users is smaller compared to a ODS and OLTP system
Granularity	Granular. Intended to capture all attributes required by the system	Can be designed to store data to a less granular extent, but several historical snapshots can be stored	DW is optimized to go aggregate analysis, and hence, we do not need granularity
Retention	Not all historical data needs to be stored in real time. For performance reasons, historical data can be archived	Depending on requirements, the snapshot can be limited to a few ETLs	Usually, DW tends to be the "black hole" holding everything
Size	Small/medium sized, measured in a few hundred megabytes to gigabytes	Measured in a few hundred gigabytes	Large. Range from hundreds of gigabytes to terabytes

(continued)

Table 3.4 (continued)

Criterion	OLTP	ODS	DW
Transaction size	Small transactions. Last a few milliseconds. Usually involve a large number inserts and updates	Larger than OLTP. Can last a few seconds. More selects are involved	Range from a few seconds to hours. Involve large aggregations
Model	Normalized relational model	Hybrid model	Start or snowflake, supporting aggregations
Data source	Direct data entry (usually from users using a front end)	ETL processes	ETL from OLTP or ODS

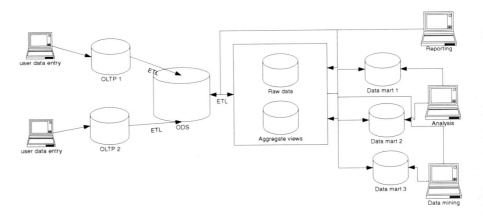

Fig. 3.10 Data architecture with data marts

3.13 Modeling Data with a Time Dimension

How we account for time in our model is a particularly important issue. Let us consider a simple example: a patient whose age changes with every encounter with a health-care professional. Is this fact something that we need to be concerned about? If the encounters are days or even a small number of weeks apart, the answer may be no; if the encounters are months or years apart, the answer may be yes. We review patient ages in a number of different ways. For example, we may consider a patients' age to see if they comply with our exclusion/inclusion criteria for a particular study. We may look at a patients' age when categorizing patients for statistical analysis: we will typically categorize patients in (say) 5-year groupings.

For clinical testing purposes, we may need to look at time at the days-hours-minutes level, depending on the tests we are interested in.

Incorporating a robust time dimension in our model allows us the opportunity to analyze our data at a level of aggregation as well as at a granular level and allows us to mine data such as PK/PD data where test results are captured over time and to see what patterns emerge. As we aggregate up and drill down, however, we have to carefully ask ourselves whether moving between layers of time affect the model we are building or not? Do we need to have different models as we travel between these levels so as to keep our conclusions consistent? We already know that the answer is yes, because this is at the heart of the multiscale integration issue that we discussed earlier in this chapter.

But even without the multiscale issue, time itself has to be dealt with coherently. But it also has to have a common semantic (sic). Specifically, if we have data in our dataset that needs time as a characteristic, such as might be found in microbiological time-kill studies, or pharmacological data capture where we need to capture drug concentrations at specific time instances, it is very important to be consistent when we integrate and aggregate our data.

Consider an example where we are interested in a particular blood-borne pathogen concentration along with the therapy concentration, we may obtain that information from a single blood sample taken at a particular time interval (say every 2 h). In this case, time is a consistent characteristic because of the single source. However, where data elements were captured at different time points, we must ask how and where they can be correlated. For example, if a patient is given an oral drug once per day at the same time, can we safely use a simple interpolation of how the drug concentration changes in that patient's body to cross-reference with other test results, even if we didn't directly measure the drug concentration? Does it matter?

How time fits into our models – whether it is relevant, and if so, how relevant – is an important consideration. In today's data environments, temporal information is almost always captured. How and where you use it for your analysis should be an explicit question you should ask at the very beginning of your endeavor. Also, if it happens to be missing, what do you need to do, or can you afford to ignore it?

3.14   Historical Data and Archiving: Another Temporal Issue?

As we have already discussed, an OLTP model deals in (pseudo) real time from the perspective of its "data freshness," whereas a data warehouse contains data that is older and invariant. It might seem, therefore, that the subject of historical data and the process of archiving may be relevant only to the OLTP, or even the ODS arena. However, this is more of a philosophical argument than one which deals with a particular architecture.

Historical data is important for many reasons. Often, *how* the data changes is as important and valuable as the change itself. If we received a test result, for example that had one value, why might it have changed? Was it a misreading on the part of the operator, or was something else behind it? Data is updated for myriad different reasons, in every system in the world. The majority of the time is of no consequence. However, knowing how and why it changed may be very important indeed. How we store and handle historical data, therefore, can have a valuable effect on our models – both where it is available and where it is not!

Let's consider a concrete example – one we have considered before: data from multiple sources. We may elect to store every feed of data that comes from external sources, such as from investigators, so that we can see every change which occurred. Why might we do this? If we saw that a particular source of data had (say) five times the average number of updates that were seen across the universe of sources, would that tell us anything about the source of the data? Possibly. It might, for example, highlight that that particular site may have a manual operational system, or might have very poor quality control procedures. If, at some time later, the number of updates drops dramatically, that can provide us with some information also.

Historical data also, by its very nature, allows us to trend and predict how things might occur in the future. Extrapolating from the data we have received may allow us to alleviate problems in the future.

The allied issue of archiving then raises the question of when should we consider "eliminating" data from our dataset? If having access to historical data provides value, wouldn't eliminating this same data reduce the value? Once again, the answer is "possibly." While history may be valuable, it can also be noise and only introduce complexity into our models. As we have discussed elsewhere in this book, dimensionality – the number of attributes – is a problem, but so is data volume. The more data we include in our data mining dataset, the more overt the balancing act becomes. We have to be careful that any history included in the dataset for our mining efforts is really valuable. Including it for the sake of including it, because we have it, does not necessarily help.

3.15 Data Management

In any organization of any size, the data environment you will be using for your data mining efforts will likely be shared with other users, or be populated from a shared source of data. In either case, managing the data and the environment itself is important if we are to have any confidence in the conclusions drawn from our models.

These management activities cover the gamut of processes and procedures for the Data Management group and include such things as:

- Maintenance, cleanup, documentation, and reconciliation of issues highlights during the day-to-day operation of such large-scale data environments
- Making sure that data loads occur correctly and are processed completely

- Scheduling of processes such as data loads to ensure that they occur when expected and as expected
- Ensuring that the turn-around time for resolving production issues is both timely and reasonable from the perspective of users
- Defining proper protocol(s) for communication between everyone involved in managing, administering, and using the data environment so that miscommunication does not introduce complexity into the process
- Implementing effective QA/QC/curation procedures to ensure that data integrity in the data environment is maintained at all times
- Balancing the need for effective security so that data integrity cannot be compromised while ensuring that those people who are both authorized and need access to the data can get access
- Pursuing change management procedures for both the data and the environment so that continuous improvement of data quality and data structure of the data warehouse is effected

From our perspective, that of mining data, we need to be comfortable that all of the above management activities and processes are in place and positively contribute to what we are trying to achieve. If not, too many of these issues can cause us problems and prevent us from fulfilling our goals and objectives.

3.16 Agile Modeling, Adaptive Data Warehouses, and Hybrid Models

Unlike traditional modeling techniques where requirement gathering and design stages are separate, *agile modeling* encourages collaboration between design teams and business users. Modeling is done in small iterations, with each iteration providing an incremental set of new features. With each version, the business user is continuously in the loop, providing valuable feedback.

In most systems, we find that requirements change over time. Hence, in a data driven system, it is imperative that the base model is continuously enhanced to allow data architects and system integrators to keep up with the evolving changes. Hence, it is important to ensure that each system is designed to fit into/with other pieces. This *evolving model* allows the environment to be resilient in the face of fundamental business change. One way to think about this is to use the lego™ analogy. We attempt to ensure those changes.

While transactional systems by nature operate on relational models, data mining applications tend to perform well with a dimensional model. However, there are several cases where we want to utilize the flexibility of a relational model and the performance of the dimensional model (an example would be clinical trial data, where patient data is required to be maintained for regulatory purposes, while requiring a data warehouse for analysis while maintaining current up-to-date data). In this case, we start out with the relational model and add dimensional constructs when implementing the physical model. This *hybrid data model* balances the precision provided by the relational aspect and the fast navigation provided by the dimensional aspect.

3.17 Gene Ontology Database

At various points throughout this text, the concept of an *ontology* as a necessary concept for effective research into the future as the volume of data generated continues to increase. In this section, we introduce the *Gene Ontology* (GO), a significant and broad initiative aimed at unifying the representation of gene and gene product attributes across all species.

In general, ontology is a formal representation of the knowledge by a set of concepts within a domain and the relationships between those concepts: a structured controlled vocabulary. We can immediately see the value of such a representation in many domains, and in fact, many different ontological projects do exist, as can be seen from a simple Google search.[16]

Researchers will often waste valuable time and effort when conducting searches in an often very small area of research. Since many variations in terminology may also exist – some of which change over time – such searches become even more onerous. If we just use a simple example, you might be interested in gene products involved in protein synthesis. This may be referred to as *protein synthesis* in one repository, whereas another will use the term *translation*. In such cases, your search algorithm, or your search person, needs to be able to understand what are, and what are not, functionally equivalent terms.

The Gene Ontology (GO) initiative has developed three ontologies – cellular component, biological process, and molecular function – describing genes and gene products in a species-independent manner.

The primary tool that a user would employ to interact with the GO database is the AmiGO browser,[17] the home page of which is shown in Fig. 3.11.

As can be seen from Fig. 3.11, the GO database can be searched using GO terms, defined as part of the ontology, or using gene or protein definitions. An example GO term is "heart contraction" and clicking "Submit Query" results in the page shown in Fig. 3.12 being displayed.

In our simple search, we allowed for this term to occur in any of the ontologies, but as shown in the header part of the page, we can limit to any of the specific ontologies, if that more meets our needs. Also, we clicked on "[show def]" for GO:0060048, which provides any additional definition information contained in the database. Selecting this same entry drills down to show Fig. 3.13.

---

[16] See also http://www.obofoundry.org/

[17] http://amigo.geneontology.org/

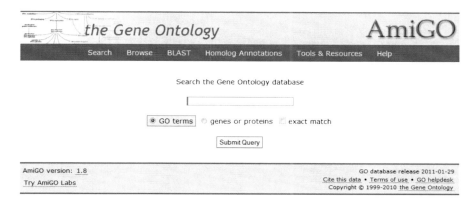

Fig. 3.11 AmiGO browser home page

Term Search Results

34 results for **heart contraction** in terms fields **term accession, term name and synonyms**

▼ **Filter search results** ⏺

Ontology

All	Set filters
biological process	
cellular component	Remove all filters
molecular function ▼	

Results are sorted by **relevance**. To change the sort order, click on the column headers.

| | Select all | Clear all | Perform an action with this page's selected terms... ▼ | Go! |

rel ↓   **Accession , Term**   **Ontology**

☐ GO:0060047 : **heart contraction** [show def]   802 gene products   biological
                                                          view in tree   process

☐ GO:0060048 : cardiac muscle contraction [hide def]   136 gene products   biological
                                                          view in tree   process
Muscle contraction of cardiac muscle tissue.

Query matches synonym "**heart** muscle **contraction**" [exact synonym]

☐ GO:0008016 : regulation of **heart contraction** [show def]   370 gene products   biological
                                                          view in tree   process

☐ GO:0045823 : positive regulation of **heart contraction** [show def]   94 gene products   biological
Query matches synonyms "up regulation of **heart contraction**" [exact synonym],   view in tree   process
and 4 more

Fig. 3.12 AmiGO search results for GO term "heart contraction"

Behind the scenes, GO terms are structured, as shown in Fig. 3.14.

Annotations about a gene or gene product use GO terms in order to provide such annotations and include the *reference* used to make the annotation, an *evidence code* that denotes the type of evidence on which the annotation is based, and the date and creator of the annotation. These can be seen in the example shown in Fig. 3.15.

cardiac muscle contraction

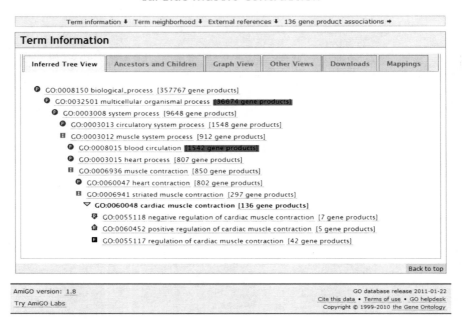

Fig. 3.13 GO entry for GO:0060048, including inferred tree view

```
id:         GO:0000016
name:       lactase activity
namespace:  molecular_function
def:        "Catalysis of the reaction: lactose + H2O = D-glucose + D-galactose." [EC:3.2.1.108]
synonym:    "lactase-phlorizin hydrolase activity" BROAD [EC:3.2.1.108]
synonym:    "lactose galactohydrolase activity" EXACT [EC:3.2.1.108]
xref:       EC:3.2.1.108
xref:       MetaCyc:LACTASE-RXN
xref:       Reactome:20536
is_a:       GO:0004553 ! hydrolase activity, hydrolyzing O-glycosyl compounds
```

Fig. 3.14 Example GO term

```
Gene product:    Actin, alpha cardiac muscle 1, UniProtKB:P68032
GO term:         heart contraction ; GO:0060047 (biological process)
Evidence code:   Inferred from Mutant Phenotype (IMP)
Reference:       PMID:17611253
Assigned by:     UniProtKB, June 6, 2008
```

Fig. 3.15 Example GO annotation

3.18   Broadening Our Concept of Data: Images, Structures, and so on

Throughout this text, we will typically highlight *transactional data elements* as a primary type of data; elements that are simple text, character, or numeric values. However, as techniques generating different data types have become commonplace within different scientific disciplines, image data and large-scale textual data, such as scientific papers, have become a fertile source of data for analytical purposes, and we shall consider some of these types of data in more detail elsewhere in this text.

As is the case with any type of data, issues specific to the data type come into play. If we consider the objective of text mining, of exploiting the information within documents, discovering patterns, trends, associations, and predictive rules, an obvious challenge is simply how we can effectively elicit this information.

Let's consider the pattern finding aspect of this: for nontextual data, the type that we will use throughout this text as the primary type of data we will encounter, we can use the general data mining methods we describe, such as clustering, classification, statistical techniques, etc., whereas for textual data, we need to use *computational linguistics* to aid us in pattern discovery.

For textual documents, where we are encountering *"free text,"* the data is not well organized and, at best, could be considered semistructured. Further, natural language text contains ambiguities on many levels: lexical, syntactic, semantic, and pragmatic. Since any learning methods we employ typically require annotated training examples, *bootstrapping methods* offer us some valuable techniques to apply to the problem.

Exploratory data analysis uses text to form hypotheses, and an example of its application of this domain to disease can be seen in Swanson and Smalheiser (1997). *Information extraction* attempts to automatically create domain-specific knowledge bases which can then have more traditional data mining techniques applied to the knowledge bases. Riloff and Jones (1999) illustrated an example of applying bootstrapping methods to this problem. *Text classification* is a technique that is a useful intermediary step for information extraction. Nigam et al. (2000) used bootstrapping methods, along with expectation maximization (EM), to illustrate an approach to this problem. As we can see, bootstrapping methods are a common technique set to use.

Diving just a little deeper, consider Swanson and Smalheiser (1997). Article titles in biomedical literature were analyzed to see if any fragments could be elicited; fragments, such as "stress is associated with migraines," "stress can lead to loss of magnesium," "calcium channel blockers prevent some migraines," and "magnesium is a natural calcium channel blocker," are some examples that their techniques extracted. They then went and combined their findings with human medical expertise to define novel hypotheses such as "magnesium deficiency may play a role in some kinds of migraine headache."

Readers with a familiarity with this type of technique will immediately see a major challenge: how to ensure that valid inference links can be determined without there being a combinatorial explosion of possible links. An answer, maybe the answer, is that we definitely need better models of the lexical relationships between terms along with semantic constraints. These are not easy problems to overcome.

But let us assume we have solved these problems; there is then another challenge: how the information is presented to the human experts so that data exploration is facilitated?

Unlike techniques such as exploratory data analysis and information extraction, text classification does not lead to the discovery of new information, but is targeted toward tagging documents as members of one of some set of predefined classes, and has seen application in many different disciplines including domain grouping of documents, which is useful for domain-specific information extraction, automatically sorting documents, such as email, and new event detection.

However, lots of labeled training instances are required, as is the case for information extraction. For example, using a training set of 1,000 USENET news articles resulted in an accuracy of approximately 50% when selecting articles of interest to the reader.

Oda et al. (2008) wrote about the challenges of associating literature with pathways and highlighted three main challenges:

1. Identification of them aping position of a specific entity or reaction in a given pathway
2. Recognizing the causal relationships among multiple reactions
3. Formulating and implementing required inferences based on biological domain knowledge

Their approach to solving these problems involved constructing new resources to link the text with model pathways (GENIA pathway corpus with event annotation and NF-kB pathway) and, through detailed analysis, determine "bioinferences" as well as identify differences between the textual and pathway representations. Their objective was to provide a starting point to accelerate the automatic construction of pathway information from text.

Dai et al. (2010) looked to the next decade and characterized a number of challenges that need to be addressed, as well as several opportunities for text mining in general. As more and more publishers move from paper-based to online mechanisms for accessing technical publications, the challenge for researchers is the sheer volume of literature: it is increasingly difficult to locate the information required by the researcher. Recent text mining systems (TMSs), along with publishers making articles available in XML format, allow more automatic techniques to be applied, curating the articles and maintaining the integrity of information while ensuring links to other data and resources are accurately maintained. However, new challenges have emerged that relate to full-text analysis, the terminology used in the life sciences, complex relationships and how to extract and maintain them, along with information fusion. Traditionally, abstracts have been the main textual entity used as the target of a TMS, due mainly to the fact of their availability and their short form. Since they summarize the content of the article, they provide a good launching point. However, there is much more information contained in the full-text article that highlighted several issues:

1. Errors in conversion from one electronic format (e.g., PDF, HTML) to plaintext
2. Difficulties in processing tables and figure legends
3. Multiple references to organisms and the resulting interspecies ambiguity in gene/protein normalization
4. Sentence boundary detection errors
5. Difficulties in extracting the associations and handling the coordination of multiple interaction pairs in single sentences
6. Phrases used to describe interactions in legends or titles that do not correspond to grammatically correct sentences in the text
7. Errors in shallow parsing and POS (part-of-speech)-tagging tools trained on general English text collections when applied to specific expressions and abbreviations found in biomedical texts

Issues 1 and 2 above are being helped by publishers who are making their articles available in XML format. But this is only a part of the challenge set, and in the future, for TMSs to really come into their own, they need to be much more user-focused, see much more integration, communication, and collaboration, and the level of information fusion must be much higher than is currently seen.

Changing tack, image-based data has become ubiquitous in the sciences over the last several decades, and probably more data is generated as image dataset than is the case with traditional elemental data. Here, we are not so much considering visualization as a product or output, but instead think about images as input to the mining effort itself. Ferreira de Oliveira and Levkowitz (2003) provided a good survey of visualization techniques on the output side of the equation. One technique that has seen broad acceptance as a scientific tool is *fluorescence microscopy*.

Fluorochromes are stains that attach themselves to visible or subvisible structures within the tissue or pathogen, and are often highly specific in their attachment targeting. In turn, the ratio of photon absorption to emission, the quantum yield, can be significant. Combine this with the development of new fluorophores – synthetic and natural – with known excitation and emission intensity profiles, along with well-understood biological targets, and we have an explanation as to why this technique has seen such widespread use in the biological sciences.

Visualization techniques for turning data into pictures have long been a staple of publications, combining this with techniques such as that above, means that images are with us for the long haul, and Wu et al. (2007) had developed a system – Datascope – that allows relational data to be mapped into 2D maps that can be viewed a la Google Maps.

Visual data mining research typically falls into one of two broad categories: visual data exploration systems or techniques to support knowledge extraction (or specific mining task), or visualization to display the results of a data mining algorithm. As we've indicated, our interest here is in the former of these categories.

Image data, in the form of X-rays, CT scans, MRI scans, and microarray outputs, has become more and more the norm. Our nature is to want to have the ability to visually inspect large amounts of data. While visualization is on the output side of the equation, processing image data on the input side is as important. If we use microarrays as an example, processing the raw image, ensuring quality control, and normalizing the data have to be completed before we can perform quantitative comparison of the image(s).

Readers interested in further details on image processing are referred to Burger and Burge (2008) or Acharya and Ray (2005) for a general approach, and Kamberova and Shah (2002) for specifics of dealing with microarray images. The RapidMiner Image Processing Extension tool (Burget et al. 2010) provides a broad range of capabilities, including local image feature extraction, segment feature extraction, global image feature extraction, extracting features from single/ multiple image(s), image comparison, and noise reduction, among other capabilities.

One novel data type that we are completely ignoring is the *stream data* type. This is the data that enters or exits the system as a real-time stream and is usually in a vast volume of data that changes dynamically, is possibly infinite, and is characterized by multidimensional features. Audio and video data are archetypal examples of streams of data. Traditional data repositories cannot handle this type of data, and in fact, the data may only be available for processing once in a sequential ordering. Many challenges exist in processing this type of data and its treatise is beyond the scope of this text.

3.19 Conclusion

Our foundation is our data architecture, providing access to all of the data we will use in our analyses. Ensuring that we have the most comprehensive and valid foundation possible is therefore an imperative if we wish to be able to effectively analyze and mine the data contained therein. In the majority of cases, the data environment available, or even mandated, will already be in place. We will have to work within the constraints already built into the model. Even in such cases, understanding the architecture itself will allow us to gain insight into how to best leverage the environment to our best advantage.

In cases where the data environment has not already been defined, our understanding will allow us to be active participants in designing the environment to meet not only our current needs but hopefully our future needs as well.

References

Acharya T, Ray AK (2005) Image processing: principles and applications. Wiley, Hoboken
Burger W, Burge MJ (2008) Digital image processing: an algorithmic introduction using Java. Springer, New York

Burget R et al (2010) RapidMiner image processing extension: a platform for collaborative research. International conference on telecommunications and signal processing, Baden, Austria

Chen PPS (1976) The entity-relationship model: toward a unified view of data. M.I.T. Alfred P. Sloan School of Management, Cambridge

Codd EF (1970) A relational model of data for large shared data banks. Commun ACM 13:377–387

Dai H-J et al (2010) New challenges for biological text-mining in the next decade. J Comput Sci Technol 25:169–179

Date CJ (2004) An introduction to database systems. Pearson/Addison Wesley, Boston

Ferreira de Oliveira MC, Levkowitz H (2003) From visual data exploration to visual data mining: a survey. IEEE Trans Vis Comput Graph 9:378–394

Kamberova GL, Shah SK (2002) DNA array image analysis: nuts & bolts. DNA Press, Eagleville

Leach AR, Gillet VJ (2003) An introduction to chemoinformatics. Kluwer Academic Publishers, Dordrecht/Boston

Martone ME (2007) Multiscale integration of brain data: new insights into glial architecture in health and disease. In: Gulliver multiscale bioimaging workshop, Berkeley, USA

Nigam K et al (2000) Text classification from labeled and unlabeled documents using EM. Mach Learn 39:103–134

Oda K et al (2008) New challenges for text mining: mapping between text and manually curated pathways. BMC Bioinformatics 9:S5

Riloff E, Jones R (1999) Learning dictionaries for information extraction by multi-level bootstrapping. In: Proceedings of the sixteenth national conference on artificial intelligence and the eleventh innovative applications of artificial intelligence conference innovative applications of artificial intelligence. American Association for Artificial Intelligence, Orlando, Florida, United States, pp 474–479

Swanson DR, Smalheiser NR (1997) An interactive system for finding complementary literatures: a stimulus to scientific discovery. Artif Intell 91:183–203

Tramontano A (2005) The ten most wanted solutions in protein bioinformatics, Chapman & Hall/CRC mathematical biology and medicine series. Chapman & Hall/CRC, Boca Raton

Wu T et al (2007) DataScope: viewing database contents in Google Maps' way. In: Proceedings of the 33rd international conference on very large data bases. VLDB Endowment, Vienna, Austria, pp 1314–1317

Chapter 4
Representing Data Mining Results

Abstract How many different ways can we represent our data in order to convey its meaning to its intended audience? What is the most effective approach? Is one technique better than another? The answer depends on your data, your audience, and the message you are trying to convey. In this chapter, we provide context for the output of our analyses, discussing very traditional representation methodologies, including tables, histograms, graphs, and plots of various types, as well as some of the more creative approaches that have seen increasing mindshare as vehicles of communication across the Internet. We also include an important technique that spans both the algorithmic and representation concepts – trees and rules – since such techniques can be valuable for both explanation and input to other systems and show that not all representations necessarily need to be graphical.

4.1 Introduction

Displaying results of an analysis in tabular form is a standard technique widely used in scientific and business communications. This makes it very simple for us to look at our results: we simply use the primary input attributes we are interested in and read off the output.

For example, if we consider a table containing MIC information, the rows and columns of our table will display the organisms and drugs. To determine the MIC for a particular drug/organism combination, we simply look at the intersection of the respective row and column on our table. This form of output is often referred to as a *decision table*.

We often refine this further by identifying attributes which are irrelevant and omitting them from the table. However, the question often becomes one of determining which attributes should be omitted. Alternately, we may summarize the underlying raw data, providing a valuable abstraction of the underlying data. Here, the question becomes one of determining the "correct" summarization. Although both of these issues are relatively simple to resolve, tabular representations are not

R. Sullivan, *Introduction to Data Mining for the Life Sciences*,
DOI 10.1007/978-1-59745-290-8_4, © Springer Science+Business Media, LLC 2012

always the best tool to use. Other representations will often provide a much more effective mechanism for communicating the output from our analysis.

In this chapter, we consider different representations of the results we obtain from our data mining investigations. The reader may be a little surprised by our considering output representations in this chapter while the next chapter looks at how we provide input into our mining environment: isn't this upside down? We consider these before we look at the input to our investigations, or even the models we might use, since the output can have a significant impact on our overall approach to building our model, to directing our investigation, and even to what data we may want to capture in the first place.

But there is another reason. Most organizations will already have developed a data warehouse or some other environment against which the investigator will develop models and hypotheses for mining. In such cases, obtaining the input will become a different issue. We return to this in the next chapter. There is a method to this madness – honest! While our ultimate objective would be to completely disconnect the input data from the output, this isn't always possible. In fact, in many cases, we will need to preprocess our data to support not only the raw dataset creation but also for the specific models we wish to implement. A major part of this latter activity will depend upon the various ways in which we want to represent our results. Keep with us; it will make sense in the end... possibly!

This is not to say that the choice of output representation should be the only, or even primary, criteria. It does, however, give us a mechanism for considering the transformation processes that need to be included within our models in order that we ensure that the output representation we are interested in does occur from our model.

In this chapter, we will primarily describe a number of representation mechanisms that can be used to review and communicate results generated from our models and analyses. Each of the representations and techniques described in this chapter overlaps with both the models we build since they often require the model to satisfy certain constraints, and with some of the underlying modeling techniques themselves. Further, the output representations themselves may best be used in combination to communicate your findings.

4.2   Tabular Representations

The most basic and intuitive way to represent our data is through a simple tabular representation. This might simply list our raw data, if the dataset is manageable enough, or it might provide some level of summarization. The biggest challenge is that for datasets containing more than 10–15 instances, or 10–15 attributes, simple tabular representations lose their effectiveness. We can use techniques such as sorting the data to make it a little easier to comprehend, and possibly even allow a few more instances/attributes to be included before the table becomes unwieldy, but even here, the representation quickly bogs down our understanding of what it is trying to represent. Trying to extract trends and patterns from such tables is often

Table 4.1 ALL summary information

	Male	Female	Total
Age (0–16)	8	3	11
Age (17–19)	14	7	21
Age (20–29)	21	9	30
Age (30–39)	15	4	19
Age (40–49)	10	10	20
Age (50+)	13	9	22
Totals	81	42	123

challenging and frequently impossible. Where tabular representations can be very valuable, however, is in providing summarized views of our data or where we are looking at a subset of the attributes in our dataset.

Contingency tables[1] provide a mechanism for looking at the relationship between two variables. The variables in question must be categorical or have been transformed to an equivalent categorical variable. Often, one of the variables has a binary domain, but this is not mandatory. An example contingency table, using the age and gender information from the ALL dataset (Table 4.1).[2]

We can make some determinations on the information from the data in the table, such as the total number of instances and how they are segmented between the age groups. (Note that we converted the age into a categorical variable.) Contingency tables can thus be used to aid in understanding the relationship between two categorical variables, which, as we shall see later, can be further quantified using the chi-square test, but they can also be useful for determining how good the predictions from our models are, a subject we shall also return to later.

A very common tabular representation is the *summary table* which, as its name suggests, summarizes the data in our dataset. We might, for example, create a summary table that shows us the number of patients excluded from studies by visit. Similar to the contingency table, we will normally use a single variable to group together the instances, with each row in our table representing a count of the number of instances which match that group: all other attributes included on that row must naturally pertain to the same grouping method and thus contain summary information. We will often use some of the fundamental descriptive statistics in these tables, such as the mean, sum, standard deviation, minimum, or maximum.

4.3   Decision Tables, Decision Trees, and Classification Rules

As its name suggests, a decision tree comprises a set of *nodes*, each of which is typically a comparison of an attribute with a constant, although this may be complicated by testing a group of attributes, or using a function. Each subsequent

---

[1] These are also known as cross classification tables.

[2] Data of T- and B-cell acute lymphocytic leukemia from the Ritz Laboratory at the DFCI and available from the Bioconductor web site.

node then tests another attribute *within the context of the attributes higher up in the tree*. Decision tree classifiers therefore repeatedly dive our instance space until the regions are as homogeneous as possible.

Leaf nodes of decision trees classify all instances which reach that leaf node, a set of classifications, or a probability distribution over all possible classifications. This can be particularly valuable if the instance we are considering is a previously unknown instance since the tests (nodes) higher in the tree will be used to classify the instance and, when the leaf node is reached, it will be classified automatically using the classification assigned to the leaf node.

For any given node, the number of child nodes is an important factor. This is referred to as the *branching factor*. For a nominal attribute, the number of children is often the same as the possible number of values the attribute can take. This will ensure that the same attribute is not tested again further down the tree because it will be completely tested due to there being one child for each possible value. For example, the interpretive MIC value generated through breakpoint identification uses a susceptible, intermediate, resistant (S, I, R) assignment.

If the attribute is numeric, the condition usually results in a two- or three-way split. If *missing value* is considered as a separate value, the number of splits will be one more (three way or four way). Although these are by far and away the most common methods, there is nothing preventing an *n*-way decision. However, this can often lead to more complication and obfuscation, as we shall see below. Often, a three-way split of *less than*, *equal to*, and *greater than* is used and thus generates a three-way split (or four way if the missing value option is included). This three-way categorization can be easily, and valuably, extended to consider testing against an interval rather than a single value. For example, *below*, *in*, and *above* may be used instead. Numeric attributes are often tested multiple times in any given *path* through the tree, with each test being against a different value or interval.

We can alleviate this multiple testing of a single attribute by increasing the branching factor for the specific node and having it branch on a larger number of values. However, as mentioned, this can result in the tree being significantly broader than would otherwise be the case, as well as complicating matters. We may not be interested in all of the different possible values. For example, a standard clinical test such as blood urea nitrate (BUN), while returning a continuous numeric value, we may only be interested in whether it is inside the normal range or not, or whether it is an abnormal value, or whether it is a critical value. Having a separate branch for each value within these ranges would not necessarily add anything to the analysis.

Consider an example given in Neapolitan (2003 #81) of the causal relationship between smoking, fatigue, bronchitis, chest X-ray results, and lung cancer. We might begin by developing a decision tree as shown in Fig. 4.1.

Several decisions (sic) have been made in developing the tree shown above. Each such decision can significantly affect the results which are generated. For example, we have separated the "fatigued" test from the subtree on the left-hand side; this could be due to our belief that a persons' state of tiredness is secondary if they are a smoker, and we evaluate them for bronchitis. We have also made the

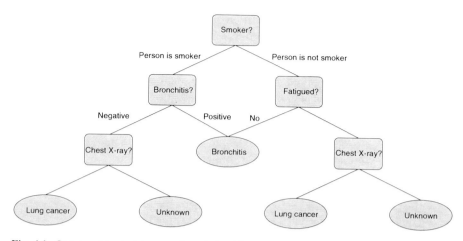

Fig. 4.1 One possible decision tree for relationship between lung cancer and other indications

decision to evaluate the patient for bronchitis before ordering a chest X-ray. This is due to our belief that the initial evaluation would occur at a physician's office and that the physician would then subsequently order an X-ray.

This naïve example illustrates that we can affect the outcome by our hypotheses and biases. This is important to keep in mind as we develop our tree structure. We return to decision trees in much more detail in Chap. 15.

Note that the chest X-ray test is performed at two places in our tree.

Although we suggested a missing value as an additional branch, this is not necessarily the most appropriate approach: it may not even make sense. Where is a missing value significant? Thus, we may want to treat a missing value as a special case. One simple approach is to keep track of the number of instances in the training set that go down each branch and then use this to guide the instance with the missing value to go down the most common branch. An alternate approach is to split the instance into parts and send each part down a different branch using weights (between 0 and 1 and chosen according to the proportion of the instances going down each branch). The sum of all weights is 1. Once all the parts reach their leaf nodes, the results must then be recombined using the weights which have percolated down the tree.

4.4 Classification and Regression Trees (CARTs)

As we have said elsewhere, *regression* is defined as the process of predicting the values of continuous variables, whereas *classification* is defined as the equivalent process for categorical variables. It is a very simple step, therefore, to intuitively defining CART as building classification trees and regression trees for predictive purposes.

Although we consider the classification and regression algorithms elsewhere in this book, we will summarize the problems here so that we can discuss how these trees are used to represent our results.

Regression problems can be generically defined as trying to predict the values of a continuous variable from one or more other predictors (continuous or discrete). For example, we may be interested in predicting the total cholesterol levels of patients from other continuous variables such as body mass index and various test results, as well as categorical variables such as gender and ethnicity.

Classification problems are the analogous problems for categorical variables. For example, we may be interested in predicting whether or not a patient will unilaterally terminate their enrollment in a clinical trial based upon various demographic variables we are capturing.

As we shall see later, there are numerous methods and algorithms that can be used to address these types of problems, such as generalized linear models (GLM), regression, generalized nonlinear models, generalized additive models (GAM), and log-linear analysis, to name a few.

At their most fundamental, classification and regression trees, built via tree-building algorithms, attempt to determine a set of logical conditions (if-then clauses) that permits us to accurately classify or predict cases.

We shall use some nomenclature from graph theory as it relates to any tree (which is a type of graph). The *root* of the tree is one node of the tree designated as such and which naturally defines a direction for the tree's edges. Another way of thinking of this is that the root is the single node of the tree composed of all observations and is the location of the first decision (or split). For our purposes, it has no parent nodes and one or more child nodes. A *node* is any point at which a decision (or split) occurs and which has a single parent and one or more child nodes. A *leaf node* is a node which has a single parent and no child nodes. Intuitively, therefore, we traverse the tree beginning at the root node (which comprises our first decision point), down a hierarchy of nodes (each of which comprises a separate and distinct decision point) to the leaf nodes (which define our final decision points). An example tree is shown in Fig. 4.2.

We have purposely left two of the boxes blank to highlight the leaf-node classifications and will return to these later.

Consider an example where we have a simple dataset of patient information that contains attributes about the patient's BMI, whether they are a smoker or not, and the results of a set of five tests $(X_1, X_2, X_3, X_4, X_5)$. An example of the information for one patient might be

29.4, $Y, X_1, X_2, X_3, X_4, X_5$.

Using this data, we need to make decisions on how our CART model will be built. For example, do we test first whether the patient is a smoker or test their BMI? Or do we use one of the tests as the first step? If, for example, our first test measured the patient's lung capacity, this may make our tree more manageable, or less. These are important decisions because they can affect both the complexity and success of the tree classification method: when such methods work, they provide very accurate results with a very few logical conditions (if-then-else).

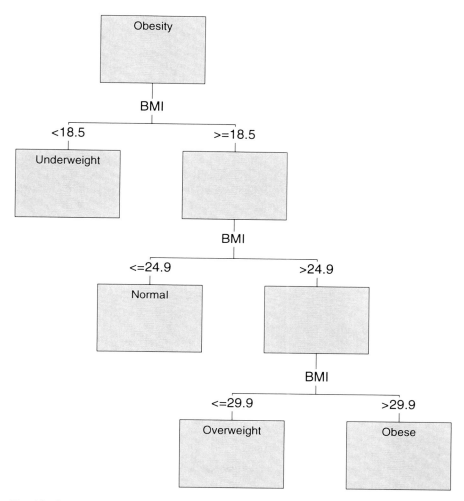

Fig. 4.2 Classification tree

If we assume that the person's lifestyle habits (i.e., whether they are a smoker or not) is the first factor we need to consider, our tree will have a rule at the root node as follows:

```
if patient-is-smoker then … else …
```

Note that we explicitly include the "else" clause in our notation since it provides a more complete textual notation for the rules and because we believe it aids in communicating the results to other interested parties.

Interpreting the results from a tree is very simple, which is valuable not only for quickly incorporating new instances into the tree but also for providing a much simpler definition for the model by explaining why instances were classified/ predicted as they were. It is much simpler to explain a small number of if-then-else rules than a slew of equations, for example.

It is also worthwhile noting that tree methods do not care about the underlying relationships between the variables. That is, whether there is a linear or nonlinear relationship between predictor variables and dependent variables (or explanatory and response variables), or any other relationship between them. This makes this type of method particularly useful in data mining because we often know little to nothing about the variables and their interrelationships *a priori*. This type of method can, therefore, highlight relationships using only a few variables that may not be so obvious through other analytical methods.

One factor that we need to be concerned about, however, is when do we stop splitting the tree? Or, equivalently, when do we stop the tree-building process? This can be of particular concern in the real world when noise is encountered in the dataset. On one extreme, if we have n instances in our dataset and perform $n - 1$ splits, this would allow us to predict each case. In general, we would want to split a *sufficient* number of times in order to validate our model by reproducing the original dataset. However, this will not typically generalize and be valuable when new instances are introduced to the rule engine: this will typically extract all of the information available in our current dataset but perform badly in the face of new data being introduced.

This issue is an example of the more general case and is generically discussed in Chap. 2. The heuristic we often use is to take an (informal) measure of the improvement gained as a result of introducing more splits into our model. Going from a prediction level of 90%, say, with n splits, to 91% with $n + 1$ splits may be worthwhile; going from 90% to 90.01% is not. There are many criteria which can be used for automatically stopping the tree-building process, a full description of which is beyond the scope of this text. Interested readers are recommended to texts such as Hall (2001).

Once we have a stable tree, using a different set of instances, that is, a set which was not used in the initial building phase, to evaluate the quality of the prediction capability of the tree is a very valuable activity as it may allow us to prune the tree to a simpler structure: a structure with less branches but the same predictive power for correctly predicting or classifying previously unseen instances.

One method we can use is the process of *cross-validation*. This is where we take a tree built from a set of instances and apply it, as mentioned above, to a completely independent set of instances. If the branches of the tree were developed because of random noise in the first set of instances, rather than on real classifications/ predictions, then the tree's ability to predict/classify in the second, independent set of instances will be relatively poor and not very useful. This shows us that the tree itself is not composed of the correct branches and needs to be reconsidered.

An enhancement to this concept, referred to as *v-fold cross-validation*, repeats the above analysis n times with different, randomly drawn sets of instances (samples), for every tree structure, starting at the root of the tree. Each subtree is then applied to predicting results from randomly selected samples. The tree which shows the best accuracy, averaged across all of the predicted outputs, will be accepted as the "best" tree. This approach provides a powerful method for selecting a smaller tree from a larger tree and can be very useful when smaller datasets are being used.

Trees can quickly become very large and unwieldy when trying to present the trees to data analysts, management, or scientific personnel. The size of the tree, however, does not comprise a computational problem since the branches are very simple computational structures typically, and so, implementing trees within traditional programming constructs or within specialty software such as PHYLIP[3] or Geneious[4] does not typically suffer significant performance issues due to the size of the tree – although the dataset size is a definite factor.

4.4.1 Process

Building on our above discussion, we can think of the process for developing CARTs as comprising the following steps:

• Determining the criteria for predictive accuracy
• Building the tree – identifying the branches
• Pruning the tree – determining when to terminate branching
• Selecting the correct ("right-sized") tree

In the next sections, we will refer to a *learning dataset*. This is a subset of our dataset that we elect to use to develop our tree. Obviously, the end result of this will be a tree which completely and accurately classifies each of the instances in our learning dataset. However, our intent, as is the case in every learning methodology, is to generate a model (tree) which will effectively classify or predict previously unknown instances from our larger dataset.

4.4.1.1 Predictive Accuracy

Theoretically, CART algorithms aim to achieve the best possible predictive accuracy (with a minimum rate of misclassification), but in practice, this is usually tempered by striving for the best accuracy at minimum cost. While cost may relate to computational processing, time, or other characteristics of the model, in this context, it is usually considered to mean the lowest rate of misclassification. However, in cases where some misclassifications are much more significant (i.e., more catastrophic) than others, we will often expand the concept of cost accordingly.

---

[3] http://evolution.genetics.washington.edu/phylip.html
[4] http://www.geneious.com/

In classification problems, where we are dealing with categorical responses, we can use *prior probabilities* to help us minimize costs. These priors are assumed to be proportional to the class sizes, and misclassification costs are assumed to be equal for each class. Care must be taken in using *a priori* probabilities since they can significantly affect the classification process itself. Priors are not required for regression problems.

4.4.1.2 Building the Tree – Branching

As mentioned above, we could introduce branches until every case in our dataset is perfectly processed. This would not make sense since the end result would be a tree that is as complex as the original dataset, and it would be highly unlikely that the tree would be useful in predicting or classifying any new instances that are presented to it. We return to this overfitting issue below.

To build our tree, we recursively branch the nodes of the tree so that each resulting node is assigned a class for the data based on the distribution of the classes from our learning dataset which would occur at that node. Note that we assign this class to the node irrespective of whether a subsequent step branches the current node into child nodes.

We begin with the root node of the tree, which includes all of the data in our learning dataset. We evaluate all of the variables to determine the "best" possible variable to split the dataset into two child nodes. When evaluating which variable would be the "best," we typically attempt to maximize the average purity (homogeneity) of the child nodes. Several methods may be used to accomplish this, including information gain, Gini branching, Twoing rule, *t* test, and entropy, which are described below. Each of these methods provides us with a measure of the impurity of the node under consideration.

Gini Branching

Gini branching looks for the largest class in the dataset and isolates all of the data that falls into that class into a single node. For example, if our dataset comprised four classes of data, where class A comprised 40% of the data, class B comprised 30%, class C comprised 20%, and class D comprised 10%, Gini would separate class A into one child node, while classes B, C, and D would comprise the other child node.[5]

Now, the Gini branching method will continue to split the data that requires further segmentation. In our artificial example, this will be the second child node

---

[5] We are, of course, making an assumption that the data can be easily split accordingly. This may not be possible given the data in our learning dataset. However, if it is, Gini branching will choose this split.

which currently contains classes B, C, and D. In this case, the algorithm will partition class B into a child node, leaving classes C and D in the other child node. Continuing, it will create a subsequent branching to put class C into a child node and class D into the other child node, as shown below.

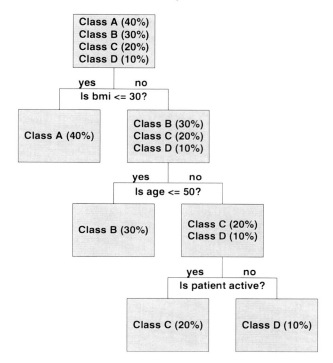

The real world, unfortunately, will rarely allow us to get such a pure tree from our methodology. It is much more usual to find, say, that the majority of our "class A" will be segmented into its own node, but that some small number of "class A" instances will find their way into our second node.

Thus, the Gini branching method partitions the data by focusing on a single class at a time. It will always tend toward the largest class in the dataset or, if weighting or costing is employed, the class deemed the most important class when the costs/ weights are applied. While this may at first seem naïve, the performance of Gini branching and its resulting accuracy not only make this a technique that should be considered; it is worth trying just to see how good a job it does.

Mathematically, the Gini index for a given node t is defined as

$$\text{Gini}(t) = 1 - \sum_{i=1}^{n} [p(i|t)]^2, \tag{4.1}$$

where $p(i|t)$ denotes the relative frequency of the class i at the node t.

Table 4.2 Gini allocation output

C_1	C_2	C_3	C_4	Gini
0	0	12	0	0
1	2	4	5	0.681
2	3	4	3	0.736
3	3	3	3	0.75

We can see that the maximum value occurs when $\sum_{i=1}^{n} [p(i|t)]^2$ is at its minimum. This occurs when the data is equally distributed among all of the classes at that node, implying the *least interesting information* is obtained. The minimum value, however, occurs when $\sum_{i=1}^{n} [p(i|t)]^2$ is at its maximum. This situation occurs when the data all belongs to a single class at that node, implying the *most interesting information* is obtained.

Consider this illustration where we have a dataset of 12 instances distributed across 4 classes (C_1, C_2, C_3, C_4) at our node of interest.

Implementing (4.1) in R gives us

```
gini <- function(classAllocation) {
      1 - sum((classAllocation/sum(classAllocation))^2)
}
```

We will use four simple class allocations:

```
classAllocation1 <- c(0, 0, 12, 0)
classAllocation2 <- c(1, 2, 4, 5)
classAllocation3 <- c(2, 3, 4, 3)
classAllocation4 <- c(3, 3, 3, 3)
```

The results of running `gini(classAllocationn)` where n is 1–4 is shown in Table 4.2.

When any given node t is split into k children, we can compute the quality of the branching using the following equation:

$$\text{Gini}_{\text{split}} = \sum_{i=1}^{n} \frac{n_i}{n} \text{Gini}(i), \tag{4.2}$$

where n_i is the number of instances we have at the child node and n is the number of instances at node t.

For example, consider our second class allocation $(1, 2, 4, 5)$ with Gini $= 0.681$. Assuming a binary branch, we may have the following partitioning of our 12 instances among the two child nodes:

	Child$_1$	Child$_2$
C_1	1	0
C_2	1	1
C_3	2	2
C_4	3	2
	7	5

```
childNode1Allocation <- c(1 ,1, 2, 3) # total = 7
childNode2Allocation <- c(0, 1, 2, 2) # total = 5
gini(childNode1Allocation)
0.6938776
gini(childNode2Allocation)
0.64
7/12*gini(childNode1Allocation) + 5/12*gini(childNode2Allocation)
0.6714286 # gini branch quality measure
```

So how do we use this information to make decisions? As we have said above, our goal is to extract the most interesting information we can with any of the techniques we use. Therefore, we are interested in looking at the smallest Gini index when we use this technique.

Twoing Rule

The Twoing rule takes a very different approach to Gini branching. Twoing attempts to find a group of classes which, when taken together, add up to 50% of the dataset under consideration. It then attempts to find a branching to separate the two subgroups. In our above example, it would split the data so that class A and class D are in one child node, while class B and class C are in the other node.

As is the case with any technique, such a perfect partitioning is highly unlikely, but if it does exist, the Twoing rule will attempt to find it.

Entropy

This rule is based upon calculating the information gained by splitting the current node. It is similar to the Twoing rule. In essence, for the variables under consideration, we calculate which attribute has the highest *information gain* and use that variable to determine the branching. This variable will minimize the information needed to classify the data in the resulting partitions and therefore indicates the least "impurity" in the partitions. Taking this approach will minimize the expected number of tests needed to classify a given instance. It will also guarantee that a simple tree results, but it will not necessarily guarantee that the resulting tree is the simplest possible tree.

Mathematically, given a partition of data D, with m possible distinct classifications C_i, where $i = 1, \ldots, m$, then the information needed to classify an instance in our partition is given by

$$I_D = -\sum_{i=1}^{m} p(i|t)\log_2 p(i|t),$$

where $p(i|t)$ is the relative frequency of an arbitrary instance of D belonging to class C_i and is estimated by $|C_{i,D}|/|D|$. I_D is also called the *entropy* of D.

I_D measures the level of homogeneity of a node. As with the Gini method, the maximum value occurs when the instances are equally distributed among the classes – least information – and the minimum occurs when all the instances belong to one class – most information.

The calculations are similar to the calculations for the Gini index.

Information Gain

We can define the *information gain* at a branch as

$$\text{Gain} = I_D(t) - \left(\sum_{i=1}^{k} \frac{n_i}{n} I_D(i) \right),$$

where I_D is our entropy measure, as defined above; t is our parent node; k is the number of partitions at the branch; n_i is the number of instances in partition i; and n is the total number of instances at node t.

Information gain measures the reduction in entropy which occurs because of the branching. We typically use this measure to select the split which achieves the *most* reduction in entropy, that is, the split which maximizes the gain.[6]

There is a downside to using this measure, however, and that is that the calculation tends to favor branching options that result in a larger number of smaller, but pure, partitions. This may not always be valuable to us. To overcome this disadvantage, we can use a different calculation, the *gain ratio*.

Here, we divide the value of the information gain by the entropy of the branching, as shown below:

$$\text{Gain}_{\text{ratio}} = \frac{I_D(t) - \left(\sum_{i=1}^{k} \frac{n_i}{n} I_D(i) \right)}{I_D(t)},$$

where $I_D = - \sum_{i=1}^{m} p(i|t) \log_2 p(i|t)$.

Thus, higher values of I_D, which imply a larger number of smaller partitions, will result in lower values for the $\text{Gain}_{\text{ratio}}$. This is used in C4.5.

Branching Based on Classification Error

The intent of branching in our trees is to improve our ability to partition our dataset into some k different classes, hopefully where each partition is a pure as possible.

---

[6] This measure is used in ID3 and C4.5.

We have seen several approaches to doing this. If we reconsider the nature of the term pure, in this context, we are interested in minimizing misclassification errors wherever possible; we can measure this by considering the "majority class" at each node. Above, we use the term $p(i|t)$ to denote the relative frequency of class i at node t. We could, therefore, consider node t's purity by comparing the relative frequencies for each class and consider that the class with the maximum value of $p(i|t)$ at this node be our basis for misclassification. Consider, without loss of generality, that class 1 has the maximum value of $p(i|t)$. We could say that any instance *not* classified into class 1 has been misclassified and define the following measure

$$\text{error}_t = 1 - \max_i (p(i|t)),$$

which says that the misclassification error made at node t is 1 minus the maximum value of $p(i|t)$. This measure has a maximum when the instances are equally distributed among all classes (least interesting information) and a minimum when all the instances belong to a single class (most interesting information).

The value is most easily seen from an example. Consider the class allocations we used to illustrate the Gini method:

```
classAllocation1 <- c(0, 0, 12, 0)
classAllocation2 <- c(1, 2,  4, 5)
classAllocation3 <- c(2, 3,  4, 3)
classAllocation4 <- c(3, 3,  3, 3)
```

Our misclassification function, in R, is

```
mcError <- function(classAllocation) {
        1 - max(classAllocation/sum(classAllocation))
}
```

Running each of our examples through gives us the following results:

```
> classAllocation1
[1]  0  0 12  0
> mcError(classAllocation1)
[1] 0
> classAllocation2
[1] 1 2 4 5
> mcError(classAllocation2)
[1] 0.5833333
> classAllocation3
[1] 2 3 4 3
> mcError(classAllocation3)
[1] 0.6666667
> classAllocation4
[1] 3 3 3 3
> mcError(classAllocation4)
[1] 0.75
```

Comparison of Branching Methods

It is instructive to review the nature of the different branching methods we have
discussed above. For this purpose, we shall look at the problem where we have two
classes to consider. In fact, we shall assume that the response values have the form
p, $1 - p$ and that each method will be parameterized with such pairs of class
allocations. That is, we shall pass pairs of values of the form p, $1 - p$ to each of
the methods as

entropy($c(p,\ 1 - p)$),
gini($c(p,\ 1 - p)$),
mcError($c(p,\ 1 - p)$),

where the functions are as defined in the above sections.
    We shall create three variables to hold the values of applying the pairs of
response variable values to the three methods and create two sequences c1 and c2
to hold the values of p, $1 - p$, respectively, as shown below.

```
c1 <- seq( 0, 10,  0.1)    # = p
c2 <- seq(10,  0, -0.1)    # = 1-p
cEntropy <- numeric(length(c1))
cGini    <- numeric(length(c1))
cError   <- numeric(length(c1))
```

    We can now iterate through our class allocations to create Gini, entropy, and
misclassification error values as shown below.

```
for (i in seq(1, length(c1))) {
      cEntropy[i]  <- entropy(c(c1[i], c2[i]))
      cGini[i]     <- gini(c(c1[i], c2[i]))
      cError[i]    <- mcError(c(c1[i], c2[i]))
      if(!is.finite(cEntropy[i])) {
            cEntropy[i] = 0 # Yeah, we know, this is bad!!!
      }
}
```

    Before any mathematically inclined reader jumps up in horror, we know! We
know! The value of $0 \times \log(0) = 0$ in the entropy calculation, but mathematically,
$\log(0)$ is $-\infty$.
    Now we can plot the various lines to obtain the output in Fig. 4.3.

```
plot(c(0,1), c(0,1), type="n", xlab="p", ylab="")
title(main="Comparison of Branching Method Criteria")
p <- c1/10
lines(p, cEntropy)
text(0.15,0.8, "Entropy")
lines(p, cGini, col="red")
text(0.3,0.5, "Gini")
lines(p, cError, col="blue")
text(0.45,0.2, "Misclassification Error")
```

Fig. 4.3 Comparison of branching method criteria

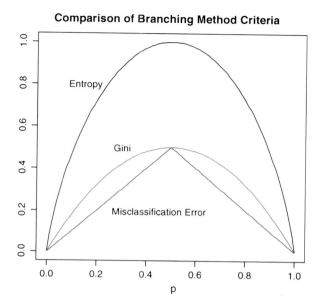

Continuous Variables: Sum of Squared Errors

Where we are undertaking regression analysis through regression trees, we are dealing with continuous target data that needs a different technique. The most widely used is the sum of squared errors.

We are interested in finding the branching that produces the greatest separation in

$$\sum_{i=1}^{n} [y - E(y)]^2,$$

which means that we are interested in finding those nodes with minimal *variance within* the node and maximum *variance between* nodes.

Minimum *n* and Fraction of Objects

We allow branching to continue until the leaf nodes are pure (homogeneous) or contain at most a minimum number of cases: the *minimum n* case. In the *fraction of objects* case, we again allow branching to continue until the leaf nodes are pure or contain at most a minimum fraction of the sizes of one or more classes.

Whichever method is used, the tree building process will continue until it is impossible to branch any further. This terminating condition occurs when:

(a) Each node contains only a single instance.
(b) All of the instances in each child node have the same distribution of the classification/predictor variables.
(c) The user has predetermined a maximum tree depth.

Upon terminating, we need to refine the tree since, as we've mentioned above, the tree created by this automatic process will invariably suffer from overfitting: every nuance and idiosyncrasy of the data will be incorporated into the tree. As might be expected, the level of overfitting is higher in the later branching choices than in the earlier choices. If we refer back to our abstract example for Gini branching, we see that one part of the tree (the left part in our figure) required very few branching levels, but the other part needed a larger number of levels to fit the dataset.

4.4.1.3   Pruning the Tree

By this step, we have generated a tree that will typically overfit the information that is contained within our dataset. The tree as it currently stands is often referred to as the *maximal* tree. As we have discussed elsewhere, overfitting is a problem that we often encounter in data mining. To eliminate this problem, we undertake an activity to prune the tree. Essentially, this consists of creating a sequence of ever more simple trees by eliminating ever more important nodes of the tree.

The methodology used to prune the tree uses some measure of *cost*, typically denoted by a parameter, α, that takes on an increasing value during the pruning process. At the leaf node level, the child nodes are pruned if the resulting change in misclassification cost is less than α times the change in the tree's complexity. With this definition, we can see that α is actually a measure of how much additional accuracy must be introduced into the tree to warrant the additional complexity that results from a branch being introduced.

As we iterate up through the tree, the value of α is increased which results in nodes of increasing importance being pruned from the tree, thus resulting in simpler trees being generated from the pruning activity.

Obviously, there is a trade-off between the simplicity of the tree and the misclassification which occurs because of the pruning activity. The question becomes where and how do we determine the optimal tree?

4.4.1.4   Selecting the "Correct" Tree

We now have a series of trees – the sequence of pruned trees – from which we will select one that fits the information from our learning dataset but doesn't suffer from the overfitting problem – the optimal tree. Although we cannot provide definitive rules for what constitutes the "correct" tree to be selected, there are a couple of heuristics that we can consider:

• While being as simple as possible, the tree must be sufficient to account for all the known facts.
• It should leverage information that improves its predictive/classification accuracy and ignore information that does not.
• It should increase our understanding of the phenomena it describes.

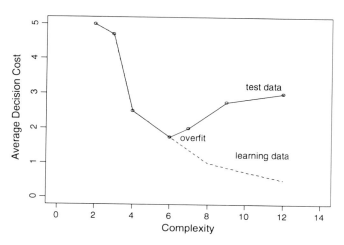

Since we will have used a particular part of our dataset to develop the tree, there is a definite issue with the balance of the tree and its value for a more general dataset. Consider the figure to the right. As the number of nodes increases (denoted by the complexity axis), the decision cost reduces. This is the fact that we stated earlier: the maximal tree will always give the best fit to the learning dataset. However, for an independent dataset, labeled "test data," we would expect the decision cost to decrease to some minimum and then increase thereafter as the complexity increases. Thus, an overfitted tree will not typically perform well against some as yet unseen set of data.

4.4.2 Cross-validation

One of the issues that we encounter with CART is the need for an independent validation dataset, as alluded to above. Once we have selected our optimal tree, we need to determine that it does, in fact, perform as expected. Sometimes it is not feasible to obtain a validation dataset. In such cases, we can use the technique of cross-validation.

Essentially, cross-validation consists of taking our learning dataset and randomly splitting it into n smaller sections, stratified by the variable of interest. This will ensure that each of the n subsets of data contain a similar distribution of the outcomes of interest. We select one of these subsets and reserve it for use as an independent test set. The other $n - 1$ are combined and used as our learning dataset for building our model. We repeat this process n times, with a different subset of the data being reserved as the test set on each iteration. We thus develop n models, each of which is tested against an independent set of data. The average performance of these n models is found to be a surprisingly accurate estimate of the performance of the original model, produced using the complete set of data, on a future independent dataset.

An area that is seeing much interest in CART is in developing reliable clinical decision rules. The relative simplicity of this method, when compared with traditional statistical approaches, allows scientists to develop such rules that can be useful in classifying new patients into clinically important categories such as risk categories from which appropriate treatment decisions may be made.

As might already be understood, creating any clinical decision rule will need a large dataset. This large dataset can, when used with statistical methods, be part of the challenge since there are often many different variables which could be used for our prediction or classification activity and selecting the "correct" one is often nontrivial. Since many clinical variables do not conform with a normal (Gaussian) distribution, and since different groups, for example different ethnic groups, may have significantly different characteristics (e.g., variances), complex methods may be necessary to effectively integrate them into a simple set of clinically relevant rules. Adding to these issues, the data itself may manifest complex patterns or, since it is one of the goals of data mining, may **not** manifest such patterns – patterns which may nonetheless exist. Such patterns will often be difficult to model, and, as the number of (possible) interactions increases, the complexity may increase so quickly as to make it impossible to use. In cases such as these, CART provides an effective analytical tool that generates easily usable models of surprisingly high quality and value.

The CART approach has several advantages over other classification methods, including:

- It is a nonparametric method (i.e., no assumptions are made about the underlying distribution of predictor values).
- It can handle skewed data, categorical data, or multimodal data.
- Variables used for branching are identified through an exhaustive search of all possibilities since the algorithms used by CART implementations tend to be highly efficient; all possible variables can be searched.
- Relatively little input/analysis is required *a priori* since CART's learning methodology is relatively automatic.
- CARTs are relatively simple to interpret by anyone.

However, there are some disadvantages that should be kept in mind when considering CART for your mining efforts:

- CART is not widely known and so subject to resistance to accepting the methodology.
- Earlier tree-based methodologies suffered from performance issues.

4.4.3   Summary

Table 4.3 provides a summary of CART techniques.

Table 4.3 Classification and regression tree techniques

	Classification trees	Regression trees
Branching methods	Gini, entropy, Twoing	Sum of squared errors
Goodness of fit	Misclassification rate	Misclassification rate
		Sum of squared errors
Prior probabilities and misclassification costs	Model parameters	Not applicable

4.5 Association Rules

4.5.1 *Context*

The very concept of a pattern is fundamental to data mining and can take many different forms. Associations and correlations flow through much of data mining since they form two important classes of pattern that we are interested in.

A *frequent itemset* is defined as a set of items which occurs frequently (sic) together in a dataset. An example that is often touted, but is probably more of an urban legend than a real example, is the "diapers and beer" story in which an analysis of the behaviors of supermarket shoppers found that both of these products were purchased together more often than would be accounted for by random chance. The story is that on further analysis, it was found that customers (presumably young fathers) would often buy beer when they went to the store to buy diapers.

Irrespective of its correlation to reality, the above apocryphal(?) story does illustrate some of the characteristics that we talk about with association rules:

- We are interested in any interesting correlation between data in our dataset.
- Associations may be between items that, at first blush, appear to have no relationship to each other.[7]
- The relationship is typically an *implication* relationship, denoted by $\Rightarrow$, such as $A \Rightarrow B$, which is read as "A implies B" or "if A is true then B is true."[8]
- We typically identify the *support*[9] and *confidence* of our association. These are measures we use to determine how interesting the association really is. Support measures how much of our dataset includes the two attributes A and B in the same instance; confidence measures the percentage of cases in which if we find A in the instance, then we will find B. For example, an association rule of the form

$$A \Rightarrow B \ [\text{support} = 2\%, \text{confidence} = 60\%]$$

---

[7] An interesting example relates to the drug Viagra which was initially clinically tested as a heart drug but which...well, you know how that ended up.

[8] We shall return to this form of the rule later.

[9] Witten and Frank (2005 #11) used the term *coverage* synonymously with support.

means that 2% of the instances in our dataset contain both A and B and that in 60% of the cases when A occurred, B was also found.

We can think of the attributes in our universe as a set of Boolean values that, for each instance, indicates the presence or absence of that value *in some context*. The context is, initially, our dataset of interest. We can then analyze the Boolean vectors within our dataset to identify patterns which reflect attributes which are frequently associated with each other. For example, we might find elevated triglycerides whenever we see low levels of LDL cholesterol.

If we take a brief step back at this point, it is pretty obvious that formulating association rules based upon the above definition would often result in a huge number of rules being identified. This is, actually, one of the downsides of association rule mining. In the extreme case, every attribute has an association to every other attribute, but the vast majority are as interesting to us as a colonoscopy without the sedative! Thankfully, we rarely have rules of the form $A \Rightarrow B$. Instead, our rules typically have more attributes on the left-hand side: $[X_1, X_2, \ldots, X_k] \Rightarrow Y$. In this type of rule, the simple fact that we are associating several attributes together to develop an implication will typically reduce the number of associations identified. However, there are also two other measures that we use. The *minimum support threshold* is used in combination with the *support* value for any given rule: if the support for that rule is below the minimum support threshold, then that rule is discarded as being "uninteresting." The *minimum confidence threshold* similarly acts as a baseline for the *confidence* for any given rule: if a rule's confidence falls below this value, the rule is discarded. These values can be set by users or domain experts to help weed out the noise.

We shall see how such thresholds can help us to process very large sets of data, as is usually the case with data mining, when we look at the *Apriori algorithm* (see Agrawal and Srikant 1994 #93; Han (2006 #14; or Witten and Frank 2005 #11) below.

Consider our universe of attributes (or items) to be a set $I = \{I_1, I_2, \ldots, I_n\}$ and our dataset, D, to be a set of instances[10] where each instance T is, in turn, a set of items such that $T \subseteq I$. That is, we have a universe of items of interest, denoted by I, from which our dataset, D, is taken. Each instance of D is a transaction T that is made up of some (sub)set of attributes from I. This is an important first checkpoint because we have possibly already made our first important decision: which members of I to omit, assuming that $T \subset I$.

Let A be some other set of items. T is said to *contain* A if and only if $A \subseteq T$. This is where our second decision point comes in. If $A = T$, then we are saying we are interested in rules where every attribute in our dataset must be considered. Although this is obviously true, in practice, we are usually more concerned with proper subsets of the attributes.

---

[10] This is also often referred to as a *transaction*. We have elected to continue with our definition of our dataset being analyzed as comprising a set of instances.

We define an association rule to be of the form $A \Rightarrow B$ where $A \subset I$, $B \subset I$, and $A \cap B = \phi$. That is, we are looking at cases where some subset of I being true implies that some other subset of I is (possibly) true. (We'll return to the "possibly" part below.) We are also saying that the sets of items A and B have no items in common (the $A \cap B = \phi$ part). Since we are making this assertion, A, B must be proper subsets of I, respectively, otherwise they would have some item in common. We discuss the limiting case in the box below, but this can be skipped by the reader without any significant impact.

We say that the rule $A \Rightarrow B$ holds in D with support s and confidence c, where s is the number of transactions (typically denoted by a percentage) that contain both A and B, $A \cup B$ and is typically measured as the probability $P(A \cup B)$. The measure of confidence, c, is the percentage of D containing A that also contains B. That is, the subset of D that contains B, where we know that the subset already contains A. This is similarly measured as a probability and is the conditional probability $P(B|A)$.

To illustrate this last concept, consider a set T of 100 instances each containing a set of attributes, such that $T = \{I_1, I_2, \ldots, I_k\}$. We select some subset of these attributes $A = \{I_1, I_2, \ldots, I_i\}$ and discover that 60% of T contain A – $P(A) = 0.60$. Denote this set of 60 instances by T_A. We now consider only T_A when looking for the confidence. We **know** that 60% of our dataset contain A; now we want to know what the probability is that any instance of T_A also contains our other set of attributes, $B = \{I_{i+1}, I_{i+2}, \ldots, I_k\}$. Since any instance of T **must** contain A, we can simply look at T_A. We look at conditional probability in Appendix A and also in Chap. 6, as well as below.

To summarize the above discussion,

$$\text{support}(A \Rightarrow B) = P(A \cup B),$$

$$\text{confidence}(A \Rightarrow B) = P(B|A).$$

For the sake of completeness, we discuss the limiting situation. This is the case in which $A \cup B = T$. Note that, in turn, $T = I$ may be true. What does $A \cup B = T$ mean? In the context of our data mining efforts, we are saying that every attribute in our dataset can be associated with each other. Ignoring the context of support and confidence for the moment, this means that for at least one instance in our dataset, we can find an association that relates every one of the attributes together, and that association is meaningful. Isn't this a good thing? Obviously, but it also implies that we have selected our set T with more knowledge than is necessarily valuable. Remember that our goal is to uncover both known and unknown patterns. If $T = \{I_1, I_2, \ldots, I_k\}$, where $k \leq n$, then this says that for some i, $A = \{I_1, I_2, \ldots, I_i\}$ and $B = \{I_{i+1}, I_{i+2}, \ldots, I_k\}$. In such a case, we are limiting our analysis in that we don't know what we might find in the subset of items $\{I_{k+1}, I_{k+2}, \ldots, I_n\}$ that we have omitted.

(continued)

Ok, so what are we saying? The limiting situation is most likely one that we can identify and understand without the need for a significant data mining effort. The value of data mining for associations really comes into play when we judiciously use our knowledge of the data. In this limiting case, we are really constraining our models by what we know. Thus, from the perspective of the authors, we consider the limiting case where we are looking at all of the attributes in T or even in I as an exception that could typically be supported without need to mine the data.

4.5.2   The Apriori Algorithm

The *Apriori* algorithm (Agrawal et al. 1993 #147; Agrawal and Srikant 1994 #93) operates on a set of transactions within a database and so has direct applicability to our concept of a dataset as a collection of instances. We introduce the term *itemset*, which is defined as a set of items; a *k-itemset* is an itemset containing k items. The term itemset is used when discussing the Apriori algorithm. Essentially, the algorithm tries to find common subsets in the dataset that are common to at least a minimum number C of the instances. C is called the *cutoff*, or *confidence threshold*. We also use a value *min_sup*, the *minimum support threshold*, with the meaning already defined for support. The Apriori algorithm is used to mine frequent itemsets from our dataset for Boolean association rules.

The algorithm uses the concept of a "bottom-up" approach by extending frequent itemsets one item at a time – to generate *candidates* – and test groups of candidates against the data. When no successful extensions are found, the algorithm terminates. The algorithms' breadth-first search and hash tree structure is used to count the instance sets. As noted above, each candidate set of length k attributes is generated from sets of length $k - 1$. At each stage, candidates that have an infrequent subpattern are pruned and discarded.[11]

Another way of thinking about this is that *k-itemsets* are used to explore k + 1-*itemsets*. The algorithm begins by identifying the set of frequent *1-itemsets*, denoted *L1*. *L1* is then used to find the set of frequent *2-itemsets*, denoted *L2*. This, in turn, is used to find the set of *3-itemsets*, *L3*, and so on until no more *k-itemsets* can be found (Fig. 4.4).

In step 2, we refer to the *Apriori property* to reduce the search space. This reduction of the search space to avoid finding each L_k requires a full scan of our dataset. If a given itemset I does not satisfy min_sup, we discard I because I is not

---

[11] The algorithm suffers from a number of inefficiencies and trade-offs that have resulted in many other algorithms being proposed. For more details, see the articles cited or search "Apriori algorithm."

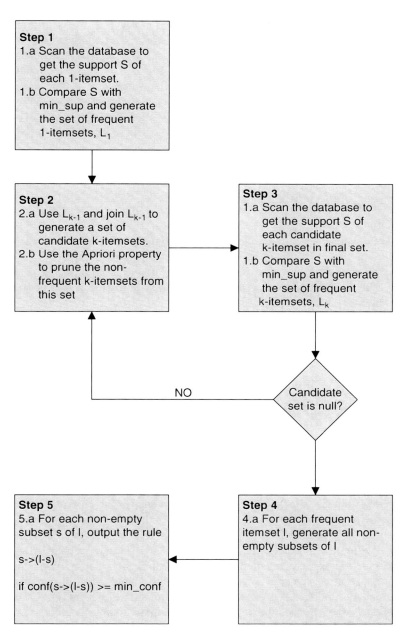

Fig. 4.4 Apriori algorithm

frequent ($P(I)<min\_sup$). Note that if we add an item A to I, the resulting itemset ($I \cup A$) cannot be any more frequent than I and so $P(I \cup A)<min\_sup$ also.

The *join* step is intended to generate a set of candidate itemsets and is accomplished by joining L_{k-1} with itself, to form the candidate set denoted C_k. The *prune* step, as its name suggests, eliminates itemsets using the Apriori property noted above. In step 5, the function conf(s->l-s) is defined as

$$\text{conf(A - >B)} = \text{support(AB)/support(A)}, \quad \text{where support(A - >B)}$$
$$= \text{support(AB)}.$$

4.5.3 *Rules, Rules, and More Rules*

Rules are a natural way of representing knowledge. In our everyday lives, we use structures such as "if it's raining, I'd better take an umbrella" implicitly as well as explicitly. In microbiology, for example, we might say "if the dosage given shows toxicity, the bug-drug combination interpretation is 'intermediate'" as opposed to susceptible or resistant.

But such natural language definitions do not provide a mechanism that can easily be incorporated into a systems-based environment. Systems such as RuleML or the Rule Definition Language (RDL) provide a generic approach. Products such as Blaze Advisor® include their own methods for defining rules. For general-purpose environments, rule engines such as Jess (for Java) provide a complete and generic foundation for implementing rule-based systems. In addition to the actual definition, an associated rule engine interprets the rules and applies them, typically, to our data. The artificial intelligence discipline of rule-based systems, also historically referred to as expert systems, is one of the more widely known areas of application.

But rules can play an important part in mining our data – especially when used to define the knowledge elicited from subject matter experts. This is where rules can become an even more powerful tool for mining, as they allow us to capture not only the definitive but also the heuristics that subject matter experts use on a daily basis. A challenge herein is that many times, these rules of thumb are not explicit. They can, however, be very powerful, if we can identify them. How effective our knowledge elicitation activities are can be directly correlated to how effective our rules are.

Rule constraints, implemented as clauses within the rules, provide much of the power of rules. We can use them as precondition predicates for our rules such as "patient_age > 55" to allow us to filter the data we are analyzing. We can use them as conclusion predicates which allow us to "define" new data, such as "patient_category is senior."

So where, and how, can we best use rules in our mining efforts? Herein, we'll assume that some rule engine and specific definition language are available within your organization. If not, consider if this is really the place to begin to introduce them. Rules take a lot of time to define, verify, and implement, and so they are not for the faint of heart. Defining the rules at the correct level of granularity is vitally important: too abstract a level and you run the risk of painting with too broad a brush. For example, a rule such as

if patient_age > 65 then hypertension_factor = 0.65

would be of little use. We need to consider a more granular approach and include other constraints, such as

if patient_age > 65
and systolic_bp_average > 120
and diastolic_bp_average > 80
and family_history = true
and bmi > 25,
then hypertension_factor = 0.65.

As this simple and not necessarily realistic example shows, rules can include a significant amount of knowledge. But this knowledge has to be specific, which in turn leads to rule bases that contain large numbers of rules. This illustrates the challenge of effectively and accurately eliciting knowledge from experts. In order to be most effective, these rules **have** to include the heuristics that experts use, as we stated above, but how do we best accomplish this? Consider yourself: you are an expert in some number of domains. How would you define your knowledge as a set of facts and rules? How many would you need to specify even a small subject area? At RuleML 2008, one presenter cited a rule base containing over 65,000 rules for "disease event analysis" (Zacharias 2008).[12]

Once the rules have been defined, the next challenge is one of verification. It is very easy, for example, to end up with a rule base where one rule can negate another or, at the very least, lead to conflicting results. Most rule-based environments available today have some level of verification tools built in to try and help with this issue, but this often iterative approach can be time-consuming, cumbersome, and error prone. Particular care must be taken to ensure that dichotomies that are identified are appropriately resolved. Further, this verification step must occur every time a new rule is added to our rule base.

As rules are added to the rule base, we have another challenge: to ensure that our rule base is internally consistent and doesn't result in rules that cause cycles of the form "A implies B,..., B implies A." This can require a significant amount of effort to avoid this problem.

We talk further about rules elsewhere in this text, but caution the investigator to consider whether using this technique provides specific value that cannot be accrued from techniques described elsewhere. The opportunity for generating new knowledge is particularly attractive, but the complexity and challenges in using this technique to its fullest extent can lead to less than desirable results. We recommend those embarking on mining for the first time to be very cautious.

---

[12] Valentin Zacharias, "Development and Verification of Rule-Based Systems – A Survey of Developers", http://www.cs.manchester.ac.uk/ruleML/presentations/session1paper1.pdf.

4.5.3.1 Say What?

Some readers may be wondering why the previous sections have been included here rather than with other algorithms that we discuss later. This is a valid question because much of the discussion is about the method of developing them rather than purely on the representational aspects. However, we felt that the context was needed in order to fully appreciate what these methods are really all about and so would help to put them into context.

But there is another reason: these representations can provide a bridge to be inputs to other systems. Rules, for example, can be used as an input to an automated reasoning system or knowledge-based system. While we talk about these later in this text, a complete treatise is outside the scope of this text. Googling "knowledge-based systems" is a good starting point, or the Knowledge-Based Systems[13] journal is an interesting resource for the interested reader. We shall look at the intersection with ontologies such as the Gene Ontology (GO), along with systems such as OpenCyc, RACER, and FaCT later under our discussion of systems biology.

4.6 Some Basic Graphical Representations

So far, we haven't introduced any representations that we could consider *visual*, or graphical. Let's begin to address that with some of the simple representations widely used in scientific and business communication.

4.6.1 Representing the Instances Themselves

In this and the next section, we consider a few of the innumerable ways of representing the data we are dealing with: the instances themselves. It is beyond the scope of any text to provide a complete inventory of all the ways in which this representation can be effected, and we do not intend to try. Instead, we've included several that the investigator can be expected to encounter from the start of their mining efforts, as well as those which are commonly used.

This being said, it is very important to always consider what we are intending to communicate and to let that be our guide. It may well be that a less commonly used technique actually happens to be the most effective means of communication, and this remains a primary objective. We have to be able to communicate the conclusions we have reached, and the way in which the conclusions are drawn will similarly

---

[13] http://www.sciencedirect.com/science/journal/09507051

add much to the equation of how we represent the instances and our results: remember, we must still be able to show enough to allow others – possibly ourselves – to replicate our process.

Thus, we also need to be careful not to overcomplicate our representation. If nobody can understand what we are talking about, why did we go to all of the effort in the first place?

Different scientific disciplines tend to use their own subset of representation techniques. If this is the case, be careful about bucking the trend too much: once again, clear, concise, and crisp communication is half the battle. . . the other half is everything else we need to do (grin). For this reason, we try and include the common, and probably therefore, most valuable, representation approaches you will encounter on a daily basis.

In this section, we're covering only a few of the basic, standard representations. Throughout the text, we consider some of the more refined representations in the sections where we describe their theory. For example, network-based representations will be discussed in the systems biology section of this text.

4.6.2   Histograms

Histograms provide a very widely used representation of data in a dataset and provide a visualization of the frequency distribution for a variable. The length of each bar is proportional to the size of each group. What is very valuable is that variables which are not continuous can also be represented by histograms. Consider the ALL dataset used earlier. In R, the built-in function hist(ALL$age) can be used to generate the following histogram

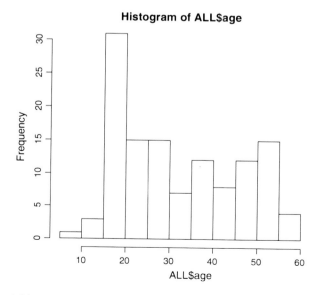

where the variable ALL$age is a variable in the ALL dataset.

We can identify some information immediately from the histogram. For example, approximately 25% of the total patient population (of 128) lies in the third group. Central values, the shape, range of values, and even outliers are immediately discernable.

4.6.3   Frequency Polygrams

As the name suggests, frequency polygrams denote the number of instances which correlate to each value, or range of values, to be plotted. For example, we might show how an individual's cholesterol results vary year by year. (Not a very valuable example, we agree).

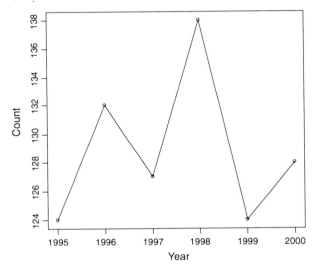

4.6.4   Data Plots

There are innumerable ways of plotting data. Some of the more common, specific plots, such as boxplots and scatterplots, are described in their own sections below due to their widespread use. Prior to considering each of these, we consider some of the more general aspects of graphically plotting data through a two-dimensional representation.

Categorical data is often represented using a histogram or polygonal representation as described above. But it is often valuable to view data as simple data points or even as "distance" measures. Consider a dataset such as the following:

```
sampleData <- c(5, 7, 12, 6, 4, 11, 15, 8, 3, 14, 9)
```

We can simply plot this dataset using, for example, the plot function in R – `plot` (`sampleData`) – to create a display as shown below.

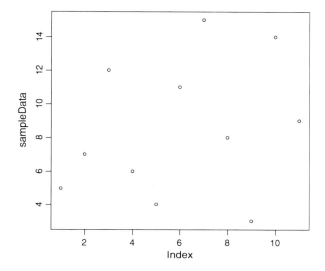

As a display, it is not as meaningful as we would like. The values of our dataset are displayed on the y-axis, with an index value – actually the position in our dataset – being used in place of any real data for the x-axis. If our data consisted of two sets of (related) data values, as below, our plot would be more meaningful, as seen in the following figure.

```
xSampleData <- c(60, 55, 78, 92, 45, 66, 81, 85, 40, 72, 95)
ySampleData <- c(68, 56, 72, 84, 55, 81, 79, 97, 45, 81, 96)
```

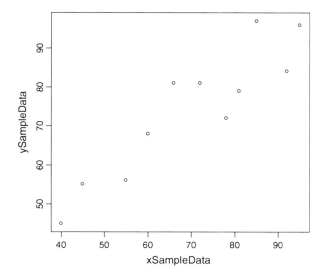

Our simple plot function – plot(xSampleData, ySampleData) – immediately provides a more meaningful representation and, intuitively, we see a pattern in the data that we shall discuss in more detail when we consider regression.

Returning to our sampleData dataset, how can we obtain a more meaningful graphical representation of our data? One way is to consider the *variability* of the data. For example, we can see that the data varies between 3 and 15,[14] and that the mean is 8.545455 (from the mean(sampleData) function). We could plot the mean value across our dataset and link each specific data value to the mean using code such as shown in the box below.

```
plot(sampleData, xlab="", ylab="Sample Data")
lines(seq(1, length(sampleData)), rep(mean(sampleData),
length(sampleData)))
for(i in seq(1, length(sampleData))) {
        lines(c(i, i), c(sampleData[i], mean(sampleData)))
}
```

This provides the graphical representation shown in the figure below.

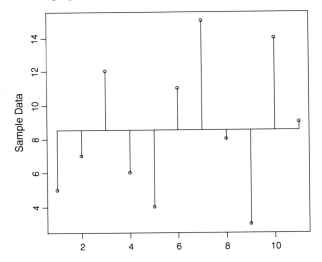

The above figure will be used again in Chap. 6 when we discuss statistical methods in more detail, especially when we look at the concept of variance.

---

[14] We can use the R function range(sampleData) to obtain this information.

Returning now to our two-dimensional dataset, depicted by xSampleData and ySample Data, we can annotate our plot in other ways. A simple and widely used technique is to apply a regression line (or curve) to the plot, as shown below.

```
plot(xSampleData, ySampleData)
z <- lm(ySampleData~xSampleData)
abline(z)
```

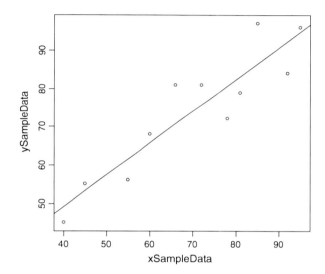

The lm function provides us with a linear model of our dataset, and the abline function draws a straight line of the form $y = a + bx$ on top of our plot. We describe these concepts in more detail in Chap. 6. At this point, we simply point out that this is a widely used technique for looking at two-dimensional data.

As we have already mentioned, and will discuss in more detail below, scatterplots provide an immediate visual representation and value for many types of data. Consider, for example, the following subset of the data from the acute lymphoblastic leukemia (ALL) dataset:

```
library(ALL)
data(ALL)
ageDiagCr <- data.frame(ALL$age, ALL$diagnosis, ALL$date.cr)
names(ageDiagCr)[1] <- "Age"
names(ageDiagCr)[2] <- "DiagDate"
names(ageDiagCr)[3] <- "RemissionDate"
plot(ageDiagCr)
```

which produces the following output:

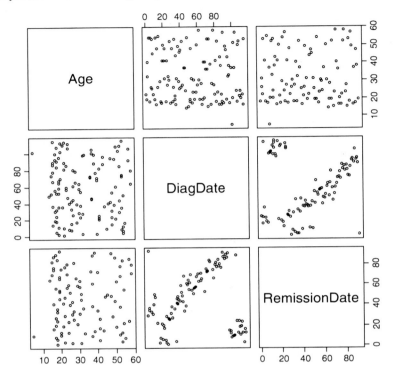

This representation allows us to see the interactions between various pairs of values in our dataset. For example, there is no obviously interesting relationship between the patient's age and date of diagnosis or remission date. This is not surprising since we would not expect a relationship between them: why would a person's age be related to the date on which they were diagnosed, for example? We see that there does seem to be something interesting going on between the data of diagnosis and the remission date. But is this really interesting or not?

4.7 Representing the Output from Statistical Models

A number of other standard representations are more often associated with statistical model output, and, for simplicity, we have grouped them together here.

Statistical models, or, more specifically, statistical distributions that arise from models, are a very common component of data mining efforts since we are rarely interested in specific outputs but rather in the pattern of the relationships between variables and sets of variables.

Within this context, our output representations should allow us to clarify and simplify the large amount of data into an instructional output format. However, we must be careful to not overly simplify. Later in this book, we consider an important concept called *principal component analysis* (PCA). This is one technique for reducing the dimension (i.e., number of variables) in our dataset by identifying the most important (i.e., the principal components). While there is much more to this technique, this definition will suffice us for the moment. One facet of the technique we must be careful about is oversimplifying by eliminating components which provide us with valuable insight into the overall dataset. The same is true with any simplified representation of a distribution or model.

All this being said, there are a number of representations that have become *de facto* standards across a wide range of communications. As is always the case, there are myriad different forms, and the reader is cautioned to consider which, if any, are applicable to the focus of your current study. Also, a lot of inventive work is being undertaken in how to communicate different types of information. Authors such as Tufte (1990 #531) (see also Tufte (1997 #538, 2001 #535, 2003 #528, 2006 #525) are one of the best-known proponents of effective communication of data, but readers are recommended to keep an eye on the web: a lot of innovation is seen there.

4.7.1   Boxplots

A boxplot provides a valuable summary of the distribution of a variable. It displays five points for the distribution of the variable along with the mean ($\bar{x}$):

- The lowest value for the variable (L)
- The lower quartile value for the variable (LQ)
- The median value for the variable (M)
- The upper quartile for the variable (UQ)
- The highest value for the variable (H)

where the values in parentheses are shown on Fig. 4.5.

Consider a set of data such as

```
height <- c(62,62,64,65,67,69,71,71,71,72,72,72,72,73,73,73,74,74,75,76)
```

We can generate a boxplot using the R `boxplot` command, `boxplot (height)`, to generate the output shown in Fig. 4.6.

Boxplots are a very valuable representation when looking at distributions over time. For example, consider a dataset where we are capturing the total cholesterol levels of patients over a multiyear study. We can use a boxplot to show us how the frequency distributions vary over time, as illustrated in Fig. 4.7.

```
boxplot(bpdata, xlab="Year", ylab="Total Cholesterol")
```

Fig. 4.5 Boxplot values

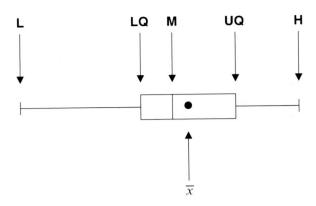

Fig. 4.6 Boxplot

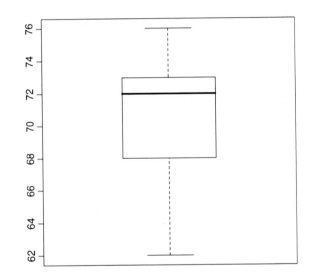

Fig. 4.7 Boxplot of
cholesterol data

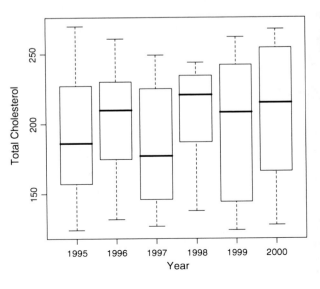

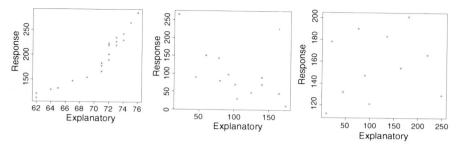

Fig. 4.8 Positive, negative, and no associations

4.7.2   Scatterplots

A scatterplot is a very valuable graphical representation of the relationship, if one exists, between two variables, based on ratio or interval scales. We introduce this representation here, for representing linear models, but this representation is valuable for **any** two variables, whether they have a linear relationship or not. We plot one of the variables – the explanatory variable – on the x-axis and the other – the response variable – on the y-axis. Each point on the scatteplot will be a single instance, or observation, from our dataset. Almost every data mining or analysis tools will have built-in functionality to create a scatterplot quickly and easily. In our discussions below, we will use functionality available within the graphics package of the R data analysis environment. The value that the visual representation provides will help us with our interpretation of the correlation coefficient or regression model.

   We continue to use our explanatory/response (or explanatory/dependent) terminology and say that there is a *positive association* between the two variables if our scatterplot depicts a positive slope, or upward trend, between the variables. That is, an increase in the value of our explanatory variable shows an increase in our dependent, or response variable. Similarly, a *negative association* is where the scatterplot has a negative slope, or downward trend: increasing values of our explanatory variable show decreasing values for the dependent variable. However, we should be prepared for our scatterplot to show no discernable pattern at all, in which case we have *no association* between the two variables. This nonassociation can provide as much value as seeing an explicit association. Examples of these three cases are shown in Fig. 4.8.

   In R, the plot command can be used to generate a scatterplot. Consider two simple sets of data as shown in the table to the right. This data shows the height and weight of a set of individuals. A simple visual inspection of the data shows increasing height data (from 62 to 76), and increasing weights (from 112 up to 285). This cursory view is enough to give us a sense that there is some relationship between the data. If we assume that this data is in a data frame called HeightWeight,[15] we can use the plot command to generate the scatterplot for this dataset, as shown in Fig. 4.9.

---

[15] We return to this dataset in Chap. 6.

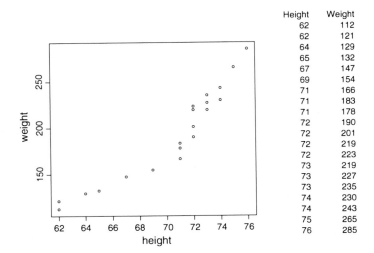

Height	Weight
62	112
62	121
64	129
65	132
67	147
69	154
71	166
71	183
71	178
72	190
72	201
72	219
72	223
73	219
73	227
73	235
74	230
74	243
75	265
76	285

Fig. 4.9 Scatterplot

This visual representation definitely provides a much clearer view of the relationship between the two variables, but the question now is whether there is a *linear* or *nonlinear* relationship between the two variables. Looking at Fig. 4.9 above, it **looks** like there is a linear relationship, but there is enough "curvature" to question whether this is true or not.

4.7.3   Q-Q Plots

We will often be interested in determining whether or not two datasets come from populations with a common statistical distribution. One method for accomplishing this and providing a graphical representation is to plot the quantiles of the first dataset against the quantiles of the second dataset.

A quantile is defined as the percentage of the dataset that lies below a given value. For example, the 0.45 quantile (45% quantile) is the value at which 45% of the data in the dataset falls below and 55% of the data falls above.

We plot the quantiles for one dataset across the x-axis and the quantiles for the other across the y-axis. We typically plot a 45-degree reference line on the graph: if the two datasets do in fact come from a population with the same distribution, then intuitively the plotted points should fall approximately along this reference line. If the data does not approximately distribute along this reference line, their distance from the line also provides valuable information since the greater the distance from this line, the greater is the evidence to support the conclusion that the two datasets come from populations with different distributions.

We have already identified the core question that we can use a Q-Q plot (quantile-quantile plot) to answer, but there are some other important questions that can also be addressed:

- Do two datasets come from populations with a common distribution?
- Do two datasets have common location and scale?
- Do two datasets have similar distributional shapes?
- Do two datasets have similar tail behavior?

Q-Q plots have several advantages as an output representation and as a technique:

1. The sample sizes of the two datasets do not need to be equal.
2. We can test many different aspects of the distribution(s) simultaneously.

The second advantage listed above deserves further explanation. Differences between the two datasets that are due to a shift in scale, a shift in location, or a change in symmetry can all be directly identified using a Q-Q plot. Let us consider two datasets whose distributions differ only in the fact that one has undergone a shift in location with respect to the other: in such a case, the points we plot will lie on a straight line, but that straight line will be displaced on one side or the other from our reference line. Furthermore, any outliers will also be immediately visible on the plot.

To plot points on the Q-Q plot, we typically plot the *estimated* quantile for one dataset on one axis (say the vertical axis) and the *estimated* quantiles for the second dataset on the other axis. The units for each of the axes are for their respective datasets. Note from these statements that we are not plotting the actual quantile levels – since any given point on the plot is at the same quantile level, we can determine this, but we cannot determine what the actual quantile value for either of the datasets is. Note that the quantiles we use are the ones which coincide with the members of the sample themselves. Thus, if we have a dataset containing 9 members, we would calculate the quantiles at $0.1, 0.2,\ldots$, and 0.9. These same quantiles will be calculated for our second sample set.

If the sizes of the two datasets are the same, the Q-Q plot essentially plots the sorted datasets against each other. If the datasets are not of the same size, the smaller dataset is typically selected with quantiles calculated from its sorted data, and quantiles for the larger dataset interpolated therein.

Checking to see if two datasets have a common distribution is an important and valuable technique, but we need to know if the assumption of their having a common distribution is actually justified or not. If they do have the same distribution, then we can use some of our estimators (location and scale, for example) and pool the datasets and obtain estimators common to both datasets. As we shall see later, we can use techniques such as the chi-square test or the Kolmogorov-Smirnov test, but the visual representation afforded by the Q-Q plot will often provide us with more insight.

We can also use the Q-Q plot to diagnose difference in the distributions of a population from which a random sample has been taken. One important use is to determine nonlinearity of the distribution. In such cases, we would plot the sample's quantiles on the vertical axis and the comparison distribution (e.g., the normal distribution) on the horizontal axis. In the case where there are substantial deviations from a linear representation, we reject the hypothesis of sameness (which is often stated as the null hypothesis). This technique is often described as a *probability plot*.

We again use R functions for our illustrations. R contains the function `qqnorm` to plot the values in a single dataset and `qqplot` to plot the data in two datasets. A third function, `qqline`, adds a line which passes through the first and third *quartiles*. For this example, we shall use another function to generate two sets of data: the random Student's *t* test function, `rt`.

```
y <- rt(200, df = 5)

x <- rt(300, df = 5)
```

The above statements generate two random datasets of different sizes, but with the same number of degrees of freedom (see Chap. 6).

We can now generate a Q-Q plot of one of the datasets, say *y*, using the `qqnorm` (`y`) function to produce the output in the figure below.

Normal Q-Q Plot

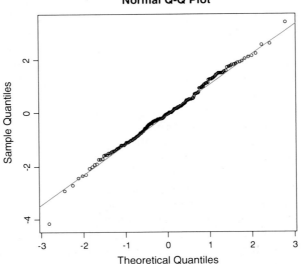

We actually used the `qqline(y, col = 2)` function to overlay the red line displayed on the output.

To generate a Q-Q plot for both datasets, we simply use the `qqplot(y, x)` function to produce the output below. Again we used the `qqline(x, col = 2)` to overlay the red line.

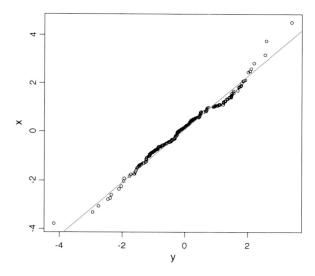

Consider the following similar code fragment:

```
y <- rt(200, df = 5)

x <- rnorm(300)

qqplot(y, x)

qqline(x, col = 2)
```

This produces the output shown below.

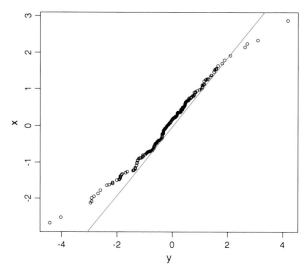

We can see in this case that there is a more pronounced deviation from the straight line we saw in the previous example. This is not surprising since we artificially generated the *x* dataset from a different distribution.

As we have already indicated, we use the Q-Q plot to determine whether or not our sample has come from a specific target population, in the one sample case. This target population could be anything we want it to be, although it is typically a normal distribution. Usage of Q-Q plots are most often seen in ANOVA and regression (see Chap. 6) since the underlying theory assumes normality, even though this may not be the case in practice.

4.8 Heat Maps

Visually oriented as we are, color is a very effective way of communicating subtle differences and not-so-subtle differences in values. The *heat map* visualization methodology uses colors to represent the different values of a variable. Using the thermal analogy, colors might be shades of red, for example, or even range from blue to red. In molecular biology, heat maps have probably been most widely used to represent gene expression level across a number of comparable samples, such as cells in different states, or samples from different patients, as the expression levels are obtained from cDNA or oligonucleotide arrays.

We'll walk through an example[16] which uses expression profile data of adults with T-cell acute lymphocytic leukemia from Chiaretti et al. (2004 #543) to recreate some of the figures in Gentleman et al. (2004 #89).

```
library(ALL)

data("ALL")

# remove samples returning a negative value

eset <- ALL[,ALL$mol.biol %in% c("BCR/ABL", "ALL1/AF4")]

heatmap(exprs(eset[1:100,]))
```

The result of running this code is shown in Fig. 4.10. In the heatmap function call, we are restricting the heat map to only the first 100 features, rather than all 12,625 gene expression levels.

We can now use the lmFit method (from limma package) to look for genes differentially expressed between the two groups (Fig. 4.11).

---

[16] http://www2.warwick.ac.uk/fac/sci/moac/students/peter_cock/r/heatmap/

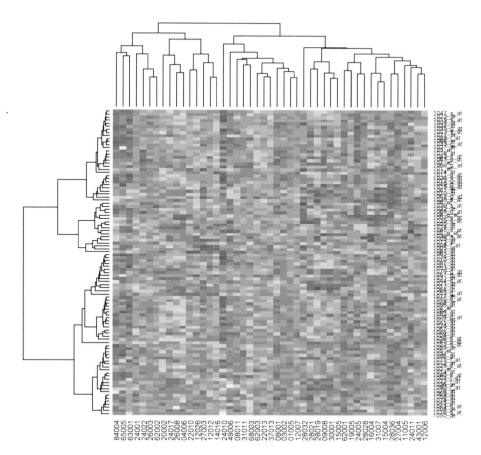

Fig. 4.10 Heat map of subset of ALL molecular biology test results

```
library(limma)

f <- factor(as.character(eset$mol.biol))

design <- model.matrix(~f)

fit <- eBayes(lmFit(eset, design))

topTable(fit, coef=2)    # figure 1 from {Gentleman, 2004 #89}

selected <- p.adjust(fit$p.value[,2]) < 0.05

esetSel <- eset[selected,]

heatmap(exprs(esetSel))
```

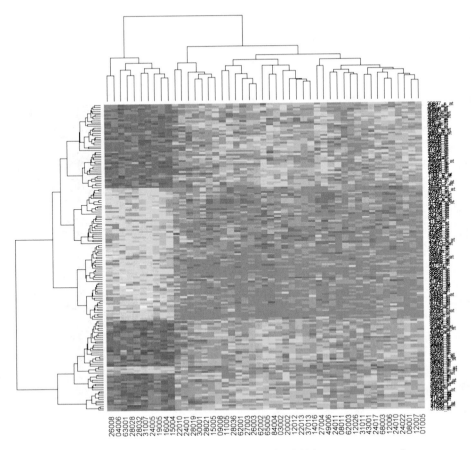

Fig. 4.11 Heat map of genes differentially expressed (Fig. 4.10 input postprocessed)

The red-yellow color scheme happens to be R's default color scheme. We can produce other color schemes using a `col=topo.colors(N)` parameter. For example,

```
heatmap(exprs(esetSel), col=topo.colors(100))
```

would use a yellow-green-blue color scheme.

Cock's article that we have used for this example was illustrating how to use R to recreate some of the figures from Gentleman et al. (2004 #89), while we are interested in illustrating heat maps as a representation option. As we can see by visual inspection of Fig. 4.11, there does seem to be something interesting going on, dividing the expression levels at column n (which happens to be where the clustering split the data into two groups of patients – one containing 10 patients; the other 37). We can highlight this further by incorporating another attribute into our `heatmap` function call (Fig. 4.12).

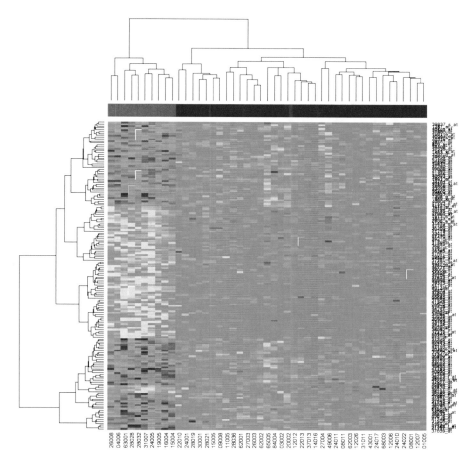

Fig. 4.12 Heat map with clustering emphasis

```
color.map <- function(mol.biol) {if (mol.biol=="ALL1/AF4") "#FF0000" else "#0000FF"}
patientColors <- unlist(lapply(esetSel$mol.biol, color.map))
heatmap(exprs(esetSel), col=topo.colors(100), ColSideColors=patientColors)
```

From the discussion above, we can see that heat maps have a very close correlation to clustering, and in fact, this is by far and away the most common context for using heat maps: cluster the genomic data and then visualize using the heat map. However, clustering isn't always the best technique to use, as we shall discuss later, as it sometimes hides the intrinsic relationships in the underlying data, certainly something that is anathema to our objectives in data mining. Dimension-reducing techniques such as principal component analysis (PCA) can sometimes provide more value by respecting the underlying data topology; however, part of the challenge is how to best visualize the output. Rajaram and Oono (2010 #545) has taken this challenge and developed some visualization methods based on the heat map concept that can be better used with techniques such as PCA.

4.9   Position Maps

Genome mapping is typically segmented into *genetic mapping* techniques that use genetic techniques to construct maps showing the position of genes and other sequence features on a genome and *physical mapping*, which uses molecular biology techniques to examine DNA molecules directly in order to construct maps showing the positions of sequence features, including genes.

Graphical maps of DNA sequence features allow us to quickly view and communicate specific characteristics of the genome under study. Incorporating the annotations from different analyses onto these maps further enhances the value of the visualization by allowing us to see the juxtaposition of features within the genome. We could, for example, use these characteristics to consider the reliability of gene prediction results in a particular region of the genome, and, if that segment of the genome showed an increased level of conservation across species, we may denote the segment as being "more reliable." Maps can also be very effective at visualizing the gene's context, which can, for example, be used to identify candidate operons in bacterial species.

A key aspect of research in genetics is associating sequence variations with heritable phenotypes, and the most common variations are single nucleotide polymorphisms (SNPs), which occur approximately once every 100–300 bases. Because SNPs are expected to facilitate large-scale association genetics studies, there has recently been great interest in SNP discovery, detection, and analysis. Thus genome mapping provides a set of tools that allows us to effectively analyze the (hidden) interrelationships through either *genetic mapping* (using genetic techniques to construct maps showing the positions of genes and other sequence features on a genome) or *physical mapping* (using molecular biology techniques to examine DNA molecules directly in order to construct maps showing the positions of sequence features, including genes). Genome position maps, highlighting gene, and/or SNP positions in chromosomes can offer valuable insight for this key area of research.

We highlight just a few of the many software packages that can produce graphical sequence maps, although there are many more than this in the domain.

4.9.1   Microbial Genome Viewer

The Microbial Genome Viewer, (Kerkhoven et al. 2004 #571), is a web-based application wherein the user can interactively combine complex genomic data. Scalable vector graphics (SVG) outputs can then be generated for chromosome wheels and linear genome maps using annotation data stored in a relational database. The application can also be used to superimpose other gene-related data such as transcriptome or time-course microarray experiment results.

4.9.2   GenomePlot

GenomePlot, (Gibson and Smith 2003 #572), is a Perl/Tk-based application with modules to display different types of information simultaneously and print or save the resulting image to a file to produce publication-quality figures.

4.9.3   GenoMap

GenoMap, (Sato and Ehira 2003 #573), is a Tcl/Tk-based application for viewing genome-wide maps of microarray expression data within circular bacterial genomes.

4.9.4   Circular Genome Viewer

CGView, (Stothard and Wishart 2005 #570), is a Java application that can generate static and interactive maps of circular DNA molecules. Output forms can be customized with annotations, and the images can be zoomed interactively. This application also has an application programming interface (API) to allow it to be incorporated with other applications. Input can be provided in XML format or tab-delimited formats, for example, and outputs can be generated in PNG, JPG, or SVG format.

4.10   Genotype Visualization

Single nucleotide polymorphism (SNP) markers are becoming central for studying genetic determinants of complex diseases since much of the variation in human DNA is due to SNPs, but one of the challenges is that this type of study collects large amounts of SNP data, which calls for the development of specialized analysis tools and techniques. These types of studies investigate the associations across the complete genome; such genome-wide association studies (GWAS) are now a widely used technique for investigating complex human disease genetics.

   To provide a brief context for readers who may not be as familiar with this concept, the density of SNPs differs between different populations and also different regions of the genome, but on average, the frequency of variation is estimated to be in the 1:200–600 base pairs. Risch and Merikangas (1996 #575) highlights how important SNPs are in various areas of medicine. Practice has identified association studies that use a polymorphic marker such as SNPs in genome-wide scans as being a very effective and efficient way of identifying regions within the genome, or even specific genes, that may be correlated to complex diseases and traits. Pharmagenomic studies, for example, may reveal (sets of) SNPs that separate phenotypically distinct classes of samples according to genotypic signatures.

A critical facet of GWAS is to ensure the quality of the study itself and to ensure that associations are sensible; genome cluster plots can be used to help in this area, but the normalized intensity data generated by the GWAS and from which, in turn, genotype cluster plots are generated is often hundreds of Gb in size. Hence, tools that can help us to generate informational outputs and visualization methods, such as cluster maps, that can help us easily make meaningful conclusions are obviously necessary.

An example application, Evoker, (Morris et al. 2010 #576), is a Java application that supports two (binary) data formats and allows remote connectivity to data sources. SNPs of interest can be loaded into the program; for example, a set for which some evidence of association exists; cluster maps can then be generated to help determine the level of association, including visualizing the impact of excluding samples (e.g., where the quality control results are borderline): what is the impact on the quality of the clusters?

Another application, Flapjack, (Milne et al. 2010 #574), similarly provides capabilities to aid in graphical genotyping. As we have already stated, the large data volumes generated by high-throughput SNP architectures are a challenge, but this is also true with other techniques used in this discipline such as genotyping by sequencing. We need tools and visualization methodologies to help in this ever-burgeoning data generating arena. Flapjack has the ability to render visualizations in real time as well as sort, search, navigate, and compare subsets of the data very efficiently.

Visualization of genotypes, identification and analysis of (sub-)genome variations, and loss of heterozygosity (LOH) regions for SNP array analysis offer valuable insights for the future. The majority of human cancers are characterized by genetic instabilities, and chromosomal anomalies can sometimes be identified by LOH. Genome maps provide a valuable visualization to help us identify such abberations.

4.11 Network Visualizations

Networks occur throughout every discipline and are not just restricted to some of the types of networks we encounter in the life sciences. For example, protein-protein interaction and signaling pathway visualization are two techniques where forms of

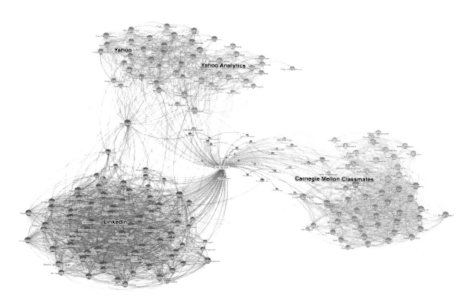

Fig. 4.13 LinkedIn InMap representation forAli Imam (http://blog.linkedin.com/2011/01/24/linkedin-inmaps/)

network visualization have been very effective in communicating the information contained in the sea of data. But it is not only in scientific disciplines that this form of representation has proved to be useful. Business contact services such as LinkedIn™, for example, see a value in the network of relationships you have and now provide a visualization of your links using their InMap tool (Fig. 4.13).

At the time of writing, an interesting website[17] described some network interactions in areas such as relationships, similarity of Ph.D. theses, and global agenda organizations (who should work together), as examples.

Networks provide information in and of themselves; not only does each *node* have a meaning but the *connections* between the nodes have meaning also. Consider the network representation in Fig. 4.13 above as an example. We can see at a glance which nodes have the most links, how the nodes are grouped, where nodes are contained in more than one group, and which nodes appear "isolated" in comparison to others.

Thus, visualizing networks, especially networks with many nodes, can provide a plethora of information that is otherwise lost in the mass of data. Within the life sciences, two areas where network visualization is very valuable are for protein interaction maps and gene interactions.

We consider some of the theory underlying networks, graphs, and maps elsewhere in this text and so constrain ourselves here to discussing how such networks can be visualized.

---

[17] http://flowingdata.com/category/visualization/network-visualization/

Table 4.4   Network types

Hierarchical graphs or networks represent dependency relationships, where some nodes precede others. For example, a simple phylogenetic tree is often represented in this manner

Undirected graphs are used when there is no inherent ordering of the nodes. Examples of this type often arise in communication and online social networks

Circular layouts depict connections of nodes closely related to one another, such as those on a local area network

Radial layouts depict networks focused on some central node, as arises in some social networks

Taken from http://www.research.att.com/articles/featured_stories/2009/200910_more_than_jus t_a_picture.html

What are the most common network or graph[18] types we encounter? Table 4.4 briefly describes the most common types.

Consider the image in Fig. 4.14.

This visualization was created using the Circos software package (Krzywinski et al. 2009 #568) and uses a circular layout to depict the interactions between nodes in a network. This tool was used to great effect in "Big Science: The Cancer Genome Challenge" (Ledford 2010 #569), published in Nature.

---

[18] We're going to take some artistic license here. "Network" and "graph" are often used interchangeably in the literature.

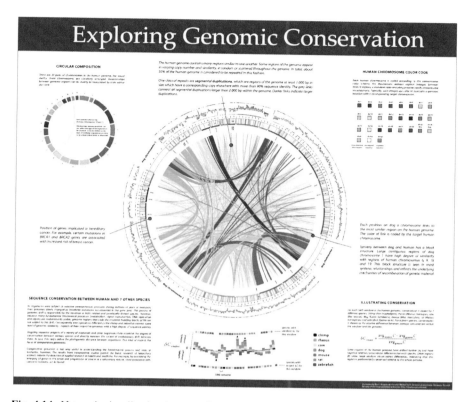

Fig. 4.14 Network visualization in genomic research (Krzywinski et al. 2009 #568)

4.12 Some Tools

There are a wide range of tools available that can help represent data, be it visually or otherwise, and, as we seem to keep saying, a complete review of these tools would require a much larger text than this just to list them. Also, we mention several tools throughout this text that provide a broad range of data representation capabilities. In this section, we include a couple that we haven't explicitly mentioned elsewhere but which provide valuable tools. The interested reader is recommended to their favorite search site as a starting point to find other packages and, in fact, for other visualization approaches.

Well, not quite a starting point. We include a couple of sites below, as well as in an appendix to this text, that we think provide value and which are freely available. This last constraint is important to highlight: there are many valuable commercial analytical tools that provide data representation capabilities, and your organization may have them available to you, along with support resources should you need them. We are avoiding commercial tools not for any intrinsic reason other than that of cost.

4.12.1 Cytoscape

In many areas of biological research, interaction networks prove to be an important tool, but visualizing such networks is often a challenging activity. Cytoscape is an open source bioinformatics software platform for visualizing these molecular interaction networks and biological pathways and integrating these networks with annotations, gene expression profiles, and other data. Cytoscape was originally designed for biological research; now it is a general platform supporting complex network analysis and visualization. Its use of plug-ins to provide additional features supporting new file formats, profiling analysis, layouts, scripting, or database connectivity, to name but a few domains, allows this tool to be a more general-purpose tool.

The tool supports many standards, including the simple interaction format (SIF), systems biology markup language (SBML; see below), OBO, delimited text files, and Microsoft Excel™, to name a few. Data from other systems platforms such as expression profile, gene ontology (GO; see elsewhere in this text) annotations, and other data can also be imported. As an example, you can input a set of custom annotation terms for your proteins and create a set of confidence values for your protein-protein interactions.

It also works as a web service client, directly connecting to external databases, allowing us to import network and annotation data directly. Currently, Pathway Commons, IntAct, BioMart, NCBI Entrez Gene, and PICR are supported.

In the illustration below, we use one of the examples from the Cytoscape website, (Rual et al. 2005 #567), which use the RUAL.SIF interaction file and the RUAL.NA node attribute file, which comprises a network of 1,089 interactions observed between 419 human proteins, and is a small subset of a large human interaction dataset. This subset of interactions consists of proteins that interact with the transcription factor protein TP53. The result of viewing this interaction network using the spring-embedded layout is shown in Fig. 4.15.

We can select a specific node from our network, in this case the TP53 node, and highlight its position in the network itself, as shown in Fig. 4.16 (zoomed in).

From this network, we can easily create a new network of only the highlighted nodes (and their edges) from the simple File > New > Network > From Selected Nodes, All Edges command to give us a more targeted network of interest, as shown in Fig. 4.17.

Importing node attributes allows us to obtain additional information such as the official HUGO symbol name shown in the data panel of Fig. 4.17.

The simple, and partial, example above does not even begin to scratch the surface of this valuable and widely used tool, and the interested reader is recommended to the Cytoscape website for more information. As of the time of writing, there are over 120 plug-ins in areas such as analysis, network and attribute I/O, network inference, functional enrichment, communication/scripting, and the ubiquitous "other" category. The GoogleChartFunctions plug-in, for example, contains functions that create image URLs from attribute values using the Google Chart API.

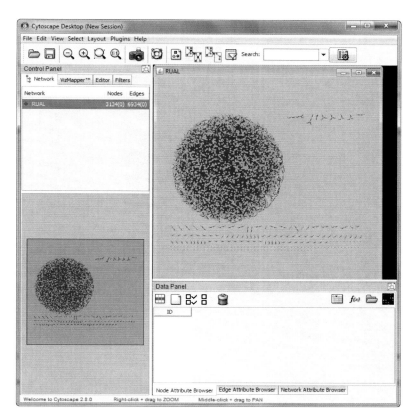

Fig. 4.15 Cytoscape primary user interface displaying the interaction network from Rual et al. (2005 #567) using the spring-embedded layout

4.12.2   TreeView: Phylogenetic Tree Visualization

TreeView is probably the classic software program, last updated in 2002, for graphically browsing the results of clustering and other analyses from the cluster software. It supports tree-based and image-based browsing of hierarchical trees and produces multiple output formats for generation of images for publications (Fig. 4.18).

In addition to TreeView, various other applications, such as Dendroscope (see Fig. 4.19), provide analogous phylogenetic tree visualization capabilities.

Many phylogenetic tree visualization software are available, some as stand-alone, some as functions within larger visualization tools, and, like many functional areas, changes. A quick web search performed at the time of writing returned 11 applications (BayesTrees, Dendroscope, ETE, FigTree, Geneious Pro, MultiDendrograms, NJPlot, TreeDyn, TreeGraph 2, TreeView, and UGENE) and 11 online systems (Archaeopteryx, Hypergeny, InfoViz Tree Tools, iTOL, jsPhyloSVG,

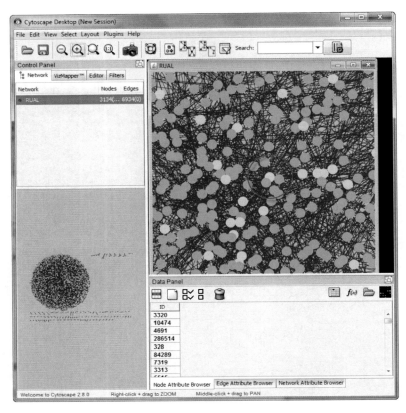

Fig. 4.16 Cytoscape interaction network with TP53 node highlighted (*yellow node circled in red*) and all nodes directly interacting with TP53 (*yellow nodes*)

Phylodendron, PhyloExplorer, Phyloviewer, PhyloWidget, TRED, and TreeViz) capable of visualizing tree structures. We also use TreeView as an example elsewhere in this text.

4.12.3   Systems Biology Markup Language

The systems biology markup language (SBML) is a free and open interchange format for computer models of biological processes that provides a machine-readable format for representing models. SBML is oriented toward describing systems involving biological entities that are modified by processes, occurring over time, such as in a network of biochemical reactions. The SBML framework is suitable for representing models commonly found in areas of research such as cell signaling pathways, metabolic pathways, biochemical reactions, and gene regulation, along with many others.

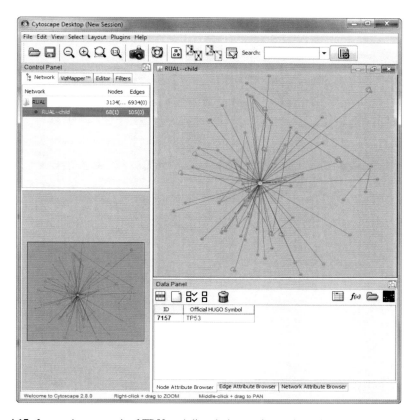

Fig. 4.17 Interaction network of TP53 and directly interacting nodes only

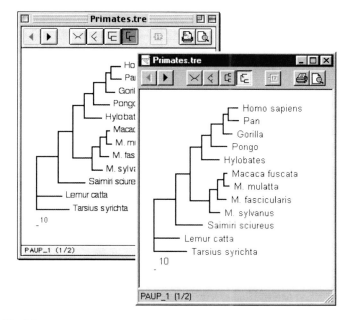

Fig. 4.18 TreeView

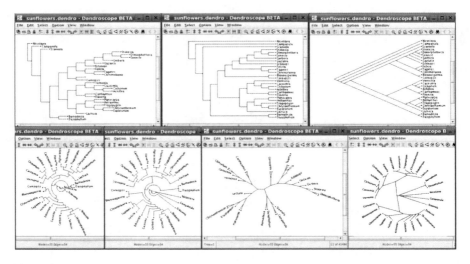

Fig. 4.19 Dendroscope

As its name suggests, it is a markup language (XML) that can be written by one system and read by another, allowing the same model to be used in multiple different areas.

We'll take an example from the SBML website.[19] Consider the enzymatic reaction

$$E + S \underset{k_{off}}{\overset{k_{on}}{\rightleftharpoons}} ES \overset{k_{cat}}{\rightarrow} E + P.$$

An SBML representation is shown in Fig. 4.20.

An SBML model, as shown above, can contain any number of different component lists, each being optional:

Function definition	A named mathematical function that may be used throughout the rest of a model.
Unit definition	A named definition of a new unit of measurement or a redefinition of an existing SBML default unit.
Compartment type	A type of location where reacting entities such as chemical substances may be located.
Species type	A type of entity that can participate in reactions. Common examples of species types include ions such as Ca^{2+}, and molecules such as glucose or ATP, but there is no reason why other kinds of entities cannot be mapped to an SBML "species type."
Compartment	A well-stirred container of a particular type and finite size where SBML species may be located. A model may contain multiple

(continued)

---

[19] http://sbml.org/More_Detailed_Summary_of_SBML

	compartments of the same compartment type. Every species in a model must be located in a compartment.
Species	A pool of entities of the same *species type* located in a specific *compartment*.
Parameter	A quantity with a symbolic name. In SBML, the term *parameter* is used in a generic sense to refer to named quantities regardless of whether they are constants or variables in a model. A parameter defined at the top level is global to a model. It is also possible to define parameters that are local to a single reaction.
Initial assignment	A mathematical expression used to determine the initial conditions of a model.
Rule	A mathematical expression added to the set of equations constructed based on the reactions defined in a model. Rules can be used to define how a variable's value can be calculated from other variables or used to define the rate of change of a variable. The set of rules in a model can be used with the reaction rate equations to determine the behavior of the model with respect to time. The set of rules constrains the model for the entire duration of simulated time.
Constraint	A means of detecting out-of-bounds conditions during a dynamical simulation and optionally issuing diagnostic messages. Constraints are defined by an arbitrary mathematical expression computing a true/false value from model variables, parameters, and constants.
Reaction	A statement describing some transformation, transport, or binding process that can change the amount of one or more species. For example, a reaction may describe how certain entities (reactants) are transformed into certain other entities (products). Reactions have associated kinetic rate expressions describing how quickly they take place. In SBML, the rate expressions can be arbitrary mathematical functions.
Event	A statement describing an instantaneous, discontinuous change in a set of variables of any type (species quantity, compartment size, or parameter value) when a triggering condition is satisfied.

Another important feature of SBML is that every entity can have machine-readable annotations attached to it which can be used to express relationships between the entities in a given model and entities in external resources such as databases. The BioModels database, for example, has every model annotated and linked to relevant data resources such as publications, databases of compounds and pathways, controlled vocabularies, and more.

4.12.4 R and RStudio

Since we've used R at many points in this text, we'll say no more than we find this a very useful general-purpose, extensible tool for both data mining and analytical purposes.

```
<?xml version="1.0" encoding="UTF-8"?>
<sbml level="2" version="3" xmlns="http://www.sbml.org/sbml/level2/version3">
  <model name="EnzymaticReaction">
    <listOfUnitDefinitions>
      <unitDefinition id="per_second">
        <listOfUnits>
          <unit kind="second" exponent="-1"/>
        </listOfUnits>
      </unitDefinition>
      <unitDefinition id="litre_per_mole_per_second">
        <listOfUnits>
          <unit kind="mole"   exponent="-1"/>
          <unit kind="litre"  exponent="1"/>
          <unit kind="second" exponent="-1"/>
        </listOfUnits>
      </unitDefinition>
    </listOfUnitDefinitions>
    <listOfCompartments>
      <compartment id="cytosol" size="1e-14"/>
    </listOfCompartments>
    <listOfSpecies>
      <species compartment="cytosol" id="ES" initialAmount="0" name="ES"/>
      <species compartment="cytosol" id="P"  initialAmount="0" name="P"/>
      <species compartment="cytosol" id="S"  initialAmount="1e-20" name="S"/>
      <species compartment="cytosol" id="E"  initialAmount="5e-21" name="E"/>
    </listOfSpecies>
    <listOfReactions>
      <reaction id="veq">
        <listOfReactants>
          <speciesReference species="E"/>
          <speciesReference species="S"/>
        </listOfReactants>
        <listOfProducts>
          <speciesReference species="ES"/>
        </listOfProducts>
        <kineticLaw>
          <math xmlns="http://www.w3.org/1998/Math/MathML">
            <apply>
              <times/>
              <ci>cytosol</ci>
              <apply>
                <minus/>
                <apply>
                  <times/>
                  <ci>kon</ci>
                  <ci>E</ci>
                  <ci>S</ci>
                </apply>
                <apply>
                  <times/>
                  <ci>koff</ci>
                  <ci>ES</ci>
                </apply>
              </apply>
            </apply>
          </math>
          <listOfParameters>
            <parameter id="kon"  value="1000000"
                         units="litre_per_mole_per_second"/>
            <parameter id="koff" value="0.2"     units="per_second"/>
          </listOfParameters>
        </kineticLaw>
      </reaction>
      <reaction id="vcat" reversible="false">
        <listOfReactants>
          <speciesReference species="ES"/>
        </listOfReactants>
        <listOfProducts>
          <speciesReference species="E"/>
          <speciesReference species="P"/>
        </listOfProducts>
        <kineticLaw>
          <math xmlns="http://www.w3.org/1998/Math/MathML">
            <apply>
              <times/>
              <ci>cytosol</ci>
              <ci>kcat</ci>
              <ci>ES</ci>
            </apply>
          </math>
          <listOfParameters>
            <parameter id="kcat" value="0.1" units="per_second"/>
          </listOfParameters>
        </kineticLaw>
      </reaction>
    </listOfReactions>
  </model>
</sbml>
```

Fig. 4.20 SBML representation of an enzymatic reaction

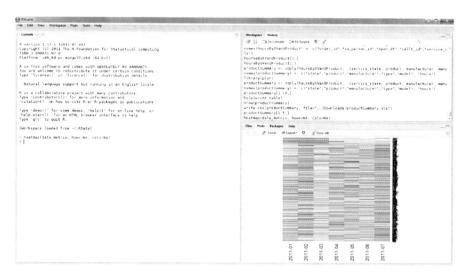

Fig. 4.21   RStudio (www.rstudio.org)

One companion product that we will mention in passing is the RStudio open source initiative that puts a user-friendly graphical user interface in front of R. See the appendices for more details and Fig. 4.21.

4.12.5   Weka

Weka is a collection of machine-learning algorithms for data mining tasks. The algorithms can either be applied directly to a dataset or called from your own Java code. Weka contains tools for data preprocessing, classification, regression, clustering, association rules, and visualization. It is also well suited for developing new machine-learning schemes. Weka is an open-source system developed and maintained by the University of Waikato, New Zealand. Upon starting the application, the GUI Chooser is displayed; selecting the Experimenter GUI puts you into the main Explorer window for Weka, shown in Fig. 4.22.

We use Weka to illustrate the naïve Bayes classifier elsewhere in this text (Bayesian statistics), and so, leave the walkthrough until that point. Appendix B (and the accompanying website) provide links to allow the interested reader to download Weka. Highly recommended by the authors!

4.12.6   Systems Biology Graphical Notation

The systems biology graphical notation (SBGN) initiative, Novere et al. (2009 #566) is an effort to standardize the graphical notation used in maps of biochemical and cellular processes studied in systems biology – a visual notation for network diagrams in systems biology. It comprises three languages: a *Process Description*

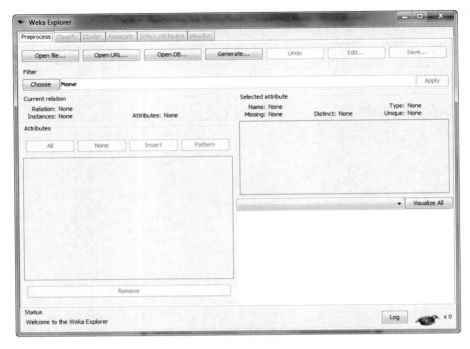

Fig. 4.22 Weka Experimenter Explorer main window

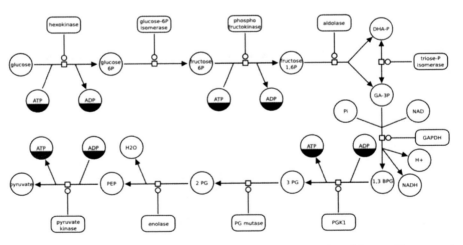

Fig. 4.23 SBGN PD language example for glycolysis (http://sbgn.org/Documents/PD_L1_Examples)

Language, showing the temporal courses of biochemical interactions in a network; an *Entity Relationship Language*, showing all the relationships in which a given entity participates, regardless of the temporal aspects; and an *Activity Flow Language*, depicting the flow of information between biochemical entities in a network. Figures 4.23, 4.24, and 4.25 show examples of maps using each of these languages.

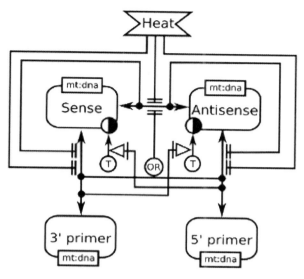

Fig. 4.24 SBGN ER language example for PCR (http://sbgn.org/Documents/ER_L1_Examples)

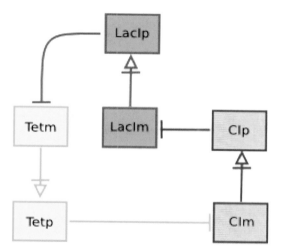

Fig. 4.25 SBGN AF language example for repressilator (http://sbgn.org/Documents/AF_L1_Examples)

4.13 Conclusion

Although we've covered a lot of ground, much has been left out, even though this is one of the longest chapters of the text. The breadth of representations is huge and challenging to cover every form. What we've tried to do is provide a number of the representations commonly used by authors as a starting point. Effective communication of our results and conclusions is of paramount importance, and using novel approaches to displaying results can have an immense impact on your analysis.

Topics such as Bayesian networks deserve chapters (or books) of their own, while further discussion on techniques such as correlation analysis, such as its use in organic chemistry, is beyond the scope of this introductory text, and we recommend the interested reader to a text such as Cohen et al. (2003).[20]

What we hope we've provided is an overview of a wide range of common representations that researchers can consider, and use, when undertaking a data analysis or data mining initiative. Being able to effectively communicate our results to anyone from a knowledgeable expert to a lay person is of paramount importance, and much confusion occurs when this important task is ineffectively accomplished. Much has been written about alternative methods of visualizing information – especially by authors such as Edward Tufte (1990 #531) – which are beyond the scope of this book. Exploring such methods can provide significant benefit in specific instances. How and where nontraditional methods of representing output might be useful is specific to the data under study, and we do not address this issue here.

In the majority of cases, some combination of tabular representations, pie charts, line charts, bar charts, case format (text based, explanation), and their variants will satisfy the majority of needs, and, in fact, for many specific activities, standard representations may already be defined by your organization, your audience (e.g., scientific publications), or regulatory agencies, and these should obviously be considered as a primary output representation.

However, the conclusions you reach must be a major factor in the representations you use. This should be as much a consideration as any standardized approach to which you must adhere. The worst thing that can happen is to reach a conclusion and not be able to crisply and clearly communicate that to others. Not only can your message be lost, erroneous conclusions may be reached by others. This being said, if your conclusions require such a specialized form of representation, this alone might cause confusion or even skepticism over your results: a fine line to balance.

There are an ever-growing number of tools that can be used to help you to represent your data, tools such as Cytoscape, Treeview, and the like, along with concepts such as the systems biology markup language (SBML) that we'll return to later in this text. These tools can provide a solid and consistent way of visualizing the data for your audience. However, and we're getting into a very subjective area, always ask if there's a better way of communicating your results.

For example, extending the concept of the mind map, we can represent a broad range of concepts. For example, this technique has been used to provide a very interesting, and widely used, representation of the web superimposed onto the Tokyo subway system, as shown in Fig. 4.26.

---

[20] Applied Multiple Regression/Correlation Analysis for the Behavioral Sciences, 3rd edn. Cohen, et al.

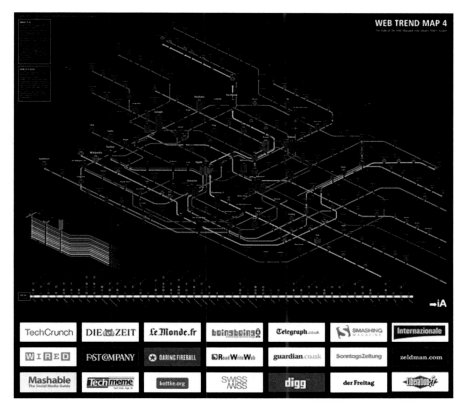

Fig. 4.26   Web Trend Map 4 (Copyright Information Architects, http://informationarchitects.jp/en/wtm4)

This type of representation is being used extensively to communicate signaling pathways, for example.

As mentioned elsewhere, Edward R. Tufte (1990 #531, 1997 #538, 2001 #535, 2006 #525) provides a wealth of stimulating thoughts on how to better display information for audiences. But the Internet can also be a very valuable source of ideas also.

Representing phylogenetic results, or even the results of clustering, a hierarchical tree has been a staple method of displaying the interrelationships between the data nodes, and most people are familiar with the Treeview software tool.[21] Tree representations provide a quick, intuitive visualization of the data. A typical representation will be the rooted tree, as depicted in Fig. 4.27.

---

[21] Treeview is now available from Google code at http://code.google.com/p/treeviewx/ for the Linux/Unix variant and http://taxonomy.zoology.gla.ac.uk/rod/treeview.html for the Windows and Mac versions.

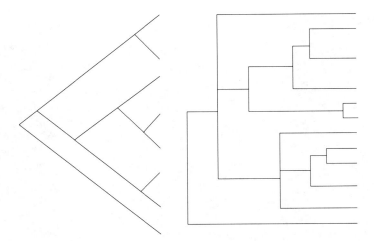

Fig. 4.27 Rooted tree representations

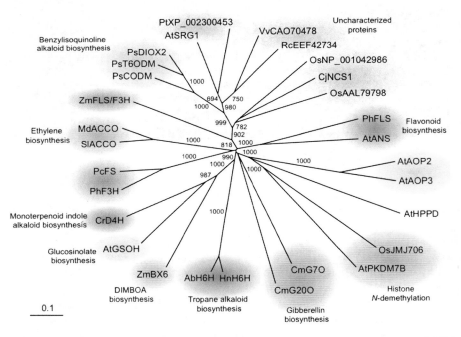

Fig. 4.28 Unrooted neighbor-joining phylogenetic tree for selected plant 2-oxoglutarate (2OG)/ Fe(II)-dependent dioxygenases (Hagel and Facchini 2010 #542)

But an increasingly widely used representation, the unrooted tree, can provide valuable insight into your data, as shown in Fig. 4.28.

But there are many other ways to represent data, with new ones being imagined every day. Whatever our approach, the objective is to inform and communicate.

Visualizing data in the "correct" way can aid this quest tremendously, just as an incorrect approach can make the report, article, presentation, or other communication vehicle a mental pain.

For interested readers, a fun way of seeing a wide range of different visualization methods is at Visual Literacy.[22] Another interesting site is Visual Complexity[23] which has over 50 different visualizations that have been used in the biological sciences. Some other sites to consider are FlowingData[24] and Smashing Magazine.[25]

David McCandless gave a talk at TEDGlobal 2010 that's well worth viewing.[26]

References

Agrawal R, Srikant R (1994) Fast algorithms for mining association rules. In: Bocca JB, Jarke M, Zaniolo C (eds) Proceedings of the 20th international conference on very large data bases, {VLDB}. Morgan Kaufmann, San Francisco, pp 487–499

Agrawal R, Imielinski T, Swami AN (1993) Mining association rules between sets of items in large databases. In: Proceedings of the 1993 ACM SIGMOD international conference on management of data, Washington DC, pp 207–216

Cohen W, Ravikumar P, Fienberg S (2003) A comparison of string distance metrics for name-matching tasks

Chiaretti S et al (2004) Gene expression profile of adult T-cell acute lymphocytic leukemia identifies distinct subsets of patients with different response to therapy and survival. Blood 103:2771–2778

Gentleman RC et al (2004) Bioconductor: open software development for computational biology and bioinformatics. Genome Biol 5:R80

Gibson R, Smith DR (2003) Genome visualization made fast and simple. Bioinformatics 19:1449–1450

Hagel J, Facchini P (2010) Biochemistry and occurrence of O-demethylation in plant metabolism. Front Physiol 1:14

Hall BG (2001) Phylogenetic trees made easy : a how-to manual for molecular biologists. Sinauer, Sunderland, Mass

Han X (2006) Inferring species phylogenies: a microarray approach. In: Computational intelligence and bioinformatics: international conference on intelligent computing, ICIC 2006, Kunming, China. Springer, Berlin/Heidelberg, pp 485–493

Kerkhoven R et al (2004) Visualization for genomics: the Microbial Genome Viewer. Bioinformatics 20:1812–1814

Krzywinski MI et al (2009) Circos: an information aesthetic for comparative genomics. Genome Res 19:1639–1645

Ledford H (2010) Big science: the cancer genome challenge. Nature 464:972–974

Milne I et al (2010) Flapjack – graphical genotype visualization. Bioinformatics 26:3133–3134

---

[22] http://www.visual-literacy.org/periodic_table/periodic_table.html

[23] http://www.visualcomplexity.com/vc/index.cfm

[24] http://flowingdata.com/

[25] http://www.smashingmagazine.com/2007/08/02/data-visualization-modern-approaches/

[26] http://www.ted.com/talks/david_mccandless_the_beauty_of_data_visualization.html

Morris JA et al (2010) Evoker: a visualization tool for genotype intensity data. Bioinformatics 26:1786–1787

Neapolitan RE (2003) Learning Bayesian networks. Prentice Hall, Harlow

Novere NL et al (2009) The systems biology graphical notation. Nat Biotechnol 27:735–741

Rajaram S, Oono Y (2010) NeatMap – non-clustering heat map alternatives in R. BMC Bioinformatics 11:45

Risch N, Merikangas K (1996) The future of genetic studies of complex human diseases. Science 273:1516–1517

Rual J-F et al (2005) Towards a proteome-scale map of the human protein-protein interaction network. Nature 437:1173–1178

Sato N, Ehira S (2003) GenoMap, a circular genome data viewer. Bioinformatics 19:1583–1584

Stothard P, Wishart DS (2005) Circular genome visualization and exploration using CGView. Bioinformatics 21:537–539

Tufte ER (1990) Envisioning information. Graphics Press, Cheshire

Tufte ER (1997) Visual explanations: images and quantities, evidence and narrative. Graphics Press, Cheshire

Tufte ER (2001) The visual display of quantitative information. Graphics Press, Cheshire

Tufte ER (2003) The cognitive style of PowerPoint. Graphics Press, Cheshire

Tufte ER (2006) Beautiful evidence. Graphics Press, Cheshire

Witten IH, Frank E (2005) Emboss European molecular biology open software suite. In: Data mining – practical machine learning tools and techniques with Java implementations. Morgan Kaufmann, San Francisco

Zacharias V (2008) Development and Verification of Rule-Based Systems – A Survey of Developers, http://www.cs.manchester.ac.uk/ruleML/presentations/session1paper1.pdf

Chapter 5
The Input Side of the Equation

Abstract The data we will analyze will typically come from multiple places – both internal repositories and external databases. Even when all of the data is in one place, it is highly unlikely that our needs are met in its current form. Preparing the data for analysis takes an appreciable amount of time and can often be the most complex part of the analytical effort. So what do we need to do so that the data is in the right format, with the right content, so that our analysis is not skewed by incorrect, inadequate, or invalid data? Here, we focus on some of the physical data manipulation activities we may (or will) need to undertake in order to transform the data into the structure and content we need to be able to effectively analyze it. Is each piece of data relevant? What do we do about data elements missing from our dataset? Can we enforce consistency on the data without changing its meaning? Extracting the data from its source(s), transforming it, and then loading it into our analytical repository (ETL) can be a significant effort: what techniques can we use? How do we update our dataset when new data is generated? We will also consider techniques to help us standardize, normalize, transform data, eliminate and reduce unwanted data, and on how we deal with noisy data.

How do we get data into our mining environment? What forms can this data take? Do we need to perform any data cleansing or transformation activities on the data before we can begin to analyze it? These questions, and questions like them, are significant topics in their own right, and we try to address getting the data ready for our mining efforts in this chapter.

We attempt to provide some insight into the importance of preparing the data that goes into our data repository – typically a data warehouse – so that it can be effectively used in data mining efforts and be consistent and accurate so that our results are built on a solid foundation. Many readers, especially Data Architects, will now be choking on their coffee because of the dichotomy that is often present between building an enterprise data warehouse *generic* enough for any future data analysis effort and the *specific* requirements for any given data mining effort. This is obviously a valid concern and one we recognize. In fact, many of the topics

R. Sullivan, *Introduction to Data Mining for the Life Sciences*,
DOI 10.1007/978-1-59745-290-8_5, © Springer Science+Business Media, LLC 2012

we describe in this chapter may be used in the initial design of the data warehouse as well as in developing a specific dataset for the purposes of a particular data mining initiative.

Preparing the input for a data mining effort often consumes the largest part of the overall effort because we have to not only perform the physical tasks involved in getting the data prepared, such as cleaning the data, but also make decisions about the data, such as what to aggregate, that may require us to backtrack as we discover more about our data later in the process. We suggest the following rule of thumb when dealing with any data: *assume the data is very low quality, has lots of holes, and needs a **lot** of preparation.*

As we discuss managing the input data, we assume that for any significant analytics environment, we are dealing with data which originates in more than one repository of data external to our analytics environment: A single environment **should** already contain consistent and coherent data. Thus, much of our consideration will be given over to ensuring that we identify and hopefully eliminate any *incompleteness* in the data under study, that any *inconsistencies* are minimized (or eliminated), and that any *noisiness* in the data is extracted. Each of these issues may require multiple techniques to completely address. Further, these issues are not totally independent of each other, as we shall see forthwith.

We should also consider that the source systems may vary greatly in the amount of data they contain, in the cleanliness of the data, in how well the data has been curated to ensure its accuracy, and in how current the data is. To give an example of a class of problem that is prevalent, what would be contained in an attribute labeled "source"? A transactional system we encountered contained a surprising range of different information domains in this single field including:

- Specimen source (e.g., blood, wound, sputum)
- Patient source (e.g., inpatient, outpatient)
- Notes to clinicians

We term this issue the *internal consistency* issue. Ensuring that the data we feed into our analytics system is consistent and coherent can be a significant challenge for any organization. We have alluded to one type of issue in the example above, but this is by no means the only issue we need to deal within this area. We discuss each type of issue in the next sections.

Prior to this, we introduce some terms we shall use throughout this chapter. These terms are consistent with those used by Witten and Frank (2005 #11), which we have found valuable.

Accurately representing data is, of course, fundamental to data mining and is not necessarily as intuitive or as obvious as we would like it to be, as we shall discuss in this chapter. That being said, determining the most appropriate representation has a dramatic impact on the accuracy and effectiveness of the model we are building. Consider, as an example, test result ranges, and in particular, consider the total cholesterol test. Tietz (1995 #80) provided reference ranges in 5-year increments from age 0 through age 69, along with cord blood and a > 70 category. This provides 16 categories of value ranges that we can use. Our patients' ages would range over 70+ categories (years). So which is more accurate? Which is more appropriate? Is there some other representation that is more valuable for our model?

These three questions underpin much of the work we perform in preparing our data for the model we are building, and the answers will often depend on many factors including ones about the data, the model, and our objectives. In the above example, we may say that the answer to our first question is "it doesn't matter." Do we really care that, for example, the reference range for a 49-year-old male is 4.09–7.15 mmol/L and that for a 50-year-old male it is 4.09–7.17 mmol/L? In the vast majority of cases, the answer is no: the difference of 0.02 mmol/L on the upper end of the range is at too granular a level for us to consider; introducing such a level of discretization into the model will typically inundate us with noise. However, grouping together all males between the ages of 20 and 65 would cause us to merge the two appropriate reference ranges of 3.21–5.64 mmol/L and 4.09–7.10 mmol/L to give, for example, a pseudo-reference range of 3.21–7.10 mmol/L, which loses too much granularity.

We will discuss several techniques for representing the data and preparing it for our model that enable us to easily incorporate data – old and new – into our model.

The atomic level of data we deal with will be referred to as *attributes*. An attribute will typically map to a single data element (column, field, etc.) that we are interested in including in our analytics environment. For example, "patient date of birth" may be an element we wish to use as an analytical driver.[1]

It is not unusual for an analytics environment to contain hundreds or even thousands of individual attributes that are of interest to the enterprise. Each of these attributes has direct and indirect relationships which permeate the whole model. In fact, many relationships will not be understood at the outset; learning systems and general datamining approaches will always highlight these "unrecognized" relationships.

We introduce a definition above those used by Witten and Frank (2005 #11): the *analytical entity*. The analytics environment, as described elsewhere in this book, comprises a data architecture that will pragmatically be used for a wide range of purposes. This structure, therefore, will contain a set of *entities* that will have been defined with the intent of supporting the different perspectives and goals of different groups of users. (We discuss this in more detail in Chap. 3.) Logically, the data architecture will define a set of entities which will be physically manifested within the physical data architecture (transactional model, star schema, snowflake, etc.). Each entity in the logical model is what we define as the *analytical entity*.

An *instance* is defined as a set of attributes which have a discrete and obvious relationship with each other. Instances typically map to rows, records, etc., within our source systems. Using this definition, instances comprise a set of

---

[1] This example highlights an interesting point relevant to the following question: Do we include calculated values such as age in our analytics environment or do we calculate "on the fly"? This issue will be considered later in this chapter.

attributes that provide us with complete information about a single example of an *analytical entity.*

The abstraction of the analytical entity is important as we model our data mining processes and systems. If and when the underlying physical implementation is changed, we may be able to limit changes to our systems.

Using the above framework, we can now consider the fundamental intent of any data mining system: to learn something about the data we have captured. To maximize the leverage we hope to gain, we want to be able to learn many different things about the data, the patterns within the data, and the relationships between the various attributes and analytical entities, and hope to generate new knowledge. Each of the things we hope to learn is called a *concept* by Witten and Frank (2005 #11). We also use their terminology of an *instance*[2] to identify each separate input item.

5.1   Data Preparation

In the previous chapter, we mentioned that preparing the data prior to feeding it into any model we build is an important, nontrivial task that includes several different, interrelated dimensions:

- Data cleansing
  In this dimension, we are interested in eliminating as much *noise* from the input as we possibly can and the elimination of missing data. While normalization and even standardization can help with the noise issue, we can also apply smoothing techniques and other such approaches to make the data more deterministic for the models we build. For missing data, various approaches such as using the most common value, or a value based on a simple statistical technique, can be used.
- Data transformation
  Normalization and standardization are two very common techniques used to transform the input data and provide value to the overall mining efforts.
- Data reduction
  Not all the data we have is valuable for any specific mining activity. As we show below, techniques such as relevance analysis have tremendous value for reducing the data we process. Other techniques such as principal component analysis, discretization, and clustering also have merit and should be considered to optimize the input data.
- Relevance analysis
  Is each attribute in our dataset actually relevant to the analysis? Do we have any redundant data attributes in our dataset? We can use techniques to identify whether there are relationships between pairs of attributes, such as *correlation*

---

[2] Sample, record, and input are often used in the literature.

analysis, and also look at using *feature subset selection*, also referred to as *attribute subset selection* which allows us to find a smaller set of attributes with a probability distribution that is close to the probability distribution of the original, larger attribute set.

It is important to state, however, that any manipulation of the input must be considered carefully to ensure that the resulting dataset has not been skewed in any way, or reduced to such a state as to invalidate the model we use. For example, if gender is not available for a significant percentage of the input population, using a default value – even NA – could potentially make any results using this attribute useless. Conversely, eliminating the age attribute for the input population may be a worse choice than using a set of values based on a normal distribution. Suffice it to say there is a definite *caveat emptor* moment here!

As we'll discuss in this chapter, there are many important questions that need to be considered between initially receiving the data and starting your analysis; many of these decisions can impact your analysis for better or for worse, so spending time now, but thinking about the implications, is worth the time and effort.

Each and every data element that is included in your dataset is there for a reason. However, the reason is unlikely to be to support analysis *per se*. Even if this was the case, the quality of the data may well be suspect, which leads us to the recognition that we need to (a) determine what data elements are important, (b) ensure that the quality of the contents of the data is accurate, and (c) validate the consistency across the dataset.

5.2 Internal Consistency

We define *internal consistency* to be the challenge of ensuring that all values in the *domain of an attribute* are consistent with each other. Using our "patient date of birth" example, we need to ensure that the data values allow us to process across the whole domain of values. Which date does 4/6/2006 refer to? April 6, 2006 or June 4, 2006?

This issue also rears its ugly head when disparate sources are considered (see *External Consistency*), but can also occur within a single system if care is not taken.

This is a particularly obvious example of this issue. However, there are others which may not be quite as obvious. For example, the microbiology test of *minimum inhibitory concentration* (MIC) has, as its domain of values, doubling dilutions for microbroth dilutions ($\log_2$ values) and half-doubling dilutions for E-Test. If a half dilution is included incorrectly in a source of data, we may not notice until later in the process, if ever!

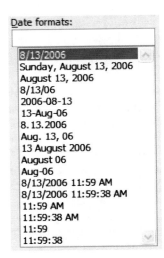

To address this issue, we approach the problem by insisting that an attribute be further defined as comprising a *single domain of values*. This domain may be further constrained by locale (for dates of birth), *de facto* standard (where we might define a date as MM/DD/YYYY and convert any other formats to this single format), or introduce additional attributes or constraints to ensure consistency. For example, using the MIC values, we may either separate out the two test method types into "broth MIC" and "E-test MIC" attributes, or use an additional column/ entity to address this issue through normalization techniques.

Date attributes cause particular problems in any system since dates can be accepted in multiple different formats. Consider, for example, the figure to the right, which shows the various different formats of dates which Microsoft Word™ supports. These are compounded when we consider that different parts of the world can use different orderings for the day and month components.

Our first consideration has to do with consistency that we discuss generically below. We could, for example, convert all of our date fields to a single YYYYMMDD format. If the operations we wish to perform on dates are limited to simple comparisons, this would definitely be sufficient. However, many of the methods and algorithms we would want to use will require our being able to look at *intervals* of dates so that we can define rules, for example, which include clauses such as

$$Date > X \text{ and } Date < Y.$$

In order to accomplish this, we need to convert our date attributes to a format which preserves interval consistency; the YYYYMMDD format does not support this, for example, $20060601 - 20060531 \neq 20060602 - 20060601$. We must be very careful that our choice of date representation does not introduce bias into our models.

Many operating systems, database management systems, and application systems use a starting point for dates and times and increment any subsequent date/time from that point. For example:

- UNIX variants typically use January 1, 1970 as their starting point.
- SAS Institute's SAS™ uses January 1, 1960.

This type of format would definitely work; however, it is not intuitive: What does it mean when we see a clause such "Date >1,155,471,299"? This so happens to be the number of seconds since January 1, 1970 at the time of writing (Sun 13 Aug 2006 12:14:59 GMT -0400). Without converting between the two, the values are nonobvious. Even more, the insights that we wish to gain in order to discover patterns and knowledge are certainly not as intuitive as we would like. One format which offers a compromise is the KSP date format.

This format uses the year of the date and adds the date within the year as a fraction. That is,

$$KSPdate = YYYY + \frac{Ndays - 0.5}{365 + IsLeapYear},$$

where *IsLeapYear* is 1 if the current year is a leap year, and 0 otherwise, and *Ndays* ranges from 1 for January 1 through 365 (or 366 in a leap year) for December 31.

For example, August 13, 2006 would be $2006 + (225 - 0.5)/365 = 2006.615068$.

This format does preserve intervals between days. However, the intervals are slightly smaller during leap years due to the denominator being 366 rather than 365. This format has a couple of other advantages in that the year is obvious, and it can be extended to include the time.

5.3 External Consistency

With *external consistency*, we are typically dealing with the same type of information being supplied from multiple sources. For example, we may receive data transfers from each of our investigator sites for an international clinical study. In such a case, we have several issues to deal with:

- Consistency of format (e.g., MM/DD/YYYY, DD/MM/YYYY)
- Consistency of value domain (e.g., reported units for specific clinical tests)

We characterize this issue as the problem of *mapping "n" attributes to a single domain of values*.

As we shall see later, this will allow us to perform longitudinal analysis of the data.

5.4   Standardization

Ensuring that each data attribute within our dataset complies with a consistent usage of the data format as well as the domain of values is of paramount importance in any analytical activity. A single format and single domain of values means that we can undertake longitudinal analysis across the data capture/creation sources without fear of misinterpretation.

As an example, consider a clinical trial in which a panel of tests has been defined for the screening visit.[3] Individual patient results are often published to the investigator in standard and local units, such as plasma hemoglobin can be reported as mg/dL or in μmol/L (see, e.g., Tietz 1995 #80, p. 312).

Often, as in the above case, standardization is simply a case of converting from one unit to another. In the above case, $mg/dL \times 0.155 = \mu mol/L$ gives the appropriate conversion. However, we often see other issues, especially in categorical data, where more processing is required.

For example, how many forms are in (widespread) use when labeling the organism formally known as *Streptococcus pneumoniae*? The following lists just some of the forms encountered by the authors.[4]

* *Streptococcus pneumoniae*
* *S. pneumoniae*
* *S. pneumo*

Although human beings intuitively recognize that each of the above names is essentially interchangeable, computational environments are not so forgiving.

Standardization is a formal process to standardize various representational forms so that expressions that have the same meaning will be recognized by computer software as synonymous in the dataset.

5.5   Transformation

Depending upon our objectives and the methods we intend to use, the value ranges for our attributes may not be as valuable to us as they might be. For example, if we are interested in using the *k-nearest neighbor* (k-NN) algorithm that we describe later in the book, we need to calculate a distance measure for each of our input instances: how do we measure the "distance" between the genders of two patients? For these reasons, we consider some approaches that can be used to *transform* the attribute values of our instances. We do not include normalization in this section

---

[3] Elsewhere in this book we use the generic term "encounter" to cover any encounter (sic) between a patient and a health-care worker.

[4] We are not even including the more colloquial nomenclatures!

since it has applicability both to this issue and in other areas and consider that topic in the next section. Instead, we focus on the concept of measuring "distance" as our motivation. This is not the only reason for considering transforming data, but for readers who have not been previously exposed to this subject; this provides a good context to the issue.

Our ultimate purpose is to transform attribute data to make it more usable in different contexts. If we consider our example of distance, this typically means to transform to numeric values.

5.5.1 Transforming Categorical Attributes

Consider the example of color. An attribute containing data labeling something by color may have values such as black, white, red, blue, green, yellow, orange, and so forth. What does it mean to measure the "distance" between blue and white? Further, what is the meaning of "distance" between blue and white when compared to the "distance" between red and white?

For categorical data, we can begin by considering a very simple approach: *if two labels are the same, assign them a numeric value of 0; if they are different, assign them a numeric value of 1*. For example, when comparing the gender of two patients, if they are both female, or both male, the value of the gender's attribute will be 0; if one is male and one is female, the value of the gender's attribute will be 1.[5] This approach works well in a wide range of cases. Before considering any more complex schemes, the question of value should be very carefully considered.

If this binary transformation is not sufficient, we need to consider some mechanism for *differentially grading* the untransformed values, or the transformed comparisons. For example, we may consider mapping colors to some numeric scheme where the lighter colors have smaller values and darker colors have larger values.

The above discussion assumes that we have two values that we can use for comparison purposes. However, as we have discussed elsewhere, the issue is often more problematic if we have to deal with missing data. If both values are missing, we typically assign it the maximum value of our transformed range. If we have transformed our categorical attribute and normalized it to the range [0,1], for example, then we would set the result to 1.

We can use this same rule if only one of the values is missing also. However, we can also consider temporarily assigning the one missing value to either 0 or 1 and then taking the absolute difference between it and the transformed value we *do* have. If the value we have for one of our instances is v', say, then we can use either $|1 - v'|$ or $|0 - v'|$ as our difference.

---

[5] We will use the prime suffix to identify the transformed attribute and its value.

5.6   Normalization

What is the normal range of values expected for total hemoglobin in an adult between the ages of 18 and 44? Tietz (1995 #80, p. 314) gave these as:

$$\text{Male}: \quad 13.2 - 17.3 \text{ g/dL}$$
$$\text{Female}: \quad 11.7 - 15.5 \text{ g/dL}$$

Actually, we must clarify that these are *reference* ranges. While many clinical trials will use these as their normal ranges, there are reasons why a particular trial may use a slightly different range. This becomes a problem when we need to be able to mine the data across studies, in our example, where different ranges have been used.

Normalization is a formal process which adjusts for difference among data from varying sources in order to create a common basis for comparison. For any given attribute, we want a single domain of values to be used.

There are various ways in which this can be accomplished, some of which are described below.

Consider a scenario where we have a data matrix of probability values, p, that we wish to analyze. (Statistical analysis will be considered in more detail in later chapters). If these p values are expressed in different units, it would ease the complexity to transform them into a single measurement unit. By doing this, we also ensure that the different measurement scales do not affect our results in any way. We could do this using a linear transformation, nonlinear Box-Cox transformation, or one of many other such transformations. (We will encounter several other techniques later in this text).

5.6.1   Averaging

We use the term *averaging* to cover a number of techniques that use some central measure – typically the mean or median – and *weight* the value accordingly. For example, we may take the median values of our ranges and use these to adjust our raw data values.

This should not be done lightly, however. The impact of this has to be considered and understood.

5.6.2   Min-Max Normalization

Min-max normalization is used to transform the data values for a numeric attribute into the range [0,1]. This is accomplished by taking the attribute's numeric value,

v_A, subtracting the minimum value for the attribute, min_A, and dividing by the range of values for the attribute, as shown below:

$$v'_A = \frac{v_A - min_A}{max_A - min_A}.$$

In this equation, v'_A is the normalized value in the range [0,1].

5.7 Denormalization

At its most basic level, denormalization is the dual of normalization. That is, it introduces redundant data into the dataset with the primary intent of improving performance when processing large sets of data. More formally, denormalization is the process of moving a data model from a higher normal form (e.g., third normal form) to a lower normal form (e.g., first normal form). There are many techniques which can be used for denormalization. A complete discussion is beyond the scope of this book, and the reader is referred to any good reference on this subject. However, we do identify some of the more common approaches.

5.7.1 Prejoining Tables

The relational model, as described in Chap. 3, stores data in physical entities, or tables, through a normalized model. When accessing data for any purpose, the likelihood is that the data you are requesting is stored in multiple tables. As described elsewhere, we need to *join* together tables in order to return that data. The performance challenge is that the cost of the join may be significant, and the overall cost of querying the data again, and again, may be prohibitive. In such cases, one solution is to create tables that are structurally identical to the tables which would be joined: to prejoin the tables.

Prejoined tables should not contain any redundant columns and should only contain those columns absolutely necessary. Such tables will need to be populated (or even created) periodically from the underlying normalized tables; the advantage, however, is that the join (which will still be incurred) will only be incurred once when the prejoined table is created. This *periodic refresh* of the data into the prejoined table should be minimally invasive in the environments typically used for data mining. They can, however, cause significant challenges in transactional systems. In either case, there is a potential for the prejoined table to be out of sync with the underlying data, and care must be taken in using this technique.

5.7.2   Report Tables

Reports pose a particular problem in any system. Not only do they typically involve significant processing to obtain and manipulate the data (aggregations, sorts, and the like), but they often require formatting. One approach that is sometimes used is to create a report that directly represents the needed report. The reporting engine can then directly access this table, which is usually created through an offline process, where the data has been loaded into the report in the sequence required for the report.

In such cases, the table should contain a column that maps to the analogous column in the report, be indexed according to the report data's sequence, and no subvert the underlying relational tenets of the integrity of the data model.

Such tables are of particular value when the results being generated require outer joins or complex processing; the complexity can be hidden by the offline process with much simpler logic used to retrieve the results.

Report tables are not typically used in the data mining environment where the nature of investigating the data is much more dynamic and the outcomes much less static. It has been included here for completeness of the discussion.

5.7.3   Mirroring Tables

For very dynamic transactional systems with very high availability requirements, it may be necessary to partition the application into two or more distinct processing components. For systems with very large data processing requirements, this technique allows for a level of parallel execution that might not be feasible within a single processing environment. In such cases, the underlying data model implementation may need to be duplicated in order to allow the processing to occur. In the former example of high availability requirements, this duplication would allow data interrogation and data updates to occur with a manageable level of impact on each type of processing. Without managing this type of interaction, frequent timeouts and database deadlocks could occur, making the system unusable during those times.

Creating mirror tables, where one set exists to handle one type of data (or for one processing system) and the other to meet the needs of the second type of data processing, would alleviate this problem. As is the case with prejoining tables, a process to periodically refresh, or update, one set of tables from the other is necessary.

As indicated for the prejoining case, this technique does not typically occur in the data mining environment and is included here for completeness.

5.7.4 Splitting Tables

Data environments will often contain entities, or tables, which contain data needed by multiple groups of users, or by multiple systems. In such cases, the data queries being performed may be significantly different and cause deadlocks and timeouts to occur. Another technique we can use is to split the table up into multiple denormalized tables, with one table for each distinct type of processing. Taking this approach does necessitate making a decision as to whether the original table should be maintained or not. In certain cases, the original table can be replaced by another object within the database management system – the view.

Splitting the table could occur horizontally, according to some ordering of the rows of data – often called a *partition* – or vertically, by separating columns of the table into the splits. In the latter case, the *primary key* needs to be maintained in every split. The vertical split case requires that one of the splits be designated the *parent* for referential integrity purposes: this parent ensures that if a row is deleted, it is deleted from all the other splits in a coherent manner. This situation is a good candidate to retain the original table and use it as the parent. There is one other consideration when splitting a table vertically: each split should contain a row for each primary key in each split table to avoid overly complicating the associated update process.

5.7.5 Combining Tables

As we describe elsewhere, there are several types of relationships between tables. If two or more tables are related in a one-to-one relationship, a performance improvement can be achieved through combining the tables into a single table.[6]

5.7.6 Copying Data Across Entities

One of the techniques used in data modeling is to separate out commonly used data into *reference tables*. For example, the names of organisms and drugs are often used throughout a system. Rather than duplicating the often long names of organisms or compounds, a shortened code, often an integral value, can be used that is included as the primary key of the row in another table. Thus, 12345 may refer to *Staphylococcus aureus* and permeate through the database wherever necessary, with the full

---

[6] It should be noted that this type of operation can also be accomplished for tables in a one-to-many relationship, but the update process is significantly more complicated due to the fact that there will be much more redundant data to handle. Discussion of this scenario is out of the scope of this book.

name being stored in only one place.[7] If a data inquiry often requires the names of organisms (or compounds, or . . .) to be accessed whenever other core data needs to be accessed, we will often consider duplicating these columns in our core table; they will be *redundant* data. However, by including these columns, the speed of data retrieval can be improved since joins will be eliminated.

This technique introduces a level of complexity into the environment that should only be considered in the event that normal methods of accessing the data are causing a debilitating effect on the system. If this technique is implemented, only the columns absolutely necessary should be duplicated, and they should contain data that is very rarely updated – the columns should be stable. Further, the universe of users of this data should either be very large or should be a very small community (typically of very important users).

5.7.7   Repeating Groups

One of the core normalization rules described in Chap. 3 deals explicitly with the concept of repeating groups of data and how to extract them into their own tables. While this can be very efficient from the online transactional perspective, which typically deals more with inserting, updating, and deleting data, it will often result in inefficiencies when retrieving the data.[8]

Sometimes we can gain significant performance improvements by storing the data back into the original table as columns. However, like every one of the techniques, there is a trade-off, in this case with flexibility. Normalizing repeating groups into their own tables means that an infinite number of the repeating groups can be accommodated; denormalizing them back into columns restricts the number of instances of the repeating group which can be supported due, in large part, to the limitations of the relational database management system.

Consideration should be given to several factors before considering using this technique (answers which make this option feasible are in parentheses):

1. Is the data rarely (or never) aggregated, averaged, compared within the row? (Yes)
2. Does the data occur according to a statistically well-behaved distribution? (Yes)

---

[7] This also has a significant impact on the amount of storage taken up by the data since storing a numeric value such as 12345 takes 2 or 4 bytes of storage, whereas *Staphylococcus aureus* takes up 21 bytes of storage.

[8] Recall that normalizing for repeating groups takes groups of columns (which repeat) and makes them distinct rows in different tables. This results in typically larger disk storage requirements (if only because of the overhead of the table itself) and requires the query to process more rows of data – using joins – to satisfy the query.

3. Does the data have a stable number of occurrences or does it change dynamically? As a corollary: does every instance of the data have the same or similar number of occurrences? (Stable and yes)
4. Is the data primarily accessed as a collection or is the repeating group selectively included? (As a collection)
5. Is the insertion (and deletion) pattern of the data predictable? (Yes)

If these criteria are not met, the underlying query code will be more complicated, or very difficult to generate, essentially making the data less available – an outcome to be avoided since the whole intent of using denormalization techniques is to make the data more readily available for us to analyze, not to make it less available!

5.7.8 Derived Data

Consider the body mass index (BMI) for an individual. This value can be derived using a readily available formula based upon the individual's height and weight – two values typically captured at every encounter between the individual and a health-care specialist. The BMI is an example of a data element *derived* from other data. This example is relatively simple to derive. However, the cost of deriving data during an interrogation can be prohibitive is the formula needed to calculate it is very complicated. In such cases, we can consider storing the derived data as columns instead of calculating it on the fly.

The challenge we have to consider is to ensure that when the underlying data changes, the derived data is consistently changed. If this doesn't occur, it is very easy to retrieve inconsistent data, resulting in reduced reliability of the dataset and impacted effectiveness of the dataset.

5.7.9 Hierarchies of Data

We discuss hierarchies, specifically *concept hierarchies*, in several places in this book (specifically, in Chap. 2) and introduce them here only in the context of denormalization and use the intuitive definition of a hierarchy.

Hierarchies can be easily implemented in the relational model, but efficient retrieval is difficult. For this reason, hierarchies are very often denormalized to improve query efficiency. The terms for such denormalized entities vary, but a widely used term is to describe these entities as *speed tables*.

The challenge with hierarchies is the fact that by their very nature they will have n levels, but that the value of n is neither known *a priori* and also changes as the hierarchy grows. Technically, a hierarchy of n levels will require n-1 UNION operations to accomplish.[9]

---

[9] Two notes: first, a UNION is an operation in Structured Query Language (SQL) which is the underlying relational data manipulation language. Second, you would need to know the value of n in order to code the n-1 UNIONs!

"Speed" tables contain the whole hierarchy: the parent (at any given level) and all children underneath it, irrespective of the level at which the child actually appears. It will also include other pertinent information such as the level of the hierarchy, whether the node of the hierarchy is a leaf node or the root node, the sequence of the nodes at a given level of the hierarchy, and any other information necessary to enable the query to be developed without knowing the levels of the hierarchy explicitly and to aid performance.[10]

The subject of concept hierarchies and implementing hierarchies in the relational model are dealt with elsewhere in this book.

5.8   Extract, Transform, and Load (ETL)

Fundamentally, ETL is concerned with ensuring that data to be included in a system, analysis, data submission, or other coherent data environment has the internal and external consistency that we describe elsewhere. In order to accommodate this, we use a wide variety of techniques, some of which we have considered above, and some others we consider later.

In this section, we consider in more depth the process of bringing data from external environments into a single, coherent data definition so that the data can be incorporated into our data mining effort. This could arguably be considered to be the most common ETL activity as most of the data that we mine will originate in databases and sources outside of our mining environment. Fundamentally, therefore, we are interested in **extract**ing the data from various external sources, **transform**ing it to meet our business needs, and **load**ing it into our mining environment.

We have described the necessary concepts underlying ETL above, but as is the case in many areas of information systems, iterative consideration of the "best" way to accomplish something has caused many companies and organizations to consider how they might improve the process. Such improvements often come through developing more robust products to ease the pain of the tasks involved, but it can also come from taking a look at the underlying process itself.

In this context, an initially innocuous looking change can enable, or complicate, the process significantly. As has been said, the transform step is typically accomplished outside of either the source environments or the destination environment (the data mining environment, in our case). Some advocates consider that extracting the data from the source environments and loading it into an intermediary

---

[10] SQL alone is not typically used to build the table due to the complexity of the logic, the inefficiency of SQL, and because the number of levels in the hierarchy is either unknown or constantly changing.

environment, if not directly into the target environment, and then transforming the data is a more effective approach (ETL). Coupling this with a business-rules-driven approach to the transformation step adds significant value.

This has some very attractive possibilities. For a wide variety of organizations, the relational data platform has become the standard. Loading the untransformed data into such an environment not only allows us to leverage the existing data architecture and resources to help but also typically opens up a wider range of products – both third party and developed by the organization – to help us in transforming our data.

There are many third-party products available that are either specifically designed for this activity or which have extensive capabilities to support ETL. These include Informatica, SAS, Pervasive-Data Junction, Sunopsis, and Cognos. But a quick search on the Internet will highlight many others. Your enterprise may well have one of these products in place already since ETL is a necessary evil of many distributed application portfolios, a quotidian part of the enterprise platform of many companies today. However, as mentioned above, custom-developed code may be necessary (or preferable) than using a third-party product. This is especially true in circumstances where the transformation tasks (in particular) require almost as much effort to develop within an ETL tool as they do outside.

5.8.1   Integrating External Data

With the plethora of databases available to the scientific community today, a common problem for data mining, and most other data analysis efforts, is that your data warehouse may not contain all of the data you need for the problem under study. This is particularly so in the informatics space as many gene, protein, transcriptome, and other sequence data may need to be incorporated from outside the organization. The same issues we discuss in this chapter relate to that external data as well as the data collected by the organization. *Integrating* this data with the data already in the data warehouse can often be very challenging. One reason for this relates to the method used for uniquely identifying the data. In an external database, this might be a unique accession number which, by and large, will not correlate to any identification scheme within your data warehouse. If it does, there is a high likelihood that a one-to-many relationship will occur, as discussed in Chap. 3.

Another factor to bear in mind is that the quality of this external data may be no better, or worse, than the data collected in the data warehouse. In either case, cleansing of the data will still be required. This external data is sometimes called *overlay data*.

Fig. 5.1 Overlap of Protein
Information Resource (*PIR*)
ID between PIR and
Universal Protein Resource
(*UniProt*)

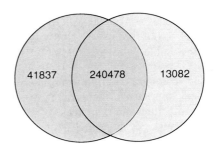

5.8.2   Gene/Protein Identifier Cross-Referencing

Gene and protein data occupies an ever-increasing importance in life science research and thus also in mining of biological data. However, one of the biggest challenges encountered today is that our knowledge of these entities is spread across multiple databases maintained by different groups of researchers. This means that a single gene or protein may have multiple identifiers across these data repositories.

Compounding this, biological terms associated with different gene identifiers for the same gene could be collected in different levels across different repositories; we need a way to be able to bring these together for our analytical efforts, so that we can look across this *distributed* data repository. In order to do this, we need to have some means for transforming the identifier in one repository to another.

One widely used tool is the *Database for Annotation, Visualization, and Integrated Discovery* (DAVID) that provides a comprehensive set of functional annotation tools for investigators to understand biological meaning behind large lists of genes.

Most gene-functional annotation databases are in a gene-associated format where the annotation contents are usually directly associated with the corresponding gene or protein identifiers. For example, consider two of the most widely used repositories – the Protein Information Resource (PIR) and the Universal Protein Resource (UniProt) – and consider the PIR identifier (PIR ID), a widely used protein identifier. The Venn diagram in Fig. 5.1 depicts a point-in-time overlap, at the time of writing, for just this one identification scheme.

On the DAVID web site,[11] a more extensive comparison, using four popular types of protein identifiers – PIR ID, UniProt Accession, RefSeq Protein, and GenPept Accession – is depicted, and reproduced below, showing the partial coverage by NCBI Entrez Gene (EG), UniProt UniRef100 (UP), and PIR NRef100 (NF).

---

[11] http://david.abcc.ncifcrf.gov/helps/knowledgebase/DAVID_gene.html#gene

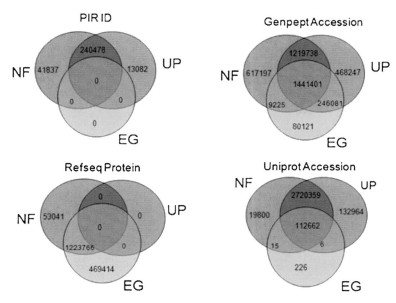

Fig. 5.2 Identifier coverage of popular gene/protein identifiers across widely used repositories (Taken from http://david.abcc.ncifcrf.gov/helps/knowledgebase/DAVID_gene.html#gene)

If we are able to cross-reference the identifiers at different repositories, this allows us to aggregate the annotations included at each of the different repositories we are accessing, providing a super-set of information about the genes and proteins we are analyzing, and further increasing our data mining opportunities (Fig. 5.2).

DAVID is by no means the only identifier cross-reference mechanism available, others include Babelomics, g:Profiler, and MatchMiner. Some are provided in Appendix B, but the interested reader is recommended to search for those available at their time of need: more will likely be available then.

5.9 Aggregation and Calculation

5.9.1 Aggregation

How much should we aggregate our data during this preparation step? How often would an attribute calculated from, say, two other attributes be more appropriate for our mining efforts? These two simple questions can have a dramatic impact on our efforts – to the good and the bad. We'll use an example from a different industry – the telecommunications industry – to illustrate this. When we use a cell phone, a record is captured at the start and end of a call, as well as every time we switch cells.[12] Instead of (potentially) having multiple instances in our dataset, we might aggregate this into a single instance that contains the start and end time and a Boolean value that might indicate whether the caller traveled outside their "home" region.

Correctly selecting the level of aggregation is vital to a successful mining effort. As we discuss elsewhere, our conclusions may be inaccurate in the best case and dangerous in the worst case scenario if we get it wrong. However, we should add that in many cases we **do** get it wrong, the first time. This is part of the reason for the preparation stage taking so much time and effort.

Hard and fast rules for when to aggregate, and to what level, are almost impossible to define. We have used several rules of thumb in our work to guide us:

- What is the impact of aggregating this instance?
  In considering our raw data, we will often find occasions where we have captured many individual instances that might, for example, vary in only a small number of ways. We have often seen datasets where, with the exception of one or two attributes, the remaining attributes contain the same values, or where the different values for individual attributes range over a small interval. We may be able to aggregate such a subset of our input data so that we have a single instance rather than multiple. We will return to this below when we talk about attribute-driven aggregation.
- How does time affect/not affect our mining efforts?
  We will often find that the temporal dimension generates raw data. That is, we will often collect the same data but at different time points. In such cases, one obvious method of aggregation is to take some time interval and aggregate all of the raw instances into a single instance. For example, we may collect data daily but may be able to aggregate it to a monthly summary. Obviously, we need to consider what we will be losing when we aggregate by time. What is our most important time interval? Is there one?
- What is the impact of aggregating this attribute?
  Aggregation will often be driven by one or more attributes. For example, we may find that a particular attribute's range of values covers an interval that is insignificant for our particular mining efforts: if we see that the range of our patients' blood pressure fluctuates insignificantly and within generally accepted normal ranges, we may not be too worried about averaging the values and driving our aggregation from this perspective. Obviously, we need to be very careful since the amount of change for one attribute may be insignificant, whereas for another may be significant and this is where we return to the question of instance-level aggregation. For example, a range of values for blood pressure between, say, 105/75 and 120/80 may not be significant for our current purposes; a corresponding fluctuation of pH between, say, 7.30 and 7.51 for the same subset of data may be significant.

---

[12] Of course, this assumes our call does not get dropped as we switch cells! Some readers familiar with the telecommunications industry may also be aware that additional data is captured on a periodic basis – such as every 6 s – but we avoid this over-complication for our illustration.

5.9.2 Calculation

Earlier in this book, we considered the body mass index (BMI), a value calculated from a person's weight and height. Consider a person's body surface area (BSA), a value used in determining medication doses and also based on a person's weight and height. One of the calculations, (DuBois and DuBois 1916 #144), is

$$BSA\ (m^2) = 0.20247 \times height\ (m)^{0.725} \times weight\ (kg)^{0.425}.$$

These attributes are examples of calculated fields with which we may be interested in augmenting our dataset.

What constitutes a valuable addition to the dataset will depend upon our objectives and the conclusions we wish to reach. As we discuss elsewhere, increasing the number of attributes in our dataset can have a deleterious effect on the models and algorithms we wish to use, but they can also add valuable insight depending on their importance. For example, if our goal is to improve our prediction of dosing for patients, including the BSA may be very valuable indeed.

As well as adding to the dimensionality of the dataset, calculated values can also reduce the number of attributes in the dataset. If we include the BSA in our dataset, for example, do we also need the height and weight? Do they add any value above and beyond the calculated value?

In the general case, introducing calculated attributes into our dataset can have a number of benefits, but we also need to be conscious of the fact that if we simply add them, the impact on our models may be to reduce their effectiveness and accuracy.

5.10 Noisy Data

In almost every data element we capture, some degree of random error or variance will be introduced into the data. This could be because of data entry errors, instrument capture, or data entry error. Noise can adversely impact the performance or our models as well as the quality of our results. We now look at some techniques we can use to remove the impact of noise on our models and results. Typically, the term *smoothing* is used since what we are really trying to do is *smooth* out the noise from our data.

The most common methods of dealing with noisy data are *binning methods*, *regression methods*, and *clustering methods*, which we describe further below. But what are we really accomplishing through the process of smoothing? Obviously, we are trying to exclude noisy data; in many cases, this means excluding outliers from our dataset. That is, data values which are patently not part of the "normal" data we wish to process.

As we shall see below, techniques for dealing with noisy data are also methods for data reduction – through discretization of the data. Typically, this is through reducing the number of distinct values for the data. We will conclude this section by describing some areas in which this can be a very valuable technique to include in our models.

For our discussions, we will consider the example of some laboratory test for which we are capturing the results as part of our mining dataset.

Data (sorted): 27, 33, 38, 49, 62, 81, 94, 99, 107, 126, 127, 145, 152, 161, 178

5.10.1   Regression

One way in which we can smooth the data is to fit the data to a function, as is accomplished using regression techniques. We discuss regression in detail elsewhere, but for our example data above, we can use *linear regression* to fit the data to a "best line" based upon a secondary variable: linear regression uses one variable or attribute to predict another. The explanatory variable is typically the observed variable; the dependent variable is the one output by the linear regression relationship. More generally, our equation would be $Y = a + bX$, where X is the explanatory variable and Y is the dependent variable. Think of this as a set of idealized values that provide a value s_i, the smoothed value, given the data value x_i, where $i = 1, ..., n$, with n being the number of elements in our data. The linear regression relationship $s_i = a + bx_i$ denotes the general relationship.

5.10.2   Binning

Binning takes a set of sorted attribute values and uses information about the values around it to determine what the *locally* smoothed values should be. The values under consideration are first sorted and then separated into individual bins or partitions. Each bin is then considered independently, hence the local smoothing, to determine what the smoothed values should be. Obviously, the first question we need to answer is how many bins should we use? We'll answer this independent of the method we shall employ for smoothing, initially.

We have 15 values for our attribute, and if we want to create partitions with equal *frequency*, we can create either 3 bins of 5 values or 5 bins of 3 values. We'll actually do both, as shown in Fig. 5.3.

Now we choose the smoothing method itself. There are many ways in which we can smooth each individual bin:

- Means – each value in the bin is replaced by the mean of bin values (Fig. 5.4):
- Medians – each value in the bin is replaced by the median of the bin values (Fig. 5.5):

3-by-5		5-by-3	
Bin 1	27, 33, 38, 49, 62	Bin 1	27, 33, 38
Bin 2	81, 94, 99, 107, 126	Bin 2	49, 62, 81
Bin 3	127, 145, 152, 161, 178	Bin 3	94, 99, 107
		Bin 4	126, 127, 145
		Bin 5	152, 161, 178

Fig. 5.3 Binning data

3-by-5		5-by-3	
Bin 1	42, 42, 42, 42, 42 [13]	Bin 1	33, 33, 33
Bin 2	101, 101, 101, 101, 101	Bin 2	64, 64, 64
Bin 3	153, 153, 153, 153, 153	Bin 3	100, 100, 100
		Bin 4	133, 133, 133
		Bin 5	164, 164, 164

Fig. 5.4 Binning data – smoothing (means)

3-by-5		5-by-3	
Bin 1	38, 38, 38, 38, 38	Bin 1	33, 33, 33
Bin 2	99, 99, 99, 99, 99	Bin 2	62, 62, 62
Bin 3	152, 152, 152, 152, 152	Bin 3	99, 99, 99
		Bin 4	127, 127, 127
		Bin 5	161, 161, 161

Fig. 5.5 Binning data – smoothing (medians)

---

[13] In this tables we have rounded up to the nearest integer value.

3-by-5		**5-by-3**	
Bin 1	27, 27, 27, 62, 62	Bin 1	33, 33, 33
Bin 2	81, 81, 81, 126, 126	Bin 2	64, 64, 64
Bin 3	127, 127,127, 178, 178	Bin 3	100, 100, 100
		Bin 4	133, 133, 133
		Bin 5	164, 164, 164

Fig. 5.6 Binning data – boundary values

- Bin boundaries – each value in the bin is replaced by the boundary value to which they are nearest (Fig. 5.6):

As we can see from the above example, there are a couple of factors that we must consider. The first, and obvious, is how many bins to create. This isn't necessarily a simple matter. If we consider our smoothing by mean, we can calculate the mean and variance, as shown below using R:

```
> datasetSmoothByMean <- c(42, 42, 42, 42, 42, 101, 101, 101, 101, 101, 153, 153,
153, 153, 153)
> mean(datasetSmoothByMean)
[1] 98.66667
> var(datasetSmoothByMean)
[1] 2203.095
> datasetSmoothByMean <- c(33, 33, 33, 64, 64, 64, 100, 100, 100, 133, 133, 133,
164, 164, 164)
> mean(datasetSmoothByMean)
[1] 98.8
> var(datasetSmoothByMean)
[1] 2349.171
```

We can see that the means are relatively similar, but the variances show a larger difference. This may or may not be significant, depending upon your goals.

The second question is what approach should we take? Above we have illustrated the mean, median, and boundary approaches, and while these are commonly used, other surrogate values could be used.

A third question that can be asked is whether or not the overall approach to partitioning is the correct approach. In our example, we decided to partition the values so that each bin, or partition, had the same number of values (frequency). Alternatively, we could elect to take a different approach, such as partitioning the values so that each partition had values where the interval range for each partition was a constant size.

To conclude our discussion, these techniques can be valuable in reducing or eliminating noise that might have seeped into our data, but they can also be value due to the data reduction nature of the techniques themselves. For example, if we build a model using decision trees, a technique which compares values of sorted data repeatedly, these techniques can be of significant value from both a simplicity and performance standpoint. Further, if we consider building concept hierarchies, we may develop one which maps our test result values into abnormal-low, normal, and abnormal-high, so that our model does not have to deal with a possibly infinite number of values.

We consider data reduction and discretization techniques at various points within this book – in the context of the methods and techniques to which they apply.

5.10.3   Clustering

Clustering is a topic that receives significant attention elsewhere in this book, and we only mention it in passing here. As we shall see, we can use clustering techniques to allow us to smooth data where it might be missing.

5.11   Metadata

Metadata, or data about data, allows us to build up a comprehensive description of the data we are studying. This is vitally important as it provides us with significant insight into the dataset itself, but also allows us to make informed decisions as we implement the methods of choice. For example, we may recognize a field as being a nominal field and one which is made up of a series of codes. This piece of metadata may help us to build a translation capability so that users can see a more meaningful description of the fields' contents rather than the (cryptic) code itself.

5.11.1   Attribute Type

Individual attributes will obviously be represented by different attribute *types*. Typically, we consider binary, nominal (categorical), ordinal, ratio (real, integer), and text to comprise the most common types of data we encounter in practice. Here, we omit special types such as binary large objects (BLOBs) and consider them separately elsewhere in this book. Further, our definition of text does include sequence data, as encountered in genomics and proteomics, and also to include text as encountered in document form – although this is also deferred to a later part of the book and not considered in the mainstream methods we describe herein.[14]

---

[14] This is because the challenge of mining unstructured documents requires their own special techniques and we consider these separately.

Each data type will have its own challenges and opportunities to deal with. How we deal with the data, based on its type, will also be dependent on the techniques we use. For example, some of the techniques we employ – such as regression – will only work on ratio data that allows us to compute a *distance* metric between two instances. If the data that we need to use is ordinal, we can use a technique whereby we decide whether two instances (or even values) are the same or different. If they are the same, we can use a value of 0 to indicate "sameness" and 1 to indicate "difference." Such an encoding now allows us to use learning methods, regression, or any other technique which requires ratio data types. Thus, we can use this method to, for example, convert gender into ratio data. An interesting nuance here is to ask what do we do if we allow an "unknown" (or "not provided") value for gender? One option might be to use ± 1 for male and female and to use 0 for unknown. Obviously, this should not be used without careful consideration as to how that might affect our models and results.

This specific example can also be expanded into a more general sense: that of converting an encoding to some numeric value set. As we see from the question of the "unknown" value for gender, there are definitely questions we need to consider. The first is why we would consider converting ordinal data in the first place. Yes, it definitely opens up our model set to a much broader set of models, but those models may be overly complex for the problem at hand.

One example of an encoding scheme that has shown value in a number of areas is the binary encoding of nucleotides, as seen in Chen (2002 #123) and Lippert et al. (2005 #124).

Minimum/maximum values for numeric fields – these can be used as part of the data checking activity.

Nominal fields containing codes – generate/acquire tables to translate codes into full text descriptions for presentation to users.

5.11.2   Attribute Role

The role of an attribute can be a very valuable characteristic to consider. For each of the attributes in our dataset, we can ask the questions:

1. Is it an input attribute which will be used for modeling?
2. Is it an output attribute?
3. Is it an attribute we can safely ignore? How do we know?
4. Is it a weight?

Question 1 is an intuitive one that we have discussed elsewhere. The relevance of an attribute to the problem at hand must be considered so that we can begin to determine its relevance and impact on our model. Question 2 is important in a number of areas. For example, if our model involves the supervised learning paradigm, an output attribute will be provided to the model for validation purposes. Question 3 relates to question 1 in that if we can ignore an attribute, we are reducing its dimensionality, and, also, excluding it from the modeling activity. The corollary, however, is extremely important: how **do** we know? We have to be careful when excluding attributes. If we're not sure, we may need to include it until some other information comes our way to allow us to exclude it.

Question 4 is an interesting one in that it partially addresses the issue of relative importance, a qualitative aspect to the dataset, as opposed to a qualitative attribute. Does the attribute introduce a weighting factor on the model? Is it more important to the conclusions than other attributes? What would happen if we excluded it? This is important to consider since this allows us to see into the data and begin to formulate our plans a little more succinctly. Attributes which act as weights can direct our efforts along particular lines of inquiry and affect our model selection. However, we need to be sure that it really is important – in fact, more important than other attributes – otherwise it can lead us down the wrong path. Careful analysis of the attribute's domain of values and its affect on other attributes in our dataset needs to be performed before we rely too heavily on some subset of our data.

5.11.3   Attribute Description

Attribute descriptions are useful for understanding the data as well as for output to users. In this role, they act as supporting documentation. While there may be valuable content in descriptive fields, they often require preprocessing to extract the information. In this regard, we may actually create additional attributes to contain the data in the descriptive attribute, unless we are undertaking text mining as part of our data mining project. Text mining is outside the scope of this book, and we assume that descriptive attributes will be explicitly preprocessed and any relevant attributes added to our dataset.

One issue that we need to be careful about under this scenario is that the number of instances where we populate data may actually be very small and the issue of missing value that we discuss below becomes very pertinent. It might be better to exclude the attribute from consideration completely, therefore.

5.12   Missing Values

We touched upon missing data in Chap. 2, but return to it here in greater depth due to the impact it can have on the accuracy and validity of both the dataset we are studying and the results we obtain from the methodologies we use. This problem of missing data in large datasets is a well-recognized problem and has been the subject of much research and discussion, especially in statistics, data analysis, and, of course, data mining.

Missing data can occur in several different forms:

- It just does not exist.
  Here, there is simply no value whatsoever. This might appear as NULL in database systems, or as NA in systems such as R, or ? as in Weka. This situation requires that we make decisions about the (physically) missing data: do we ignore it, ignore the instance itself, or do we use a *default value*?
- It exists as a default value.
  Here, the data exists in a default form. For example, numeric data may default to 0 or 1, typically. The default value is often prescribed by the database management system or source application(s). However, if the data in the dataset being studied has come from several discrete source systems, it is very possible that different systems have used different default values. In many data environments, it is the database management system itself which defines the default value at the time that the entity containing the data is created. This issue is discussed in Chap. 3.

We need to handle missing data carefully as incorrect consideration can quickly lead to chaos. As a simple example, consider missing numeric data. Using 0 means that any "counting" or "averaging" operations will not include this data; any operation where this attribute is used as the denominator in an algorithm will immediately be an issue. There are several approaches we can use to handle missing data:

- Ignore instances with missing values.
  We rarely want to do this, unless many attributes in the instance are missing. Excluding any data should be considered very carefully since this not only reduces the size of our sample, but may skew the sample so that it is no longer representative. This could, in turn, lead to the model over-fitting issue.
- Consider the missing value as a separate value.
  Here, we add a value to the domain of values for the field. For example, with gender we may have "Male," "Female," and add "Not Reported" to cover any missing values. We need to consider what percentage of the instances under study would have this value for the attribute. If a majority of the instances would end up having this value, we might be better off excluding this attribute from our dataset. We return to this question below. We also need to consider the cause of the missing data: is it because of one circumstance, or set of circumstances, or is it because of several different reasons? If the latter, we may need several distinct codes, depending on the reason. For example, if we have a "is a smoker?" attribute, we may need "Not Reported" and "Not Applicable" if we have a mixture of data on children and adults.[15]
- Replace the missing value.
  If we determine that it is important to populate the attribute with a value, what might that value be? We can certainly consider 0 or 1, but the questions we have

---

[15] Assuming we don't have chain-smoking children.

raised above come back into play. We could consider, instead, mean or median values. Depending upon our methods and algorithms, one or other of these might be more appropriate. Alternatively, we could try and *impute* or estimate the missing value from other information in the instance in which it appears, or in the datasets itself; the latter option of which often leads us back to the 0, 1, mean, or median result.

The above techniques allow us to "fill-in-the-blanks" but don't completely address the case where the "blanks" outnumber the values. How do we handle attributes with a majority of "missing" values? As various locales introduce extensive data protection legislation and as companies continually introduce more robust security policies and procedures, many pieces of data – especially health-care data – may become inaccessible.

The first question we should ask ourselves is how important is the attribute itself? Information such as gender and age information may be vitally important, but is it as important to know if the person is a smoker? Using this example may be a surprise, but if our objectives have nothing to do with whether a person is a smoker or not, then why worry about it? But, we can counter, the whole intent of mining data is to find previously unknown patterns in the data, so there may be a correlation with whether a person is a smoker or not that we have not yet deduced. This may be true (and the reason why we chose this example). So how do we handle such cases?

Consider the reality of **any** data environment: we are capturing data that is a *sample* of some *population*. Further, any model we develop, as we discuss elsewhere, is a model from which we want to extrapolate items of interest in the overall population from the sample we have taken through our trials, experiments, or other data collection activities. One approach we can take, therefore, is to look for an independent source for information on our missing data. That is, can we find independent information on smokers in some other comparable sample or population?[16]

Consider the data in Table 5.1. This provides a breakdown of smokers in the USA between the years of 2000 and 2004, by age, and goes further to provide us with an indication of how the relative percentages of smokers change over time (using the former smoker category). Using this data, we could estimate how many people in our sample **may** be smokers.

Using this data, we can generate a statistical model that allows us to populate the attribute for which the values are largely missing.

However, we must be careful about how we interpret the results from our model. The above data was *not* collected during the trial or experiment, and we must consider what we are deducing from our model. Did the missing data become an

---

[16] Statisticians reading this will immediately raise a red flag about the data we have already collected, since the underlying population may be different to the "independent" population we are looking for to eliminate our missing data. This is true, and we return to this in Chap. 6.

Table 5.1 Smoking statistics – US population 2000–2004

Smoking status	Gender (years)	Current			Former			Never		
		All	Male	Female	All	Male	Female	All	Male	Female
All[a]	18+[b]	21.5	23.8	19.4	21.9	26.2	18.4	56.6	50.1	62.3
	18–44	25	27.8	22.3	12.4	12.6	12.2	62.6	59.6	65.5
	18–24	25.2	28	22.5	7.2	7.3	7.1	67.6	64.7	70.4
	25–44	25	27.7	22.3	14.2	14.5	13.9	60.9	57.8	63.9
	45–64	22.4	24.5	20.4	28.4	34	23.2	49.2	41.5	56.5
	65+	9.1	10	8.4	39.9	54.6	29.1	51.1	35.4	62.5
White	18+[b]	22	23.8	20.2	23	27.1	19.8	55	49.1	60
	18–44	26.1	28.4	23.8	13.6	13.4	13.8	60.3	58.2	62.5
	18–24	26.9	29.5	24.3	8.3	8.4	8.2	64.8	62.1	67.5
	25–44	25.8	28	23.6	15.3	15.1	15.6	58.9	56.9	60.8
	45–64	22.3	24	20.5	29.6	34.8	24.6	48.2	41.1	54.9
	65+	8.8	9.4	8.4	41.1	55.9	30.1	50.1	34.7	61.6
Black	18+[b]	20.8	25	17.6	15.6	20.2	12.3	63.6	54.8	70.2
	18–44	21.1	24.8	18.1	6.7	7.3	6.2	72.2	67.9	75.7
	18–24	17	19.8	14.5	3.2	3.1	3.2	79.9	77.1	82.3
	25–44	22.7	26.9	19.4	8.1	9	7.4	69.2	64.1	73.3
	45–64	25.5	29.7	22.1	22.1	29.1	16.5	52.3	41.2	61.4
	65+	11.5	17.1	8	31.8	44.9	23.8	56.7	38	68.2
American Indian/ Alaska Native	18+[b]	31.7	34.4	28.9	21.1	22.1	20.1	47.2	43.5	51.1
	18–44	36.2	38.9	33.7	11	10.2	11.8	52.8	50.9	54.5
	18–24	42.5	50	36.2	*	*	*	54.5	49.4	58.7
	25–44	33.3	34.1	32.6	14.6	14.3	14.9	52.1	51.6	52.5
	45–64	33	36	29.1	29.5	31.2	27.3	37.4	32.8	43.6
	65+	15.2	*	*	37.6	*	33	47.2	*	53.7
Asian	18+[b]	11.5	17	5.8	14	22.3	5.7	74.5	60.6	88.5
	18–44	13.7	20.6	6.4	7.7	12.4	2.8	78.6	67	90.8
	18–24	14.3	16.4	11.6	*	*	*	84.2	81.1	88
	25–44	13.5	22	5	9.5	15.6	3.5	77	62.4	91.5
	45–64	11.1	15.5	6.3	19.5	30.5	7.3	69.4	54	86.4
	65+	5.6	*	*	23.8	39	11.8	70.6	52.4	85
Native Hawaiian/ Pacific Islander	18+[b]	31.9	37.2	*	16.4	15.6	*	51.7	47.2	57.4
	18–44	27.8	*	*	*	*	*	59.4	50.5	*
	18–24	*	*	*	*	*	*	*	*	*
	25–44	*	*	*	*	*	*	61.7	51.6	*
	45–64	*	*	*	*	*	*	*	*	*
	65+	*	*	*	*	*	*	*	*	*
Multiple race	18+[b]	31.3	33.3	29.5	22.3	25.4	19.8	46.5	41.3	50.7
	18–44	34.8	38.9	31	13.1	13.9	12.4	52.1	47.1	56.6
	18–24	35.8	40.6	30.8	*	*	*	57.9	52.9	63
	25–44	34.3	38.1	31.1	16.3	17.8	15.1	49.4	44.1	53.8
	45–64	32	34.3	30.3	29	31.6	27.2	39	34.1	42.5
	65+	19.2	*	23.3	38.8	50.3	30	42	36	46.7

(continued)

Table 5.1 (continued)

Smoking status		Current			Former			Never		
	Gender (years)	All	Male	Female	All	Male	Female	All	Male	Female
Hispanic	18+[b]	15.2	19.9	10.5	15.9	21.6	10.7	68.9	58.6	78.8
	18–44	16.7	22.2	10.5	9.7	12.1	7.1	73.6	65.7	82.4
	18–24	15.9	21.3	9.7	6.6	7.4	5.8	77.5	71.3	84.6
	25–44	17	22.5	10.8	10.9	13.8	7.6	72.2	63.7	81.6
	45–64	17.2	21.3	13.2	20.5	27.7	13.7	62.3	51	73.1
	65+	7.4	10.2	5.4	26.8	40.3	16.9	65.8	49.5	77.7
Puerto Rican	18+[b]	23	28.8	17.7	17.2	21	13.9	59.8	50.2	68.4
	18–44	25.6	28.9	22.4	12.6	15	10.2	61.8	56.1	67.4
	18–24	27.7	33	21.7	*	*	*	61.8	59.1	64.8
	25–44	24.9	27.3	22.6	13.3	17.7	9.2	61.8	55	68.3
	45–64	24.8	36.3	14.5	20	22.3	17.8	55.2	41.4	67.7
	65+	11.6	*	*	26.5	37.2	18.8	62	47.3	72.6
Mexican	18+[b]	14.6	19.4	9.3	15.4	20.9	10	70	59.7	80.7
	18–44	15.8	22	8.4	9	11.3	6.4	75.2	66.6	85.2
	18–24	14.1	20.2	7	6.2	7.1	5.2	79.7	72.7	87.8
	25–44	16.4	22.8	8.9	10.2	13	6.8	73.4	64.3	84.2
	45–64	16.8	20.2	13.4	20	27.9	12.5	63.2	52	74.1
	65+	7.2	9.9	4.9	26.9	38.5	16.9	65.9	51.5	78.3
Non-Hispanic White	18+[b]	23.3	24.8	21.9	23.9	27.6	21	52.7	47.6	57.1
	18–44	28.2	30	26.6	14.5	13.7	15.2	57.3	56.3	58.3
	18–24	29.7	31.8	27.5	8.6	8.5	8.7	61.7	59.7	63.7
	25–44	27.8	29.4	26.2	16.4	15.4	17.2	55.9	55.2	56.5
	45–64	22.8	24.3	21.3	30.5	35.6	25.7	46.7	40.1	53
	65+	8.9	9.4	8.5	42	56.9	31	49.1	33.8	60.5
Non-Hispanic Black	18+[b]	20.8	24.9	17.7	15.6	20.2	12.3	63.6	54.9	70
	18–44	21	24.4	18.1	6.7	7.3	6.3	72.3	68.3	75.6
	18–24	16.8	19.3	14.7	3.1	3.1	3	80.1	77.6	82.3
	25–44	22.6	26.6	19.4	8.1	9	7.5	69.3	64.4	73.2
	45–64	25.8	30.1	22.3	22.1	28.9	16.6	52.1	41	61.1
	65+	11.6	17.2	8.1	31.9	44.9	23.8	56.6	37.9	68.1

Source: NHIS via CDC Health Data for All Ages (http://www.cdc.gov/nchs/health_data_for_all_ages.htm)
[a] Race/Ethnicity
[b] Age adjusted
* Unknown data

important driver for our results, or is it ancillary? If the latter, we may be safe in ignoring its impact on the results. If the former case occurs, however, we have to question the validity of our results. Using our above example, results which show a high correlation to whether a person was guessed to be a smoker cannot be relied on. If we randomly selected patients based upon a statistical model of smoking in the general population, the individual we selected to be a smoker may not have been one in real life. This will give us a false positive.

Thus, the question that this discussion raises is where, if ever, is this technique valid? The answer is twofold. First, we have actually identified value even where the results are in error. Huh? We have identified that there **could** be a relationship which includes smoking. In such a case, this would provide us with a very good rationale to see if we can obtain the missing data, or provide the model to a third party to run against the data. The second valid scenario is where we are investigating *aggregate* level results. That is, if we are making deductions about a subpopulation. In such cases, the issue is less pronounced – but not necessarily eliminated.

Many environments provide a separate and distinct encoding for missing data. For example, the R environment uses NA, and Oracle™ and many other relational database environments use NULL. However, the lack of standardization across environments causes an associated problem, that of *disguised missing data* (Pearson 2006 #83). With this problem, we can encounter situations where unknown data, inapplicable data, and even nonspecified responses are included as valid data.

This problem can be very serious. Pearson (2006 #83) used the FDA's Adverse Event Reporting System (AERS) as an example of this and cited that gender (7.2%), age (25.8%), and weight (42.0%) are each missing from the data reported from 2001 Q1 through 2003 Q4, according to the percentages in parentheses. Such examples identify a number of archetypes that we need to consider as missing data can occur for many different reasons:

- Poorly designed questionnaires
- Interviewer errors (e.g., omitted questions)
- Data entry errors
- Nonresponses
- Assemblage of datasets from multiple sources
- Blinding, or censoring of data (often unavoidable, especially with medical data)
- Cost/difficulty of obtaining certain data (e.g., nonroutine clinical results)
- Complementary attributes or features (i.e., attributes which correspond to measurements of the same or closely related quantities but which use different methods)[17]

In reality, the issues around missing data are very source-dependent. This, in turn, leads to "highly heterogeneous patterns of missing data" (Pearson 2006 #83). Horton and Lipsitz (2001 #84) highlighted three important issues relating to missing data:

1. Loss of efficiency
2. Complication in data handling and analysis
3. Bias due to differences between the observed and unobserved data

---

[17] From Pearson (2006 #83) once again, the National Institute of Diabetes and Digestive and Kidney Diseases (NIDDK) liver transplant database includes cyclosporine (CSA) levels and FK506 measurements but states that if one is recorded for a given patient at a given time, the other will be omitted.

For many techniques, the inclusion of explicitly encoded missing data can have unexpected consequences and force us to modify our analysis. Such modifications often result in one of the following generic approaches:

- Exclude incomplete instances
  The obvious issue with this approach is it immediately reduces the size of the dataset and can impact the effectiveness of our techniques as well as skewing the remaining dataset. For example, many of the univariate processes we use decay inversely with the sample size.
- Impute missing values
  This approach is very widely used, and we will include several approaches in this book which fall into this category. However, even this is fraught with challenges, as described elsewhere in this chapter. One example which characterizes this can be seen in a nonclinical setting: any capture of income information tends to fall off at the higher end of the scale; the average income is therefore underestimated. This is referred to as *nonignorable missing data*.
- Computational modification
  Here, we use methods such as the *Expectation-Maximization (EM) algorithm* with an iterative process that imputes missing values, estimates model parameters using these imputed values, then reestimate and loop until convergence occurs.

Thus, the key to addressing the problem of missing data is to first recognize that such data is, in fact, missing. While this sounds obvious, and is under many scenarios, missing data is sometimes not explicit: the data is coded with values which can be misinterpreted as valid data.

5.12.1   Other Issues with Missing Data

Data used for a data mining effort may come from more than one source. In such cases, as we've already seen, we need to integrate the data together. How we do this is dependent upon the data we receive. When integrating data from several sources, there is an increased likelihood of introducing missing data because of data existing in one source, but not in the other. As an example, consider data from two different studies being brought together into a single repository: if one study used drug A as a comparator and the second study didn't, we would have to deal with missing data in the integrated dataset. Since this issue is very source-dependent, we may end up having to spend a lot of time and effort on effectively integrating the data.

Developing a set of heterogeneous patterns – somewhat specific to individual sources of data – rather than a set of homogeneous patterns across the integrated dataset may be our recourse, but this can introduce its own challenges.

5.13   Data Reduction

We now turn our attention to the topic of reducing the dataset under study. At the very beginning of Chap. 1, we referenced some of the work of Lyman and Varian (2003 #70) that estimated that data being stored in some electronic fashion was of the order of 5 exabytes in 2002. It is definitely true that data is being generated and stored at ever-increasing rates for various business, legal, and strategic reasons. Nowhere is this truer than in the life sciences. Nowhere is this impact being seen more than in the data mining arena.

It is not unusual for the data to be captured for a single clinical trial to be in the hundreds of megabyte realm. For the complete pharmaceutical development process, hundreds of gigabytes or even a terabyte of data is not unusual. It would therefore be interesting to consider whether or not we can identify a subset of the data that could act as a surrogate for the whole but which allows us to obtain the same analytical results.[18]

There are many techniques we can use for the purpose of reducing the size of the dataset under study, and we consider several of them here, in no particular order. Some we leave for other chapters where they more rationally fit.

We offer up caution to anyone considering these techniques. Before applying them, think very carefully about how they might affect your model and results. For example, the very powerful technique of *principal component analysis* (PCA) is described later in the book and has a wide range of applicability. By its very nature, it aims to reduce a large number of dimensions (think of these as attributes in our dataset) to a smaller number – the principal components. The challenge with this is to ensure that the attributes which fall out of the model as being secondary really are secondary and that their effect is inconsequential *within our current area of consideration*. If they happen to have an important effect, eliminating them means that our results will not be the same (or very similar).

5.13.1   Attribute Subsets

As mentioned above for PCA, there are many occasions where we do not need all of the data in our dataset. Returning to our patient dataset example, we may not be interested in their intracountry geography and so may be able to eliminate the information about their specific address. This is a fairly banal example, however, since this type of elimination is intuitive. We can also exclude irrelevant attributes by performing a correlation analysis and determining whether any attributes act as surrogates for other attributes.

---

[18] We are being fast and loose with the use of the word "same." Here only, we use it to mean identical or similar to the point that any variances in the results are so small as to be inconsequential for our analysis.

5.13.2   Data Aggregation

As its name suggests, we reduce the amount of data we are considering by *aggregating* the data in some consistent manner. For example, if some of our data contains timestamp values,[19] we may be interesting in aggregating the data to some higher unit such as hour, day, week, month, or the like, or we might combine several locations (e.g., US states) into regions (e.g., the Mid-Atlantic region). When we group the data by an attribute, or subtotal the data, or use cross-tab functionality, we are aggregating the data.

A widely used technique in data mining is to create a *data cube*. A data cube can be thought of as a multidimensional hierarchy of aggregate values that allows us to look at an (somewhat) abstract level and as the entry point to drill down into increasing levels of detail until we can see the raw data underneath (Fig. 5.7).

In the simple cube example of Fig. 5.1 above, we have the ability to look at an aggregate level by gender, visit, or test result, and drill down by the pairs, such as the data for male patients across all visits or to the underlying raw data.

The above example is a very simple example of a cube and is used as an *aide-memoire* to the more detailed discussion of cubes from Chap. 3. We also remind the viewer that for any dataset with d dimensions (attributes), the d-dimensional base cube will have 2^d subcubes (cuboids) associated with it.

5.13.3   Dimensional Reduction

We've already briefly introduced the concept of PCA as a means of dimensional reduction, and this is a prime example of how we might go about reducing the number of attributes within our dataset. This is not, by any means, the only approach that can be used. Techniques such as minimum length encoding and wavelets are other methods we can use.

5.13.4   Alternate Representations

There will often be times when we can look at the data in our dataset and replace some subset of it by an alternate representation. Typically, clusters and parametric models provide us with the most useful representations. However, there are a myriad different encoding schemes and algorithms which might also provide value. For example, one algorithm – the Soundex algorithm – has been available

---

[19] A timestamp is a data value that includes both a date component and a time component (typically down to some subset of a second, such as millisecond).

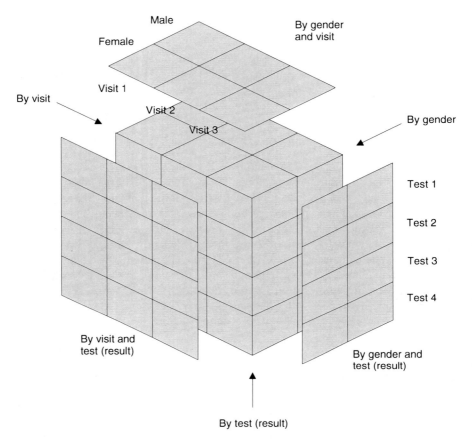

Fig. 5.7 Data cube

for almost one hundred years and is probably the most well-known phonetic algorithm. It has been widely used to encode a person's name based upon its phonetic structure. This can provide significant value when dealing with people's names as it allows us to encode their names – even where they may have been misspelled – and take some of the error out of the data capture. In analyzing the data, we may encode the name using this algorithm, for instance, and be a little more confident that we are dealing with a single patient rather than two.

5.13.5   *Generalization*

We have already introduced an example of generalization in our discussion of the data cube above; we took a smaller geographic region (in this case the US state)

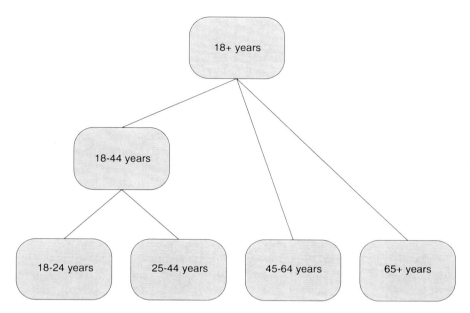

Fig. 5.8 Simple concept hierarchy

and generalized it to a region. This is an example of *concept hierarchies* where we organize an attribute or concept into a hierarchy with varying levels of abstraction.

Using the age information in Table 5.1, we can see a simple example of a concept hierarchy that is shown pictorially in Fig.5.8.

Note that in the above depiction, we have elected to show the leaf nodes at the same level.

5.13.6   Discretization

Discretization is a technique to reduce the number of values that a given attribute has into a set of intervals. We have already seen an example of discretization in Table 5.1 where the ages of individuals have been grouped into intervals. The interval labels can then be used instead of the actual ages. For example, we can use "18–24" as the value for anyone whose age falls into the sequence 18, 19, 20, 21, 22, 23, or 24. Thus, here we have reduced 7 values to 1.

From the above description, we can see there is a relationship with concept hierarchies in that these provide a natural and recursive mechanism for discretization.

5.14   Refreshing the Dataset

Data being mined rarely remains static. To put it another way, our underlying dataset and the data environment within which it resides constantly sees change – typically by the addition of more data, or by corrections being made to erroneous or missing data. How does this affect our models and the results obtained from those models? Do we even have to care?

We definitely have to be aware of how changes in data affect our results. In fact, we've already seen some examples of this in our discussions earlier in this chapter and in earlier chapters. Even simple measure such as the mean can be adversely affected by data being changed; even more concerning is if such changes did not materially change the model's results – we may not know until it is too late! If this occurs, however, should we even care since the changed dataset provides the same results: the data added (or changed) did not affect the results? We could assume that the changes had no impact on the model and move on to the next problem, could not we?

As with everything in life, the answer isn't cut and dried. It depends. Let's use our simple measure – the mean. The mean of the set 100, 300, 500, 700, and 900 is obviously 500, as is the mean of the set 498, 499, 500, 501, and 502. The difference, however, is in the size of the distribution. Typically, the underlying model is as important as the results themselves. Being able to identify that the distribution of data, in our example, is different does have bearing on the model. What if the set started off as 100, 300, 500, 700, and 900, but was extended to 100, 300, 498, 499, 500, 500, 501, 502, 700, and 900? Its mean is still 500.

Originally, we thought that we could separate highly volatile data from static data by placing the former into *transactional* databases and the latter into *data warehouse*.[20] In fact, one of the ways of describing what would be placed into a data warehouse was to describe it as any relevant data element that was static. We rapidly recognized that very little valuable data fell into the domain of being completely static, if only because of data errors. If we uncovered a data error, we certainly wanted to correct it. But how to do this in a "static" environment was the question. Without stepping through every step and nuance of the analytical infrastructure discussions, we now recognize that changes to data occur with almost any dataset of value.[21]

We can identify four major categories of change that we need to think about:

1. Addition of data to our underlying dataset
2. Removal of data from our underlying dataset
3. Correction of data in our underlying dataset
4. Changing the data in our dataset by significantly affecting its underlying distribution

---

[20] We are purposely using the term data warehouse as a generic label at this time.

[21] In the last several years, Bill Inmon, one of the leading figures in the data warehousing world, has defined *exploration warehouse* and *adaptive data mart* as parts of an infrastructure and model designed to support such change in a (somewhat) deterministic manner.

5.14.1   Adding Data to Our Dataset

Let's first consider the scenario that is most likely to occur. After all, in many projects, we will be building our model before all of the data has been captured and prepared; the opportunity to serialize the overall process has vanished as more and more organizations are expected to reach conclusions and decisions, and act upon those decisions in the most efficient manner possible.

Models built upon an initial influx of data will only be as accurate as that initial base of data is an accurate representation of the dataset once all data has been accumulated. If the original subset of data has a skewed distribution when compared to the larger dataset, our model will output different results. So one of the first tests we can make is to determine whether there is a significant change between the dataset as it was, which we'll call the *before* dataset, and the dataset as it is with the new data applied, which we'll call the *after* dataset. Ingenious, huh? If the underlying distributions of the before and after datasets are very similar, our model should be relevant. However, there are a couple of interesting questions that this paragraph brings to light: what does similar mean? How easy is it to compare the distributions of two datasets? Is comparing the distributions enough?

5.14.2   Removing Data from Our Dataset

In one sense, this is simply the converse of the addition case we discussed above: removing data that, for whatever reason, is no longer required or desired. However, beyond this simple statement are some complexities that need to be carefully considered.

First, we believe it is fair to say that very few data administrators will allow data to be physically deleted. Although we use this term liberally, we assume that any excluded data is *logically deleted* from the dataset. Perhaps *excluded* is the more accurate term.

Secondly, the underlying motive for excluding data from our dataset needs to be elucidated: are we introducing bias into our model by excluding this data? Is it being excluded because the data are not correlating to our hypothesis? Is our hypothesis incorrect? Were any of our baseline assumptions incorrect? These are all questions to carefully consider before excluding any data whatsoever. The authors recommend that an impartial reviewer be used to exercise these questions and offer an independent sign-off before the dataset is changed in this way.

If the above sounds ominous, it is because this is something that can fundamentally change the nature of the whole data mining effort. For example, excluding data for patients who did not have the expected results in the intent-to-cure group of a clinical trial may be the correct action to take; conversely, this could have the effect of making your overall results look much more positive than is really the case. Discovering this after person-months of effort, and, typically elapsed months of effort, does nothing for the psyche!

5.14.3 Correcting the Data in Our Dataset

The term "correcting the data" conjures up a gamut of scenarios as causes. We often do not have all of the data when we begin our analysis: much data may not be available until we receive the case report forms or patient diaries days, weeks, or even months after we begin our modeling efforts. Data may have been reported erroneously: two distinct patients may well turn out to be the same patient. However, the salient data used to identify them, such as patient initials, date of birth, and the like, may have been entered incorrectly, and we now have the correct data. In these and many other cases, we will want and require that the dataset be corrected.

The impact on such corrections may be minor, or they may be very significant. Further, what may have had a minor impact previously may turn out to be very significant this time around.

One of the advantages of today's data environments is the ubiquitous *temporal dimension*. Almost every data warehouse will be set up with a time dimension that can be used for many different purposes. One such use is to allow the data to be entered while retaining the previous version of the data. If this capability is available in your environment, leverage it to perform a *differential analysis* on how your model reacts to the corrected data.

A differential analysis is, as its name suggests, an analysis on what has changed between two states, and is a very powerful tool to use in many areas of data analysis. By focusing only on what has changed, we can more surgically examine how our model is holding up. The exact steps to perform a differential analysis will depend on how your data environment is set up and what tools are available to you. At a most basic level, extracting a copy of your dataset into, say, a text-based format such as coma-separated value (CSV) format and doing the same once the data has been changed will allow you to use even basic tools such as a simple file comparison tool. Obviously, this will not provide an understanding of how your model will react to the changed datasets, but it can provide a good starting point. In reality, however, this simple analysis will often be insufficient for our needs, and we return to this topic in the next section.

Whatever method we use, identifying what has changed is not an intractable problem – even our simple technique above will allow us to determine the extent of the change in the dataset. We now need to determine how the model changes in the face of such change. In order to do this, we do need to examine the changes we have identified in the context of the whole dataset so that we can understand the *nature* of the differences.

For example, if we identify that a significant amount of the change is restricted to one part of our dataset – say the data provided by a single investigator site that is part of a large phase III clinical trial – the impacts might be relatively minor if that site is representative of the whole population. However, if that site has a number of patients whose demographics cause them to be at (one of) the tails of the patient population distribution, the impact could be very significant.

Table 5.2 Risk factors for drug-induced liver injury

- Race: some drugs appear to have different toxicities based on race. For example, blacks and Hispanics may be more susceptible to isoniazid (INH) toxicity
- Age: elderly persons are at increased risk of hepatic injury because of decreased clearance, drug-to-drug interactions, reduced hepatic blood flow, variation in drug binding, and lower hepatic volume[a]
- Sex: for reasons unknown, hepatic drug reactions are more common in females
- Alcohol ingestion: alcoholic persons are susceptible to drug toxicity: alcohol induces liver injury and cirrhotic changes that alter drug metabolism and causes depletion of glutathione (hepatoprotective) stores
- Liver disease: patients with chronic liver disease are not uniformly at increased risk of hepatic injury. Patients with HIV infection who are coinfected with hepatitis B or C virus are at increased risk for hepatotoxic effects when treated with antiretroviral therapy. Patients with cirrhosis are at increased risk of decompensation by toxic drugs
- Genetic factors: a unique gene encodes each P450 protein, and genetic differences in the P450 enzymes can result in abnormal reactions to drugs, including idiosyncratic reactions[b]
- Other comorbidities: persons with AIDS, persons who are malnourished, and persons who are fasting may be susceptible to drug reactions because of low glutathione stores
- Drug formulation: long-acting drugs may cause more injury than shorter-acting drugs

From http://www.emedicine.com/med/topic3718.htm

[a]In addition, poor diet, infections, and multiple hospitalizations are important reasons for drug-induced hepatotoxicity

[b]Debrisoquine is an antiarrhythmic drug that undergoes poor metabolism because of abnormal expression of P450-II-D6. This can be identified by polymerase chain reaction amplification of mutant genes. This has led to the possibility of future detection of persons who can have abnormal reactions to a drug

The question of *significance* is interesting in its own right because this is significantly (sic) affected by the model, the underlying dataset semantics, and the overall objectives of the data mining effort, the purpose for capturing the data, and the general intent that will be pursued once conclusions have been drawn.

For example, we may be capturing data elements that measure hepatotoxicity levels in our patients. If patient evaluation includes a set of liver function tests, our data elements may include some or all of total protein (TP) [6.0–8.0 g/dL], albumin (Alb) [3.4–4.8 g/dL], alanine transaminase (ALT) [7–35 U/L (female); 10–40 U/L (male)], aspartate transaminase (AST) [10–20 U/L (female); 11–26 U/L (male)], alkaline phosphatase (ALP) [32–92 U/L], and total bilirubin (TBIL) [0.3–1.2 mg/dL], for example, where reference ranges are provided in the square brackets as per Tietz (1995) #80. If we do not have this subset of data for a set of patients under a single investigator, for whatever reason, we can still mine the data but consider this subset to be missing and leverage some of the missing data techniques described in this book. If the data arrives later, and is integrated in, we may see our results change. If all the patient results are within the normal ranges shown above, the likelihood is that our model and the results obtained will not be affected. However, if the patient subpopulation seen by this investigator were to have a significantly higher proportion of individuals with some of the factors related to drug-induced liver injury (see Tables 5.2 and 5.3), the test results may be at the distributions tails than in the median area and thus significantly skew our results once this data is included in the dataset.

Table 5.3 Host factors that may enhance susceptibility to drugs, possibly inducing liver disease

- Female – Halothane, nitrofurantoin, sulindac
- Male – amoxicillin-clavulanic acid (Augmentin)
- Old age – acetaminophen, halothane, INH, amoxicillin-clavulanic acid
- Young age – salicylates, valproic acid
- Fasting or malnutrition – acetaminophen
- Large body mass index/obesity – halothane
- Diabetes mellitus – methotrexate, niacin
- Renal failure – tetracycline, allopurinol
- AIDS – dapsone, trimethoprim-sulfamethoxazole
- Hepatitis C – ibuprofen, ritonavir, flutamide
- Preexisting liver disease – niacin, tetracycline, methotrexate

From http://www.emedicine.com/med/topic3718.htm

What to do in such instances will be dependent on decisions within the mining effort and without the mining effort. From our example above, if our model and results have been so significantly impacted due to the corrected data replacing missing data, we may go back and change the techniques we used to handle the missing data. If we used a simple Gaussian distribution to estimate what we thought the data would be, is this assumption still valid? Does the corrected data give us more insight into what the distribution *should* be? Alternatively, we may have to go back to square one and revisit our assumptions completely.

External to our model, we should ask ourselves how significantly the corrected data affects our overall goal. Typically, the answer will be that it does affect what we are trying to do. However, it may be that certain changes are actually ancillary and may be documented, but left as is. We have to state that while this is an alternative that should be considered – especially due to time and cost constraints – the underlying premise of data mining, being one of uncovering hidden patterns in the data, makes this last option a very dangerous one to pursue as we do not know how this might affect our model: it may cause some important patterns to be ignored, or it may promote insignificant patterns to significance.

5.14.4 Data Changes that Significantly Affect Our Dataset

In the above sections, we have discussed several of the more common ways in which our dataset can be significantly affected by data changes. Even in the most stable of environments, data change is inevitable and desirable. After all, if the data doesn't change in the face of new input, it won't be very valuable. In the face of changing data, we have two objectives: (a) to understand *what* has changed and (b) to determine *how* our model will react to such changes.

The first of these goals is relatively simple to execute, so long as we have some mechanism within the data environment that allows us to pinpoint all such changes.

We discussed this subject in more detail in Chap. 3; some of the more common ways to do this include some form of differential analysis function, and storage of *versions* of the data.

The second step is a much more intractable challenge. Knowing how our model will change in the face of this new data is almost, but not quite, the objective of the data mining effort itself. We can leverage a technique that we will discuss at various points later and run several iterations of the model and compare the "before" and "after" versions of the output. In this way, we can perform some level of backtracking to determine the impact that the changed data had on the model.

5.15 Conclusion

As noted by Refaat (2007 #135), preparing the data and assuring its quality can account for up to 80% of the overall data mining effort. The significance of this is not lost on anyone who has undertaken a data mining effort only to find themselves continually returning to the input data and iteratively cleaning it up, or enhancing it in some manner. It is very true to say that this is the foundation for the whole effort, and if we don't get this right, our modeling efforts and the conclusions we draw from our models are suspect.

Taking the time to understand your input, dealing with the issues that may lie within the data, and cleaning it to ensure its accuracy has the dual benefit of allowing us to better understand the data as well as to better understand the conclusions we draw from our models.

One project that the authors worked on involved a large amount of clinical data from several studies. Each of the studies seemed to have had enough differences in the data management strategy to require a significant amount of integration effort. The personnel who had originally worked on the studies were no longer available for consultation. However, at the end of the effort, we were able to not only integrate the data effectively to allow program-wide analysis but also understand the data to be able to track back the conclusions drawn from the models to the underlying data.

What can often happen is that we get partway, or all the way, through our analysis only to find that we've missed some crucial data elements that would have allowed us to extend our model, conclusions, or recommendations further, or, at the other extreme, tells us that our model or results may not be valuable without that data. This issue of effectively scoping the project, ensuring we have the correct data elements, is an important activity to exercise up-front.

References

Chen LYY et al (2002) Single nucleotide polymorphism mapping using genome wide unique sequences. J Genome Res

DuBois D, DuBois E (1916) A formula to estimate the approximate surface area if height and weight be known. Arch Intern Med 17:863–871

Horton NJ, Lipsitz SR (2001) Multiple imputation in practice: comparison of software packages for regression models with missing variables. Am Stat 55:244–254

Lippert R, Mobarry C, Walenz B (2005) A space-efficient construction of the Burrows-Wheeler transform for genomic data. J Comput Biol 12:943–951

Lyman P, Varian HR (2003) How much information. University of California, Berkeley, pp. 100

Pearson RK (2006) The problem of disguised missing data. SIGKDD Explorations Newsl 8:83–92

Refaat M (2007) Data preparation for data mining using SAS. Morgan Kaufmann Publishers, San Francisco

Tietz NW (1995) Clinical guide to laboratory tests. W.B. Saunders Co, Philadelphia, pp. xxxix, 1096

Witten I, Frank E (2005) Emboss European Molecular Biology Open Software Suite. In: Data mining: practical machine learning tools and techniques with Java implementations. Morgan Kaufman, Amsterdam/Boston

Chapter 6
Statistical Methods

Abstract Virtually all analytical methods involving data incorporate some form of statistical analysis, and well it should. Statistical methods offer a complete and robust infrastructure for quickly understanding our dataset, giving us insight into the data itself. Statistical analysis methods are very important in data mining applications in the life sciences and are used in many areas as the primary mechanism for analytical work, such as when analyzing differentially expressed gene selection in control and disease groups; and significance analysis is widely used in biological studies. Our objective for this chapter is to provide an overview of many of the concepts and techniques that are used in analytical initiatives. The basic inferential methodology and hypothesis testing are described, along with the ubiquitous p value, as well as a discussion on type I and type II errors and how we identify and handle those circumstances. Test statistics are discussed using the t test as an example. How we can use confidence intervals to provide an interval estimator for a population parameter and how it can be used as an indicator for the reliability of our estimate are then described. We then describe regression analysis, an invaluable tool in analysis, along with two widely used estimation methods: maximum likelihood estimation (MLE) and maximum a posteriori (MAP) estimation. Finally, we discuss statistical significance and its relevance in the clinical setting as an application context for some of the challenges we encounter.

6.1 Introduction

We now introduce some of the basic statistical methods used to mine and analyze data in real-world situations. Statistical methods range from the very simple, to the very complex, and constitute the most common techniques used when mining data. After all, even a very simple statistical analysis – to determine the mean, variance, and quartile values – can provide insight.

There are, however, a vast number of approaches which can be used on any given dataset, and it is very easy to become overwhelmed. A very common problem

R. Sullivan, *Introduction to Data Mining for the Life Sciences*,   235
DOI 10.1007/978-1-59745-290-8_6, © Springer Science+Business Media, LLC 2012

is, in fact, to know where to begin. We typically, however, also have the problem: where do we stop? This might well be the more common problem for many of us.

We will often use a number of different methods in concert to fully explore the dataset. These may be different statistical methods, or statistical methods along with other techniques, which allow us the opportunity of gaining insight through applying a broad range of tools, techniques, and concepts.

Statistics has a long history of creating methods to effectively analyze data and remains an important set of tools for data mining. If we compare statistical methods with machine-learning methods, we can see that methods in either category are developed with reference to the data being analyzed, but where they differ is in their underlying reference paradigms. The paradigm underlying statistical methods has made them exceedingly rigorous and coherent but has also slowed adaptation in the face of new machine-learning applications, for example.

We believe it is safe to say that statistical analysis is what many think of as being synonymous with data mining and constitutes the first set of activities that people tend to perform. In many ways, this is a reasonable starting point. Basic statistical measures such as the mean and variance provide us with simple indications of how the data we are studying vary from a central point, how it is distributed, and whether it fits into any standard models that are widely used. Thus, statistical analysis forms an important set of tools in our arsenal, but as we show elsewhere, many nonstatistical approaches are also valuable tools.

As we relate statistics to data mining, we need to address two issues that arise out of the rigorous science of statistics. The first relates to the underlying reference model, or models: there is not one model to which everyone can ascribe, but instead there are several competing models. The "appropriate" model is chosen in reference to the data being modeled. Thus, it is always possible to find an "appropriate" model which will adapt itself to the data. However, this model may be irresponsibly complex. The second issue, which we have already discussed, relates to the fact that with such large amounts of data, nonexistent relations between data attributes may be found.

Since, however, much focus is placed on the ability to *generalize* the models and results, complex models quickly become unattractive and thus tend to exorcise themselves during the process. We have to recognize, however, that many of the findings which data mining can elucidate are not known ahead of time. In fact, a primary intent of data mining – to uncover hidden patterns – would preclude this from being a tautology and prevent such findings from being used to develop a research hypothesis.

Statistical analysis has traditionally been used to analyze the primary data collected to check a specific research hypothesis; data mining can also be used to analyze secondary data – data collected for other reasons and purposes. Statistical data is also typically experimental data whereas data used in data mining is typically observational.

In this chapter, we focus on those methods of the classical, or *frequentist* school of statistics. Bayesian statistics is important enough that we devote the next chapter to this subject.

We do not provide a complete treatise on probability, distribution theory, or statistical inference. The interested reader is referred to any good statistical reference book.[1] However, Appendix A includes a summary of the basic theory of probability. This being said, we describe many basic statistical techniques as they often provide valuable insight into the data and can be used for exploratory data mining activities if not used on their own.

In Chap. 2, we considered a simple method, the 1R method, which uses a single attribute as the basis for the method. Although this often provides surprisingly good results, there are many cases where it is too simplistic. Instead, we could use all of the attributes in our dataset and allow each attribute to make a contribution to our analysis and, thus, our decisions.

We have to recognize that different attributes have different levels of *importance* in our model and that some of the attributes may be *dependent* on other attributes in our dataset. These facts make the datasets we process interesting. However, it does not necessarily mean we need to introduce significant complexity into our model; as we shall see, there are simple methods which allow us to analyze the data and get remarkably useful and accurate results.

We begin, however, by looking at some of the theoretical underpinnings of statistical modeling and analysis. However, we assume that the reader is familiar with descriptive statistics, probability theory, and distribution theory. For a primer, the reader is referred to Appendix A or to Bolstad (2004 #18) and Gelman (1995 #24), or a standard statistics reference for more details.

6.1.1   Basic Statistical Methods

Table 6.1 provides a quick reference for the most commonly used measures we encounter in statistics.

As anyone with a little statistical knowledge will attest, Table 6.1 doesn't even come close to providing a quick reference. For example, we often use particular methods of analysis based on the type of response and explanatory variables we are dealing with, as shown in Tables 6.2 and 6.3.

We're going to assume readers have had some exposure to statistics prior to reaching this point. If not, we highly recommend a text such as Glantz (2005 #140) to fill in the blanks.

---

[1] A particular favorite of the authors is *Statistics: An Introduction Using R* by Michael Crawley.

Table 6.1 Basic statistical measures and methods

Location (Central tendency)	Mode: most common value
	Median: middle value
	Mean: $\bar{x} = \dfrac{\sum\limits_{i=1}^{n} x_i}{n}$
Variation	Range: high-low
	Quartiles: Q1 (25%), Q2 (50%), Q3 (75%)
	Variance: $s^2 = \dfrac{\sum\limits_{i=1}^{n}(x_i-\bar{x})^2}{n-1}$
	Standard deviation: $s = \sqrt{\dfrac{\sum\limits_{i=1}^{n}(x_i-\bar{x})^2}{n-1}}$
	z-score: $z = \frac{x_i-\bar{x}}{s}$
Confidence levels	Mean (>30 observations): $\bar{x} \pm z_C \frac{s}{\sqrt{n}}$
	Mean (<30 observations): $\bar{x} \pm t_C \frac{s}{\sqrt{n}}$
	Proportion: $p \pm z_C \sqrt{\frac{p(1-p)}{n^n}}$
Heterogeneity	Gini index: $G = 1 - \sum\limits_{i=1}^{n} p_i^2$; normalized: $G' = \frac{G}{(k-1)/k}$
	Entropy: $E = -\sum\limits_{i=1}^{n} p_i \log p_i$; normalized: $E' = \frac{E}{\log k}$
Asymmetry or skewness	Skew: $\gamma_1 = \frac{m_3}{\sigma^3} = \dfrac{\frac{\sum (y-\bar{y})^3}{n}}{\sigma^3} = \frac{1}{n}\sum \frac{(y-\bar{y})^3}{\sigma^3}$
	Measure of how long the tail of the distribution on one side or the other. $\gamma_1 < 0$ means the distribution skews to the left; $\gamma_1 > 0$ means a skew to the right
Kurtosis	Kurtosis: $\gamma_2 = \frac{m_4}{\sigma^4} - 3 = \dfrac{\frac{\sum (y-\bar{y})^4}{n}}{\sigma^4} = \frac{1}{n}\sum \frac{(y-\bar{y})^4}{\sigma^4} - 3$
	Measure of "peakyness" (leptokurtic) or "flat-toppedness" (platykurtic) of the distribution. Normal distribution has $\gamma_2 = \frac{m_4}{\sigma^4} = 3$, hence the "$-3$" value
Hypothesis test	1. Specify the null hypothesis (e.g., $H_0 : \mu = \mu_0$) and the alternate hypothesis (e.g., $H_a : \mu > \mu_0$)
	2. Select significance level (e.g., $\alpha = 0.05$)
	3. Compute the test statistic (t or z)
	4. Determine the critical value for t or z using $\frac{\alpha}{2}$ for two-sided tests
	5. Reject the null hypothesis if the test statistic falls into the "reject H_0" region
Comparing (more than 2) groups	Categorical data: chi-square test
	Continuous data: one-way ANOVA
Comparing variables	Correlation coefficient (r): $r = \dfrac{\sum_{i=1}^{n}(x_i-\bar{x})(y_i-\bar{y})}{(n-1)s_x s_y}$

Table 6.2 Standard methods based on the explanatory variable

Explanatory variable	Method
Continuous	Regression
Categorical	Analysis of variance (ANOVA)
Both	Analysis of covariance (ANCOVA)

Table 6.3 Standard methods based on the response variable

Response variable	Method
Continuous	Regression, ANOVA, or ANCOVA
Proportion	Logistic regression
Count	Log linear methods
Binary	Binary logistic
Time-at-death	Survival analysis

6.2 Statistical Inference and Hypothesis Testing

Statistical inference is a problem in which data have been generated in accordance with some unknown probability distribution which must be analyzed and some inferences about the unknown distributions have to be made. There may, therefore, be more than one probability distribution that could have generated the data. By analyzing the data, we attempt to learn about the unknown distribution, make some inferences about certain properties of the distribution, and to determine the relative likelihood that each possible distribution is actually the correct one.

Note that this situation, of making statements about some population based on data collected from samples, is almost always the situation in which we find ourselves. Not only is it typically too costly to collect data for the whole population, it is normally impossible to do. But putting these aside, it is simply not necessary since our objective is to get a reasonably accurate estimate of the population: if we take an *unbiased* random sample of the population, we can usually do pretty well.

We can take this concept one step further. Let's consider the above process of taking an unbiased random sample and calculate its mean. Now let's repeat the random sampling a second time, and calculate its mean. What is the likelihood of these two means being the same? Let's repeat this process several more times. Each sample will result in a different mean because the random sample is different each time. This is the *sampling error*. We could expect to see the mean for most of the samples to be close to the mean of the population if we generate many samples. There would still be a few aberrant values since our random sampling could include any outliers, but these would constitute a smaller percentage of our samples as the number of samples increases. In fact, where the sample size is larger than 30, the distribution of the *mean values* follows a normal distribution and is referred to as the *sampling distribution*.[2]

The traditional approach taken is that of *hypothesis testing*, a form of proof by contradiction. We develop evidence to support our theory by demonstrating that the data is unlikely to be observed if the postulated theoretical model were false.

---

[2] In fact, the reason why this is the case is due to the *central limit theorem*, which is not discussed here. Interested readers are recommended to any statistics or biostatistics reference such as Glantz (2005 #140).

Epistemologically, hypothesis testing rests on the following foundations:

- There exists one and only one process that generates the actions of a population with respect to some variable.
- There are many examples of long accepted scientific theories losing credibility. Once objective "truths" are rejected.
- If we cannot be sure that a theory is "true," then the next best thing is to judge the probability that a theory is true.

The first bullet point above raises the question of accuracy: is it *really* the case that one and only one process is responsible? In Bayesian statistics, the answer to this question is an emphatic **no**! For it to be the case, the knowledge involved would have to be purely objective; Bayesian approaches, as we shall see, consider all knowledge to be subjective. In fact, this is the key difference between frequentist and Bayesian approaches. This being the case, there cannot be one and *only* one process in general.

The third bullet point above raises a different question: how do we express the probability that a theory is true? Using standard conditional probability, we would like to express this as

$$P(\text{Model is true} \mid \text{Observed Data})$$

However, based upon the epistemological foundations identified above, we cannot state that a model is true *with a probability P*; our foundations say that a model is either true or not true. Instead, we are limited to expressing our conditional probability as

$$P(\text{Observed Data} \mid \text{Model is true})$$

So now the question becomes one of how do we interpret $P(\text{Observed Data} \mid \text{Model is true})$? If $P(\text{Observed Data} \mid \text{Model is true})$ is close to one, then the data is consistent with the model. We can comfortably consider it to be an objective interpretation of reality. For example, given the hypothesis

Men have higher wages than women

and given the data

Median wages for men:	$38,000
Median wages for women:	$29,000

we can say that the data is consistent with the model $P(\text{Observed Data} \mid \text{Model is true})$ is close to one.

Conversely, if $P(\text{Observed Data} \mid \text{Model is true})$ is not close to one, we say that the data is inconsistent with the model's predictions, and we reject the model; that the model is not a useful representation of reality.

The classical hypothesis testing process is

1. Define the research hypothesis.
   A *research* or *alternate hypothesis* is a statement derived from theory about what the researcher expects to find in the data.
2. Define the null hypothesis.
   A *null hypothesis* is a statement of what you would not expect to find if your research or alternative hypothesis was consistent with reality.
3. Perform an analysis of the data to determine whether or not you can reject the null hypothesis with some predetermined probability.

   a. If we can reject the null hypothesis with some probability, then the data is consistent with the model.
   b. If we cannot reject the null hypothesis with some probability, then the data is not consistent with the model.

Although we will study Bayesian statistics later, it is useful to digress and identify where the Bayesian and frequentist, or classical, approaches differ. Bayesian approaches try to make inferences based on all the information we have at our disposal. As new data becomes available, we incorporate this into our inferences to see how this new data affects current inferences. Importantly, we try and identify all the hypotheses (states) that may be true. This allows us to know what each hypothesis predicts what we will observe. Using all of this information, we now look to update our inferences in light of our observations, a subject which will be explored later. This approach provides a close correlation with the way in which scientists think.

We return to our concept of the *model*, discussed in Chap. 2 within the context of statistical analysis. In particular, we consider the Bayesian approach which provides significant value within the data-mining arena.

Hypothesis testing can also be used to compare different statistical models to give us a measure of "bestness" for our problem at hand. When looking at any problem, we will discover that solutions can be developed using any number of different approaches. We can, in one sense, consider using regression models or neural network models as being *equivalent* modeling approaches to tackle the problem of predictive classification. But determining the "best" in any specific context requires us to undertake some level of comparative analysis. We shall return to this important subject in more detail later.

6.2.1   What Constitutes a "Good" Hypothesis?

This question and its corollary – what constitutes a bad hypothesis? – is actually both a simple and complicated issue. Intuitively, we can consider a hypothesis as something that can be *falsified* or rejected. Karl Popper, a leading philosopher of the twentieth century emphasized falsifiability as a criterion of empirical statements in science. We can leverage this by saying that any "good hypothesis is a falsifiable hypothesis" (Crawley 2005 #98).

Consider these examples:

(a) *There is a direct correlation between smoking and lung cancer.*
(b) *There is no direct correlation between smoking and lung cancer.*

We can see that both of these statements are related to the linkage between lung cancer and smoking. However, the important difference between them involves their value to us as hypotheses. In the first case, we may undertake a series of trials, scouring of publications, and a significant data-mining effort, at the end of which we determine that there is no direct link between the two. The problem with this is that, as Carl Sagan said *"absence of evidence is not evidence of absence."* That is, we may simply not have the data that allows us to link the two, or our study may have included some flaw, or any other host of reasons. Thus, we cannot definitively reject the hypothesis based on our first version even if we find no evidence – it may still be out there, somewhere.

In the second case, however, we can easily see that finding just one item of correlation will allow us to reject the hypothesis. Until that time, we assume our hypothesis is true – that there is no correlation between lung cancer and smoking – but reject it as soon as we see a correlation.

When defining a hypothesis, the key, therefore, is to define a hypothesis for which we can clearly see a falsifiable condition.

6.2.2   The Null Hypothesis

We introduced the null hypothesis above with the statement:

> A *null hypothesis* is a statement of what you would not expect to find if your research or alternative hypothesis was consistent with reality.

Another, clearer way of stating this is that "nothing is happening."

Ok, if your head isn't spinning, it's because you are not trying hard enough! Consider this example: we have two sets of data and we compare their means. The null hypothesis may be stated as "the means are the same." Our alternate hypothesis may be "the means are different." If the reality is that the means are different, then we would not expect the means to be the same. Clear, huh? The core fact to bear in mind is that the null hypothesis is *falsifiable* and we reject it when our data shows that the null hypothesis is unlikely.[3]

---

[3] We return to the concept of "unlikely" later when we discuss statistical significance and clinical relevance. For the moment, consider "unlikely" as meaning that the event happens less than 5% of the time.

6.2.3   *p Value*

We can never discount the possibility that the results we obtain may have occurred simply by chance. More specifically, we can never discount the possibility that the results we obtain, or results *more extreme* than the results we obtain could have occurred by chance *if the null hypothesis were true*. Remember that the alternate hypothesis is the one of real interest to us; the one we have crafted based upon our beliefs.

We would therefore like to be able to measure how plausible the null hypothesis is; the *p* value gives us this measure. The *p* value measures how much evidence we have against the null hypotheses: the smaller the *p* value, the more evidence we have against H_0. It also measures how likely we are to get a certain result or a result that is "more extreme," assuming that H_0 is true. The type of hypothesis we are making – right tailed, left tailed or two tailed – will determine what the term "more extreme" means.

As we shall see later, if an event is very unlikely to have occurred by chance, we will refer to it as statistically significant and assign it a *p* value, say $p < 0.002$. In general, therefore, a low *p* value means that the null hypothesis is unlikely to be true and that any difference will be statistically significant. Conversely, a large *p* value means that there is no compelling evidence that will allow us to reject the null hypothesis.

Consider an example of where an investigator is interested in whether an investigational drug alters a person's blood pressure. An experiment may be designed where two groups of people, as similar as possible, are administered either a placebo or the investigational drug, and various vital statistics, including blood pressure measurements, are taken. If these sets of data are available to us, we may then compute the means and standard deviation of the two groups. As we shall see below, the mean of the two groups will very likely be different irrespective of whether the drug had any effect for the same reason that any two random samples from a single population will compute different estimates for the mean. Given this inevitability, the question now becomes one of whether the observed difference in the mean blood pressure value is likely to be because of random factors (or chance) or because of the effect of the drug.

To answer this question, we first quantify the difference between the values using a *test statistic* such as *t* (or *F*, or *q*, or ...). Since test statistics have the characteristic that the larger the difference between the samples, the greater their value, if the drug had no effect, then the test statistic will be small. Recall that we have our null hypothesis concept; we can use this to say that the drug has *no* effect on blood pressure. If this is the case, then the two groups are essentially random samples from a single population: since the drug has no effect on blood pressure, for our purposes, and *in this context*, the drug acts as a placebo, therefore we can consider the two groups to be from a single population.

Theoretically, we could repeat our experiment for all possible samples of people and compute the test statistic for each experiment. Because of our discussion above, each experiment would likely produce a different value of the test statistic; most will be similar in value, but there will likely be a few values which are not representative of the population as a whole.[4] Our repeating the experiment will produce only a few of the values of the test statistic – say 5% – that are above some cutoff point. That is, 5% of our test statistic values will be larger than a value that we designate as the cutoff point.

We could now perform an experiment on a (different) drug that has unknown properties and similarly compute the test statistic. Let us assume that the results are "large." We can say that there is a less than 5% chance of our observing data that would lead to the computed value of the test statistic *assuming that the drug having no effect is true.*

The 5% heuristic is typically used in reality. If the chances of observing the test statistic are below this threshold, we will reject the (null) hypothesis and assert the alternate hypothesis – in our example, we reject the hypothesis that the drug has no effect and assert that it *does* have an effect. We should, however, recognize that this approach and its concomitant assertion may be wrong – 5% of the time. Theoretically, our 5% p value (also known as *significance level*) could be any value; traditionally we use 5%.

The p value is the probability of obtaining a test statistic value that is as large, or larger than one computed from the data when the null hypothesis is correct (i.e., no difference between the two populations). Or stating it another way, the p value is the probability of obtaining a result at least as extreme as a data point, assuming that the data point was the result of chance alone.

The significance level is often represented as α, and one rejects the null hypothesis if the p value is smaller than α. If $\alpha = 0.05$, as in our above example, we know that we can expect to get a more extreme result 5% of the time, given the null hypothesis is true. If the p value exceeds α, the null hypothesis is not rejected and is often noted in publications as being "*not statistically significant at the 5% level.*" If the value is less than α then we would say that our findings are "*statistically significant at the 5% level.*"

We need to make several statements about the p value since these are often points of confusion in use:

- The p value is not the probability of the null hypothesis being true: we cannot attach probabilities to hypotheses in frequentist statistics.[5]
- The p value is not the probability that the result is a random result or a fluke – recall that our definition of the p value is that the result itself is due to random chance so it cannot simultaneously be used to measure the probability of the assumption being true.

---

[4] Remember that we are taking random samples from a population. In any population there will be individuals on either end of the distribution; if our random sample contained, say, everyone who naturally had high blood pressure, the resulting sample would not be representative. Such samples would produce large values of the test statistic irrespective of whether the drug had an effect.

[5] The Jeffreys-Lindley paradox shows that even when a p value is close to zero, the posterior probability (see the next chapter) can be close to 1.

- The p value is not the probability of falsely rejecting the null hypothesis.
- The p value is not the probability that upon our replicating the experiment again we would get a different result.
- One p value is not the probability of the alternate hypothesis being true.
- The significance level of a test is not determined by the p value. The significance level should be determined *before* analyzing the data; we compare it against the p value *after* the data has been analyzed and the p *value* computed.

We take a moment to ask the question what's so special about $p = 0.05$? This traces its history and genesis back to the work of R.A. Fisher. He suggested this value in the 13th edition of his *Statistical Methods for Research Workers*. If we look at his tables, we see that the value for which $p = 0.05$ is 1.96 – close to 2 – and it is convenient to take this point as the limit in determining whether a deviation is significant or not. Thus, any value which deviates by more than 2 standard deviations is considered to be significant.

Some readers may consider the 1:20 ratio to be artificially low. There is nothing to stop you using $p = 0.01$ (1%), or even lower values. However, recognize that this may be much more accurate than is either warranted or realistically achievable. In fact, the 5% level is a feasible level for research: we can usually, but maybe with some difficulty, set up an experiment which will show effects large enough to be of interest to us. A level such as 1% (or more extremely 0.1%, or ...) may not be attainable and thus we would have very little to report as our experiments would not identify anything of value. In fact, we typically use $p = 0.01$ as a strong indication that the hypothesis fails to account for the facts.

So, as we can see, p value is based upon a somewhat arbitrary level, typically 5%, and looks at the probability in terms of chance alone. Killeen (2005 #99) proposed a slightly different measure, p-rep, or p_{rep} that looks at the probability to replicate the effect rather than just its relationship to chance. Some disciplines, such as in psychology, are beginning to use this measure instead of the p value.

6.2.4 Type I and Type II Errors

As we interpret our models, we can obviously make errors in interpretation. If we consider the null hypothesis (H_0) and alternate hypothesis (H_1) form our standard hypothesis testing methodology described above, we can see the following error conditions may occur:

1. We can reject the null hypothesis when it is true (type I error)
2. We can accept the null hypothesis when it is false (type II error)

Null Hypothesis	Reality True	False
Accept	✔	Type II
Reject	Type I	✔

Later in this text, we will consider some examples in more detail, but for the moment, let's consider how this might manifest itself in a study:

Conclusion from observations	Actual situation Treatment has an effect	Treatment has no effect
Treatment has an effect	✔	False positive (α)
Treatment has no effect	False negative (β)	✔

We have used the same labels that we might use with a diagnostic test – false positive and false negative[6] – to highlight the analogy. Obviously, we want to minimize instances in both shaded cells, if possible.

In statistical terms, α is used to denote a false positive error and a good starting rule of thumb is to try and keep the chances of making such an error below 5%.

Relating the false negative value, β, to the statistical test, we ask ourselves what is the probability of this occurring? We can use the concept of the *power* of the test, which quantifies the probability of detecting a real difference of a given size.

6.2.5   An Example: Comparing Two Groups, the t Test

We are going to briefly jump ahead in our discussion and introduce a specific statistical test.

By far and away the most common analysis that we perform is in comparing two groups. Within this context, we are most interested in determining what the differences are between those two groups, if there are any. The *t* test, also known as *student's t test*, is the most common test to use. In fact, this test has been shown to appear in more than 50% of papers in the medical literature (Glantz 2005 #140). As also mentioned in this same source, in addition to being used to compare two groups, it is often incorrectly applied to compare multiple groups by pairwise comparison. Once again Glantz (2005 #140) provided a good example from the clinical journal *Circulation*, in which a review of 142 articles identified that 27% of articles used the *t* test correctly, whereas 34% used the test incorrectly.

Let's define our example scenario.

Consider a new drug that may be effective at reducing blood pressure in patients. We identify 20 patients and randomly place them into one of two groups: a control group and a treatment group. The control group will receive a placebo, whereas the treatment group will receive the new drug. We measure their cholesterol levels, specifically for our purposes, the LDL cholesterol levels, for the next 8 weeks.

Table 6.4 shows the raw test result data for both groups.

[6] False positive: concluding that a treatment has an effect when it really does not. False negative: concluding that a treatment does not have an effect when it really does.

Table 6.4 LDL cholesterol data (shaded group is control group)

Patient	Group	Week1	Week2	Week3	Week4	Week5	Week6	Week7	Week8
1	A	182	180	183	179	181	183	181	181
2	A	165	169	167	180	165	164	164	163
3	A	97	97	95	99	100	96	95	96
4	A	91	93	91	91	92	91	93	91
5	A	105	109	110	111	109	115	115	115
6	A	133	133	134	134	133	132	132	132
7	A	127	127	121	126	127	129	131	129
8	A	145	144	145	147	147	151	153	153
9	A	111	115	114	115	115	116	115	115
10	A	175	177	176	177	179	179	176	181
11	B	166	158	151	143	141	140	137	135
12	B	121	119	120	118	121	117	117	118
13	B	171	173	171	169	170	168	170	170
14	B	157	149	143	138	133	131	128	126
15	B	96	96	94	95	94	95	94	93
16	B	142	138	133	131	127	126	124	123
17	B	135	131	127	124	123	121	119	118
18	B	98	96	95	93	92	91	89	89
19	B	181	180	182	179	179	178	177	177
20	B	183	181	175	171	169	167	166	166

Let's begin by taking a look at the data. We'll use the following R code fragment to produce Fig. 6.1.

```
# get data
workingData <- read.csv("chapter 6 - t Test Example Data.csv",
header=TRUE, sep=",", quote="\"", dec=".", fill=FALSE)
# setup plot area
plot(c(0,9),c(80,190),type="n",xlab="Week",ylab="LDL Cholesterol
Reading")
# process data set
for(i in 1:20) {
    for(j in 1:length(workingData)) {
        points(i,workingData[i,j])
    }
}
```

In Fig. 6.1, we make no separation between the two groups. By simply separating out the two groups, as shown for group A in the box below, we can plot the data for each group separately, as shown in Fig. 6.2.

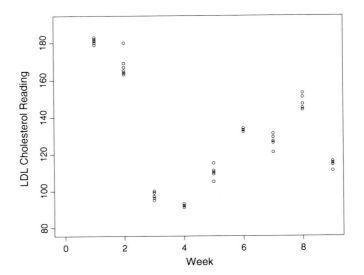

Fig. 6.1 LDL cholesterol dataset

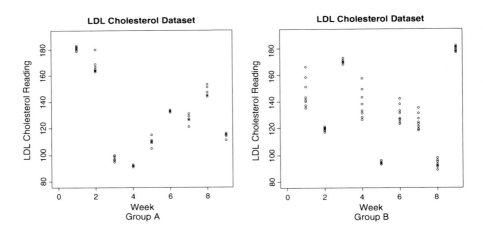

Fig. 6.2 LDL cholesterol dataset – separation by group

```
# plot the two groups separately

groupAWorkingData <- workingData[workingData$Group=='A',]

plot(c(0,9),c(80,190),type="n",main="LDL Cholesterol Dataset",

sub="Group A",xlab="Week",ylab="LDL Cholesterol Reading")

for(i in 1:10) {

      for(j in 1:length(groupAWorkingData)) {

            points(i,groupAWorkingData[i,j])

      }

}
```

```
> summary(groupAWorkingData)
   Patient        Group         Week1             Week2              Week3             Week4
 Min.   : 1.00   A:10    Min.    : 91.0    Min.    : 93.0    Min.    : 91.0    Min.    : 91.0
 1st Qu.: 3.25   B: 0    1st Qu.:106.5     1st Qu.:110.5     1st Qu.:111.0     1st Qu.:112.0
 Median : 5.50           Median :130.0     Median :130.0     Median :127.5     Median :130.0
 Mean   : 5.50           Mean    :133.1    Mean    :134.4    Mean    :133.6    Mean    :135.9
 3rd Qu.: 7.75           3rd Qu.:160.0     3rd Qu.:162.8     3rd Qu.:161.5     3rd Qu.:169.5
 Max.   :10.00           Max.    :182.0    Max.    :180.0    Max.    :183.0    Max.    :180.0
      Week5               Week6             Week7             Week8
 Min.   : 92.0   Min.    : 91.0    Min.    : 93.0    Min.    : 91.0
 1st Qu.:110.5   1st Qu.:115.2     1st Qu.:115.0     1st Qu.:115.0
 Median :130.0   Median :130.5     Median :131.5     Median :130.5
 Mean    :134.8  Mean    :135.6    Mean    :135.5    Mean    :135.6
 3rd Qu.:160.5   3rd Qu.:160.8     3rd Qu.:161.2     3rd Qu.:160.5
 Max.    :181.0  Max.    :183.0    Max.    :181.0    Max.    :181.0
> summary(groupBWorkingData)
   Patient        Group         Week1             Week2              Week3             Week4
 Min.   :11.00   A: 0    Min.    : 96.0    Min.    : 96.0    Min.    : 94.0    Min.    : 93.0
 1st Qu.:13.25   B:10    1st Qu.:124.5     1st Qu.:122.0     1st Qu.:121.8     1st Qu.:119.5
 Median :15.50           Median :149.5     Median :143.5     Median :138.0     Median :134.5
 Mean   :15.50           Mean    :145.0    Mean    :142.1    Mean    :139.1    Mean    :136.1
 3rd Qu.:17.75           3rd Qu.:169.8     3rd Qu.:169.2     3rd Qu.:166.0     3rd Qu.:162.5
 Max.   :20.00           Max.    :183.0    Max.    :181.0    Max.    :182.0    Max.    :179.0
      Week5               Week6             Week7             Week8
 Min.   : 92.0   Min.    : 91.0    Min.    : 89.0    Min.    : 89.0
 1st Qu.:121.5   1st Qu.:118.0     1st Qu.:117.5     1st Qu.:118.0
 Median :130.0   Median :128.5     Median :126.0     Median :124.5
 Mean    :134.9  Mean    :133.4    Mean    :132.1    Mean    :131.5
 3rd Qu.:162.0   3rd Qu.:160.2     3rd Qu.:158.8     3rd Qu.:158.2
 Max.    :179.0  Max.    :178.0    Max.    :177.0    Max.    :177.0
> |
```

Fig. 6.3 Summary information for LDL cholesterol subsets

We can immediately see differences between the two groups of data using a quick visual inspection. But let us look a little further. We will next use the sum-mary function to look at summary (sic) information about each subset of data, as shown in Fig. 6.3.

We can see that the mean values for our cholesterol measure start off with some difference (133.1, 145.0) for group A versus group B, but end up being much closer to each other (135.6, 131.5). Is this a real difference, or simply due to random sampling?

Let's now suppose that we try this again with another set of patients – say 50 patients in each group – and we see mean responses that are in line with our smaller samples. Most of us would feel more comfortable basing our conclusions on the larger set of patients, the total set of 100 with 50 in each group, than the smaller set of 20, with 10 in each group. However, both appear to reasonably represent the underlying population. One of the reasons is that as sample sizes increase, our ability to estimate population means improves, with lowered error, and so we can begin to better discern differences between our two groups.[7] The obvious outcome

---

[7] As we mentioned earlier, this is due to the *standard error of the mean*. This decreases according to the relationship $\sigma_{\bar{X}} = \frac{\sigma}{\sqrt{n}}$, where n is the sample size and σ is the standard deviation of the population from which the sample was drawn.

of this is more confidence in the drug actually having an effect, or less confidence in the null hypothesis of the drug having no effect. In this latter case, the corollary is that the two groups could be considered as simply two random samples drawn from a single population.

How do statisticians quantify this discussion? By considering the ratio

$$t = \frac{\text{difference in sample means}}{\text{standard error of difference of sample means}}.$$ (6.1)

When the ratio in (6.1) is small, we conclude that the data is compatible with the hypothesis that both samples were drawn from a single population. When this ratio is large, we conclude that it is unlikely that the samples were drawn from a single population and in turn assert that the drug had an effect.

In order to compute t, we need to be able to calculate the difference between the sample means, and also the standard error of this difference.

For two populations, the distribution of all possible values of $X - Y$ (or $X + Y$) will have the variance $\sigma_{X-Y}^2 = \sigma_{X+Y}^2 = \sigma_X^2 + \sigma_Y^2$. For our scenario, the estimates of the variances for our two samples, denoted s_X and s_Y can replace the population variances in this equation to produce

$$s_{X-Y}^2 = s_X^2 + s_Y^2, \text{ or } s_{X-Y} = \sqrt{s_X^2 + s_Y^2}.$$

Placing this all into (6.1) gives

$$t = \frac{\bar{X}_1 - \bar{X}_2}{s_{\bar{X}_1 - \bar{X}_2}} = \frac{\bar{X}_1 - \bar{X}_2}{\sqrt{s_{\bar{X}_1}^2 + s_{\bar{X}_2}^2}} = \frac{\bar{X}_1 - \bar{X}_2}{\sqrt{\left(\frac{s_1^2}{n}\right) + \left(\frac{s_2^2}{n}\right)}}.$$

If our hypothesis that the two samples are in fact drawn from the same population, then we can see that the variances s_1^2 and s_2^2 would be estimates for the same population variance, and so we could use this single estimate, s^2, averaging the two estimates

$$s^2 = \frac{1}{2}\left(s_1^2 + s_2^2\right)$$

and put this into our equation for t

$$t = \frac{\bar{X}_1 - \bar{X}_2}{\sqrt{\left(\frac{s^2}{n}\right) + \left(\frac{s^2}{n}\right)}}.$$

The t test statistic is based on this concept – the *pooled-variance estimate*.

So what does this all mean? A couple of things. First, hopefully, this provides some insight into one of the more commonly used test statistics. Second, we can now draw a number of conclusions from this relatively simple equation. First, our value of t is going to be affected not only by whether or not the samples are drawn from different populations (i.e., whether or not there actually *is* a difference between the means), but also on the specific instances that happened to be selected for the samples. Second, this means that t can have a range of possible values even when the samples are drawn from the same population. Third, if the samples are drawn from the same population, the means computed will tend to be close to the mean of the population, and so the numerator will tend to be small, hence so will t. Thus, to use t we compute the value, assuming that the samples were drawn from the same population if the value is "small"; conversely, rejecting the hypothesis that the samples were drawn from the same population if the value of t is "big," which brings us to the question of "what is big." By convention, we typically use the 5% cutoff ($p < 0.05$) in our analysis.

Almost all tools available today have built-in functions to support these standard tests. In R for example, the function t.test allows us to easily compute the information we need.

```
> var.test(workingDataTTest$LDLLevel ~ workingDataTTest$Group)

        F test to compare two variances

data:  workingDataTTest$LDLLevel by workingDataTTest$Group
F = 1.0907, num df = 79, denom df = 79, p-value = 0.7007
alternative hypothesis: true ratio of variances is not equal to 1
95 percent confidence interval:
 0.6994584 1.7006328
sample estimates:
ratio of variances
          1.090652

> t.test(workingDataTTest$LDLLevel ~ workingDataTTest$Group, var.equal=T)

        Two Sample t-test

data:  workingDataTTest$LDLLevel by workingDataTTest$Group
t = -0.4064, df = 158, p-value = 0.685
alternative hypothesis: true difference in means is not equal to 0
95 percent confidence interval:
 -11.500107    7.575107
sample estimates:
mean in group A mean in group B
       134.8125        136.7750
```

Here are a couple of comments about the output in the figure above. First, we denormalized the data into a more convenient form where each reading was placed on its own record, along with its grouping (e.g., 185, "A"). Second, the reader can see that the results of this test do not conclude that the data came from two different distributions, which is not surprising when you look at the original data: a visual inspection will show that patients in both groups cover the gamut of "normal" readings through "very high" readings. Thus, we wouldn't necessarily expect the t test to identify them as different. What do we do?

6.2.6 Back to Square One?

This situation is not unusual in analysis of data. Although we might begin with a hypothesis, the whole purpose is to conclude or refute that hypothesis. Our information to date indicates that we have to rethink our starting position.

However, when we saw the two groups of data visually, in Fig. 6.2, it appeared that we should see a more definitive difference between the two groups.

Let us explore this one step further. Let us add a new, calculated piece of data to our dataset:

```
for(i in 1:20) {

        workingData$Difference <- abs(workingData$Week8 -

workingData$Week1)

}
```

The result of this can be seen below, where we now have a magnitude of the change, if any, from the first week's reading, to the last. If we had simply looked at the difference, we would have seen a number of reductions – the intent of the drug, if it works – but we are more interested in just the magnitude of the change.

```
-1   -2   -1    0   10   -1    2    8    4    6  -31   -3   -1  -31   -3  -19  -17   -9   -4  -17
```

```
> workingData
   Patient Group Week1 Week2 Week3 Week4 Week5 Week6 Week7 Week8 Difference
1        1     A   182   180   183   179   181   183   181   181          1
2        2     A   165   169   167   180   165   164   164   163          2
3        3     A    97    97    95    99   100    96    95    96          1
4        4     A    91    93    91    91    92    91    93    91          0
5        5     A   105   109   110   111   109   115   115   115         10
6        6     A   133   133   134   134   133   132   132   132          1
7        7     A   127   127   121   126   127   129   131   129          2
8        8     A   145   144   145   147   147   151   153   153          8
9        9     A   111   115   114   115   115   116   115   115          4
10      10     A   175   177   176   177   179   179   176   181          6
11      11     B   166   158   151   143   141   140   137   135         31
12      12     B   121   119   120   118   121   117   117   118          3
13      13     B   171   173   171   169   170   168   170   170          1
14      14     B   157   149   143   138   133   131   128   126         31
15      15     B    96    96    94    95    94    95    94    93          3
16      16     B   142   138   133   131   127   126   124   123         19
17      17     B   135   131   127   124   123   121   119   118         17
18      18     B    98    96    95    93    92    91    89    89          9
19      19     B   181   180   182   179   179   178   177   177          4
20      20     B   183   181   175   171   169   167   166   166         17
```

In viewing the difference alone, we can see a marked difference (sic) between group A and group B. Does this tell us anything (Fig. 6.4)?

As we can see from the t test results, there is now conclusive evidence that these come from different populations.

```
> var.test(workingData$Difference ~ workingData$Group)

        F test to compare two variances

data:   workingData$Difference by workingData$Group
F = 0.0905, num df = 9, denom df = 9, p-value = 0.001417
alternative hypothesis: true ratio of variances is not equal to 1
95 percent confidence interval:
 0.02248274 0.36441437
sample estimates:
ratio of variances
        0.09051537


> t.test(workingData$Difference ~ workingData$Group, var.equal=T)

        Two Sample t-test

data:   workingData$Difference by workingData$Group
t = -2.6737, df = 18, p-value = 0.01549
alternative hypothesis: true difference in means is not equal to 0
95 percent confidence interval:
 -17.857810  -2.142190
sample estimates:
mean in group A mean in group B
          3.5             13.5
```

Fig. 6.4 Testing for differences

This may be but we need to ask ourselves: was it was valid to create the difference data? A good consultant would say "it depends." And it does. We began our example by looking at the cholesterol readings taken over an 8 week period and progressed our analysis using the raw data. However, if we had taken a few minutes and visually inspected the data at a lower level than we did in Fig. 6.2, then we would have noticed that the patients were spread across all of the same categories of readings. That is, we had patients with normal, slightly elevated, and high readings in both groups. This would have been very evident if we had looked carefully at some of the descriptive statistics for the dataset, which we discuss below.

But this is also a good example of how simple statistics can help us in looking for hidden patterns that is at the core of data mining. In this instance, we returned to our data and asked: "what are we really interested in?" In this case, we were interested in validating or refuting whether the drug affected the LDL cholesterol values of our patients in any meaningful way: meaningful being in comparison to no overt therapy. Clinically, the way in which we measure this is in whether or not the readings alter. We elected, therefore, to look at the difference between the study's endpoint (at week 8) and the reading at the start of the study. By doing this, we excluded any transient fluctuations. As we can see below, one patient (patient 2) actually had two large intrastudy fluctuations (with opposite sign).

Patient	Group	Week1	Week2	Week3	Week4	Week5	Week6	Week7	Week8	Difference	Difference2	Difference3	Difference4	Difference5	Difference6	Difference7	Difference8
1	A	182	180	183	179	181	183	181	181	1	-2	3	-4	2	2	-2	0
2	A	165	169	167	160	165	164	164	163	2	4	-2	13	-15	-1	0	-1
3	A	97	97	95	99	100	96	95	96	1	0	-2	4	1	-4	1	-2
4	A	91	93	91	91	92	91	93	91	0	2	-2	0	1	-1	2	-2
5	A	105	109	110	111	109	115	115	115	10	4	1	-2	6	0	0	0
6	A	133	133	134	134	133	132	132	132	1	0	1	0	-1	-1	0	-2
7	A	127	127	121	126	127	129	131	129	2	0	-4	5	1	2	4	-2
8	A	145	144	145	147	147	151	153	153	8	-1	1	1	0	4	2	0
9	A	111	115	114	115	115	116	115	115	4	4	-1	1	0	1	-1	0
10	A	175	177	174	177	179	179	176	181	6	2	-1	2	0	-3	-3	-2
11	B	166	158	151	143	141	140	137	135	31	-8	-1	-4	-2	-1	-3	-2
12	B	121	119	120	118	121	117	117	118	3	-2	1	-2	3	-4	0	1
13	B	171	173	171	169	170	168	170	170	1	2	-2	-2	1	-2	2	0
14	B	167	149	143	138	133	131	128	124	31	-8	-6	-5	-5	-2	-3	-4
15	B	96	96	94	95	94	95	94	93	3	0	-2	1	-1	1	-1	-1
16	B	142	135	133	131	127	126	124	123	19	-4	-5	-2	-4	-1	-2	-1
17	B	135	131	127	124	121	121	119	118	17	-4	-4	-3	-3	-1	-2	-1
18	B	98	96	95	93	92	91	89	89	9	-2	-1	-2	-1	-1	-2	0
19	B	181	180	182	179	179	178	177	177	4	-1	2	-3	0	-1	-1	0
20	B	183	181	175	171	169	167	166	166	17	-2	-6	-4	-2	-2	-1	0

Is this valid? For this instance, we would say yes. Is this valid in general? That's impossible to say. Each analysis has to be considered on its own merits. What we can say, in general, however, is that it is not unusual to have to retrace our steps, rethink our analysis, and reframe our objectives. We have more to say about this elsewhere.

6.2.7 Some Other Hypothesis Testing Methods

In the section above, we used the *t* test as our testing method for walking through an example. Needless to say, there are many other testing methods that we could use, a number of which are listed in Table 6.5.[8]

Generalizing the hypothesis testing methodology:

1. State your null hypothesis (H_0) and your alternate hypothesis (H_A) to be mutually exclusive.
2. Formulate an analysis approach: how to use sample data to accept or reject H_0, specifying:

   - The significance level (e.g., 0.01, 0.5, 0.1, or another value that makes sense).
   - The test method (involving a test statistic and a sampling distribution).
     The test statistic is computed from the sample data and may be the mean, proportion, difference between means, difference between proportions, *z*-score, *t*-score, chi-score, rank sum, or any other appropriate measure.

   Given a test statistic and its sampling distribution, we can calculate probabilities associated with the test statistic. If the test statistic probability is less than the significance level, the null hypothesis is rejected.

3. Analyze our sample data by computing the calculations identified in our analysis plan:

   - If H_0 involves a mean or proportion, we typically use one of the following equations:
     Test statistic = (statistic − parameter)/(standard deviation of statistic), or
     Test statistic = (statistic − parameter)/(standard error of statistic)

---

[8] Even this table is not exhaustive. To illustrate, just take a look at the http://en.wikipedia.org/wiki/ Category:Statistical_tests Wikipedia page: Whether this is exhaustive or not, we will leave it to the reader to decide. Alternatively, see http://www.itl.nist.gov/div898/handbook/eda/section3/eda35. htm

Table 6.5 Some commonly used statistical tests

Name	Formula
z-test (1 sample)	$z = \frac{\bar{x}-\mu_0}{(\sigma/\sqrt{n})}$
z-test (2 samples)	$z = \frac{(\bar{x}_1-\bar{x}_2)-d_0}{\sqrt{\frac{\sigma_1^2}{n_1}+\frac{\sigma_2^2}{n_2}}}$
t test (2 samples pooled; equal variances)	$t = \frac{(\bar{x}_1-\bar{x}_2-d_0)}{s_p\sqrt{\frac{1}{n_1}+\frac{1}{n_2}}}$, $\quad s_p^2 = \frac{(n_1-1)s_1^2+(n_2-1)s_2^2}{n_1+n_2-2}$, $\quad df = n_1 + n_2 - 2$
t test (2 samples unpooled; unequal variances)	$t = \frac{(\bar{x}_1-\bar{x}_2-d_0)}{\sqrt{\frac{s_1^2}{n_1}+\frac{s_2^2}{n_2}}}$, $\quad df = n\frac{\left(\frac{s_1^2}{n_1}+\frac{s_2^2}{n_2}\right)^2}{\frac{\left(\frac{s_1^2}{n_1}\right)^2}{n_1-1}\frac{\left(\frac{s_2^2}{n_2}\right)^2}{n_2-1}}$
z-test (1 proportion)	$z = \frac{\hat{p}-p_0}{\sqrt{\frac{p_0(1-p_0)}{n}}}$
z-test (2 proportions; pooled for $d_0 = 0$)	$z = \frac{(\hat{p}_1-\hat{p}_2)-d_0}{\sqrt{\hat{p}(1-\hat{p})\left(\frac{1}{n_1}+\frac{1}{n_2}\right)}}$, $\quad \hat{p} = \frac{x_1+x_2}{n_1+n_2}$
z-test (2 proportion; unpooled for $|d_0| > 0$)	$z = \frac{(\hat{p}_1-\hat{p}_2)-d_0}{\sqrt{\frac{\hat{p}_1(1-\hat{p}_1)}{n_1}+\frac{\hat{p}_2(1-\hat{p}_2)}{n_2}}}$
Chi-square test (1 sample)	$\chi^2 = \frac{(n-1)s^2}{\sigma_0^2}$
F-test (2 sample; equality of variances)	$F = \frac{s_1^2}{s_2^2}$

df degrees of freedom, $\hat{p} = \frac{x}{n}$, d_0 hypothesized population mean difference, p_0 hypothesized population proportion

("Parameter" is the value appearing in H_0 and "statistic" is a point estimate of "parameter.")

- If H_0 involves categorical data (with parameter), then use the chi-square statistic.
- Calculate the p value; the probability of observing a sample statistic as extreme as the test statistic, assuming H_0 is true.

4. Interpret our results: do they make sense? Are the sample findings unlikely, given H_0? If so, reject H_0. (Typically we do this by comparing the p value to the significance level and reject if the p value < the significance level).

6.2.7.1 Rank-Sum Test

Although the t test is the standard for testing the difference between population means for two samples, if the underlying populations are not normal, or if the samples are small, then the t test may not be valid. In general, is our distributional assumptions are suspect, we may use the *rank-sum*[9] test instead. The (Wilcoxon) rank-sum test is a

---

[9] This test is also commonly referred to as the Mann–Whitney rank-sum test, or the Mann–Whitney test, even though it was developed by Wilcoxon.

Fig. 6.5 Native American
and Caucasian MSCE data
(stripchart)

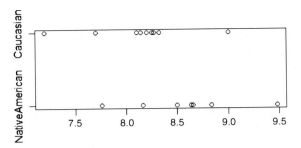

nonparametric alternative to the *t test* which is only based on the order in which the
observations from the two samples occur. However, we must be careful because the
rank-sum test is not as powerful as the *t test* when our assumptions are valid.

To use the rank-sum test, we rank the combined samples and compute the sum of
the ranks for our first sample, R_1, and compute the sum of the ranks of the second
sample, R_2. If our sample sizes are equal, which is typically assumed to be the null
hypothesis – $H_0 : R_1 = R_2$, that the two samples have the same distribution – the
rank-sum test statistic is $T = \min(R_1, R_2)$. If our sample sizes are unequal
($H_A : R_1 \neq R_2$), then we take the sum of the ranks for the smaller sample (say
R_1) and then compute $R_2 = n_1(n_1 + n_2 + 1) - R_1$. The test statistic is then $T =
\min(R_1, R_2)$ as before. Note that if the values are very small, it can cause rejection
of the null hypothesis even when the sample means are equal. Significance levels
for small values of n_1 and n_2 are available in tabulated form; for large values, a
normal approximation is used.

The rank-sum test is based on ranking the $n_1 + n_2$ observations from our
combined sample, giving each observation a rank from 1 upward. We'll walk
through the details in a few moments but for now we'll say that T will have mean
and variance given by $\mu_T = \frac{n_1(n_1+n_2+1)}{2}$, and $\sigma_T^2 = \frac{n_1 n_2}{12}(n_1 + n_2 + 1)$, respectively.

The Process

We'll use a simple example for illustration taken from the original work of
Margolin and Shelby (1985 #577). *Mean sister-chromatid exchange* (MSCE)
values were elicited for two ethnic groups:

Native American	8.50	9.48	8.65	8.16	8.83	7.76	8.63		
Caucasian	8.27	8.20	8.25	8.14	9.00	8.10	7.20	8.32	7.70

If we plot these two sets of data, we can see there are differences between them:

```
NativeAmericanPlotData <- c(8.50, 9.48, 8.65, 8.16, 8.83, 7.76, 8.63, NA, NA)

CaucasianPlotData      <- c(8.27, 8.20, 8.25, 8.14, 9.00, 8.10, 7.20, 8.32, 7.70)

msce=data.frame(NativeAmerican=NativeAmericanPlotData, Caucasian=CaucasianPlotData)

stripchart(msce, pch=1)
```

Note that we added two "NA" values to make both sets of data the same length to
make using the `stripchart` function simpler for the image shown in Fig. 6.5.

```
                  [,1]   [,2]   [,3]  [,4]   [,5]  [,6]   [,7]
NativeAmerican    8.5    9.48   8.65  8.16   8.83  7.76   8.63
                  11.0  16.00  13.00  6.00  14.00  3.00  12.00
[1] 75
                 [,1]  [,2]  [,3]  [,4]  [,5]  [,6]  [,7]   [,8]  [,9]
Caucasian 8.27   8.2  8.25  8.14     9   8.1   7.2   8.32   7.7
               9.00   7.0  8.00  5.00    15   4.0   1.0  10.00   2.0
[1] 61
[1] 1.587768
[1] 1.693620
              [,1]        [,2]
[1,] 0.05616936 0.9548312

  Wilcoxon rank sum test

data:  NativeAmerican and Caucasian
W = 47, p-value = 0.1142
alternative hypothesis: true location shift is not equal to 0
```

Fig. 6.6 Rank-sum test

The R code we used to generate this figure is shown below.

```
> NativeAmerican <- c(8.50, 9.48, 8.65, 8.16, 8.83, 7.76, 8.63)
Caucasian       <- c(8.27, 8.20, 8.25, 8.14, 9.00, 8.10, 7.20, 8.32, 7.70)

NativeAmericanPlotData <- c(8.50, 9.48, 8.65, 8.16, 8.83, 7.76, 8.63, NA, NA)
CaucasianPlotData      <- c(8.27, 8.20, 8.25, 8.14, 9.00, 8.10, 7.20, 8.32, 7.70)

msce=data.frame(NativeAmerican=NativeAmericanPlotData, Caucasian=CaucasianPlotData)
stripchart(msce, pch=1)

n1 <- length(NativeAmerican);
n2 <- length(Caucasian)
n <- n1 + n2

> n
[1] 16
> |
```

Now let's compute the various variables we need, as shown in blue below, with the output following in black (Fig. 6.6).

```
> R <- rank(c(NativeAmerican, Caucasian))
rbind(NativeAmerican, R[1:n1])
T1 <- sum(R[1:n1]); T1
rbind(Caucasian, R[(n1+1):n])
T2 <- sum(R[(n1+1):n]); T2
z11 <- (T1 - n1*(n+1)/2 - 1/2)/sqrt(n1*n2*(n+1)/12); z11
z12 <- (T1 - n1*(n+1)/2 + 1/2)/sqrt(n1*n2*(n+1)/12); z12
cbind(1-pnorm(z11), pnorm(z12))
wilcox.test(NativeAmerican, Caucasian, alternative = "t")
```

Now we have our conclusion: are they the same or different populations?

Rank-Sum or *t*? Or Something Else?

The rank-sum test is useful in many of the same domains as the *t* test, so the natural question is which test should be used in what situations? For ordinal data that is not interval scaled, the rank sum is the usual choice. Since we are comparing sums of ranks, as opposed to specific values, the rank sum is less likely to indicate significance because of outlier values.

Use of the *t* test relies critically on the assumption that the two populations follow a normal distribution as well as having independent samples. However, if $N = n_1 + n_2 \geq 30$, that is, reasonably large, then we can continue to use the *t* test even if the original populations do not have normal distributions so long as the level of skewness is not too dramatic and where there are no outliers present.

Where the rank-sum test becomes a preferred choice is where we want to test whether two populations are different, when we have small sample sizes, and where the data is skewed or has heavy tails.

Classically, the *t* test is widely used, there is no doubt of that, and that is why we used it as an example earlier in this section, but as we've seen, nonparametric methods such as the rank-sum test are equally valid. For example, if we look at data such as the following, from Del Greco and Burgess (1973 #578), for patients who have undergone surgery for the removal of a kidney,

Patient	1	2	3	4	5
BP before surgery	107	102	95	106	112
BP after surgery	87	97	101	113	80

there are a set of assumptions underlying our use of the *t* test, namely that the statistic follows a *t* distribution if the differences are normally distributed (which indicates a parametric method), that the observations are independent (so that the selection of any given patient does not influence the chance of any other patient being included), that the populations must have the same variances (two sample case), and that the variables must be measured on an interval scale (so as to allow us to interpret the results). A challenge is that these assumptions may not be tested, but simply accepted, and this is not uncommon.

We can use nonparametric methods instead, which follow the same general methodology (state hypotheses, calculate test statistic, reject/accept H_0 based on magnitude of the test statistic) and relieve some of the constraints without sacrificing our objective. Since nonparametric methods typically use ranking, sensitivity to measurement error is often far less than with parametric tests.

But in fact, there are many methods we can use based upon our objective, as is shown in Table 6.6.

So although we've only discussed a couple of tests in the text, the actual choice of the test statistic should depend on the design of the study: how many groups do we have? Are the samples dependent or independent? Can we construct ordered alternative hypotheses?

Table 6.6 Analysis objectives and some methodological options

Objective	Approach
2 independent samples	t test
	Wilcoxon rank-sum test
More than 2 independent samples	ANOVA
	Kruskal-Wallis test
2 dependent samples	Paired t test
	Sign test; Signed-rank test
Randomized block design	Mixed models
	Friedman test
Ordered treatments	Regression
	Jonckheere-Terpsta test

With parametric tests, we make assumptions about the distribution in the population and have conditions that are not often tested. The test depends on the validity of the assumptions, and so it is the most powerful test if all the assumptions are met.

With nonparametric tests, we make fewer assumptions about the distribution in the population and in cases of small sample sizes, they are often the only alternative, unless the nature of the population distribution is known exactly. Since they are less sensitive to measurement error because of their use of ranks, they can be used for data which are inherently in ranks, even for data measured in a nominal scale. Lastly, they are often considered easier to learn.

6.2.8 Multiple Comparisons and Multiple-Testing Correlation

In this text, when we use the term comparisons, we are typically referring to comparisons between two groups of data, such as might be seen in a traditional clinical trial comprising a control group and a treatment group. The extension of this to multiple comparisons is therefore the intuitive one where we conduct several two-group comparisons and where we focus on the "strongest" differences between the multiple comparisons (sic) made.

Multiple comparisons, or multiple-testing problems occur when we consider a set of statistical inferences simultaneously. Errors can be introduced in the inference process. For example, including confidence intervals where we have failed to include their corresponding population parameters, or hypothesis tests that have incorrectly rejected the null hypothesis can occur.

Consider this a little further: suppose we are analyzing the efficacy of a new drug in terms of how it affects (specifically, reduces) any of a number of different symptoms of a particular disease. As we include more symptoms in our analysis, it becomes more likely that the drug will appear to be an improvement over existing drugs in terms of at least one of the symptoms we consider. (Why?) This case can be similarly made in terms of different side effects (as opposed to symptoms): as we consider more side effects, the new drug will appear to be less safe than existing drugs in terms of at least one side effect. (Again, why?) Intuitively, as we continue to increase the number of comparisons, the likelihood that the compared groups will appear to be different (in terms of at least one attribute) will similarly increase. The question, however, is whether this between-group difference will generalize to an independent sample of data. A logical conclusion would be that our confidence in a result generalizing to independent data should be weaker if the analysis involved multiple comparisons, stronger if it only contained a single comparison.

Confidence intervals or hypothesis tests, or both, can occur in multiple comparison analysis. Let's briefly illustrate the problem using a confidence interval (CI). Having a CI of 95% (i.e., 95% coverage probability level) means that in the long run the true population parameter that we're interested in will be included in 95% of the confidence intervals. If we consider 100 CIs simultaneously, each with a coverage probability of 0.95, it is likely that some number of them, possibly only one, will not contain the population parameter. We would expect five of these intervals to not contain the population parameter; for independent intervals, this probability is actually 99.4%!

Correlation coefficients between biological measurements and clinical scales are a staple of statistical analysis within scientific research, and calculating numerous correlations increases the risk of a type I error, that is, to erroneously conclude the presence of a significant correlation. To address this, we may need to adjust the level of statistical significance of the correlation coefficients.

Publication of Vul et al. (2009 #817) issued a challenge for the field of cognitive neuroscience since Vul's analysis demonstrates, in rigorous detail, how the too-good-to-be-true results of fMRI studies are often the result of complex statistical errors and biases. Since its publication, there has been much "robust" discourse on its contents and accuracy. But this is not the only source to have suggested challenges in statistical analysis, a foundation of many techniques outside of statistics as much as within. Glantz (2005 #140), for example, made claims that many published analyses often use incorrect methodologies or contain errors. Anyone in research, who is not a statistician or data-analyst on training, can attest that this is often a challenging part of the overall research.

In one response to Vul et al. (2009 #817) and Jabbi et al. (2009 #819), the authors argue that "correcting for multiple comparisons eliminates the concern by Vul et al. that the voxel selection 'distorts the results by selecting noise exhibited by the effects being searched for.'" Why we included this example is not to single out social neuroscience, but simply to show that all disciplines encounter issues in this arena.

Lindquist and Gelman (2009 #818) had weighed into the above debate and, for our purposes, provides an interesting addition:

> *Huizenga, Winkel, Grasman, and Waldorp argue that if* **adequate corrections for multiple comparisons** *are performed, it is not warranted to label high correlations as being "voodoo" and that "the correlations simply are high because they survive more conservative thresholds." Both Jabbi et al. and Huizenga et al. argue that the* **focus should be on the statistical testing and not on the magnitude of the correlations**: *as Jabbi et al. write, "a key question is often not how strongly two measures were correlated, but whether and where in the brain such correlations may exist." (Emphasis ours)*

A common use of multiple comparison is in analysis of variance (ANOVA). A resulting significant test, such as the ANOVA F-test, often suggests rejecting H_0, which states that the means are the same across the compared groups. We can use multiple-comparison techniques to determine which of the means actually differ: if we perform ANOVA on data with n group means we'll have $n(n - 1)/2$ pairwise comparisons.

6.2.8.1 Multiple-Testing Correction

Consider a situation where we repeat a statistical test multiple times, such as might arise from retaining a prescribed family-wise error rate in an analysis that involves more than one comparison. We need to consider *multiple-testing correction* when we recalculate probabilities multiple times.

In a situation where the type I error rate for each comparison is $\frac{\alpha}{n}$, the total error rate will not be greater than α; this is one of the most commonly used approaches for multiple comparisons and is called the *Bonferroni correction*, and we shall describe it here.

If the test statistics are highly dependent, the Bonferroni correction can be very conservative and provide a family-wise error rate significantly less than α. Using an example from fMRI, the Bonferroni method would require p values $< 0.05/100,000$ for there to be significance, assuming 100,000 voxels. Adjacent voxels tend to be highly correlated, making this threshold to stringent a value. Given this scenario, alternative techniques have been considered whereby the false positive rates are balanced without causing the false negative rates to increase unnecessarily.

In general, such methods can be thought to fall into one of the following general types:

- Proof that $\alpha \leq x$ and never exceeds this value ($x = 0.05$ or some other chosen value). Such methods offer control against type I error, even if the null hypothesis is only partially correct.
- Proof that $\alpha \leq x$ and never exceeds this value ($x = 0.05$ or some other chosen value), except under certain defined conditions. This is a corollary to the first category.
- Cases which rely on an omnibus test (ANOVA, Tukey's range test) prior to proceeding to multiple comparisons. This type of method has only weak control of type I errors.
- Empirical methods, controlling the type I errors using adaptive techniques such as correlation and the distribution characteristics of the observed data. Computerized resampling methods (such as Monte Carlo simulations and bootstrapping) have given rise to many techniques in this category.[10]

The Bonferroni method is a widely known, and stringent method, but can increase the number of false negatives we encounter. In an attempt to address this

---

[10] It should be noted that exhaustive permutation resampling can give us much control over type I errors; other methods, such as bootstrapping, give us only moderate control over the type I error.

Fig. 6.7 Multiple-testing
correction methods

issue, the Bonferroni step-down (Holm) correction method was developed; a less
stringent method that reduces the potential for false negatives. In addition to this,
many other methods have been developed including the Westfall and Young
permutation method and the Benjamin and Hochberg false discovery rate method,
which have the challenge of potentially encountering more false positives.

Figure 6.7 shows the relative stringency of several multiple-testing correction
methods, with the Bonferroni method discussed above being the most stringent. As is
always the case, no individual technique is a panacea and we still have to be careful.
Note that we could have added a fifth method – the "no method" – to this list, which
would necessarily potentially introduce the most false positives of all the methods listed.

Many analytical products now contain techniques to support testing correction,
so you'll not always have to build them from scratch. For example, the examples
given in Fig. 6.7 above are available from within the GeneSpring product, from
Agilent Technologies.

We will briefly describe each of the above four methods in the context of
analyzing a set of $n = 1,000$ genes and assume an error rate of $\alpha = 0.05$.

Bonferroni Correction

To use this method, we simply take the p value of each gene and multiply it by the
number of genes in our analytical set. If the *corrected p* value < error rate then the
gene is significant.

$$Corrected\, p - value = (p - value \times n) < \alpha$$

As we can see in this example, and from our discussion above, the largest p value
we can accept from an individual gene is 0.00005. *A family error rate of 0.05, which
indicates we can expect at least an error in the family, the expected number of false
positives will be 0.05.*

Bonferroni Step-Down (Holm) Correction

As its name suggests, this method is similar to the Bonferroni method, but is a less
stringent. In this method, we rank the individual gene p values from smallest to
largest and compare the p value divided by k (where k runs from n to 1) against α.

So, the first comparison will use the smallest p value (say $p = 0.005$) divided by $k = 1{,}000$ and compare it against α, which in our analytical set is $0.05/1{,}000 = 0.00005$. If our variable quotient is less than α, we reject the associated null hypothesis. The next p value (say $p = 0.01$) would be divided by 999 and compared. The next value for p would be divided by 998, and so on until we obtain a quotient which is not less than α, at which point we stop and accept that H_0 and all subsequent H_0.

The table below depicts a more concrete example.

Gene	p Value	Rank	Correction	Significant?
A	0.00002	1	$0.00002 \times 1{,}000 = 0.02$	$0.02 < 0.05$? Yes
B	0.00004	2	$0.00004 \times 999 = 0.039$	$0.039 < 0.05$? Yes
C	0.00009	3	$0.00009 \times 998 = 0.0898$	$0.0898 > 0.05$? No

We can see that as the p value increases, the correction becomes less and less conservative. However, the family-wise error rate is still very similar to the Bonferroni correction.

6.2.8.2   Westfall and Young Permutation

The two methods discussed above both correct the p values independently, and are thus single-step procedures. Westfall and Young's permutation method leverages the fact that there is a dependence structure among genes and permutes all the genes at the same time. Similar to the Holm method, it uses a step-down procedure but combines this with a bootstrapping method in order to compute the p value distribution. Briefly, the method is as follows:

1. Calculate p values for each gene in the analytical set and rank them.
2. Create a pseudoanalytical set by dividing the data into artificial treatment and control groups.
3. Calculate p values for all genes on the pseudodata set.
4. Successive minima of the new p values are retained and compared to the original ones.
5. Repeat N (a large number) of times. The proportion of resampled datasets where the minimum pseudo-p value $<$ original p value is the adjusted p value.

The permutation process makes this method very computer intensive (a.k.a. slow). The family-wise error rate is similar to that of the Bonferroni and Holm methods.

We'll consider an R example, using the data from Golub et al. (1999 #77) and consider the first 100 genes in the dataset, along with the default number of permutations (10,000).[11]

---

[11] This example can be found at http://rss.acs.unt.edu/Rdoc/library/multtest/html/mt.maxT.html

We begin with the typical setup:

```
> library(multtest)
data(golub)
smallgd<-golub[1:100,]
classlabel<-golub.cl
Loading required package: Biobase

Welcome to Bioconductor

    Vignettes contain introductory material. To view, type
    'openVignette()'. To cite Bioconductor, see
    'citation("Biobase")' and for packages 'citation(pkgname)'.
```

The `golub` dataset is contained within the `multtest` library, and since we're only going to use the first 100 genes, we'll split them out into our `smallgd` variable and also extract our class labels.

```
> classlabel
 [1] 0 0 0 0 0 0 0 0 0 0 0 0 0 0 0 0 0 0 0 0 0 0 0 0 0 0 0 0 0 0 0 0 1 1 1 1 1 1 1 1 1 1 1
```

Next we'll permute the unadjusted *p* values as well as the adjusted *p* values using the `maxT` and `minP` procedures, in turn using Welch *t*-statistics.

```
> resT<-mt.maxT(smallgd,classlabel)
resP<-mt.minP(smallgd,classlabel)
rawp<-resT$rawp[order(resT$index)]
teststat<-resT$teststat[order(resT$index)]
b=100 b=200 b=300 b=400 b=500 b=600 b=700 b=800 b=900 b=1000
b=1100 b=1200 b=1300 b=1400 b=1500 b=1600 b=1700 b=1800 b=1900 b=2000
b=2100 b=2200 b=2300 b=2400 b=2500 b=2600 b=2700 b=2800 b=2900 b=3000
b=3100 b=3200 b=3300 b=3400 b=3500 b=3600 b=3700 b=3800 b=3900 b=4000
b=4100 b=4200 b=4300 b=4400 b=4500 b=4600 b=4700 b=4800 b=4900 b=5000
b=5100 b=5200 b=5300 b=5400 b=5500 b=5600 b=5700 b=5800 b=5900 b=6000
b=6100 b=6200 b=6300 b=6400 b=6500 b=6600 b=6700 b=6800 b=6900 b=7000
b=7100 b=7200 b=7300 b=7400 b=7500 b=7600 b=7700 b=7800 b=7900 b=8000
b=8100 b=8200 b=8300 b=8400 b=8500 b=8600 b=8700 b=8800 b=8900 b=9000
b=9100 b=9200 b=9300 b=9400 b=9500 b=9600 b=9700 b=9800 b=9900 b=10000
B=10000
b=100 b=200 b=300 b=400 b=500 b=600 b=700 b=800 b=900 b=1000
b=1100 b=1200 b=1300 b=1400 b=1500 b=1600 b=1700 b=1800 b=1900 b=2000
b=2100 b=2200 b=2300 b=2400 b=2500 b=2600 b=2700 b=2800 b=2900 b=3000
b=3100 b=3200 b=3300 b=3400 b=3500 b=3600 b=3700 b=3800 b=3900 b=4000
b=4100 b=4200 b=4300 b=4400 b=4500 b=4600 b=4700 b=4800 b=4900 b=5000
b=5100 b=5200 b=5300 b=5400 b=5500 b=5600 b=5700 b=5800 b=5900 b=6000
b=6100 b=6200 b=6300 b=6400 b=6500 b=6600 b=6700 b=6800 b=6900 b=7000
b=7100 b=7200 b=7300 b=7400 b=7500 b=7600 b=7700 b=7800 b=7900 b=8000
b=8100 b=8200 b=8300 b=8400 b=8500 b=8600 b=8700 b=8800 b=8900 b=9000
b=9100 b=9200 b=9300 b=9400 b=9500 b=9600 b=9700 b=9800 b=9900 b=10000
r=1 r=2 r=3 r=4 r=5 r=6 r=7 r=8 r=9 r=10
r=11 r=12 r=13 r=14 r=15 r=16 r=17 r=18 r=19 r=20
r=21 r=22 r=23 r=24 r=25 r=26 r=27 r=28 r=29 r=30
r=31 r=32 r=33 r=34 r=35 r=36 r=37 r=38 r=39 r=40
r=41 r=42 r=43 r=44 r=45 r=46 r=47 r=48 r=49 r=50
r=51 r=52 r=53 r=54 r=55 r=56 r=57 r=58 r=59 r=60
r=61 r=62 r=63 r=64 r=65 r=66 r=67 r=68 r=69 r=70
r=71 r=72 r=73 r=74 r=75 r=76 r=77 r=78 r=79 r=80
r=81 r=82 r=83 r=84 r=85 r=86 r=87 r=88 r=89 r=90
r=91 r=92 r=93 r=94 r=95 r=96 r=97 r=98 r=99 r=100
```

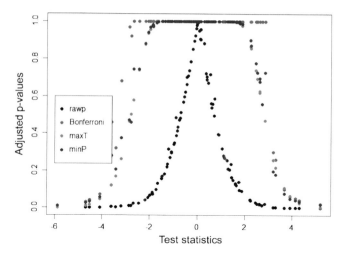

Fig. 6.8 Westfall and Young permutation comparison with Bonferroni method

Now we'll plot the results and compare them with the Bonferroni procedure, as shown in Fig. 6.8.

6.2.8.3   Benjamini and Hochberg False Discovery Rate

The Benjamin and Hochberg method offers a less stringent option to the methods described above and thus will tolerate more false positives. We should not that there will also be less false negatives.

1. Rank the *p* values of all genes from smallest to largest.
2. Keep the largest *p* value as it is.
3. Multiply the second largest *p* value by the total number of genes in our dataset and divide by its rank. If the adjusted *p* value $< \alpha$, it is significant.

$$Adjusted\,p - value = p - value \times (n/n - 1)$$

4. The next *p* value is computed and compared as per step 3.
5. Repeat step 4 until dataset is exhausted.

Gene	p Value	Rank	Correction	Significant?
A	0.1	1,000	None	0.1 < 0.05? No
B	0.06	999	1,000/999 × 0.06 = 0.06006	0.06006 < 0.05? No
C	0.04	998	1,000/998 × 0.04 = 0.04008	0.04008 < 0.05? Yes

Thus, the correction becomes more and more stringent as the *p* value decreases in value, which is similar to the Holm method. This method provides a good alternative to family-wise error rate methods.

6.3 Measures of Central Tendency, Variability, and Other Descriptive Statistics

6.3.1 Location

We are often interested in measuring the "center" of a set of data within the data-mining process. For example, we described cluster analysis earlier in this book and figure X-Y showed the center of each cluster as a red dot. Measuring the center, however, can be accomplished in several different ways.

The most common method of measuring location is to compute the arithmetic mean of a set of data. Typically, the data we compute, the set of observations, will be numeric and constitute the values of some single attribute, such as age. If we have n values for an attribute $x_1, x_2, \ldots, x_n$, then we can compute the mean using the formula

$$\bar{x} = \frac{1}{n} \sum_{i=1}^{n} x_i. \tag{6.2}$$

Almost every database management system and statistical software system includes a built-in function for this function. Under the SQL92 standard, the function **avg()** allows you to compute this value for a particular column of data. In R, the function **mean()** accomplishes the same.

Often, the values we wish to find the center of will be *weighted* in importance, a fact we have to take into account. In this case, we compute the average as

$$\bar{x} = \frac{\sum_{i=1}^{n} w_i x_i}{\sum_{i=1}^{n} w_i}. \tag{6.3}$$

As we can see from the above description, the arithmetic mean is a linear operator on the data in that even if our data elements are described as a linear combination such as $a + bx_i$, we find that $\frac{1}{n} \sum (a + bx_i) = a + b\bar{x}$. The arithmetic mean also provides us with some other useful properties. Since it is a measure of central tendency, we can use it to look at the deviations of our data values about that central measure. In fact, the sum of the deviations of each data value about the mean is zero, that is, $\sum (x_i - \bar{x}) = 0$. Additionally, it is the value which minimizes the sum of the squares of the deviations of each data element from the mean itself, that is, $\min_a \sum (x_i - a) = \bar{x}$. We shall have cause to use this property in several areas of analysis, as we shall see later.

We can also look at other descriptive information which provides us with significant initial value when examining data, including measure such as:

- Quartiles
- Minimum and maximum values

```
      cod                diagnosis              sex              age                    BT
Length:128            Length:128          F   :42      Min.   : 5.00      B2     :36
Class :character      Class :character    M   :83      1st Qu.:19.00      B3     :23
Mode  :character      Mode  :character    NA's: 3      Median :29.00      B1     :19
                                                       Mean   :32.37      T2     :15
                                                       3rd Qu.:45.50      B4     :12
                                                       Max.   :58.00      T3     :10
                                                       NA's   : 5.00      (Other):13
 remission        CR                  date.cr            t(4;11)
CR   :99     Length:128          Length:128         Mode  :logical
REF  :15     Class :character    Class :character   FALSE:86
NA's:14      Mode  :character    Mode  :character   TRUE :7
                                                    NA's :35


  t(9;22)          cyto.normal           citog              mol.biol
Mode :logical    Mode :logical      Length:128         ALL1/AF4:10
FALSE:67         FALSE:69           Class :character   BCR/ABL :37
TRUE :26         TRUE :24           Mode  :character   E2A/PBX1: 5
NA's :35         NA's :35                              NEG     :74
                                                       NUP-98  : 1
                                                       p15/p16 : 1

  fusion protein       mdr                   kinet         ccr
p190      :17      Length:128          dyploid:94     Mode :logical
p190/p210: 8       Class :character    hyperd.:27     FALSE:74
p210     : 8       Mode  :character    NA's   : 7     TRUE :26
NA's     :95                                          NA's :28


  relapse          transplant            f.u               date last seen
Mode :logical    Mode :logical      Length:128         Length:128
FALSE:35         FALSE:91           Class :character   Class :character
TRUE :65         TRUE :9            Mode  :character    Mode  :character
NA's :28         NA's :28
```

Fig. 6.9   Descriptive statistical information from R "summary"

- Missing values (designated as "NA" in R output)
- Median
- Mode

Executing the following R command against the acute lymphoblastic leukemia (ALL) dataset from the Ritz Laboratory and made available under the Bioconductor project (Gentleman et al. 2004 #89)

```
data(ALL)
```

```
print(summary(pData(ALL)))
```

provides a wealth of information in one place, as shown below.

We can see from Fig. 6.9 that the dataset contains approximately twice the number of male patients compared to female patients. We can also identify that approximately twice as many patients have relapsed as those that haven't but only a small percentage have been positively identified as having transplants (7%) – but a higher percentage are unknown (21.88%).

Such information not only provides value in and of itself, but also provides valuable information to drive our subsequent analytical efforts.

Above, we consider the most common measure of location, the mean, $\bar{x}$, which is a very valuable and easy to calculate measure and can provide quick insight into the data under consideration. However, like all measures and techniques, it also has some issues and must be used cautiously. For example, if our dataset has very large observations as well as very small observations, not only do they counterbalance each other, but the very large ones can significantly affect the computed value. This is particularly noticeable with outliers, which we return to later.

The *mode* is a second simple measure that we can use for all kinds of data and is typically defined as the value associated with the greatest frequency. This is not quite the whole story since while this definition works well for discrete quantitative data and for qualitative data, we typically use a slight variant for continuous data: create intervals for the data (to create a histogram) and use the value whose interval has the greatest value (height in the histogram).

A third simple measure, the *median*, is defined for a set of N data elements in monotonically increasing order as either the observation which occupies the $(N + 1)/2$ position (N odd), or the mean of the values which occupy the positions $N/2$ and $N/(2 + 1)$ if N is even.

We describe these measures for completeness, although virtually every environment (R, SAS, etc.) provides built-in functions to support calculating these values.

6.3.2 Variability

One factor that is often interesting to us is how the data varies within a distribution, or how the data is dispersed around (say) the mean. As we indicated in our list above, the difference between the maximum and minimum values (the range), or the difference between the third and first quartiles (interquartile range, or IQR), can also provide us with simple, rapid insight into the data we are studying. However, as with every other measure, we need to recognize that the IQR is very sensitive to outlying observations, as we shall see below.

Consider a set of n observations, $x_1, \ldots, x_n$, of a variable X, with mean as defined by Eq. 6.2 and variance defined by

$$\sigma^2(X) = \frac{\sum_{i=1}^{n} (x_i - \bar{x})^2}{n},$$

(6.4)

which defines the variance as the average squared deviation from the mean value. We note here that when the sample is used, instead of the population, it is also denoted by s^2. We also note, in passing, that using a denominator of $n-1$ instead of n provides us with an unbiased estimate of the population variance.

A complete discussion of estimators is outside the scope of this book, although we provide a brief overview in Appendix A.[12] Here we highlight a couple of core conclusions:

1. The sample mean $\bar{X} = \frac{1}{n}\sum_{i=1}^{n} X_i$ is always an unbiased estimator of the population mean μ.
2. The sample variance $S^2 = \frac{1}{n}\sum_{i=1}^{n}(X_i - \bar{X})^2$ is a biased estimator of σ^2, but $S^2 = \frac{1}{n-1}\sum_{i=1}^{n}(X_i - \bar{X})^2$ is an unbiased estimator and the one typically used.
3. $MSE(\hat{\theta}) = E[(\hat{\theta} - \theta)^2]$ and $MSE(\hat{\theta}) = Var(\hat{\theta}) + [bias(\hat{\theta})]^2$. Thus, the mean square error comprises two components which typically require us to trade off between them since as one increases the other decreases.

6.3.3 Heterogeneity

One of the issues with the above measures is that they cannot be used with qualitative data, an important type of data that we encounter a lot in the data we collect in the life sciences. In the general sense, a qualitative variable will have some number n levels, each with its own relative frequency. Consider each level to be represented by the modalities $x_1, \ldots, x_n$ with respective relative frequencies of $p_1, \ldots, p_n$. We define the extreme cases of the distribution to be as follows:

- *Null heterogeneity* is when all the observations fall into the same level. That is, for some level i, $p_i = 1$ and $p_j = 0 \; \forall j \neq i$.
- *Maximum heterogeneity* is when the observations are equally distributed among the n levels. That is, $p_i = \frac{1}{n} \; \forall i = 1, \ldots, n$.

We have already encountered two measures of heterogeneity in Chap. 4: the Gini index and entropy. We include their mathematical formulae here for completeness.

$$G = 1 - \sum_{i=1}^{n} p_i^2$$

As we computed in Chap. 4, the range of values that the Gini index can take ranges from 0 (null heterogeneity or perfect homogeneity) to $1 - \frac{1}{k}$ (maximum

---

[12] The reader is recommended to any good reference book on statistical inference for a more complete discussion of this important subject.

heterogeneity). There are times, however, when computing a normalized range –
[0,1] – would be preferable. The above equation can be easily rescaled using the
maximum value to give us a normalized Gini index, G', as below:

$$G' = \frac{G}{(k-1)/k}.$$

Recall that the computation of entropy is as shown below:

$$E = -\sum_{i=1}^{n} p_i \log p_i.$$

Similarly, this can be normalized by rescaling by its maximum value, as shown
below:

$$E' = \frac{E}{\log k}.$$

6.3.4 Concentration

Concentration is the inverse of heterogeneity. A frequency distribution is said to be
maximally concentrated when it has null heterogeneity and minimally concentrated
when it has maximal heterogeneity. This measure has found particular value in
areas where variables measure some transferrable item (usually of fixed amount),
and typically a quantitative or ordinal qualitative variable.

Consider the case with n quantities measuring some characteristic,
$0 \leq x_1 \leq \ldots \leq x_n$, placed in nondecreasing order. We are interested in understanding the concentration of the characteristic among the n quantities that correspond to
different observations. Since $\bar{x} = \frac{1}{n}\sum_{i=1}^{n} x_i$, then $n\bar{x} = \sum_{i=1}^{n} x_i$, which defines the total
amount available. Not that this would be a real-life example, but consider that we
have a (fixed) amount of a compound we are investigating and using for in vitro
testing, where we might use doubling dilutions of the compound to test against an
organism. We have two boundary conditions to consider:

- *Minimum concentration* where $x_1 = x_2 = \cdots = x_n = \bar{x}$.
- *Maximum concentration* where, without loss of generality, $x_1 = x_2 = \cdots = x_{n-1} = 0$, $x_n = n\bar{x}$, the "winner takes all" condition.

However, our interest usually lies somewhere in between these two boundary
conditions; we need a measure of concentration.

Define $U_i = \frac{i}{n}$, to be the cumulative percentage of units up to the ith unit.

Define $C_i = \frac{x_1+x_2+\cdots+x_i}{n\bar{x}} = \frac{\sum_{j=1}^{i} x_j}{n\bar{x}}$, for $i = 1, \ldots, n$, to be the cumulative percentage
of the characteristic we are measuring for the same i units. We can intuitively see

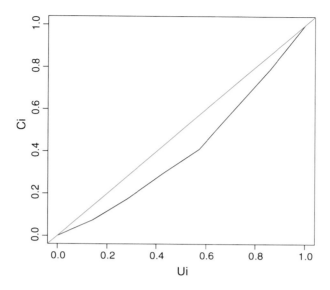

Fig. 6.10 Concentration curve

that U_i and C_i range in values as follows: $0 \le U_i \le 1$, $0 \le C_i \le 1$. In addition, for any given values of U_i and C_i, $U_i \le C_i$, and also that $U_n = C_n = 1$. When developing a graphical representation, we usually include the nonpoint $U_0 = C_0 = 0$ to give us an origin. We can then plot points of the form (U_i, C_i), $i = 0, \ldots, n$, to form the concentration curve.

Consider the example in the table below where we have nine concentrations (sic) of a compound along with the calculations for U_i and C_i, respectively.

Concentration	U_i	C_i
	0	0
13	1/7	13/175
18	2/7	31/175
21	3/7	52/175
24	4/7	76/175
29	5/7	105/175
33	6/7	138/175
37	1	1

Plotting this curve gives us the figure below, which also includes the 45° line (in red) that is the minimal concentration curve (Fig. 6.10).

We have already encountered one use of concentration – the Gini concentration index – elsewhere in this book, which is based on the differences between our measures: $(U_i - C_i)$. To conclude, we can identify several facts about concentration measures:

1. $(U_i - C_i) = 0$, $i = 1, 2, \ldots, n$ gives us **minimal concentration**.
2. $(U_i - C_i) = U_i$, $i = 1, 2, \ldots, n - 1$, and $U_n - C_n = 0$ gives us **maximum concentration**.

3. $0 < U_i - C_i < U_i$, $i = 1, 2, \ldots, n - 1$ with increasing differences as we approach maximum concentration.

We can use the above steps to define the concentration index as

$$R = \frac{\sum_{i=1}^{n-1} (U_i - C_i)}{\sum_{i=1}^{n-1} U_i} . \tag{6.5}$$

In this, we have the ratio of the quantity $\sum_{i=1}^{n-1} (U_i - C_i)$ and the maximum value $\sum_{i=1}^{n-1} U_i$. R is the Gini concentration coefficient and has a value of 0 for minimum concentration and 1 for maximum concentration. The data in the above table has a value of 0.163, indicating a relatively low level of concentration.

6.3.5 Asymmetry

Symmetric distributions will intuitively have a "balance" to them, most easily seen when graphed. This balance comes from the mean and median measures: if they are coincident, the distribution can be described as symmetric.

We can therefore use these same measures to determine whether or not a distribution is *asymmetric*, or skewed:

Mean > median	Positive asymmetry	(Skewed to the right)
Median < mean	Negative asymmetry	(Skewed to the left)

Figure 6.11 depicts negative asymmetry, symmetry, and positive asymmetry, respectively, with the mean highlighted in red and the median highlighted in blue.

Another technique we can use, which we have already described and will not repeat here, is the boxplot which uses the median value, the first quartile (25th percentile, lower quartile, or Q1) and the third quartile (75th percentile, higher quartile, upper quartile, or Q3), and the interquartile range (IQR). For a symmetric distribution, the median value is equidistant from Q1 and Q3, that is, $d(Q1, \text{median}) = d(Q3, \text{median})$.[13]

For asymmetric distributions,

---

[13] We are using our measure of distance, analogous to the measure we shall use in high-dimensional datasets later on when we consider machine-learning techniques. In this discussion, the distance is a simple difference since the data is one-dimensional, and we take the absolute value.

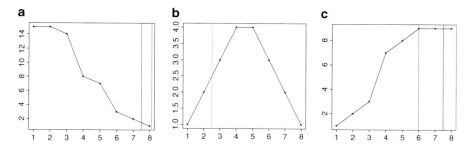

Fig. 6.11 Asymmetry and symmetry: (**a**) positive asymmetry (mean > median), (**b**) symmetry, and (**c**) negative asymmetry (mean < median)

$d(Q3, \text{median}) > d(Q1, \text{median})$	Positive asymmetry	(Skewed to the right)
$d(Q1, \text{median}) > d(Q3, \text{median})$	Negative asymmetry	(Skewed to the left)

We can determine a measure of asymmetry by using the third central moment of the distribution:

$$\mu_3 = \frac{\sum_{i=1}^{n} (x_i - \bar{x})^3}{N}.$$

We define the asymmetry index as

$$\gamma = \frac{\mu_3}{\sigma^3},$$

which, in turn, gives us

(a) $\gamma = 0$, symmetric distribution
(b) $\gamma < 0$, left asymmetric distribution
(c) $\gamma > 0$, right asymmetric distribution

This measure can only be calculated for quantitative data, but it can assume any value – so we do not need to normalize the data or prepare it in any special way.

This simple measure allows us to quickly begin gaining insight into our data.

6.3.6   Kurtosis

Kurtosis is the degree of peakedness of a distribution and is often used to identify where the variance is due to extreme deviations (higher values for kurtosis) as opposed to more frequent and more modestly sized deviations. Or, alternatively, a distribution with a high kurtosis value has a sharper peak and longer, fatter tails, while one with a low kurtosis value has a more rounded peak and shorter thinner tails. If our dataset has a high kurtosis value, it will tend to have a distinct peak near the mean, decline rather rapidly, and have heavy tails. Conversely, datasets with low kurtosis values tend to have a flat top near the mean rather than a sharp peak. Using this last explanation, we can see that a dataset conforming to the uniform distribution would be the extreme case.

As shown above, kurtosis is defined as

$$\gamma_2 = \frac{m_4}{\sigma^4} - 3 = \frac{\frac{\sum (y-\bar{y})^4}{n}}{\sigma^4} = \frac{1}{n}\sum \frac{(y-\bar{y})^4}{\sigma^4} - 3.$$

The normal distribution has $\gamma_2 = \frac{m_4}{\sigma^4} = 3$, and the "$-3$" value results in a value of zero for the normal distribution.

So why would we be interested in values for skewness and kurtosis? For many of the traditional statistical tests, an underlying assumption is that they conform to some semblance of normality. High values for skewness and kurtosis moments indicate that the data is not normal, and so we would be advised to consider our tests very carefully. Further, high values would recommend that we transform our data first, using something such as the Box-Cox transformation to try and make the data normal, or near to normal.

6.3.7 Same Means, Different Variances – Different Variances, Same Means

We now consider an application that is often encountered in the real world where we have two datasets that we are investigating. One of the first questions we are interested in answering is whether the two datasets have the same means or not, and whether they have the same variances or not. The answers to these questions allow us to leverage some very powerful techniques, or eliminate some of these techniques from our arsenal of tools.

The table below shows sets of blood glucose levels for 10 patients in 3 groups.

	Group A	Group B	Group C
1	72	111	96
2	75	106	91
3	85	106	97
4	79	69	72
5	90	68	97
6	82	66	88
7	90	65	101
8	89	67	91
9	87	66	76
10	83	108	71

If we calculate the means for each group, we find that groups A and B have the same mean values:

Mean	83.2	83.2	88
	Subtracting mean (differences)		
1	−11.2	27.8	8
2	−8.2	22.8	3
3	1.8	22.8	9
4	−4.2	−14.2	−16
5	6.8	−15.2	9
6	−1.2	−17.2	0
7	6.8	−18.2	13
8	5.8	−16.2	3
9	3.8	−17.2	−12
10	−0.2	24.8	−17
	Squares of differences		
1	125.44	772.84	64
2	67.24	519.84	9
3	3.24	519.84	81
4	17.64	201.64	256
5	46.24	231.04	81
6	1.44	295.84	0
7	46.24	331.24	169
8	33.64	262.44	9
9	14.44	295.84	144
10	0.04	615.04	289
Sum of squares	355.6	4045.6	1,102
Degrees of freedom	9	9	9

If we take the values in each group and subtract their respective mean values, to obtain three sets of differences, we can square and sum these values to obtain sums of squares for each group. As we have seen above, dividing the sum of squares by the degrees of freedom ($10 - 1 = 9$, since we have estimated one parameter, the mean, in calculating the sum of squares), we can calculate the variances:

Variance (SS/df)	39.51111	449.5111	122.4444
Numerator Denominator	A	B	C
A		11.37683	3.098988
B	0.087898		0.272395
C	0.322686	3.671143	
F-test: Numerator Denominator	A	B	C
A		0.001264	0.107324
B	0.001264		0.066059
C	0.107324	0.066059	

So, to summarize, groups A and B have the same mean, and groups B and C have the same variance.[14] Below is the code to generate the above information using R.

```
groupAbgl <- c( 72,  75,  85,79,90,82,  90,89,87,  83)
groupBbgl <- c(111,106,106,69,68,66,  65,67,66,108)
groupCbgl <- c( 96,  91,  97,72,97,88,101,91,76,  71)
groupAmean <- mean(groupAbgl)
groupBmean <- mean(groupBbgl)
groupCmean <- mean(groupCbgl)
groupAvar <- sum((groupAbgl-mean(groupAbgl))^2)
groupBvar <- sum((groupBbgl-mean(groupBbgl))^2)
groupCvar <- sum((groupCbgl-mean(groupCbgl))^2)
```

So are the different variances for groups A and B significant? An F-test can be calculated by dividing the larger variance by the smaller variance and obtaining the cumulative probability of the F-distribution. This latter value can be computed using the pf function in R, passing the variance ratio, degrees of freedom for the numerator of the ratio, and degrees of freedom of the denominator:

```
fTest <- 2*(1-pf(groupBvar/groupAvar,9,9))
```

which gives a value of 0.001263796. Since this value is significantly less than 5%, we conclude that there is a significant difference between these two variances.

```
var.test(groupAbgl, groupBbgl)
```

6.4   Frequency Distributions

Summarizing data by counting the number of times a particular attributes' value occurs is a natural way for us to analyze data. Such *frequency distributions* allow us to get a sense of the data quickly and easily. However, as is the case with any summarization, data is lost.

We have already considered the issue of the number of attributes in our instance set – the dimensions for our analysis – and considered how complexity increases as the number of attributes increases. Frequency distributions are a simple way of summarizing the data by the co-occurrence of their values. It is also a technique by which we can reduce the amount of data we are looking at. However, by its very nature, a frequency distribution leads to a loss of information.

To generate a frequency distribution for a univariate (single variable) distribution, we need to know the number of times that each particular value occurs in our dataset (its absolute frequency). The values, and their frequencies, directly produce the frequency distribution.

Consider again the acute lymphoblastic leukemia (ALL) dataset.

Figure 6.12 shows the default frequency distribution for the 128 data points in the ALL package using the following R function:

```
hist(ALL$age, main='Frequency Histogram for Age (ALL Dataset)')
```

---

[14] We are taking a small liberty by saying that the 0.333 difference is insignificant.

Fig. 6.12 Frequency
histogram

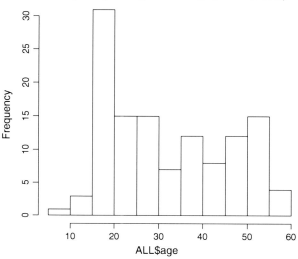

We can begin to make inferences about this dataset even from this very limited analysis: between the ages of 20 and 55, for example, the proportions of patients are between 5 and 15 for each category, whereas the numbers rapidly reduce on either end. We could therefore subset our data only to include those patients between 20 and 55, feeling comfortable that the relative frequencies will not significantly skew our results.

Multivariate frequency distributions provide a means for us to examine more than one variable at the same time. For example, we may be interested in looking at the combination of age and transplant as a joint distribution. We can develop a contingency table for the combination of variables we are interested in, where each variable creates a dimension in the contingency table. If we consider the two variables of age and transplant, the variables will generate a bivariate distribution and the contingency table will have two dimensions.

Consider the general bivariate case where our variables are X and Y, collected for N data points. If we were to generate a frequency distribution for X, we would have i categories of values for X, $x_1, \ldots, x_i$ and j categories for Y, $y_1, \ldots, y_j$. In our contingency table, we are interested in seeing what the total number of occurrences are for each pair of values (x_i, y_j), a value we represent as $n_{xy}(x_i, y_j)$. Thus, our table will comprise the pairs $\{(x_i, y_j), n_{xy}(x_i, y_j)\}$. $n_{xy}(x_i, y_j)$ is the absolute joint frequency for the pair of values (x_i, y_j) and is often simplified to the symbol n_{ij}. Our contingency table is depicted in Table 6.7.

Since $N = \sum_i \sum_j n_{xy}(x_i, y_j)$ is the total number of classified units in our distribution, $p_{xy}(x_i, y_j) = \frac{n_{xy}(x_i, y_j)}{N}$ gives us the relative joint frequencies. From the joint frequencies, we can get the univariate frequencies using

$$n_X(x_i) = \sum_j n_{xy}(x_i, y_j),$$

$$n_Y(y_j) = \sum_i n_{xy}(x_i, y_j).$$

Table 6.7 Bivariate contingency table

X\Y	y_1	$\cdots$	y_d	$\cdots$	y_j	
x_1	$n_{xy}(x_1, y_1)$	$\cdots$	$n_{xy}(x_1, y_d)$	$\cdots$	$n_{xy}(x_1, y_j)$	$n_x(x_1)$
$\vdots$	$\vdots$	$\vdots$	$\vdots$	$\vdots$	$\vdots$	
x_f	$n_{xy}(x_f, y_1)$	$\cdots$	$n_{xy}(x_f, y_d)$	$\cdots$	$n_{xy}(x_f, y_j)$	$n_x(x_f)$
$\vdots$	$\vdots$	$\vdots$	$\vdots$	$\vdots$	$\vdots$	
x_i	$n_{xy}(x_i, y_1)$	$\cdots$	$n_{xy}(x_i, y_d)$	$\cdots$	$n_{xy}(x_i, y_j)$	$n_x(x_i)$
	$n_y(y_1)$		$n_y(y_d)$		$n_y(y_j)$	N

Many software tools provide functions to directly generate joint and univariate frequencies, including R, SAS, and SPSS, to name a few.

6.5   Confidence Intervals

Consider a situation where we have a single statistic of some sort. If we were to use this as a *point estimate* for our population, what level of confidence would we have in its accuracy? For example, if we have the blood pressure measurement from one patient, what is our confidence in its use as the mean for our population? Intuitively, our level of confidence in its accuracy would be low, or nonexistent. Say that we now have a sample of patients and their associated blood pressures. Based on these figures, we might feel reasonably confident that the mean blood pressure is somewhere between 100/65 mmHg and 110/65 mmHg. Such a range of values is referred to as a *confidence interval*. If, however, our sample is smaller, we would have to increase our range of values to give us a comparable level of confidence. This naturally leads to the question of degree, or level, of confidence. We are typically interested in calculating the estimate at some *confidence level*. How we calculate this is the subject of this section. Since the methods we use are slightly different depending on the type of data, we shall consider continuous data and categorical data separately.

6.5.1   Continuous Data Confidence Levels

By far and away the most common statistic used for population estimation in continuous data is the mean, a statistic that we have already defined earlier in this chapter. In order for us to calculate a confidence interval, we begin by calculating the mean and then the range above and below the mean (the confidence interval) that we are looking for based on our desired level of confidence. In addition to the level of confidence, our range will also depend on the standard error of the mean. We will begin by discussing the process for a sample that contains 30 or more

Fig. 6.13 Normal
distribution with 95%
confidence interval

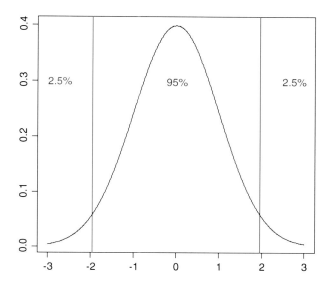

observations, typically referred to as a large sample. The calculation of our range is
given by the following equation:

$$\bar{x} \pm z_c \frac{s}{\sqrt{n}}.$$

In the above equation, $\bar{x}$ is our sample mean and $\frac{s}{\sqrt{n}}$ is our standard error of the
mean, where s is the standard deviation of the sample and n is the number of
observations in the sample. This provides one of the two dependencies for the
confidence interval, namely the standard error of the mean, and gives a static range
based upon a particular sample. z_c *z-score* gives us the variability based upon the
level of confidence we wish to use. Common confidence levels are 90%, 95%, and
99%, and the *z-score* is calculated by looking at the area under the normal
distribution curve at the specified confidence level. This is illustrated in Fig. 6.13
for a 95% confidence interval.

```
nd <- seq(-3, 3, 0.01)
y <- dnorm(nd)
plot(nd, y, type="l", xlab="", ylab="")
cl95 <- qnorm(c(0.025, 0.975))
abline(v=cl95[1], col="blue")
abline(v=cl95[2], col="blue")
text(0,0.3,"95%", col="blue")
```

In R, the function qnorm(c(0.025, 0.975)) gives us the quartiles for the
normal distribution, in this case for 95%, and we have drawn these on the graph,
their values for the particular example distribution used above are −1.959964 and
1.959964. This means that we would expect to see values falling between these

Fig. 6.14 Common
confidence intervals

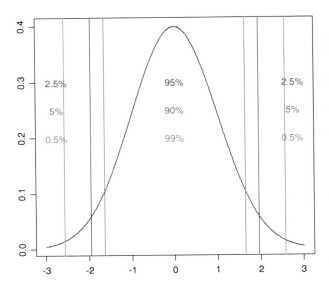

values 95% of the time. Figure 6.14 illustrates the three most common confidence
intervals encountered in practice.

```
nd <- seq(-3, 3, 0.01)
y <- dnorm(nd)
plot(nd, y, type="l", xlab="", ylab="")

cl90 <- qnorm(c(0.05, 0.95))
cl95 <- qnorm(c(0.025, 0.975))
cl99 <- qnorm(c(0.005, 0.995))

abline(v=cl95[1], col="blue")
abline(v=cl95[2], col="blue")
text( 0   ,0.3,"95%", col="blue")
text(-2.75,0.3,"2.5%", col="blue")
text( 2.75,0.3,"2.5%", col="blue")

abline(v=cl90[1], col="red")
abline(v=cl90[2], col="red")
text( 0   ,0.25,"90%", col="red")
text(-2.75,0.25,"5%", col="red")
text( 2.75,0.25,"5%", col="red")

abline(v=cl99[1], col="green")
abline(v=cl99[2], col="green")
text( 0   ,0.2,"99%", col="green")
text(-2.75,0.2,"0.5%", col="green")
text( 2.75,0.2,"0.5%", col="green")
```

We are often interested in looking at particular data elements and asking questions
such as "is this randomly selected instance less than X," or "is this randomly selected

instance greater than Y," or even "does this randomly selected value lie between X and Y"? We shall use these examples to discuss the specifics of z-scores.

Consider the following (made-up) weight dataset:

```
weight <- seq(110, 185, 0.01)
plot(weight, dnorm(weight, mean(weight),
    sd(weight)), type="l", xlab="Weight", ylab="Density")
```

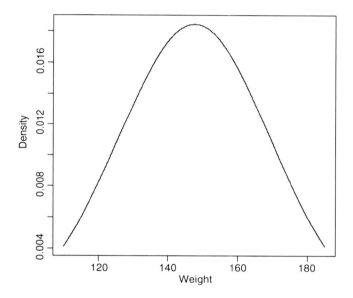

Consider a particular value, say 170 kg; we are interested in knowing what the probability is that a randomly selected person from our dataset will weigh less than 170 kg. In order to do this, we need to convert our weight into a z value. That is, the number of standard deviations from the mean.

The area under a normal curve is exactly 1, since the tails extend to infinity in both directions, which is not particularly useful to us. However, we know that the standard normal distribution has a mean of 0 and standard deviation of 1. Using this information, we can convert any value from a distribution $N(\bar{x}, s)$ to $N(0, 1)$ by using

$$z = \frac{(y - \bar{y})}{s}.$$

Our weight dataset has a mean of 147.5 and a standard deviation of 21.65497. Using our 170-kg example, we can calculate the z value as follows:

$$z = \frac{(170 - 147.5)}{21.65497} = 1.039022.$$

Now, we simply find $P(X \leq 1.039022)$, the probability of a value in the standard Normal distribution having a value less than or equal to 1.039022. We will use the R function `pnorm(1.039022)` to give us the value 0.8506027, or just over 85%.

Returning to our *z-score* equation $\bar{x} \pm z_c \frac{s}{\sqrt{n}}$, if we have a distribution with a mean of 147.5 and a standard deviation of 21.65497, with 75 observations, and we are interested in a 95% confidence interval (where `qnorm(c(0.025, 0.975))` gives us ± 1.96), we calculate

$$\bar{x} \pm z_c \frac{s}{\sqrt{n}},$$

$$147.5 \pm 1.96 \frac{21.65497}{\sqrt{75}},$$

$$147.5 \pm 4.9.$$

Thus, at a 95% confidence level, the weights will range between 2.6 and 152.4. We will briefly introduce the concept of linear models at this point.

6.6   Regression Analysis

Regression analysis using linear models is a technique very commonly used for predicting numerical data, and logistic regression is commonly used to perform linear classification. We now introduce these techniques and describe how and where they can help us in mining our dataset.

The core concept orbits around modeling the class of the data as a linear combination of the attributes in our instances, using a set of *weight* values as:

$$c = a_0 + a_1 x_1 + a_2 x_2 + \ldots + a_n x_n, \tag{6.6}$$

where $\mathbf{x} = (x_1, \ldots, x_n)$ denotes our data-instance attributes, and the $a_0, a_1, \ldots, a_n$ denote the weights. c is our class.

We generate the weights using training data, just as we do for many other techniques. Taking the first training instance, $\mathbf{x}_1 = (x_{11}, x_{12}, \ldots, x_{1n})$, and using Eq. 6.6, we would create the predicted value as

$$a_0 x_{1,0} + a_1 x_{1,1} + \ldots + a_n x_{1,n} = \sum_{j=1}^{n} a_j x_{1,j}, \tag{6.7}$$

where $x_{1,j}$ denotes the *j*th attribute in (training) instance 1.

It is important to note that this value is the *predicted* value for this training instance, not the actual value and, as we have discussed elsewhere, we are interested in the difference between the predicted and actual values. We discuss this topic elsewhere in this book and so will not duplicate that discussion here. Instead, we will simply consider the sum of squares of the differences between the actual value (which is denoted by x_i) and the predicted value generated in (6.7), to give

$$\sum_{i=1}^{t} \left(x_i - \sum_{j=1}^{n} a_j x_{i,j} \right)^2 .$$

We discuss linear regression in more detail in the following section, but prior to that, we note that while this is a very powerful technique and has been used in statistical analysis for many years, it does depend on the underlying data having a linear relationship: if a straight line is not a good estimate of the data, this model will not provide a good interpretation of the data.

6.6.1 Linear Regression

As its name suggests, our intent is to model the relationship between two variables using a linear relationship between the observed data. We often use the term *explanatory* variable to refer to one of the variables, X, and *response* (or sometime dependent) variable to refer to the other variable, Y.

An obvious first step is to determine whether or not there is a relationship between the variables at all. That is, is there any *significant association* between the variables? This association does not imply a *causal* association, but simply any association. We can use any number of simple techniques to determine this: one such technique, the scatterplot, see Chap. 2, provides a valuable graphical technique that also provides us with a measure of the *strength* of the relationship. For a more formal measure of the association, we can determine the *correlation coefficient* between the variables (see below).

Given our two variables X, Y, the equation for a linear regression line is

$$Y = a + bX, \tag{6.8}$$

where X, Y, are the explanatory and dependent variables, respectively, b is the gradient of the line and a is the *y-intercept* (the value of y when $x = 0$).

We consider a dataset of height and weight data for a group of individuals, as shown below.

Height	Weight
62	112
62	121
64	129
65	132
67	147

(continued)

69	154
71	166
71	183
71	178
72	190
72	201
72	219
72	223
73	219
73	227
73	235
74	230
74	243
75	265
76	285

```
csvFileName <- "c:/data/HeightWeight.csv"
hw <- read.csv(csvFileName, header = TRUE, sep = ",")
names(hw)[1] <- "weight"
names(hw)[2] <- "height"
```

As we mentioned above, a useful technique is to use a scatterplot to summarize a set of two variables prior to calculating the correlation coefficient or fitting a regression line to the data. We digress to describe this valuable technique.

6.6.1.1   Scatterplot

As we described in Chap. 4, a scatterplot is a very valuable graphical representation of the relationship, I one exists, between two variables, based on ratio or interval scales. We plot one of the variables – the explanatory variable – on the x-axis, and the other – the response variable – on the y-axis. Each point on the scatterplot will be a single instance, or observation, from our dataset. Almost every data-mining or data-analysis tools will have built-in functionality to create a scatterplot quickly and easily. In our discussions below, we will use functionality available within the graphics package of the R data analysis environment. The value that the visual representation provides will help us with our interpretation of the correlation coefficient or regression model.

We continue to use our explanatory/dependent (or explanatory/response) terminology and say that there is a *positive association* between the two variables if our scatterplot depicts a positive slope, or upward trend, between the variables. That is, an increase in the value of our explanatory variable shows an increase in our dependent, or response variable. Similarly, a *negative association* is where the scatterplot has a negative slope, or downward trend: increasing values of our explanatory variable show decreasing values for the dependent variable.

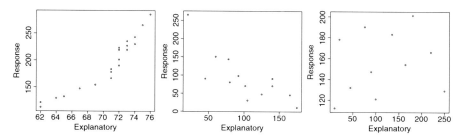

Fig. 6.15 Positive, negative, and no associations

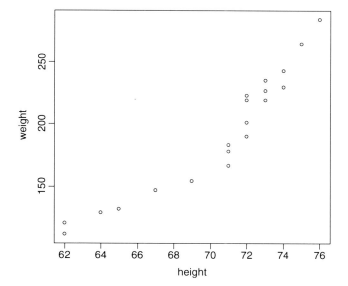

Fig. 6.16 Weight and height scatterplot

However, we should be prepared for our scatterplot to show no discernable pattern at all, in which case we have *no association* between the two variables. Examples of these three cases are shown in Fig. 6.15.

We now return to the linear regression discussion on our dataset.

If we plot the complete dataset (see Fig. 6.16), we can see that there is a relationship between the two variables. Our R data frame HeightWeight can be plotted using the command

```
plot(HeightWeight)
```

Now we can plot the regression line on top of this. If we begin by eyeballing the line, we can deduce some of its characteristics. First, it will intuitively go from the bottom left corner to the top right. Since the two values, a and b, the intercept and the slope, completely define the line, we can guesstimate what they should be. Recall that a is the value when $x = 0$. Visually inspecting the data tells us to expect a negative value for a since any value of $a \geq 0$ will not be able to provide a good representation of the relationship for the variables of our dataset. Since the data values for our explanatory variable (height) generally increase, we would expect $b > 0$. Taking this a step further, we can see that the y value, our response variable, ranged from a value from 112 to 285, so the change in y, denoted as δy ("delta y") is +173. Similarly, the value of x, our explanatory variable, ranged from a value of 62 to 76, so $\delta x = 14$. We already guessed that the value of y when $x = 0$ is a negative value, but cannot really visually inspect it for a value since a person of zero height would not exist. However, we can use the other data to tell us that the slope is $\frac{\delta y}{\delta x} = \frac{173}{14} = 12.36$.

In R, we have a simple way of determining these values using the linear model function lm:

```
lm(HeightWeight$weight ~ HeightWeight$height)
```

which provides the following output:

```
> lm(HeightWeight$weight ~ HeightWeight$height)
Call:
lm(formula = HeightWeight$weight ~ HeightWeight$height)
Coefficients:
      (Intercept)  HeightWeight$height
        -590.62         11.13
```

This gives us an equation for our line of $y = -590.62 + 11.13x$. Note that our y-intercept is indeed a negative value and our slope is 11.13, not too far away from our visual guesstimate of 12.36. To plot this on top of our scatterplot, we can use the abline function in R (Fig. 6.17):

```
abline(lm(HeightWeight$weight ~ HeightWeight$height))
```

6.6.1.2 Least-Squares Regression

This is probably the most common regression method used to fit a regression line to data. It calculates the line which best fits the data by minimizing the squares of the *vertical deviations* from each data point to the line. If a point lies on the line, its vertical deviation is 0.

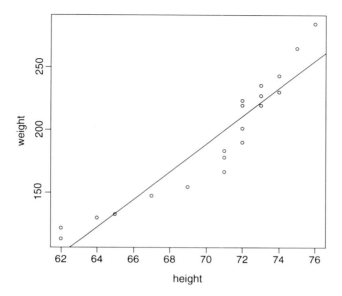

Fig. 6.17 Weight and height scatterplot with regression line

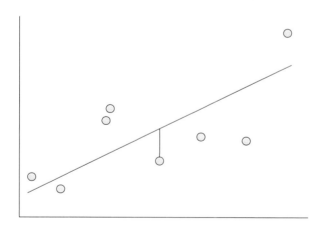

Since we take the deviations, square them, and then sum them, positive and negative deviations, arising from data points on opposite sides of the line, are not canceled out.

Consider our example dataset of height and weight data. Intuitively, we would expect taller people to be, on average, heaver than shorter people, but does our dataset bear this hypothesis out?

We are trying to find the straight line that gives us the best fit for our data. In the least-squares estimate, we rotate the line until the error sum of the squares, SSE, is at its minimum value. Using our equation for the line, we are looking for the minimum of $\sum (y - a - bx)^2$. We do this by taking the derivative of the SSE with respect to b, then setting the derivative to zero, substituting for a and applying some algebra, as shown in the box below.

$$\frac{dSSE}{db} = -2 \sum x(y - a - bx)$$

$$= -2 \sum xy - ax - bx^2.$$

Setting the derivative to zero and dividing by -2,

$$\sum xy - \sum ax - \sum bx^2 = 0.$$

$a = y = bx$ and $\sum ax$ can be written as $a \sum x$, so our equation becomes $\sum xy - \left[\frac{\sum y}{n} - b \frac{\sum x}{n} \right] \sum x - b \sum x^2 = 0$ (where we have moved all constants outside the summations),

$$\sum xy - \frac{\sum x \sum y}{n} - b \frac{(\sum x)^2}{n} - b \sum x^2 = 0,$$

$$\sum xy - \frac{\sum x \sum y}{n} = b \sum x^2 - b \frac{(\sum x)^2}{n},$$

$$b = \frac{\sum xy - \frac{\sum x \sum y}{n}}{\sum x^2 - \frac{(\sum x)^2}{n}}.$$

Thus, the value which minimizes SSE is the sum of the square of xy divided by the sum of squares of x. This is formally referred to as the *maximum likelihood estimate* of b (the slope) of the linear regression.

Referring back to Fig. 6.17, we can see that the line does tend to follow the data, but very few of the data points lie on the line itself. We recall that the least-squares method considers the *vertical deviations* between the line and the data points. This value is called a *residual* and we can see from our scatterplot that some are positive values (i.e., the data point is above the line) and some are negative (the data point is below the line).

Since the residuals provide us with a measure of the goodness-of-fit of the line to the data,

6.6.2   Correlation Coefficient

We can see from our scatterplot that there is a general association, but we cannot intuitively see how strong an association exists. The *correlation coefficient* provides a numerical method for determining the strength of the linear association between the variables.

Consider a set of instances given by $(x_1, y_1), \ldots, (x_n, y_n)$ for two variables $\mathbf{X}, \mathbf{Y}$. The correlation coefficient is defined as

$$r = \frac{1}{n-1} \sum \left(\frac{X - \bar{X}}{S_x} \right) \left(\frac{Y - \bar{Y}}{s_y} \right). \tag{6.9}$$

The range of values for r is $-1 \leq r \leq 1$, where ± 1 indicates a perfect correlation. In this case, all of the points would lie on a straight line. $r > 0$ indicates a positive correlation between the variables and means that an increase in the value of one of the variables corresponds to an increasing value in the other variable. Likewise, $r < 0$ indicates a negative correlation, with an increasing value in one variable corresponding to a decreasing value in the other variable. $r = 0$ indicates that there is no correlation between the variables.

One of the advantages of determining the value of r over the scatterplot is that the correlation coefficient formula standardizes the variables so that changes in the scale or units of measurement have no effect on its value.

When applied to linear regression, we typically use r^2, since this value represents the fraction of the variation in one variable that can be explained by the other variable. For example, if $r = 0.8$ is observed between two variables – such as what might be seen when examining height and weight data – a linear regression model that attempts to explain either of the variables in terms of the other would account for 64% $\left(r^2 = 0.8^2 = 0.64 \right)$ of the variability of the data.

The correlation coefficient also has a direct relationship to (6.8) in that $b = r \frac{S_y}{S_x}$. As we shall also see, in least-squares regression, the regression line will always pass through the means of $\mathbf{X}, \mathbf{Y}$, and thus the regression line may be specified by the means, standard deviations, and correlation of the two variables under consideration.

6.6.3   Multiple Linear Regression

In our above discussions, we have considered the case of a single explanatory variable, but in reality, we will typically need to deal with multiple explanatory variables. Consider a situation where we have a dataset containing instances of the form $(x_{i1}, x_{i2}, \ldots, x_{ik}, y_i)$, where the x_{ij} are explanatory variables and y_i is the response variable. In this case, multiple linear regression is defined by

$$y_i = a + b_1 x_{i1} + b_2 x_{i2} + \ldots + b_k x_{ik} + e_i, \tag{6.10}$$

where the x_{ij} are as defined above, a, b_i, e_i are constants. The above equation can also be written as

$$\mathbf{Y} = \mathbf{X}b + \mathbf{E}.$$

In the simple regression case, the regression model itself was represented by a straight line. In the multivariate case, it corresponds to a $k + 1$-dimensional plane. The b_i are model parameters that were estimated based on the data, and e_i are error terms.

To determine the regression plane, as we have said, we need to estimate the parameters using our available data. We can once again use the least-squares approach and obtain a solution analogously to the bivariate case, only in the multivariate case, the solution is given by

$$\hat{\mathbf{Y}} = \mathbf{X}\beta.$$

6.7   Maximum Likelihood Estimation Method

The maximum likelihood estimation method is one of the most important estimation methods available and is widely used in data analysis and data mining. Typically, we *estimate* the parameters for our probabilistic model by using a set of examples that we can trust will give us accurate parameter values. This set of examples is referred to as the *training dataset*. We might, for example, look at the distribution of amino acids by considering their relative frequencies by looking at a repository such as the protein data bank, which, at the time of writing, contains over 43,000 complete structures. We can reasonably expect the relative frequencies of the amino acids we get from a source such as the PDB to be reasonably accurate estimates of the relative frequencies for parameters in our underlying model. This approach to estimating is known as *maximum likelihood estimation* because using the frequencies we obtain from the database maximizes the total probability of all the sequences given the model. Generally, we say given a model with parameters θ, and a dataset D, the maximum likelihood estimate for θ is the value that maximizes $P(D|\theta)$. As we have discussed earlier, if the dataset we use for training is small, there is a very real danger of overfitting the model.

Such methods begin by considering the likelihood of a model. This will typically be a joint density distribution of a random variable $\mathbf{X}$ which we express as a function of the (set of) unknown parameters θ. That is, $\mathbf{X}$ has the probability density function (pdf) $p(\mathbf{x}; \theta_1, \ldots, \theta_k) = p(\mathbf{x}; \theta) = \prod_{i=1}^{n} p(x_i; \theta)$, in the discrete case, or

$f(\mathbf{x}; \theta_1, \ldots, \theta_k) = f(\mathbf{x}; \theta) = \prod_{i=1}^{n} f(x_i; \theta)$, in the continuous case. In either case,

$\theta_1, \ldots, \theta_k$ are the parameters which we need to estimate. Henceforth, we consider the continuous case without loss of generality.

The process we pursue is to design an experiment and obtain n independent observations $x_1, \ldots, x_n$ and generate the likelihood function:

$$L(x_1, \ldots, x_n | \theta_1, \ldots, \theta_k) = L = \prod_{i=1}^{n} f(x_i; \theta_1, \ldots, \theta_k), \quad i = 1, \ldots, n, \qquad (6.11)$$

with the logarithmic likelihood function given by

$$\Lambda = \ln L = \sum_{i=1}^{n} \ln f(x_i; \theta_1, \ldots, \theta_k). \qquad (6.12)$$

The maximum likelihood estimators (MLEs) of $\theta_1, \ldots, \theta_k$ are obtained by maximizing L or Λ. Λ is much simpler to work with than L. If we maximize Λ, the MLEs of $\theta_1, \ldots, \theta_k$ are the simultaneous solutions of the k equations:

$$\frac{\partial(\Lambda)}{\partial \theta_j} = 0, \quad j = 1, \ldots, k. \qquad (6.13)$$

It is a fairly common practice to plot the MLE solution using median ranks.[15] However, doing this is not totally accurate. Consider Eq. 6.13: we can see that the MLE method is independent of both any kind of rank and also any form of plotting method. This being said, we often find that the MLE solution does not correlate to the data in any probability plot we generate. This should not be a problem since the two methods are independent, but we must be careful not to discount the MLE solution because they are different.

6.7.1 Illustration of the MLE Method

Consider the problem of calculating MLE estimates for the mean $\bar{X}$ and the standard deviation $\hat{\sigma}_X$ for a population known to have the normal distribution. The pdf for the normal distribution is

$$f(X) = \frac{1}{\sigma_X \sqrt{2\pi}} e^{-\frac{1}{2} \left(\frac{x-x}{\sigma_X} \right)^2}.$$

If $x_1, \ldots, x_n$ are known {variable_type}, then the likelihood function is given by

---

[15] In fact, the most common practice is to plot points according to the median ranks and plot the lines according to MLE solutions.

$$L(x_1, \ldots, x_n | \bar{X}, \sigma_X) = \prod_{i=1}^{n} \left[\frac{1}{\sigma_X \sqrt{2\pi}} e^{-\frac{1}{2} \left(\frac{x_i - \bar{x}}{\sigma_X} \right)} \right]$$

$$= \frac{1}{\left(\sigma_X \sqrt{2\pi} \right)^n} e^{-\frac{1}{2} \sum_{i=1}^{n} \left(\frac{x_i - \bar{x}}{\sigma_X} \right)},$$

$$\Lambda = \ln L = -\frac{n}{2} \ln(2\pi) - n \ln \sigma_X - \frac{1}{2} \sum_{i=1}^{n} \left(\frac{X_i - \bar{X}}{\sigma_X} \right)^2.$$

Taking partial derivates of Λ with respect to each parameter, and setting these equal to zero gives

$$\frac{\partial(\Lambda)}{\partial \bar{X}} = \frac{1}{\sigma_X^2} \sum_{i=1}^{n} (X_i - \bar{X}) = 0 \qquad (6.14)$$

and

$$\frac{\partial(\Lambda)}{\partial \sigma_X} = -\frac{n}{\sigma_X} + \frac{1}{\sigma_X^3} \sum_{i=1}^{n} (X_i - \bar{X})^2 = 0. \qquad (6.15)$$

Solving (6.14) and (6.15) simultaneously gives

$$\bar{X} = \frac{1}{n} \sum_{i=1}^{n} X_i \qquad (6.16)$$

and

$$\hat{\sigma}_X^2 = \frac{1}{n} \sum_{i=1}^{n} (X_i - \bar{X})^2,$$

$$\hat{\sigma}_X = \sqrt{\frac{1}{n} \sum_{i=1}^{n} (X_i - \bar{X})^2}. \qquad (6.17)$$

6.7.2 Use in Data Mining

As we can see from the discussion above, the MLE method takes the statistics which make the observed data most likely under the assumed statistical model.

Although they have many positive characteristics, one common use is to derive confidence intervals for the data. To do this, we typically assume that a large sample is available – which is typically the case with the large datasets we deal with when mining the data – and then consider that the maximum likelihood estimator is (approximately) distributed as a normal distribution. The estimator can then be simply used to derive an *asymptotic confidence interval*.[16]

Consider an example where we have a maximum likelihood estimator E. Let Var (E) be its asymptotic variance. A $100(1 - \zeta)\%$ confidence interval is given by

$$\left(E - z_{\left(1 - \frac{\zeta}{2}\right)} \sqrt{Var(E)}, E + z_{\left(1 - \frac{\zeta}{2}\right)} \sqrt{Var(E)} \right),$$

where $z_{\left(1 - \frac{\zeta}{2}\right)}$ is the $100(1 - \frac{\zeta}{2})$ percentile of the standardized normal distribution where $p(X \le z_{\left(1 - \frac{\zeta}{2}\right)}) = \left(1 - \frac{\zeta}{2}\right)$. $(1 - \zeta)$ is also known as the confidence level of the interval since it gives the confidence that the procedure is correct. That is, that $100(1 - \frac{\zeta}{2})\%$ of the time, the unknown quantity will fall within the chosen interval.

Consider, again, the normal distribution. The estimator for μ is the sample mean, given by $\bar{X} = \frac{1}{n} \sum_{i=1}^{n} X_i$. Thus, assuming that we known the variance σ^2, a confidence interval for the mean is given by

$$\left(\bar{X} - z_{\left(1 - \frac{\zeta}{2}\right)} \sqrt{Var(\bar{X})}, \bar{X} + z_{\left(1 - \frac{\zeta}{2}\right)} \sqrt{Var(\bar{X})} \right), \quad \text{where} \quad Var(\bar{X}) = \frac{\sigma^2}{n}. \quad (6.18)$$

If we *know* the distribution is normal, the confidence interval of (6.18) holds for a sample of any size. This is a very valuable result for data mining because we can begin with a smaller sample and have a relatively high level of confidence that this will correlate to the full dataset size. It is very common to target a 95% confidence interval. For a normal distribution, this leads to $z_{\left(1 - \frac{\zeta}{2}\right)} = 1.96$.

6.8 Maximum A Posteriori (MAP) Estimation

An alternative method to MLE is the maximum *a posteriori* (MAP) estimation. Here, we are interested in choosing parameter values for θ that maximize $P(\theta|D)$ (the opposite of MLE, which attempts to maximize $P(D|\theta)$). However, there is a relationship between MLE and MAP, as we shall see in a moment.

We use Bayes' theorem in the form

---

[16] Asymptotic here relates in the intuitive sense to being valid for large samples.

$$P(\theta|D) = \frac{P(\theta)P(D|\theta)}{\int_{\theta'} P(\theta')P(D|\theta')},$$

to allow us to estimate parameters.[17] In the above equation, the denominator is independent of any particular value of θ, and so the maximum value is independent of it. Thus, MAP estimation essentially corresponds to maximizing the likelihood ($P(D|\theta)$) times the prior ($P(\theta)$). If the prior is flat, then MAP estimation is the same as MLE.

6.9   Enrichment Analysis

Historically, gene products have been typically studied individually, with function and roles in biological processes similarly assigned to each product in (some) isolation. Today, much of this analysis is automated, which allows investigators to look at a broader context. A widely used hypothesis is that genes showing similar experimental profiles share biological mechanisms that if understood could provide clues to the molecular processes leading to pathological events.

Centralized repositories such as the Gene Ontology (GO) database, discussed elsewhere in this text, allow us to provide prior knowledge to investigators about the genes that they are researching, assigning attributes to groups of genes as such information becomes available from experiments of data-analysis efforts. This means that we could investigate a set of genes with some common starting point such as a set of genes that were clustered together from an expression analysis experiment, a set of genes bound by the same transcription factor, or even some set of genes for which the investigators have some prior knowledge.

Given this starting point, we can now concentrate on assigning biological meaning to some group of genes: looking for larger patterns that may exist within the group and assessing whether or not some subset of this group shows a significant overrepresentation of some biological characteristic. This method, *enrichment analysis* (EA), is popular in high-throughput genomics experiments, seeks to infer if a collection of genes that we are interested in is "enriched" for a particular set of GO classes, where each of the classes is assumed independent for the purposes of statistical testing. Since genes may be annotated for more than one biological classification, the resulting test statistics may be dependent if the overlapping gene sets are large.

Gene set enrichment analysis (GSEA) further takes into account the magnitude of expression differences between conditions for each gene, thus allowing us a means of determining how significant the differences between individual conditions

---

[17] The denominator is an integral as opposed to a sum since our parameters are typically continuous.

really are. In this method, there is a reliance on approximately 1,300 predetermined gene sets from repositories such as GO and other pathway repositories. Computational studies are stored in MSigDB.[18] The MSigDB gene sets are divided into five major collections:

- C1 **positional gene sets** for each human chromosome and each Cytogenic band.
- C2 **curated gene sets** from online pathway databases, publications in PubMed, and knowledge of domain experts.
- C3 **motif gene sets** based on conserved *cis*-regulatory motifs from a comparative analysis of human, mouse, rat, and dog genomes.
- C4 **computational gene sets** defined by expression neighborhoods centered on 380 cancer-associated genes.
- C5 *GO* **gene sets** consist of genes annotated by the same GO terms.

GSEA tests for the enrichment of some group S among N background genes. An expression measure of all the genes is used to assess the correlation of each with regard to some phenotype C, assigned to each sample. Genes are then ranked based on this correlation to calculate the enrichment score $ES(S)$.

Given a set D of expression data for N genes and k samples, we use a ranking procedure to produce a gene list $L = \{g_1, \ldots, g_N\}$. This includes a ranking metric such as a correlation metric $r(g_j) = r_j$ and the expression profiles of the phenotype, or profile of interest, C, such as a "sick versus healthy" metric, as might be appropriate in the 2-category case. We also use an exponent p to control the weight of the step as well as an independently derived gene set S of N_H genes of some set taken from a repository such as MSigDB.

The GSEA evaluates the function of genes $g_j \in S$ ("hits") weighted by their correlation and the function of genes $g_j \notin S$ ("misses") that are present up for some position i in L:

$$P_{hit}(S, i) = \sum_{g_j \in S, j \leq i} \frac{|r_j|^p}{N_R}, \quad N_R = \sum_{g_j \in S} |r_j|^p,$$

$$P_{miss}(S, i) = \sum_{g_j \notin S, j \leq i} \frac{1}{N - N_H},$$

$$ES(S) = \max_i |P_{hit}(S, i) - P_{miss}(S, i)|.$$

$ES(S)$ is the maximum deviation from zero that depends on both the weight of the correlations and the positions of the genes in S relative to all the genes in L. Setting $p = 0$ reduces the expression to the Kolmogorov-Smirnov statistic, while setting

---

[18] http://www.broadinstitute.org/gsea/msigdb/index.jsp

$p = 1$ causes the score to weigh genes in S by their correlation in C normalized by the sum over all the correlations in S.

A set of scores, ES_{null}, are computed by permuting phenotypes by taking the original phenotype labels and assigning them randomly to the k samples. The genes are then sorted based on their correlations to these labels, and $ES(S)$ is then recomputed. This permutation step is repeated many times (say, 1,000) to construct a histogram of the enrichment scores. The observed $ES(S)$ values are compared to ES_{null}.

Since the distribution behaves differently on the positive and negative sides, the p value for S is estimated for ES_{null} using the portion of the distribution that corresponds to the sign of the observed $ES(S)$.

We'll use multiple-testing correction, described earlier, for the cases where we are considering many gene sets. In this scenario, the sets are normalized for size and significance, as described above, and then we calculate a false discover rate (FDR) – see next section – for each normalized score so that we can estimate the probability of a given score resulting from a false positive.

Given $ES(S)$ for each gene set,

1. For each S and each permutation π (out of the 1,000 computed above) of the phenotype labels, reorder the genes in L and determine $ES(S, \pi)$.
2. Adjust for variation in the gene set size. Normalize $ES(S, \pi)$ and $ES(S)$, separately rescaling the positive and negative scored, by dividing by the mean of $ES(S, \pi)$ to yield normalized score $NES(S, \pi)$ and $NES(S)$.
3. Compute the FDR and use this to control the ratio of false positives to the total number of gene sets by separately fixing the levels of significance for positive and negative $NES(S, \pi)$ and $NES(S)$. Create a histogram for all $NES(S, \pi)$ overall S, π, and use this null distribution to compute an FDR q-value for a given $NES(S) = \alpha \geq 0$:

$$q = \frac{|\{(S, \pi)|NES(S, \pi) \geq \alpha\}|/|\{(S, \pi)|NEW(S, \pi) \geq 0\}|}{|\{S|NES(S) \geq \alpha\}|/|\{S|NES(S) \geq 0\}|}.$$

Subramanian et al. (2005 #820) used GSEA as a method for reanalyzing results from two existing lung cancer studies, the datasets for which are referred to as "Boston" and "Michigan," both of which consisted of gene-expression profiles in tumor samples from patients with lung adenocarcinomas ($n = 62$ for Boston; $n = 86$ for Michigan). Each expression profile was classified as either "good" or "poor" outcomes. One of the conclusions was that there was very little overlap between the top 100 genes most correlated to the outcomes in each study (12 genes in common; barely statistically significant with a permutation test ($P = 0.012$)), and no genes significantly associated with a significance level of 0.05 (after multiple-testing correction). Using the GSEA method on the same data, it was found that there were 8 genes (Boston) and 11 genes (Michigan) that were significantly correlated to poor outcome (FDR ≤ 0.25). The analysis showed some of the disadvantages of the single-gene analysis approach but also showed value in the enriched gene sets: approximately 50% of the gene sets were shared between the two studies, as well as several nonidentical sets that related to the same processes, such as up-regulation by telomerase, and two different insulin-related sets.

Scanfeld (2006 #821) also used GSEA, with motif discovery software and ChIP-chip measures to predict gene sets targeted by a specific transcription factor. Among the results were some expected, such as Nanog, since the ChIP-chip screened for targets of Nanog, but there were also surprises: GSEA also highlighted genes that also belonged to the larger breast cancer gene set, as genes up-regulated in BRCA1 tumors. So this yielded a result that has implications for potential future therapies. Yang (2011 #822) also described the use of GSEA in a genome-wide association study (GWAS). Chagoyen and Pazos (2011 #823) described the Metabolite Biological Role (MBRole), a web server for carrying out overrepresentation analysis of biological and chemical annotations in arbitrary sets of metabolites (small chemical compounds) coming from metabolomic data of any organism or sample.

Although we've highlighted GSEA in this section, it is not the only EA algorithm. TANGO – Tool for Analysis of GO Classes – tests for significance by assuming that the genes in our gene set are sampled from a hypergeometric distribution, for example.

In addition, there are a number of online tools that can support EA, such as the NIAID Database for Annotation, Visualization, and Integrated Discovery (DAVID) Bioinformatics Resources,[19] the Broad Institute's GSEA site.[20]

Since we have used R packages for illustration elsewhere, we want to highlight the BioConductor and topGO[21] R packages.

6.10   False Discover Rate (FDR)

False positives are a fact of life, and occur when you get a significant difference when, in reality, none exists. Recall that the p value is the chance that this data could occur given no difference actually exists. So, choosing a cutoff of 0.05 means there is a 5% chance that we make the wrong decision. While 5% may be acceptable for one test, if we conduct many tests on the data, 5% can result in a large number of false positives. For example, if there are 200 spots on a gel and we apply an ANOVA, t test, or some other test statistic to each spot, then we would expect to get 10 false positives by chance alone. This is generally known as the multiple-testing problem.

---

[19] http://david.abcc.ncifcrf.gov/

[20] http://www.broadinstitute.org/gsea/index.jsp

[21] The paper at http://rss.acs.unt.edu/Rdoc/library/topGO/doc/topGO.pdf provides a complete gene set enrichment analysis walkthrough.

Some of our efforts will be focused on trying to control the false positives we encounter. Methods such as the Bonferroni method try and control the change of any false positive occurring, but another approach – *false discovery rate* (FDR) – attempts to control the expected proportion of false positives that occur. This threshold is determined from the observed p value distribution, which means it changes in response to the amount of signal in the data.

This more tolerant metric for determining false positives means that it is more sensitive than some other traditional methods, but in the event that there is really no signal in the data, FDR methods provide the same level of control as traditional methods. More technically, FDR methods have weak control of family-wise type I errors.

To put it another way, the majority of traditional approaches to the multiple-testing problem assign an adjusted p value to each test, or to similarly reduce the p value threshold. The challenge with this is that while they reduce the number of false positives, they also reduce the number of true positives within our data – we consider them to be too *conservative*; a good example of this is the Bonferroni method we discussed earlier.

Hence, a value of the FDR approach, which also determines adjusted p values for our tests, is that it focuses on controlling the number of false positives that result in a significant result. This means that it is less conservative than traditional methods such as the Bonferroni method and has a greater power to find significant results.

So, a p value of 0.05 implies that 5% of our tests will result in a false positive; an FDR-adjusted p value (sometimes called a q-value) of 0.05 implies that 5% of *significant* tests will result in false positives. This latter quantity is clearly a smaller quantity than the former quantity.

The term q-value, then, is result of adjusting a p value using an optimized FDR method, where optimization occurs by using characteristics of the p value *distribution* in order to generate the q-values. We'll explore this a little more and include an example.

Genomic or proteomic experiments result in our testing hundreds or thousands of spot variables, and each test will generate a p value which obviously takes on values between 0 and 1. We can easily generate a histogram of the p values to see how they are distributed, as shown in Fig. 6.18.

The light blue bar represents the significant values for a p value threshold of 0.05.

In any experiment, we're still unsure if a result with a p value < 0.05 is a true discovery or whether it is a false positive. The q-value approach tries to determine the height (of the bar) where the p value distribution flattens out and incorporates this being into the calculation of the FDR adjusted p values. We can see this in the histogram below, where the significant values that are actually false positives are highlighted in red on the light blue bar (Fig. 6.19).

Let's look at the (ordered) q-values and take the data element in location 52. This has a p value of 0.01 and a q-value of 0.0141. Using the p value, we would expect to see approximately 8 or 9 (1% of our 839 elements) false positives in our dataset. Since we have 52 elements whose p value is less than or equal to 0.01, we can assume that 8 or 9 of these values will be false positives. However, if we examine

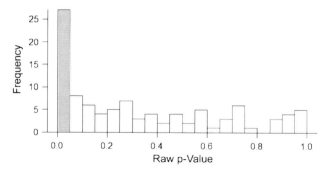

Fig. 6.18 Frequency distribution of raw *p* values for subset of Golub dataset

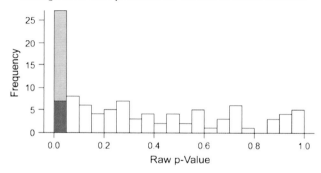

Fig. 6.19 Frequency distribution of raw *p* values for subset of Golub dataset (false positives *highlighted*)

the *q*-value of 0.0141, we should expect 1.41% of our elements to be false positives. Thus, if we have 52 elements with a *q*-value of 0.0141 or less, we should expect 0.7332 false positives.[22] Using *q*-values will not always result in a smaller number of false positives but it will give a much better indication of how many false positives we should expect, given a particular threshold value.

As a practical matter, if we are conducting a large number of tests, such as would be the case in proteomics experiments, for example, we interpret the *p* values and *q*-values across the complete dataset rather than considering each one independently so that a threshold value of 0.05 has meaning across the entire set of experiments.

---

[22] If we calculate false positives according to *p* values, we have to take into account **all** of the elements in our dataset when we determine how many false positives we expect to encounter; when using *q* values, we only need to consider those tests with *q* values less than the threshold value we choose.

Which leads us to another comment: it is tempting to stick with a widely used threshold such as 0.05 (or 0.01) but we recommend looking at the number of false positives that this will generate rather than taking a specific value and considering that everything below this value is significant.

6.11   Statistical Significance and Clinical Relevance

One challenge with large datasets, as typically used in data-mining studies, is that the large n values we deal with often result in statistically significant results – especially when using hypothesis testing – but which may or may not be clinically relevant.

When comparing two treatment groups, for example, hypothesis testing is widely used, and we typically look at simple indications of whether or not the differences are statistically significant. However, this may not always be as appropriate as we may desire. Instead, it may be more beneficial to use statistical methods which can quantify the magnitude of the differences between the treatment groups.

It has become well understood that statistical significance does not necessarily imply clinical significance. In fact, differences between treatment groups which may be so small as to be clinically irrelevant can be statistically significant by finding just the right sample size. But the reverse problem is also very real: statistically insignificant differences may be clinically relevant.

In order to develop these ideas further, we need to begin by defining what is *statistically significant*. To help us in this regard, let's look at the duality: what is statistically insignificant? Intuitively, we can say that anything which can happen by chance would be a good candidate for one definition of statistical insignificance; statisticians will often consider this to be anything which occurs less than 5% of the time. Can we therefore say that statistical significance is anything that occurs more than 5% of the time, and is also unlikely to have occurred by chance? Whether we can or not, we can definitely use this as a heuristic.

6.12   Conclusion

We describe a wide range of statistical techniques and concepts in this chapter, but only scratch the surface, as any statistician will confirm. Statistics, both descriptive and inferential, provide us with a set of tools that allow us to obtain significant insight into the data we are analyzing, and are often the starting point for many research initiatives.

A good question to address at this point is *why* we spent this amount of time focusing on statistical methods. Well, statistical methods, as we shall see elsewhere in this text, are also used in combination with many other techniques and can well be considered the foundation for data analysis and mining. For this reason, we strongly recommend gaining experience and knowledge in basic statistical analysis techniques for any data-mining effort.

Further, statistical approaches are well defined, and available in many commercial and open-source software products. These tools provide many built-in capabilities to quickly and relatively easily understand much about the data and the underlying statistical distribution for that sample, or its population. And this is a very valuable step to perform.

Combining a good set of tools, such as is available with SAS, R, Biostat, or any of a plethora of other software products will allow the investigator to not only rapidly analyze their data and gain insight, but also allow processes and fragments to be built that can be reused time and again. Many organizations already have standard products available, and the first-time investigator is strongly advised to determine the products and custom components available within their organization.

If we consider just the statistical methods that fall under the title of *descriptive statistics* – those techniques that simply describe our dataset – the information we can glean about our data may cause us to change our approach to our analysis. We may elect to use different mining techniques based simply on what we discover from the data.

Hopefully, you can see the value from using some of these techniques. Since many standard statistical tests are widely used in the literature, and sometimes misused, it is valuable to understand how to use these same tests. But they also give us insight. Are the data for two groups from the same population? Can we compare the means of the data from two groups? Such questions often help us in determining the direction our mining efforts should progress.

But finally, with a nod to William of Ockham, this may be all you need, at least, for a quick analysis of the data. It may be sufficient to determine whether or not the data is complex enough to contain potentially interesting hidden patterns. Maybe the patterns are not so hidden either.

Using standard statistical methods as an initial analytical step can often save us a lot of work later on.

References

Bolstad WM (2004) Introduction to Bayesian statistics. Wiley-Interscience, Hoboken
Chagoyen M, Pazos F (2011) MBRole: enrichment analysis of metabolomic data. Bioinformatics 27:730–731
Crawley MJ (2005) Statistics: an introduction using R. Wiley, Chichester
Del Greco F, Burgess JL (1973) Hypertension in terminal renal failure: observations pre and post bilateral nephrectomy. J Chronic Dis 26:471–501
Gelman A (1995) Bayesian data analysis. Chapman & Hall, London/New York
Gentleman RC et al (2004) Bioconductor: open software development for computational biology and bioinformatics. Genome Biol 5:R80
Glantz SA (2005) Primer of biostatistics. McGraw-Hill Medical Pub. Division, New York
Golub TR et al (1999) Molecular classification of cancer: class discovery and class prediction by gene expression monitoring. Science 286:531–537
Jabbi M et al (2009) Response to "Voodoo Correlations in Social Neuroscience" by Vul et al. – summary information for the press (search online)

Killeen PR (2005) An alternative to null-hypothesis significance tests. Psychol Sci 16:345–353

Lindquist MA, Gelman A (2009) Correlations and multiple comparisons in functional imaging: a statistical perspective (Commentary on Vul et al. 2009). Perspect Psychol Sci 4:310–313

Margolin BH, Shelby MD (1985) Sister chromatid exchanges: a reexamination of the evidence for sex and race differences in humans. Environ Mutagen 7:63–72

Scanfeld D et al (2006) Motif discovery: algorithm and application (search online)

Subramanian A et al (2005) Gene set enrichment analysis: a knowledge-based approach for interpreting genome-wide expression profiles. Proc Natl Acad Sci USA 102:15545–15550

Vul E et al (2009) Puzzlingly high correlations in fMRI studies of emotion, personality, and social cognition. Perspect Psychol Sci 4:274–290

Yang W et al (2011) Variable set enrichment analysis in genome-wide association studies. Eur J Hum Genet 19(8):893–900

Chapter 7
Bayesian Statistics

Abstract Statistical methods such as those discussed earlier in this text are familiar to a wide range of scientists; somewhat less familiar is the other school of statistics – Bayesian statistics. Bayesian statistics, based on the work of Reverend Thomas Bayes, introduces the concept of conditional probabilities, whereby we are interested in the "probability of A given B." But Bayesian reasoning and the associated statistical methods go further than this. In clinical settings, using tests for purposes such as determining the probability of a woman having breast cancer, given a positive mammography versus a woman having a positive mammography who does **not** have breast cancer is an important consideration; conditional probabilities, a staple of Bayesian statistics, provides a robust tool for such an investigation. In this chapter, we consider the fundamental theory of Bayesian statistics, including Bayes' theorem and formulations, probabilities, odds ratios, Bayes factors, and the like, and consider an example where we look at using Bayesian techniques for simple classification of proteins as intracellular or extracellular. We then consider Bayesian reasoning and Bayesian classification a little more formally, following this by considering a widely used classifier – the naïve Bayes classifier – using both the R language environment and an open source data mining tool: Weka. Bayesian belief networks provide an important tool in allowing us to represent dependencies between attributes, as well as classification, and we consider that next, along with methods for estimating parameters and then how the concept of priors and posteriors applies in the multiple dataset scenario.

7.1 Introduction

Earlier we focused on the plethora of statistical methods available for data mining that fall into the classical or Frequentist school of statistics. As we introduced those methods, we took time at various points to compare and contrast with the Bayesian school.

R. Sullivan, *Introduction to Data Mining for the Life Sciences*,
DOI 10.1007/978-1-59745-290-8_7, © Springer Science+Business Media, LLC 2012

Bayesian statistics has a long history, dating back to the fundamental rule proposed by the Reverend Bayes. However, in the last couple of decades of the twentieth century, it came into vogue in many areas of science.

The Bayesian approach differs from the Frequentist approach in the following ways:

- Parameters are considered as random variables since we do not know their true values.
- We use the rules of probability to make inferences about parameters.
- Probability statements about parameters are interpreted as *degrees of belief.*
- We revise our beliefs about parameters after receiving data through the use of Bayes' theorem.

What do we mean when we say that probability statements are interpreted as degrees of belief? As we shall see, we usually consider two distributions. The *prior distribution* is our subjective view of the problem, where each parameter is weighted by each person and measures how plausible that person views the parameter's value to be **before seeing any data**. Once data is observed, we revise our beliefs, using Bayes' theorem, to provide us with a *posterior distribution*, giving relative weights to each parameter following analysis of the data. Thus, the posterior distribution is derived from two sources: the observed data and the prior distribution.

Thus, any inferences we make using the Bayesian approach is based upon the **actual** data, not on all possible sets of data that might have occurred. With parameters being random variables, we can make probability statements about each parameter after (posterior to) the data being analyzed.

We refer readers to Appendix A for a brief review of definitions of basic probability and statistical theory concepts. For more in-depth requirements, we refer readers to any standard statistics text.

7.2   Bayesian Formulations

We have already discussed a method, the 1R method, which can offer surprisingly good results and which only considers a single attribute as being important. We now consider a method which considers all attributes. The *naïve Bayes* method assumes also that all attributes are equally important and independent of one another with respect to the class under consideration. While this method works surprisingly well in practical applications, it is somewhat unrealistic since for any real-life dataset, all attributes are not equally important, nor are they totally independent.

But since we state that this method works pretty well, does it matter that it assumes all attributes are equally important? Suppose we have a population of patients that have been examined and diagnosed as hypertensive or not (Fig. 7.1).

We'll apply the naïve Bayes classifier to this dataset, with the goal of predicting whether an instance will be hypertensive or not. We haven't recreated the complete

Fig. 7.1   Patient population

Patient Id	Hypertensive
1	Y
2	Y
3	N
...	...
90	N

dataset in the text,[1] but in the complete dataset, there are twice as many patients designated as hypertensive or not. Given this, it would not be unreasonable for us to assume that the same proportion will be seen in any future instances also. As we will explain later, in Bayesian statistics, this assumption – actually called a *belief* – is referred to as a *prior probability* (or simply a *prior*), and are usually determined based on our prior (previous) experience – not just within the context of the data or deterministic algorithms.

Side Note

This concept of introducing previous, external knowledge or experience into the mix is one area that has generated much debate between the Bayesian and Frequentist camps. By introducing this concept into our model, we are naturally directing the model – at least initially – and the question of whether this is appropriate or not is obviously subjective. Given this subjectivity, can we be confident that we are not artificially guiding the model into a particular solution (sub)space. If we recall an earlier discussion about how a solution space can be visualized as a multidimensional space with solutions being global minima, we need to be sure that we are not causing our model to miss potential solutions.

That being said, it is also a truism that in almost every area of knowledge, expertise is an important factor. If all investigations were performed ab initio, we would definitely be wasting time, knowledge, and experience. Is this really that valid to do?

We believe that using knowledge is an important part of any data mining activity and so subscribe to the view that leveraging existing knowledge is a valuable addition to the mining effort. This being said, we do have to be careful. It **is** valid to be concerned that we might miss the optimal solution.

---

[1] The companion site contains a dataset that includes a number of additional data elements that can be used for multiple purposes.

However, as we shall see, there are some safeguards built in. Further, as we have stated on several occasions, there will not typically be one approach used in a mining effort; two or more models may well be used to arrive at a conclusion, and they can provide a means of cross-validating each other.

So given this information, we can define our *priors* to be

$$\text{Prior Probability for HYPERTENSIVE} \propto \frac{\text{Number HYPERTENSIVE instances}}{\text{Total number of instances}},$$

$$\text{Prior Probability for NOT HYPERTENSIVE}$$
$$\propto \frac{\text{Number NOT HYPERTENSIVE instances}}{\text{Total number of instances}}.$$

Since we have a 2:1 ratio between hypertensive and not hypertensive in our 90 instance dataset, we can provide specific values for the above equations:

$$\text{Prior Probability for HYPERTENSIVE} \propto \frac{60}{90},$$

$$\text{Prior Probability for NOT HYPERTENSIVE} \propto \frac{30}{90}.$$

Using these prior probabilities, we can now consider what happens when we introduce a previously unseen instance into our dataset. The plot in Fig. 7.2 shows a representation of two of the data elements from our dataset: systolic blood pressure and diastolic blood pressure, with each point colored red if the instance was classified as hypertensive and green if not.

Visual inspection of the above figure shows us that the instances are in a 2:1 ratio.

We now introduce our as yet unseen instance, shown in Fig. 7.3 in blue, and draw a circle around our new point (shown in blue). Based on our dataset, it is reasonable to assume that the prevalence of green (or red) points in the vicinity of our new point will lead us to conclude that our new point also belongs to that subset of points.

We chose the size of the circle to include 12 instances, including our new instance, a priori, and to be independent of the class to which any instance belongs. We can now use this information to calculate likelihoods for this new point by calculating the number of instances that occur (inside the circle) for each class label. That is,

$$\text{Likelihood of } X \text{ given HYPERTENSIVE (red)}$$
$$= \frac{\text{Number of HYPERTENSIVE in vicinity of } X}{\text{Total number of HYPERTENSIVE cases}},$$

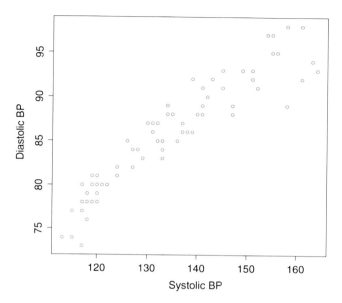

Fig. 7.2 Hypertension dataset

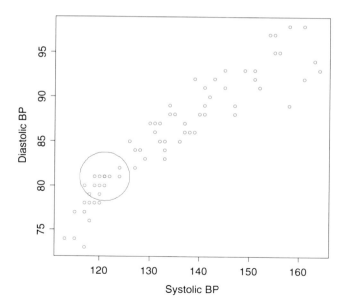

Fig. 7.3 Hypertension dataset, including new data point

Likelihood of X given NOT HYPERTENSIVE (green)

$$= \frac{\text{Number of NOT HYPERTENSIVE in vicinity of } X}{\text{Total number of NOT HYPERTENSIVE cases}}.$$

Substituting our values, we get

$$\text{Likelihood of } X \text{ given HYPERTENSIVE (red)} = \frac{3}{60},$$

$$\text{Likelihood of } X \text{ given NOT HYPERTENSIVE (green)} = \frac{8}{30}.$$

Recall that our prior probabilities

$$\text{Prior Probability for HYPERTENSIVE} \propto \frac{60}{90},$$

$$\text{Prior Probability for NOT HYPERTENSIVE} \propto \frac{30}{90}$$

suggested that our new instance would belong to the set of HYPERTENSIVE, simply due to the larger number of HYPERTENSIVE instances. However, our process suggests otherwise as more NOT HYPERTENSIVE instances occur in the vicinity of our new instance. In Bayesian analysis, the actual, or final classification, is determined by applying the Bayes' rule (see below) to the combination of the prior probability and the likelihood:

Posterior probability of X being HYPERTENSIVE
$\propto$ Prior probability of HYPERTENSIVE
$\times$ Likelihood of X given HYPERTENSIVE,

Posterior probability of X being NOT HYPERTENSIVE
$\propto$ Prior probability of NOT HYPERTENSIVE
$\times$ Likelihood of X given NOT HYPERTENSIVE.

Substituting our values, we obtain

$$\text{Posterior probability of } X \text{ being HYPERTENSIVE} \propto \frac{60}{90} \times \frac{3}{60} = \frac{3}{90},$$

$$\text{Posterior probability of } X \text{ being NOT HYPERTENSIVE} \propto \frac{30}{90} \times \frac{8}{30} = \frac{8}{90}.$$

So we would classify our new instance as NOT HYPERTENSIVE (green) based on the posterior probabilities.

7.2.1 *Bayes' Theorem*

We used Bayes' theorem in our discussion of the naïve Bayes classifier above without any prior discussion of the theory itself. We're now going to rectify this to provide the theoretical underpinnings of this fundamental theorem, one which forms a basis for the whole of Bayesian statistics.

We'll begin with the definition of conditional probability,

$$P(B|A) = \frac{P(A \cap B)}{P(A)}.$$

This states that the probability of some event B occurring, given that we know that the event A occurred, is the quotient of the probability of both events occurring simultaneously, together with the probability of event A occurring. Wow, a mouthful, if ever there was one. Let's break this down.

We know that the marginal probability of an event A is determined by summing the probabilities of its disjoint parts. For any events A, B, we can define $A = A \cap B + A \cap \bar{B}$, and since $A \cap B, A \cap \bar{B}$ are clearly disjoint, $P(A) = P(A \cap B) + P(A \cap \bar{B})$. If we substitute this into the definition of conditional probability, we get

$$P(B|A) = \frac{P(A \cap B)}{P(A \cap B) + P(A \cap \bar{B})}.$$

The multiplication rule states that $P(A \cap B) = P(B) \times P(A|B)$, and we can now use this to find each of the joint probabilities in the right-hand side of our equation:

$$P(B|A) = \frac{P(A|B) \times P(B)}{P(A|B) \times P(B) + P(A|\bar{B}) \times P(\bar{B})}.$$

In the above equations, we note that $B \cup \bar{B} = \Omega$, where Ω is the universe of events, and that B and $\bar{B}$ are disjoint, thus B and $\bar{B}$ partition the universe. Also, $B \cap \bar{B} = \phi$, the empty set.

Typically, we will have more than two events partitioning the universe. Consider the n events $B_1 \cup B_2 \cup ... \cup B_n = \Omega$, where $B_i \cap B_j = \phi \ \forall i = 1, ..., n, j = 1, ..., n$, $i \neq j$, where the B_i partition the universe. Any observed event A will therefore be partitioned according to the B_i as $A = (A \cap B_1) \cup (A \cap B_2) \cup ... \cup (A \cap B_n)$, where $(A \cap B_i)$ and $(A \cap B_j)$ are disjoint because B_i, B_j are disjoint. We can now denote the probability of A as $P(A) = \sum_{i=1}^{n} P(A \cap B_i)$ (law of total probability).

Using the multiplication rule allows us to say

$$P(A) = \sum_{i=1}^{n} P(A|B_i) \times P(B_i).$$

The conditional probability $P(B_i|A)$ for $i = 1, ..., n$ is computed by dividing the joint probabilities by $P(A)$ to give

$$P(B_i|A) = \frac{P(A \cap B_i)}{P(A)}.$$

Using both of these most recent results, we get $P(B_i|A) = \frac{P(A|B_i)P(B_i)}{\sum\limits_{j=1}^{n} P(A|B_j)P(B_j)}$ (Bayes' theorem).

There are a couple of points to note about Bayes' theorem before we move on. The first is that it is, essentially, a restatement of our conditional probability formula where we used the multiplication rule in the numerator to find the joint probability and the law of total probability and the multiplication rule in the denominator to find the marginal probability. Note how the events A and B_i are treated. The events B_i are unobservable: we do not know which one occurs. However, the marginal probabilities, $P(B_i)$, are assumed to be known and constitute our *prior probabilities*.

At first this may seem a little unnerving. If we can't observe the B_i, how can we know their probabilities? Before we begin, we assign values for each of the B_i. How we assign these initial probabilities will be discussed below. We then look at A. The likelihood of any of the events B_i is the conditional probability that A has occurred *given* B_i. Thus, the likelihood is the weight given to each B_i event given that A occurs, denoted $P(B_i|A)$, where $i = 1, ..., n$, that is, what is the probability of B_i having occurred, given that A did occur?

From Bolstad (2004 #18), we can think of the Bayesian universe as having two dimensions: an unobservable dimension (containing the unobservable B_i) and an observable dimension, containing A, represented pictorially below.

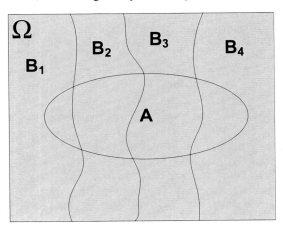

The unobservable B_i partition the universe completely. Given the observable event A, we are interested in looking at the intersections.

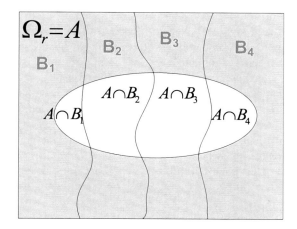

We use the multiplication rule to determine the probability of each $B_i \cap A$ by multiplying the prior probability of B_i by the probability of $A \cap B_i$. As we can see in the above diagram, the event A is the union of the (disjoint) parts $A \cap B_i$, which we simply sum to obtain the probability of A. This is referred to as the *marginal probability* of A.

The posterior probability of any B_i given A is that part (proportion) of A that is also in B_i: the probability of that particular $B_i \cap A$ divided by the sum of all $B_i \cap A$:

$$\frac{P(B_i \cap A)}{\sum_{j=1}^{n} P(B_j \cap A)}.$$

We can summarize Bayes' theorem as posterior $\propto$ prior $\times$ likelihood. This simple proportion contains an implicit requirement: that the prior be *independent* of the likelihood. That is, our choice of the prior cannot be influenced by the data we are observing. This is analogous to the case of joint probabilities of random variables being the product of the marginal probabilities – but only where the random variables are independent. In other words, each posterior probability, for any B_i given A is found by multiplying the prior probability $P(B_i)$ by the likelihood $P(A|B_i)$.

From Bolstad (2004 #18), page 68, the use of Bayes' theorem is summarized as follows:

1. Multiply the *prior* probability times the *likelihood* for each B_i to determine the probability of $B_i \cap A$ by the multiplication rule.
2. Sum the above probabilities for $i = 1,\ldots,n$ to determine $P(A)$ by the law of total probability.
3. Divide each prior $\times$ likelihood by their sum to find the conditional probability of a particular B_i given A.

We have walked through a lot of theory to get to the point of being able to use Bayes' theorem, although we used it in our naïve Bayes classifier discussion without knowing all this theory. What we haven't yet covered is how we assign probabilities in the first place. Again, referring to our naïve Bayes classifier discussion, our approach was certainly intuitive, but in a more complex scenario, how do we handle such assignments?

This question, which we attempt to answer in the next section, is actually one of the contentious points between the various schools of thought since we introduce subjectivity into the equation by leveraging our own knowledge when selecting these probabilities. That is, we are not just letting the data tell us the probabilities; we are potentially affecting them by using our "world knowledge." Again referring back to our naïve Bayes classifier example, we looked at our initial instance set (our training set?) and determined two probabilities – one for each subset of HYPERTENSIVE and NOT HYPERTENSIVE – that we subsequently referred to as *prior probabilities*:

$$\text{Prior Probability for HYPERTENSIVE} \propto \frac{60}{90},$$

$$\text{Prior Probability for NOT HYPERTENSIVE} \propto \frac{30}{90}.$$

We then used these as factors in our calculations for *posterior probabilities*, but should we have? What are the implications?

Consider, in this instance (sic) what we are saying: the probability of an instance in our dataset being classified as HYPERTENSIVE is twice that of it being classified as NOT HYPERTENSIVE. But this is in the general sense. Recall our single new as yet unseen instance. Its attribute values put it into the boundary area between the two subsets, and, in fact, it was classified as NOT HYPERTENSIVE. If we simply use these prior probabilities as our guide, this is certainly counterintuitive. However, based on our dataset, they are what they are. Would we have obtained the same result for our new instance without using these prior probabilities? These are some of the questions that are often raised in discussing the merits and demerits of the Bayesian versus Frequentist approaches, a discussion outside the scope of this text.

We do need to consider, however, our approach to "generating the circle" in our naïve Bayes classifier discussion and how we more formally determine how we determine the likelihoods and assign probabilities.

7.3 Assigning Probabilities, Odds Ratios, and Bayes Factor

7.3.1 *Probability Assignment*

By definition, any method we use for assigning a probability must obey the laws of probability. As we have discussed above, when assigning prior probabilities, the values cannot be influenced by the data we are observing; the independence of the probabilities will be compromised otherwise.

One approach we can use is the basic definition of a probability: the relative frequency (proportion) of the event occurring if an experiment were performed an infinite number of times. This is the approach used in Frequentist statistics and is a very familiar concept and is widely used in Bayesian statistics as well. In this scenario, the unobservable variable is the *parameter*, and the experiment is considered to be performed an infinite number of times, holding the parameter constant.

The parameter is also considered a random variable in Bayesian statistics. The challenge here is that we cannot use the concept of the long run frequency to assign a probability to an event such as "the parameter has value d." For an unknown random variable, with a fixed value, we need to consider a different approach – degrees of belief.

This is the second approach we can use. Essentially, we are saying that our experiences lead us to believe that the probability of an event is p. For example, my previous experience of clinical trials leads me to believe that an individual patient has equal probability of being male or female; therefore, the probability of a patient being male is 0.5. Someone else, however, may have different experiences and may assign a probability of 0.55 to the same event. This subjective view has been the cause of some debate. However, as we can see, this subjectivity is only of import at the beginning. Assigning probabilities using our degree of belief as to its merits provides a starting point. Thereafter, we wish to make inferences about our parameter given the data that we are considering. We will subsequently use the rules of probability to update our values. Note, however, that the probability statements we make about our parameters will always be subjective since the prior belief was subjective.

The question of how we specifically assign our prior probabilities is still a little fuzzy. We have said that we would use our experiences to provide prior beliefs, but how do we convert this into practice?

If we have no information at all to allow us to make an explicit determination, we can assign equal probabilities to all of the parameter values. That is, the priors form a uniform distribution.

This same distribution can be used if we want to be as objective as possible and not favor any one value over any other. Assigning each parameter value an equal probability reduces any personal beliefs we might have, but does not make it objective, for obvious reasons.

However, we may know, from our experiences, other facts about our domain. For example, if we are mining protein sequences, we know that phenylalanine, tyrosine, and tryptophan are structurally very similar and often evolutionarily interchangeable. In such cases, we would want to have a model where the priors we choose have similar probabilities for these three amino acids.

We're going to conclude this section by just mentioning that Beta distributions are used extensively in Bayesian analysis as they offer a family of conjugate priors. The general form of the family is

$$f(x; \alpha, \beta) = \frac{1}{B(\alpha,\beta)} x^{\alpha-1}(1-x)^{\beta-1}, \text{ where } B(x,y) = \int_0^1 t^{x-1}(1-t)^{y-1} dt.$$

We include this only as a launching point for interested readers but do mention that it is $x^{\alpha-1}(1-x)^{\beta-1}$ that determines the overall shape of the curve. Beta distributions are often used in circumstances where we wish to model events that are constrained within an interval explicitly defined by a minimum and maximum value. Any good statistics textbook will provide a more complete description of the Beta distribution, but a complete exposition can be found in Gupta and Nadarajah (2004, #281). For an example of using the Beta function in solving correlation problems related to gene expression levels, see Ji et al. (2005 #282).

7.3.2   Odds Ratios

When modeling uncertain events as random variables, we can also use the *odds ratio*. This is essentially the probability of an event occurring divided by the probability of it not occurring:

$$\text{odds}(A) = \frac{P(A)}{P(\bar{A})} = \frac{P(A)}{1 - P(A)}.$$

For prior probabilities, we have the *prior odds ratio*, and for posterior probabilities, we have the *posterior odds ratio*. We can solve the left- and right-hand sides of the above equation for $P(A)$ to obtain

$$P(A) = \frac{\text{odds}(A)}{1 + \text{odds}(A)}.$$

An interesting fact to note is that there is a one-one correspondence between probabilities and odds ratios.

7.3.3   Bayes Factor

So far we have talked about priors and posteriors but have not described how to get from one to the other. The Bayes factor B contains the evidence in the data D that is relevant to the question about a particular event A occurring and is the value used to multiply the prior odds by in order to get the posterior odds:

$$\text{prior odds}(A) \times B = \text{posterior odds}(A).$$

From this, we can obtain B:

$$B = \frac{\text{posterior odds}(A)}{\text{prior odds}(A)}.$$

Substituting from our earlier discussions, we obtain

$$B = \frac{P(D|A)}{P(D|\bar{A})},$$

which says that the Bayes factor is the ratio of the probability of obtaining the data which occurred given the event, to the probability of obtaining the data which occurred given the complement of the event (i.e., that the event did not occur). If $B>1$, this means that the data has made us believe that the event is more probable than we previously thought; if $B<1$, the data has convinced us that the event is less probable than we previously thought.

7.4 Putting It All Together

We'll now use some of the theory we've discussed in an example. We believe that proteins have slightly different amino acid compositions depending upon whether they are *intracellular* or *extracellular* proteins (Nakashima and Nishikawa 1994 #206). As the authors of this article state, "Segregation by sequence was found to be a more reliable procedure for distinguishing intra/extracellular proteins than methods using structural class."

To determine this, we'll use SWISS-PROT/PDB as our source of data as this is a publicly available database and contains a wide range of proteins.

Our first step will be to obtain a set of sequences from our source, incorporating them into a local database, and determining whether or not they are an "internal" protein or an "external" protein. Let's examine this a little further.

Extracting the sequences and placing them into a local database is simply for convenience. We could just as well reference them at their source, but what would be the fun in that? As we process each sequence, we're capturing information about the sequences themselves. Initially, we're going to take a naïve approach and count the various amino acid occurrences, giving us 20 data points for each sequence. Each instance in our analytical dataset will now contain this set of values, as illustrated in Table 7.1.

In Table 7.1, we have an additional column that allows us to identify the protein as (I)ntracellular, (E)xtracellular, or i(N)determinate. This third value is important as many transmembrane proteins have both intracellular and extracellular components. Wherever we come across such sequences, we identify them so that they are not used in our training set. There is actually a fourth value – (U)nclassifiable – that we will be using later in our analysis. You might be wondering where this is different to the indeterminate case. We'll explain this a little later. For this step in our analysis, it won't be used. However, we do need to explain that we will only initially use those proteins that we can classify as internal or external based upon our hypothesis.

Table 7.1 Protein dataset fragment

ID	I/E/N	Length	Ala	Arg	Asn	Asp	Cys	Glu	Gln	Gly	His	Ile	Leu	Lys	Met	Phe	Pro	Ser	Thr	Trp	Tyr	Val	Sec	Unk
3FY7	I	250	24	18	3	17	5	17	11	11	12	6	35	10	4	13	18	15	12	0	7	12	0	0
2ZFU	I	215	16	19	5	15	6	9	13	12	3	4	28	10	3	15	13	15	6	1	4	18	0	0
2JX4	I	52	6	9	0	0	1	3	1	6	2	2	4	1	0	1	3	5	3	0	0	4	0	1
2VSN	I	568	96	44	9	32	6	23	28	44	25	6	73	5	11	21	36	23	27	11	9	39	0	0
2X57	E	116	5	3	6	7	6	11	3	7	8	3	5	6	2	6	5	12	8	3	3	7	0	0
2X4S	E	275	24	23	2	18	4	22	17	20	13	4	17	10	5	8	11	14	23	10	14	16	0	0
3KJ6	E	366	25	17	17	11	14	17	24	9	30	34	14	9	25	10	25	20	8	13	33	0	0		

So now would be a good time to look at our model, specifically that part of the model that we are using to make the initial internal/external determination.

Table 7.1 gives us a set of amino acid frequencies that we designate as q_a^{int} or q_a^{ext}, where *int* and *ext* denote whether the protein is intracellular or extracellular, respectively, and a designates the specific amino acid. Our training set is included in this table, since we have identified intracellular and extracellular proteins as appropriate. We can now use this to give us "points" in the 20-dimensional protein (actually, amino acid) space and "color" them as we did in Figs. 7.2 and 7.3.

Since we know that we'll be using Bayes' theorem, we can now start to build the model. Recall above that we said we'd identify each sequence as intracellular, or extracellular (or indeterminate or unclassifiable), and so this is the subset we'll use. Given this, we will now try and estimate the probability of the sequence being intracellular or extracellular – by p^{int} and p^{ext}– respectively. Since we are only considering the intracellular and extracellular subsets, we have $p^{\text{int}} = 1 - p^{\text{ext}}$ and p^{int} and p^{ext} are our *prior probabilities*. Why? Because without knowing anything about the sequences themselves, these will be the best guess we can make about the sequence.

For both scenarios, we can write

$$P(x|\text{ext(tracellular)}) = \prod_i q_{x_i}^{\text{ext}},$$

$$P(x|\text{int(racellular)}) = \prod_i q_{x_i}^{\text{int}}.$$

Let's detour for a moment. If we look at the relative frequencies of amino acids in all vertebrate proteins, irrespective of whether they are intracellular, extracellular, or otherwise, we'll obtain a table such as the one shown in Table 7.2.

Using frequencies of DNA bases seen in nature – uracil (22.0%), adenine (30.3%), cytosine (21.7%), and guanine (26.1%) – we can calculate the expected frequency of a particular codon by multiplying the frequencies of each DNA base that comprises that codon. The expected frequency of the amino acid is then simply calculated by adding the frequencies of each codon that codes for the particular amino acid. For example, lysine has codons AAA and AAG. So we can calculate an expected frequency for lysine as follows:

$$(0.303)(0.303)(0.303) + (0.303)(0.303)(0.261) = 0.0278 + 0.0240 = 0.0518.$$

We have to apply a correction factor to this resulting frequency due to 3 of the 64 codons being stop codons, so we multiply by a factor of $64/61 = 1.047$.

These give us an initial metric for expected frequencies, and we can use this information later. We build up analogous tables to that shown in Table 7.2 for the intracellular and extracellular subsets of our protein sequence data. These will be our q_a^{int} and q_a^{ext} values. Using the same approach outlined in the previous paragraphs, we can calculate our relative frequencies, for our subsets, as shown in Table 7.3.

Table 7.2 Relative frequencies of proteins in vertebrates

Amino acids	Codons	Observed frequency in vertebrates (%)
Alanine	GCU, GCA, GCC, GCG	7.4
Arginine	CGU, CGA, CGC, CGG, AGA, AGG	4.2
Asparagine	AAU, AAC	4.4
Aspartic acid	GAU, GAC	5.9
Cysteine	UGU, UGC	3.3
Glutamic acid	GAA, GAG	5.8
Glutamine	CAA, CAG	3.7
Glycine	GGU, GGA, GGC, GGG	7.4
Histidine	CAU, CAC	2.9
Isoleucine	AUU, AUA, AUC	3.8
Leucine	CUU, CUA, CUC, CUG, UUA, UUG	7.6
Lysine	AAA, AAG	7.2
Methionine	AUG	1.8
Phenylalanine	UUU, UUC	4.0
Proline	CCU, CCA, CCC, CCG	5.0
Serine	UCU, UCA, UCC, UCG, AGU, AGC	8.1
Threonine	ACU, ACA, ACC, ACG	6.2
Tryptophan	UGG	1.3
Tyrosine	UAU, UAC	3.3
Valine	GUU, GUA, GUC, GUG	6.8
Stop codons	UAA, UAG, UGA	–

Now recall that we have

$$P(x|\text{ext(tracellular)}) = \prod_i q_{x_i}^{ext},$$

$$P(x|\text{int(racellular)}) = \prod_i q_{x_i}^{int}.$$

These tell us that for any given sequence x, we can calculate its probability, *conditional on it being a member of one subset or the other* using the product of the relative frequencies. However, since, in this part of our discussion, we are considering every sequence to be intracellular or extracellular, we can combine these to give

$$p(x) = p^{ext}P(x|\text{ext}) + p^{int}P(x|\text{int}).$$

Recall that p^{int} and p^{ext} are our prior probabilities and that we defined the relationship between them as being $p^{int} = 1 - p^{ext}$. How should we determine values for these? In our hypertensive example at the beginning of this chapter, we designated our prior probabilities as being

Table 7.3 Relative frequencies of proteins in our dataset

Amino acids	Codons	Intracellular relative frequency	Extracellular relative frequency	Vertebrate relative frequency (%)
Alanine	GCU, GCA, GCC, GCG			7.4
Arginine	CGU, CGA, CGC, CGG, AGA, AGG			4.2
Asparagine	AAU, AAC			4.4
Aspartic acid	GAU, GAC			5.9
Cysteine	UGU, UGC			3.3
Glutamic acid	GAA, GAG			5.8
Glutamine	CAA, CAG			3.7
Glycine	GGU, GGA, GGC, GGG			7.4
Histidine	CAU, CAC			2.9
Isoleucine	AUU, AUA, AUC			3.8
Leucine	CUU, CUA, CUC, CUG, UUA, UUG			7.6
Lysine	AAA, AAG			7.2
Methionine	AUG			1.8
Phenylalanine	UUU, UUC			4.0
Proline	CCU, CCA, CCC, CCG			5.0
Serine	UCU, UCA, UCC, UCG, AGU, AGC			8.1
Threonine	ACU, ACA, ACC, ACG			6.2
Tryptophan	UGG			1.3
Tyrosine	UAU, UAC			3.3
Valine	GUU, GUA, GUC, GUG			6.8
Stop codons	UAA, UAG, UGA			–

$$\text{Prior Probability for HYPERTENSIVE} \propto \frac{\text{Number HYPERTENSIVE instances}}{\text{Total number of instances}},$$

Prior Probability for NOT HYPERTENSIVE

$$\propto \frac{\text{Number NOT HYPERTENSIVE instances}}{\text{Total number of instances}}.$$

Can we use an analogous relationship here? That is, $p^{int} \propto \frac{\text{count(sequences|int)}}{\text{count(sequences)}}$ and $p^{ext} \propto \frac{\text{count(sequences|ext)}}{\text{count(sequences)}}$?

Since these are our prior probabilities, these would not be unreasonable to use. Based on our dataset, the values for these would be

$$p^{int} \propto \frac{\text{count(sequences|int)}}{\text{count(sequences)}} = ?? \quad \text{and}$$

$$p^{ext} \propto \frac{\text{count(sequences|ext)}}{\text{count(sequences)}} = ??.$$

Note that these values have been obtained using *only* the subset of protein sequences explicitly designated as intracellular or extracellular. We continue to omit the indeterminate and any unclassifiable from our consideration.

Now we can combine the above with Bayes' theorem to give us a value for $P(\text{ext}|x)$, which is the value we want:

$$P(\text{ext}|x) = \frac{p^{\text{ext}} \prod_i q_{x_i}^{\text{ext}}}{p^{\text{ext}} \prod_i q_{x_i}^{\text{ext}} + p^{\text{int}} \prod_i q_{x_i}^{\text{int}}}.$$

Remember that we are assuming $p^{\text{int}} = 1 - p^{\text{ext}}$, which easily allows us to calculate p^{int}. Conversely, we can calculate p^{ext} using

$$P(\text{int}|x) = \frac{p^{\text{int}} \prod_i q_{x_i}^{\text{int}}}{p^{\text{ext}} \prod_i q_{x_i}^{\text{ext}} + p^{\text{int}} \prod_i q_{x_i}^{\text{int}}}.$$

We now have our model that we can execute against our data in the other two classifications – indeterminate and unclassifiable – to see how they are classified.

Ok, ok. Some of you probably need a stiff drink at this stage, if only because of the cavalier way we skipped over the fact that many proteins have an intracellular and an extracellular component. Well, you caught us out. We did that on purpose. We would need to consider a more complex probabilistic model to support being able to switch from one assignment to the other to support such *transmembrane proteins*.

What about the indeterminate and unclassifiable sequences that are a part of our dataset? We can use these sequences as if they are as yet unseen instances. Let's consider the unclassifiable subset first. Any sequence in this category can truly be considered a new instance. Not only have they not been classified, by their very nature, we're saying we *can't* classify them. Running this subset of data against our model provides us with a mechanism for trying to classify them according to our model. We should also note that our model will classify a sequence as either *intracellular* or *extracellular*. Since we know that many sequences represent transmembrane proteins, we need to recognize that our classification is missing a vital piece of the puzzle.

This neatly brings us to the indeterminate category of sequences: this subset was not able to be classified as either intracellular or extracellular. But this does not necessarily mean that any such sequence is transmembrane, although it's reasonable to assume that a significant proportion does fall into that designation. Our model, however, will try and classify them according to our two classes; a misclassification, in reality. For our model to be accurate, therefore, we need to enhance it accordingly.

Here's where we weasel out. We're going to leave this to the interested reader to pursue. How might the model best be enhanced? Where would we begin? How do our classes intersect with each other? Can they be partitioned or is there overlap?

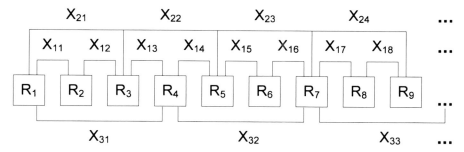

Fig. 7.4 First-, second-, and third-tier sequence-order correlation (Chou 2001 #520)

How does this affect the definitions of our model components? For example, the $p^{int} = 1 - p^{ext}$ relationship: How would this be different? How would we define p^{trans} and how would this relate to our other measures?

The data and algorithm implementations for our simplified model are available on the companion web site.

In our discussion above, we considered a protein P of length l to be represented as $P = R_1 R_2 R_3 ... R_l$, where R represents an individual amino acid residue, and the subscript identifies its location within the protein. This in turn means that we can represent P as

$$P = [\, f_1 \, f_2 \, ... f_{20}]^T,$$

where f_i for $i = 1, 2, ..., 20$ are the normalized occurrence frequencies of the 20 amino acids in the protein. (T is the transpose operator.) While being widely used in methods – especially in earlier approaches to this problem – the loss of any sequence-related composition information is a shortcoming of this method. We don't have any indication of where the residues occur in relation to each other.

This is important for obvious reasons, but a simple illustration of how having even a small amount of such information can be very valuable. In Nakashima and Nishikawa (1994 #206), single residue and residue pairs were considered. Using single residue scores, 78% of the proteins in their test set were correctly identified. However, when they used residue pairs, this improved to 86%.

To address this issue, improved models have been proposed, including the *pseudo amino acid* (PseAA) approach. In this model, a set of n discrete factors ($n > 20$) are used. The first 20 are analogous to those used in the amino acid composition model described above. The remaining factors are rank-different correlation factors or any combinations of other factors; the only constraint is that they reflect some form of sequence-order effect. For example, Chou (2001 #520) showed three additional factors that consider residues adjacent to each other (first-tier sequence-order correlation), residues separated by a single residue (second-tier sequence-order correlation), and residues separated by two residues (third-tier sequence-order correlation), as shown in Fig. 7.4, where **R** represents the amino acid residue and X_{nm} denotes the factor.

Incorporating this concept, our protein is now modeled by

$$P = [p_1, p_2, ..., p_{20}, p_{20+1}, ..., p_{20+\lambda}]^T,$$

where $\lambda < l$, the length of the protein, and where each of the p_u are given by

$$p_u = \begin{cases} \dfrac{f_u}{\sum_{i=1}^{20} f_i + w \sum_{k=1}^{\lambda} \tau_k}, & (1 \leq u \leq 20) \\[3mm] \dfrac{w\tau_{u-20}}{\sum_{i=1}^{20} f_i + w \sum_{k=1}^{\lambda} \tau_k}, & (20 + 1 \leq u \leq 20 + \lambda) \end{cases},$$

where w is the weight factor, and τ_k is the k-th tier correlation factor $\tau_k = \frac{1}{l-k} \times \sum_{i=1}^{l-k} J_{i,i+k}$ $(k < l)$ and $J_{i,i+k} = \frac{1}{\Gamma} \sum_{g=1}^{\Gamma} [\Phi_\xi(R_{i+k}) - \Phi_\xi(R_i)]^2$, where $\Phi_\xi(R_i)$ is the ξ - th function of the residue R_i, and Γ is the total number of functions.

As an additional example, amino acid composition has also been used for predicting protein-protein interactions (Roy et al. 2009 #521).

7.5 Bayesian Reasoning

Now that we've considered a number of the fundamental concepts in and around Bayesian statistics, let's step back and contemplate some generic facets of Bayesian modeling. Consider Fig. 7.5.

This depicts the iterative nature of reasoning in the Bayesian world. Once the initial theory, hypothesis, or model is defined, we use the process of *deduction* to deduce outcomes from the hypotheses. For example, if we have

If we know	If A then B
and (we know)	A
we can deduce	B

We can then use B as our basis for prediction and, gathering further data, using deduction. This simple rule will be familiar to anyone who has taken an introductory course in logic, but it is also something we can use in our day-to-day mining activities to introduce "new," explicit information into our model. We can also use a variant of this.

If we know	If A then B
and (we know)	B is not true
we can deduce	A is not true

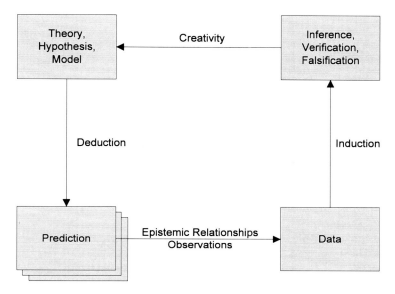

Fig. 7.5 Conceptualization of Bayesian reasoning

using the same deductive logic.

We can see from these two instances that deduction takes us from a general case to a particular case. For example, we might have the following "if two DNA samples, one from a crime scene, one from a suspect, match, then the suspect was present at the crime scene," where A = "two DNA samples, one from a crime scene, one from a suspect, match." We now need to determine whether A is true or not. Today, we have standards for determining matching DNA, such as the 13 used in the FBI's CODIS system, which makes the probability that they could have come from two unrelated people virtually zero, making DNA identification an extremely reliable test.

So using this approach, we have a tool to allow us to test some of our hypotheses against the (huge) base of data we have, so long as we can convert our hypothesis into a form that can be processed against our data. Some techniques we can use to accomplish this are described throughout this text and in many of the sources included in the bibliography. However, we cannot always define something so deterministically, as we shall discuss further below.

We are going to introduce the duality to deduction – induction – here as well. Induction allows us to go from the specific to the general.

Suppose we are told the following:

If we know	If A then B
and (we know)	A is not true

What can we now deduce? The answer is that we don't know because we could reasonably deduce both "B is true" and "B is not true" from the information,

Table 7.4 Bayesian rule calculations

Model M	Prior probability $P(M)$	Likelihood $P(D|M)$	Prior × likelihood (joint) $P(D \cap M)$	Posterior probability $(M|D)$
M_1	$P(M_1)$	$P(D|M_1)$	$P(D \cap M_1) = P(M_1) \times P(D|M_1)$	$P(D \cap M_1)/P(D)$
M_2	$P(M_2)$	$P(D|M_2)$	$P(D \cap M_2) = P(M_2) \times P(D|M_2)$	$P(D \cap M_2)/P(D)$
M_3	$P(M_3)$	$P(D|M_3)$	$P(D \cap M_3) = P(M_3) \times P(D|M_3)$	$P(D \cap M_3)/P(D)$
			$P(D) = \sum P(D \cap M)$	

although it would be more plausible to assume that "B is not true" than it was in our earlier scenario. A reason for this is that one of the ways in which B could be true is no longer an option: namely that both A and B are both true. Note, however, that we used the term "more plausible" in the above sentence. This will become more important shortly.

One of the challenges that we consistently encounter when dealing with data – especially data captured from less formal sources such as patient diaries – is that we have to deal with "degrees of belief" that are subjective as opposed to objective, quantified values. Mosteller (1990 #241), for example, studied how people use probabilistic expressions, and Kadane (1990 #242), in commenting on the study, suggested 11 terms that ranged from disbelief ("almost never"; 0–5% probability) through to belief (no label; 95–100% probability) and which could be used to quantify probability. A good example where this may be valuable is in converting the "pain scale" used in many hospital settings into some rational quantitative value. Unfortunately, although the question is often posed as "on a scale of 1–10, with 10 being the worst pain you've ever encountered, what is your current pain level?" an overabundance of "10" values is often the response. As a serious consideration, however, and as we discussed in a previous chapter, quantizing subjective data is an important concept and one which has particular import in any Bayesian analysis where we are already considering factors outside of our dataset alone.

How can we easily use Bayesian techniques in our analytical efforts? Using our initial example as a pattern, and given an analytical scenario, we need to determine an initial set of prior probabilities that constitute our *prior distribution*. Given our objective – defined above as our parameter – we can lay out a table with columns as in Table 7.4.

7.5.1 A Simple Illustration

Consider a simple model where we are interested in the outcomes associated with a single diagnostic test, say one that determines the likelihood of a patient having HPV, which gives us a simple positive or negative result. Here, we'll use two models for our example: M_1 – the patient has HPV and M_2 – the patient does not

Table 7.5 Bayesian rule calculations – step 1

Parameter value (model) M	Prior probability P(M)	Likelihood P(D|M)	Prior × likelihood (joint) $P(D \cap M)$	Posterior probability P(M|D)
M_1	0.000077			
M_2	0.999923			

Test Result	Disease Present	Disease Absent
Positive	True Positive (A)	False Positive (B)
Negative	False Negative (C)	True Negative (D)

Sensitivity $= A / (A+C)$

Specificity $= D / (B+D)$

Positive predictive value (PPV) $= A / (A+B)$

Negative predictive value (NPV) $= D / (C+D)$

Fig. 7.6 Definitions of diagnostic test sensitivity and specificity (Wallach 2007 #209)

have HPV. According to the Finnish Cancer Registry (2002 #208), prevalence is 7.7 per 100,000, which we'll use to obtain prior probabilities of $P(M_1) = 7.7/100,000 = 0.000077$ and $P(M_2) = 7.7/100,000 = 0.999923$. We can now begin to build up our spreadsheet (Table 7.5):

We now need to calculate our likelihoods, which is the probability of the observed data, assuming the respective model is correct. For our purposes, the data is the result of the diagnostic test – positive or negative. We now have two values for D, which we'll refer to as D_+ and D_- to stand for a positive test result or a negative test result, respectively. Now we need to apply these to our two models.

Any diagnostic test has two important characteristics: its sensitivity and specificity. If we look at a simple representation of the diagnostic test and the applicable disease, then we define certain attributes about the pairing. Wallach (2007 #209) described them as shown in Fig. 7.6.

If we begin with the assumption that the diagnostic test result was positive (D_+), then we need to compute what the values are for each of our models M_1 and M_2:

$P(D_+|M_1)$ = "P(Patient tested positive and has HPV)" = sensitivity
$P(D_+|M_2)$ = "P(Patient tested positive and does not have HPV)" = 1-specificity

Similarly for the negative test result scenario,

$P(D_-|M_1)$ = "P(Patient tested negative and has HPV)" = 1-sensitivity
$P(D_-|M_2)$ = "P(Patient tested negative and does not have HPV)" = specificity

Table 7.6 Bayesian rule calculations – positive HPV diagnostic test result

Parameter value (model) M	Prior probability P(M)	Likelihood P (D|M)	Prior × likelihood (joint) $P(D \cap M)$	Posterior probability P(M|D)
M_1	0.000077	0.946	0.000072842	0.001213
M_2	0.999923	0.006	0.059995380	0.998786
P(D)			0.060068322	

Table 7.7 Bayesian rule calculations – negative HPV diagnostic test result

Parameter value (model) M	Prior probability P(M)	Likelihood P(D|M)	Prior × likelihood (joint) $P(D \cap M)$	Posterior probability P(M|D)
M_1	0.000077	0.054	0.000004158	0.000004
M_2	0.999923	0.940	0.939927620	0.999996
P(D)			0.939931778	

The sensitivity of the HPV diagnostic test has been reported to be 94.6%. That is, $P(D_+|M_1) = 0.946$ and $P(D_-|M_1) = 1 - 0.946 = 0.054$. Its specificity is similar, 94%, allowing us to determine $P(D_-|M_2) = 0.94$ and $P(D_+|M_2) = 1 - 0.94 = 0.06$.

We can now complete our tables for the two scenarios: a positive diagnostic test and a negative diagnostic test. (Refer to Table 7.4).

In Table 7.6, we had assumed that the patient tested positive for HPV, and so the (posterior) probability that the patient *is infected* given that the patient previously tested positive is 0.001213 or just over 1 in 1,000. The prior probability was 0.000077 or just under 8 in 100,000. So this is much higher than the prior probability.

In Table 7.7, we are dealing with the negative case. What does this tell us about the probability that the patient is infected? Again, the prior probability is the same, approximately 8 in 100,000. However, the posterior probability is now different: it is the probability that an infected person *tests negative* – a false negative. This is the interpretation for the first row in this table. Here we can see that the probability that the patient is infected now drops to approximately 4 in 1,000,000.

There is one other fact that this example illustrates and which is often a topic of discussion. That is, the prior probabilities can never depend on the data. They are purely a person's beliefs before seeing the data. So how and where does the data start to insert itself? In the likelihoods. This is where the data itself begins to assert itself over the beliefs. Why is this important? Much is discussed about whether these prior beliefs are appropriate or not. Some people believe that they can sway our thinking, and our analysis, with the potential that our analytical results may be flawed.

We believe (sic) that such beliefs are a part of our zeitgeist and should be considered carefully. The knowledge and expertise embedded in such beliefs can lead us astray, but as the simple example above illustrates, the modeling process itself does contain safeguards. If our model were used as part of a discussion with this particular, fictitious patient, for example, we could use it as one data point to put their mind at ease. However, we should also recognize that challenge that comes with beliefs: it is often difficult to change them. This can also be a problem with the subject matter expertise that goes into quantifying the prior probabilities: we have to be willing to reconsider them if the data leads us in a different direction.

7.6   Bayesian Classification

Bayesian classifiers are statistical classifiers based on Bayes' theorem and a particular type of classifier – the *naïve Bayesian classifier* – has been shown to be comparable to certain types of neural network and decision tree classifiers when their performance profiles have been compared. Further, their accuracy against large databases has been high.

The generic process involving training, validation, and execution is depicted in Fig. 7.7.

Naïve Bayesian classifiers use a concept called *class conditional independence* which essentially assumes that the effect of an attribute value on a given class is independent of the values of other attributes. This assumption significantly simplifies the computational requirements for such models and is a factor in the performance characteristics of this type of classifier.

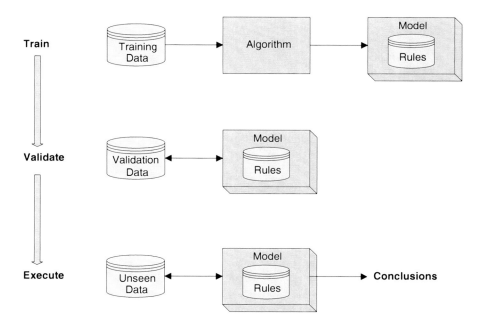

Fig. 7.7 Train, validate, execute

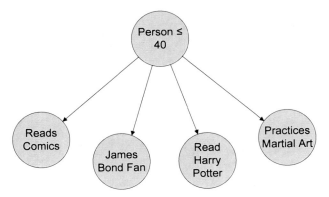

Fig. 7.8 Simple relationship network

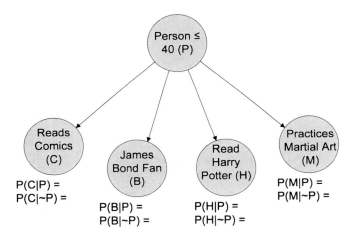

Fig. 7.9 Simple relationship network with conditional probabilities

Let's consider a simple example to illustrate this. Consider the simple network shown in Fig. 7.8.

Here, we define relationships between the "Person ≤ 40" node and the other four nodes. Thus, we can determine conditional probabilities for each of our four pieces of data – the lower nodes. Thus, we can calculate *P(Reads Comics / Person ≤ 40)* and also the converse: *P(Reads Comics / ~Person ≤ 40)* and similarly for the other nodes (Fig. 7.9).

Suppose we have a database of information captured about people: how can we use this information to estimate the values in our net? *P* would be a simple enough value to calculate: it's the number of people under 41 (sic) divided by the total number of people we have information about. Using the people who read comics (C) to illustrate the other nodes, we have

$$P(C|P) = \frac{\#\text{people} \leq 40 \text{ AND who read comics}}{\#\text{people} \leq 40},$$

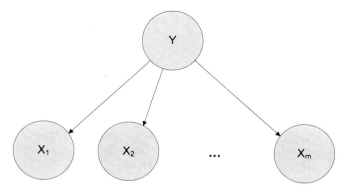

Fig. 7.10 Generalized network

$$P(C \mid \sim P) = \frac{\#\text{people}{>}40 \text{ AND who read comics}}{\#\text{people}{>}40}.$$

Given that we complete the calculations for each node, if we received an email from anon@gmail.com that said "I read HP7, Watchmen, and saw Quantum of Solace before my Shodan exam yesterday," what's the probability that they are under 41 years of age? Probably, very high!

We can see a natural correlation to survey questions that could be asked: "Do you read comics?" "Are you a James Bond fan?" "How old are you?" We can also see how this data might be used to provide us with our training data. But there are a couple of questions that we need to ask ourselves, not least of which is what are we trying to classify or predict? In the above example, we were trying to determine if the person was older or younger than 40; the challenge, as is always the case, is to determine what is most valuable to us in this particular case.

Before we look at another simple, but more relevant, example, consider the general case, as outlined by Moore (2004 #210). Y denotes the object of our classification, and $X_1, \ldots, X_m$ denote other attributes that we have captured (Fig. 7.10).

First, we want to estimate $P(Y = v)$ as a function of the instances in our dataset where the instances have the value v for attribute Y. Next, for each X_i, we want to estimate $P(X_i = u \mid Y = v)$, the function that considers only the instances in our dataset that have the value v for attribute Y **and** which also have the value u for attribute X. Given this set of estimates, we now want to take these given observations for all of the X_i and predict what our value of Y will be, given these observations

$$Y_{predict} = \arg\max_{v} \; P(Y = v \mid X_1 = u_1 \ldots X_m = u_m)$$

While we do not show the steps here, the following is also true:$Y_{predict} =$ arg max $P(X_1 = u_1...X_m = u_m|Y = v)P(Y = v)$, and can be simplified further to

$$Y_{predict} = \arg\max_v \ P(Y = v)\prod_{j=1}^{n_Y} P(X_1 = u_1...X_m = u_m|Y = v)^2.$$

In our more typical analyses, we'll be coping with many more "X_i's" than three or four, and, as we can see from the above discussion, the number of calculations can quickly become overwhelming, an issue we'll address below. A more immediate issue we have to concern ourselves with, however, is the question of what our Y variable will be. We know that this is the object of our classification, and this helps us to best determine the variable, but this can also lead to challenges. Practically, one of these is the misidentification of the appropriate attribute. However, we haven't found this to be a significant setback as this can also provide valuable insight to the underlying data. But, if we can identify the most appropriate attribute a priori, it means that we can save ourselves some iterations of effort. Elsewhere, at several points, we've mentioned the value that can be accrued from any other analysis we have performed. This is definitely true here. There is also value to considering not only our ultimate goal, but whether there are any valuable intermediary goals. For example, our ultimate goal may be to take an existing sample of people – say from previous clinical trials – and use the data previously captured to highlight any hidden patterns. Not only is this objective too nebulous, it is also much too broad. We would typically decompose this further. For example, we may be interested in any adverse effects noted in individuals. Decomposing this further, we may be interested in adverse effects in older populations. We could use this as a "> yy years of age" objective, as we did above, and then focus on mining our dataset using any test results, physiological symptoms, and signs noted by healthcare providers or the patients themselves, along with the knowledge we've built up *after the fact* to allow us to build up our Bayesian classifier. For drugs, many potential issues come to light only after the drug has been in widespread use because we don't see some of these patterns early enough in the discovery and development processes. Using this new information, we can revisit our data and possibly use it to see if there are any other patterns related to it. Using this new information can provide value by potentially highlighting other relations in existing products or provide another valuable line of research in new products. While we do not explore this here, with care, the Y of one classifier could be used as an X_i for another.

As in the previous section, D denotes our training dataset, a set of instances and their respective class labels, where each instance, $X = (x_1, x_2, ..., x_n)$, contains

---

[2] In practice, using this formulation can lead to problems because we are generating the product of probabilities, which are typically small – especially in large analyses. Multiplying such small values together can lead to problems with underflow in various systems and programming languages. This problem with floating point math can be overcome by using logs instead :

$$Y_{predict} = \arg\max_v \left(\log P(Y = v) + \sum_{j=1}^{n_Y} \log P(X_j = u_j|Y = v) \right)$$

n measurements from n attributes, respectively. We shall assume that the data may be classified into one of m classes, $C_1, C_2, ..., C_m$. For any instance X, the classifier will predict (assign) it to the class having the highest posterior probability, conditioned on X. That is, the Bayesian classifier predicts that X is in class C_i if and only if

$$P(C_i|X) > P(C_j|X) \text{ for } 1 \leq j \leq m, j \neq i.$$

C_i, for which $P(C_i|X)$ is at its maximal value, is called the *maximum posteriori hypothesis*, and, using Bayes' theorem, is

$$P(C_i|X) = \frac{P(X|C_i)P(C_i)}{P(X)}.$$

As we have already seen, the denominator, $P(X)$, is not variant across classes, so we only need to focus on maximizing the numerator, $P(X|C_i)P(C_i)$.

In the case where the prior probabilities are not known, we assume each class is equally likely – $P(C_1) = P(C_2) = ... = P(C_m)$ – and would therefore look to maximize $P(X|C_i)$. If the prior probabilities are not all equal, then we will obviously maximize $P(X|C_i)P(C_i)$, as the more general case. Recalling our discussion on estimators in Chap. 6, the class prior probabilities can be estimated using

$$P(C_i) = \frac{|C_{i,D}|}{|D|},$$

where $|C_{i,D}|$ denotes the number of instances in our training dataset D that are in class C_i.

Our datasets will typically have many attributes, which would make the computations for $P(X|C_i)$ very expensive. But as we have already stated, the naïve Bayesian classifier takes advantage of the concept of class conditional independence. This makes the assumption that there are no dependence relationships between the attributes of the instance, given the class. That is, the values of the attributes are conditionally independent of each other, given the class of the instance. Given this independence, we can use the multiplication rule and obtain

$$P(X|C_i) = P(x_1|C_i) \times P(x_2|C_i) \times ... \times P(x_n|C_i) = \prod_{j=1}^{n} P(x_j|C_i).$$

We can now easily estimate each of the probabilities $P(x_j|C_i)$ from our training dataset. We assume that the value x_j denotes a value for an attribute A_j:

- If A_j is categorical, the value for $P(x_j|C_i)$ is

$$\frac{\# \text{ tuples of class } C_i \text{ in } D \text{ with value } x_j}{|C_{i,D}|}.$$

• If A_j is continuous, the distribution is usually assumed to be a Gaussian distribution (mean μ, standard deviation σ; $g(x, \mu, \sigma) = \frac{1}{\sqrt{2\pi}\sigma} e^{-\frac{(x-\mu)^2}{2\sigma^2}}$), and the value for $P \times (x_j|C_i)$ is $g(x_j, \mu_{C_i}, \sigma_{C_i})$, where μ_{C_i} is the mean of the values of the attribute A_j for the instances of our training set in class C_i, and σ_{C_i} is the standard deviation of the values of the attribute A_j for the instances of our training set in class C_i.

The continuous case above may at first seem a little overwhelming, so we will illustrate this case. Consider a set of patient data containing an attribute *age* (our A_j). We will assume it is a continuous-valued attribute rather than it having been discretized. Let us also assume that we have a class *is smoker* (our C_i), which has values of true and false. If we look at the ages of all the patients in our dataset, we find, say, that patients who are smokers are 41 ± 11 years of age. That is, their ages range from 30 to 52. This tells us that for the attribute *age* in the class *is smoker* we have $\mu = 41$, $\sigma = 11$. If we have a particular instance $X = (\ldots, 37, \ldots)$, we can plug this age value into the equation for $g(x, \mu, \sigma)$ along with μ and σ to estimate $P(\text{age} = 37|\text{is smoker} = \text{TRUE})$. Remember that we are using our training dataset throughout to generate estimators for our mining datasets to come!

The final step is to predict the class for X. We evaluate $P(X|C_i)P(C_i)$ for each class C_i. Recall from our earlier discussions that the classifier will predict that X is a member of class C_i for the maximal value of $P(X|C_i)P(C_i)$:

$$P(X|C_i)P(C_i) > P(X|C_j)P(C_j) \ for \ 1 \leq j \leq m, j \neq i.$$

Before leaving the discussion on Bayesian classifiers, we should take a moment and consider how effective this type of classifier is in practice and how easy it is to use. We'll take the "ease of use" question first. Although we have outlined a lot of theory, the actual implementation is very simple. In fact, the mathematical functions required – calculating mean and standard deviation of the subset of our data in a particular class and calculating $g(x, \mu, \sigma)$ using those values – are typically available in any mining environment we would use. Tools such as SAS or R, for example, have all of the necessary functionality so that we really don't have to worry too much. Again, preparation is key: we are leveraging our training dataset – a dataset that contains a sufficient number (and range) of instances to allow us to feel comfortable that the model will be a good reflection of the reality we will subsequently be dealing with. With regard to the performance profile of such models, the actual processing needs are relatively small; obviously, the size of the datasets we are processing will have an impact on its operating profile, but this is no different to any other model. So what about its performance (accuracy) relative to other methodologies?

We've already mentioned that various studies looked at the naïve Bayes classifier and compared it to decision tree algorithms and neural network classifiers, for example, and found them to be comparable in various domains.[3] We are typically

---

[3] We will skip over the obvious allusion to domains in which they are not as comparable since this criticism can be applied to any methodology.

Table 7.8 Normal values

Test	Normal (a.k.a. healthy) level[a]
TC	<200 mg/dL
LDL	<100 mg/dL
HDL	>40 mg/dL
Triglycerides	<150 mg/dL

[a]https://www.health.harvard.edu/fhg/updates/update0205c.shtml

Table 7.9 Naïve Bayes classifier example – training data

Age	Smoker	Gender	TC	LDL	HDL	Trig	Class
37	N	M	163.2	80	59	121	Good
42	Y	M	165.4	91	47	137	Good
61	Y	M	164.2	75	61	141	Good
58	N	F	162.4	82	52	142	Good
49	Y	F	179.8	110	38	159	Bad
52	Y	M	189.6	123	36	153	Bad

more interested in the error rates for this type of classifier when compared to other methods. Theoretically, the error rate for this type of classifier *should* be minimal. However, this is not always the case. Care must be taken to ensure that the available data from which the probabilities are calculated is sufficient and that the class conditional independence assumption is actually valid in our area of study, and finally, as is the case with any technique, we need to make sure that the assumptions which led us to use this technique are valid.

We now consider a simple illustrative example. Our dataset will comprise a set of instances with the following subset of attributes:

$X = ($age, smoker, gender, total_cholesterol, LDL, HDL, triglycerides, lipoproteins$)$

The value for **total_cholesterol** (TC) is calculated using the formula

$$TC = LDL + HDL + \left(\frac{\text{Triglycerides}}{5} \right).$$

As a guide, we'll use the following values for our normal values (Table 7.8):

We'll also use the naïve Bayes classifier that is a part of the Weka product (see Appendix B) to illustrate the point, as well as an implementation contained in an R package (e1071). For our test dataset, we'll use the following data (Table 7.9):

In Weka, select the "Weka Explorer" from the Weka GUI Chooser and then open up your file containing the training data[4] from the "Preprocess" tab. If your dataset is properly processed, you will see the "Preprocess" window reference your data elements, as in Fig. 7.11.

---

[4] Note that as of the time of writing, the ARFF or CSV formats must be used for the file. We elected to use CSV as most people will be familiar with generating this format from an Excel spreadsheet.

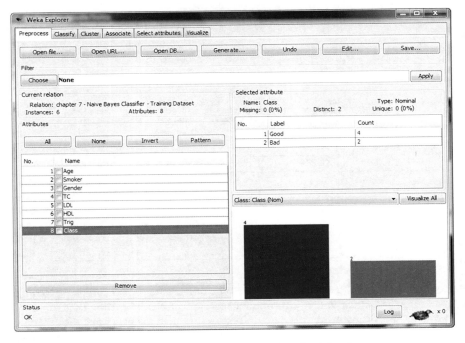

Fig. 7.11 Weka Preprocess window – successful processing of training data

We now turn to the "Classify" tab and run the classification using our training data. The results are shown in Fig. 7.12.

Note that in Fig. 7.12, we selected the naïve Bayes classifier and chose to use the training data we provided. As expected, this was able to process all of the instances successfully.

Just to provide context, we changed the classification of one of our instances, as shown in Table 7.10, to illustrate the classification step. The output is shown in Fig. 7.13.

The code fragment in Fig. 7.14 shows how to use the e1071 package, and naiveBayes() function, to accomplish the equivalent of our Weka example from above.

Figure 7.15 shows the processing step involving the training data.

Now that we have built our naïve Bayes classifier, we can use it for its intended purpose: to predict as yet unseen instances. We would obviously want to build up our classifier using more than six test instances, but the salient points can be seen even in this simple example. However, there is also a value to beginning with such as small, simple training set in that we get immediate feedback as to whether we are on the right track. This immediacy allows us to determine the probable success of our mining effort without our spending days on the problem.

To conclude, in order to use a Bayesian classifier, we need to understand the distribution over the inputs for each value Y, which will then allow us to compute

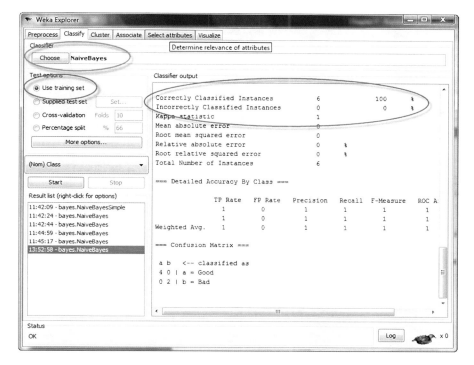

Fig. 7.12 Weka classification using the naïve Bayes classifier and training data

Table 7.10 Naïve Bayes classifier example – testing data

Age	Smoker	Gender	TC	LDL	HDL	Trig	Class
37	N	M	163.2	80	59	121	Good
42	Y	M	165.4	91	47	137	Bad
61	Y	M	164.2	75	61	141	Good
58	N	F	162.4	82	52	142	Good
49	Y	F	179.8	110	38	159	Bad
52	Y	M	189.6	123	36	153	Bad

the various $P(X_i|Y = v_j)$. In turn, this will allow us to estimate $P(Y = v_j)$ for the fraction of instances in our dataset with $Y = v_j$. Now, armed with these results from our test data, we can use $Y_{\text{predict}} = \arg\max_v P(X_1 = u_1 ... X_m = u_m|Y = v)P(Y = v)$ to make a prediction.

Why has this technique seen such support? It is inexpensive to implement and responds well in the face of large numbers of attributes – even into the many thousands!

For readers who are further interested, Lee et al. (2009 #218) illustrated an interesting use of the naïve Bayes classifier in predicting malignant renal cysts on

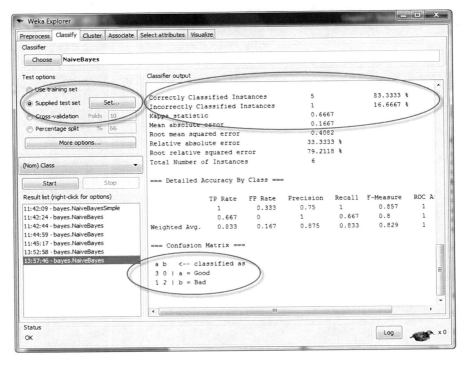

Fig. 7.13 Weka naïve Bayes classifier using modified dataset

```
# naiveBayes Classifier

# set working directory to my documents directory

workingDirectory <- getwd()
setwd("F:/Documents/nbc")

# get data
workingData <- read.csv("nbcTraining.csv", header=TRUE,
                        sep=",", quote="\"", dec=".", fill=FALSE)

library(e1071)

# model <- naiveBayes(Class ~ ., data = workingData)
model <- naiveBayes(workingData[,-8], workingData[,8])
predictors <- predict(model, workingData[,-8])
table(predictors , workingData[,8])

# reset working directory
setwd(workingDirectory)
```

Fig. 7.14 Naïve Bayes classifier example using R e1071 package

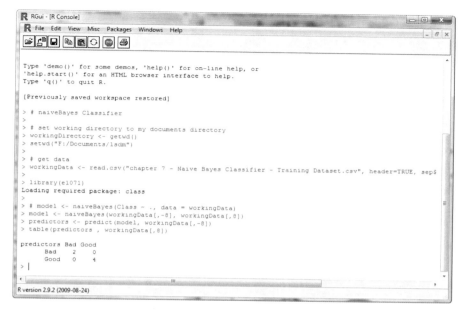

Fig. 7.15 Naïve Bayes classifier using the R e1071 package and our training data

MDCT images. De Ferrari and Aitken (2006 #219) described an approach to using a naïve Bayes classifier as an alternative to direct assay of mRNA presence across different tissues.

7.7 Bayesian Belief Networks

We can also use graphical models comprising *Bayesian belief networks* to represent the dependencies between attributes within our dataset, as well as to provide a form of classification. We now turn our attention to describing how this can provide another useful weapon in our data mining arsenal.

One of the underlying premises for the naïve Bayesian classifier was the conditional independence between attributes in the dataset. If this is indeed the case in our dataset, we can use the simple computational processing of the naïve Bayesian classifier and obtain very accurate results. However, in many cases, this conditional independence is not valid and dependencies do exist between attributes. How can we leverage this knowledge? We now turn our attention to the situation where such dependencies exist and consider how Bayesian belief networks are used to define conditional independence between subsets of the data and to specify conditional joint probability distributions. By using this technique, we explicitly encode for the dependencies, taking them into account in our model.

By their very nature, belief networks provide a visual model of the causal relationships between the attributes and thus allow learning to be built upon these

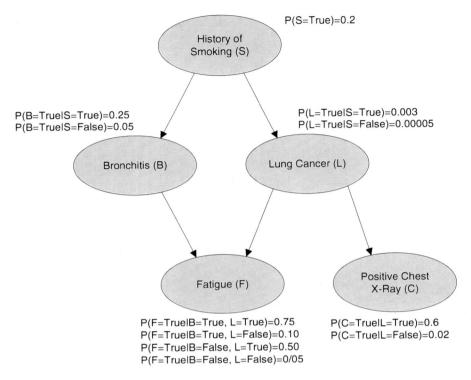

P(S=True)=0.2

P(B=True|S=True)=0.25
P(B=True|S=False)=0.05

P(L=True|S=True)=0.003
P(L=True|S=False)=0.00005

P(F=True|B=True, L=True)=0.75
P(F=True|B=True, L=False)=0.10
P(F=True|B=False, L=True)=0.50
P(F=True|B=False, L=False)=0/05

P(C=True|L=True)=0.6
P(C=True|L=False)=0.02

Fig. 7.16 Bayesian network

relationships. This graphical representation also allows us to see which subsets of attributes are conditionally independent of each other and which attributes have a dependence on one another. In addition to the graphical representation, formally a directed acyclic graph, we define a table of conditional probabilities that define the probabilities for each variable in the network (see below), given knowledge about one or more other variables. (See discussion on conditional probability in Appendix A).

Each node in our graph represents a random variable, and we place no restriction on whether these variables are discrete or continuous. The source for our variables will typically be attributes provided in our dataset. However, we will also have occasion to use *hidden* variables (Neapolitan 2003 #81; Han 2006 #14), which are causes for our observed variables that are not themselves observed. For example, we may have a syndrome which represents a number of symptoms but which is not (itself) included in our network. Each edge (linking two nodes) designates a causal relationship between the two nodes and represents a conditional relationship between the two nodes. However, this also represents that each variable is conditionally *independent* of all other nondescendent nodes in the graph, given its parents.

Consider the belief network shown in Fig. 7.16 (from Neapolitan 2003 #81, p. 47):

In this simplified example, we are stating that we have a causal relationship between history of smoking (S), and bronchitis (B), and lung cancer (L). Further, we have a similar relationship between bronchitis and fatigue (F) and lung cancer and fatigue. We finally identify a relationship between lung cancer and a positive chest X-ray. We now need to define what our conditional probabilities are for these elements. We begin by saying that the probability of there being a history of smoking is 0.2. That is, 20% of patients are identified as having been smokers at some point in their lives. This might include being a current smoker, or someone who has given up smoking at the point in time we gathered our data. We may be able to obtain this information from our mining dataset directly if such a question was asked as part of the data gathering questionnaire or on the patient history form.

We continue to iterate through our network, node by node, to obtain probabilities for each node, based upon its parents. Note that we have arrows linking nodes. The directionality of the arrows is important as it indicates that we believe there is a causal relationship between the two nodes. For example, we are stating that smoking *causes* bronchitis in the graph. A second item to note is that we have the arrows pointing in one direction only. This creates a *directed acyclic graph* (DAG).[5] Thus, for bronchitis, we are interested in the probability of bronchitis existing (for us, this is a value of True), given there being a history of smoking, and also the probability of there being bronchitis is there is no history of smoking:

P(Bronchitis present|Smoking history),
P(Bronchitis present|No smoking history).

Since we are interested in Boolean values, we have used True to represent occurrence and False to represent absence, and a single letter to represent each random variable. In our network above, the two probabilities are

$$P(B = \text{True}|S = \text{True}) = 0.25 \text{ and}$$
$$P(B = \text{True}|S = \text{False}) = 0.05.$$

We can see from our two examples that we use the definitions for conditional probability, and joint probability, along with Bayes' theorem to calculate the appropriate values.

Belief networks allow us to quantify statements such as "if a chest x-ray is positive, given a person has lung cancer, we can be confident of this 60% of the time." However, we are most interested in being able to answer questions such as "what is the probability that I have lung cancer if a chest x-ray is positive?" By applying Bayes' theorem to the results from our network, we can calculate this as follows:

$$P(L = \text{True}|C = \text{True})$$
$$= \frac{P(C = \text{True}|L = \text{True})P(L = \text{True})}{P(C = \text{True}|L = \text{True})P(L = \text{True}) + P(C = \text{True}|L = \text{False})P(L = \text{False})}.$$

---

[5] We do not discuss graph theory anywhere in this text, but the interested reader is recommended to read texts such as Wilson (1996 #193), Marcus and Mathematical Association of America (2008 #291), or Chartrand (1985 #292).

We'll once again follow Neapolitan (2003 #81) and use $P(L = \text{True}) = 0.001$, so now we can calculate

$$P(L = \text{True}|C = \text{True}) = \frac{(0.6)(0.001)}{(0.6)(0.001) + (0.2)(0.999)} = 0.029.$$

Linking this discussion to our earlier discussions, $P(L = \text{True}) = 0.001$ is an example of a *prior probability*, and $P(L = \text{True}|C = \text{True})$ is an example of a *posterior probability*. Also, consider that the posterior probabilities are values that are relative to what we know about the event, not the event itself. We don't know from this whether or not the patient has lung cancer. What we can say is that based upon the information we have about the event, we *can* say something about our *belief* as to whether or not the patient has lung cancer. This belief, and the probabilities that our belief is based on, will likely change if we determine more relevant information. For example, we may decide to return to the investigators, or the patients themselves, and obtain further data such as any family history of cancer or even the prior work environment(s) of the patients. We may incorporate these into our network.

For a complete and rigorous reference on Bayesian networks, the reader is recommended to read Neapolitan (2003 #81).

7.8 Parameter Estimation Methods

Let's turn our attention to how we use the data to determine an estimate for a parameter in our model, because that is, after all, what we are going to end up doing for a lot of our analysis. Within the Bayesian paradigm, the posterior distribution of the parameter, given the data, is the entire inference and so we are very interested in how we can generate unbiased estimators of a parameter from the distribution. An unbiased estimator is an estimator where the expected value that we calculate from the sampling distribution is the true value of the parameter.

Before we discuss how we develop the estimate, it is valuable to consider how we evaluate the "trueness" of the estimator. Typically, this is determined using the mean squared error of an estimator, a concept we have met before.

The mean squared error of an estimator $\hat{\theta}$ for a parameter θ is the averaged squared distance that lies between the estimator and its true value:

$$MSE\left(\hat{\theta}\right) = E\left(\hat{\theta} - \theta\right)^2$$
$$= \int \left(\hat{\theta} - \theta\right)^2 f\left(\hat{\theta}|\theta\right) d\hat{\theta}.$$

Although we don't prove it here, it also turns out that the

$$MSE\left(\hat{\theta}\right) = \text{bias}\left(\hat{\theta}\right)^2 + \text{Var}\left(\hat{\theta}\right).$$

So now that we have this information, let's turn our attention to the estimators themselves. At least, let's turn to them after we consider an example situation: the ubiquitous coin toss.[6]

You and a colleague work in a very small team. In fact, it's just the two of you, and so you divide up the work between you in a very egalitarian way, by tossing a coin to see who gets to work on what. But over the last several months, you notice that your colleague has been "winning" all the interesting work from your coin tossing exercises. So you think back to the last 15 examples and notice that a heads only came up 5 times. So now you are beginning to question whether or not the coin is fair.[7] We are then interested in how sure we might be that the coin was fair, if we decide that it **is** fair, and also how unfair it was if we decide it was not fair. Fair enough?

How might we go about this problem? We could proceed by considering how *biased* the coin might be by looking at the range of bias and then formulating various hypotheses. Let's assume that we are interested in the "heads" bias. If we put a value of $H = 0$, then we are talking about a coin that produces tails on every toss; $H = 1$ would denote a coin that produces heads on every toss. By extension, $H = \frac{1}{2}$ denotes a fair coin.

Using this set of definitions, we could then define hypotheses that look at $0.00 \leq H < 0.25, 0.25 \leq H < 0.50, 0.50 \leq H < 0.75$, and $0.75 \leq H < 1.01$, for example. Our knowledge about the fairness, or lack thereof, of the coin is then specified by how much we believe that these propositions are true. We can, for example, assign a high probability to one of these hypotheses, which would indicate a level of confidence in our estimate of the bias, as opposed to the case in which each hypothesis has a probability comparable to all of the others, which would tell us that we don't really know much about the coin.

As we know from our discussions in this chapter, we can summarize this whole picture with $P(H|\{\text{data}\}, I)$, where {data} is the set of coin tosses, and I, which is typically any contextual information we have, is, in this case, simply that "the coin is weird."

Note: In the remainder of this discussion, we'll use R to illustrate the concept. We can use the binomial distribution function (pbinom) to generate our plots.

[6] At least, this is ubiquitous in statistics.

[7] We're going to use the intuitive definition of fair in that over the long run, 50% of the time it would show up as "heads" and 50% of the time as "tails."

7.9   Multiple Datasets

We have discussed the fact that we may not have all of our data at the time we begin our data mining effort. We have also discussed approaches we can take and considerations which are important in order for our results to be valid. In using Bayesian techniques, these issues continue to be pertinent and should be borne in mind. In addition, we need to consider what differences, if any, occur because of our use of Bayesian techniques.

For multiple datasets, the question becomes one of analyzing each dataset individually or waiting for all the data to come in. We've touched on this before and so will not belabor the point here. However, there is an option that is particular to Bayesian analysis.

If, upon receipt of subsequent datasets, we combine them with the previously available data and revisit the analysis, the net result is a significant amount of extra work. Alternatively, we could consider each subsequent dataset separately and use the posterior probabilities from the previous dataset to be the prior probabilities of the subsequent dataset. We will not go into details here but simply state that both approaches lead to the same posterior probabilities. (See Bolstad 2004 #18 for more details.)

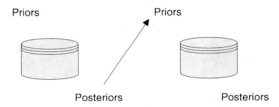

7.10   Hidden Markov Models (HMM)

Hidden Markov Models, or HMMs, have experienced an explosion in popularity in recent years across a broad range of disciplines and are especially useful in environments where changes in state are of particular interest. Natural language processing (NLP) has used this technique very effectively, and speech applications have used HMMs to great effect. A heavily cited article providing a very complete treatise on this subject is from Rabiner (1989 #825).

HMMs provide a formal foundation for generating probabilistic models of sequence problems. In this context, sequence is a more generic concept than used in life sciences, and HMMs have been used for a myriad different linear sequence labeling problems, such as in natural language processing. However, they have seen much applicability in the life sciences and have been used in diverse applications

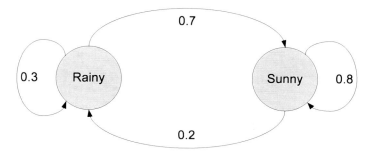

Fig. 7.17 Simple weather Markov model

such as gene finding, consensus profile searches, multiple sequence alignment, and regulatory site identification.

A core value of these models lies in their being able to develop models of almost any complexity.

Consider a set of states $\{S_1, S_2, ..., S_N\}$ and a process that moves from state to state, generating a set of states $s_{i1}, s_{i2}, ..., s_{ik}, ...$. The Markov chain property is that the probability of each subsequent state is dependent only on what was the previous state:

$$P(s_{ik}|s_{i1}, s_{i2}, ..., s_{ik-1}) = P(s_{ik}|s_{ik-1}).$$

Thus, to define a Markov model, we have to specify the initial probabilities: $\pi_i = P(s_i)$, transition probabilities: $a_{ij} = P(s_i|s_j)$.

Let's consider a very simple example before we go any further. This "weather" model will consider two states: $S_1 =$ "sunny" and $S_2 =$ "rainy." The initial probabilities of these two states are $P(S_1) = 0.6$ and $P(S_2) = 0.4$; the probability of a day being sunny is 0.6, and the probability of a day being rainy is 0.4. From here, we have to define probabilities for each of the four transition possibilities.

Probability of tomorrow being sunny (S_1), given that today was sunny (S_1)	$P(S_1|S_1) = 0.8$
Probability of tomorrow being sunny (S_1), given that today was rainy (S_2)	$P(S_1|S_2)0.7$
Probability of tomorrow being rainy (S_2), given that today was sunny (S_1)	$P(S_2|S_1) = 0.2$
Probability of tomorrow being rainy (S_2), given that today was rainy (S_2)	$P(S_2|S_2) = 0.3$

A graphical representation of this model is shown in Fig. 7.17.

Returning to the Markov property, the probability of a state sequence can be found by the formula

$$\begin{aligned} P(s_{i1}, s_{i2}, ..., s_{ik}) &= P(s_{ik}|s_{i1}, s_{i2}, ..., s_{ik-1})P(s_{i1}, s_{i2}, ..., s_{ik-1}) \\ &= P(s_{ik}|s_{ik-1})P(s_{i1}, s_{i2}, ..., s_{ik-1}) \\ &= ... \\ &= P(s_{ik}|s_{ik-1})P(s_{ik-1}|s_{ik-2})...P(S_{i2}|s_{i1})P(s_{i1}). \end{aligned}$$

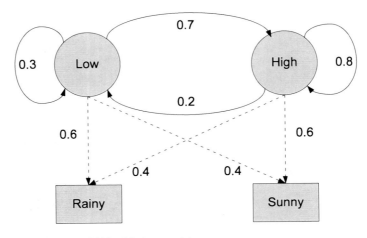

Fig. 7.18 Simple weather hidden Markov model

We can now consider situations such as determining the probability of 4 days being {"Sunny," "Sunny," "Rainy," "Rainy"}:

$$
\begin{aligned}
P(\{\text{Sunny}, \text{Sunny}, \text{Rainy}, \text{Rainy}\}) &= P(\text{Rainy}|\text{Rainy})P(\text{Rainy}|\text{Sunny}) \\
&\quad P(\text{Sunny}|\text{Sunny})P(\text{Sunny}) \\
&= 0.3 \times 0.2 \times 0.8 \times 0.6.
\end{aligned}
$$

In a *Hidden* Markov Model, the state transitions are not visible, but instead, each state randomly generates one of M observations, or visible states $\{v_1, s_2, ..., v_M\}$. Thus, to define an HMM, we define the following probabilities:

Matrix of state transition probabilities	$A = (a_{ij});\ a_{ij} = P(s_i|s_j)$
Matrix of observation probabilities	$B(b_i(v_m));\ b_i(v_m) = P(v_m|s_i)$
Vector of initial probabilities	$\pi = (\pi_i);\ \pi_i = P(s_i)$

The model is represented by $M = (A, B, \pi)$.

Returning to our simple weather model, illustrated in Fig. 7.18, we have two states – atmospheric pressure states – "low" and "high," and two observations, "rainy" and "sunny." Our probabilities are

Matrix of state transition probabilities	$P(\text{low}|\text{low}) = 0.3$
	$P(\text{high}|\text{low}) = 0.7$
	$P(\text{low}|\text{high}) = 0.2$
	$P(\text{high}|\text{high}) = 0.8$

(continued)

Matrix of observation probabilities	$P(\text{rainy}|\text{low}) = 0.6$
	$P(\text{sunny}|\text{low}) = 0.4$
	$P(\text{rainy}|\text{high}) = 0.4$
	$P(\text{sunny}|\text{high}) = 0.3$
Vector of initial probabilities	$P(\text{low}) = 0.4$
	$P(\text{high}) = 0.6$

If we consider a simple example {sunny, rainy}, then

$$P(\{\text{sunny, rainy}\}) = P(\{\text{sunny, rainy}\}, \{\text{low, low}\})$$
$$+ \; P(\{\text{sunny, rainy}\}, \{\text{low, high}\})$$
$$+ \; P(\{\text{sunny, rainy}\}, \{\text{high, low}\})$$
$$+ \; P(\{\text{sunny, rainy}\}, \{\text{high, high}\}).$$

The first term expands to

$$P(\{\text{sunny, rainy}\}, \{\text{low, low}\}) = P(\{\text{sunny, rainy}\}|\{\text{low, low}\}) \, P(\{\text{low, low}\})$$
$$= P(\text{sunny}|\text{low}) \, P(\text{rainy}|\text{low}) \, P(\text{low}) \, P(\text{low}|\text{low})$$
$$= 0.4 \times 0.6 \times 0.4 \times 0.3 = 0.0432.$$

Using HMMs poses some challenges we need to consider. First is the *evaluation problem*. Given the HMM $M = (A, B, \pi)$ and the observations sequence $O = o_1 o_2 ... o_k$, where $o_k \in \{v_1, ..., v_M\}$, calculate the probability that M has generated the sequence O.

Trying to determine the probability of the observations $O = o_1 o_2 ... o_k$ by considering all the hidden state sequences is impractical. There are N^k hidden state sequences which, as we can see, introduce exponential complexity into our problem.

We can use *forward-backward HMM algorithms* for efficient calculations where we define $\alpha_k(i)$ to be the joint probability of the partial observation sequence $o_1 o_2 ... o_k$ and let the hidden state at time k to be s_i, then $\alpha_k(i) = P(o_1 o_2 ... o_k q_k = s_i)$.

The second challenge is the *decoding problem*. Here, given the HMM $M = (A, B, \pi)$ and the observations sequence $O = o_1 o_2 ... o_k$, where $o_k \in \{v_1, ..., v_M\}$, calculate the most likely sequence of hidden state s_i that produces the observed sequence O.

We want to find the state sequence $Q = q_1 q_2 ... q_k$ that maximizes $P(Q|o_1 o_2 ... o_k)$, or equivalently $P(Q, o_1 o_2 ... o_k)$. Similarly, consideration of all paths would take exponential time, so using the *Viterbi algorithm* instead helps us to avoid this pitfall. Here, we define $\delta_k(i)$ to be the maximum probability of producing the observation sequence $o_1 o_2 ... o_k$ when progressing along some hidden state sequence $q_1 q_2 ... q_{k-1}$ to get to $q_k = s_i$. So $\delta_k(i) = \max P(q_1 q_2 ... q_{k-1} q_k = s_i, o_1 o_2 ... o_k)$, where the maximum is taken over all possible paths $q_1 q_2 ... q_{k-1}$.

The third challenge is the *learning problem*. Here we are given some training sequences O and the general structure of the HMM (number of hidden and visible states), and need to determine the HMM parameters $M = (A, B, \pi)$ that best fit the training data.

```
hmm = initHMM(
        c("Low", "High"),                    # states
        c("Rainy", "Sunny"),          # Observations
        c(0.4, 0.6),                  # initial state probabilities
        matrix(c(0.3, 0.7, 0.2, 0.8),2),    # state transition probabilities
        matrix(c(0.6, 0.4, 0.4, 0.3),2))     # Observable state (emission) probabilities
```

Fig. 7.19 HMM creation using initHMM

```
> library(HMM)

# Create HMM for Weather HMM
hmm = initHMM(c("Low", "High"),      # states
     c("Rainy", "Sunny"),      # Observations
     c(0.4, 0.6),        # initial state probabilities
     matrix(c(0.3, 0.7, 0.2, 0.8),2),  # state transition probabiliities
     matrix(c(0.6, 0.4, 0.4, 0.3),2)) # Observable state (emission) probabiliities
print(hmm)
$States
[1] "Low"  "High"

$Symbols
[1] "Rainy" "Sunny"

$startProbs
 Low High
 0.4  0.6

$transProbs
      to
from   Low High
  Low  0.3  0.2
  High 0.7  0.8

$emissionProbs
      symbols
states Rainy Sunny
  Low    0.6   0.4
  High   0.4   0.3

>
```

Fig. 7.20 Weather HMM definition in R package HMM

By best fitting the training data, we are essentially looking for parameters that maximize $P(O|M)$, but unfortunately, there is no algorithm that produces optimal parameter values. Instead, we use the *Baum-Welch algorithm*, an iterative EM algorithm that we use to maximize $P(O|M)$.

Let's return to our simple weather HMM and utilize the HMM package in R. We can now define our model using the states, observable states, and probabilities from above, defining these as parameters to the initHMM function as shown in Fig. 7.19 (reformatted).

Figure 7.20 shows the result of this definition via the print(hmm) function call, allowing us to confirm the various transition probability matrices.

Now we can define our observations, just as before, obtaining the appropriate probabilities for the sequence, as shown below.

```
>  observations = c("Rainy", "Sunny")

posterior = posterior(hmm,observations)
print(posterior)
            index
states            1          2
   Low   0.2571429 0.5714286
   High  0.7428571 0.4285714
>
```

An interesting capability of the HMM package is it includes a function, simHMM, that allows us to simulate a sequence for our HMM model of any given length. For example, below we show a simulation of a 100-step sequence.

```
> simHMM(hmm, 100)
$states
 [1] "High" "Low"  "High" "High" "Low"  "High" "Low"  "High" "High" "Low"  "High" "High" "High" "Low"  "High"
[16] "High" "Low"  "Low"  "High" "High" "High" "Low"  "Low"  "High" "High" "Low"  "High" "High" "Low"  "High"
[31] "Low"  "Low"  "High" "Low"  "Low"  "Low"  "Low"  "Low"  "Low"  "Low"  "High" "Low"  "Low"  "Low"  "Low"
[46] "High" "High" "Low"  "High" "Low"  "Low"  "Low"  "High" "High" "High" "High" "Low"  "High" "Low"  "Low"
[61] "Low"  "Low"  "Low"  "High" "Low"  "Low"  "Low"  "High" "Low"  "Low"  "Low"  "Low"  "High" "Low"  "Low"
[76] "High" "Low"  "Low"  "Low"  "Low"  "Low"  "Low"  "High" "High" "Low"  "High" "High" "Low"  "High" "High"
[91] "Low"  "High" "High" "High" "Low"  "Low"  "Low"  "Low"  "Low"  "High"

$observation
 [1] "Sunny" "Sunny" "Sunny" "Rainy" "Rainy" "Rainy" "Rainy" "Rainy" "Rainy" "Rainy" "Rainy" "Sunny" "Rainy"
[14] "Sunny" "Rainy" "Rainy" "Rainy" "Rainy" "Sunny" "Rainy" "Sunny" "Sunny" "Rainy" "Rainy" "Rainy" "Rainy"
[27] "Sunny" "Rainy" "Rainy" "Rainy" "Sunny" "Rainy" "Sunny" "Rainy" "Rainy" "Sunny" "Sunny" "Rainy" "Sunny"
[40] "Rainy" "Rainy" "Sunny" "Rainy" "Sunny" "Sunny" "Rainy" "Sunny" "Rainy" "Sunny" "Rainy" "Rainy" "Sunny"
[53] "Rainy" "Rainy" "Rainy" "Sunny" "Sunny" "Sunny" "Sunny" "Sunny" "Sunny" "Rainy" "Rainy" "Sunny" "Rainy"
[66] "Sunny" "Sunny" "Sunny" "Rainy" "Sunny" "Sunny" "Sunny" "Sunny" "Rainy" "Sunny" "Rainy" "Sunny" "Rainy"
[79] "Rainy" "Sunny" "Rainy" "Rainy" "Rainy" "Rainy" "Rainy" "Sunny" "Sunny" "Sunny" "Rainy" "Sunny" "Rainy"
[92] "Rainy" "Rainy" "Rainy" "Rainy" "Rainy" "Rainy" "Rainy" "Rainy" "Sunny"

>
```

We would like to model the statistical regularities of sequences such as genes, regulatory sites in DNA (e.g., where RNA polymerase and transcription factors bind), or proteins in a given family, and Markov models provide a flexible architecture for this type of task.

Consider a model such as shown in Fig. 7.21.

In this figure, we can see all the possible transition states between the various nucleotides, and so for any sequence such as CGGT, we can compute the probability as

$$P(CGGT) = P(C|\text{begin})P(G|C)P(G|G)P(T|G)P(\text{end}|T).$$

As described above, we need the starting probabilities, such as

$$P(A|\text{begin}) = 0.18,$$
$$P(C|\text{begin}) = 0.25,$$
$$P(G|\text{begin}) = 0.33,$$
$$P(T|\text{begin}) = 0.24,$$

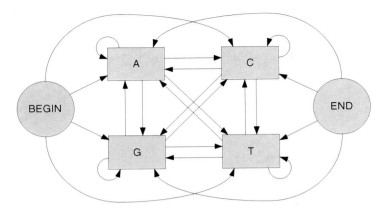

Fig. 7.21 Markov chain model for DNA

along with the various conditional probabilities, such as (for G)

$$P(s_i = A | s_{i-1} = G) = 0.16,$$
$$P(s_i = C | s_{i-1} = G) = 0.34,$$
$$P(s_i = G | s_{i-1} = G) = 0.38,$$
$$P(s_i = T | s_{i-1} = G) = 0.12.$$

In this scenario, we have one other set of probabilities, such as

$$P(s_i = \text{end} | s_{i-1} = A) = 0.23,$$
$$P(s_i = \text{end} | s_{i-1} = C) = 0.33,$$
$$P(s_i = \text{end} | s_{i-1} = G) = 0.31,$$
$$P(s_i = \text{end} | s_{i-1} = T) = 0.13.$$

From this, we can now set up our model as before.

Consider another example application of Markov models: finding genes. Based on what we've described so far, we could use a Markov Chain Model to elicit genes by:

- Building Markov models of coding and noncoding regions
- Applying the models to ORFs or to fixed-size windows of a sequence

An implementation of this is GeneMark (Borodovsky and McIninch 1993 #827; Besemer et al. 2001 #826) which is a popular system for identifying genes in bacterial genomes.

To begin concluding this section, we'll consider a further example, one from Eddy (2004 #828), that offers a very simplistic 5′ splice site recognition problem. In this example, we assume the provided DNA sequences begin with an exon, contains a single 5′ splice site, and ends with an intron. The problem therefore being to determine where the exon-to-intron switch occurred: that is, where the 5′ splice site is located.

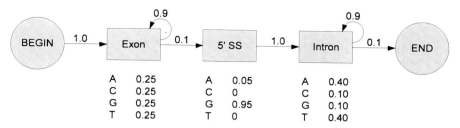

Fig. 7.22 HMM for 5'SS Problem

The first assumption, and potential challenge, is that exons, introns, and splice sites must have different statistical properties, otherwise we cannot realistically build models to determine the categorizations of the subsequences. For example, we might determine that exons tend to have a uniform distribution of the bases (say 25% of each), whereas introns tend to be more A/T rich (say 40% for each of A and T; 10% each for C and G), and let's assume that the 5' splice site (SS) is almost always a G (say 95%) with a small probability of it being an A (5%). Our HMM would look something like Fig. 7.22.

The *emission probabilities* are shown below the states, indicating the probability that it generates each of the four DNA nucleotides. The *transition probabilities* are shown on the arrows.

Let's build our HMM, using the R HMM library, as we used above:

```
hmm = initHMM(c("E", "S", "I"),
              c("A", "C", "G", "T"),
              c(1, 0, 0),
              matrix(c(0.9,0,0,0.1,0,0,0,1,0.9),3),
              matrix(c(0.25,0.05,0.4,0.25,0,0.1,0.25,0.95,0.1,0.25,0,0.4),3))
print(hmm)
```

Figure 7.23 shows the output from our definition.

Now we'll use the same sequence used in Eddy (2004 #828):

```
observations = c( "C","T","T","C","A","T","G","T","G","A","A","A",
                  "G","C","A","G","A","C","G","T","A","A","G","T",
                  "C","A")
```

and calculate the posteriors, as shown in Fig. 7.24.

We can see that position 19 provides the greatest likelihood of being the 5' SS, which coincides with the original paper.

As we mentioned at the beginning of this section, HMMs are seeing a broad range of uses. Along with this, many different software implementations are available. For example, in addition to the capabilities available from within the R community, another implementation is HMMER, an implementation used for searching sequence databases for homologs of protein sequences and for making protein sequence alignments using HMMs. A third option for readers familiar with Java is *Jahmm* (pronounced "jam"), which is a Java implementation of Hidden Markov Model (HMM)-related algorithms. Since this is such a vibrant area of research, readers are encouraged to take some time and review the available implementations just before you begin an analysis.

```
> library(HMM)
> hmm = initHMM( c("E", "S", "I"),
    c("A", "C", "G", "T"),
    c(1, 0, 0),
    matrix(c(0.9,0,0,0.1,0,0,0,1,0.9),3),
    matrix(c(0.25,0.05,0.4,0.25,0,0.1,0.25,0.95,0.1,0.25,0,0.4),3)
    )
print(hmm)

$States
[1] "E" "S" "I"

$Symbols
[1] "A" "C" "G" "T"

$startProbs
E S I
1 0 0

$transProbs
    to
from   E   S   I
   E 0.9 0.1 0.0
   S 0.0 0.0 1.0
   I 0.0 0.0 0.9

$emissionProbs
       symbols
states    A    C    G    T
     E 0.25 0.25 0.25 0.25
     S 0.05 0.00 0.95 0.00
     I 0.40 0.10 0.10 0.40
```

Fig. 7.23 HMM definition for Eddy 5'SS problem

```
> observations = c("C", "T", "T", "C", "A", "T", "G", "T", "G", "A", "A", "A", "G", "C", "A", "G", "A", "C", "G",
  "T", "A", "A", "G", "T", "C", "A")
posterior = posterior(hmm, observations)
print(posterior)
       index
states 1 2 3 4         5          6          7          8          9         10         11
     E 1 1 1 1 0.9993316483 0.9993316483 0.9794899587 0.97948996 0.94848732 0.947467495 0.9468301051
     S 0 0 0 0 0.0006683517 0.0000000000 0.0198416897 0.00000000 0.03100264 0.001019824 0.0006373898
     I 0 0 0 0 0.0000000000 0.0006683517 0.0006683517 0.02051004 0.02051004 0.051512681 0.0525325051
       index
states         12         13         14         15         16         17         18         19         20
     E 0.9464317364 0.92750923 0.92750923 0.925953099 0.85203705 0.849605596 0.8496056 0.5608710 0.560871
     S 0.0003983686 0.01892251 0.00000000 0.001556127 0.07391605 0.002431449 0.0000000 0.2887346 0.000000
     I 0.0531698949 0.05356826 0.07249077 0.072490773 0.07404690 0.147962955 0.1503944 0.1503944 0.439129
       index
states        21         22        23        24        25        26
     E 0.554934855 0.551224758 0.3749952 0.3749952 0.3749952 0.366843084
     S 0.005936155 0.003710097 0.1762296 0.0000000 0.0000000 0.008152069
     I 0.439128990 0.445065145 0.4487752 0.6250048 0.6250048 0.625004848
>
```

Fig. 7.24 HMM posterior probabilities for Eddy HMM

For readers interested in a little more detail than we've provided here, Rabiner (1989 #825) and Fonzo et al. (2007 #824) are highly recommended. Fonzo et al. (2007 #824) provided both a background to the theory of HMMs but also a survey of the areas within the bioinformatics discipline where HMMs are currently finding favor, such as in gene finding and protein family characterization. Rabiner (1989 #825) provided a very comprehensive discussion on HMMs and how they have been applied in speech recognition.

7.11 Conditional Random Field (CRF)

Conditional random fields (CRFs) are discriminative undirected probabilistic graphical models most often used for labeling or parsing sequential data such as that encountered in natural language processing or biological sequence analysis. In the life sciences, CRFs have been used to great effect in gene finding. As readers may have deduced, CRFs provide an alternative to the related HMM.[8]

The undirected graphical model (also known as a *Markov random field*) represents each random variable whose distribution is to be inferred as a vertex, with dependencies between the random variables being the edges.

So then, CRFs form a probabilistic framework for labeling and segmenting structured data such as sequences, and we define a conditional probability distribution over the label sequences, given a particular observed sequence, rather than a joint distribution over both label and observation sequences. Or, to put it another way,

A conditional random field (CRF) is a Markov random field of unobservables which are globally conditioned on a set of observables (Lafferty et al. 2001 #830).

The primary advantage of CRFs over HMMs is their conditional nature, resulting in the relaxation of the independence assumptions required by HMMs, but they also avoid the label bias problem, a weakness exhibited by maximum entropy Markov models (MEMMs) and other conditional Markov models based on directed graphical models. But a very real-world consideration is that CRFs often outperform both MEMMs and HMMs on real-world tasks in many fields, including bioinformatics, computational linguistics, and speech recognition, something which can be a very important characteristic.

Representation is a fundamental problem when labeling sequential data, and our ideal would be a model that supports tractable inference but also represents the data in such a way as to avoid independence assumptions. An approach we can use to satisfy these requirements is to look for a conditional probability model rather than the joint probability model of the HMM. We can do this by defining a conditional probability over the label sequences, given a particular sequence $\mathbf{x} - P(Y|x)$ – and avoid the joint distribution over both the label and observation sequences that we

---

[8] In fact, a CRF is a Markov random field trained discriminatively.

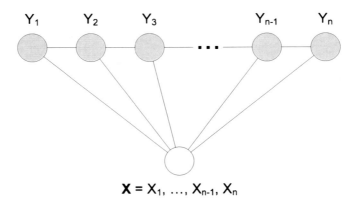

Fig. 7.25 Common CRF graph representation for sequential data

used with HMMs. We can build our conditional model to label some novel observed sequence x^* by selecting the label sequence y^* that maximizes $P(y^*|x^*)$.

Define $G = (V, E)$ to be an undirected graph[9] where V denotes the set of vertices (random variables we are interested in determining distributions for), and E denotes the set of edges (dependencies between the random variables). We can view a CRF to be an instance of this model (an undirected graphical model or Markov random field), globally conditioned on X, a random variable representing the observed sequences. Within G, therefore, there is a node $v \in V$ that corresponds to each random variable that represents an element $Y_v \in Y$. If each Y_v obeys the Markov property that we discussed with HMMs above, with respect to G, then (Y, X) is a conditional random field. While the structure of G may be arbitrary, the most common graph encountered when modeling sequences is where the nodes that correspond to Y form a simple chain, as shown in Fig. 7.25.

In an undirected graphical model, edges simply represent some form of compatibility function, or potential function, between values of the random variables, which are globally normalized to assign a probability to each graph configuration. We'll discuss this more below.

For the remainder of this section, we'll relate our discussion on the theory with gene prediction – finding subsequences of bases that encode proteins – in which CRFs have been used to great effect. In essence, in gene prediction we are presented with the sequence from an original strand of DNA and need to predict the *coding sequence* (or CDS) that will be deterministically translated into amino acids. Using CRFs allows us to incorporate arbitrary, nonindependent features of the input without having to make conditional independence assumptions about feature interaction. This can be very valuable since we can include elements from protein databases, EST data, or other data elements that can improve accuracy.

---

[9] We actually describe graphs in much more detail in Chap. 11. In this section, we simply introduce the notation with only a modicum of the necessary explanation.

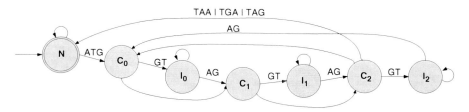

Fig. 7.26 FSM representation of a CRF (Culotta et al. 2005 #835)

HMMs model the joint probability distribution $p(\mathbf{x}, \mathbf{y})$, but in gene prediction, because $\mathbf{x}$ is known at testing time, we don't need to model the uncertainty of $\mathbf{x}$, so we can instead model the conditional probability $p(\mathbf{y}|\mathbf{x})$.

Given $G = (\mathbf{x}, \mathbf{y})$ and a set of *cliques* $C = \{\{\mathbf{x}_c, \mathbf{y}_c\}\}$, a CRF defines the conditional probability of a label sequence $\mathbf{y}$ given an observed sequence $\mathbf{x}$:

$$p_\Lambda(\mathbf{y}|\mathbf{x}) = \frac{1}{Z(\mathbf{x})} \prod_{c \in C} \Phi(\mathbf{y}_c, x_c; \Lambda),$$

where Φ is a real-valued potential function parameterized by Λ and the normalization factor $Z(\mathbf{x}) = \sum \prod_{c \in C} \Phi(\mathbf{y}_c, \mathbf{x}_c)$. The potential function can be parameterized by a set of feature functions $\{f_i\}$ over each clique, such as

$$\Phi(\mathbf{y}_c, \mathbf{x}_c; \Lambda) = \exp\left(\sum_i \lambda_i f_i(\mathbf{y}_c, \mathbf{x}_c)\right).$$

The model is parameterized by a set of weights $\Lambda = \{\lambda_i\}$, where each λ_i weights the output of feature function f_i.

Given training data D, and maximum-likelihood training, Λ is chosen to maximize the log-likelihood of the data being maximized, with $L(\Lambda) = \sum_{(\mathbf{x},\mathbf{y}) \in D} \log p_\Lambda(\mathbf{y}|\mathbf{x})$.

Because we are using a different semantic for the edges, we can add edges to our graphical model between a given label y_i and any set of observed nodes in $\mathbf{x}$ without creating further dependencies between label nodes. In addition, given an observed $\mathbf{x}$, we don't have to consider any dependencies among $\mathbf{x}$ when we model $p(y_i|\mathbf{x})$.

Given an input sequence of DNA bases $\mathbf{x} = \{x_1, x_2, ..., x_n\}$ with $x_i \in \{a, c, g, t\}$, each sequence $\mathbf{x}$ has an associated set of labels $\mathbf{y} = \{y_1, y_2, ..., y_n\}$ where $y_i \in \{C, C'\}$, which corresponds to a coding or noncoding region, respectively. Gene prediction therefore is to discover a mapping function $f(\mathbf{x}) = \mathbf{y}$. Probabilistic models such as HMMs and CRFs assume that $\mathbf{x}, \mathbf{y}$ are random variables and attempt to learn the relationship (statistical dependence) between them.

Culotta et al. (2005 #835) described a finite-state machine representation of a CRF, as illustrated in Fig. 7.26.

Table 7.11 CRF model features to predict label y_i, where b_i is the identity of the base at position i (Culotta et al. 2005 #835)

Feature type	Subtypes
Base	$b_{i-5}, b_{i-4}, b_{i-3}, b_{i-2}, b_{i-1}, b_i$
	$b_{i-4}, b_{i-3}, b_{i-2}, b_{i-1}, b_i$
	$b_{i+4}, b_{i+3}, b_{i+2}, b_{i+1}, b_i$
	b_{i-2}, b_{i-1}, b_i
	b_{i+2}, b_{i+1}, b_i
	b_{i-1}, b_i
	$b_{i+1} b_i$
	$b_{i-2}, b_{i-1}, b_i, b_{i+1}, b_{i+2}$
	b_{i-1}
	b_{i+1}
	b_i
Histogram (windowsize = 5, historysize = 40, futuresize = 10)	Frequency of base singletons, pairs, and triples; frequency of disjunctions of size 2 (e.g., G or T)
BLASTX	Number of hits, maximum score, sum of scores; conjunctions at $i-1 \wedge i$ and $i+1 \wedge i$; conjunctions with EXTERNAL features

In this model, the definition of y_i has been extended such that $y_i \in \{C, I, N\}$, where I represents an intron and N is either a noncoding exon or intergenic (not transcribed into pre-mRNA).

Since base triples, or codons, encode for proteins, output coding region lengths must be a multiple of 3, so the labels for C and I are expanded to $\{C_0, C_1, C_2\}$, $\{I_0, I_1, I_2\}$, respectively.

Further, known information such as regularities in coding region borders, for example splice sites, are also leveraged. For example, coding regions always begin with the start codon "ATG" and end with one of the stop codons "TAA," "TGA," or "TAG"; 99% of transitions from C to I begin with "GT"; and transitions from I to C end with introns "AG" (the 5' and 3' splice sites, respectively). Table 7.11 summarizes the various features of the CRF model, and we direct the interested reader to Culotta et al. (2005 #835) for a more detailed explanation. To highlight one example, examining the statistics of sequences of amino acids can be useful since coding regions consist of base triples that will be translated into amino acids. While a hierarchical model could be used for this purpose, considering the identity of the previous five bases can provide similar information.

The example outlined above, from Culotta et al. (2005 #835), documented a 10% reduction in base-level errors from using CRFs over HMMs.

Another gene predictor system – Conrad – is described in DeCaprio et al. (2007 #834). Wang and Sauer (2008 #831) described a method for predicting order and disorder in proteins using CRFs.

A drawback of the HMM is that we have to model dependent features of the input sequence that are often arbitrary, a challenge that can be particularly challenging for gene prediction because there are many external sources of evidence that may be valuable. HMMs assume that each feature is generated independently (by some hidden process), but this is not generally true. We can, however, overcome this challenge by modeling each dependency, but this becomes impractical in general. CRFs, discriminatively trained as opposed to generatively trained (as is the case for HMMs), are designed to handle nonindependent input features, which can help us significantly.

Readers interested in further details are recommended to read Bishop (2006 #211), Lafferty et al. (2001 #830), DeCaprio et al. (2007 #834), or Wallach (2004 #829) for more details on CRFs. For examples of CRFs, the reader is directed to DeCaprio et al. (2007 #834) for an example of gene finding, Wang and Sauer (2008 #831) for an example focused on predicting order and disorder in proteins, Liu et al. (2005 #832) for an example on how CRFs are being used for protein fold recognition, and Wu et al. (2009 #833) for a novel loss of heterozygosity (LOH) [in tumor evolution] inference and segmentation algorithm.

7.12   Array Comparative Genomic Hybridization

Array Comparative Genomic Hybridization (aCGH) is a technique to detect genomic copy number variations at a higher level of resolution than available using *comparative genomic hybridization* (CGH).

In summary, DNA from the test sample and a reference sample are labeled using different fluorophores and hybridized to several thousand probes.[10] The ratio of the fluorescence intensity of the test to that of the reference DNA is then calculated and used to measure the copy number changes for a particular location in the genome.

Copy number changes at a level of 5–10 kilobases of DNA can be detected using this method. Newer methods are providing even higher levels of resolution: 200 base pair resolution can be attained using *high-resolution CGH*.

A typical analysis graphs the clones/chromosomes (along the x-axis) against the copy number (y-axis). We can then smooth the data to reduce noise; detect loss, normal, or gain amplification; and perform breakpoint analysis. Naïve smoothing would have us "follow the curve," but we can also perform "discrete" smoothing, where the copy numbers are integer values, where the smoothed values average across a number of breakpoints, with corresponding levels. Using a fitness function to score each smoothing according to the fitness of the data, we deduce the smoothing that has the highest fitness score.

In the discrete case, breakpoints provide a segmentation along the clones/chromosomes, and levels identify (averaged) copy numbers for each, with an associated variance for the group of clones/chromosomes.

The fitness function typically used is a Gaussian noise process–based function along with maximum likelihood and a penalty adjustment term for model complexity.

---

[10] Current arrays contain 100,000–2,000,000 short oligonucleotide probes (approximately 45–80 nucleotides in length).

Given aCGH $x_1, ..., x_n$, breakpoints $0<y_1<...<y_N<x_n$, levels $\mu_1, ..., \mu_N$, and error variances $\sigma_1^2, ..., \sigma_N^2$, we'll have sets $(x_1, ..., x_{y_1}), (x_{y_1+1}, ..., x_{y_2}), ..., (x_{y_{N+1}}, ..., x_n)$, to give us likelihood functions:

$$\prod_{i=1}^{y_1} \frac{1}{\sigma_1 \sqrt{2\pi}} e^{-\frac{1}{2}\left(\frac{x_i-\mu_1}{\sigma_1}\right)^2}, ..., \prod_{i=y_{N+1}}^{n} \frac{1}{\sigma_{N+1}\sqrt{2\pi}} e^{-\frac{1}{2}\left(\frac{x_i-\mu_{N+1}}{\sigma_{N+1}}\right)^2}.$$

Maximum-likelihood estimators for μ and σ^2 can be found explicitly, but we need to add our penalty to the log-likelihood for control of the N breakpoints:

$$f(y_1, ..., y_N) = \sum_{i=1}^{N+1} (y_{i+1} - y_i) \log \hat{\sigma}_i + \lambda N.$$

HMMs can be used to create effect to address the computationally hard problem of maximizing fitness.

Cancer, birth defects, and other disease conditions due to chromosomal aberrations due to microdeletions or duplications can be identified using this method.

Shinawi and Cheung (2008 #838) provided a good overview of the clinical applications and implications of this method. Based on the results obtained, better tests can be performed to measure the DNA copy number for a target gene. But we can also use this method to help us monitor cancer progression and better distinguish between whether something is metastatic or not using *fluorescence in situ hybridization* (FISH) probes. The method is also seeing use in identifying regional copy number markers that are being used for cancer prediction, as well as identifying and understanding the genes involved in cancer, so that better therapies can be developed to target the genes or to avoid therapies that cause tumor resistance.

We'll walk through an example that is available with the aCGH R package. We first consider creating an aCGH object from log2.ratios and clone info files, such as is shown below.

```
> datadir <- system.file(package = "aCGH")
datadir <- paste(datadir, "/examples", sep="")

clones.info <- read.table(file = file.path(datadir, "clones.info.ex.txt"), header = TRUE, sep =
"\t", quote="", comment.char="")
log2.ratios <- read.table(file = file.path(datadir, "log2.ratios.ex.txt"), header = TRUE, sep =
"\t", quote="", comment.char="")
pheno.type <- read.table(file = file.path(datadir, "pheno.type.ex.txt"), header = TRUE, sep = "\t",
quote="", comment.char="")
ex.acgh <- create.aCGH(log2.ratios, clones.info, pheno.type)
```

This creates our aCGH object (ex.acgh) so that we can use it later.

```
> data(colorectal)
colorectal
summary(colorectal)
sample.names(colorectal)
phenotype(colorectal)
plot(colorectal)
```

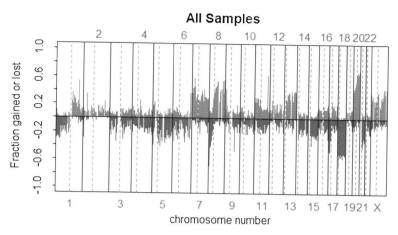

Fig. 7.27   Colorectal data

The plot output for the above command is shown in Fig. 7.27.
Now we'll subset our data

```
> colorectal[1:1000, 1:30]
aCGH object
Call: `[.aCGH`(colorectal, 1:1000, 1:30)

Number of Arrays 30
Number of Clones 1000
Warning message:
In `[.aCGH`(colorectal, 1:1000, 1:30) : subsetting the log2.ratios only
```

and impute the log2 ratios.

```
> log2.ratios.imputed(ex.acgh) <- impute.lowess(ex.acgh)
Processing chromosome   1
Processing chromosome   2
Processing chromosome   3
Processing chromosome   4
Processing chromosome   5
Processing chromosome   6
Processing chromosome   7
Processing chromosome   8
Processing chromosome   9
Processing chromosome   10
Processing chromosome   11
Processing chromosome   12
Processing chromosome   13
Processing chromosome   14
Processing chromosome   15
Processing chromosome   16
Processing chromosome   17
Processing chromosome   18
Processing chromosome   19
Processing chromosome   20
Processing chromosome   21
Processing chromosome   22
Processing chromosome   23
```

Our next step is to determine the HMM states of the clones.

```
> hmm(ex.acgh) <- find.hmm.states(ex.acgh)
sample is 1 chromosomes: 1  2  3  4  5  6  7  8  9  10  11  12  13  14  15  16  17  18  19  20  21
22  23
sample is 2 chromosomes: 1  2  3  4  5  6  7  8  9  10  11  12  13  14  15  16  17  18  19  20  21
22  23
```

Next we need to calculate the standard deviations for each array and find the genomic events for each sample.

```
> sd.samples(ex.acgh) <- computeSD.Samples(ex.acgh)
genomic.events(ex.acgh) <- find.genomic.events(ex.acgh)

Finding outliers
Finding focal low level aberrations
Finding transitions
Finding focal amplifications
Processing chromosome   1
Processing chromosome   2
Processing chromosome   3
Processing chromosome   4
Processing chromosome   5
Processing chromosome   6
Processing chromosome   7
Processing chromosome   8
Processing chromosome   9
Processing chromosome   10
Processing chromosome   11
Processing chromosome   12
Processing chromosome   13
Processing chromosome   14
Processing chromosome   15
Processing chromosome   16
Processing chromosome   17
Processing chromosome   18
Processing chromosome   19
Processing chromosome   20
Processing chromosome   21
Processing chromosome   22
Processing chromosome   23
warning messages:
1: In max(indstretch[indstretch < indaber[m]]) :
   no non-missing arguments to max; returning -Inf
2: In min(indstretch[indstretch > indaber[m]]) :
   no non-missing arguments to min; returning Inf
3: In min(indstretch[indstretch > indaber[m]]) :
   no non-missing arguments to min; returning Inf
```

From here, we can plot the HMM states as shown in Fig. 7.28.

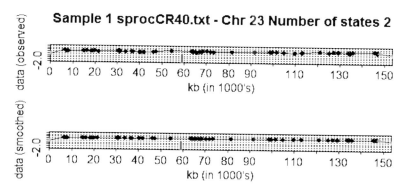

Fig. 7.28 HMM states for our aCGH analysis

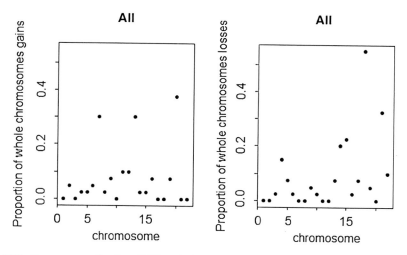

Fig. 7.29 Summary profiles for aCGH analysis

```
> plotSummaryProfile(colorectal)
warning messages:
1: In bxp(list(stats = c(0, 0.5, 4, 5, 10), n = 40, conf = c(2.87581029181014, :
   some notches went outside hinges ('box'): maybe set notch=FALSE
2: In bxp(list(stats = c(0, 0, 0, 0.5, 1), n = 40, conf = c(-0.124909967576651, :
   some notches went outside hinges ('box'): maybe set notch=FALSE
3: In bxp(list(stats = c(0, 0, 0, 0.5, 1), n = 40, conf = c(-0.124909967576651, :
   some notches went outside hinges ('box'): maybe set notch=FALSE
```

The output of plotSummaryProfile() is shown in Fig. 7.29.

Díaz-Uriarte and Rueda (2007 #842) described the ADaCGH package, and Hofmann et al. (2009 #841) provided an example using R, Bioconductor, and the snapCGH R package, two other software packages that can be used to perform array CGH analysis.

Scheinin et al. (2010 #839) described a web-based tool called CGHpower (available at http://www.cangem.org/cghpower/) that performs sample size calculations for array CGH experiments but also includes several examples, such as that from Myllykangas et al. (2008 #840).

7.13   Conclusion

The problem with any introductory text is to determine what is introductory and what is not; a very subjective question at the best of times. Some readers may consider this chapter went far beyond what would normally be considered as introductory. For Bayesian methods, however, we felt it necessary to include concepts and tools that *may* be valuable but *will* be encountered when using Bayesian methods.

So, this being said, can we skip these methods in favor of those described elsewhere? Anyone who has talked to a consultant will recognize our answer: yes. . .and no.

Bayesian methods offer considerable value in data mining. A core consideration is the inclusion of knowledge outside the data you are analyzing; knowledge that subject matter experts have about their disciplines. This knowledge can often shortcut the process. But, it can also lead us down a path that we ultimately realize didn't exist. The questions we should ask are whether this knowledge is valuable and whether this knowledge can be encoded into our model. If the answers to these questions are yes and yes, then it is definitely worthwhile incorporating Bayesian methods into your analytical toolkit.

We have only scratched the surface with our discussions in this chapter – maybe we've only scratched a part of the surface. As can be said with any of the topics we introduce in this text, each of them deserves a whole book of their own. And such books exist. For interested readers, we particularly recommend Woodworth (2005 #23) and Bolstad (2004 #18). Finally, we also highly recommend Sivia (1996 #283), a small book that is a useful handbook to have when using Bayesian techniques. Be careful, though, it can get dog-eared very quickly!

References

Besemer J, Lomsadze A, Borodovsky M (2001) GeneMarkS: a self-training method for prediction of gene starts in microbial genomes. Implications for finding sequence motifs in regulatory regions. Nucleic Acids Res 29:2607–2618

Bishop CM (2006) Pattern recognition and machine learning. Information science and statistics. Springer, New York

Bolstad WM (2004) Introduction to Bayesian statistics. Wiley-Interscience, Hoboken

Borodovsky M, McIninch J (1993) GeneMark: parallel gene recognition for both DNA strands. Comput Chem 17:123–133

Chartrand G (1985) Introductory graph theory. Dover, New York

Chou K-C (2001) Prediction of protein cellular attributes using pseudo amino acid composition. Proteins 43:246–255

Culotta A, Kulp D, McCallum A (2005) Gene prediction with conditional random fields. University of Massachusetts, Amherst

De Ferrari L, Aitken S (2006) Mining housekeeping genes with a Naive Bayes classifier. BMC Genomics 7:277

DeCaprio D et al (2007) Conrad: gene prediction using conditional random fields. Genome Res 17:1389–1398

Díaz-Uriarte R, Rueda OM (2007) ADaCGH: a parallelized web-based application and R package for the analysis of aCGH data. PLoS One 2:e737

Eddy SR (2004) What is a hidden Markov model? Nat Biotechnol 22:1315–1316

Fonzo VD, Aluffi-Pentini F, Parisi V (2007) Hidden Markov models in bioinformatics. Curr Bioinforma 2:49–61

Gupta AK, Nadarajah S (2004) Handbook of beta distribution and its applications. Marcel Dekker, New York

Han X (2006) Inferring species phylogenies: a microarray approach. Computational intelligence and bioinformatics: international conference on intelligent computing, ICIC 2006, Kunming, China. Springer, New York, pp 485–493

Hofmann WA et al (2009) Analysis of array-CGH data using the R and Bioconductor software suite. Comp Funct Genomics 2009:8

Ji Y et al (2005) Applications of beta-mixture models in bioinformatics. Bioinformatics 21:2118–2122

Kadane J (1990) Comment: codifying chance. Statistical Science 5(1):18–20

Lafferty JD, McCallum A, Pereira FCN (2001) Conditional random fields: probabilistic models for segmenting and labeling sequence data. Proceedings of the eighteenth international conference on machine learning. Morgan Kaufmann Publishers Inc., San Francisco, pp 282–289

Lee Y et al (2009) Bayesian classifier for predicting malignant renal cysts on MDCT: early clinical experience. Am J Roentgenol 193:W106–W111

Liu Y, Carbonell J, Weigele P, Gopalakrishnan V (2005) Segmentation Conditional Random Fields (SCRFs): A New Approach for Protein Fold Recognition. In S. Miyano, J. Mesirov, S. Kasif, S. Istrail, P. Pevzner & M. Waterman (Eds.), Research in Computational Molecular Biology 3500:408–422: Springer Berlin / Heidelberg

Marcus DA, Mathematical Association of America (2008) Graph theory: a problem oriented approach. Mathematical Association of America, Washington, DC

Moore AW (2004) Naive Bayes Classifiers, from http://www.autonlab.org/tutorials/naive02.pdf. Accessed on July 26, 2009

Mosteller F, Youtz C (1990) Quantifying probabilistic expressions. Statistical Science 5(1):2–12

Myllykangas S et al (2008) Integrated gene copy number and expression microarray analysis of gastric cancer highlights potential target genes. Int J Cancer 123:817–825

Nakashima H, Nishikawa K (1994) Discrimination of intracellular and extracellular proteins using amino acid composition and residue-pair frequencies. J Mol Biol 238:54–61

Neapolitan RE (2003) Learning Bayesian networks. Prentice Hall, Harlow

Rabiner LR (1989) A tutorial on hidden Markov models and selected applications in speech recognition. Proc IEEE 77:257–286

Roy S et al (2009) Exploiting amino acid composition for predicting protein-protein interactions. PLoS One 4:e7813

Scheinin I et al (2010) CGHpower: exploring sample size calculations for chromosomal copy number experiments. BMC Bioinforma 11:331

Shinawi M, Cheung SW (2008) The array CGH and its clinical applications. Drug Discov Today 13:760–770

Sivia DS (1996) Data analysis: a Bayesian tutorial. Oxford Science Publications/Clarendon Press/Oxford University Press, Oxford/New York

Wallach HM (2004) Conditional random fields: an introduction. Department of Computer and Information Science, University of Pennsylvania, Philadelphia

Wallach J (2007) Interpretation of diagnostic tests. Lippincott Williams & Wilkins, Philadelphia

Wang L, Sauer UH (2008) OnD-CRF: predicting order and disorder in proteins conditional random fields. Bioinformatics 24:1401–1402

Wilson RJ (1996) Introduction to graph theory. Longman, Harlow

Woodworth GG (2005) Biostatistics: a Bayesian introduction. Wiley-Interscience, Hoboken

Wu L-Y et al (2009) Conditional random pattern algorithm for LOH inference and segmentation. Bioinformatics 25:61–67

Chapter 8
Machine-Learning Techniques

Abstract Our ultimate objective in data mining is to identify any hidden patterns or relationships between our data elements, and in one sense, machine learning provides us with a set of techniques to do just that: techniques that allow us to learn the patterns without any outside influence (unsupervised learning). However, just as is the case with anything, that power comes at a price, but the results can be very interesting and very significant. In other cases, we have some sense on what the results should be and so can guide the learning techniques through an initial "training" phase, directing our system and honing the results (supervised learning). These two broad classifications of machine-learning methods will ground us as we discuss a broad range of techniques and where they are currently being applied in life sciences research, expanding our toolkit and enabling us to take a very different path in our analysis efforts: using an artificial intelligence discipline and letting the data tell us what it contains. As datasets grow, these techniques become more important.

8.1 Introduction

As its name suggests, machine learning is all about automated processes to gain intelligent insight into a dataset. We introduced two of the major areas of machine learning – supervised learning and unsupervised learning – with a brief informal characterization earlier in the book. In this chapter, we introduce these areas more formally, along with several others. Machine learning provides significant opportunity for us to apply rigorous, extensively researched methods to our data and extract significant and often unexpected knowledge.

Although we have mentioned this elsewhere, it is useful to reiterate some of the challenges that affect our efforts in the life sciences. In particular, the heterogeneity of the data we capture, such as clinical data (e.g., symptoms, demographics, diagnoses, images, biochemical tests, video, vital signals), logistics data (e.g., policies, guidelines, clinical trial data, charges, costs), molecular data, and bibliographical data, to name a few, are stored in numerical, image, text, sound, and video

R. Sullivan, *Introduction to Data Mining for the Life Sciences*,
DOI 10.1007/978-1-59745-290-8_8, © Springer Science+Business Media, LLC 2012

formats. Compound this with the fact that the evidence-based nature of medicine, which is often a major component of what we are studying, means that large quantities of high-quality data are typically available to us. These dimensions come together in *requiring* data mining to be a part of our efforts – whether this is through an explicit or implicit process.

Many areas of machine learning are often associated with a primary mechanism of learning: classification, association, and the like. However, each area has tremendous opportunities for us to explore and significant value in understanding patterns of interest that might otherwise be overlooked. In fact, machine learning has been successfully applied in many areas of the life sciences including diagnosis, prevention, therapeutic decision making, disease discovery, biomarker discovery, and data relationship and structure detection to name a few. Recently, such techniques have been applied to areas such as improving hospital resource utilization (Ng et al. 2006 #120). Morik et al. (2000 #121) demonstrated a more direct example of how data-mining principles and machine-learning techniques can help to improve operational protocols in the clinical setting.

A substantial amount of data mining is based upon machine-learning techniques. This discipline has been a major force in the data-mining arena for many years but has proven particularly useful as the volume of data has exponentially grown over the past few years. In fact, machine-learning techniques and their application to data mining is one of the most active areas of current research.

Techniques we have described elsewhere continue to be applicable. Researchers use association rules, feature selection, regression, neural networks, reinforcement learning, and a host of other techniques we have described, as well as some which are out of the scope of this book, including linear discriminant analysis, logic programming, and others.

Machine learning has been the subject of many books in and of itself, and is a vibrant area of applied research. It is impossible to do it justice in a single chapter, and we therefore only attempt to give an overview of some of the topics that fall into this domain. The reader interested in further readings of general applications of machine learning in the life sciences is recommended to (Enderle 2007 #122). For a more general introduction, any number of sources can be recommended, including Mitchell (1997 #30), Bishop (2006 #211), Alpaydin (2004 #22), or Witten and Frank (2005 #11). We offer some additional, and some more focused, options at the end of this chapter also.

There are several concepts that permeate our discussion on machine learning: classification learning, association learning, cluster analysis, supervised learning, unsupervised learning, and training, and we'll begin by providing some definitions for these core concepts.

The primary objective of *classification learning* is to correctly identify the outcome for an input instance. Since this type of learning is often characterized by having the correct output defined for each input instance in the training set, it is typically called a *supervised learning* method. That is, we typically train our model by providing it with the output associated with the input. We can be confident in its accuracy only when/if it successfully classifies a previously unseen instance. Thus, the process has two distinct phases: the first, *training* phase uses a dataset of instances along with each instance's correct response (or output); the second *learning* phase is where we open the model up to previously unseen instances and evaluate its performance against these instances.

With *association learning*, there is no predefined output, instead the inputs themselves are used to learn the patterns or structures within the data – anything which is interesting to us, a notion we have already considered. This type of *unsupervised* learning allows the model itself to extract information about any aspect of the instances used for the learning phase. Note that there are still two phases: training and learning.

One fact that is a valuable differentiator between the two types of learning is that association learning can be used for prediction of an attribute – any attribute – and not just the classification of the instance.

Cluster analysis is used to group instances together when there is no specified classification and occurs according to any natural groupings within the data itself.

As already indicated, a significant part of the process for any machine-learning system is to train the system using representative data. That is, to allow the system to gain *knowledge* about the datasets we will be presenting. Such training will prime the model parameters so that when the system is presented with previously unseen data, the results will (hopefully) be in line with our expectations. As we shall see, our expectations can radically affect how the system performs.

Training is often conducted in a separate phase of operation – the training phase (sic) – that is distinct from the systems' operational phase. Over time, this training may be performed again and again for reasons such as our gaining of new insight, as we recognize a need for a higher level of accuracy in our results, or because we see a degradation of its performance against previously unseen datasets.

Fundamentally, we can consider the learning activity associated with the training, since that is our real intent, as either *supervised* or *unsupervised*, and some models use a combination of these approaches. In essence, supervised learning provides both the model's input instances (the independent, or feature variables) along with their associated output values (dependent or target values). We can get immediate feedback on how well the system did, and we can apply some form of corrective action as appropriate to improve our subsequent performance. For unsupervised learning, we do not provide the output values and instead expect the model to group or classify the inputs into meaningful sets.

Consider a hypothetical example where we have a dataset containing the results of patient questionnaires – for example, these may have been used as part of the initial patient screening process for some clinical trial – that include questions on a wide range of relevant topics, one topic relating to the potential for noncompliance.[1]

---

[1] Noncompliance in this context specifically considers the situation where patients do not follow through on the complete regiment for their medications. This has been a particular challenge with anti-infective drugs where patients will often feel better before the complete course of drugs has been taken and will stop taking the drug. An impact of this is that the infective agent may not have been completely eradicated. While a full discourse is outside the scope of this text, one of the consequences of this (in)action is that the patient may have a recurrence of the outbreak, which could potentially require a different, stronger drug.

We may augment that dataset with some information from health-care professionals involved with those same patients: here the attributes indicate whether the patient *was* noncompliant or not. Making such questions too overt may result in invalid data being entered by the patient; making them too subtle could also result in unusable data. We could use this augmented dataset, including the health-care provider's input, to train a model to detect future patients that may fall into the noncompliant category. Since the health-care professionals have given us information on each patient, we can use supervised learning methods to help us by treating the data provided by the patient as the input and (some of) the data from the health-care provider as the expected output. What if we don't know which patients were noncompliant? We'd like to see who was or who wasn't compliant. In this case, our dataset would contain a smaller number of attributes, excluding the data entered by the health-care professionals, and we would use unsupervised methods to intelligently classify which patients fell into *compliant* and *noncompliant* categories. How we accomplish this is discussed later when we consider unsupervised learning approaches.

Machine-learning techniques require us to include mathematical constructs that are more rigorous and complex than we've described elsewhere in this text. Unfortunately, for some readers, this may be beyond what you encounter on a daily basis, and it may have been a while since this level of mathematics has been studied. We apologize. But stick with it. While it will definitely help if you understand the mathematics, many of the models are available in forms that don't require you to build the mathematical models themselves.

8.1.1 Missing and Erroneous Data

In Chap. 2, we spent some time considering the issue of missing data and how to handle such occurrences. We briefly return to this issue here because there is a particular nuance to this issue as relates to many machine-learning approaches: they apply no particular significance or meaning to missing data.

As we've already discussed, data may be missing for many different reasons, and we will not reiterate them here. However, we do need to be particularly careful when applying machine-learning techniques to our dataset that contains missing data because the reason may be significant and affect our models, just as is the case with other techniques.

Consider a case where we have a dataset of test result data for patients that are our training input for our model. There will likely be cases in which specific tests will not have test results. If we apply the generic "why?" question to the missing data, it may be because the automated instrument we used malfunctioned, or it could be because, for certain patients, the test was not completed. In this latter case, there is valuable information inherent in that decision. In such a case, we may be better off introducing a new value – "not tested" – than to treat it as missing data.

In some respects, taking the above approach will have the same effect as a default value. There is, however, a subtle difference: by incorporating this "additional" value, we are making a statement about this data attribute, that its value is *not* missing, it was omitted *by design*. Being able to make this determination requires knowledge of the data itself that may require you to engage a subject matter expert outside of the data-mining effort. But it has an additional value: once the model has been generated, we can see how important that attribute really was to our model.

Another problem that has particular significance with machine-learning techniques is duplicate data. This can have a major impact on our model as the presence of several instances with the same data can indicate a significance which may or may not be appropriate. We see this in life in general. If we receive a diagnosis from our physician and ask for a second opinion and receive the same diagnosis, this lends it a level of significance. The same can be the case with our models. We need to consider the data very carefully and ask ourselves whether the potential for skewing the model's conclusions exists and whether allowing duplicates in our dataset is appropriate or not.

A particular challenge we shall see as we explore machine learning, and as we go about our day-to-day analysis efforts, is that a fundamental objective of any machine-learning technique is to recognize an as-yet-unseen instance, obviously a very powerful technique. Yet, with this power comes a challenge: we need to temper this to ensure that we are not recognizing, predicting, an attribute, instance, or classification that cannot be reasonably predicted. Using our example from above, if we have a lot of missing data for a particular attribute, the resulting model may be skewed and tend to categorize that attribute incorrectly. This may not be as obvious as we might hope, and unraveling such issues can be challenging indeed.

Let's consider the challenge of ascertaining whether a patient was compliant or was noncompliant as a data-mining effort a little further than we did in the previous section. How can we make this determination if we don't have any direct data that tells us whether or not the patient was compliant? This is a twist on the subject of missing data, but one that we often have to consider.

One approach is to use some surrogate data elements. For example, we may see a relationship between a particular test result and compliance. We may see an increase, for example, in the amylase test results. If we are comfortable that this is specific enough, we could make a determination that for each patient that exhibits an increased amylase level, we will designate them as being in the noncompliant category. Conversely, anyone who doesn't exhibit such an increase will be considered to have been compliant.

An obvious challenge with using such a surrogate is that there are bound to be errors, occasions where the increase is physiologic and has nothing to do with noncompliance. In this and other such cases, we will naturally mislabel the instances. Therefore, we will always need to be cognizant of this and correct for such errors.

An alternate approach would be to see if we can elicit information from the patients themselves, or the health-care professionals who worked with the patients, to try and determine who was compliant and who was not.

Similarly, this may be infeasible, or at least, prone to error, due to timing, people's memories, or accessibility to the patients or professionals.

So do we even try? Of course, but we need to be on the lookout for the issues that could arise. It's worth trying to determine whether or not some data element, or elements, could be used as a determiner for a couple of reasons.

First, it allows us to use supervised learning techniques as alternatives to the unsupervised learning techniques we would otherwise be constrained to use. Second, even if we still elect to use unsupervised techniques, this gives us a means of comparing the effectiveness of our model.

We might, however, be able to obtain such information about a subset of our data. That is, it may be that such information is available to us, but only for some percentage (a small percentage?) of our dataset. If this is the case, we have a natural candidate for our training set – those with expected outcomes – and a natural candidate for the operational phase of the model's execution – those without expected outcomes.

Later in this chapter, we'll see why this partitioning may provide a natural and effective means of dividing our dataset into a set of instances that we can use to train our model, and another set that is usable for the operational phase, where we use our model to generate new information. As is always the case, however, we have to be careful. Would our training set overtrain our model? Are the training set and operational set of instances effectively from the same distribution? If not, we may have a well-trained model, but one which is useless for the data that we can expect to meet in the real world.

8.2   Measure of Similarity

Throughout this book, we are interested in being able to determine how similar, or different, two of our data instances (observations, etc.) are when compared against each other. Although different techniques naturally define *similarity* differently, so as to optimize the algorithms and models underlying the technique, there is a commonality to the concept that we can leverage throughout our study.

There are several points throughout this book where we could validly and appropriately introduce a formal definition of similarity, but we choose to introduce it here as it is a consideration in virtually all machine-learning techniques and, as we shall see when we consider *kernel methods*, is integral to those techniques.

What do we mean when we say that two instances are similar to each other, and what is its' intended purpose? If we answer this in the context of classification, we are saying that two instances are more alike and should thus be grouped together than two others should be. That is, instances x_1 and x_2 should be put into the same classification, but instance x_3 should be put into a different classification. In order to formally accomplish this, we need to have some quantitative measures that we can use within our models that determine this similarity (and difference).

We shall call this similarity measure the *measure of distance* (or just distance). This measure is also referred to as the *proximity* between instances in some of the literature.

Consider a dataset of patient information from a single encounter[2] for a large Phase III clinical trial which contains a value for a LDL cholesterol test. Using the 100–129 range of values to designate the normal range of values for this test, what does it mean for a patient with a value of 134? If a second patient has the value 109 and a third has 98, can we ascribe a valid meaning when we say that "98 is similar to 109?" Is it fair to also say that "134 is dissimilar, or less similar, to 109?" While these questions may at first sight seem fatuous, similarity is a somewhat ephemeral concept that we used in many areas, such as support vector machines. If we take the median value of the normal range above, 114.5, we could use this to determine a relative *distance* for each of our three values to give us values of -19.5 (134), 5.5 (109), and 16.5 (98).[3] We see from these distances that 98 and 109 are closer to each other than 109 and 134. Drawing this on a straight line would show this even more clearly. This very simple example shows the concept of distance as we use it in several machine-learning techniques. However, the challenge comes when not dealing with just a single variable but with two or more variables in combination; our concept of Euclidean distance becomes more complex but still provides a useful measure. As we shall see with support vector machines, the partitioning hyper-plane[4] (our "line" in multiple dimensions) uses this concept of distance to allow our SVM model to work.

Let us consider the Euclidean distance measure a little more formally.[5] Consider two instances from our dataset, $\mathbf{x}_1 = (x_{11}, x_{12}, ..., x_{1n})$ and $\mathbf{x}_2 = (x_{21}, x_{22}, ..., x_{2n})$. We define the distance between two such instances as

$$d(\mathbf{x}_1, \mathbf{x}_2) = \sqrt{(x_{11} - x_{21})^2 + (x_{12} - x_{22})^2 + ... + (x_{1n} - x_{2n})}.$$ [6]

Whatever measure of distance is used, we must ask ourselves what it means: what does it means for $d(\mathbf{x}_1, \mathbf{x}_2) = 2 \times d(\mathbf{x}_2, \mathbf{x}_3)$?

---

[2] We use the term encounter to identify any formal encounter (sic) between a patient and a health-care professional.

[3] Note that we have arbitrarily used *x*-value as opposed to value-*x*.

[4] We shall see later that it is called the *maximum margin hyperplane*.

[5] Other distance measures, such as the Manhattan metric, are useful in certain circumstances; however, many people find the Euclidean measure to be sufficient, and this is certainly the most common form of measure used.

[6] It is not strictly necessary to compute the square root; sometimes we will simply compare the sums of squares.

8.3   Supervised Learning

We have already given a brief, informal definition of supervised learning as being learning where we are given the target (dependent) output values for a given set of independent input values. We use this dataset to improve our model's parameters and have it learn to predict the output values for as-yet-unseen instances.

The result of such an approach is to determine values for our model. For example, in the case of a neural network, this will be to determine the number of layers, number of neurons per layer, and the weights used for each neuron-neuron connection.

However, since we are building our model from a specific starting point, it is highly unlikely that we will get the expected outputs when we start the learning (or training) phase. Thus, we will naturally have a variance between the target value provided as part of the training set and the value predicted from our model. The overall purpose of the learning phase is to minimize the difference between these two values. To aid us in this endeavor, we use an error function, typically denoted by E.

To illustrate this, let us consider a model that outputs a single value. This value could, for example, be a determination as to whether a patient has a certain condition that we are specifically interested in. Given n input instances to our model, we would have a value predicted by our model, which we shall denote as o_i, and a target value provided with the input dataset that we shall denote by t_i. If we denote the difference between these values as a measure of our "error," $o_i - t_i$, we can use the sum of squared errors to provide our error function:

$$E = \sum_{i=1}^{n} (o_i - t_i)^2$$

In the above, the squared error value is used since we are most interested in the (absolute) difference; as we have discussed elsewhere in this book, there could be a positive or negative difference between the values. Note that this is only one of a myriad different error functions, and both the choice of model and the specific problem being studied will guide us toward a particular choice of error function.

Our ideal state would be to have $E = 0$ for our model. In practice, this is not typically possible. First, the dataset being used would have to be totally *clean*, a condition that is difficult to determine at the very least. Second, our model would have to be precise enough, again difficult to achieve if only because of system constraints such as rounding. Third, the closer we get to this ideal state, the longer, typically, would be the processing cycle for each input. This elongation of the processing cycle is not usually a linear relationship between the processing time and increased accuracy. This would quickly make the model unusable. But fundamentally, is this really necessary or even desirable?

8.3.1 Classification Learning

In classification learning, as its name suggests, we wish to take a particular input and designate a specific output class to which it belongs. Our determination of which class it belongs to will be as a result of our model being *trained* using a set of well-defined, complete input instances, along with their respective associated class labels. Each input instance $X = (x_1, x_2, ..., x_n)$ comprises n attribute values, with each x_i being associated with an underlying attribute A_i.[7] Each X has a particular class label y provided to our model for training purposes. The class label is a categorical value, that is, discrete and unordered.[8]

Our first objective, therefore, is to learn from our training data what the underlying generalized mapping is between our input instances and their associated class labels. This mapping (or function), $y = f(X)$, will then be able to predict the class labels for our as-yet-unseen instances. As we shall see later, this mapping may be mathematical formulae, it may be (a set of) decision trees, or it may be classification rules.

Once we have our mapping, we wish to validate its accuracy. We *could* use the model as is without going through this step, but we would not be able to determine a very important characteristic of our model: its accuracy. Our goal is to develop a model that works for any (pertinent) data that might be presented to it. So far, we have only provided it with a set of training instances and so we have no way of determining whether or not the model has been overfit to the training data. Recalling our earlier discussion on overfitting, we want to make sure that any characteristics of the training set that may be peculiar to the training set itself and not present in the general dataset to which our model will be exposed are not evident in the model. In order to do this, we undertake a *validation* step whereby we provide to the model a second set of data which was not a part of the training data. This validation set would have associated class labels. We would use the model to generate what it believes are the correct class labels and then compare with our knowledge of the real class labels. This validation set is typically chosen from the more general population of data to which the model will be exposed but must be completely independent of the training set in order to be as valuable as possible. If we cannot generate class labels for a separate validation set, we can elect to randomly exclude instances from our training set and use those as the validation set.

Performing the validation step allows us to get a measure of accuracy for our model by providing a percentage of the validation set that it was able to correctly classify. There are several methods which can be used to measure the accuracy of classifiers which we return to in Chap. 9. If our model passes the mark of what we

---

[7] Attributes are often referred to as *features* of X.

[8] It is at this point that we introduce another point that we will discuss in much more detail later in the book. If we do not have the class label, the problem is not one of classification but is instead a *clustering* problem. That is to say that we do not know what the classes are and instead rely on the data itself to generate the classes for us.

consider its required accuracy, we can use it in its normal execution mode to classify the as-yet-unseen data in our mining dataset.

As we discuss elsewhere, if we are interested in identifying a numeric output rather than a categorical output, the problem is not one of classification but of prediction. We conclude this section by mentioning that our mapping, $y = f(X)$, changes only in that y is now a continuous or ordered value. We expand upon the similarities and differences between these two concepts in Chap. 9 also.

8.4   Unsupervised Learning

8.4.1   Association Learning

One challenge we encounter with the association learning method relates to the sheer number of association rules which may be defined. This can become overwhelming and may, in actuality, obfuscate what we are trying to uncover. We use various heuristics to help us to manage the number of rules. For example, we may use only rules which apply to a larger proportion of the dataset we are processing, or we may only retain those rules which meet a minimum level of accuracy, or we may use a combination, or any other heuristic.

Elsewhere we introduced the terms support (also referred to as *coverage*) as a measure of the number of instances correctly predicted and *confidence* (also referred to as *accuracy*) as a measure of the proportion of instances to which the rule applies as methods of eliminating rules that will not provide us with the value we are looking for. However, if we were to use only this approach, the problem would quickly become infeasible.

We have also discussed the *Apriori* algorithm as a method for association learning earlier in this text, an alternate method of approaching this problem. Since we did discuss this earlier, we refer the reader back to Chap. 4.

8.4.2   Clustering

Within the context of machine learning, clusters correspond to hidden patterns in the data, and searching for clusters is typically an unsupervised learning activity. Thus, the obvious challenge is to first identify a set of appropriate clusters themselves and then associate the instances with their representative cluster. As we shall see in this chapter and in a later chapter dedicated to clustering, we have to be careful with our algorithm so that we don't end up on one end of the spectrum with one cluster for every input or, on the other, to have a single cluster that covers everything. While admittedly extreme cases, pragmatically, we can easily end up with too many or too few clusters. We may find, for example, that one or more of our clusters are naturally subdivided due to subtypes of the inputs. The question, therefore, is how do we measure whether we have sufficient clusters and successfully associate inputs with those clusters?

Subjective measurements, such as how useful the results are to users, are often sufficient.

We may append a classification step to allow us to give a description of how new instances should be placed into a cluster so that we can ascertain how this segmentation occurred.

8.5 Semisupervised Learning

Intuition leads us to the correct conclusion that semisupervised learning (SSL) falls somewhere between supervised and unsupervised learning. In this approach, we identify target (output) values with a small amount of our training data, leaving the larger amount with no output/target values.

Since there is a cost to identifying output values – typically this assignment requires human subject matter expertise – the cost may be too great for us to label every instance in our training set. Conversely, leaving every training instance unlabeled may not be desirable. In fact, researchers have found that taking this mixed-mode approach can lead to considerable improvement in learning accuracy.

In short, in SSL, the unlabeled data is used to modify or prioritize the hypotheses that are made from using the labeled data alone. Using statistical notation, although not all techniques are probabilistic, if the unlabeled data is represented by $p(x)$ and hypotheses are represented as $p(y|x)$, then we are looking at techniques which assume that these two models share parameters.

Zhu (2005 #551) provided an interesting survey into many of the techniques and suggested an approach to selecting an appropriate SSL technique:

> Do the classes produce well clustered data? If yes, EM with generative mixture models may be a good choice; do the features naturally split into two sets? If yes, co-training may be appropriate; is it true that two points with similar features tend to be in the same class? If yes, graph-based methods can be used; Already using SVM? Transductive SVM is a natural extension; is the existing supervised classifier complicated and hard to modify? Self-training is a practical wrapper method.

In this section, we'll describe EM and cotraining, and discuss graph-based methods, but these are only islands in the ocean of algorithms which include self-training, generative models, S2VMs, the larger collection of graph-based algorithms, and multiview algorithms. The class of graph-based methods is seeing good application in motif discovery. We ignore transductive methods, which are typically defined as those methods that work only on the labeled and unlabeled data and cannot handle unseen data since our focus is to investigate approaches that can then be used with such data. Again, from Zhu (2005 #551), "people sometimes use the analogy that transductive learning is take-home exam, while inductive learning is in-class exam."

The example methods discussed in this section are by no means exhaustive. For more information on semisupervised learning, the reader is recommended to Zhu and Goldberg (2009 #550).

The most common classes of SSL algorithms are bootstrapping (cotraining latent variables with (domain) side information), graph regularization, and structural learning (entity recognition, domain adaptation, theoretical analysis) and has seen much use in canonical natural language processing (NLP) (tagging, chunking, parsing), entity-attribute extraction, sentiment analysis, and link spam detection, to name but a few areas.

8.5.1   Expectation Maximization

The expectation-maximization (EM) algorithm was first described by Dempster et al. (1977 #844) and has become a popular tool in statistical estimation problems involving incomplete data or in problems which can be posed in a similar form, such as mixture estimation, and is a method for finding maximum likelihood (or maximum a posteriori (MAP)) estimates of parameters in statistical models, where the model depends on unobserved latent variables.

EM is a method that iterates between an expectation step (E-step), where we compute the expectation of the log-likelihood using the current estimate for our unobserved (latent) variables, and a maximization step (M-step) that computes parameter values maximizing the expected log-likelihood found from the E-step. These parameter values are then used in the subsequent E-step.

Consider a statistical model with a set $\mathbf{X} = (x_1, x_2, ..., x_n)$ of observed data, a set $\mathbf{Z} = (z_1, z_2, ..., z_n)$ of unobserved (latent) data, or missing values, and a vector $\boldsymbol{\theta}$ of unknown parameters. Assume the likelihood function is $L(\theta; \mathbf{X}, \mathbf{Z}) = p(\mathbf{X}, \mathbf{Z}|\theta)$ and is the maximum likelihood estimate (MLE) of $\boldsymbol{\theta}$ and is determined by the marginal likelihood of $\mathbf{X}$,

$$L(\theta; \mathbf{X}) = p(\mathbf{X}|\theta) = \sum_{\mathbf{Z}} p(\mathbf{X}, \mathbf{Z}|\theta).$$

Since this is often difficult to determine, we can use the EM algorithm to find the MLE through

E-step: $Q(\theta|\theta^{(t)}) = E_{\mathbf{Z}|\mathbf{X}, \theta^{(t)}}[\log L(\theta; \mathbf{X}, \mathbf{Z})]$, which is the expected value of the log-likelihood function with respect to conditional distribution of $\mathbf{Z}$ given $\mathbf{X}$ under the current estimate for the parameters $\theta^{(t)}$.

M-step: $\theta^{(t+1)} = \arg\max_{\theta} Q(\theta|\theta^{(t)})$

If we know the values of θ, we can typically determine the values for $\mathbf{Z}$ by maximizing the log-likelihood over all possible values for $\mathbf{Z}$ by iterating over $\mathbf{Z}$ or by using some algorithm such as the Viterbi algorithm or hidden Markov models (HMMs). Conversely, if we know $\mathbf{Z}$, we can find an estimate for θ by grouping $\mathbf{X}$

according to the values of the associated unobserved (latent) variables and averaging the values of the points in each group, or averaging some function of the values of the points in each group.

Algorithmically,

1. Initialize θ to some random values.
2. Compute (the best value for) $\mathbf{Z}$ given these parameter values.
3. Use $\mathbf{Z}$ from step 2 to compute a better estimate for θ.
4. Return to step 2 and continue until convergence.

This form of EM is typically referred to as *hard EM*, and an example of this class of algorithm is the *k-means* algorithm. There is an alternative to step 2:

2. Determine the probability of each possible value of $\mathbf{Z}$, for each data point, and use the probabilities associated with a particular value of $\mathbf{Z}$ to compute a weighted average over the entire set of data points.

This alternative version, *soft EM*, is the version most normally associated with EM.

The EM algorithm and a faster form called *ordered subset EM* are widely used in medical image reconstruction, such as positron emission tomography (PET) and single-photon emission computed tomography (SPECT).

8.5.1.1   Gaussian Mixture Example

Consider a mixture of two multivariate normal distributions (Gaussian mixture) of dimension n, with $\mathbf{X} = (x_1, x_2, ..., x_n)$ being a sample of independent observations and $\mathbf{Z} = (z_1, z_2, ..., z_n)$ being the unobserved variables that determine the distribution (or component) from which the observation originates. Then, $X_i|(Z_i = 1) \sim N_d(\mu_1, \sigma_1)$, $X_i|(Z_i = 2) \sim N_d(\mu_2, \sigma_2)$, and $P(Z_i = 1) = p_1, P(Z_i = 2) = p_2 = 1 - p_1$.

We want to estimate the unknown parameters (θ) that represent the "mixing" value between the Gaussians and the means and covariances of each, $\theta = (p, \mu_1, \mu_2, \sigma_1, \sigma_2)$, where the likelihood function is

$$L(\theta; \mathbf{X}, \mathbf{Z}) = P(\mathbf{X}, \mathbf{Z}|\theta) = \prod_{i=1}^{n} \sum_{j=1}^{2} I(z_1 = j) p_j f(x_i; \mu_j, \sigma_j),$$

where I is an *indicator function* (or *characteristic function*)[9] and f is the *probability distribution function* (pdf) of a multivariate Gaussian, which can be written as

$$L(\theta; \mathbf{X}, \mathbf{Z}) = \exp\left\{ \sum_{i=1}^{n} \sum_{j=1}^{2} I(z_i = j) \left[\log p_j - \tfrac{1}{2}\log|\sigma_j| - \tfrac{1}{2}(x_i - \mu_j)^T \sigma_j^{-1}(x_i - \mu_j) - \tfrac{n}{2}\log(2\pi) \right] \right\}^{10}.$$

---

[9] The indicator function of a subset A of X is $I_A : X \to \{0, 1\}$ where $I_A(x) = \begin{cases} 1 & \text{if } x \in A \\ 0 & \text{if } x \notin A \end{cases}$.

[10] This is the exponential family form.

We can now use this information to define our E-step and M-step formulae.

Given the current estimate of the parameters, $\theta^{(t)}$, $\mathbf{Z}_i$ is determined by Bayes' theorem as the proportional height of the normal density, weighted by T, where

$$T_{j,i}^{(t)} = P\left(\mathbf{Z}_i = j | \mathbf{X}_i = x_i; \theta^{(t)}\right) = \frac{p_j^{(t)} f\left(x_i; \mu_j^{(t)}, \sigma_j^{(t)}\right)}{p_1^{(t)} f\left(x_i; \mu_1^{(t)} \sigma_1^{(t)}\right) + p_2^{(t)} f\left(x_i; \mu_2^{(t)} \sigma_2^{(t)}\right)},$$

resulting in

$$Q\left(\theta | \theta^{(t)}\right) = E[\log L(\theta; \mathbf{X}, \mathbf{Z})]$$

$$= \sum_{i=1}^{n} \sum_{j=1}^{2} T_{j,i}^{(t)} \left[\log p_j - \tfrac{1}{2}\log|\sigma_j| - \tfrac{1}{2}(x_i - \mu_j)^T \sigma_j^{-1} (x_i - \mu_j) - \tfrac{n}{2}\log(2\pi) \right].$$

We can see that p, (μ_1, σ_1), and (μ_2, σ_2) can be maximized independently:

$$p^{(t+1)} = \arg\max_{p} Q\left(\theta | \theta^{(t)}\right) = \arg\max_{p} \left\{ \left[\sum_{i=1}^{n} T_{1,i}^{(t)}\right] \log p_1 + \left[\sum_{i=1}^{n} T_{2,i}^{(t)}\right] \log p_2 \right\},$$

which has the same form as the MLE for the binomial distribution and can be rewritten as

$$p_j^{(t+1)} = \frac{\sum_{i=1}^{n} T_{j,i}^{(t)}}{\sum_{i=1}^{n}\left(T_{1,i}^{(t)} + T_{2,i}^{(t)}\right)} = \frac{1}{n}\sum_{i=1}^{n} T_{j,i}^{(t)}.$$

For $\left(\mu_j^{(t+1)}, \sigma_j^{(t+1)}\right)$,

$$\left(\mu_j^{(t+1)}, \sigma_j^{(t+1)}\right) = \arg\max_{\mu_j, \sigma_j} Q\left(\theta | \theta^{(t)}\right),$$

$$= \arg\max_{\mu_j, \sigma_j} \sum_{i=1}^{n} T_{j,i}^{(t)} \left\{ -\tfrac{1}{2}\log|\sigma_j| - \tfrac{1}{2}(x_i - \mu_j)^T \sigma_j^{-1}(x_i - \mu_j) \right\},$$

which has the same form as a weighted MLE for a Gaussian distribution and so can be rewritten as

$$\mu_1^{(t+1)} = \frac{\sum_{i=1}^{n} T_{1,i}^{(t)} x_i}{\sum_{i=1}^{n} T_{1,i}^{(t)}}, \qquad \sigma_1^{(t+1)} = \frac{\sum_{i=1}^{n} T_{1,i}^{(t)}\left(x_i - \mu_1^{(t+1)}\right)\left(x_i - \mu_1^{(t+1)}\right)^T}{\sum_{i=1}^{n} T_{1,j}^{(t)}},$$

and similarly for $\mu_2^{(t+1)}$ and $\sigma_2^{(t+1)}$.

This form of mixture modeling is very useful. For example, we could use this approach to model the wait time versus consultation time in ERs.

8.5.1.2 EM and HMMs

We'll now briefly relate EM to our earlier discussion on HMMs.

Consider a scenario where we observe one sequence x of length n, $x = (x_1 x_2 ... x_n)$ where x_i is (say) the ith base of a DNA sequence (A, C, G, T) and is a realization of a random sequence X. Although in reality we may have N independent and identically distributed (i.i.d.) sequences, since we only need one observed sequence to learn an HMM, that's what we'll use in this discussion.

As we saw in our HMM discussion, there is a corresponding hidden-state sequence $Z = (z_1 z_2 ... z_n)$, and that given Z, elements of X are conditionally independent. For our example, the hidden state z_i might specify whether x_i is part of a gene or not (or, in reality, a more granular segmentation). For our discussion, we'll assume that the hidden states can take one of G fixed values, such that $Z_i \in \{1, 2, ..., G\}$, and that in an HMM, $p(Z_i = g | z_{i-1}, z_{i-2}, ..., z_1) = p(Z_i = g | z_{i-1})$ and $p(Y_i = y_i | z, y_1, y_2, ..., y_{i-1}, y_{i+1}, ..., y_n) = p(y_i | z_i)$.

Parameters into the HMM are:

- The initial probability distribution over the G possible hidden states, $\rho = [\rho_1 ... \rho_G]^T$; $\rho_i = P(Z_1 = g)$
- A hidden-state probability matrix[11] $P \in \mathbb{R}^{G \times G}$ that specifies the probability of transitioning from a state a to a state b: $P_{a,b} = P(Z_i = b | Z_{i-1} = a)$

This gives us our parameter set $\theta = \{\rho, P, b\}$, where $b = \{b_g\}_{g=1}^{G}$. We omit the calculation steps here as they are similar to our discussion above and refer the interested reader to Gupta and Chen (2010 #846), Bilmes (1998 #847), and Rabiner (1989 #825), among others.

8.5.2 Cotraining

The original paper describing cotraining was published by Avril Blum and Tom Mitchell in 1998, (Blum and Mitchell 1998 #552), and has been cited close to 2,000 times, as of the time of writing. The algorithm has been very effectively used for text mining for search engines, and the original paper illustrated this with an experiment in which 95% of 788 web pages were correctly classified using only 12 labeled web pages as examples.

---

[11] Here, we're assuming time homogeneity so that the matrix is not dependent on t.

This technique ideally requires two views of the data and assumes that each given example is described using two distinct feature sets which provide different but complementary information about the instance. These two views are described as *conditionally independent* (the feature sets are conditionally independent given the class) and *sufficient* (the class can be predicted from either view alone).

In Krogel and Scheffer (2004 #553), Krogel and Scheffer further identified that the method is beneficial only where classification datasets are independent. If one of the classifiers correctly labels a piece of data that the other classifier previously misclassified, then cotraining can work effectively. If both classifiers agree on all the unlabeled data, they are not independent, labeling the data does not create new information. This technique has been used in functional genomics applications, and one of the challenges is that cotraining made the results worse when classifier dependence was above 60%.

8.5.2.1 Cotraining in Functional Genomics

Bioinformatics includes the objective of generating models describing the relationship between genetic information and the underlying cellular processes. These models not only have to explain experimental data but are often derived from said experimental data. This data, as we've discussed, resides in a broad range of disparate repositories including gene interaction repositories (often relational databases), documentary repositories (such as MEDLINE), and other repositories containing unlabeled data, including gene data with unknown functional properties. Being able to elicit knowledge from these different types of data is of particular interest in *functional genomics*.

Abstracts of scientific papers contain information that, if we could effectively elicit it, could be valuable when building our models. As noted above, MEDLINE is a particularly widely used repository containing scientific papers, and there is an active area of research in algorithms that extract information from literature (Hirschmann et al. 2002; Leek 1997; Fukuda et al. 1998; Craven et al. 2000; Hahn et al. 2002). Even dictionary-based extractors, a somewhat simpler approach, can provide valuable support for functional genomics models.

In the functional genomics domain, unlabeled data is typically an instance identifying a gene and some unknown function (or localization), or a gene whose deletion has some effect, as yet unknown. Such unlabeled data is readily available and usually reasonably inexpensive. Krogel and Scheffer (2004 #553) showed that using propositionalization[12] for learning and using dictionary-based extraction algorithms to generate attributes both improved model definition and, among other things, demonstrated a system to solve a range of functional genomics problems using these available data sources.

---

[12] This is the methodology of transforming a relational representation of a learning problem into a propositional (feature-based, attribute-value) representation.

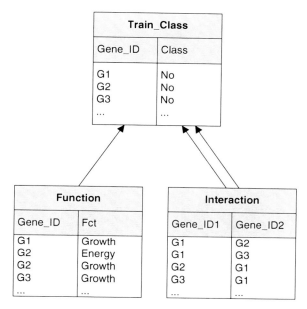

Fig. 8.1 Simplified gene interaction model

The RELAGGS algorithm, RELational AGGregationS, Krogel and Wrobel (2001 #554), uses database entities (tables) and a particular attribute of one entity (the target) as input. The target table describes each instance (as a row in that target table) and uses foreign key relationships between the input entities to compute result sets that always include the target table. Recall from our earlier discussions (Chap. 3) that these result sets will often (typically?) include multiple rows for each instance due to differences in several attributes. The algorithm will then resolve these multiple rows into a single output row for each instance using aggregation functions.

In order to understand this process, consider an example from Krogel and Scheffer (2004 #553) where we have a table *Train_Class* with attributes *Gene id* and the target attribute *Class*. Furthermore, we have a table *Interaction* with *Gene id1* and *Gene id2* and, slightly simplified, a table *Function* with attributes *Gene id* and *Fct*, depicted in Fig. 8.1.

The algorithm generates intermediate results from joining *Train_Class* and *Function* (Join1) as well as a result set depicting the functions of all genes interacting with a given gene (Join2), as depicted in Fig. 8.2. Note that there are multiple rows for a single entry of the target table in the intermediary results, such as is the case with *G1* that interacts with *G2*, which has multiple functions, as well as with *G3*, which only has a single function.

The results generated by the aggregation step, which are depicted in Fig. 8.3, take care of this by collapsing the intermediary results into a single row for each target.

Join1	
Gene_ID	Fct
G1	Growth
G2	Energy
G2	Growth
G3	Growth
...	...

Join2		
Gene_ID1	Gene_ID2	Fct
G1	G2	Energy
G1	G2	Growth
G1	G3	Growth
G2	G1	Growth
G3	G1	Growth
...	...	...

Fig. 8.2 Intermediate RELAGGS step

RELAGGS_Result_Set						
Gene_ID	Class	Fct_Growth_1	Fct_Energy_1	Fct_Growth_2	Fct_Energy_2	...
G1	No	1	0	2	1	
G2	No	1	1	1	0	...
G3	No	1	0	1	0	
...	...	...	...	...	...	

Fig. 8.3 Resulting relation from RELAGGS

Krogel and Scheffer (2004 #553) showed that the additional interaction attributes generated by RELAGGS can have a significant (positive) impact on performance of decision functions for recognition, in certain cases one or two standard deviations' worth.

Reutemann et al. (2004 #848) described an implementation of a toolkit for using RELAGGS directly against a relational database.

Propositionalization has already been shown to be a particularly promising approach for robustly and effectively handling relational datasets for knowledge discovery. In multirelational learners that are based on propositionalization, instead of searching the first-order hypothesis space directly, a transformation is used to first compute a large number of the propositional features; this is then used as propositional learner.

While the theoretical underpinnings post that such an approach is less powerful in principle than systems that directly search the full first-order hypothesis space, in many cases, searching the fixed subspace that can be defined by feature transformations is not only sufficient, but also learning based on such transformations offers a potential for enhanced efficiency, a factor that is becoming more and more important with the ever-increasing size of the data repositories used for large applications in data mining. But there is another value to performing a transformation of multirelational data into a single table (entity) format: we can directly use all propositional learning systems, increasing the number of algorithms available to us.

For the interested reader, Krogel et al. (2003 #849) described a comparative evaluation of three different multirelational learning systems based on propositionalization: RSD, SINUS, and RELAGGS.

8.5.3   Graph-Based SSL Methods

If we consider the problem of gene-function classification, including the concept of gene-gene interaction, which we briefly touched on above, we can see just from the problem itself that there is likely to be a much larger amount of data available to us where the *labeling* (either the function or interaction) is unknown than there will be where the function of a gene or the interaction between two specific genes is known. This is, in fact, a much broader situation than just the life sciences, but is seen across many disciplines and application domains.

Consider document classification. Many organizations have thousands upon thousands of documents and often only a small number have been accurately classified, the rest totally unclassified. Can we use the small number of labeled (classified) documents along with the much larger number of unclassified documents to help us? This is where semisupervised learning (SSL) techniques become valuable since such algorithms combine unlabeled data with a small labeled training set to train better models.

Since large amounts of unlabeled examples can often be gathered cheaply, there has been a great deal of work in recent years on how unlabeled data can be used to aid classification (Ratsaby and Venkatesh 1995 #850; Castelli and Cover 1996 #851; Nigam et al. 1998 #852; Blum and Mitchell 1998 #552; Bennett and Demiriz 1998 #854; Hofmann 1999 #855; Zhang and Oles 2000 #856; Schuurmans 1997 #857). One such method, using graphical models and *cuts* is described here, although this is by no means the only approach being pursued, and we shall provide some further references for the interested reader at the end of this section.

We consider an algorithm based on finding minimum cuts in graphs, which uses pairwise relationships among the examples in order to learn from both labeled and unlabeled data (Blum and Chawla 2001 #858). Our algorithm uses a similarity measure between data to construct a graph and then outputs a classification corresponding to partitioning the graph in a way that minimizes (roughly) the number of similar pairs of examples that are given different labels. This method is also seen to be robust to noise on the labeled examples.

Originating in vision literature, (Greig 1989 #860; Roy 1998 #861; Boykov 1998 #862; Snow 2000 #863), the problem of improving a noisy image by minimizing an appropriate "energy function" was identified as being approachable by applying a graph mincut algorithm. Blum and Chawla (2001 #858) further showed that this method could similarly be applied to the problem of combining labeled and unlabeled data within the machine-learning paradigm, where the graph created on a dataset containing labeled and unlabeled instances is constructed in such a way as to yield an optimal binary labeling of the unlabeled data, according to certain optimization functions from the minimum cut on the graph. Kleinberg and Tardos (2002 #864) influenced Blum and Chawla's work in that they connected the work from the vision discipline to the more general classification problem through their *metric labeling problem*.

The high-level idea underlying the method is to assign values to unlabeled instances so as to optimize the associated objective function. In the context of our discussion here and Blum and Chawla (2001 #858), the kinds of functions that can be optimized are limited to depend on pairwise relationships among the instances. However, for functions which *can* be approached, this method provides a polynomial-time algorithm that is able to find the true *global* optimum. Comparing this to methods such as EM which can be applied in a much more general context, but may only detect a local optimum, in cases where the mincut approach is pertinent, it has some very real, interesting advantages. Chief among these is its ability to use unlabeled data but also because the algorithm appears to be robust to random noise.

So what type of optimization problem can the mincut algorithm actually be used for? Probably the best answer is the one that Blum and Chawla used as an example:

> *Given a set of (positive and negative) labeled example* **L***, and a set of unlabeled example* **U***, find a labeling of the points in* **U** *that minimizes the leave-one-out cross-validation (LOOCV) error of the nearest-neighbor algorithm, when applied to the entire dataset* $L \cup U$.

This type of problem is a good candidate for any iterative-relabeling style algorithm, or a greedy local optimization algorithm, for that matter. Since the goal of the algorithm is to assign labels to the unlabeled instances so that the learning algorithm moves toward its goal, the graph mincut approach relates to nearest-neighbor style algorithms in an analogous way to how transductive SVM relates to the standard SVM algorithm.

Now to the algorithm. Given a set L of labeled instances and a set U of unlabeled instances, and assuming a binary classification where the labels are positive or negative, we use L_+ to denote positive instances in L and L_- to denote negative instances in L. The algorithm steps are as follows:

1. Construct a weighted graph $G = (V, E)$, where $V = L \cup U \cup \{v_+, v_-\}$ and $E \subseteq V \times V$. Associated with each edge $e \in E$ is a weight $w(e)$. v_+ and v_- are called *classification vertices*, whereas all other vertices are *example* (*instance*) *vertices*.
2. Classification vertices are connected by edges of infinite weight to the labeled instances having the *same* label: $w(v, v_+) = \infty \ \forall v \in L_+, w(v, v_-) = \infty \ \forall v \in L_-$.
3. Edges between example (instance) vertices are assigned weights based on some relationship between the instances, such as similarity (distance) between them, via an *edge weighting function* **w**.
4. We determine a minimum (v_+, v_-) cut for the graph by determining the minimum total weight set of edges whose removal disconnects v_+ from v_-, using a max-flow algorithm in which v_+ is the source, v_- is the sink, and the edge weights are treated as capacities. Removing the edges in the cut partitions the graph into two sets of vertices, V_+ and V_-, with $v_+ \in V_+$ and $v_- \in V_-$.

5. Assign a positive label to all unlabeled instances in V_+ and a negative label to all unlabeled instances in V_-.

If edges between instances that are similar to each other are given a large weight value, it is reasonable to assume that the two instances are likely to be placed in the same vertex subset that results from the mincut, which conforms to the premise of many learning algorithms such as the nearest-neighbor family of algorithms: that similar instances should be classified similarly.

Thus, if we have a concept of distance between instances, such that nearby instances generally have the same label, as we might achieve by an L_0 distance (Hamming) or L_2 distance (Euclidean), then a natural weighting function should put high-weight edges between nearby instances and low-weight edges between farther-away instances.

Blum and Chawla (2001 #858) used several variants of the mincut algorithm, differing in weight functions, and compared with the ID3 and 3-nearest-neighbor algorithms, using the UC Irvine Machine Learning Repository for datasets. The $Mincut - \delta_{opt}$ algorithm, where the value of δ corresponds to the least classification error (in hindsight), proved to outperform the other algorithms in the experiments performed.

Taking an approach of assigning values to unlabeled instances such that it optimizes consistence, in a nearest-neighbor sense, allows for an algorithm that cannot only execute in polynomial time but also provides for some level of generative model and also minimizes LOOCV while performing well against algorithms that do not use unlabeled data.

8.5.4   Is This Type of Approach Always Helpful?

Not always because we have to make strong assumptions about the underlying joint probability distribution P(X,Y) – the relation of P(X) and P(Y|X) – because of the small amount of labeled data we use. That being said, the empirical success of semisupervised learning methods certainly shows that using unlabeled data can significantly improve performance, so it does merit considering, especially as *big data* analysis problems become more and more the norm.

Semisupervised learning is being used in many areas and provides an important tool in our repository. Basu (2004 #859), for example, investigated how SSL applies in the clustering domain, an important technique for life science data mining.

8.6   Kernel Learning Methods

We have already introduced the concept of similarity as a measure within patterns. Intuitively, we would expect a (sub)set of instances in our dataset to have some set of characteristics that lead us to believe that this subset has something in common. We now introduce this concept more formally and describe the concept of a *kernel* as a measure of similarity. We further discuss how this can be useful and how the discipline of kernel methods, and in the next section, support vector machines in particular, provide a valuable set of tools that we can use to extract patterns, represent patterns, and analyze patterns within our data-mining efforts.

As we discuss throughout, our dataset of interest consists of a set of input instances that, in this section, we shall denote by X. Each x_i that is a part of X is typically received as a tuple along with a target value y_i, (x_i, y_i). In the literature, the x_i are typically referred to as *patterns* and the y_i as *labels, targets,* or *observations*.[13] Formally, we say that

$$(x_1, y_1), ..., (x_n, y_n) \in X \times \{\pm 1\}$$

We have assumed in this simple case that the labels represent two classes, denoted by +1 and −1, respectively.

So far, we have made no assumptions about the patterns x_i, which, as we shall see, is an important point to keep in mind. These patterns could be gene sequences, test results, or anything else we might be interested in. We shall return to this later.

In any learning paradigm, we want to be able to generalize our model so that for any unseen x_i, we can accurately predict its corresponding label, y_i. In order to accomplish this, we need the concept of similarity in X (and also in $\{\pm 1\}$)![14]

As described in Schölkopf and Smola (2002 #82), we consider a similarity measure of the form

$$k : X \times X \to \mathbb{R},$$
$$(x, x') \mapsto k(x, x'),$$

where we define a function that accepts two patterns as input and provides a real number as an output: the real number giving us a measure of the similarity between the two patterns. We assume that the function k is symmetric so that $k(x, x') = k \times (x', x)$ and call k a *kernel*.[15]

To illustrate, we shall consider the commonly used kernel of a dot product,[16] which is defined as

$$\langle \mathbf{x}, \mathbf{x}' \rangle = \sum_{i=1}^{n} [\mathbf{x}]_i [\mathbf{x}']_i, \tag{8.1}$$

where $\mathbf{x}, \mathbf{x}' \in \mathbb{R}$ are two vectors and $[\mathbf{x}]_i$ denotes the ith entry of $\mathbf{x}$.

---

[13] This is where things get tricky. In keeping with kernel method literature, we shall use *pattern* instead of our typical *instance* and *label* for the output or target.

[14] We shall ignore the concept of similarity for $\{\pm 1\}$ since it is trivial: either two values are identical or they are different. As we consider more than two classifications of pattern, we shall see that our notion of similarity as we shall define it for the input patterns will be applicable to the output labels also.

[15] Put simply, a *kernel* computes the similarity of two points.

[16] Also known as the canonical dot product, inner product, or scalar product and is often denoted as $(x \cdot x')$. We shall simply use the term "dot product" to refer to (8.1). We should note at this point that although we will use the dot product for illustration, it does not have sufficient generality for us to deal with many of the problems we shall encounter. More on this anon.

Geometrically, the dot product computes the cosine of the angle between $\mathbf{x}, \mathbf{x}'$ if they are normalized to a length of 1. We can also use this to compute the length (also referred to as the *norm*) of a vector $\mathbf{x}$ as

$$\|\mathbf{x}\| = \sqrt{\langle \mathbf{x} \cdot \mathbf{x}' \rangle}$$

Similarly, we compute the distance between two vectors as being the length of the difference vector.

Given all of this, we can construct the geometric interpretations for anything that can be defined in terms of angles, lengths, and distances. We shall see the importance of this shortly.

Returning to our input patterns, we note that we have made no assumptions on their composition: even to the point of determining whether they even exist in some dot product space. They could be any kind of object we like. However, to use a dot product as a measure of similarity between such patterns, we must be able to represent them in some dot product space H.[17] In order to accomplish this, we use a map[18]

$$\Phi : X \rightarrow H,$$
$$x \mapsto \mathbf{x} := \Phi(x). \tag{8.2}$$

What does this process do for us? First, it allows us to define a similarity measure using the dot product in H so that

$$k(x, x') := \langle \mathbf{x}, \mathbf{x}' \rangle = \langle \Phi(x), \Phi(x') \rangle,$$

and second, it allows us to process patterns using a set of analytical geometry tools and linear algebra techniques. Third, Φ allows us to design a wide range of similarity measures and learning algorithms.

8.7   Let's Break for Some Examples

In this section, we'll briefly digress from our mathematical discourse and mention a few areas in which the model theory we've discussed so far is being used actively. We will not expand upon any of the specifics but instead provide just a brief description and some references, along with some models available that allow us to execute some of the models without having to build them by hand.

---

[17] H does not need to coincide with $\mathbb{R}^N$. H is referred to as a *feature space*.

[18] Even if our patterns exist in a dot product space, we may still find it useful to apply a map such as denoted in (8.2).

8.7.1   String and Tree Matching

A common representation of data that we can use machine-learning techniques to classify is a set of discrete structures, for example, the string of discrete instances (characters). A prime example of this is the gene sequence or the protein sequence. In such instances, we might be interested in the similarity between such strings where these strings may be tens, hundreds, or thousands of characters in length. We can define a measure of similarity between the structures (the feature map), and where the dot products lead to kernels, $k(x, x')$, where x and x' are members of our set of structures.

Stafford Noble's SVM package is one of many SVM implementations that can be used to classify such source data, and there is a web-based interface available for classifying (relatively) small datasets.[19]

A more complete exposition can be found in many references; one that we particularly wish to highlight is Durbin (1998 #128). Vishwanathan and Smola (2003 #293) outlined a method for an algorithm that will match discrete objects, such as strings or trees, in linear time. Gribskov and Robinson (1996 #294) used the receiver operating characteristic (ROC) analysis and applied this to matching sequences. In Lewis et al. (2006 #295), the challenge of combining large amounts of heterogeneous data in order to effect a comprehensive analysis is considered.

8.7.2   Protein Structure Classification and Prediction

Many readers will be familiar with proteins being represented by a sequence of amino acids, encoded by a gene, and how current techniques make it easy to generate the protein sequence, but obtaining the structure of a protein is still a challenge. One of the areas of research is how we can *classify* protein sequence data into families and superfamilies that are defined by structure-function relationships (Fig. 8.4).

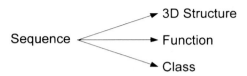

We know that the primary structure is deterministically definable from the DNA sequence through the process of *translation*. The challenge comes from the way in which the proteins, as identified within the primary protein structure, then fold into the

---

[19] See http://svm.sdsc.edu/cgi-bin/nph-SVMsubmit.cgi

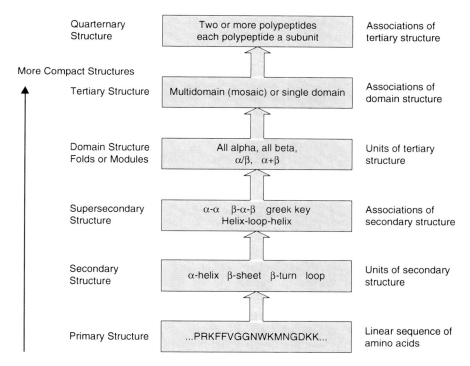

Fig. 8.4 Protein structure hierarchy

higher-level structures. As we go up the hierarchy, the three-dimensional folding, which has a major impact on the protein's behavior, becomes more and more intractable. But even when looking at classification using sequence homology, the challenge is substantial. Simplicity, computational efficiency, training complexity (and time), and predictive capacity all come together in this problem, as highlighted by the use of support vector machines (SVMs) to attack this problem.

Techniques aimed at classifying proteins have used a wide range of techniques to try and effectively and efficiently attack the problem. Some of these techniques are described elsewhere in this text, but some are outside the scope of this text. Approaches include among others:

- Pairwise sequence similarity (Waterman et al. 1991 #863; Altschul et al. 1997 #864)
- Protein family profiling, Gribskov et al. (1987 #865)
- Consensus patterns using motifs, Bairoch et al. (1996 #866), Attwood et al. (1998 #868)
- Hidden Markov models, Krogh et al. (1982 #869), Eddy (1995 #870), Baldi et al. (1994 #871)

Researchers have therefore looked to combining approaches to gain traction with these issues. Leslie et al. (2004 #862), for example, introduced a class of string kernels called *mismatch kernels* which measure sequence similarity based on shared occurrences of fixed-length patterns in the data. In this way, they can be combined with SVMs to support both protein classification and remote homology detection, all while allowing for mutations between the patterns. This is an alternative approach to those which use family-based generative models (e.g., hidden Markov models) to compare sequences. The kernels are computed using a mismatch tree structure where the contributions of all patterns within the data are calculated in one pass which, when used with an SVM, mean that the kernels enable fast prediction of protein classification.

Discriminative approaches appear to have good performance profiles and involve seeing protein sequences as labeled instances – positive if they are in the family and negative otherwise. Our learning algorithm is then responsible for learning the decision boundary between the classes. Successful techniques use these sequences to train a support vector machine classifier (see Haussler et al. (1998 #872), Liao and Noble (2002 #873), Leslie et al. (2002 #874)).

We'll use the *mismatch kernel* of Leslie et al. (2004 #862) as an example approach to protein classification. However, this is a very vibrant area of research, and the interested reader is recommended to any number of references, including Wang et al. (2000 #384), Weston (2006 #866), Dong et al. (2006 #877), any of the other references in this section, and the ubiquitous online search for "protein classification" or "protein structure classification."

Using SVMs for remote homology detection has been very successful. Leslie et al. (2004 #862) described using a family of kernel functions called mismatch kernels. As we describe below, kernel functions measure similarity between pairs of input instances, defining an inner product within a feature space for the SVM optimization problem. The features used for the mismatch kernel functions are the set of all possible amino acid sequences of length k within the two inputs. If the two inputs contain many k-length subsequences that differ at most by some number m mismatches, then the inner product defined from the mismatch kernel function will be large. That is, the mismatch kernel is calculated using shared occurrences of (k, m)-patterns in the data, where the (k, m)-patterns generated by a fixed k-length sequence (called k-mers) consist of all the k-length sequences differing from it by at most m mismatches. Computation of the (k, m)-patterns is further optimized by using a mismatch tree data structure so that the computations are completed in a single pass, which is important for use on real datasets. Further, when combined with SVMs, the algorithm is proposed to be able to make linear-time prediction.

Sequences are represented in an l^k-dimensional vector space (feature space), where $l = |A|$, and A is the alphabet of our character set ($|A| = 20$ for amino acids), where coordinates are indexed by the set of all possible k-mers. For example, for each input sequence x and each k-mer α, the coordinate indexed by α is the number of times α occurs in x, giving a k-spectrum feature map $\Phi_k(x) = (\phi_\alpha(x))_{\alpha \in A^k}$, where $\phi_\alpha(x)$ is the number of occurrences of α in x. The k-spectrum kernel for x and y is $K_k(x, y) = \langle \Phi_k(x), \Phi_k(y) \rangle$.

As of the time of writing, the authors of Leslie et al. (2004 #862) had made the software available at http://cbio.mskcc.org/leslielab/software/string-kernels.

Automated classification is going to continue to be an important capability for us to have in our arsenal of tools. A significant percentage of proteins, possibly as much as 50% (at time of writing), in sequenced genomes currently have no assigned functionality, and direct observation of the function of proteins is still costly, time-consuming, and difficult. Yona et al. (1999 #876) described ProtoMap, a site that offers a comprehensive classification of SWISS-PROT proteins based on analysis of all pairwise similarities among protein sequences. Since the domains within the tertiary structure of a protein often have a separate function to perform for the protein, such as ligand binding, membrane spanning, DNA binding, or the site of the catalyst, for example, each domain may be encoded by a separate exon in the encoding gene sequence. But sometimes, we don't know where the domains are, although it is generally accepted that two sequences that match to 30% or more are likely to have the same folding, and homologous proteins are likely to have the same function, and since homology is a transitive property, being able to automatically classify proteins provides a valuable tool for the scientist. Interested readers may also find (Zaki et al. 2003 #878) interesting as it offered a comparison of several different approaches to homology detection.

8.8   Support Vector Machines

Support vector machines (SVMs) are a set of supervised learning methods used for classification and regression, and belong to the family of *generalized linear classifiers*. Because they simultaneously minimize the classification error[20] and maximize the geometric margin, they are also referred to as *maximum margin classifiers*.

In essence, SVMs will map input instances to a higher-dimensional space wherein we can construct a *maximal separating hyperplane*. In order to accomplish this, two parallel hyperplanes are constructed, one on either side of the hyperplane separating the data. The maximal separating hyperplane is the hyperplane that maximizes the distance between the two parallel hyperplanes. The assumption is that the larger the distance between the parallel hyperplanes, the better the generalization error of the classifier will be. Thus, we wish to find the optimal hyperplane that correctly classifies our data points (as much as it is possible to do so) and which separates the points of two classes (as far as possible). As is the case with any powerful (and useful) technique, there are also potentially significant issues to consider, including VC dimension, linear separability, the feature space, and multiple classes.

---

[20] See the discussions on classification.

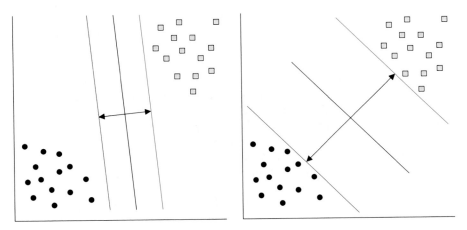

Fig. 8.5 Separating hyperplane

We've already mentioned the separating hyperplane between two sets of data without describing it, and this is a good place to begin. Consider the illustration in Fig. 8.5.

We can see that the distance between the red and blue hyperplanes in the left-hand figure is much smaller than the distance in the right-hand figure; the wider margin[21] in the right-hand figure proposes that we can expect a better generalization for our model. This generalization capability is closely related to both the capacity of our model – the functions it can represent – as well as the dataset that is used for training.

In essence, given a set of data that is separated into two classes, a SVM will find the hyperplane that will result in the largest possible number of points of the same class on the same side of the hyperplane while maximizing the distance between each class and the hyperplane. Being able to determine this optimal separating hyperplane, we minimize the risk of misclassifying any of our test data as well as any as-yet-unseen data.

If we can't effectively determine this optimal separation, we can potentially end up with a model that could misclassify instances or has limited generality.

For the remainder of this section, we'll typically use a linearly separable dataset as our example since it is easy to understand and diagram. However, the technique is obviously applicable to much more complex datasets than this.

The points nearest to the separating hyperplane are called *support vectors*, and they are the only points that determine the position of the hyperplane. This is an important concept: no other points in the datasets have influence over the position-ing of the hyperplane. For mathematically inclined readers, the weighted sum of the support vectors is the *normal vector* of the hyperplane.

---

[21] Formally, the term *margin* is used as a measure between the black line and one of the red or blue lines, as depicted in our figure. The black line is the separating hyperplane.

This is all well and good – *if* our datasets are separable, but in reality, this is not necessarily the case. We can use the same concept of linear separation between the two datasets, but recognize that there will be errors in our training efforts, as well as when the model is implemented in a production environment. We can compute a penalty for each instance that is misclassified by introducing an error cost, C, and multiplying this by the distance to the hyperplane.

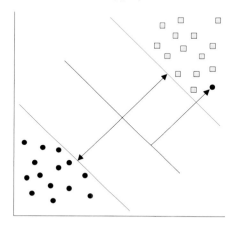

Linear learning is of particular interest since it typically has unique, optimal solutions, has fast learning algorithms, and has a broad range of statistical analysis tools available. However, it typically has insufficient capacity for many real-world problems. As far back as the 1960s, this issue was highlighted by Marvin Minsky when analyzing perceptrons (a simple form of neural networks).

In the current kernel methods context, we stay with linear functions but work in a higher-dimensional feature space where we expect this much higher-dimensional space (than the input space) to allow us to leverage the linearity of the functions.

Returning to the dataset in Fig. 8.5, let x_1 represent the subset of data depicted by the black circles and x_2 represent the subset of data depicted by gray squares. In the input space, we may not be able to easily separate these, as illustrated in Fig. 8.6.

We might consider a mapping to some feature space such as $(x_1, x_2) \rightarrow (x_1^2, x_1 x_2, x_2 x_1, x_2^2)$ and consider a linear equation such as $ax_1^2 + bx_2^2 = c$ in this feature space, which is actually an elliptical figure, allowing us to use this to separate the two subsets of our dataset, as shown in Fig. 8.7.

An interesting nuance to the separation problem is that it might be easier to separate our datasets in higher dimensions, using the separating hyperplane, than in lower dimensions. Our feature mapping may allow us to move from that high-complexity/low-dimension space to the lower-complexity/high-dimension space. If this is indeed the case (for our problem), then we would like to develop a maximal marginal hyperplane in some higher-dimension feature space but still be able to use it in any dimensional space that's applicable. . .if we can. The challenge is that the construction of this hyperplane depends on our ability to compute inner products in

Fig. 8.6 Non–linearly
separable dataset

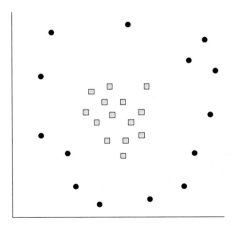

Fig. 8.7 Non–linearly
separate dataset (feature
space separation)

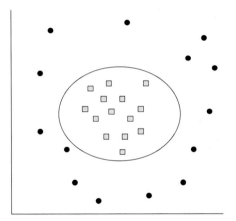

the feature space, which can be computationally intractable when the number of
dimensions is too large.

This is where the *kernel trick* comes into play. We use a kernel function that
exists in low dimensions but behaves just like an inner product when the number of
dimensions is large.[22]

---

[22] Our objective is to determine an appropriate function to provide us a measure of similarity, so
we don't really need to know what the feature space looks like. Thus, we don't know what happens
inside the kernel: we are more interested in its output values. That being said, we're not talking
about a black box in the way we do when talking about neural networks since we *do* have a
geometric interpretation for the hyperplane. Think of it as more of a dark-gray box than a black
box. What this does give us is *equivalence between nonlinear separation of vectors in the gene
space using kernel functions and linear separation of vectors in the feature space using inner
products*.

Consider two expression profiles, $p = (p_1, p_2, ..., p_n) \in \mathbb{R}^n$ and $q = (q_1, q_2, ..., q_n)$ $\in \mathbb{R}^n$, generated from microarrays. A similarity measure in the *gene space*, where we are looking at the comparisons between each element, is an inner product

$$\langle p, q \rangle = p_1 q_1 + p_2 q_2 + ... + p_n q_n,$$

whereas in the feature space, it is some form of kernel function $\kappa(p, q)$, which might be a

linear function: $\kappa(p, q) = \langle p, q \rangle$,
polynomial function: $\kappa(p, q) = (\gamma \langle p, q \rangle + c_0)^d$,
radial basis function $\kappa(p, q) = e^{-\gamma \|p - q\|_2^2}$, or some other form of function.

In the above, γ is the width of the radial basis function coefficient in the polynomial, d is the degree of the polynomial, and c_0 is an additive constant. Missing from these examples is our error cost, C, that we mentioned above.

Using our expression analysis example, we can see that a support vector machine is a maximal margin hyperplane in (gene) feature space built using a kernel function in gene space.

The above description, from Markowetz (2004 #859), is extended to include some practical examples of using SVMs to classify tumor samples using R and the e1071 and pamr packages. Using an archive of expression profiles, with classes (labels) defined by an expert, the information was passed into the svm function, which was used (posttuning) to predict the cancer type of unseen patients.

We mentioned that one of the challenges relates to the capacity of our model or, more specifically, the capacity of the feature space, which is proportional to the dimension. See Vapnik (2000 #157), Shawe-Taylor and Cristianini (2004 #42), or others for more details on the following theorem: *given $m + 1$ examples in general position in an m-dimensional space, we can generate every possible classification with a thresholded linear function.*

This can provide a very powerful technique for our mining efforts. Kernel methods let us use linear functions in the feature space, such as $x \mapsto \langle \mathbf{w}, \phi(x) \rangle$ for regression or $x \mapsto \mathrm{sgn}(\langle \mathbf{w}, \phi(x) \rangle + b)$ for classification (with thresholding).

However, we're not let off the hook so easily. It is very easy for the capacity to become too large, leading to overfitting, and thus a lack of generalization. Also, as our dimensions increase, the computational costs of processing large vectors can become problematic. One way we can try and control the generalization issue is to force as large a margin as possible on our training data, which is the equivalent of minimizing the *norm* of the weight vector (keeping outputs above a specific value). This approach is a little different to *structural risk minimization* (see below) in that the hierarchy depends on the data.

Just to provide a simple example, in relation to the mapping $(x_1, x_2) \rightarrow$ $(x_1^2, x_1 x_2, x_2 x_1, x_2^2)$, illustrated in Figs. 8.6 and 8.7, if we apply this to a 20 $\times$ 30 pixel image, we have approximately 180,000 dimensions to deal with, an unrealistic standard practice using the typical computational power available in 2011.[23]

---

[23] Yeah, yeah, yeah, we know. This *could* be accomplished by many processing environments, but we're assuming that your organization has already looked at you weirdly for suggesting some of these techniques and is not necessarily going to give you the go-ahead to take over the whole of their computational environment. . . or will they?

All this being said, there are mathematical approaches to overcoming some of the obstacles associated with dimensionality. Using our quadratic mapping example from above, we can use a shortcut whereby we compute an inner product and square the result – a $20 \times 30 = 600$ dimensional inner product, nonetheless – and we can even consider the *Gaussian kernel*[24] to allow us to consider infinite dimensional spaces.

However, we still have to be concerned with the data fit. This is crucial but also can lead to overfitting, so care must be taken.

We mentioned structural risk minimization (SRM) (Vapnik and Chervonenkis 1974 #860) above and now discuss this important principles for selecting models for learning from finite training datasets. Why this is an important technique is that it describes a general model of capacity control, providing a trade-off between the dimensional complexity and the fitting issues we described above.

Sewell (2008 #861) provided a succinct definition of the procedure as follows:

1. Using a priori knowledge of the domain, choose a class of functions, such as polynomials of degree n, neural networks having n hidden layer neurons, a set of splines with n nodes, or fuzzy logic models having n rules.
2. Divide the class of functions into a hierarchy of nested subsets in order of increasing complexity. For example, polynomials of increasing degree.
3. Perform empirical risk minimization on each subset (this is essentially parameter selection).
4. Select the model in the series whose sum of empirical risk and VC confidence is minimal.

Approximating functions of a learning machine are ordered according to their complexity, forming a *nested structure*, as shown in Fig. 8.8.

Support vector machines use the concept of SRM within their architecture. SRM considers a set of models that are ordered in terms of their complexity, often defined by the number of parameters or, as we discussed above, a dimensional complexity measure. Model selection by SRM is then a problem of finding the simplest model, in terms of order, and best, in terms of empirical error on the data.

Saigo et al. (2002 #879) offered a comparison of SVM-based methods for remote homology detection.

8.8.1 Gene Expression Analysis

When, where, and under what conditions are genes expressed? What triggers this expression, or, conversely, what prevents this expression? Gene expression, the process by which information from genes is used in the synthesis of functional gene

---

[24] $\kappa(\mathbf{x}, \mathbf{z}) = \exp\left(-\frac{\|\mathbf{x}-\mathbf{z}\|^2}{2\sigma^2}\right).$

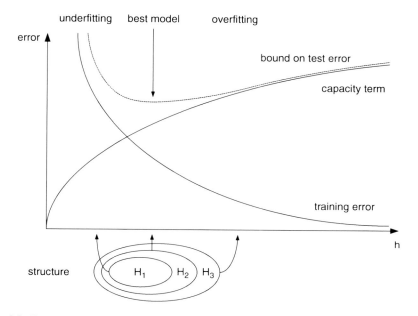

Fig. 8.8 Structural risk minimization (SRM)

products, is used by all known life forms: the surprisingly wide range of products of
transcription and translation, and how these different expression products determine the growth and health of an organism, is obviously important to understand.
The functional gene products are typically proteins, but in the case of non-protein-
coding genes, products include ribosomal RNA (rRNA), transfer RNA (tRNA), and
small nuclear RNA (smRNA). Many techniques have been developed to allow us to
measure gene expression, including Northern blot, Western blot, fluorescence in
situ hybridization (FISH), serial analysis of gene expression (SAGE), and
microarrays, to name a few. Thus, information on the functional state of an
organism is largely determined by the information on gene expression.

Gene expression analysis is used for many purposes within the life sciences,
including[25]:

- Differential analysis (or marker selection): the search for genes that are differentially expressed in distinct phenotypes
- Class prediction: the search for a gene expression signature that predicts class
  (phenotype) membership, which uses supervised learning techniques

---

[25] From http://www.broadinstitute.org/cancer/software/genepattern/desc/expression.html

- Class discovery: the search for a biologically relevant unknown taxonomy identified by a gene expression signature or a biologically relevant set of coexpressed genes, which uses unsupervised learning techniques
- Pathway analysis: the search for sets of genes differentially expressed in distinct phenotypes

Due to the complexity and data volume, many tools are available to the investigator, such as Bioconductor (Gentleman et al. 2004 #89), GenePattern (Reich et al. 2006 #909), and Genevestigator (Zimmermann et al. 2005 #908). This common characteristic – large volume data generation – necessitates many of the techniques inherent to data mining. Although it has been said before, it is worthwhile considering this issue again:

> But can we really expect to construct a detailed biochemical model of, say, an entire yeast cell with some 6,000 genes (only about 1,000 of which were defined before sequencing started, and about 50% of which are clearly related to other known genes), by analyzing each gene and determining all the binding and reaction constants one by one? Likewise, from the perspective of drug target identification for human disease, we cannot realistically hope to characterize all the relevant molecular interactions one-by-one as a requirement for building a predictive disease model.

(D'haeseleer et al. 1999 #911)

A single microarray experiment, for example, can generate millions of discrete pieces of data, and in order to draw meaningful inferences, we have little choice but to use tools, such as cluster analysis, correlation analysis, or many of the predictive tools that comprise data mining.

Ihmels et al. (2005 #912) used differential clustering to characterize phenotypic variations on a genome-wide scale to reveal conserved and diverged coexpression patterns. Applying these techniques across different levels of organization provides a framework for analysis of open reading frames and *cis*-regulatory elements.

Mehta (2010 #910) described the use of gene expression analysis to identify important genes and pathways relevant to several clinical parameters in the identification and treatment of breast cancer, identifying novel genes that were not previously associated with ER-related pathways in cancer. This work further developed an artificial neural network (back-propagation model) to help predict clinical outcomes, which was able to predict relapse with 97.8% accuracy.

Kittleson et al. (2005 #914) used a microarray-based prediction algorithm differentiating nonischemic (NICM) from ischemic cardiomyopathy (ICM) using nearest shrunken centroids, using this to test the hypothesis that NICM and ICM would have both shared and distinct differentially expressed genes relative to normal hearts.

Gene expression analysis has also been used in the area of drug discovery (Walker 2001 #915).

From these areas of research, it can be seen that algorithms and methods are being used to focus on applications such as clustering gene expression patterns to identify genes that are coexpressed and possibly coregulated, predict gene function based on expression patterns, discover statistically significant associations between expression patterns of a chosen gene and a subset of other genes, and infer unknown genetic signaling networks from gene expression time series data.

The techniques we describe elsewhere in this text, as well as in the references given, apply to this important bioscience technique.

The datasets generated from gene expression experiments are typically *gene-sample* (or *gene-condition*) where the data is a numeric or discretized set of expression levels for each appropriate combination of gene and sample,[26] *gene-time*, where the data is a time series of expression values, or *gene-sample-time*, which is a combination of both.

Using such large datasets would allow us, for example, to develop a classifier to differentiate between different subtypes of *acute lymphoblastic leukemia* (ALL), where the different subtypes tend to respond differently to the same therapy, where they visually look similar, and where conventional diagnostic methods, such as immunophenotyping, cytogenetics, and molecular diagnostics may not be readily available. Wong (2006 #916) described how combining gene selection using χ^2 with a classifier on the emerging pattern using prediction by collective likelihood (PCL) for future diagnosis has an interestingly low error rate when compared to other techniques.

In Jiang et al. (2004 #917), the problem of cluster analysis for gene expression data is further described, segmenting the problem into three distinct categories: gene-based clustering, sample-based clustering, and subspace clustering (capture clusters formed by a subset of genes across a subset of samples).

For a concise general overview of gene expression analysis of microarray data, the interested reader is referred to Slonim and Yanai (2009 #918) as a very short introduction.

Gene expression analysis techniques, as hinted above, can be thought of within a standardized flow, a simplified version of which is shown in Fig. 8.9.

From the perspective of the techniques that fall within the area of gene expression analysis, Committee on Applications of Toxicogenomic Technologies to Predictive Toxicology and Risk Assessment (2007 #920) provided some interesting commentary on the various techniques available, as shown in Fig. 8.10.[27]

---

[26] Just as a data point, it is not unusual for an experiment to range between 100 and 500 samples and from 1,000 to 100,000 genes.

[27] Note that these comments, published in 2007, are already becoming inaccurate, as is shown, for example, by the commentary on EST/SAGE.

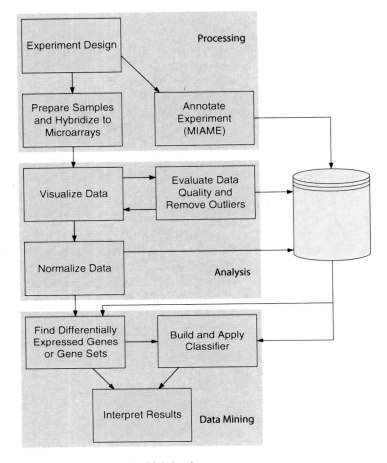

Fig. 8.9 Gene expression analysis – high-level context

Method	Throughput	Comments
• Northern blot	1 gene	• Standard procedure; low throughput
• Substractive cloning		• Not always comprehensive
• Differential display	Increasing data density	• Follow up full-length cloning required; potential to identify rare mRNSa
• EST/SAGE		• "Expensive" and requires a dedicated sequencing facility
• Gridded filters		• Cannot multiplex probes derived from two different tissue samples
• High density arrays	10^4 gene	• Identification of differentially expressed genes dependent on arrayed elements

Fig. 8.10 Gene expression analysis methods (commentary, Committee on Applications of Toxicogenomic Technologies to Predictive Toxicology and Risk Assessment)

8.9 Artificial Neural Networks

8.9.1 Introduction

Artificial neural networks, or ANNs, are parallel computational models that comprised and interconnected groups of processing units – called *neurons* – each of which processes knowledge that is stored in the interconnection strengths – the (*synaptic*) *weights*. The neurons are organized into *layers* of neurons, with interconnections between the layers and, sometimes, within each layer. The synaptic weights are generated through the *learning algorithm* associated with the ANN. Although such models have some characteristics in common with biological neural networks, as we shall indicate at various points below, there are some important differences.

From the above we can see that an ANN can be characterized by the pattern, or structure, of the interconnections between the neurons, the architecture, and the learning algorithm used for the ANN. The learning algorithm is also referred to as the training algorithm and is used to update the synaptic weights, based on the data presented to the ANN. The choice of architecture and learning algorithm thus allows for much flexibility and also different performance characteristics. We shall explore some of the more common architectures and algorithms below.

Before discussing the details further, ANNs have been used to address many different types of problem in business, biology, engineering, and finance, to name a few. Pattern classification and pattern recognition have seen particular value from these models. It is also instructive to point out that while the inspiration for ANNs came from areas of neuroscience, the practical application of this technology is more closely related to statistical models.

There are two fundamental types of learning associated with ANNs, and we have already come across them: supervised learning and unsupervised learning. To reiterate, with supervised learning, we provide the "answer" along with the input; with unsupervised learning, we let the model guess at the "answer" and modify its output based upon the data presented. We shall return to learning below as we look at example models which have provided particular value in different disciplines.

8.9.2 Neurons

The basic processing unit within an ANN is the artificial neuron, typically depicted by a circle (or sometimes a square or dot). The ANN architecture consists of groups of neurons that are organized into layers. Pictorially, we might represent an ANN as shown in Fig. 8.11.

Each of the circles in the above figure represents a single neuron. Conventionally, ANNs are drawn with the left-most layer depicting the *input* layer and the right-most layer being the *output* layer, and we shall adhere to this convention

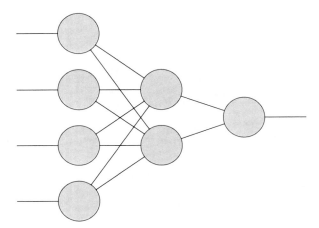

Fig. 8.11 ANN generic representation

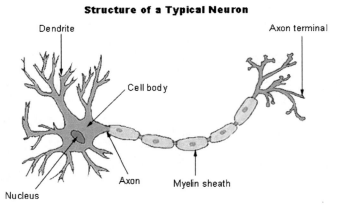

Fig. 8.12 Biological neuron

unless explicitly stated otherwise. The information flow, therefore, is from left to right, and although arrows are not necessarily used, this will be assumed. Such ANNs are referred to as *feed-forward* networks for obvious reasons. Since the inspiration for ANNs came from neuroscience, many of the terms originate from that discipline. Consider, therefore, a typical neuron as depicted in Fig. 8.12.

In comparison, our representation of the artificial neuron is shown in Fig. 8.13 with the biological terms in parentheses.

We can see that our representation is a very gross, approximate representation of its biological equivalent. This is important because there are some fundamental differences that underscore the models we use.

Fig. 8.13 Artificial neuron

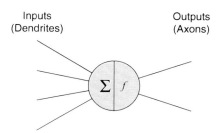

Every neuron has some internal processing capability that takes the input signals and generates an associated output signal. This is where some fundamental differences also manifest themselves. The biological neuron is a series of fixed amplitude pulses whose frequency changes in the face of the input signals received by its dendrites; an artificial neuron outputs a numeric value in response to the input. The output from a biological neuron constantly changes with time; the artificial neuron outputs a value in discrete time – only when its inputs change.

We can represent an artificial neuron as $O = f(I)$ where O is the output and I is the set of inputs. The function f, however, typically comprises two specific functions: the first is some form of summation of the inputs, while the second is some form of thresholding, which transforms the output based on the value of the summation step. Before we consider these functions in more detail, we consider how artificial neurons are connected.

We have already mentioned that the knowledge for the system is stored in the synaptic weights associated with the connections between artificial neurons. Thus, each connection needs to be able to store an associated value, typically denoted as w_i or w_{xy}. In the former notation, the i is a simple counter, and each neuron is counted according to some ordering (e.g., top to bottom in each layer, left to right for the layers). In the latter notation, the x and y values typically indicate the "from" and "to" neurons. In this book, we will use the notation w_{xy}.

8.9.3 Neuronal Functions

We have already indicated that an artificial neuron will typically have two functions that together comprise its internal functionality: some form of summation function and some form of thresholding function.

The summation function takes the inputs to the neuron, multiplying each of them by their synaptic weights (their connection strengths) and then summing them up, as shown in the equation below:

$$\Sigma = \sum_{i=1}^{n} x_i w_{ij}.$$

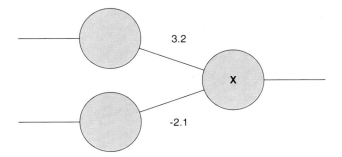

Fig. 8.14 ANN weights

The subscript j indicates some specific neuron. The subscript i runs from 1 to n, where n is the number of neurons connected to the neuron j (i.e., the number of inputs into the neuron). Consider a simple ANN of three neurons, with the identified connection strengths representing the ANN at a discrete point as shown in Fig. 8.14.

If we assume that the upper neuron in the left column has an activation level of +1 and the lower one has an activation level of −1, then $\Sigma = +1 \times 3.2 + (-1) \times (-2.1) = 5.3$ for neuron X. The second function, the thresholding function, takes the output from the summation function and determines the output value for that neuron. An artificial neuron's output value could theoretically be any value between $\pm \infty$, but in practice, the range of values is typically between 0 and 1, or even just the values 0 and 1.

We might begin with considering a very simple function that outputs 1 if the value is greater than or equal to zero and 0 if it is less than zero:

$$t(x) = \begin{cases} 1 & x \geq 0 \\ 0 & x < 0 \end{cases},$$

where $t(x)$ is our notation for the thresholding function and x is the output from the summation function. Here, we have used 0 as our threshold, or activation level. More generally, we would state

$$t(x) = \begin{cases} 1 & x \geq \theta \\ 0 & x < \theta \end{cases},$$

where θ is our threshold (activation level). This second form of equation can be rewritten as

$$t(x) = \begin{cases} 1 & \Sigma - \theta \geq 0 \\ 0 & \Sigma - \theta < 0 \end{cases},$$

Fig. 8.15 Heaviside function

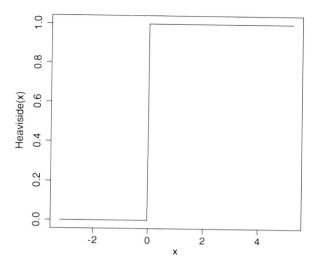

which is an implementation of the Heaviside step function (or unit step function),

$$H(x) = \begin{cases} 0 & x < 0 \\ \frac{1}{2}x = 0 \\ 1 & x > 0 \end{cases}$$

However, in practice, the form of equation used is

$$H(x) = \begin{cases} 0 & x < 0 \\ 1 & x \geq 0 \end{cases}$$

A different notation, $H_c(x) = H(x - c)$, is also sometimes used.

The R fSeries library contains the Heaviside function as shown in Fig. 8.15.

```
library(fSeries)
x = sort(round(c(-1, -0.5, -0.01, 0, 0.01, 0.5, 1, 5*rnorm(5)), 2))
plot(x, Heaviside(x), type="l")
```

Using Heaviside(x, a = 2), for example, will move the vertical line to the right. Any thresholding function will *squash* the range of values from the summation function into a relatively small range of output values, and we shall see this further when we consider the sigmoid function below.

We introduced the term θ above and referred to it as our threshold, or activation level. The reason for this is that it determines the level at which the neuron's output value is produced. That is, above this value, the output tends toward 1, whereas below this value, the output tends toward 0. This value, therefore, *biases* the output and is in fact the term widely used: the neuron's bias.

Note that the bias is specific to a particular neuron – or potentially different for each neuron – and is independent of the inputs to that neuron. In order to compute using the bias, we will often define an additional "input" with a value of -1 (or sometimes $+1$) and use the associated weight to be the value of the bias. That is, for our jth neuron

$$\Sigma = \sum_{i=1}^{n} x_i w_{ij} = x_1 w_{1j} + x_2 w_{2j} + \ldots + x_n w_{nj} - \theta$$

Or, using $x_0 w_{0j}$ where $x_0 = -1$ and $w_{0j} = \theta$, we use

$$\Sigma = \sum_{i=0}^{n} x_i w_{ij} = x_0 w_{0j} + x_1 w_{1j} + x_2 w_{2j} + \ldots + x_n w_{nj}$$

One point we make at this stage relates to neurons in the input layer. We typically pass the input value through to the next layer without any form of modification. Since these neurons will only have a single input – their respective input – the summation function is irrelevant, and the thresholding function is simply 1.

The Heaviside step function has a fundamental problem that mathematicians would prefer to avoid dealing with: it is discontinuous and so it does not have a continuous derivative, which is crucial for many training methods, as we shall see later. Instead, the logistic (or sigmoid) function is used. The logistic function has the form

$$f(x) = \frac{1}{1 + e^{-x}}$$

We typically use it in the form

$$f(x) = \frac{1}{1 + e^{-\Sigma}}$$

where Σ is the output from our summation function. We can see how this function compares with the Heaviside function by the four plots shown in Fig. 8.16.

We can see that the logistic function quickly becomes comparable to the Heaviside function. Other functions which have been used successfully include the hyperbolic tangent function ($\tanh(x)$) or even Gaussian functions (in radial basis function neural networks).

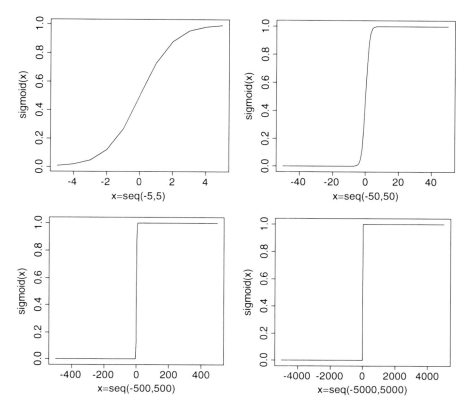

Fig. 8.16 Logistic function and Heaviside function comparison

Summarizing the above discussion, we can see that there are several ANN
characteristics that drive the performance and success of our model:

- ANN architecture: connections between neurons, number of layers, and
  connections between layers
- Neuronal functions
- Learning algorithm (and training methods)
- Applications of/for the ANN

The choices we make in each of these dimensions have a significant
impact on how successfully our model solves our problem.

We have not as of yet considered all of the characteristics listed above. These
will be considered in the sections below. We conclude this section with a few
comments about ANNs in general. Research in this discipline has been around for
half a century, and many valuable results have been generated from this research.
Although the inspiration for ANNs came from neuroscience, the highly simplified

1. Select a (random) set of initial weights

2. Apply a set of inputs to the ANN and compare its performance with what we

   expect.

3. If the results of step 2 are poor – that is, they do not meet our predefined

   criteria for acceptable performance – modify the weights and return to step 2.

Fig. 8.17   Generic ANN training method

model of the brain that has been used does not mean that ANNs are a panacea and, to be fair, shouldn't be judged in this light.

ANNs can be validly used to represent the real world in many different contexts and have been used to successfully approximate, classify, predict, and generalize our understanding across a wide range of disciplines and applications.

8.9.4   Encoding the Input

In our discussions so far, we have made the implicit assumption that the input to an ANN can be any numeric value, and this is in fact the case. However, for reasons of practicality, it is usual to scale the input values to the range $[0.0, 1.0]$. Thus, one of the first steps we need to take is to perform this mapping of values. This concept – normalization – was a topic we discussed in Chap. 5, and we will not repeat this discussion here.

8.9.5   Training Methods

In essence, the goal of training an ANN is to ensure that the ANN represents the data it has seen and is likely to see "correctly." In order to accomplish this, we typically perform the procedure shown in Fig. 8.17.

The term *epoch* is used to denote a training cycle that uses every instance of our input dataset. Although we could change the weights (step 3) after each individual instance is presented, we typically change them at the end of each epoch.

There are some natural questions that arise from our above procedure.

How do we modify the weights? The algorithm for accomplishing this is typically tightly coupled with the ANN model or architecture, and we shall look at some of these later.

How do we determine whether or not the performance is good? Here, we begin to get to the heart of the difference between supervised and unsupervised learning methods. The data we use for training will consist of a set of variables. For supervised learning, these will be independent variables analogous to the regression problem we considered earlier in the book. With supervised learning methods, we have been provided with the target we would like our ANN to hit (or get close to) – the dependent variable – so we can immediately see how close we got to the "correct" answer. In the unsupervised learning case, we have no such output; we are expecting the ANN to cluster the input instances in some meaningful manner. However, this only raises another question: what is meaningful in this context?

Can we "intelligently" set the initial weights? This is a particularly interesting question and requires that we consider the error space for our ANN results

8.9.5.1   Supervised Learning Methods

In this section, we will build on our earlier discussions and focus on specific training methods for specific models. Intuitively, supervised methods are those where the instances used to train our model have explicitly defined expected outputs. For example, if we expect to obtain a particular value as a result of feeding a particular test instance to our model, then we can measure the model-derived response with our expected response, giving us an *error measure*, and take action based upon the difference through some form of feedback loop.

Perceptrons

This provides one of the simplest learning methods. We start with an initial set of weights and iteratively test each input instance against our model. If the output matches our target, we move onto the next input instance. If the output is larger than our target, we reduce the weights and try the same instance again; if the output is less than our target, we increase the weights and try the same instance again. Continue this across our complete set of input instances until we make no more changes to the weights.

We show the formal algorithm in Fig. 8.18, but first highlight a couple of factors. The first relates to how we select our initial weights. Are these selections important? What effect can they have on our model? Typically, we initialize our weights to small random values. Typically, the values chosen are in the range 0–1. The values selected can have an impact on the speed of convergence of the model to our desired level of accuracy. As we can see in the perceptron learning rule in Fig. 8.18, the rate of change is governed by the current value of the weight and the input value for the associated attribute, since this is the increment (or decrement) of change. We can affect this by introducing an additional parameter δ, the *learning rate*, to make the equations $w_i \Leftarrow w_i + \delta x_i$ and $w_i \Leftarrow w_i - \delta x_i$, respectively. This form is referred to as the *Widrow-Hoff delta rule*.

The perceptron learning algorithm, or perceptron learning rule, has been proven to converge to a solution for any linearly separable problem in a finite number of

1. Randomly initialize weights and threshold values

2. Apply an input instance $\mathbf{X} = (x_1,...,x_n)$, with associated target output t, to the

    network and calculate the network output o for this instance.

3. If $t=o$, select another input instance and return to 2.

    If $t>o$ increase each weight $w_i \Leftarrow w_i + x_i$.

    If $\mathbf{t}<\mathbf{o}$ reduce each weight $w_i \Leftarrow w_i - x_i$.

4. Iterate through 2 and 3 until there are no more changes to be made for each

    input instance.

Fig. 8.18 Perceptron learning algorithm

iterations by the *Perceptron Convergence Theorem* (Rosenblatt 1962 #105; Minsky and Papert 1969a, b #102).

Example

Let us consider an example application. Consider a hypothetical situation where we have a set of data values for a group of patients that have been diagnosed as either having or not having a particular condition. We have identified two measures that, individually, do not provide a good indicator of whether the patient has the disease or not, but, when taken together, they show a clear distinction between patients who have the condition and patients who do not, as shown in Fig. 8.19.

For this example, we are using the EasyNN-plus software.[28] Our input file of data, which is plotted in Fig. 8.19, is shown in Box 8.1 below.

We have a total of 14 examples with which we wish to train our network. The network associated with this problem is shown in Fig. 8.20.

The product, like many others, provides a mechanism for us to test our network on as-yet-unseen data. If we test using 0.25 and 0.95 as our input, our network predicts that the patient will have the condition (Fig. 8.21). For our hypothetical example, this is the correct response.

Stormo et al. (1982 #106) used a perceptron to distinguish translational initiation sites in *Escherichia coli* in a library of mRNA sequences. In this case, the nucleotide sequence was encoded such that each nucleotide was denoted by a binary sequence as shown in Table 8.1.

---

[28] We refer the reader to Appendix B for more information on this product.

Fig. 8.19 Linearly separable
patient dataset

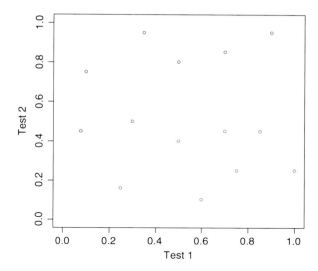

Box 8.1 Perceptron Classification

	Test1	Test2	HasCondition
[1]	0.25	0.16	0
[2]	0.50	0.40	0
[3]	0.60	0.10	0
[4]	0.70	0.45	0
[5]	0.75	0.25	0
[6]	0.85	0.45	0
[7]	1.00	0.25	0
[8]	0.08	0.45	1
[9]	0.10	0.75	1
[10]	0.30	0.50	1
[11]	0.35	0.95	1
[12]	0.50	0.80	1
[13]	0.70	0.85	1
[14]	0.90	0.95	1

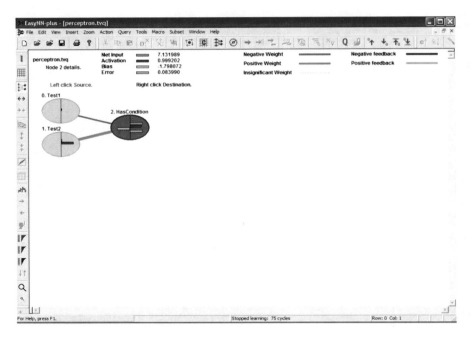

Fig. 8.20 EasyNN-plus network

Day 1	Test1	Test2	HasConditi+
0:0	0.2500	0.9500	true
[1]	0.2500	0.1600	false
[2]	0.5000	0.4000	false
[3]	0.6000	0.1000	false
[4]	0.7000	0.4500	false
[5]	0.7500	0.2500	false
[6]	0.8500	0.4500	false
[7]	1.0000	0.2500	false
[8]	0.0800	0.4500	true
[9]	0.1000	0.7500	true
[10]	0.3000	0.5000	true
[11]	0.3500	0.9500	true
[12]	0.5000	0.8000	true
[13]	0.7000	0.8500	true
[14]	0.9000	0.9500	true

Fig. 8.21 Network query

Table 8.1 Nucleotide encoding

A	C	G	T
1	0	0	0
0	1	0	0
0	0	1	0
0	0	0	1

Table 8.2 Sequence encoding

A	C	G	G	T	A	C
1	0	0	0	0	1	0
0	1	0	0	0	0	1
0	0	1	1	0	0	0
0	0	0	0	1	0	0

Thus, four-bit encodings can be used for each nucleotide. Using this encoding, the sequence would be encoded as shown in Table 8.2.

The network developed by Stormo et al. included hundreds of input units, but the encoding above illustrates how data such as a nucleotide sequence could be encoded for a neural network, each bit being provided as input to a separate input unit.

This area of research has provided a number of interesting models, including identifying cleavage sites in protein sequences (Schneider et al. 1993 #107).

Multilayer Perceptrons

As the name suggests, multilayer perceptrons are perceptrons with more than the input and output layer of perceptrons, as exemplified in Fig. 8.22. These have one, or more, "middle" layers – called *hidden layers* – which are not directly connected to both (or even either) of the input and output layers. Information flow in these networks is only in the feed-forward direction.

In these networks, the transfer functions must be differential everywhere; this is essential to training such networks but is outside the scope of this book. Multilayer perceptrons can solve nonlinear problems in addition to linearly separable problems solvable by perceptrons, which makes them much more flexible and usable.

Since functions such as the hyperbolic tangent or sigmoid functions are typically used, the binary values of 1 and 0 to indicate activation and inhibition no longer apply since the output will be a value on the continuous interval [0.00, 1.00] (to two decimal places). Thus, we need to consider the threshold at which activation occurs. A threshold of 0.50 is often selected (at least initially), but it can obviously be set (or changed) to any value, such as 0.80 or 0.25. However, it is important to realize the implications of this. Setting the threshold to 0.80, for example, requires "more" to switch the neuron on; the result is that the neuron will be less sensitive. Conversely, setting the threshold to 0.25 will require "less" to switch the neuron on, thus making the neuron more sensitive to the input. Each layer in the network will now typically have its own bias neuron (+1 or −1).

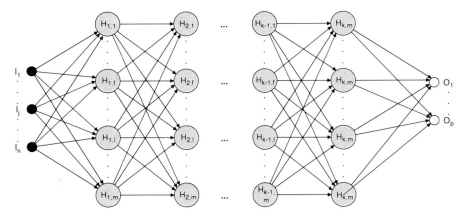

Fig. 8.22 Multilayer feed-forward artificial neural network

At this point, we introduce some heuristics for designing networks. First, the number of input layer neurons (or units) will be determined by the number of *features* used in the input vector. In our example network above, we had two test results, which correlated to two input neurons. The number of neurons in the output layer will correlate to the number of *classes* of output we are interested in.

The challenge, however, comes when trying to determine the number of hidden units – and, in fact, the number of hidden layers. Although work has been done in this area, such as Hornik et al. (1989 #109), which shows that a network with one hidden layer can represent any transformation from input to output, given a sufficient number of units, the number of units in the hidden layer can be large. This being said, most applications *do* use a single hidden layer. For the interested reader, we recommend Ripley (1996 #37) as a resource for further discussion on this subject. But be warned: while thorough, this is not for the faint of heart.

Back Propagation

Training of multilayer perceptrons, as we have said above, does not correlate to training of perceptrons: we can't use the perceptron training rule. Instead, we typically use the *back-propagation* (backprop) method (Rumelhart et al. 1986a, b #108). The rule is so-called because once the error (difference between the target and actual value) is computed, this value is propagated backward through the network, layer by layer, so that the weights can be modified in a manner similar to the delta rule.

Let's build up our model from the beginning. First, as we have discussed above, the typical ANN comprises some n number of inputs and some p number of outputs connected by hidden layers[29] of neurons in the middle. In Fig. 8.22, we have a total

---

[29] Recall that the *hidden* nature is that we don't have any visibility to the values apportioned to each neuron and how these change over the training phase(s).

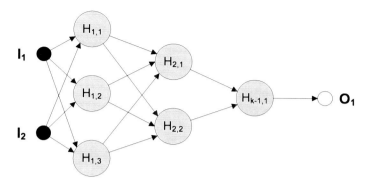

Fig. 8.23 Simplified feed-forward network

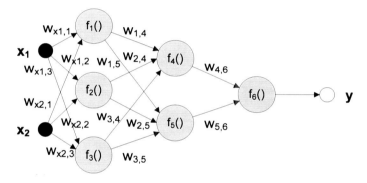

Fig. 8.24 Simplified feed-forward network – alternate representation

of k layers. Each layer of units, in our example, comprises m units, or neurons, and each layer is fully connected to the next layer in the network.

As we'll later see, it has been shown that if certain constraints are accepted, for most applications, a feed-forward network with a single layer of hidden units can be used with a sigmoid activation function for the units. In the remainder of our discussion, we'll use the simplified network shown in Fig. 8.23.

We can see that this network has two inputs I_1, I_2 and one output O_1. We're going to refer to these as x_1, x_2, and y in our discussions below. Further, we're going to label each $H_{i,j}$ unit in our network with a function, $f_p\left(\sum_i input_i \times weight_i\right)$, where p is simply an integer value, but where the function f is the nonlinear output function, typically a sigmoid function. Our network now looks as shown in Fig. 8.24.

Now we would typically use our training data to teach the network. As we've described elsewhere, this consists of the tuple of input values $(x_{1,i}, x_{2,i})$ and a corresponding output value, y_i, for some number, i, of available training instances.

As we propagate our input values, $(x_{1,i}, x_{2,i})$, through the first layer of the network, we will determine values for the connection strengths (weights) between the units, and then propagate to the next layer, determine connection strength values, and so on until we produce some output $\hat{y}_i$. We can now compare this value against our expected output, y_i, and calculate an error value, $\delta = \hat{y}_i - y_i$. Δ is called the *error signal* of the output layer.

Let's walk through this, assuming we only have a single training instance, so we don't introduce another subscript into our notation, which will only serve to complicate matters. Before we do that, however, we're going to explain the notation used in Fig. 8.24 for the connection strengths between the units, otherwise known as the *weights*. The subscripts serve to show the origin and destination nodes, thus $w_{4,6}$ denotes the connection strength between unit 4, denoted by $f_4()$, and unit 6, denoted by $f_6()$. We'll see how these are used momentarily. We didn't label every node.

We would first determine values for our first layer of units, $f_1()$ through $f_3()$, by calculating outputs according to the delta rule:

$$y_1 = f_1\left(w_{x1,1}x_1 + w_{x2,1}x_2\right),$$

$$y_2 = f_2\left(w_{x1,2}x_1 + w_{x2,2}x_2\right),$$

$$y_3 = f_3\left(w_{x1,3}x_1 + w_{x2,3}x_2\right).$$

These values will then be used as inputs to calculate the outputs for $f_4()$ and $f_5()$:

$$y_4 = f_4\left(w_{1,4}y_1 + w_{2,4}y_2 + w_{3,4}y_3\right),$$

$$y_5 = f_5\left(w_{1,5}y_1 + w_{2,5}y_2 + w_{3,5}y_3\right).$$

Likewise, the values for y_4 and y_5 are used as input to the next layer:

$$y_6 = \hat{y} = f_6\left(w_{4,6}y_4 + w_{5,6}y_5\right).$$

In this last equation, our output y_6 is our network output $\hat{y}$.

Using our relationship from above – $\delta = \hat{y}_i - y_i$ – we calculate the error $\delta = \hat{y} - y$ and then propagate this backward to the previous layer in our network by multiplying by the appropriate connection strength:

$$\delta_4 = w_{4,6}\delta$$

$$\delta_5 = w_{5,6}\delta$$

where the subscripts refer to the specific unit, analogous to the function subscript introduced above. Essentially, we have determined a unit-specific error value for the two units connected to the output of our network. We do this for the next prior layer using a similar approach but introducing all of the appropriate connection strengths. In our example, this results in the following:

$$\delta_1 = w_{1,4}\delta_4 + w_{1,5}\delta_5,$$

$$\delta_2 = w_{2,4}\delta_4 + w_{2,5}\delta_5,$$

$$\delta_3 = w_{3,4}\delta_4 + w_{3,5}\delta_5.$$

At this stage in the back-propagation algorithm, we now have an error value that is specific to each unit and specific to the actual input instance. Obviously, if we have i training instances, we would have values $\delta_{1,i}, \delta_{2,i}, \delta_{3,i}, \delta_{4,i}, \delta_{5,i}$, and $\delta_{6,i}$ for each of our training instances. But how do we apply these values to update our network?

Each connection strength in our network will be updated using a combination of the input to the unit and the errors we have just calculated. For the first layer in our network, the updated values are

$$w'_{x1,1} = w_{x1,1} + \eta\delta_1 \frac{df_1(X)}{dX} x_1,$$

$$w'_{x2,1} = w_{x2,1} + \eta\delta_1 \frac{df_1(X)}{dX} x_2,$$

$$w'_{x1,2} = w_{x1,2} + \eta\delta_2 \frac{df_2(X)}{dX} x_1,$$

$$w'_{x2,2} = w_{x2,2} + \eta\delta_2 \frac{df_2(X)}{dX} x_2,$$

$$w'_{x1,3} = w_{x1,3} + \eta\delta_3 \frac{df_3(X)}{dX} x_1,$$

$$w'_{x2,3} = w_{x2,3} + \eta\delta_3 \frac{df_3(X)}{dX} x_2$$

In the above equations, $\frac{df_i(X)}{dX}$ denotes the derivative of the nonlinear, neuron activation function. η is a parameter that determines the speed of learning for the network. The appropriate selection of this value significantly impacts the network and should be carefully considered. Many times, the approach used is to begin the learning phase with a large value, gradually decreasing the value as the connection strengths or weight coefficients are being established. An alternative approach is to begin with a small value, gradually increase it during the learning phase, and decrease it toward the end of the learning phase. A major reason for choosing one approach over the other is that an initial small value helps determine the signs of the coefficients quickly.

Table 8.3 Common forms of radial basis functions, where $r = \|x - x_i\|$

Gaussian	$\phi(r) = e^{-(\varepsilon r)^2}$
Multiquadric	$\phi(r) = \sqrt{1 + (\varepsilon r)^2}$
Inverse quadratic	$\phi(r) = \frac{1}{1+(\varepsilon r)^2}$
Inverse multiquadric	$\phi(r) = \frac{1}{\sqrt{1+(\varepsilon r)^2}}$

We're going to conclude this section with a couple of observations. One of the criticisms leveled at ANNs is their lack of transparency, and this can be seen in the description of the back-propagation algorithm above. Once the model has been created, it is difficult to see what is happening during the training phase. Once the training has been completed, information about the model is contained in the connection strengths, and this doesn't really provide us with much insight into the validity of what we've just generated. That being said, ANNs have been deft at providing valuable and accurate solutions to problems.

We mentioned that some of the research into the back-propagation algorithm has been shown that for networks where the inputs are binary, only one layer of hidden units is required to approximate many functions to an arbitrary level of precision. Interested readers can find the proofs for this, along with other constraints such as the nonlinear activation functions that are necessary on the hidden units, in Hornik et al. (1989 #109), Funahashi (1989 #253), Cybenko (1989 #254), and Hartman et al. (1990 #255).

Radial Basis Functions

As its name suggests, a radial basis function (RBF) is a real-valued function whose value depends only on the distance from some origin or center:

$$\phi(x) = \phi(\|x\|) \text{ or } \phi(x, c) = \phi(\|x - c\|)$$

The norm is usually Euclidean distance, but other distance measures can be used. Some common types of RBFs are shown in Table 8.3.

RBFs are typically used to develop function approximations of the form

$$y(x) = \sum_{i=1}^{N} w_i \phi(\|x - x_i\|)$$

where $y(x)$ is a sum of N RBFs, each of which is associated with a different center x_i and weighted by a coefficient w_i. This type of RBF has seen use in time series prediction and nonlinear system control.

This form of function can also be interpreted as a simple, single-layer ANN called an RBF network where individual RBFs are the activation functions for the network and form a linear combination of RBFs.

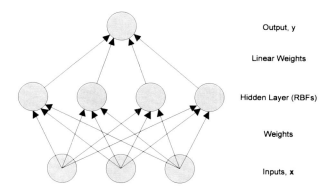

Fig. 8.25 Radial basis function network

The general architecture is shown in Fig. 8.25.

More formally, the output $y : \mathbb{R}^n \to \mathbb{R}$ and is $y(x) = \sum_{i=1}^{N} a_i \rho(\|x - c_i\|)$, where N is the number of neurons in the hidden layer, c_i is the center vector for neuron i, and a_i are the weights of the linear output neuron. As we mentioned above, the norm is typically a Euclidean distance, and the basis function is taken to be Gaussian.

One of the reasons for interest in RBFs is that they are *universal approximators* on a compact subset of $\mathbb{R}^n$, meaning that if we specify enough hidden neurons, the network can approximate any continuous function with arbitrary precision.

The R package frbf (flexible RBF) provides a nice simple illustration.

The first step is to segment our dataset into training and classification subsets

```
> library(frbf)
> # Example data will be split into training and classification groups
data(iris)
samp <- sample(1:150, 75)

# the training matrix will be use 75 random points
training_matrix <- iris[samp, ]
# the matrix to classify will use all the other points
classification_matrix <- iris[-samp, ]
>
```

from which we can build our RBF network model

```
> model <- frbf(training_matrix, weighting_function="mahalanobis", class_name = "Species",
number_clusters = 3, scale_variance = TRUE)
warning messages:
1: In finds(training_matrix, kernels, model_lambda, config) :
  niter parameter has been calculated, value is 4
2: In finds(training_matrix, kernels, model_lambda, config) :
  niter was too low, it has been redefined to 10
```

The various components of our model instance, depicting the configuration, model, lambdas, and kernels, are shown in Fig. 8.26.

Now we can use our classification subset to predict some values (Fig. 8.27).

Self-Organizing Maps

A *self-organizing map* (SOM), sometimes called a *Kohonen map*,[30] is an ANN that
uses unsupervised learning to produce a low(er)-dimensional, discretized representation of the input space of the training instances (a map) and uses a neighborhood
function to preserve the topological properties of the input space.

```
> print(model@config)

configuration
  class_name (class name): species
  number_clusters (number of clusters): 3
  clustering_algorithm (k-means algorithm):
  weighting_function (weighting function): mahalanobis
  niter (number of iteractions): -1
  niter_changes (number of iterations without change allowed): 5
  perform_sum (perform cluster sum): TRUE
  scale_variance (scale variance): TRUE
  s: 0.2
  d: 0.23
  epsilon: 0.01
  verbose: no

> print(model@model)
        class size        s centroid sepal.Length sepal.width petal.Length petal.width
1      setosa   27 0.400000        1     4.988889    3.429630     1.448148    0.262963
2  versicolor   22 0.594336        1     6.027273    2.800000     4.336364    1.350000
3   virginica   26 0.492000        1     6.611538    2.996154     5.584615    2.007692

> print(model@lambda)
$setosa
$setosa[[1]]
             sepal.Length sepal.width petal.Length petal.width
sepal.Length   1.89213774  -0.8732785   -0.6053354   0.01471003
sepal.width   -0.87327848   1.5365958    0.2045275  -0.11324227
petal.Length  -0.60533543   0.2045275    1.3617701  -0.28570686
petal.width    0.01471003  -0.1132423   -0.2857069   1.11481889


$versicolor
$versicolor[[1]]
             sepal.Length sepal.width petal.Length petal.width
sepal.Length   1.19995732  -0.06283117   -0.5001636   0.1624831
sepal.width   -0.06283117   1.21015347   -0.1893689  -0.2809519
petal.Length  -0.50016362  -0.18936890    1.8655615  -0.8140253
petal.width    0.16248313  -0.28095193   -0.8140253   1.6245789


$virginica
$virginica[[1]]
             sepal.Length sepal.width petal.Length petal.width
sepal.Length   1.51459773  -0.2368397   -0.7326171   0.01865172
sepal.width   -0.23683971   1.1143006    0.1508817  -0.24483310
petal.Length  -0.73261705   0.1508817    1.5194278  -0.23654043
petal.width    0.01865172  -0.2448331   -0.2365404   1.13285559
```

Fig. 8.26 Model instance

---

[30] Tuevo Kohonen was the first to describe this type of model.

```
> print(model@kernels)
$setosa
Kernels
  class_name: setosa
  eigen_values:
    1.56814 0.9484738 0.7257639 0.3385282

  eigen_vector:
    -0.5837387 -0.5010265 -0.5004353 -0.3972229 0.3111807 0.5487774 -0.3718903 -0.6809607 -0.1596685
  0.3830338 -0.6784368 0.6062298 0.7327494 -0.5487266 -0.3885686 0.1048425

  centroids:
  Sepal.Length Sepal.Width Petal.Length Petal.Width
1     4.988889    3.42963     1.448148    0.262963

  size: 27

  clusters:
28 35  5  1 22 42 44 14 47 30 29 16 11 13 34  9  6 39 41 43  3 24 18 21 27 23 19
 1  1  1  1  1  1  1  1  1  1  1  1  1  1  1  1  1  1  1  1  1  1  1  1  1  1  1

  cluster_points:
   Sepal.Length Sepal.Width Petal.Length Petal.Width
28          5.2         3.5          1.5         0.2
35          4.9         3.1          1.5         0.2
5           5.0         3.6          1.4         0.2
1           5.1         3.5          1.4         0.2
22          5.1         3.7          1.5         0.4
42          4.5         2.3          1.3         0.3
44          5.0         3.5          1.6         0.6
14          4.3         3.0          1.1         0.1
47          5.1         3.8          1.6         0.2
30          4.7         3.2          1.6         0.2
29          5.2         3.4          1.4         0.2
16          5.7         4.4          1.5         0.4
11          5.4         3.7          1.5         0.2
13          4.8         3.0          1.4         0.1
34          5.5         4.2          1.4         0.2
9           4.4         2.9          1.4         0.2
6           5.4         3.9          1.7         0.4
39          4.4         3.0          1.3         0.2
41          5.0         3.5          1.3         0.3
43          4.4         3.2          1.3         0.2
3           4.7         3.2          1.3         0.2
24          5.1         3.3          1.7         0.5
18          5.1         3.5          1.4         0.3
21          5.4         3.4          1.7         0.2
27          5.0         3.4          1.6         0.4
23          4.6         3.6          1.0         0.2
19          5.7         3.8          1.7         0.3
```

Fig. 8.26   (continued)

This provides a very valuable data visualization technique by reducing the high-dimensional data to a one- or two-dimensional map, plotting similarities in the data by grouping those similar data instances together.

Learning in the SOM model is a competitive process aimed at causing different parts of the network to respond similarly to certain input patterns, similar to how sensory information is handled in separate parts of the human cerebral cortex.

Neuron weights are typically initialized to small random values. However, taking the two largest principal component eigenvectors and sampling from the subspace so spanned can speed up learning since the initial values will already be reasonable approximations to the eventual SOM weights.

During the learning process, training instances must be provided to the network in large numbers, representing, as close as possible, the types of instance it will see in the mapping phase of its life cycle.

```
points_per_cluster:
  point_index Sepal.Length Sepal.width Petal.Length Petal.width
1          28         5.2          3.5          1.5          0.2
2          35         4.9          3.1          1.5          0.2
3           5         5.0          3.6          1.4          0.2
4           1         5.1          3.5          1.4          0.2
5          22         5.1          3.7          1.5          0.4
6          42         4.5          2.3          1.3          0.3
7          44         5.0          3.5          1.6          0.6
8          14         4.3          3.0          1.1          0.1
9          47         5.1          3.8          1.6          0.2
10         30         4.7          3.2          1.6          0.2
11         29         5.2          3.4          1.4          0.2
12         16         5.7          4.4          1.5          0.4
13         11         5.4          3.7          1.5          0.2
14         13         4.8          3.0          1.4          0.1
15         34         5.5          4.2          1.4          0.2
16          9         4.4          2.9          1.4          0.2
17          6         5.4          3.9          1.7          0.4
18         39         4.4          3.0          1.3          0.2
19         41         5.0          3.5          1.3          0.3
20         43         4.4          3.2          1.3          0.2
21          3         4.7          3.2          1.3          0.2
22         24         5.1          3.3          1.7          0.5
23         18         5.1          3.5          1.4          0.3
24         21         5.4          3.4          1.7          0.2
25         27         5.0          3.4          1.6          0.4
26         23         4.6          3.6          1.0          0.2
27         19         5.7          3.8          1.7          0.3

$versicolor
Kernels
  class_name: versicolor
  eigen_values:
    1.619194 0.8863327 0.6821191 0.3568438

  eigen_vector:
    0.3953707 0.4760455 0.576785 0.5332745 0.8464809 -0.3803813 0.07169591 -0.3655679 -0.1810707 -
0.792273 0.3415411 0.4720875 0.3071898 -0.03153215 -0.7385989 0.5992594

  centroids:
  Sepal.Length Sepal.width Petal.Length Petal.width
1     6.027273         2.8    4.336364         1.35

  size: 22

  clusters:
  54  93  72  88  59  96  64  83  97  70  57  95  69  53  92  71  52  85  63 100  98  66
   1   1   1   1   1   1   1   1   1   1   1   1   1   1   1   1   1   1   1   1   1   1

  cluster_points:
     Sepal.Length Sepal.width Petal.Length Petal.width
54           5.5          2.3          4.0          1.3
93           5.8          2.6          4.0          1.2
72           6.1          2.8          4.0          1.3
88           6.3          2.3          4.4          1.3
59           6.6          2.9          4.6          1.3
96           5.7          3.0          4.2          1.2
64           6.1          2.9          4.7          1.4
83           5.8          2.7          3.9          1.2
97           5.7          2.9          4.2          1.3
70           5.6          2.5          3.9          1.1
57           6.3          3.3          4.7          1.6
95           5.6          2.7          4.2          1.3
69           6.2          2.2          4.5          1.5
53           6.9          3.1          4.9          1.5
92           6.1          3.0          4.6          1.4
71           5.9          3.2          4.8          1.8
52           6.4          3.2          4.5          1.5
85           5.4          3.0          4.5          1.5
63           6.0          2.2          4.0          1.0
100          5.7          2.8          4.1          1.3
98           6.2          2.9          4.3          1.3
66           6.7          3.1          4.4          1.4
```

Fig. 8.26 (continued)

```
  points_per_cluster:
    point_index Sepal.Length Sepal.Width Petal.Length Petal.Width
1           54          5.5         2.3          4.0          1.3
2           93          5.8         2.6          4.0          1.2
3           72          6.1         2.8          4.0          1.3
4           88          6.3         2.3          4.4          1.3
5           59          6.6         2.9          4.6          1.3
6           96          5.7         3.0          4.2          1.2
7           64          6.1         2.9          4.7          1.4
8           83          5.8         2.7          3.9          1.2
9           97          5.7         2.9          4.2          1.3
10          70          5.6         2.5          3.9          1.1
11          57          6.3         3.3          4.7          1.6
12          95          5.6         2.7          4.2          1.3
13          69          6.2         2.2          4.5          1.5
14          53          6.9         3.1          4.9          1.5
15          92          6.1         3.0          4.6          1.4
16          71          5.9         3.2          4.8          1.8
17          52          6.4         3.2          4.5          1.5
18          85          5.4         3.0          4.5          1.5
19          63          6.0         2.2          4.0          1.0
20         100          5.7         2.8          4.1          1.3
21          98          6.2         2.9          4.3          1.3
22          66          6.7         3.1          4.4          1.4


$virginica
Kernels
  class_name: virginica
  eigen_values:
    1.484827 1.013405 0.7724566 0.4142589

  eigen_vector:
   -0.5803434 -0.3704711 -0.5617733 -0.4586541 0.3385723 -0.6960463 0.462391 -0.4325309 -0.3274966
  -0.5634129 0.09554336 0.7524516 0.6643165 -0.2466509 -0.6793209 0.1907095

  centroids:
  Sepal.Length Sepal.width Petal.Length Petal.width
1     6.611538     2.996154     5.584615     2.007692

  size: 26

  clusters:
121 131 135 132 111 109 141 101 139 138 129 104 128 119 127 105 144 134 125 145 133 143 142 103
  1   1   1   1   1   1   1   1   1   1   1   1   1   1   1   1   1   1   1   1   1   1   1   1
150 130
  1   1

  cluster_points:
     Sepal.Length Sepal.width Petal.Length Petal.width
121           6.9         3.2          5.7          2.3
131           7.4         2.8          6.1          1.9
135           6.1         2.6          5.6          1.4
132           7.9         3.8          6.4          2.0
111           6.5         3.2          5.1          2.0
109           6.7         2.5          5.8          1.8
141           6.7         3.1          5.6          2.4
101           6.3         3.3          6.0          2.5
139           6.0         3.0          4.8          1.8
138           6.4         3.1          5.5          1.8
129           6.4         2.8          5.6          2.1
104           6.3         2.9          5.6          1.8
128           6.1         3.0          4.9          1.8
119           7.7         2.6          6.9          2.3
127           6.2         2.8          4.8          1.8
105           6.5         3.0          5.8          2.2
144           6.8         3.2          5.9          2.3
134           6.3         2.8          5.1          1.5
125           6.7         3.3          5.7          2.1
145           6.7         3.3          5.7          2.5
133           6.4         2.8          5.6          2.2
143           5.8         2.7          5.1          1.9
142           6.9         3.1          5.1          2.3
103           7.1         3.0          5.9          2.1
150           5.9         3.0          5.1          1.8
130           7.2         3.0          5.8          1.6
```

Fig. 8.26 (continued)

```
points_per_cluster:
    point_index Sepal.Length Sepal.width Petal.Length Petal.width
1       121          6.9          3.2          5.7          2.3
2       131          7.4          2.8          6.1          1.9
3       135          6.1          2.6          5.6          1.4
4       132          7.9          3.8          6.4          2.0
5       111          6.5          3.2          5.1          2.0
6       109          6.7          2.5          5.8          1.8
7       141          6.7          3.1          5.6          2.4
8       101          6.3          3.3          6.0          2.5
9       139          6.0          3.0          4.8          1.8
10      138          6.4          3.1          5.5          1.8
11      129          6.4          2.8          5.6          2.1
12      104          6.3          2.9          5.6          1.8
13      128          6.1          3.0          4.9          1.8
14      119          7.7          2.6          6.9          2.3
15      127          6.2          2.8          4.8          1.8
16      105          6.5          3.0          5.8          2.2
17      144          6.8          3.2          5.9          2.3
18      134          6.3          2.8          5.1          1.5
19      125          6.7          3.3          5.7          2.1
20      145          6.7          3.3          5.7          2.5
21      133          6.4          2.8          5.6          2.2
22      143          5.8          2.7          5.1          1.9
23      142          6.9          3.1          5.1          2.3
24      103          7.1          3.0          5.9          2.1
25      150          5.9          3.0          5.1          1.8
26      130          7.2          3.0          5.8          1.6
```

Fig. 8.26   (continued)

```
> classification <- predict(model, classification_matrix)
> print(classification)
 [1] "setosa"     "setosa"     "setosa"     "setosa"     "setosa"     "setosa"     "setosa"
 [8] "setosa"     "setosa"     "setosa"     "setosa"     "setosa"     "setosa"     "setosa"
[15] "setosa"     "setosa"     "setosa"     "setosa"     "setosa"     "setosa"     "setosa"
[22] "setosa"     "setosa"     "versicolor" "versicolor" "versicolor" "versicolor" "versicolor"
[29] "versicolor" "versicolor" "versicolor" "versicolor" "versicolor" "virginica"  "versicolor"
[36] "versicolor" "versicolor" "versicolor" "virginica"  "versicolor" "versicolor" "versicolor"
[43] "versicolor" "virginica"  "versicolor" "versicolor" "versicolor" "versicolor" "versicolor"
[50] "versicolor" "setosa"     "virginica"  "virginica"  "versicolor" "virginica"  "virginica"
[57] "virginica"  "virginica"  "virginica"  "virginica"  "virginica"  "virginica"  "virginica"
[64] "virginica"  "virginica"  "virginica"  "virginica"  "virginica"  "virginica"  "virginica"
[71] "virginica"  "virginica"  "virginica"  "virginica"  "virginica"
```

Fig. 8.27   Model instance predictions

The competitive learning underlying training is driven by the distance metric between that training instance and all the weight vectors. The neuron with the weight vector most similar to the training instance – the *best matching unit* (BMU) – and the neurons in close proximity to the BMU in the SOM lattice have their weights adjusted toward the value of the training instance by some determined value. The change delta decreases with time and the distance from the BMU. Given a neuron i with weight vector $\mathbf{w}_i(t)$ at (training) time interval t, with a monotonically decreasing learning coefficient $\alpha(t)$, and input training instance $I(t)$, the update formula is

$$\mathbf{w}_i(t+1) = \mathbf{w}_i(t) + \theta(i,t)\alpha(t)(I(t) - \mathbf{w}_i(t))$$

The neighborhood function $\theta(i,t)$ depending on the lattice distance between the BMU and neuron i and a Gaussian function is a common choice. Initially, the self-organizing takes place across the whole of the SOM, but the neighborhood will shrink with time, resulting in weights converging to local estimates.

Let's consider a simple example using colors represented by the triad of intensity data *(red, green, blue)*, where each value is a real value between 0 and 255. Let's assume we have two units with "values" of $(255,0,0)$ (red) and $(102,255,0)$ (green). Our input is $(153,255,51)$, light green, and we can intuitively see that "green" will

be our BMU. Using the Euclidean distance measure of $\sqrt{\sum_{i=0}^{n} x_i^2}$, we have

$$ \text{Red} = \sqrt{(255-153)^2 + (0-255)^2 + (0-51)^2} = 78030, $$
$$ \text{Green} = \sqrt{(102-153)^2 + (255-255)^2 + (0-51)^2} = 5202. $$

8.9.5.2   Unsupervised Learning Methods

As per our discussion on supervised methods, unsupervised methods do not provide an expected response to instances provided as input for the testing phase but instead define their own responses in a "black box" mode of operation: the model itself determines the nature of each instance, in comparison to other instances it has seen, and generates a response.

8.9.5.3   Issues

We alluded to the fact that perceptrons are very adept at solving any *linearly separable* problem but quickly moved on. It should be noted that this is a very significant limitation and, in fact, was one of the reasons why little research occurred with perceptrons between the publication of Minsky and Papert (1969a, b #102) in 1969 and Rumelhart et al. (1986a, b #108) in 1986, which introduced the concept of back propagation and multilayer perceptrons, to overcome the linear separability.

Multilayer perceptrons themselves are only suited to problems where training data for supervised learning is available. For unsupervised learning situations, these are not appropriate models to use. Further, for problems which require training across the entire training set, that is, where learning has to occur using the complete training set and generalization is not possible, the multilayer perceptron is not a valid model. The reader may notice that when we discussed multilayer perceptrons, we did not discuss convergence. While it may have been assumed that the Perceptron Convergence Theorem may be applicable, it should be noted that multilayer perceptrons are not guaranteed to converge. This is obviously a major limitation. It also highlights the difficulty of training which will be associated with the lack of guaranteed convergence. This being said, the multilayer perceptron is the most common form of neural network architecture used in practice.

8.9.6   ANN Architectures

We have considered a number of the characteristics of ANNs and considered a few of the many models, or architectures, which have been developed in this discipline. As has been mentioned in several places in this chapter, the inspiration for ANNs came from neuroscience. It is therefore instructive to make a comment about a biological neural network, the neocortex. Consider that the neocortex has approximately 30 billion neurons arranged in 6 layers (Hawkins 2007 #101).

8.9.7   Application to Data Mining

It's been a long time coming, but we now turn our attention to how ANNs can be applied to data mining. As we discuss the merits and demerits, the value and constraints, of ANNs, it is important to bear in mind that ANNs may be valuable approaches, but they may not be the only, or even the most desirable, approach to take. For example, if we can accurately describe the problem using a set of formulae, a more traditional development approach may be recommended. Keep this in mind, especially if this domain is new to you.

8.9.7.1   Back Propagation

The back-propagation model can be very valuable in circumstances where a large amount of data – both data that can be used as input and data that might be considered "output" – is available but where it is not completely clear how to correlate the input and output to each other. Second, this might provide value in cases where the problem is extremely complex but where it is clear that a solution exists – or should exist.

Can we create examples of the correct behavior that we would expect from an ANN? If so, this provides us with a cause to consider using back propagation; if not, consider alternatives. If the outputs we are looking at are either nonnumeric, or if they are somewhat fuzzy, this model can be very valuable.

And not so finally, does the solution change over time? If so, this model may be very beneficial. This definitely needs a little explanation. Consider a simple example: the window of values that we think of as the normal range of values for a specific diagnostic test. Suppose our objective is to provide a guideline for what should be expected as normal for a brand new test. We would normally expect this to change over time, but only within reasonable bounds; those bounds would be somewhat driven by the input and output parameters we use. This variability is easily managed by the back-propagation algorithm and so makes this a good candidate in such circumstances.

8.10   Reinforcement Learning

Taking its inspiration from behavioral psychology, the fundamental concept underpinning *reinforcement learning* is to consider how an *agent* should take *action* in some *environment* such that some form of cumulative *reward* is maximized. As we can see from this simplified description, the problem statement is very general, leading to this technique being used in a wide range of disciplines. Within machine learning, the environment is often defined as a Markov decision process (MDP), and algorithms often show their relation to dynamic programming. However, the major difference between the two is that the reinforcement learning algorithm does not need to *know* the MDP, and so these techniques can be a useful alternative to an MDP if the MDP becomes infeasible to compute due to its size.

   In contrast to the supervised learning paradigm, correct input/output instance pairs are never presented to the algorithm. Further, resulting actions that are suboptimal are similarly not explicitly corrected within the algorithm itself. However, due to its focus on providing a real-time performance characteristic, it provides a valuable approach to problems where the exploration (of the unknown) and exploitation (of the known facts) are important.

   In this text, we only mention reinforcement learning in passing since its applicability to date has primarily been outside the domain of data mining as we discuss it herein. The interested reader is recommended to Sutton and Barto (1998 #31) for a robust explanation of this learning paradigm. But we do want to point out its success in such diverse areas as robot control, elevator scheduling, games (e.g., chess and backgammon), and telecommunications.

8.11   Some Other Techniques

The myriad techniques available to help us in our mining efforts are far beyond the scope of this text to include completely. That a technique has been included should not necessarily mean it is more important, or even more widely used, than some other technique that has not been included. Instead, the criteria for inclusion have been very subjective. This being said, there are some techniques that we wish to highlight to the reader. The techniques identified in this section will only be presented in summary form, with references for the interested reader.

8.11.1 Random Walk, Diffusion Map, and Spectral Clustering

In certain cases, our data may exist on a low-dimensional manifold, for which the shape is unknown but is known to be nonlinear. Using a technique such as principal component analysis (PCA) to reduce the dimensions would not provide coherent results since the manifold is nonlinear. Instead, we can use the concept of spectral clustering as a nonlinear dimensionality reduction scheme.

The mathematics is similar to what we have seen elsewhere. Given N data points $\{x_i\}_{i=1}^N$, where each $x_i \in \mathbb{R}^p$, the similarity (distance) measure between points x_i and x_j is given by

$$L_{i,j} = k(x_i, x_j) = \exp\left(-\frac{\|x_i - x_j\|^2}{2\varepsilon}\right),$$

given a Gaussian kernel of width ε and a diagonal normalization matrix $D = Diag([D_1 ... D_N])$, where $D_i = \sum_{j=1}^N L_{i,j}$.

If we then solve the normalized eigenvalue problem $L\varphi = \lambda D\varphi$, or $M\varphi = \lambda\varphi$, where $M = D^{-1}L$, we can use the first several eigenvalues of M for a reasonable low-dimensional representation of our data and good coordinates for our clustering model.

More detailed background on the spectral clustering technique can be found at Roweis and Saul (2000 #880) or Belkin and Niyogi (2003 #881). For further explanation on regularization of manifolds, the interested reader is directed to Belkin et al. (2006 #882).

Many software components are available to support this. In R, for example, the igraph package provides a function to calculate the Laplacian, as shown in Fig. 8.28.

Meila and Shi (2001 #884) considered an alternative view of clustering and segmentation by pairwise similarities where they interpret the similarities as edge flows in a random walk on the graph, showing that spectral methods for clustering and segmentation have a probabilistic foundation, and use the normalized cut method of Jianbo and Malik (2000 #885) as their basis, showing that several other methods are subsumed by this algorithm.

A diffusion map is a mapping between our original (data) space and the first k eigenvectors[31] $\Psi^t(x) = \left(\lambda_1^t \Psi_1(x), \lambda_2^t \Psi_2(x), ..., \lambda_k^t \Psi_k(x)\right)$, where, for any two points x_i, x_j in the diffusion map space, the distance between them is defined as $D_t^2(x_i, x_j) = \|\Psi^t(x_i) - \Psi^t(x_j)\|^2$. This *diffusion distance* D is a distance measure at time t between two probability mass functions.

---

[31] Since the eigenvectors have the relationship $\lambda_1 \geq \lambda_2 \geq ... \geq \lambda_{N-1} \geq 0$, we can stop at any appropriate k with an error of order $O\left((\lambda_{k+1}/\lambda_k)^t\right)$.

```
> library(igraph)
> g <- graph.ring(10)
> g
Vertices: 10
Edges: 10
Directed: FALSE
Edges:

[0]  0 -- 1
[1]  1 -- 2
[2]  2 -- 3
[3]  3 -- 4
[4]  4 -- 5
[5]  5 -- 6
[6]  6 -- 7
[7]  7 -- 8
[8]  8 -- 9
[9]  0 -- 9
> graph.laplacian(g)
       [,1] [,2] [,3] [,4] [,5] [,6] [,7] [,8] [,9] [,10]
 [1,]     2   -1    0    0    0    0    0    0    0    -1
 [2,]    -1    2   -1    0    0    0    0    0    0     0
 [3,]     0   -1    2   -1    0    0    0    0    0     0
 [4,]     0    0   -1    2   -1    0    0    0    0     0
 [5,]     0    0    0   -1    2   -1    0    0    0     0
 [6,]     0    0    0    0   -1    2   -1    0    0     0
 [7,]     0    0    0    0    0   -1    2   -1    0     0
 [8,]     0    0    0    0    0    0   -1    2   -1     0
 [9,]     0    0    0    0    0    0    0   -1    2    -1
[10,]    -1    0    0    0    0    0    0    0   -1     2
> graph.laplacian(g, norm=TRUE)
       [,1] [,2] [,3] [,4] [,5] [,6] [,7] [,8] [,9] [,10]
 [1,]   1.0 -0.5  0.0  0.0  0.0  0.0  0.0  0.0  0.0  -0.5
 [2,]  -0.5  1.0 -0.5  0.0  0.0  0.0  0.0  0.0  0.0   0.0
 [3,]   0.0 -0.5  1.0 -0.5  0.0  0.0  0.0  0.0  0.0   0.0
 [4,]   0.0  0.0 -0.5  1.0 -0.5  0.0  0.0  0.0  0.0   0.0
 [5,]   0.0  0.0  0.0 -0.5  1.0 -0.5  0.0  0.0  0.0   0.0
 [6,]   0.0  0.0  0.0  0.0 -0.5  1.0 -0.5  0.0  0.0   0.0
 [7,]   0.0  0.0  0.0  0.0  0.0 -0.5  1.0 -0.5  0.0   0.0
 [8,]   0.0  0.0  0.0  0.0  0.0  0.0 -0.5  1.0 -0.5   0.0
 [9,]   0.0  0.0  0.0  0.0  0.0  0.0  0.0 -0.5  1.0  -0.5
[10,]  -0.5  0.0  0.0  0.0  0.0  0.0  0.0  0.0 -0.5   1.0
```

Fig. 8.28 Calculating the Laplacian

$$D_t^2(x_i, x_j) = \left\| p(t, y, x_i) - p(t, y, x_j) \right\|_w^2 = \sum_{y=x_1}^{x_N} \left(p(t, y, x_1) - p(t, y, x_j) \right)^2 w(y),$$

where $w(y) = \frac{1}{\phi_0(y)}$.

For our matrix M, we can derive a symmetric matrix $M_s = D^{\frac{1}{2}} M D^{-\frac{1}{2}}$, where $M_{i,j} = \frac{k(x_i, x_j)}{\sum_{j=1}^{N-1} k(x_i, x_j)}$, where M and M_s have the same eigenvalue set and with left eigenvectors $\phi_k = \varphi_k D^{\frac{1}{2}}$ and right eigenvectors $\Psi_k = \varphi_k D^{-\frac{1}{2}}$, and $\langle \phi_k, \varphi_{k'} \rangle = \delta_{k,k'}$. These equations allow us to build the random walk representation of M for time step ε:

$$p\left(x^{t+\varepsilon} = x_j | x^t = x_i\right) = M_{i,j} = \frac{k(x_i, x_j)}{\sum_{j=1}^{N} k(x_i, x_j)}, \quad k(x_i, x_j) = \exp\left(-\frac{\|x_i - x_j\|^2}{2\varepsilon}\right).$$

An interesting note is that ε has both a time step representation and also a kernel width representation. This now allows us to determine the probability of landing at some location y, from an initial location x_i, after some number r time steps:

$$p(t = r\varepsilon, y|x_i) = p\left(x^t = y|y^0 = x_i\right) = e_i M^r$$

where e_i is a row vector, all zeros, with 1 at the ith position.

The $\lim\limits_{t\to\infty} p(t, y|x_i) = \lim\limits_{r\to\infty} e_i M^r = \phi_0(y)$, which is the left eigenvector of M with eigenvalue $\lambda_0 = 1$ and $\phi_0(x_i) = \frac{D_i}{\sum_{j=1}^{N} D_j}$. The eigenvector represents both the probability of landing at location x after infinite steps of the random walk (regardless of the starting position) and is also the density estimate at x.

We've touched on the mathematical theory but haven't explicitly defined where spectral clustering fits into the bigger picture nor, to any great extent, how it is being effectively used in data mining today. We've discussed the concept of clustering elsewhere in this text. Spectral clustering is the name given to a class of clustering algorithms that take pairwise similarities of data points as inputs and use the eigenvectors and eigenvalues of the similarity matrix (or a related matrix) in clustering the data points. A useful way to think about spectral clustering is to consider it in terms of a random walk on the set of vertices of a graph, where the vertices are our data points (hence our discussion above).

Using this analogy, we can consider the process of clustering the data points as partitioning the vertices into disjoint, nonempty sets, thus introducing *cuts* into the graph. One of the most widely used clustering approaches is the *multiway normalized cut* (MNCut).

Given a set of data points V (vertices of our graph) and a clustering $C = \{C_1, C_2, ..., C_k\}$ that partitions V,

$$MNCut(C) = \sum_{k=1}^{K} \sum_{k' \neq k} \frac{Cut(C_k, C_{k'})}{Vol\, C_k}$$

where $Vol\, C_k$ is an aggregated similarity measure[32] and $Cut(A, B) = \sum_{i \in A} \sum_{j \in B} s_{ij}$.
If we have a binary clustering problem, then *MNCut* reduces to

$$MNCut(\{C_1, C_2\}) = \frac{Cut(C_1, C_2)}{Vol\, C_1} + \frac{Cut(C_1, C_2)}{Vol\, C_2}.$$

Looking at this expression, a minimal value is achieved when the two clusters are very different from each other (balanced volumes and a small value for

---

[32] For the ith vertex $(i \in V)$, $D_i = Vol\, V_i = \sum_{j \in V} s_{ij}$, where s_{ij} is the similarity between the ith and jth points. For a set of vertices A, $Vol\, A = \sum_{i \in A} D_i$.

Fig. 8.29 Spectral clustering process

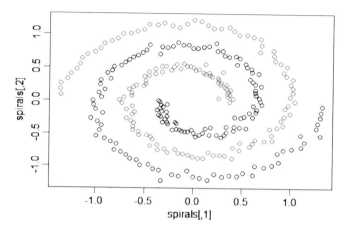

Fig. 8.30 Spectral clustering example

$Cut(C_1, C_2)$). This balancing is important as it helps us to determine the best place to cut the graph. The mincut objective function that we mentioned above is only one method we can use: the *ratio cut*, *normalized cut*, and *min-max-cut* are three popular objective functions that we can consider. When the clusters are well separated from each other, each of these objective functions provides similar accuracy. When the clusters are marginally separated, the normalized cut and min-max-cut tend to provide better results. If there is significant overlap among the clusters, the min-max-cut tends to provide a better balance of the clusters as well as more compact clusters.

Essentially, to partition the graph, solve the mincut problem using the Laplacian. The complete process is depicted in Fig. 8.29.

However, a wide range of software is available to support this technique. Using R as our example environment, the `kernlab` package includes the `specc` function. Figure 8.30 shows a simple example using the `spirals` dataset provided with the package.

The `sc` object created by the `specc` function provides detail on the cluster membership and methods used (Fig. 8.31).

Another interesting package is the SCUBA package, an R package for performing spectral clustering on a data matrix using an MCMC uncertainty algorithm.

A very nice overview on the spectral clustering technique can be found in von Luxburg (2006 #887). Jing et al. (2008 #888) explored performance improvements

```
> sc
Spectral Clustering object of class "specc"

Cluster memberships:

1 1 2 2 1 2 2 2 1 2 2 1 1 2 2 1 1 1 1 1 2 2 1 2 2 2 2 1 1 1 2 1 2 2 1 2 1 2 1 1 2 2 2 2 1 1 1
1 1 2 1 2 1 1 2 2 2 1 1 1 1 1 2 2 1 2 1 1 1 2 2 1 2 2 2 1 1 1 1 2 1 2 1 2 1 1 1 1 1 1 2 1 1 2
2 2 1 2 2 2 2 1 1 1 2 2 1 2 2 2 2 1 2 1 1 1 1 2 2 1 1 2 1 1 1 2 1 2 1 1 1 1 1 2 2 2 2 2 1 1 1 2
2 1 2 1 1 1 2 2 2 1 2 2 2 2 2 2 1 1 1 1 2 1 2 1 1 1 2 1 1 1 1 2 1 2 1 1 1 2 2 1 1 1 2 2 2 1 1
2 2 2 2 2 2 2 2 1 1 1 1 2 1 2 2 1 2 1 2 2 2 2 2 1 2 1 2 1 2 1 1 1 2 2 2 2 1 1 1 2 1 1 2 2 2 2
2 1 1 2 2 2 2 1 1 1 2 2 2 2 2 1 1 2 2 1 1 1 1 1 1 1 2 2 2 2 1 2 1 2 1 1 2 2 2 1 2 1 1 1 1 2
2 1 2 1 2 2 2 2 1 2 1 2 2 1 1 2 2 2 1

Gaussian Radial Basis kernel function.
 Hyperparameter : sigma =  342.590151048389

Centers:
            [,1]        [,2]
[1,]  0.01997201 -0.1761483
[2,] -0.01770984  0.1775137

Cluster size:
[1] 150 150

Within-cluster sum of squares:
[1] 117.3429 118.1182
```

Fig. 8.31 R spectral clustering object

for spectral clustering on multicore processors and GPUs. Two popular graph partitioning packages are Metis, from the University of Minnesota, and Chaco, from Sandia National Labs.

For some further applications, see Patrikainen and Meilă (2005 #886) for applications of Netscan data and the use of dendromatrices. Ding (2004 #889) provided an example of using spectral clustering for DNA gene expression analysis. Ng et al. (2001 #890) provided some valuable examples using Matlab code. Pentney and Meila (2005 #892) provided another example of using this technique on biological sequence data, considering how to deal with asymmetric affinities such as alignment scores and how to deal with imbalanced cluster sizes. Nepusz et al. (2010 #893) described SCPS, a fast implementation of a spectral method for detecting protein families on a genome-wide scale. Paccanaro (#894) considered the automatic clustering homologous proteins when only sequence information is available.

Spectral clustering has shown itself to be a very successful technique for partitioning data of any kind and has seen an increase in popularity[33] thanks in main to advances in computation that now make the well-established graph-theoretic underpinnings implementable. It includes a family of algorithms with tunable parameters that provide a wide range of opportunities for its use in data mining.

The use of matrix factorization, eigenvectors, etc., to solve problems in data mining is a fast-growing trend in part because the techniques are relatively simple, the underlying theory is well established, and many mature, widely available software components are available to support the theory.

---

[33] Googling "spectral clustering gold-rush 2001" will show 9 original papers published in that year alone.

To finish, we refer the reader to Filippone et al. (2008 #891) as an example of how multiple techniques are being used together to great effect for particular problems: kernel methods and spectral analysis for clustering.

8.11.2   Network (Graph)-Based Analysis

As the previous section exemplifies, network-based (graph-based) methods have become a widely used set of techniques for analyzing complex sets of data where such data has a natural mapping to some graph structure. A good example of this is protein interaction networks (sic). Elsewhere in this text, we consider graph-based techniques in much more detail, but make mention of this here since we have already used this concept. A particular area of interest in graph-based techniques is network motif discovery.

8.11.3   Network Motif Discovery

A *network motif* is a subgraph (or connectivity pattern) that occurs more often than is the case in a random network. Where this becomes of significant interest in the life sciences is that many networks studied have been found to include a relatively small set of such network motifs where the larger network seems to be composed of reoccurring instances of these motifs. Further, different types of networks appear to have their own types of characteristic motif: gene regulation networks having a different set of motifs to ecological networks, for example. We can consider these motifs to be akin to building blocks of the larger network, an idea first described in Milo et al. (2002 #931) and later in Alon (2007a #924) and Alon (2007b #925), among others.

Gene regulatory networks, where genes are expressed in the cell in response to biological signals, have been the subject of much research into network motifs. In this case, genes are the nodes of the graph, and edges represent the control of one gene by a transcription factor encoded by another gene: network motifs are therefore patterns of genes regulating the transcription rates (via regulatory proteins that bind DNA) of other genes. Protein-protein interaction (PPI) is important for the majority of biological functions. Signals from the exterior of cells to the interior are mediated by protein-protein interactions. This process of *signal transduction* plays a fundamental role in both normal cellular processes as well as in many diseases. Thus, being able to model and mine the complex networks that occur as a result of this is a very important capability for researchers.

What has been shown is that the same network motifs exist across a diverse range of organisms – from bacteria to humans – leading to the hypothesis that such motifs are independently selected by evolutionary processes (Babu et al. 2004 #926, Conant and Wagner 2003 #927). Just to provide one example, the transcription network is, basically, almost fully defined by three motif families!

Several different types of common network motifs have been elicited from transcription networks and have been the subject of interest due to their functions. These include

- Negative autoregulation (NAR): a transcription factor (TF) represses its own transcription (Rosenfeld et al. 2002 #928)
- Positive autoregulation (PAR): a TF enhances its own rate of production (Maeda and Sano 2006 #929)
- Feed-forward loop (FFL): involves three genes and three regulatory interactions, where some gene G_1 is regulated by two TFs, T_1, T_2, and where T_2 is also regulated by T_1. Each of the regulatory interactions may be positive or negative, resulting in a possible eight types of FFL motif (Mangan and Alon 2003 #930) (Table 8.4).[34]
- Coherent type 1 FFL (C1-FFL): have a function of a "sign-sensitive delay" element and a persistence detector (Mangon and Alon 2003).
- Incoherent type 1 FFL (I1-FFL): is a pulse generator and response accelerator and can serve as response accelerator in a way which is similar to the NAR motif, with the difference being that the I1-FFL can speed up the response of any gene and not necessarily a transcription factor gene.
- Multiple-output FFLs: in some cases, the same regulators T_1 and T_2 regulate several genes $G_1, G_2, ...$ of the same system. By adjusting the strength of the interactions, this motif was shown to determine the temporal order of gene activation.
- Single-input modules (SIM): occurs when a single regulator regulates a set of genes with no additional regulation and is useful when the genes are cooperatively carrying out a specific function and always need to be activated in a synchronized manner.
- Dense overlapping regulons (DOR): occurs when several regulators combinatorially control a set of genes with diverse regulatory combinations.

Network motifs therefore provide an important tool for understanding the modularity and the large-scale structure of networks and also allow one to classify networks into "superfamilies," such as is described in Milo et al. (2004 #932), and have been used with machine-learning techniques to determine the most appropriate network model for a given real-world network, such as is described in Middendorf et al. (2005 #933).

One of the challenges with many of the methods developed is the limited size of motifs discoverable by those methods, with subgraphs of single-digit node counts being the norm (Milo et al. 2002 #931, Kashtan et al. 2004 #937, Kashtan et al. 2004 #936, Baskerville and Paczuski 2006 #935, Middendorf et al. 2005 #933).

---

[34] Four configurations are termed *coherent*, meaning that the sign of the direct regulation path (T_1 to G_1) is the same as the overall sign of the indirect regulation path (T_1 to T_2 to G_1); the other four are termed *incoherent* and have opposite signs for the direct and indirect regulation paths.

Table 8.4 Coherent FFL types and their abundance in transcription databases of *E. coli* and *S. cerevisiae*

Species	Coherent Type 1 Structure	Coherent Type 1 Abundance	Coherent Type 2 Structure	Coherent Type 2 Abundance	Coherent Type 3 Structure	Coherent Type 3 Abundance	Coherent Type 4 Structure	Coherent Type 4 Abundance
E. coli	X→Y→Z (FFL)	28	X⊣Y⊣Z (FFL)	2	X→Y⊣Z (FFL)	4	X⊣Y→Z (FFL)	1
S. cerevisiae	Z	26	Z	5	Z	0	Z	0
Z Logic →	AND	OR	AND	OR	AND	OR	AND	OR
Steady-state $Z(S_x, S_y)$	$S_x \wedge S_y$	S_x	$\bar{S}_x \wedge S_y$	$\bar{S}_x$	$\bar{S}_x$	$\bar{S}_x \wedge \bar{S}_y$	S_x	$S_x \wedge \bar{S}_y$
Steady-state								
S_x on step	Delay	–	–	Delay	–	Delay	Delay	Delay
S_x off step	–	Delay	Delay	–	Delay	–	–	–
inverted out	No	No	Yes	Yes	Yes	Yes	No	No

$Z(S_x, S_y)$: steady-state Z expression of coherent FFLs for the four combinations of S_x and S_y on and off levels ($\wedge, \vee, \_$ represent AND, OR, NOT).
Response: response delay of coherent FFLs to on and off S_x steps in the presence of S_y. –, not delayed
Inverted out means that Z goes off in response to Sx on step (From (Mangan and Alon 2003 #930))

```
FindSubgraphInstances(H,G) # Find all instances of query graph H in network G
Start with an empty set of instances.
[Find Aut(H). Let Hᴇ be the equivalence representatives of H.]
[Find symmetry-breaking conditions C for H given Hᴇ and Aut(H).]
Order nodes of G by increasing degree and then by increasing neighbor degree sequence.
For each node g of G
For each node h of H [Hᴇ] such that g can support h # (Note)
Let f be the partial map associating f(h) = g.
IsomorphicExtensions(f,H,G[,C(h)]) # Find all isomorphic extensions of f [up to symmetry]
Add the images of these maps to the set of all instances.
Remove g from G.
Return the set of all instances.
```

Fig. 8.32 Find subgraph instances within a network (Grochow and Kellis 2007 #934). Note: with the symmetry-breaking logic included, this would iterate over a set of equivalence class representatives, not over all nodes of H

Grochow and Kellis (2007 #934) presented an algorithm that exhaustively assesses the significance of a single query subgraph as a potential motif, which can then be applied to all subgraphs of a given size to emulate the behavior of previous exhaustive algorithms, but with an exponential speedup due to a novel symmetry-breaking technique and are able to find motifs of up to 15 nodes, to find all instances of subgraphs of 31 nodes, and potentially even larger subgraphs. This algorithm takes a motif-centric approach to the problem. To avoid the increased complexity of subgraph enumeration, the algorithm works by exhaustively searching for the instances of a single query graph in a network and, through several optimization factors, enables this search to be effective even though the subgraph isomorphism problem[35] is known to be NP-complete, allowing for subgraphs up to 31 nodes. Rather than enumerating all connected subgraphs of a given size and testing to see whether each is isomorphic to the query graph, the algorithm tries to map the query graph onto the network in all possible ways. Another feature is the avoidance of multiple subgraph acquisition due to subgraph symmetry, probably one of its most valuable features, since subgraph isomorphism is one of the biggest hurdles to finding matches.

Consider a search graph G within which we want to determine whether a particular query subgraph H exists. A node $g \in G$ *supports* a node $h \in H$ if we cannot rule out a subgraph isomorphism from H into G which maps h to g based on the degrees of h, g, and their neighbors. The core subgraph search algorithm is shown in Fig. 8.32 but without the symmetry-breaking capability.[36]

The IsomorphicExtensions function finds all isomorphisms from H to G and uses the most constrained neighbor to eliminate any maps that cannot be isomorphisms. Each call to IsomorphicExtensions extends f, the partial map associating $f(h) = g$ by one node, ensuring that this newly mapped node is appropriately connected to existing (mapped) nodes. Hence, any returned map is

---

[35] Finding a given graph which is a subgraph of a larger graph (network)

[36] Implementing this algorithm as stated would result in the algorithm spending time in finding several distinct maps to a single subgraph.

```
IsomorphicExtensions(f,H,G[,C(h)])      # Find all isomorphic extensions of partial
                                        # map f: H → G [satisfying C(h)]
Start with an empty list of isomorphisms.
Let D be the domain of f.
If D = H, return a list consisting solely of f. (Or write to disk.)
Let m be the most constrained neighbor of any d ∈ D    # constrained by degree, neighbors
                                                       # mapped, etc.
For each neighbor n of f(D)
If there is a neighbor d ∈ D of m such that n is not neighbors with f(d),
or if there is a non-neighbor d ∈ D of m such that n is neighbors with f(d)
[or if assigning f(m) = n would violate a symmetry-breaking condition in C(h)],
then continue with the next n.
Otherwise, let f' = f on D, and f'(m) = n.
Find all isomorphic extensions of f'.
Append these maps to the list of isomorphisms.
Return the list of isomorphisms.
```

Fig. 8.33 Find all isomorphisms (Grochow and Kellis 2003.)

```
SymmetryConditions: # Finds symmetry-breaking conditions for H given H_E, Aut(H)
Let M be an empty map from equivalence representatives to sets of conditions.
For each  n ∈ H_E
Let C be an empty set of conditions.
n' ← n , and  A ← Aut(H).
Do until |A| = 1:
Add "LABEL(n') < MIN {LABEL(m) | m~_A n' and m ≠ n'}" to C.
A ← {f ∈ A | f(n') = n'}
Find the largest A-equivalence class E.
Pick n'∈E arbitrarily.
Let M(n) = C.
Return M.
```

Fig. 8.34 Symmetry-breaking function (ibid.)

guaranteed to be an isomorphism. Note that the implication of this is that
IsomorphicExtensions is responsible for the isomorphism testing, which
allows the test to abort early if necessary, which introduces significant efficiency
into the algorithm (Fig. 8.33).

Symmetries of H are known as automorphisms (self-isomorphisms) and denoted
by $Aut(H)$ in Fig. 8.32 and is used to help with efficiency since starting a map from
two equivalent nodes, equivalence defined using an automorphism from one node
to the other, is inefficient.

We don't describe the symmetry-breaking conditions here but refer the interested reader to the original paper, Grochow and Kellis (2007 #934), for more
information, since the basic algorithm is described above. However, Fig. 8.34
does include the SymmetryConditions logic for completeness.

Given this method, finding network motifs is a case of enumerating candidate
subgraphs H, either exhaustively or via sampling, and then evaluating each case.

This isn't by any means the only algorithm available that attacks this problem.

Kashani et al. (2009 #939) presented a new algorithm for finding k-size network
motifs that uses less processing resources than many other algorithms, and it is
based on counting all k-size subgraphs of a given graph (directed or undirected).
The algorithm was evaluated on biological networks of *E. coli* and *S. cerevisiae*,

so its performance can be compared with that of Grochow and Kellis (2007 #934), and its source code is available per the paper's authors.

Omidi et al. (2009 #941) described another algorithm that incorporates a pattern growth approach, among other techniques, to the problem of extracting larger motifs efficiently. Its source code is available per the paper's authors.

The interested reader is referred to Ling (1996 #938) as another example of an algorithm focused on addressing the core subgraph isomorphism problem. Wong and Baur (2010 #940) presented a survey study of current network motif discovery tools, including discussions of algorithms, experimental data, limitations, and the various pros and cons of the included tools. Ribeiro et al. (2009 #942) provided a review and runtime comparison of current motif detection algorithms in the field. Alon et al. (2008 #943) used the "color coding" technique and implemented an algorithm that can count all occurrences of some motif H with k vertices in a network G with n vertices in polynomial time with n, provided $k = O(\log n)$. Sandve and Drablos (2006 #944) presented a survey of methods for motif discovery in DNA, based on a structured and well-defined framework that integrates all relevant elements and shows that although no single method takes all relevant elements into consideration, much progress can be made through a combination of approaches.

A different approach to this problem, using neural networks, is described in Blekas et al. (2005 #945). They described the issue of the encoding sequence necessary to feed the neural network and proposed an approach of mapping proteins into numerical feature spaces, using sequence matching scores to group conserved patterns (motifs) into protein families.

8.11.4   Binary Tree Algorithm in Drug Target Discovery Studies

For readers who may not be familiar with tree structures, a binary tree is a very common construct and comprises a set of *nodes* where each node has 0, 1, or 2 *child nodes*. In the example binary tree in Fig. 8.35, we show the tree root (which is often omitted), the *root node*, and two small *subtree* instances.

While it can be slightly different among authors and users, this is a reasonably standard notation. Each node has a *key* value, and every left subtree of the node contains only nodes with key values less than that node's value; likewise, every right subtree contains nodes with key values greater than that node's values. Using our figure above, we can see that the root node contains a key value of 8, so every node in its left subtree has to contain key values less than that: value of 1–7.

Stavrovskaia (2006 #895) described the ClusterTree-RS algorithm, developed for clustering regulatory signals using binary trees, and discussed its value in identifying groups of coregulated genes as part of studying transcriptional regulation.

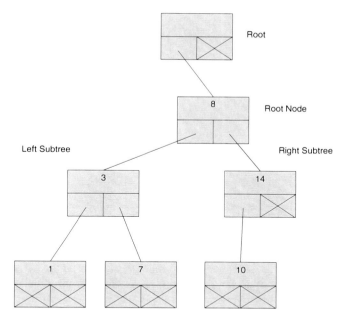

Fig. 8.35   Binary tree

8.11.5   *Petri Nets*

Petri Nets (PNs) were originally conceived as a language to describe distributed systems by Carl Adam Petri (1962 #899), but over the years, the technique has been used in any area that can be described graphically. However, this generality leads to one of its limitations via complexity: PN-based models tend to become too large for effective analysis. This being said, almost every organization using PNs will have their own toolsets to help with this complexity. The figures in this section were generated using PIPE 3.0, originating from Bonet et al. (2007 #897), which is a freely available example.

PNs have been used in a number of biological studies, such as can be seen in Chaouiya (2007 #902), which illustrates how extensions allow different abstraction levels – from qualitative to quantitative – while preserving the underlying graph, which depicts the interactions between biological components.

Chemical processes have been modeled with PNs from the beginning, so we'll use the simple chemical process $2H_2 + O_2 \rightarrow 2H_2O$ and create a PN, as shown in Fig. 8.36.

In Fig. 8.36a, our PN depicts two initial places, labeled *H2* and *O2*, that respectfully denote the H_2 and O_2 molecules from the left-hand side of our chemical equation. The *H2O* place similarly denotes the H_2O molecule.

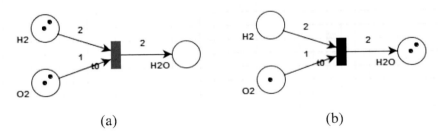

Fig. 8.36 Petri Net for a simple chemical process (**a**) shows the initial marking, (**b**) shows postfiring of the transition

The *H2* and *O2* places each contain two tokens, represented by black dots. The arcs from each of the left-hand places to the transition *t0* are weighted with 2 (from *H2*) and 1 (from *O2*). If we animate this (in PIPE), the step forward animation results in the PN shown in Fig. 8.36b which shows two tokens in the *H2O* state, modeling two molecules of H_2O, and one token remaining in the *O2* state.

Now that we've seen a simple example, we need to provide some formal definitions. There are a few similar notations in use, so your favorite PN reference may use a slightly different version to the one we use in this text; however, the differences are likely to be minimal and so mapping between texts should not be a problem.

PNs are directed, bipartite graphs whose nodes represent *transitions* (events) that are denoted by bars and *places* (conditions) that are denoted by circles. Tokens, represented by dots, move between places as a result of executing actions. We shall see in a few moments that weights can be assigned to arcs. The PN has an initial state, typically denoted M_0, and, in general, a *marking* (or state) assigns to each place a nonnegative integer value k. We say that a *place p is marked with k tokens* and initially place k black dots (tokens) into the circle denoting place p.

So we can now denote the PN graph by the tuple (P, T, F, W, M_0) where

- $P = \{p_1, p_2, ..., p_m\}$, the (finite)set of places
- $T = \{t_1, t_2, ..., t_n\}$, the (finite) set of transitions
- $F \subseteq (P \times T) \cup (T \times P)$, the set of arcs (flow relations)
- $W : F \rightarrow \{1, 2, 3, ...\}$, the weight function
- $M_0 : P \rightarrow \{0, 1, 2, 3, ...\}$

We also note that $P \cap T = \emptyset$ and $P \cup T \neq \emptyset$. Sometimes the PN is denoted by the tuple $N = (P, T, F, W)$, without the initial marking, and if an initial marking is provided, you may see it denoted (N, M_0).

A marking M is an m-vector where m is the total number of places. The pth concept of M, denoted $M(p)$, is the number of tokens in place p.

Places and transitions comprise fundamental entities in PNs, and Murata (1989 #896) provided the following example interpretations for these concepts (Table 8.5).

Table 8.5 Petri Net interpretations of places and transitions (Murata 1989 #896)

Input places	Transition	Output places
Preconditions	Event	Postcondition
Input data	Computational step	Output data
Input signals	Signal processor	Output signals
Resources needed	Task or job	Resources released
Conditions	Clause in logic	Conclusions
Buffers	Processor	Buffers

A change in marking (change in state) occurs as a result of the transition rule (firing rule):

1. A transition t is *enabled* if each input place p of t is marked with at least $w(p,t)$ tokens, where $w(p,t)$ is the weights of the arc from p to t.

   In our simple chemical process above, $H2$ is enabled because it is marked with 2 tokens, and the arc between $H2$ and $t0$ has a weight equal to 2. Similarly, $O2$ is enabled because it is also marked with 2 tokens, and the arc between $O2$ and $t0$ has a weight equal to 1.

2. An enabled transition may or may not fire. (This depends on whether or not the event actually takes place.)

3. A firing of an enabled transition t removes $w(p,t)$ tokens from each input place p of t and adds $w(t,p)$ tokens to each output place p of t, where $w(t,p)$ is the weight of the arc from t to p.

   Using our simple example again, transition $t0$ removes $w(H2,t0) = 2$ tokens from place $H2$ and $w(O2,t0) = 1$ token from place $O2$ and places $w(t0,H2O) = 2$ tokens in place $H2O$. Note that because $w(O2,t0) = 1$, one token remains at place $O2$.

A transition without any input place is called a *source transition* and is unconditionally enabled. A transition without any output place is called a *sink transition*, and the firing of a sink transition consumes tokens but does not produce any tokens.

The transition (firing) rule is a very simple rule that can be used for a wide range of purposes, but this is where a lot of the complexity comes into play. Murata (1989 #896) provided a more detailed overview of Petri Nets, along with a broader discussion of the issues around analysis and applications. Knottenbelt et al. (2009 #898) discussed Generalized Stochastic Petri Nets (GSPNs) in the context of computational performance.

As we've already mentioned, groups using PNs in their research will invariably use some tool to aid their modeling and analysis activities. While we have used PIPE in this text, other tools are available, some of which can be found in Appendix B or at the companion web site. In the example we describe below, *Cell Illustrator*[37] has been used as part of the researcher's toolkit. We wanted to point that out to avoid any confusion.

---

[37] At the time of writing, *Cell Illustrator* can be found at https://www.cellillustrator.com/ and was formerly known as *Genomic Object Net*.

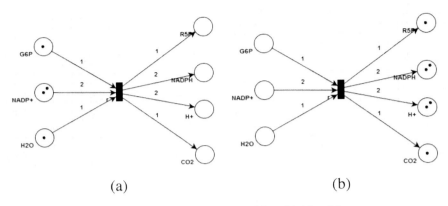

Fig. 8.37 Pentose phosphate pathway PN (**a**) Before firing, (**b**) After firing

PNs have been used in research into many areas, including gene regulatory networks, signal transduction pathways, and metabolic pathways.

Consider the pentose phosphate pathway $G6P + 2NADP^+ + H_2O \rightarrow R5P + 2NADPH + H^+ + CO_2$, where $G6P$ denotes glucose-6-phosphate and $R5P$ denotes ribose-5-phosphate. Figure 8.37a shows the PN before firing of the network, with Fig. 8.37b depicting the state after firing (Figure is from Koch and Heiner (2004 #903)).

Figure 8.38, taken from Voss et al. (2003 #905), illustrates the power of PNs in depicting complex pathways. For the interested reader, Koch and Heiner (2004 #903) provided a more in-depth tutorial on the use of PNs in the modeling and analysis of biochemical pathways.

Further examples and details can be found in many sources, including Heiner et al. (2003 #906) and Doi et al. (2004 #901), the latter illustrated online at Doi (#900). Baldan et al. (2010 #907) provided a review of research in this area.

8.11.6 Boolean and Fuzzy Logic

We've segmented this section into three so that readers familiar with Boolean logic or fuzzy logic can skip over these sections. Of necessity, the overview of the logics will be very cursory, and as usual, we provide references for readers interested in a more detailed understanding of these interesting topics.

8.11.6.1 Boolean Logic

In this section, we're going to provide a *very* short discussion on the underlying theory of logic and where it's used within data mining and specifically within life sciences research. In a sense, logic in its various forms can be seen to be a foundation stone of the majority of methods and algorithms we use.

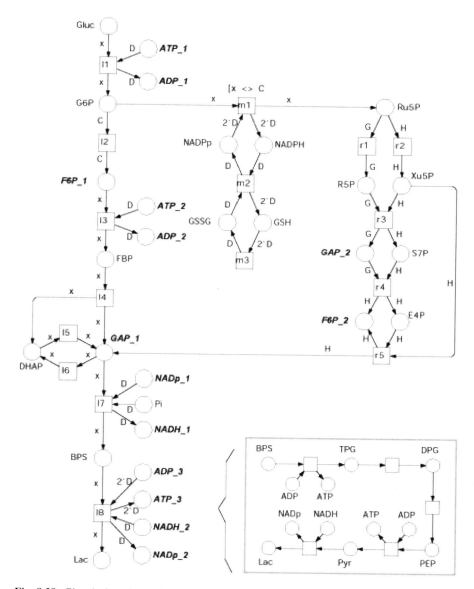

Fig. 8.38 Glycolysis pathway for erythrocytes (Voss et al. 2003 #905)

Boolean logic or Boolean algebra deals with *truth values* of 0 and 1, along with a set of operators *conjunction* ($\wedge$), also denoted as AND; *disjunction*($\vee$), also denoted as OR; and *negation* ($\neg$), also denoted as NOT or the *complement*, and was developed in 1854 by George Boole (1854 #946), and has been applied to a wide range of disciplines including logic, programming, set theory, and statistics.

The basic Boolean operations can be seen in the following *truth tables* (Fig. 8.39).

AND (both must be 1)			OR (either must be 1)			NOT (invert)	
x	y	$x \wedge y$	x	y	$x \vee y$	x	$\neg x$
0	0	0	0	0	0	0	1
0	1	0	0	1	1	1	0
1	0	0	1	0	1		
1	1	1	1	1	1		

Fig. 8.39 Basic Boolean algebra truth tables

Table 8.6 Boolean algebra laws

Associativity of $\vee$	$x \vee (y \vee z) = (x \vee y) \vee z$	Idempotence of $\vee$	$x \vee x = x$
Associativity of $\wedge$	$x \wedge (y \wedge z) = (x \wedge y) \wedge z$	Idempotence of $\wedge$	$x \wedge x = x$
Commutativity of $\vee$	$x \vee y = y \vee x$	Absorption 1	$x \wedge (x \vee y) = x$
Commutativity of $\wedge$	$x \wedge y = y \wedge x$	Absorption 2	$x \vee (x \wedge y) = x$
Distributivity of $\wedge$ over $\vee$	$x \wedge (y \vee z) = (x \wedge y) \vee (y \wedge z)$	Distributivity of $\vee$ over $\wedge$	$x \vee (y \wedge z) = (x \vee y) \wedge (y \vee z)$
Identity for $\vee$	$x \vee 0 = x$		
Identity for $\wedge$	$x \wedge 1 = x$		
Annihilator for $\wedge$	$x \wedge 0 = 0$	Annihilator for $\vee$	$x \vee 1 = x$
Complementation 1	$x \wedge \neg x = 0$	De Morgan's law 1	$(\neg x) \wedge (\neg y) = \neg(x \vee y)$
Complementation 2	$x \vee \neg x = 1$	De Morgan's law 2	$(\neg x) \vee (\neg y) = \neg(x \wedge y)$
Double negation	$\neg\neg x = x$		

Arithmetically, we can define these three relationships as follows:

$$x \wedge y = xy$$

$$x \vee y = x + y - xy$$

$$\neg x = 1 - x$$

Associated with these basic principles are a number of (Boolean) algebraic laws that we list in Table 8.6 but do not intend to prove in this text.

Using these simple rules, surprisingly complex structures can be developed. Probably the most ubiquitous application is in logic circuits that are embedded in the device you are using to read this text, assuming you are not holding a physical book!

We can also build out more connectives from just this simple set. How would we define exclusive-or (XOR) from the above connectives?

In the above descriptions, we've used x and y and assigned them "true" (1) and "false" (0) values. However, this concept is extended to sets in an analogous way. "The Boolean algebra $b(A)$ of a set A is the set of subsets of A that can be obtained by means of a finite number of set operations (AND, OR, NOT)" (Comtet 1974 #954), as described above.

8.11.6.2 Fuzzy Logic

We can think of fuzzy logic as a logic concerning continuous variables. With Boolean logic, we have the black-and-white "true or false" scenario, using discrete variables and can answer questions such as "is that e-mail spam or nonspam," whereas with fuzzy logic, we can consider imprecise or fuzzier (sic) concepts such as high risk (of getting a disease), what constitutes a "long duration," what we mean when we say that something is "increasing rapidly," or even be able to develop systems where we can say:

> if   the adverse_reaction_risk is low
> then our drug_safety must be reasonably high

One of the fundamental concepts of fuzzy logic is the *set*, just as it is in Boolean logic. The major difference between the two, however, is that whereas there is a definite boundary to set membership in Boolean logic, this is obviously not the case with fuzzy logic. In fact, Boolean sets are often described as *crisp sets*, and fuzzy sets are described as...uh...*fuzzy sets*.

In order to aid us in this, we consider a value called the *alpha cut threshold* that truncates *set membership*, or a rule predicate, at a particular (truth) value such that any value below is considered equivalent to zero. Alpha cuts therefore have two forms: a comparison that is simply less than (called the strong form),or a comparison that is less than or equal to (called the weak form).

We used the term set membership above, which leads us to the recognition of a *membership function* being necessary. By the very nature of our defining a fuzzy set, elements of that set have a natural *degree of membership*, which is where the membership function really comes into play, since it defines the relationship between a value in the set's domain (the explicit range of values over which the fuzzy set's membership function is defined, which is generally the same as the *support set*) and its degree of membership:

$$t = f(s, x)$$

where t is a truth membership value (degree of membership)
s is the (fuzzy) set
x is a value from the set's domain

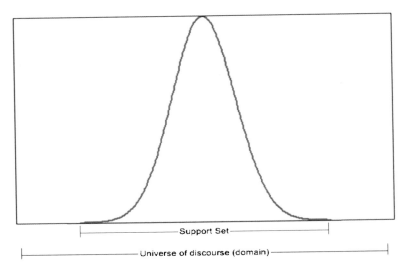

Fig. 8.40 A fuzzy set

The support set we mentioned above is the region of the membership function where the truth values $t > 0$. The complete range of values over which a variable can assume a value is referred to as the *universe of discourse*.

If we visualize a fuzzy set as a circular region, we can think of membership as having a maximal value at the center of the region, reducing as we move toward the edge of the region, with a value of zero (because of the alpha cut threshold) at the boundary.[38] We might draw this visually as a bell curve. The term *expectancy* is used to mean the width of a fuzzy number, usually measured from the center of the fuzzy set. (This does lead to the realization that the larger an expectancy value, the more imprecision that *fuzzy number* encapsulates. This isn't necessarily a bad thing as relaxing this precision may make the system more tolerable to change.) And so now we come to the fuzzy number, which is essentially a representation of a fuzzy set.

We'll introduce a few other terms quickly that are used in the fuzzy logic literature. A *fuzzy quantifier* is used to define a set that is not a number. A concept such as risky, for example, is an example of a fuzzy quantifier. Often associated with this is the concept of a *hedge*, which is akin to an adverb. Very is an example of a hedge. Bringing the hedge and fuzzy quantifier together allows us to consider concepts such as "very risky" when applied to a fuzzy set membership function. Figure 8.40 depicts a fuzzy set, per our discussion so far.

Consider a fuzzy set for some fuzzy quantifier, say "elevated." We would likely define some underlying range of values that matches that range. For example, if we are dealing with total cholesterol levels, we might say that the "elevated" range

---

[38] Before anyone jumps up and down and calls for our heads, we are using this for illustration purposes only and not trying to indicate that this is the only visualization.

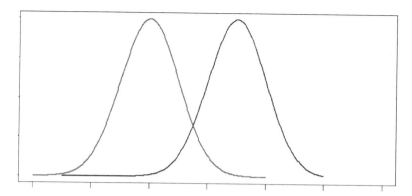

Fig. 8.41 Overlapping fuzzy numbers

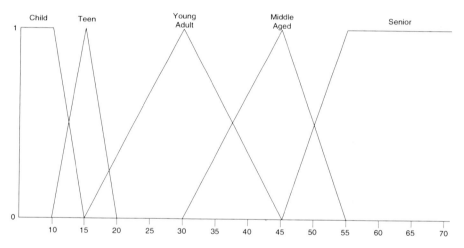

Fig. 8.42 Age

is 190–240. However, we might also define a second quantifier, say "high," that ranges from 230 upward. Here, the fuzzy numbers have an overlap, as might be shown by Fig. 8.41.

We can also see some other aspects of the fuzzy set where if we were to draw a vertical line from the highest point in each set, we can now see the expectation and would also need to consider that alpha cut threshold to determine where membership stops. On the blue set, we have a longer tail that we would definitely need to work with.

Figure 8.42 shows a more familiar fuzzy set, related to age. Here we can see a *term set* associated with various linguistic features that we encounter in real life all the time.

```
Library(e1071)
x<-rbind(matrix(rnorm(150,sd=0.3),ncol=3),
         matrix(rnorm(150,mean=1,sd=0.3),ncol=3),
         matrix(rnorm(150,mean=2,sd=0.3),ncol=3))
cl<-cmeans(x,6,20,verbose=TRUE,method="cmeans")
print(cl)
```

Fig. 8.43 Fuzzy c-means (FCM) clustering

With a basic understanding of the definitions, we can now think about implementing our model, and the whole complement of techniques that we've discussed elsewhere in this text are at our disposal. The only difference is the inherent fuzziness that we now get to play with. Consider one such technique, cluster analysis, where we use methods such as the k-nearest-neighbor method that calculates the distance from some hypothetical central point of a cluster and then assigns an instance to a specific cluster. In the fuzzy case, we do a similar thing, but an instance is allowed to belong to several clusters, with a different degree of membership in each cluster. Thus, clustering in this sense means taking the distance between some point $X_m = (x_{k1}, x_{k2}, ..., x_{km})$ and each of the clusters $C_1, ..., C_k$ as (say) the sum of the differences between the point X_m and the cluster centers:

$$distance_{k \rightarrow C} = \sum_{i=1}^{n} (X(x_i) - C(x_i))^2,$$

where n is the number of attributes in a cluster, $X(x_i)$ is the ith data point in X, and $C(x_i)$ is the ith data point in a cluster's centroid.

The most well-known fuzzy clustering algorithm is the fuzzy c-means algorithm (Bezdek 1981 #955) which is available in many different language implementations. Figure 8.43 is an example that can be executed in R.

Given p specified clusters and k data points, with x_i being the ith data point and $\mu_j(\bullet)$ being a function that returns the membership of x_i in the jth cluster, FCM imposes the following constraint on the fuzzy membership function associated with each point:

$$\sum_{j=1}^{p} \mu_j(x_i) = 1, \quad i = 1, 2, \ldots, k.$$

The total cluster membership (for a point) must add up to 1.

Since the goal of FCM is to assign data points into clusters with varying degrees of membership in each of those clusters, we need to have a mechanism whereby the membership correlates to the representativeness of the point within each cluster. That is, if a point is more representative of the points in cluster C_i than it is of points that exist in cluster C_j, then our membership function should reflect this fact, and so we attempt to minimize a loss function

$$\sum_{k=1}^{p}\sum_{i=1}^{n}[\mu_k(x_i)]^m\|x_i - c_k\|^2$$

where m is some fuzziness parameter, and c_k is the centroid for the kth cluster, and all other parameters are as above. To calculate the centroid for a cluster, we use

$$c_j = \frac{\sum_i [\mu_j(x_i)]^m x_i}{\sum_i [\mu_j(x_i)]^m},$$

and $d_{ji} = \|x_i - c_j\|^2$ denotes the Euclidean distance between the data point and the cluster centroid, which allows us to determine cluster membership using

$$\mu_j(x_i) = \frac{\left(\frac{1}{d_{ji}}\right)^{\frac{1}{m-1}}}{\sum_{k=1}^{p}\left(\frac{1}{d_{ki}}\right)^{\frac{1}{m-1}}}.$$

A highly recommended text for the reader interested in a much broader and deeper exposition than we can provide here is Nguyen and Walker (2006 #952). For readers who would like more details, but at a slightly more user-friendly level, Cox (2005 #953) provides a gentler and valuable introduction as well as a plethora of examples.

8.11.6.3   Application to Data Mining

Anekritmongkol and Kasamsan (2010 #947) described the use of Boolean algebra in overcoming the major drawback of the Apriori algorithm: the amount of time taken to read data in the database for each candidate generated. They use Boolean algebra and the compression technique for association rule mining (B-Compress) to reduce the amount of time necessary to scan the database. In Ruczinski et al. (2003 #948), the application of Boolean logic to regression and analysis of microarray SNP data is described and how, given a set of binary predictors, the truth of new predictors can be determined. More specifically, the authors try to fit regression models of the form $g(E[Y]) = b_0 + b_1L_1 + ... + b_nL_n$, where L_j is any Boolean expression of the predictors, and L_j and b_j are estimated simultaneously using a simulated annealing algorithm.

We already discussed one application of fuzzy logic, to cluster analysis, and refer the interested reader to Hofmann (1999 #65) or Cox (2005 #953) for further details.

8.12   Conclusion

Machine learning continues to be a very active, vibrant area of both theoretical and applied research which, as we can see from just the limited subset of techniques described, can provide valuable approaches to data mining in bioinformatics.

The breadth and depth of techniques and research areas even within this discipline cannot be adequately covered in a single text, let alone a single chapter, and we acknowledge that omitting many of the techniques will be curious to some readers. We haven't explicitly touched on Boolean logic and fuzzy logic – a set of techniques that can be very valuable – although these have been implicitly incorporated into many of the techniques described throughout this text.

On one level, k-means and EM algorithms can be considered to be iterative optimization algorithms in that they (re)assign data points, either hard or soft, and then update some combined model. Kalton 2001 (#234) extended this concept to form a generalized framework linking predictive mining and clustering. Liu (2000 #235) combined supervised learning with decision trees to address challenges of clustering including adding data points to trees, problems with uniform distributions in higher dimensions, and how to avoid making physical additions to the dataset under study.

Application of gradient descent to clustering issues has similarly been a fertile area of research, such as with Marroquin (1993 #236) in the context of vector quantization and in Bottou (1995 #237) who investigated the behavior of convergence of the k-means algorithm.

There is one widely used algorithm from the machine-learning realm that we have not described in this chapter: AdaBoost (Freund and Schapire 1996 #207). AdaBoost, short for *adaptive boosting*, can be used to boost the performance of many other machine-learning algorithms. The adaptive part comes into play in that subsequent classifiers are "tweaked" in order to favor instances that were misclassified by previous classifiers. In a sense, this can be considered a meta-algorithm, and as such we considered it to be beyond the scope of the intent of this text. However, it is a very powerful algorithm, and readers are recommended to read Freund and Schapire (1996 #207) for a description.

For the interested reader, several other texts have been included in the bibliography, such as Kononenko and Kukar (2007 #213), that can serve as solid foundations for furthering your knowledge and expertise of this domain of study and its intersection with data mining.

As has been the case with all of the other chapters of this text, what has been left out far exceeds what has been included. Furthermore, the application of machine-learning techniques into data mining is probably one of the most dynamic areas of all.

References

Alon U (2007a) An introduction to systems biology: design principles of biological circuits, Chapman & Hall/CRC mathematical and computational biology series. Chapman & Hall/CRC, Boca Raton

Alon U (2007b) Network motifs: theory and experimental approaches. Nat Rev Genet 8:450–461

Alon N et al (2008) Biomolecular network motif counting and discovery by color coding. Bioinformatics 24:i241–i249

Alpaydin E (2004) Introduction to machine learning, Adaptive computation and machine learning. MIT Press, Cambridge

Altschul SF et al (1997) Gapped BLAST and PSI-BLAST: a new generation of protein database search programs. Nucleic Acids Res 25:3389–3402

Anekritmongkol S, Kasamsan MLK (2010) Boolean algebra and compression technique for association rule mining. In: Proceedings of the 6th international conference on advanced data mining and applications – Volume Part II. Springer, Chongqing, pp 150–157

Attwood TK et al (1998) The PRINTS protein fingerprint database in its fifth year. Nucleic Acids Res 26:304–308

Babu MM et al (2004) Structure and evolution of transcriptional regulatory networks. Curr Opin Struct Biol 14:283–291

Bairoch A, Bucher P, Hofmann K (1996) The PROSITE database, its status in 1995. Nucleic Acids Res 24:189–196

Baldan P et al (2010) Petri nets for modelling metabolic pathways: a survey. Natural Computing 9:955–989

Baldi P et al (1994) Hidden Markov models of biological primary sequence information. Proc Natl Acad Sci 91:1059–1063

Baskerville K, Paczuski M (2006) Subgraph ensembles and motif discovery using a new heuristic for graph isomorphism. Phys Rev E 74:13

Basu S, Bilenko M et al (2004) A probabilistic framework for semi-supervised clustering. Proceedings of the Tenth ACM SIGKDD International Conference on Knowledge Discovery and Data Mining (KDD-2004). Seattle, WA:59–68

Belkin M, Niyogi P (2003) Using manifold structure for partially labeled classification. Neural Inform Process Syst 15(2002):929

Belkin M, Niyogi P, Sindhwani V (2006) Manifold regularization: a geometric framework for learning from labeled and unlabeled examples. J Mach Learn Res 7:2399–2434

Bennett KP, Demiriz A (1998) Semi-supervised support vector machines. In: Kearns MJ, Solla SA, Cohn DA (eds) Advances in neural information processing systems 11. MIT Press, Denver, pp 368–374

Bezdek JC (1981) Pattern recognition with fuzzy objective function algorithms, Advanced applications in pattern recognition. Plenum Press, New York

Bilmes J (1998) A gentle tutorial of the EM algorithm and its application to parameter estimation for Gaussian mixture and hidden Markov models. International Computer Science Institute, Berkeley

Bishop CM (2006) Pattern recognition and machine learning, Information science and statistics. Springer, New York

Blekas K, Fotiadis DI, Likas A (2005) Motif-based protein sequence classification using neural networks. J Comput Biol 12:64–82

Blum A, Chawla S (2001) Learning from labeled and unlabeled data using graph mincuts. In: Proceedings of the eighteenth international conference on machine learning. Morgan Kaufmann, San Francisco, pp 19–26

Blum A, Mitchell T (1998) Combining labeled and unlabeled data with co-training. In: Proceedings of the eleventh annual conference on computational learning theory. ACM, Madison, pp 92–100

Bonet P et al (2007) PIPE v2.5: a Petri net tool for performance modelling. In: 23rd Latin American Conference on Informatics (CLEI'07), San Jose, Costa Rica

Boole G (1854) An investigation of the laws of thought. Prometheus Books, New York

Bottou L, Bengio Y (1995) Convergence properties of the KMeans algorithm. Advances in Neural Information Processing Systems. Denver, MIT Press. 7

Boykov Y, Veksler O et al (1998) Markov random fields with efficient approximations. Computer vision and pattern recognition, 1998. Proceedings. 1998 IEEE Computer Society Conference on

Castelli V, Cover TM (1996) The relative value of labeled and unlabeled samples in pattern recognition with an unknown mixing parameter. IEEE Trans Inform Theory 42:2102–2117

Chaouiya C (2007) Petri net modelling of biological networks. Brief Bioinform 8:210–219

Committee on Applications of Toxicogenomic Technologies to Predictive Toxicology and Risk Assessment, NRC (2007) Applications of toxicogenomic technologies to predictive toxicology and risk assessment. The National Academies Press, Washington, DC

Comtet L (1974) Advanced combinatorics: the art of finite and infinite expansions. Springer, Dordrecht

Conant GC, Wagner A (2003) Convergent evolution of gene circuits. Nat Genet 34:264–266

Cox E (2005) Fuzzy modeling and genetic algorithms for data mining and exploration, The Morgan Kaufmann series in data management systems. Elsevier/Morgan Kaufmann, Amsterdam/Boston

Craven M, DiPasquo D et al (2000) Learning to construct knowledge bases from the World Wide Web. Artif. Intell. 118(1–2):69–113

Cybenko G (1989) Approximation by superpositions of a sigmoidal function. Math Cont Sig Syst (MCSS) 2:303–314

D'haeseleer P, Liang S, Somogyi R (1999) Gene expression data analysis and modeling (Tutorial). In: Pacific symposium on biocomputing, 1999 (PSB99), Hawaii, US

Dempster AP, Laird NM, Rubin DB (1977) Maximum likelihood from incomplete data via the EM algorithm. J Roy Stat Soc Ser B 39:1–38

Ding C (2004) Tutorial on spectral clustering. International conference on machine learning, Alberta

Doi A (2011) Glycolytic pathway and lac operon of E. coli, from http://www.csml.org/models/csml-models/glycolytic-pathway-and-lac-operon-of-e-coli/. Accessed 7/17/2011

Doi A et al (2004) Constructing biological pathway models with hybrid functional Petri nets. In Silico Biol 4:271–291

Dong Q-w, Wang X-l, Lin L (2006) Application of latent semantic analysis to protein remote homology detection. Bioinformatics 22:285–290

Durbin R (1998) Biological sequence analysis: probabalistic models of proteins and nucleic acids. Cambridge, UK New York, Cambridge University Press

Eddy SR (1995) Multiple alignment using hidden Markov models. In: Intelligent systems in molecular biology. AAAI Press, Menlo Park, pp 114–120

Enderle JE (2007) Machine learning in the life sciences. IEEE Eng Med Biol 26:86–93

Filippone M et al (2008) A survey of kernel and spectral methods for clustering. Pattern Recogn 41:176–190

Freund Y, Schapire RE (1996) Experiments with a new boosting algorithm. In: Machine learning: proceedings of the thirteenth international conference. Morgan Kaufmann, San Francisco

Fukuda K et al (1998) Toward information extraction: identifying protein names from biological papers. Pac Symp Biocomput 98:707–718

Funahashi K (1989) On the approximate realization of continuous mappings by neural networks. Neural Netw 2:183–192

Gentleman RC et al (2004) Bioconductor: open software development for computational biology and bioinformatics. Genome Biol 5:R80

Greig DM, Porteous BT et al (1989) Exact maximum a posteriori estimation for binary images. J Roy Stat Soc Ser B Methodological 51(2):271–279

Gribskov M, Robinson NL (1996) The use of receiver operating characteristic (ROC) analysis to evaluate sequence matching. Comput Chem 20:25–33

Gribskov M, McLachlan AD, Eisenberg D (1987) Profile analysis: detection of distantly related proteins. Proc Natl Acad Sci 84:4355–4358

Grochow JA, Kellis M (2007) Network motif discovery using subgraph enumeration and symmetry-breaking. In: Proceedings of the 11th annual international conference on research in computational molecular biology. Springer, Oakland, pp 92–106

Gupta MR, Chen Y (2010) Theory and use of the EM algorithm. Found Trend Sig Process 4:223–296

Hahn U, Romacker M et al (2002) Creating knowledge repositories from biomedical reports: the MEDSYNDIKATE text mining system. Pac Symp Biocomput: 338–349

Hartman E, Keeler JD, Kowalski JM (1990) Layered neural networks with Gaussian hidden units as universal approximations. Neural Comput 2:210–215

Haussler D, Diekhans M, Jaakkola T (1998) A discriminative framework for detecting remote protein homologies. J Comput Biol 5:211–221

Hawkins J (2007) Why can't a computer be more like a brain? IEEE Spectr 44:21–26

Heiner M et al (2003) Model validation of biological pathways using Petri nets – demonstrated for apoptosis. In: Proceedings of the first international workshop on computational methods in systems biology. Springer, London, p 173

Hirschman L, Morgan AA et al (2002) Rutabaga by any other name: extracting biological names. J Biomed Informat 35(4):247–259

Hofmann T (1999) Probabilistic latent semantic analysis. In: Laskey K, Prade H (eds) Fifteenth conference annual conference on uncertainty in artificial intelligence (UAI-99). Morgan Kaufmann, Stockholm, pp 289–296

Hornik K, Stinchcombe M, White H (1989) Multilayer feedforward networks are universal approximators. Neural Netw 2:359–366

Ihmels J et al (2005) Comparative gene expression analysis by a differential clustering approach: application to the *Candida albicans* transcription program. PLoS Genet 1:e39

Jianbo S, Malik J (2000) Normalized cuts and image segmentation. IEEE Trans Pattern Anal Mach Intell 22:888–905

Jiang D, Tang C, Zhang A (2004) Cluster analysis for gene expression data: a survey. IEEE Trans Knowl Data Eng 16:1370–1386

Jing Z et al (2008) Parallelization of spectral clustering algorithm on multi-core processors and GPGPU. In: Computer systems architecture conference, 2008. ACSAC 2008. 13th Asia-Pacific, Busan, pp 1–8

Kalton A, Langley P et al (2001) Generalized clustering, supervised learning, and data assignment. Proceedings of the seventh ACM SIGKDD international conference on Knowledge discovery and data mining. San Francisco, California, ACM:299–304

Kashani Z et al (2009) Kavosh: a new algorithm for finding network motifs. BMC Bioinforma 10:318

Kashtan N et al (2004) Topological generalizations of network motifs. Phys Rev E 70:031909

Kittleson MM et al (2005) Gene expression analysis of ischemic and nonischemic cardiomyopathy: shared and distinct genes in the development of heart failure. Physiol Genomics 21:299–307

Kleinberg J, Tardos E (2002) Approximation algorithms for classification problems with pairwise relationships: metric labeling and Markov random fields. J ACM 49(5):616–639

Knottenbelt WJ, Dingle NJ, Suto T (2009) Performance trees: a query specification formalism for quantitative performance analysis. In: Parallel, distributed and grid computing for engineering. Saxe-Coburg Publications, Kippen, pp 165–198

Koch I, Heiner M (2004) Qualitative modelling and analysis of biochemical pathways with Petri Nets (Tutorial Notes). In: 5th international conference on systems biology – ICSB 2004, Heidelberg, Germany

Kononenko I, Kukar M (2007) Machine learning and data mining: introduction to principles and algorithms. Horwood Publishing Limited, Chichester

Krogel MA, Scheffer T (2004) Multi-relational learning, text mining, and semi-supervised learning for functional genomics. Mach Learn 57:61–81

Krogel M-A, Wrobel S (2001) Transformation-based learning using multirelational aggregation. In: Rouveirol C, Sebag M (eds) Inductive logic programming. Springer, Berlin/Heidelberg, pp 142–155

Krogel MA et al (2003) Comparative evaluation of approaches to propositionalization. In: Inductive logic programming: 13th international conference, ILP'2003. Springer, Szeged, pp 197–214

Krogh A et al (1982) Hidden Markov models in computational biology. Computer Research Laboratory, Santa Cruz

Leek TR (1997) Information extraction using hidden Markov models

Leslie CS, Eskin E, Noble WS (2002) The spectrum kernel: a string kernel for SVM protein classification. In: Pacific symposium on biocomputing, CSH Press, pp 566–575

Leslie CS et al (2004) Mismatch string kernels for discriminative protein classification. Bioinformatics 20:467–476

Lewis DP, Jebara T, Noble WS (2006) Support vector machine learning from heterogeneous data: an empirical analysis using protein sequence and structure. Bioinformatics 22:2753–2760

Liao L, Noble WS (2002) Combining pairwise sequence similarity and support vector machines for remote protein homology detection. In: Proceedings of the sixth annual international conference on computational biology. ACM, Washington, DC, pp 225–232

Ling Z (1996) An effective approach for solving subgraph isomorphism problem. IASTED International Conference

Liu Y, Yao X et al (2000) Evolutionary ensembles with negative correlation learning. IEEE Transactions on Evolutionary Computation 4:380–387

Maeda YT, Sano M (2006) Regulatory dynamics of synthetic gene networks with positive feedback. J Mol Biol 359:1107–1124

Mangan S, Alon U (2003) Structure and function of the feed-forward loop network motif. Proc Natl Acad Sci 100:11980–11985

Markowetz F (2004) Classification by support vector machines. practical DNA microarray analysis (Bioconductor course). Online (Max Planck Institute)

Marroquin JL (1993) Deterministic interactive particle models for image processing and computer graphics. Graphical Models and Image Processing 55(5):408–417

Mehta JP (2010) Gene expression analysis in breast cancer. Dublin City University, Dublin

Meila M, Shi J (2001) A random walks view of spectral segmentation. AISTATS 2001:8–11

Middendorf M, Ziv E, Wiggins CH (2005) Inferring network mechanisms: the Drosophila melanogaster protein interaction network. Proc Natl Acad Sci USA 102:3192–3197

Milo R et al (2002) Network motifs: simple building blocks of complex networks. Science 298:824–827

Milo R et al (2004) Superfamilies of evolved and designed networks. Science 303:1538–1542

Minsky ML, Papert S (1969a) Perceptrons: an introduction to computational geometry. MIT Press, Cambridge/London

Minsky ML, Papert S (1969b) Perceptrons: an introduction to computational geometry. MIT Press, Cambridge/London

Mitchell TM (1997) Machine learning. McGraw-Hill, New York

Morik K et al (2000) Knowledge discovery and knowledge validation in intensive care. Artif Intell Med 19:225–249

Murata T (1989) Petri nets: properties, analysis and applications. Proc IEEE 77:541–580

Nepusz T, Sasidharan R, Paccanaro A (2010) SCPS: a fast implementation of a spectral method for detecting protein families on a genome-wide scale. BMC Bioinforma 11:120

Ng AY, Jordan MI, Weiss Y (2001) On spectral clustering: analysis and an algorithm. In: *Neural Information Processing Systems*. MIT Press, Cambridge, pp 849–856

Ng S-K, McLachlan GJ, Lee AH (2006) An incremental EM-based learning approach for on-line prediction of hospital resource utilization. Artif Intell Med 36:257–267

Nguyen HT, Walker E (2006) A first course in fuzzy logic. Chapman & Hall/CRC, Boca Raton

Nigam K et al (1998) Learning to classify text from labeled and unlabeled documents. In: Proceedings of the fifteenth national/tenth conference on artificial intelligence/innovative applications of artificial intelligence. American Association for Artificial Intelligence, Madison, pp 792–799

Omidi S, Schreiber F, Masoudi-Nejad A (2009) MODA: an efficient algorithm for network motif discovery in biological networks. Genes Genet Syst 84:385–395

Paccanaro A, Casbon JA, Saqi MAS (2006) Spectral clustering of protein sequences. Nucleic Acids Res 34:1571–1580

Patrikainen A, Meilă M (2005) Spectral clustering for Microsoft Netscan Data, Washington (state), USA, p 74

Pentney W, Meila M (2005) Spectral clustering of biological sequence data. National conference on artificial intelligence, Pittsburgh, pp 845–850

Petri CA (1962) Kommunikation mit Automaten. In: Institut für Instrumentelle Mathematik. Institut für Instrumentelle Mathematik, Bonn

Rabiner LR (1989) A tutorial on hidden Markov models and selected applications in speech recognition. Proc IEEE 77:257–286

Ratsaby J, Venkatesh SS (1995) Learning from a mixture of labeled and unlabeled examples with parametric side information. In: Proceedings of the eighth annual conference on computational learning theory. ACM, Santa Cruz, pp 412–417

Reich M et al (2006) GenePattern 2.0. Nat Genet 38:500–501

Reutemann P, Pfahringer B, Frank E (2004) A toolbox for learning from relational data with propositional and multi-instance learners. In: 17th Australian joint conference on artificial intelligence (AI2004). Springer, Berlin

Ribeiro P, Silva F, Kaiser M (2009) Strategies for network motifs discovery. In: Proceedings of the 2009 fifth IEEE international conference on e-science. IEEE Computer Society, Oxford, pp 80–87

Ripley BD (1996) Pattern recognition and neural networks. Cambridge University Press, Cambridge/New York

Rosenblatt F (1962) Principles of neurodynamics; perceptrons and the theory of brain mechanisms. Spartan, Washington, DC

Rosenfeld N, Elowitz MB, Alon U (2002) Negative autoregulation speeds the response times of transcription networks. J Mol Biol 323:785–793

Roweis ST, Saul LK (2000) Nonlinear dimensionality reduction by locally linear embedding. Science 290:2323–2326

Roy S, Cox IJ (1998) A maximum-flow formulation of the N-camera stereo correspondence problem. ICCV:492–502

Ruczinski I, Kooperberg C, LeBlanc M (2003) Logic regression. J Comput Graph Stat 12:475–511

Rumelhart DE, McClelland JL, University of California San Diego, PDP Research Group (1986a) Parallel distributed processing: explorations in the microstructure of cognition, Computational models of cognition and perception. MIT Press, Cambridge

Rumelhart DE, McClelland JL, University of California San Diego, PDP Research Group (1986b) Parallel distributed processing: explorations in the microstructure of cognition, Computational models of cognition and perception. MIT Press, Cambridge

Saigo H et al (2002) Comparison of SVM-based methods for remote homology detection. Genome Inform 13:396–397

Sandve G, Drablos F (2006) A survey of motif discovery methods in an integrated framework. Biol Direct 1:11

Schneider G, Rohlk S, Wrede P (1993) Analysis of cleavage-site patterns in protein precursor sequences with a perceptron-type neural network. Biochem Biophys Res Commun 194:951–959

Schölkopf B, Smola AJ (2002) Learning with kernels: support vector machines, regularization, optimization, and beyond, Adaptive computation and machine learning. MIT Press, Cambridge

Schuurmans D (1997) A new metric-based approach to model selection. In: Fourteenth national conference on artificial intelligence (AAAI-97). MIT Press (for AAAI Press), Providence, pp 552–558

Sewell M (2008) Structural risk minimization. University College London, London, p 3

Shawe-Taylor J, Cristianini N (2004) Kernel methods for pattern analysis. Cambridge University Press, Cambridge/New York

Slonim DK, Yanai I (2009) Getting started in gene expression microarray analysis. PLoS Comput Biol 5:e1000543

Snow D (2000) Exact voxel occupancy with graph cuts

Stormo GD et al (1982) Use of the 'Perceptron' algorithm to distinguish translational initiation sites in E. coli. Nucleic Acids Res 10:2997–3011

Sutton RS, Barto AG (1998) Reinforcement learning: an introduction, Adaptive computation and machine learning. MIT Press, Cambridge

Vapnik VN (2000) The nature of statistical learning theory, Statistics for engineering and information science. Springer, New York

Vapnik VN, Chervonenkis AY (1974) Theory of pattern recognition (In Russian)

Vishwanathan SVN, Smola AJ (2003) Fast kernels for string and tree matching. In: Advances in neural information processing systems 15. MIT Press, Cambridge, pp 569–576

von Luxburg U (2006) A tutorial on spectral clustering. Online (Max Planck Institute)

Voss K, Heiner M, Koch I (2003) Steady state analysis of metabolic pathways using Petri nets. In Silico Biol 3(31):367–387

Walker MG (2001) Drug target discovery by gene expression analysis cell cycle genes. Curr Cancer Drug Targ 1:73–83

Wang JTL et al (2000) Application of neural networks to biological data mining: a case study in protein sequence classification. In: Proceedings of the sixth ACM SIGKDD international conference on knowledge discovery and data mining. ACM, Boston, pp 305–309

Waterman MS, Joyce J, Eggert M (1991) Computer alignment of sequences. In: Phylogenetic analysis of DNA sequences. Oxford University Press, New York, pp 59–72

Weston J, Kuang R et al (2006) Protein ranking by semi-supervised network propagation. BMC Bioinformatics 7(Suppl 1):S10

Witten IH, Frank E (2005) Data mining: practical machine learning tools and techniques. Morgan Kaufmann, Amsterdam/Boston

Wong L (2006) Knowledge discovery techniques for bioinformatics, Part IV: Gene expression analysis. National University of Singapore, Singapore

Wong EA, Baur B (2010) On network tools for network motif finding: a survey study. Online

Yona G, Linial N, Linial M (1999) ProtoMap: automatic classification of protein sequences, a hierarchy of protein families, and local maps of the protein space. Protein Struct Funct Bioinform 37:360–378

Zaki NM, Deris S, Illias RM (2003) A comparative analysis of protein homology detection methods. J Theor 5:7

Zhang T, Oles FJ (2000) The value of unlabeled data for classification problems. In: Seventeenth international conference on machine learning. Morgan Kaufmann, San Francisco, pp 1191–1198

Zhu X (2005) Semi-supervised learning literature survey. University of Wisconsin, Madison

Zhu X, Goldberg AB (2009) Introduction to semi-supervised learning. Synth Lect Artif Intell Mach Learn 3:1–130

Zimmermann P, Hennig L, Gruissem W (2005) Gene-expression analysis and network discovery using Genevestigator. Trends Plant Sci 10:407–409

Chapter 9
Classification and Prediction

Abstract Assigning our input instances to one of some number of distinct classes is one of the fundamental data-mining activities, allowing us a plethora of techniques to address the question "how similar are X and Y?" Once we have a sense of what characterizes such differences (or similarities), it is natural to then ask how we can predict what will come next. There are some specific data preparation challenges that we need to consider and once we have these in mind, we can focus on some of the common methods that are used by researchers. Linear regression is by far the most common method used for prediction, but decision trees and a very simple algorithm, 1R, provide valuable insight into our datasets without a huge amount of work being necessary. As we increase the sophistication of our models, the concept of the nearest neighbor becomes more important, and, following that, we discuss some aspects of Bayesian modeling and neural networks. The AutoClass algorithm has proven itself many times, and this is included as a practical method that is readily available in several implementation technologies, allowing it to be used somewhat out-of-the-box. Feature representation using alphabet sets is an obvious application area and we discuss that next before considering the k-means method and a discussion on some of the different distance measures we can use in our classification and prediction efforts. Finally, we hone in on the question of accuracy: how we measure it, what it means, and how to improve it. We include the widely used receiver operating characteristic (ROC) technique at this point also. Accuracy is directly coupled with our ability to accurately (sic) separate instances in different classes from each other.

9.1 Introduction

Classification and prediction are some of the most common approaches used to mine data. This is not surprising since our primary goal is to understand the data, and one of the best ways to do this is to understand how similar to each other two sets of data are. In each of these cases, we are interested in making intelligent

R. Sullivan, *Introduction to Data Mining for the Life Sciences*,
DOI 10.1007/978-1-59745-290-8_9, © Springer Science+Business Media, LLC 2012

decisions and where classification is used to predict categorical data; prediction predicts (sic) continuous data. Clustering, another fundamental objective, while very similar, has one important difference: we do not have to know what the categories are when clustering – the data itself is allowed to tell us – whereas with classification, we need to label the categories a priori. We shall see how this important difference allows us significant latitude but also important constraints as we mine our data. From this we can not only build models which describe important categories within the current dataset but also be able to predict how the data will trend under the influence of new data being encountered.

In this chapter, we focus on the efforts involved in classification/prediction[1] and consider clustering elsewhere. We will use many of the techniques we have previously discussed to support the investigation of our data, and we will see that research in a wide range of disciplines has created techniques which can be applied to this (fundamental) problem: we can apply machine-learning techniques, statistical techniques, Bayesian techniques, neural networks, and support vector machines, to name a few.

Consider an example: We may be interested in analyzing leukemia data in order to predict which particular therapy out of a set of optional therapies is best for a particular patient. This is an obvious case for classification. In order to accomplish this classification activity, we would develop a classifier model with the goal of predicting the "correct" outcome. In this particular example, the outcome will be a categorical label of some kind, such as "therapy 1," "therapy 2," or "therapy 3." This type of classifier model, which predicts categorical labels, has no implied ordering between the outputs. That is, there is no meaning to saying that "therapy 1" $\leq$ "therapy 2." If we want such a model, we instead develop a predictor model, which will allow us to predict ordered value ranges since the model predicts continuous-valued functions instead of discrete categorical labels.[2, 3] An important question we glossed over in the above example, however, is what constitutes our definition of "correct"? The nature of this question will obviously have a significant impact on our model.

A wide variety of techniques can be used to support classification and prediction efforts, and many of the same techniques that can be used elsewhere are valuable tools in our arsenal here. As we have mentioned above, techniques from machine learning

---

[1] We will use "classification/prediction" as a generic term to allow us to talk about concepts and techniques applicable to both categorical and continuous data. Where items are specific to one data type or the other, we will use the specific term.

[2] Using our example, we may further postprocess the output to give us ranges of values that are groups so that 0–0.5 may be considered "unsafe," 0.51–0.75 may be "safe," and ≥ 0.75 may be "preferred," but this categorization is simply for convenience rather than the output of a model itself and is certainly subjective.

[3] In much of the literature, prediction of the form described is often synonymously labeled as regression analysis, due to this technique being the most common approach taken to numeric prediction. However, many different techniques can be used for prediction, and, in common with Han (2006 #14), we do not use these terms synonymously.

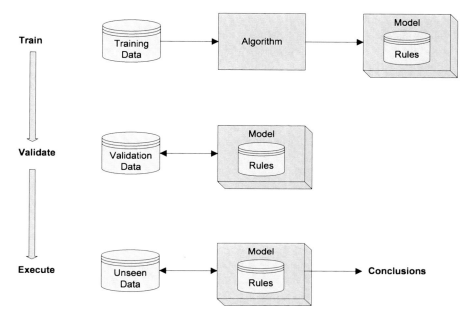

Fig. 9.1 Train, validate, and execute

have had particular success in this area, as have models from traditional statistics and pattern recognition, to name a few. Initially, many of these techniques required that the implementation of the model(s) be resident in memory, requiring that the dataset be relatively small. However, this constraint has become less and less an issue as refinements and new research have produced much more scalable algorithms and techniques which now allow us to process "unlimited" amounts of data.

Classification and prediction techniques we will discuss involve leveraging techniques such as decision trees, support vector machines, neural networks, Bayesian classifiers and nets, as well as rule-based approaches, k-nearest neighbor, case-based reasoning, genetic algorithms, fuzzy modeling, neural networks, and regression-based methods. Regression analysis, in particular, is probably the most widely used technique for predicting numeric values, although we shall also consider some alternates that have value in specific areas.

Some of these important disciplines have been separated into their own chapters to provide a more in-depth view of these valuable techniques, and we refer the reader to those areas at the appropriate places in this chapter. We apply these techniques in a generalized setting to provide a broad foundation, and apply them later to microarray data analysis, an area seeing much interest in recent years.

For many of the approaches we discuss in this chapter, the abstract process, depicted in Fig. 9.1, can be used as a guide, a figure we introduced in the previous chapter. We begin with some level of training of the algorithm we are interested in. This training data will typically comprise a set of instances that are numerous enough, and complete enough, to prevent overfitting of the model that we then generate. Once we have a model (algorithm and rules/parameters) that provides sufficient accuracy for our purposes, we typically then use a separate set of instances to validate that the model's ability to generalize has not been compromised. If our model passes the validation, we can then feel comfortable in using it for our mining purposes.

Although not made explicit in the above figure, there is an implicit feedback loop between the various phases so that knowledge gained during the training and validation stages can be incorporated into the model to provide higher-value conclusions generated.[4]

Consider a case where we have access to a large database of patient information (including specimen data) from many different clinical oncology programs. We may be particularly interested in a class of drugs called tyrosine kinase inhibitors (TKIs) and be interested in which of (say) Iressa, Tarceva, Tykerb, or Herceptin may be the best therapy for a patient. We have already identified this type of classification problem above. We know that this type of compound inhibits the epidermal growth factor receptor (EGFR) kinase and that they have been used to treat cancers that have activating mutations in the EFGR gene. A significant percentage of cancers treated using EFGR inhibitors develop resistance to the treatments (Engelman et al. 2007 #131). We would like to determine whether or not a secondary mutation in EFGR exists for each patient, which accounts for a significant portion of the resistance in published research. Does this allow us to classify as yet unknown patients according to which therapy may be the most appropriate?

Alternately, we may be interested not in which therapy would be considered the "best," but, given a particular therapy, what dose would be optimal? In this case, rather than a classification application, we would undertake a regression analysis since the conclusion we wish to reach is a numeric value as opposed to a categorical value.

With this context, we'll discuss some techniques and concepts specific to the classification and prediction objective, but we'll also see that many of the topics we've already discussed are relevant to this subject also. For this reason, as we've indicated before, we won't duplicate the discussion, if we can avoid it, but simply refer to the relevant points at which the topic is described elsewhere in this text.

An important subtype of this problem is the *unsupervised* case that is often referred to as *clustering* or *unsupervised learning*. This is where we leave the system to determine what the "natural" classes may be within the data. We put quotes around natural because as we've discussed elsewhere, we have to be careful since the classes within the data may not be valuable for our domain of study. However, one of the interesting aspects of this is that these classifications reflect

---

[4] The training and validation stages are often considered one and the same. We have explicitly separated them in our discussion since there are important features of each stage that we wish to highlight.

some of the underlying causal relationships that make instances look like each other. The challenge is to discern those relationships that might be simple biases within the data from those that might represent a new insight or discovery in the domain under study. In any automated approach, the classification scheme that results may be known to subject matter experts in the field or may not be known (Cheeseman and Stutz 1996 #336). As also mentioned in this reference,

> Such discovery of previously unknown structure occurs most frequently when there are many relevant attributes describing each case, because humans are poor at seeing structure in a large number of dimensions. (Cheeseman and Stutz 1996 #336)

This reality is both a value and a challenge for any data-mining effort, and while automated approaches may offer valuable insight, they are not a panacea. Further, it is rarely a single iteration through the data, nor is it completely automated. Interactions with subject matter experts will be an important part of the data-mining process. Since classification is used in two contexts – assigning an instance to one of a number of existing classes or as the identification of classes as defined by the data – both cases at least need an evaluation step to ensure validity. Classifications found through an unsupervised learning approach may then be used in the former sense as the set of existing classes for classifying new instances. This tie-in between the two general forms of classification provide a powerful set of tools for analyzing data – especially in the life sciences where, as we've already mentioned, many high-throughput techniques generate large volumes of data that we want to investigate.

In this chapter, we will explore several techniques that allow us to classify and predict outcomes from the input instances available to us. Throughout this discussion, the notion of a *distance* between instances will keep occurring, a central theme that we use to allow us to determine whether two instances should be classified together or separately. The concept of distance has a multitude of implementations, although the Euclidean definition of instance is probably the most common form used. While we touch upon some of the different forms that can be used, most of our examples will use Euclidean distance. The choice of distance, however, shouldn't be left to chance: the nature of your data, as well as the analysis objectives, will be a major determiner of the most appropriate choice, be it Euclidean, Manhattan, Hamming, maximum norm, or any of the other distance measures that researchers have devised over the years. If you find that the measure you have selected doesn't seem to work, search for "distance measure" or "similarity measure" to get an idea of what other researchers have used for problems similar to the one you are investigating.

9.2   Data Preparation

In Chap. 5, we discussed techniques which can be used to ensure that the dataset we are processing is as valid as possible. For example, what value(s) to use for missing data. We refer the reader back to that chapter and emphasize its importance by highlighting one technique here that can have a significant impact on the classification and clustering effort: relevance analysis.

We can use the technique of correlation analysis along with feature subset selection to identify attributes that will not materially contribute to classification or prediction. Further, such attributes may have a negative impact on the classification/clustering effort by leading the model to false conclusions. At the very least, processing unnecessary attributes will have a performance impact on the model, and if the dataset is very large, this can be significant.

Han (2006 #14) identified five criteria against which we can measure the effectiveness of a classification or prediction approach:

- The *accuracy* of the model. How well does our model do against data not yet seen? Further, how well do we *need* it to do? It may well be that our requirements or expectations are too high and our model just cannot be used.
- The *speed* with which the model generates the output. We focus here on the speed in use rather than the speed of developing the model itself. It is true that the process of generating the model may make it unusable, but this would manifest itself early enough during the development effort that we can make an informed decision as to whether to continue with this model or to consider an alternative. During use, the issue may be compounded. For example, if a classifier takes 2 s to perform the classification, we can only process 43,200 in any given day. Is this throughput sufficient?
- How *robust* is our model in the face of noisy or missing data? During the training stage, we would typically have provided all the attributes necessary for the model to classify/predict the output, as appropriate. Did we consider which attributes are absolutely necessary during validation? Did we incorporate instances where certain attributes were missing to see how it performed? Did we deliberately introduce noise into the validation set to measure its accuracy? Did it even run?
- As the volume of data increases, how *scalable* is the model? Does it have a linear performance profile or is it exponential? As more and more data is provided from our mining dataset, does the performance characteristic become the limiting factor?
- Can we improve our understanding of the data through the model? Does it allow us to *interpret* the model and its conclusions so that we can leverage them in other areas? For example, can we elicit understanding from a model developed in one technology (e.g., neural networks) and implement it in another technology (e.g., decision rules)?

9.3 Linear Regression

Since regression is by far the most common technique used for numeric prediction, it's fitting that we begin with this technique. Statistically speaking, regression refers to examining the relationship between two sets of variables, where one set depends on the other. For example, our sets may simply consist of one variable each, and we may have a relationship where one variable, denoted as x, is related to another variable, denoted as y. As an example, we may be interested in modeling a person's weight based on their height, or vice versa, where one is known. This one-to-one correspondence is the most simplistic instance. In real-life situations, the relationship typically involves more than one variable. For example, we might model the BMI using weight and height:

$$BMI = \alpha\, weight + \beta\, height.$$

More generally, if we are given a dataset $\left\{y_i, x_{1i}, x_{2i}, ..., x_{pi}\right\}_{i=1}^{n}$, we denote the relationship as

$$y_i = \beta_1 x_{1i} + \beta_2 x_{2i} + ... + \beta_p x_{pi} + \varepsilon_i.$$

Here, we've added a term – ε – that is often referred to as the error, noise, or even "disturbance term" and provides a vehicle for introducing some noise into the relationship. If we consider our dataset as $\{bmi_i,\ weight_i,\ height_i\}_{i=1}^{n}$, and exclude the ε from our model, we are effectively saying that there is nothing else that can or does affect the dependent term (the BMI) other than the independent terms (the weight and the height). While this may be so in very specific cases, we cannot rule out other factors in the more general case.[5] Given this, our simple example model would be defined as

$$bmi_i = \beta_1\, weight_i + \beta_2\, height + \varepsilon_i.$$

Using standard notation, a linear regression model is given by

$$y_i = \alpha + \beta x_i + \varepsilon_i.$$

In general, the ε_i are assumed to be independent and $N(0, \sigma^2)$. If we exclude the ε_i from our model equation, we also see that it describes the y_i as lying on a straight line, with the gradient given by β and the y-intercept being given by α. We can estimate α, β, and σ^2 using the method of least squares that we discuss elsewhere in this text.

Before we go any further, we should take a few moments to consider α and β just a little more. We will generate estimates for these values, $\hat{\alpha}$ and $\hat{\beta}$, from our data. Taking several samples will naturally generate different values for $\hat{\alpha}$ and $\hat{\beta}$ which will deviate from α and β. We've seen this issue before, where the mean and

---

[5] For completeness, we'll remind the reader of some terms. y terms are often called *regressands*, *dependent variables*, *endogenous variables*, *response variables*, or *measured variables*. The x_i are called *regressors*, *exogenous variables*, *explanatory variables*, *covariates*, *input variables*, *predictor variables*, or *independent variables*.

Fig. 9.2 Classes of data with
overlapping (outlier) points

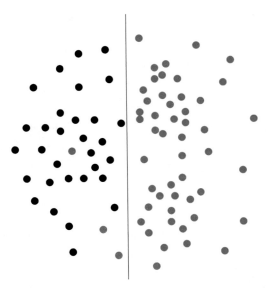

standard deviation estimated by any one sample will differ, if only slightly, from
that estimated by any other sample.

Using a slightly different notation and considering a different aspect of linear
regression, we are interested in computing weights w_i for the hyperplane which
corresponds to an equation of the form

$$w_0 + w_1 x + \dots + w_i y \geq 0 \tag{9.1}$$

that will be parameterized to best separate the classes. In the two-dimensional case,
that is, where we want to separate two classes, this corresponds to an equation of
the form

$$w_0 + w_1 x + w_2 y = 0. \tag{9.2}$$

However, this is not typically flexible enough for real-world problems, as can be
seen from Fig. 9.2.

But before dismissing linear regression as too simplistic, we need to ask a few
questions about our dataset. For example, in the above dataset we can see that while
there are going to be a few false negatives for the data classified as "red," the linear
model would correctly classify data in the "black" category: how representative is
the training set we used for the model? If it's *very* representative, the complexity
and effort involved in using more complex models may not be worth the investment. Further, we need to ask "how 'accurate' are we trying to be?" This question is
fundamental to any data-mining effort.

Linear regression is so widely used that most environments have some form of
model already available into which you can plug your data to obtain estimates for

Fig. 9.3 Linear model definition in R

α and β. Using the *thuesen* data frame described in Dalgaard (2002 #296), we can see just how simple this can be using the R environment, as shown in Fig. 9.3.

The lm function is the *l*inear *m*odel function. This tells us that the best linear relationship, that is, the best-fitting straight line, is given by the equation short.velocity $= 1.098 + 0.022 \times$ blood.glucose. Remember that these are the *estimates* for the real α and β. We included a summary of the linear model to illustrate that much more information can be calculated from a linear regression model, much of which may be available in the toolset at your disposal.

9.4 Decision Trees

As we describe in Chap. 4, decision trees repeatedly divide our instance space until the remaining regions are as homogeneous as possible. Our overall goal is to have a set of leaf-node classifications for which membership is as discrete as possible. That

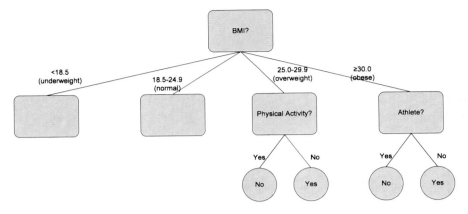

Fig. 9.4 Decision tree

IF x_bmi ≥ 30.0 AND x_isAthlete = FALSE THEN x_dyslipidemia_risk = HIGH

IF x_bmi ≥ 30.0 AND x_isAthlete = TRUE THEN x_dyslipidemia_risk = AVERAGE

IF x_bmi > 25.0 AND x_bmi < 30.0 AND x_isActive = TRUE

    THEN x_dyslipidemia_risk = AVERAGE

IF x_bmi > 25.0 AND x_bmi < 30.0 AND x_isActive = FALSE

    THEN x_dyslipidemia_risk = ELEVATED

Fig. 9.5 Decision tree implementation as classification rules

is, where the members of each class, defined at a specific leaf node of the tree, is as similar to each other member of that class as possible. From this description, we can see that a decision tree has similarities with flowchart representations.

Too loose a similarity between the members of a class means we have not balanced the sensitivity-specificity conundrum. Using the tree from Fig. 9.4, we can see that we made many decisions, some of which are very questionable, in developing the decision tree. In this section, we introduce some heuristics for developing decision trees and also more detail behind them.

So, to summarize, each nonleaf node represents a test on an attribute, each branch represents an outcome of the test, and each leaf node is a class label.

Consider the following simple decision-tree fragment which might be built to ask whether an individual has a higher risk of dyslipidemia (Fig. 9.5)[6]:

---

[6] This could also be used as a fragment for any of the conditions associated with obesity such as type 2 diabetes, coronary heart disease, stroke, etc.

```
For each attribute,

        For each value of the attribute, make a rule as follows:

                count how often each class appears

                find the most frequent class

                make the rule assign that class to this attribute-value

        Calculate the error rate of the rules

Choose the rules with the smallest error rate
```

Fig. 9.6 1R pseudocode

Here we use some of the findings from Prentice and Jebb (2001 #85) to build our fragment. We have taken some latitude with this fragment for purposes of illustration. Note that for an individual in the obese category (BMI $\geq$ 30.0), we ask whether or not they are an athlete. Prentice and Jebb (2001 #85) identified that professional football players and Olympic shot-putters have high BMI values but actually have low body fat percentages.

In this fragment of a decision tree, we have encoded several questions:

? What is the individual's BMI?
? Is the individual physically active?
? Is the person an athlete?

These questions obviously provide only a very gross classification of people; for any real-world application, we would take many other factors into account. For example, Prentice and Jebb (2001 #85) also highlighted that the BMI and body weight remain relatively constant with age, but the actual percentage of fat increases, along with diminished muscle mass. Thus, we may introduce age into our larger decision tree in order to obtain a lower level of granularity.

Given an input, **X**, for which the associated class is unknown, we can apply it as input to our decision tree and trace a path down the tree from the root node to a particular leaf node. Using our simple example, an individual with a BMI of 32.3 who is not a (professional) athlete would have an elevated risk of dyslipidemia.

We can also use our decision trees to create classification rules. Rules we can deduce from our decision tree fragment above are shown in Fig. 9.6.

Notice that in creating the set of classification rules from our decision tree fragment, we have made some further refinements to our yes/no risk outputs. In the rules, we have identified HIGH, ELEVATED, and AVERAGE values. Assuming we would also include a LOW value, we can return to our decision tree and refine it to include such classifications.

This iterative approach is a valuable tool for our data-mining activities since it allows us to begin with a very simple model, providing some validation of our hypotheses, and then allowing us to refine it by introducing the (undeniable) complexity that is a by-product of more insight. As we have repeated many times in this text, and we repeat once again here, the challenge of knowing when to stop – when it is "good enough" – and the challenge of overfitting, require us to be cautious and challenge our assumptions at each point in the process.

However, as stated by Occam's razor, simplicity is best. . .if it can be made to work.

9.5 1R

Recall the 1R method from earlier in the book. This is a very widely used technique to create decision trees and was discussed in great detail elsewhere. We return to it here, somewhat briefly, to discuss some of the algorithm's aspects specific to classification. As we recall, this is a very simple algorithm, which is both a strength and a weakness, that generates a 1-level decision tree, a rule-based system where the rule tests one particular attribute. However, this simplicity offers us a lot. As determined by O'Donnell (2005 #297), decision trees tend to have an influential variable: combining this with the 1R algorithm provides us with an opportunity to develop a simple, fast, and efficient classifier, a very interesting proposition indeed.

For any rule-based system, rules can be generically thought of as a set of *antecedents* that, when evaluated together, generate a *consequent*:

$$r : \{x_1, ..., x_n\} \rightarrow y$$

The antecedents $x_1, ..., x_n$ are usually *conjuncts* since they are usually "ANDed" together.

In 1R, our objective is to extract the single *best* rule that covers the current set of training instances. This seemingly simple statement hides several complex questions: How do we *grow* the antecedent clauses? How do we evaluate the new version of our rule, that is, once we have grown the rule? How do we determine how we stop the growth process? How do we *prune* the rule when generalizing the rule for use beyond our training set?

Before we address these questions further, we recall that our goal is to find a rule, or set of rules, that identify the instances of a specific class. For example, we may be interested in those patients in our dataset who fall into a "high-risk" category based upon some attribute in our dataset. So we want to generate the "best" rule. Typically, we measure this by optimizing the classification probability, which is in turn determined by looking at our various candidate attribute-pairs and selecting the best one for this purpose.

Note: This type of algorithm is often referred to as a *covering* algorithm because generated rules attempt to *exactly cover* a specific class of our data.

The general approach can be simply summarized as follows:

1. Generate a rule using our training data T.
2. Remove the training data covered by our rule.
3. Repeat.

Essentially, our algorithm will generate rules that are constrained to test a single attribute and branch for all values of that attribute. For every branch in the tree, the class with the test classification (i.e., supported by our rule) is the class being covered.

Let's begin to put this all together and answer the questions from a couple of paragraphs ago.

The 1R algorithm can be encapsulated in pseudocode[7] as shown in Fig. 9.7.

In this algorithm, we assume that a missing value is exactly that, an additional attribute value. Further, the error rate is defined as the proportion of instances that do not belong to the majority class.

Exploring this a little further, although we chose the rules with the smallest error rate, this is essentially being determined only by our training dataset. As we've discussed elsewhere, we need to be careful so that we don't end up with a model overfitted to our training data. As we evaluate our rules, we definitely want to consider coverage and accuracy, but also consider the entropy in the rules (similar to those used in the C4 algorithm) as we look outside of our training data. This is particularly important as we generalize our model.

The core of the 1R algorithm is the concept of the attribute-value pair: one value for each attribute. Our rule can naturally leverage multiple of these attribute-value pairs to provide more granular classifications as we "grow" our rule. Before we address this, the obvious question of how we establish our termination criteria is important to think about. We can evaluate our individual conjuncts, the attribute-value pairs, but we can also do the same for our rule by comparing it to the performance of the previous rule.

When we think about the rule itself, we are typically considering using a specific set of training data and moving to the more generalized case, although the opposite can be considered by choosing a positive instance as an initial seed for the rule and then iterate through a conjunct refinement function until our termination criteria are met. However, in looking to generalize, we might initially assume that an empty rule is a good first step, $r : \{\} \rightarrow y$, adding conjuncts to the rule until we have arrived at our termination criteria. Using our discussion so far, we would add conjuncts from our attribute-value pairs into our rule, comparing at each point with the previous version to see if we are doing better. If so, we can use the new rule; if not, then we can consider the prior rule.

---

[7] For readers not familiar with the concept of pseudocode, this is a structured-English representation for describing an algorithm in a form that is (hopefully) understandable to people who are not (hard-core) programmers. http://users.csc.calpoly.edu/~jdalbey/SWE/pdl_std.html has a nice introduction to the concept.

Input: D= {X$_1$,...,X$_n$}, X$_i$: {X$_{i1}$,...,X$_{ik}$}
              Distribution underlying the data (e.g. gaussian)

Prep: AutoClass generates a list of pseudo-random
              numbers as the number of classes (J)

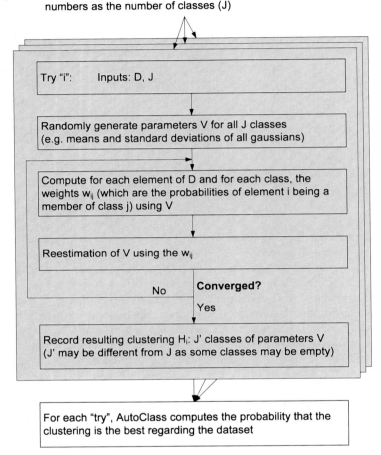

Try "i":   Inputs: D, J

Randomly generate parameters V for all J classes
(e.g. means and standard deviations of all gaussians)

Compute for each element of D and for each class, the
weights w$_{ij}$ (which are the probabilities of element i being a
member of class j) using V

Reestimation of V using the w$_{ij}$

                         No   **Converged?**

                              Yes

Record resulting clustering H$_i$: J' classes of parameters V
(J' may be different from J as some classes may be empty)

For each "try", AutoClass computes the probability that the
clustering is the best regarding the dataset

Output: The best clustering (J, V, w$_{ij}$ for each element and class

Fig. 9.7 AutoClass algorithm

If we consider this last statement a little further, we have to ask ourselves how
we can *know* that the prior version of our rule is better: could we create a better
rule if we prune one or more conjuncts out of our rule? What about if we take this to
the logical extreme and ask whether we would uncover a better rule by starting
over, from our empty rule once again? We have met these two scenarios elsewhere.
In the first, that of *rule pruning*, we are interested in seeing the effect of removing
one of the conjuncts and then testing the resulting rule against some (different) set
of data that will be our validation dataset. If we have multiple conjuncts in our rule,

we may elect to do this for each one in turn and look at the results in each case. Our rule can now grow *or* contract in each cycle. It may well be that adding conjunct x_7 to our rule and then testing without conjunct x_4 may give us the same performance, or even better, than leaving x_4 in. What about if we want to start from scratch again? If we decide that we want to see if a different rule would be generated if we start from the beginning, how can we do this? If we simply start again with the same training data, the deterministic nature of the 1R algorithm would result in the same rule being generated. Thus, in order to generate a different rule, we need to eliminate one or more instances from our training set. If we have created a training set and validation set from a larger base of instances, we could remove one or more positive instances after each rule is extracted, or randomly associate each instance with either the training set or validation set at the beginning of each rule generation process.

   Why did we spend more time talking about the 1R algorithm? First, because it is a simple algorithm and performs as effectively, typically, as more complex algorithms do. Second, because simplicity is often a good leader into our mining effort, if not good for the mining effort itself. But thirdly, it is because we can see many of the classification-related issues in this simple algorithm. Although this algorithm is typically used for nominal values, it can also be used for continuous data (i.e., for prediction) and, in fact, considers all numerically valued attributes as continuous. But as Holte himself says, there is a real potential for overfitting. For readers further interested in the 1R algorithm, see (Holte 1993 #318).

9.6   Nearest Neighbor

Many methods used for classification are referred to as *eager learners* because they construct a classification model before receiving any new instances to classify. Examples of this type of method include Bayesian classification, decision-tree induction, support vector machines, and back propagation, to name a few. An alternative approach is the *lazy learner* where no model is constructed until late in the process. Instead, training instances perform minimal (if any) processing on the training instances and wait until they receive a test instance. It is at this point that the generalization occurs to classify the new instance based upon its base of stored knowledge. Since this type of method stores the instances, they are also referred to as *instance-based learners*.[8] Instance-based learners need lots of examples to be effective. A possible drawback of instance-based learning is that most of the computation happens when the test example is presented. Thus, efficiency is very important in selecting an example that matches the test case. Also, this type of learning method offers very little insight into the structure of the data, but they do allow for incremental learning. One of their major advantages is

---

[8] This is a bit of a misnomer since all methods of learning are based on instances.

that they can model very complex decision spaces that may not be as easily described using other methods.

In this section, we shall describe one of the more common instance-based methods, the *k-nearest neighbor* (k-NN) classifier. However, this is by no means the only such method, and the reader is directed to many of the references in the bibliography, or the Internet, for more information about these other methods.

We shall use the concept of *neighbor* or *closeness*, without detailed discussion since this is closely related to concepts of similarity that we describe elsewhere. That being said, nearest-neighbor classifiers rely on learning by analogy; a new instance is compared with our existing base of instances and is classified according to the instances which are most similar to it.

Consider our instances as comprising a set of *n* attributes, $\mathbf{X}_i = (x_{i1}, x_{i2}, ..., x_{in})$. We can use this definition and represent each instance, $\mathbf{X}_i$, by a point in an *n*-dimensional pattern space. When the model receives an instance that it has not seen before, the pattern space is searched for the training instances that are closest to the new instance presented to the model. If we are interested in only the training instance that is closest to our new instance, we have the *1-nearest neighbor* (1-NN) algorithm. In general, however, we are interested in some number of nearest neighbors – the *k-nearest neighbors*.

For our purposes in this section, we will define our notion of closeness to be a Euclidean distance measure.[9] For two instances, $\mathbf{X}_1 = (x_{11}, x_{12}, ..., x_{1n})$ and $\mathbf{X}_2 = (x_{21}, x_{22}, ..., x_{2n})$, the distance measure $dist(\mathbf{X}_1, \mathbf{X}_2)$ is defined as

$$dist(\mathbf{X}_1, \mathbf{X}_2) = \sqrt{\sum_{i=1}^{n} (x_{1i} - x_{2i})^2}$$

An important point to consider in the above equation is that attributes which have large value ranges can swamp those with small ranges. For example, the difference between two values of an attribute containing white blood cell counts will be measured in thousands, whereas a binary representation for gender will have a difference of 0 or 1. Since we usually want to ensure that such variability does not adversely affect our model, we will typically normalize the data values prior to using the $dist(\mathbf{X}_1, \mathbf{X}_2)$ equation.

In k-NN, the new instance is assigned the class that is most common among its *k*-nearest neighbors. For 1-NN, it will be assigned the class of its nearest neighbor.

If the labels associated with the instances are real valued, k-NN can also be used for prediction purposes. In this case, the normal approach is to return the average of the label values of the nearest neighbors.

We refer the reader to Chap. 5 to recall our conversation about data transformation, where we used the example of measuring distance to discuss various approaches for handling categorical data.

We have so far avoided a question that we now must face: what is the value of *k*?

---

[9] We discuss this in much more detail in Chap. 8.

9.7 Bayesian Modeling

Recall from our previous discussions in Chap. 7 that Bayesian modeling involves statistical inference in which observations (evidence) are used to update the probability that an hypothesis H may be true through the use of Bayes' theorem.

The scientific method involves our positing a hypothesis and collecting data in order to support or refute our hypothesis. This data allows our degree of belief in the hypothesis to change. This degree of belief, considered as a probability, means that our belief should become very high or very low.

If we accept this interpretation, a hypothesis with a very high level of support should be accepted as true; with a very low level of support, it should be rejected as false. However, as we discussed elsewhere, concern has been raised that this inference may be biased because of an investigator's initial beliefs: beliefs held from before data is collected.

Also recall from our earlier discussions that we use Bayesian techniques to estimate a probability – our degree of belief – before evidence has been observed, so that we can estimate a probability for the hypothesis that we should expect to see *after* evidence has been observed – also a degree of belief. We do this, for as many iterations as is reasonable, using Bayes' theorem

$$P(H|E) = \frac{P(E|H)P(H)}{P(E)}$$

where $P(H)$ is the *prior probability* of H that we inferred for the hypothesis (H) before any/new evidence E was observed. $P(E|H)$ is the *conditional probability* of observing E *if H is true*. This is also called a *likelihood function* when we consider it as a function of H when E is fixed. $P(E)$ is the *marginal probability* of E, the a priori probability of observing E under all possible H: $P(E) = \sum P(E|H_i)P(H_i)$. Finally, $P(H|E)$ is the posterior probability of H given (i.e., after observing) E.

Rewriting Bayes' theorem just slightly,

$$P(H|E) = \frac{P(E|H)}{P(E)} \times P(H)$$

we can more clearly see the impact that any evidence we observe will have on our belief in H. If it is likely that we would observe E when our hypothesis is true, then the factor $P(E|H)/P(E)$ would be large because of the value of $P(E|H)$, and therefore, multiplying the prior probability, given here by $P(H)$, will result in a larger posterior probability, $P(H|E)$. Conversely, if it is unlikely that we would observe the evidence E for our hypothesis but, a priori, is likely that the evidence will be observed, then the factor will be small, resulting in a smaller posterior probability. Thus, Bayes' theorem measures the amount by which the belief in our hypothesis H should change given the observation of a new set of evidence. So, to summarize, we are interested in finding the most probable set of classifications for our instances, given that set of instances and some set of prior expectations.

Let's begin to look at how Bayesian inference can help with our mining activities. Consider a medical test with the following characteristics:

- If a patient has a disease, a positive result is returned 99.5% of the time.
- If a patient does not have the disease, a positive result is returned 7.5% of the time.

Suppose that 0.25% of the population has the disease; a randomly selected patient has a 0.0025 prior probability of having the disease.

We want to calculate the probability that a positive result is a false positive.

Let D be the condition in which the patient has the disease and let R be a positive test result. We can calculate the probability that a patient has the disease, given a positive test result, as

$$P(D|R) = \frac{P(R|D)P(D)}{P(R|D)P(D) + P(R|\neg D)P(\neg D)}$$

where $\neg$ symbolizes the "not" condition, that is, $P(\neg D)$ is the probability that a patient does not have the disease:

$$P(D|R) = \frac{0.995 \times 0.0025}{0.995 \times 0.0025 + 0.075 \times (1 - 0.0025)} = 0.0322$$

Therefore, the probability that a positive result is a false positive is $1 - 0.0322 = 0.9678$.

This might seem counterintuitive. There are a couple of comments we need to make at this stage. First, the test itself was deemed to have a very high degree of accuracy: 99.5%. The prevalence of the disease, however, was very low: 2.5%. This means that the vast majority of patients will not have the disease. Given this, we would naturally expect the probability of a person actually having the disease, given a positive test result, would be low and that the majority of patients with a positive test result would not have the disease.

To offset this issue of false positives, any test should be very accurate for negative results when a patient does not have the disease. Let's assume our test has a probability of 0.999 for the probability of a negative result given that the patient does not have the disease:

$$\frac{0.995 \times 0.0025}{0.995 \times 0.0025 + 0.001 \times 0.999} \approx 0.71$$

The probability of a false positive is $1 - 0.71 = 0.29$.

To complete this part of our discussion, we need to discuss the concept of a false negative: where the test reports a negative result, but the patient really does have the disease. Using our notation from above,

$$P(D|\neg R) = \frac{P(\neg R|D)P(D)}{P(\neg R|D)P(D) + P(\neg R|\neg D)P(\neg D)}$$

$$= \frac{0.005 \times 0.0025}{0.005 \times 0.0025 + 0.925 \times 0.9975}$$

$$= 1.355 \times 10^5,$$

$P(D|\neg R)$ is about 0.001355%, which tells us that false negatives will not be a problem for our test for a disease as rare as our fictitious example. What about in a situation where a much larger portion of the population had the disease? Let's consider a case where 75% of the population had this disease:

$$P(D|\neg R) = \frac{0.005 \times 0.75}{0.005 \times 0.75 + 0.925 \times 0.25} \approx 0.01596$$

Now we can see that false negatives could account for close to 1.6% of cases, a much different situation.

Now that we've revisited the basis of Bayesian inference, let's briefly recall that *supervised learning* is where we have a set of input training instances, labeled with their intended classifications, that are used to predict the class memberships for as yet unseen instances, whereas *unsupervised learning* uses training instances that are unlabeled. Since we are not providing our model with any form of direction in this latter case, we often think about the unsupervised learning case where the best classification is one in which the model is least "surprised" by any new instances it receives. In its purest sense, unsupervised learning is closest to our goal of data mining – that of uncovering hidden patterns in the data – and can be used in exploratory analysis where we avoid, or have, preconceptions about the data and what it might contain.

Recently, several studies, both theoretical and applied, have shown that Bayesian analysis – especially unsupervised classification – have particular relevance to biological studies. See, for example, (Medvedovic and Sivaganesan 2002 #324; Medvedovic et al. 2004 #325; Yeung et al. 2001 #326; Ng et al. 2006 #327; Qin 2006 #328; Xiang et al. 2007 #329; Fraley and Raftery 1998 #330; Haughton et al. 2009 #331; Tadesse et al. 2005 #332; Baladandayuthapani et al. 2008 #333).

A good example of this is AutoClass (Cheeseman 1988 #319) that uses Bayesian methods to cluster instances into groups (sic) that we'll discuss further here to provide a basis for further research into Bayesian methods for classification and clustering by the interested reader.

AutoClass incorporates an unsupervised classification system using Bayesian inference. As we've already seen, this delegates the determination of how many classes, along with their composition, to the system itself: The Bayesian approach

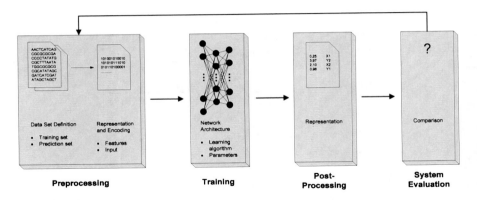

Fig. 9.8 Neural network design approach

will search the model space for what it considers to be the "best" class descriptions based on the data. Typically, this will result in a trade-off between predictive accuracy and class complexity, but will also not usually overfit to the data. One other factor to mention is that with such systems, an instance is not so much assigned a class as assigned a probability of being a member of each and every class in our system. The highest probability "wins out." Thus, AutoClass has some valuable features, broadly applicable to many disciplines within the biological sciences. It determines the number of classes that best fit the data automatically. This is a tremendous value as it does not rely on the investigator trying to guesstimate the number of classes ahead of time, but allows the data (and algorithm) to select them for us – at least, initially. It allows the user to mix discrete and real valued data together. One of the challenges with mixing such data comes from the complexity of the sums (discrete data) and integrals (real or continuous data) that comprise the models. It handles missing data. Need we say more?

Figure 9.8 shows a representation of the AutoClass algorithm.[10]

Berger (1993 #322) provided a solid foundation, well tested, to illustrate the value of Bayesian theory as a basis on which to build valuable processes for analyzing data. The theory also defines a procedure whereby we can deal with myriad different problems. The underlying machinery of the Bayesian approach trades off model complexity against that model's fit to new data that comes into our environment without our needing to include anything explicit to deal with it, excluding overfitting of the data and the problems concomitant with that challenge. We obviously have to be explicit about the model space that our models are searching, which are often very large, and the models themselves quickly involve complex sums or integrals (when the data is continuous). Cheeseman (1990 #323) provided an interesting discussion on some of the perceived disadvantages of the

---

[10] This is taken from the supplemental information available at Nucleic Acids Research (NAR) at http://nar.oxfordjournals.org/cgi/data/gkp430/DC1/1.

Bayesian approach, including issues in the ambiguities in choosing a prior and how they are generally manageable since any of the possible selections do not typically disagree strongly with the region of the model's space we are interested in, and how we can use this type of model to step outside what is traditionally regarded as statistical data to models more aligned with real-world descriptions.

More recently, AutoClass has been used within a freely available environment – AutoClass@IJM to classify heterogeneous biology data. An example of its use in the genomic space is described in Cheeseman and Stutz (1996 #336) where it was applied to DNA intron data. As a result of the investigation, several conclusions were reported:

- The class of a donor site was highly correlated with the corresponding acceptor site. For the C-rich class, the donor site, acceptor site, and entire intron between them were all C rich. (This was similarly the case for the other classes.)
- The same classes were observed in mouse genes, and where the corresponding genes exist in mice and humans, they have the same classes, indicating that the patterns observed have persisted for millions of years.
- Base-frequency patterns extend into flanking exons, but not as strongly as that observed in introns.
- If one intron is (say) TA rich, there is a high probability that any neighboring introns will also be TA rich.

Considering the underlying Bayesian theory, taking into account the summations and integrals that come along with it, applying the theory can be difficult, sometimes resulting in our using approximations to make what are sometimes mathematically intractable calculations realistic in our models. When taken together with our modeling efforts, the end result is somewhat less than optimum from a descriptive standpoint, but is often more than valid from an analytical, real-world standpoint.

For example, simple prior distributions are often preferred so that the integrals (when dealing with continuous data) can be approximated. Making the prior as broad (think uninformative) as possible will broaden (sic) the applicability of the model to other contexts. That being said, the question of value comes into play: if we make the prior more specific to our domain of study, we can expect to obtain a "better" result, but as we keep saying, this definition of "better" needs to be considered carefully as the added complexity may not translate to added value. If the prior can predict the different parameters of the model independently – through a product of terms for each parameter – this will help also. Another point made by Hanson et al. (1991 #321) that can be very valuable is to consider a prior that is somewhat independent of the complexity of the various models under consideration, that is, a prior that provides a similar weight to different levels of complexity. This can be used as a type of significance test for the models. Remember that adding model parameters will require a significantly better fit in order for the more complex model to be preferred over a simpler one. Once again, we see a trade-off that requires careful consideration.

By this point, readers may be turned off by the Bayesian approach. For readers not familiar with some of the mathematics underpinning the subject, it can be daunting.

However, many algorithms already have freely available implementations, hiding some of the mathematics and allowing us to focus on the analytics. The underlying Bayesian theory is well founded and has been well tested, and the procedure itself is applicable and consistent across a wide domain of problems. The procedure itself also automatically manages the model complexity-fit to the evidence dual, eliminating the need for us to continually concern ourselves with (some of) the issues of overfitting and increasing model complexity. But one of its most valuable advantages is its ability to incorporate contextual information in the input, if we wish.

Countering this, our search space for the models has to be explicitly defined. This can often be a challenging and daunting task. That being said, it is also good discipline to do so. Once we have defined our search spaces, another challenge that manifests itself is the size of the search spaces, although this is not specific to Bayesian approaches. We have already mentioned the issue of integral and sum complexity. To offset this, many numerical implementations are available for many of the environments we might use for our analysis such as MATLAB, Mathematica, R, SPSS, and SAS, to name a few.

Naturally, AutoClass is not the only implementation of Bayesian inference techniques, and interested readers can obtain information about other approaches, such as COBWEB (Fisher 1987 #334), on which several systems have built on this work, and Geiger et al. (1990 #335), which focuses on the induction of Bayesian inference networks, to provide just a couple of staring points for further research. For a nice general introduction to classification using Bayesian inference, see (Hanson et al. 1991 #321) and (Cheeseman 1990 #323). As an alternative, we also want to highlight (Duda et al. 2001 #28) as recommended reading: many researchers have been stimulated by the pattern recognition and classification work of Duda and Hart.

Readers may have recognized our focus on *unsupervised* techniques in our discussion, especially with our use of AutoClass as our example, and wonder about this. To some extent, (pure) data mining is an unsupervised discipline (bad joke) in that we are very interested in those *hidden* patterns. Rather than our knowing, or suspecting, classifications and rather than our predicting clusters, using techniques that can provide us with "surprises" can be very valuable. Bayesian approaches are not the only subject area to provide a wealth of tools, techniques, and concepts to help us with this type of learning: as we saw in the last chapter, and look at in the next section, machine learning allows for some valuable approaches to the clustering/prediction challenge.

We close this section by addressing a concept that we mentioned in passing during our discussion above and which might be a little confusing to some readers: balancing of the complexity of the model versus overfitting of the model to the data.[11] If we consider that model complexity is directly related, among other things, to the introduction of parameters into that model, we can see how one model would

---

[11] This is the application of Occam's razor to the Bayesian approach.

be less complex than another based upon the parameters that are needed to define it. But each parameter, in turn, will affect the joint probability by bringing its own prior probability to the party – a prior probability that is *multiplicative* – the impact of which is to always *lower* the marginal probability. Thus, if the (additional) parameter fails to raise the marginal probability by increasing the direct probability more than the prior probability lowers the marginal probability, then the model incorporating the additional parameter will be rejected.

9.8 Neural Networks

We discussed neural network technologies in some detail earlier in this text and focus here more on its application than the underlying theory. However, as a reminder, the general architecture and approach is depicted in Fig. 9.9.

As is the case with many of the concepts and technologies of machine learning, they have applicability to a broad range of problems.

In our earlier discussion, we separated supervised and unsupervised learning of the system and differentiated between those occasions where we wanted to force any as yet unseen instances into a predetermined set of buckets, or where we wanted to let the system itself determine what the partitioning scheme (i.e., classes) should be.

Neural network approaches provide a robust set of tools to support separating input patterns from each other, and as we've discussed, much progress that is generalized to problem domains such as those seen in the life sciences has come from pattern recognition. From the simplest type of system such as the perceptron, and its ability to distinguish between any linearly separable instances, through networks involving backpropagation and counterpropagation, feedforward nets, associative memories, Hopfield nets, adaptive resonance theory (ART), and incorporation of statistical techniques such as linear regression and principal component analysis (PCA), neural network research has brought together many concepts to provide a robust platform for data mining.

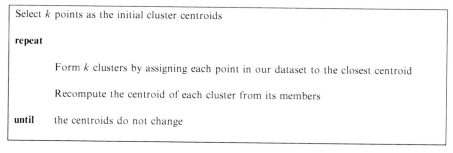

Select k points as the initial cluster centroids

repeat

        Form k clusters by assigning each point in our dataset to the closest centroid

        Recompute the centroid of each cluster from its members

until   the centroids do not change

Fig. 9.9 k-Means clustering algorithm

A seminal work in this arena is Bishop (1995 #16), and readers are strongly recommended to obtain a copy. This is not the only reference to this important intersection of research areas, and several have been provided earlier in this text, along with some which will be provided below. As is the case in every other area of data mining we have considered, it is impossible to do justice to the depth and breadth of neural networks and their applicability to data mining – particularly classification, which we consider in this section – and so any reader whose interest is piqued has to pick up some of the references we cite.

Readers familiar with the theory, including our discussion of it earlier in this text, will probably have some trepidation: how do I begin? Do I have to build my network from scratch? How do I even determine whether or not I'm making positive progress? These are just some of the challenges that researchers face when considering using neural networks. Thankfully, there are many tools available to the researcher that abstracts some of the complexity, allowing us to focus on our objective rather than the mechanics of the network itself. We have listed a number of tools available as of the time of writing, and readers are referred to Appendix B for more details.

The "black-box" nature of neural networks requires both a level of trust and a rigorous validation step to ensure that the results are copasetic with both our expectations and the reality of the data. This can be challenging without a level of familiarity and expertise with neural networks. These incomprehensible models, and the often long training times required for the models, are primary reasons why neural network methods are not commonly used for data mining.

So, with such challenges, we should ensure we ask ourselves whether the neural network approach is appropriate for the problem at hand. Researchers have concluded that it is in cases where there is an inadequate knowledge base surrounding the problem, or where such knowledge is very volatile, where the subject area is extremely data intensive, where standard technologies have shown themselves to be inadequate, where the data is noisy, or where complex quantitative or qualitative reasoning is required.

The data-related characteristics we mention in the previous paragraph should be particularly considered: the size and noise associated with the data, its representation in the knowledge domain and how the input is coded, whether there is sufficient data, and how to generate both the training dataset and the test dataset.

We'll consider an example from Wang et al. (2000 #384). Therein, the problem is defined as determining whether some unlabeled protein sequence S is a member of a known superfamily[12] F, where F is referred to as the *target class* and the set of sequences not in F is the nontarget class. If S is determined as belonging to F, then its structure and function can be inferred because of this membership. This can be very important for many areas of research. For example, in drug discovery, if S is obtained from some disease D, and subsequently determined to be a member of F, then a potential treatment for D may be some combination of drugs already available for F.

For neural networks of any sort, representing the input in such a way that the neural network is able to recognize the underlying regularities in the input – recognizing the patterns – is vital.

---

[12] A superfamily is a set of proteins that share some level of similarity in structure and function.

Table 9.1 Common data-mining alphabets

Name	Size	Subject area	Membership
Gene sequence	4	Sequence identity	A, C, G, T
Amino acid identity	20	Sequence identity	A, C, D, E, F, G, H, I, K, L,M, N, P, Q, R, S, T, V, W, Y
Exchange group	6	Conservative substitution	{HRK}, {DENQ}, {C}, {STPAG}, {MILV}, {FYV}
Charge polarity	4	Charge and polarity	{HRK}, {DE}, {CTSGNQY}, {APMLIVFW}
Hydrophobicity	3	Hydrophobicity	{DENQRK}, {CSTPGHY}, {AMILVFW}
Mass	3	Mass	{GASPVTC}, {NDQEHILKM}, {RFWY}
Structural	3	Surface exposure	{DENQHRK}, {CSTPAGWY}, {MILVF}
2D propensity	3	2D structure propensity	{AEQHKMLR}, {CTIVFYW}, {SGPDN}

To calculate global similarity, the 2-g encoding method outlined in Wu and McLarty (2000 #63) was used, which extracts occurrences of patterns of two consecutive amino acids in a sequence. For example, in the sequence KLEQKLPQTV, the results would be KL=2, LE=1, EQ=1, QK=1, LP=1, PQ=1, QT=1, and TV=1.

Evolution supports a set of conservative replacements of amino acids, and so we can take our amino acid alphabet $A = \{A,C,D,E,F,G,H,I,K,L,M,N,P,Q,R,S,T,V,W,Y\}$ and create conservation or exchange groups $e_1 \in \{H,R,K\}$, $e_2 \in \{D,E,N,Q\}$, $e_3 \in \{C\}$, $e_4 \in \{S,T,P,A,G\}$, $e_5 \in \{M,I,L,V\}$, and $e_6 \in \{F,Y,W\}$. If we take our example sequence KLEQKLPQTV from above, it would be encoded as $e_1 e_5 e_2 e_2 e_1\ e_5 e_4 e_2 e_4 e_5$, with a 2-g exchange group encoding of 2 for $e_1 e_5$ and one for each of the other pairs.

Alphabet Sets for Feature Representation

We're going to take a brief side trip here to elaborate a little on the use of alphabet sets as they relate to feature representation. We identified six discrete *exchange groups* that themselves form a specialized alphabet that we can use during our preprocessing step to better represent features in our input that we wish to highlight as a focus for our neural network architecture.

The following table (adapted from Wu and McLarty (2000 #63)) identifies some of the alphabet sets you are likely to encounter in data mining (Table 9.1).

As we shall see in our example, understanding the relationships between the data that we are dealing with as input is important so that we can determine whether there really are patterns within the data or not, something we have discussed already.

This may seem like a catch-22 position: we need to understand the patterns in the data. . .to identify patterns in the data. This is not our intent. Instead, when we consider the data that constitutes our input, the *domain* of that data is important to understand. If it is comprised of amino acid residues, for example, knowing that the residues H, R, and K may stand in for each other can allow us to eliminate false patterns or identify patterns whose only differences are the result of conservative substitutions.

Applying both the 2-g amino acid encoding and the 2-g exchange group encoding results in 436 possible 2-g patterns,[13] and if each pattern were used as a feature of the neural network, the result would be a significant number of weight parameters and training data, which would make the training effort a difficult challenge. In fact, this is a good example of the dimensionality issue that we discussed earlier. To address this, (Wu and McLarty 2000 #63) select relevant features (2 g) using a distance measure, denoted by $D(X)$.[14] One factor that is important to consider with this approach, and one that they discuss, is the effect that random pairings can have on the distance result.

Addressing the dimensionality issue, Wu and McLarty (2000 #63) selected a subset of the possible 436 features by selecting the ones with the largest values of $D(X)$. This set of $N_g \geq 30$ features will occur more frequently in the positive training dataset and less frequently in the negative training dataset, intuitively providing us with a separation into our binary classes. The issue of the possible loss of information is also addressed within the paper by considering a linear correlation coefficient that the reader is encouraged to review in the original paper.

An available tool – *Sdiscover* (Wang et al. 1994 #386) – that was originally developed to find regular expression motifs was used in combination with the *minimum description length* (MDL) principle to calculate the significance of the motifs.

The Bayesian neural network (BNN) originally described in MacKay (1992 #387) forms the basis of the BNN used to classify the protein sequences provided as input and consists of a single hidden layer with multiple units, an output layer with a single unit whose activation function is based on the logistic function, and is fully connected between adjacent layers.

Using data from the Protein Information Resource (PIR)[15] for both training and subsequent analysis, the precision – the number of correctly classified sequences divided by the total number of sequences – was over 98%.

The performance of the BNN classifier was also compared to BLAST and SAM – the latter of which is built on hidden Markov models, as well as developing an ensemble of the three called COMBINER – and the precision was found to be greater than 99%.

As this example illustrates, neural networks provide an effective approach to data mining that is at least comparable with other approaches. The complexities are in different aspects of the model and, depending on the resources available to you, may be more effective for your particular problem at that particular time. However, it also illustrates a value to using neural networks as an independent approach to classification and prediction, thus providing a sanity check on your work or, more valuably, as a part of an integrated program where it is incorporated along with

---

[13] $20 \times 20 + 6 \times 6$,

[14] The reader is recommended to Wu and McLarty (2000 #63) for further details.

[15] http://www-nbrf.georgetown.edu/

other approaches to provide a system where the combination of models provides more value than the individual models can do on their own.

Some general references that provide more contexts to neural network use in data mining include Lu et al. (1996 #383).

For readers interested in further exploring the application of neural network technologies, Zheng et al. (2009 #382) describe the use of an artificial neural network to analyze affinity of the N-n-alkylnicotinium salts for the $\alpha 4\beta 2^*$ nicotinic acetylcholine receptor.

Neural networks have actually been used across many application areas within the genomics space including coding recognition, splice site prediction, ribosome binding site determination, *E. coli* promoter prediction, clustering and prediction, phylogenetic classification, rRNA classification, and tRNA gene recognition, to name a few. Protein structure prediction and folding determination have also fertile research areas in which this architecture has provided valuable insight and momentum, and, together with their use in family classification, as we described above, cleavage site determination, and signal peptide prediction, neural networks are proving to be a valuable tool in the arsenal of the researcher across a number of domains.

9.9   k-Means

The k-means clustering algorithm was originally developed by MacQueen (1967 #388), and is one of the simplest of the unsupervised learning algorithms in clustering, and one that we have described earlier in this text. So herein, we'll consider a simple example of how we might apply this approach to a problem.

Consider a dataset containing information about tumors. This dataset might contain a set of attributes such as those depicted in Table 9.2.

For our example, we'll use only a subset of these attributes to allow us to visualize in three dimensions: curvature, texture, and blood consumption.[16]

Consider the following subset of our input data (Table 9.3):

Tumor type is an obvious classification, and we'll use this as our mechanism for determining how well our model does. For this example, we'll use the other three attributes, which conveniently allows us to visualize the information in three dimensions, although our discussion will intuitively extend to higher-dimensional spaces!

---

[16] We are not suggesting that such a method of reducing the dimensionality of the dataset would be applicable in the real world. Obviously, we are using this to better illustrate as three dimensions allow us to show the pertinent details.

Table 9.2 Tumor attribute dataset

Attribute	Domain
Classification	Lung, head & neck, esophagus, thyroid, stomach, duodenum & small intestine, colon, rectum, anus, salivary glands, pancreas, gallbladder, liver, kidney, bladder, testis, prostate, ovary, corpus uteri, cervix uteri, vagina, breast
Patient_Age	<16, 16–30, 30–59, ≥60
Patient_Gender	Male, female, unknown
Histologic_Type	Epidermoid, adeno, anaplastic
Degree_of_Differentiation	Well, fairly, poorly
Bone	Yes, no
Bone_Marrow	Yes, no
Lung	Yes, no
Pleura	Yes, no
Peritoneum	Yes, no
Liver	Yes, no
Brain	Yes, no
Skin	Yes, no
Neck	Yes, no
Supraclavicular	Yes, no
Axillar	Yes, no
Mediastinum	Yes, no
Abdominal	Yes, no
Curvature	Numeric
Texture	Numeric
Blood_Flow[a]	Categorical: A, B, C, D
Tumor_Type	Benign, malignant, undetermined

[a] Tumor blood flow is proportional to the pressure differences between the arterial and venous sides and inversely proportional to the viscous and geometric resistances (Jain 1988 #389). We've elected to oversimplify this for illustrative purposes and readers are encouraged to consider (Jain 1988 #389 and Hori et al. 2008 #390) as good points for extending your knowledge of this important characteristic of tumors and why it is important

Table 9.3 Sample subset of tumor characteristics

Curvature	Texture	Blood flow	Tumor type
0.85	1.30	A	Benign
0.91	1.40	A	Benign
0.74	1.20	B	Benign
0.79	1.30	A	Benign
0.83	1.10	B	Benign
0.32	0.50	D	Malignant
0.40	0.45	D	Malignant
0.29	0.40	D	Malignant
0.23	0.50	D	Malignant
0.28	0.30	D	Malignant

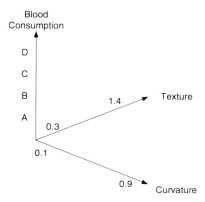

Using the attributes from our dataset, we can plot the points in our *n*-dimensional space, using each individual attribute as representative of a single dimension. In the figure to the left, we have arbitrarily chosen blood consumption to represent what we traditionally consider to be the y-axis in graphical representations, although there is nothing significant about these choices. In our example, we are also plotting the points with no effort to alter the value ranges. We will often need to map the range of values differently to meet our needs. For example, we may collect the data as numeric values but be better served by mapping them to categorical values, without our losing any significant amount of information. Whether this is pertinent or not depends on the specific analysis being undertaken.

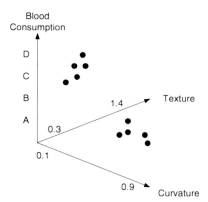

Plotting our dataset onto our axes allows us to see how and where the points group together on the graph and whether or not there are any natural groupings to our data; in this case, we can see that there are two such groupings. If we plot the rest of our data, there would more likely be a greater number of groups and also more overlap between them. This is where the k-means method of clustering provides us with value. If we draw n-dimensional circles – spheres in our three dimensional case – around our groups of points, we can identify the *centroid* value for that cluster. This centroid value can then be used as that cluster's representative.

```
curvature  <- c(0.82, 0.91, 0.74, 0.79, 0.83, 0.32, 0.40, 0.29, 0.23, 0.28)

texture    <- c(1.30, 1.40, 1.20, 1.30, 1.10, 0.50, 0.45, 0.40, 0.50, 0.30)

blood_flow <- c(   1,    1,    2,    1,    2,    4,    4,    4,    4,    4)


x <- cbind(curvature, texture, blood_flow)

colnames(x) <- c("x", "y", "z")

(cl <- kmeans(x, 2))

plot(x, col = cl$cluster)

points(cl$centers, col = 1:2, pch = 8, cex=2)

draw.circle(cl$centers[2,1], cl$centers[2,2],0.13,border=2)

draw.circle(cl$centers[1,1], cl$centers[1,2],0.105,border=1)
```

Fig. 9.10 k-Means example

In our example, we can then replace our two groups of 5 points with these two distinct points. The only information missing is how close to the centroid the actual points lie; for that we need a distance measure.

The magnitude of the distance measure will obviously be key to our model's accuracy since a value that is too large has the possibility of subsuming multiple discrete clusters into one. However, the converse is also a concern as a value that is too small will result in a larger number of clusters than the data really represents.

We typically begin by selecting the number of clusters, k, that we think accurately represents the data. Each cluster is then associated with its own centroid value, and each point in our dataset is assigned to the cluster with the closest centroid. So how do we select the centroids?

We typically begin by selecting k points as our centroids and then form the clusters by assigning all the points near to each centroid to their respective cluster. Once we have completed this for our dataset, we then recomputed the centroid using the points in each cluster. If the newly computed centroid is different to the one initially selected, we use this new value as the centroid and then assign the points to the clusters as above. This process is continued until the centroids do not change (Fig. 9.10).

Using the R stats package, we can very quickly build out model (Fig. 9.11):

The plot (and points) provide a visualization of the x and y dimensions as shown in Fig. 9.12.

Our data was generated to allow us to illustrate a distinct separation, but even so, we can show some interesting facets of the k-means algorithm. We altered our code fragment as shown below:

```
k <- 3

(cl <- kmeans(x, k))

plot(x, col = cl$cluster)

points(cl$centers, col = 1:k, pch = 8, cex=1)
```

Fig. 9.11 2D Output from
k-means clustering

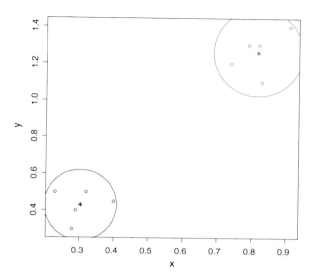

which provided the following visualization:

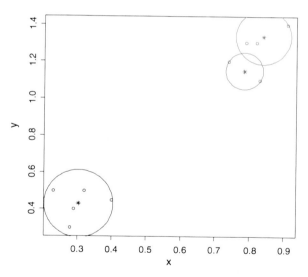

Note the separation of the single cluster in the top right-hand corner into two clusters.[17] So, are there two or three clusters? Have we asked for too granular a separation by using $k=3$ rather than $k=2$? Does it matter? These questions, and others like them, are dependent upon the data, model, and intent of the analysis, as

---

[17] We've drawn circular regions around the centroids to highlight them. Recall that the regions are not necessarily circular in the general case.

Fig. 9.12 ROC curve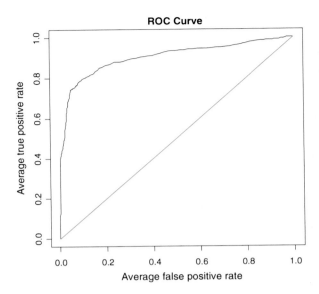

ROC Curve

we have said before, and may require exploring the results and, if they are unsatisfactory, iterating back through the model with different parameters.

9.10   Distance Measures

In clustering, as in many other mining techniques, we are often interested in metrics which quantify differences between the instances in our dataset. If we consider the concept of similarity in data, the question becomes one of determining (measuring) that similarity, and the difference between two values is an intuitive way of thinking of how similar two values are. We can obviously use either *similarity* metrics or *dissimilarity* (or *distance*) metrics as our vehicle for determining whether two things look alike or not. But the choice of such a measure can drastically alter the simplicity and capability of our model, and/or alter its performance profile and mean the difference between a model running to completion in a reasonable amount of time, or not completing at all (in the worst case).

Many models built into analytical environments will contain algorithms to allow the user to select one of a number of different distance measures. Some of the more common include the Euclidean, Maximum, Manhattan, Canberra, Binary, Pearson, Correlation, Spearman, Kendall, and Cosine similarity measures.

We briefly provide a summary of some of these measures, but this table is not exhaustive by any measure (sic) (Table 9.4).

Algorithms of all kinds can be measured to provide an understanding of their performance profile and how that will change as the magnitude of data increases. The so-called "big O" notation is used widely; it measures the execution of an

Table 9.4 Distance measures (not exhaustive)

Name	Definition	Use
Euclidean	$D(a,b) = \sqrt{\sum_{i=1}^{n}(a_i - b_i)^2}$	Normalized datasets, or datasets that have no special distribution
Manhattan	$D(a,b) = \sum_{i=1}^{n}|a_i - b_i|$	Especially relevant to discrete data Also known as the "city-block distance" as it sums the distances along each dimension (i.e., walking around the block)
Canberra	$\sum_{i}|x_i - y_i|/|x_i + y_i|$	Used where elements are always nonnegative. Note that elements are usually omitted if $|p_i| = |q_i|$
Binary	$s(x,A) = \max\{s : \forall I \subseteq [n], |I| \leq s, \exists y \in A,\ y|_I = x|_I\}\ s(x,\varnothing) = 0\forall x$	$x \in \{0,1\}^n$ is a vector where each entry represents the presence or absence of some factor of interest (e.g., a medical symptom). We are interested in the similarity of x and $A \subseteq \{0,1\}^n$
Pearson	$1 - \dfrac{\sum_i x_i y_i}{\sqrt{\sum_i x_i^2 \sum_i y_i^2}}$	Based on the Pearson correlation coefficient: calculated from instance values and their standard deviations. r takes values from -1 (large, negative correlation) to $+1$ (large, positive correlation)
		Effectively, the Pearson distance – dp – is computed as $dp = 1 - r$ and lies between 0 (when correlation coefficient is $+1$, i.e., the two samples are most similar) and 2 (when correlation coefficient is -1)
		Data is centered by subtracting the mean, and scaled by dividing by the standard deviation
		Note: the absolute value of the Pearson correlation coefficient can also be used; the corresponding distance lies between *0 and 1*, as for the correlation coefficient. Taking the absolute value gives equal meaning to positive and negative correlations, which causes anticorrelated samples to be clustered together
Correlation	$1 - r$ $1 - |r|$	This is the same as the Pearson correlation, except means are set to zero in the expression for

(continued)

Table 9.4   (continued)

Name	Definition	Use
		uncentered correlation. The uncentered correlation coefficient lies between -1 and $+1$, and the distance lies between **0 and 2**
		Similarly, the absolute correlation distance is the same as the Absolute Pearson correlation, except sample means are set to zero in the expression for uncentered correlation. The uncentered correlation coefficient lies between **0 and +1**; hence the distance lies between **0 and 1**
Spearman	$d_{ij} = \sum_{k=1}^{n} \left\| x_{ik} - x_{jk} \right\|$	Measures the absolute distance between two rank vectors
Kendall	$K(\tau_1, \tau_2) = \begin{vmatrix} (i,j) : i<j, \\ (\tau_1(i)<\tau_1(j) \wedge \tau_2(i)>\tau_2(j)) \\ \vee\, (\tau_1(i)>\tau_1(j) \wedge \tau_2(i)<\tau_2(j)) \end{vmatrix}$ $K(\tau, \tau) = 0$ $K(\tau, reverse(\tau)) = n(n-1)/2$	Useful in identifying samples with a huge deviation in a given dataset
Cosine similarity	$\dfrac{A \times B}{\|A\|\|B\|}$	Considers the relative differences between two instances, assuming that the scale is uniform. A type of Pearson measure. Can sometimes provide better results, especially if the data is not normally distributed
Mahalanobis	$D_M(x) = \sqrt{(x-\mu)^T S^{-1}(x-\mu)}$ $x = (x_1, ..., x_N)^T$ from a group of values with mean $\mu = (\mu_1, ..., \mu_N)^T$ and covariance matrix S	Often used to detect outliers, especially in developing linear regression models. It takes into account the correlations of the dataset and is (measurement) scale invariant

algorithm as the problem size – usually denoted by n – increases. The measure is typically in terms of time (or memory).

An exposition of performance is beyond the scope of this text, and the interested reader is directed to any good computer science text, which will include a full discussion on this topic. We raise it here only to point out it is one facet of the problem of building your model and one that can become important when we implement one or other similarity measure in our model. Selecting an appropriate measure is both a matter of functional appropriateness and performance issues.

9.11 Measuring Accuracy

Once we have designed, built, and trained our model, we are ready to put it into a production mode and allow it to process as yet unseen input instances. Say our model is aimed at classifying a person as having lung cancer or not based on chest radiographs: We now want to present it with information about patients that have not been used for training purposes so that it can help us in patient diagnosis. But we need to ask ourselves a question: if it diagnoses a patient as either having cancer, or not having cancer, how much can we rely on its conclusions?

In order to answer this question, we need to consider a methodology for defining an *accuracy* measure for our model. But first we need to consider the question of how accurate our model needs to be. This might seem an odd question because the intuitive answer is obviously as accurate as it can be, and this is our objective. However, we might be willing to accept a model that is 90% accurate if, for example, our analysis problem goal is to improve the accuracy surrounding the prostate-specific antigen test,[18] but we would want something significantly higher if our model is being used to diagnose a life-threatening medical condition.

Different models and different applications of the models will require different levels of accuracy. Thinking about this up front will aid us as we look at measuring the accuracy of our model and as we consider its sensitivity and specificity.

9.11.1 Classifiers

For any classifier model[19] C, we need to determine how accurate the model is. Our intuitive definition of accuracy is the percentage of cases that are appropriately classified. However, the obvious problem is how we get a measure of accuracy a priori. Further, if we have two classifier models, how can we determine which one is the "better" model? Since we can't wait until the end of its life, any measure we have will only be an estimate of its true accuracy, since that will not be known until we have stopped using the model, we now have the question of how do we define an appropriately accurate *estimate* of its accuracy (sic)?

We are really interested in determining an accuracy measure before we use the model in our real-world environment. This means that our measure of accuracy will typically be based upon what we discover during the training period. Our challenge here is that any such accuracy will be an optimistic estimate of the model's real performance since the model will not have been tried with any yet unseen input. For this reason, we often use a separate and distinct set of instances that were not used to train the model and use these to determine an accuracy measure.

---

[18] The current PSA test has 86% sensitivity, 33% specificity, and 41% predictive value (Hoffman et al. 2002 #337).

[19] This also applies to predictor models.

Table 9.5 Confusion matrix

		Predicted class	
		C_1	C_2
Actual class	C_1	True positive	False negative
	C_2	False positive	True negative

Using our intuitive statement above, we define the accuracy of a model C as the percentage of instances that it correctly classified. We will normalize this value so that we can define the error rate as $1 - \text{Accuracy}(C)$.

As mentioned above, if we use the training set to measure $\text{Accuracy}(C)$, the value we would get is going to be an optimistic value. Since the training set was used for...training, the model will have already been tuned, through the training process itself, to correctly classify the class of each of the input instances in the training set. Since we are concerned with ensuring that the model is not overfitted to the data, we would not expect 100% accuracy, however, we would expect a high value – higher than would be seen once it is put into a production mode. Thus, rather than using this value – sometimes referred to as the *resubstitution error* – we use the independent set of instances that we mentioned above. We call this independent instance set the *validation set* for the model.

Since we can select the instances for the validation set, we will also know the classification for each instance. In this case, our accuracy measure will be closer to reality. As is the case with the training set, we need to ensure a valid cross section of values so that the accuracy measure is not skewed far from the distribution of instances we would expect to see in the future.

Correctly classifying values naturally results in four possible values for any given model C and instance I:

- C correctly positively classifies I.
  I is a true positive. For example, a patient is **correctly** classified as **having** a particular condition.
- C incorrectly positively classifies I.
  I is a false positive. For example, a patient is **incorrectly** classified as **having** a particular condition.
- C correctly negatively classifies I.
  I is a true negative. For example, a patient is **correctly** classified as **not having** a particular condition.
- C incorrectly negatively classifies I.
  I is a false negative. For example, a patient is **incorrectly** classified as **not having** a particular condition.

We can depict this generically in Table 9.5, for two classes C_1 and C_2.

Let us consider an example. In Oken et al. (2005 #137), chest radiographs were used to detect lung cancer. A total of 5,991 radiographs identified anomalies that required further examination, at which time 126 were found to actually have lung cancer. If *"has lung cancer"* is our C_1 class, the number of true positives is 126, and

Table 9.6 Confusion matrix (partial completion)

		Predicted class	
		Lung cancer	No lung cancer
Actual class	Lung cancer	126	a
	No lung cancer	5,865	8
	Total	5,991	

[a] We cannot fill in this column since the data on how many people were not predicted to have lung cancer but which subsequently were found to have lung cancer was not published in Oken et al. (2005 #137)

the number of false positives is $5991 - 126 = 5865$. We can use this information to fill in part of our confusion matrix for this study, as shown in Table 9.6.

In general, for m classes, our confusion matrix will be an $m \times m$ table. We would ideally want the majority of our instances to be represented in the leading diagonal (top left to bottom right), with the remaining entries being as close to zero as possible. Where this is not the case, it is a good visual indicator of the (lack of) accuracy of the model.

As most readers will already be thinking, this is not the end of the story. A model that has an accuracy measure of, say, 90% will, at first blush, appear to be reasonably accurate. For example, if our lung cancer model was able to accurately classify patients as having, or not having cancer, to the tune of 90%, we might be tempted to think of it as being reasonably accurate. However, if a very small percentage of our training instances were actually instances of patients that had cancer, we have to question whether our model is acceptable. It may well be, for example, that our model is only correctly classifying instances where the patient does *not* have cancer, a definitely unacceptable situation.

We have already met the concepts of sensitivity, specificity, and precision, and they come into play when measuring accuracy here as well. These measures are defined as

$$sensitivity = \frac{true\,positives}{positives}$$

$$specificity = \frac{true\,negatives}{negatives}$$

$$precision = \frac{true\,positives}{(true\,positives + false\,positives)}$$

Using these measures, we typically define *accuracy* as

$$accuracy = sensitivity \frac{positives}{(positives + negatives)} + specificity$$
$$\times \frac{negatives}{(positives + negatives)}$$

Before we leave the discussion about accuracy, there is one more important fact we need to be cognizant of: incorrectly classifying a cancerous patient as not cancerous (false negative) is much more concerning that of classifying a noncancerous patient as cancerous (false positive). In the latter, more conservative case, the patient's condition will typically be followed up on; in the former case, it may go undetected. This distinction is often taken into account by weighing the risks/gains (costs/benefits) of the model and weight false negatives and false positives to provide us with a better sense as to the merits of the model.

9.11.1.1 Receiver Operating Characteristic (ROC) Analysis

We can see that *sensitivity* and *specificity* provide us with measures that describe our classifier model's performance with greater clarity than *accuracy*. However, this also means that for any given classifier model, we have two measures to consider: one for positive cases and one for negative cases. We can generate a compound measure by using Receiver Operating Characteristic (ROC) analysis from signal detection theory.

We use *confidence thresholds* as part of our definition for the classification task. For a *strict* threshold, we are looking for **high** specificity and **low** sensitivity. For a not so strict threshold, we lower the specificity and allow the sensitivity to rise. Thus, we can compare two classifier models over as wide a range of thresholds as we like and generate an ROC curve that plots the true positive rate against false positive rates, or by plotting *sensitivity* against $1 - specificity$. The straight line going from the bottom left to the top right represents performance expected due to pure chance. A perfect classifier would follow the y-axis and the upper axis. The reality is somewhere in between and is located above the chance performance line.

From Sing et al. (2005 #138), using their ROCR.hiv dataset[20] from the ROCR package for R, the following ROC curve is obtained.

In addition to the R package (ROCR), Bioconductor and Weka are two other environments that provide functionality to produce ROC curves. For more details on these software projects, see Appendix B.

9.11.2 Predictors

Prediction models differ from classifiers, as we have seen, since they provide a continuous value as opposed to a classification label. If our model returns a value of 0.5, say, how accurate is this value? If our test dataset comprises n instances of the form $(\mathbf{X}_i, y_i)$, where y_i is the response variable value for the ith instance, we can

---

[20] Linear support vector machines and neural networks applied to predict usage of the coreceptors CCR5 and CXCR4 based on sequence data of the third variable loop of the HIV envelope protein.

look at the difference between this value and the value predicted by our model, which we will denote by y'_i. In the figure below, the gray points are the values predicted by our model (the y'_i), whereas the black points are the response variable values (the y_i).[21] Measuring the difference between these two values is accomplished using a *loss function*. The most common loss functions used are measured using *absolute error* or *squared error*. *Absolute error* is, as its name suggests, the difference between the response variable value and the predicted value with any minus sign removed: $|y_i - y'_i|$. *Squared error* squares the difference between the response variable value and the predicted value: $(y_i - {}'_i)^2$.

We can use these functions to determine the *generalization error* or the *test error* by averaging the loss function over the complete test set to give us the *mean absolute error* or the *mean squared error*:

Mean absolute error: $\dfrac{\sum\limits_{i=1}^{n} |y_i - y'_i|}{n}$

Mean squared error: $\dfrac{\sum\limits_{i=1}^{n} (y_i - y'_i)^2}{n}$

We often use a variation on the second equation above since it has a tendency to exaggerate any outliers in our dataset due to the squaring function by taking the square root to form the *root mean squared error*:

Root mean squared error: $\sqrt{\dfrac{\sum\limits_{i=1}^{n} (y_i - y'_i)^2}{n}}$

There may be valid reasons for considering the error relative to the mean value for the y_is. In such cases, we can divide the mean error by the appropriate loss incurred if we compared against the mean value. That is,

Mean absolute error: $\dfrac{\sum\limits_{i=1}^{n} |y_i - y'_i|}{\sum\limits_{i=1}^{n} |y_i - \bar{y}|}$, and

Mean squared error: $\dfrac{\sum\limits_{i=1}^{n} (y_i - y'_i)^2}{\sum\limits_{i=1}^{n} (y_i - \bar{y})^2}$, respectively, where $\bar{y} = \dfrac{\sum\limits_{i=1}^{n} y_i}{n}$.

9.11.3 *Evaluating Accuracy*

Armed with our discussion above, we can now consider how we can use these measures in order to obtain a valid and valuable measure of the accuracy of our model. We'll discuss three common techniques for assessing accuracy of models: random subsampling, cross-validation, and bootstrap. There is, in fact, a fourth common technique that we have already discussed: holdout. *Holdout* is where we

---

[21] We have joined the pairs by lines simply for identification.

create a training dataset (or test dataset) and a separate validation dataset, typically by randomly partitioning our available dataset into two. The validation set will typically be significantly smaller than that used for training, for obvious reasons. One interesting fact is that the accuracy estimate generated by the validation set is actually a pessimistic estimate of its accuracy. Why?[22]

In *random subsampling*, we take the above concept further by performing the holdout method some number of times. Each time we randomly select the subset of instances to be used as the validation set. Note that through this technique, we are effectively generating a new classifier or predictor each time since we are using a different subset of the available data for training in each iteration. Also note that the test datasets are independent and randomly selected in this method.

In *cross-validation*, we extend our ideas of partitioning the test dataset a little further. Here, we take the complete training dataset and partition it into some number, say k, of mutually exclusive subsets, each of which is of (approximately) equal size. We then perform k iterations of training and validation, using one of the partitions for validation and the other k-1 for testing. If we have our dataset partitioned into subsets $D_1, ..., D_k$, on iteration 1, we might reserve D_1 for validation and train using $D_2, ..., D_k$; for iteration 2, we might reserve D_2 for validation and train using $D_1, D_3, ..., D_k$, and so on for the remaining k-2 iterations. The end result is that each partition is used k-1 times for training and once for validation. We then denote the accuracy of the classifier by taking the number of correct classifications from all k iterations and divide it by the number of instances in the original dataset. For predictors, we divide the total loss by the number of instances. A special case of this is the so-called *leave-one-out* where only one instance is left out at any given time. This technique provides an unbiased estimator for the classifier or predictor. However, the variance can be very high – especially for small sample sizes.

Cross-validation is somewhat computationally expensive, which is ever becoming less of a problem, but should be borne in mind if you decide to use this technique.[23] This is a superior approach and is well documented (see Kohavi 1995 #377; Picard and Cook 1984 #378; Efron and Tibshirani 1997 #379, among others), and is an almost unbiased estimator of the true error rate of a classifier. Thus, over many different sample sets, the estimate will tend toward the true error rate.

---

[22] Since we are actually reducing the training data available for training the model, the model will not be able to take advantage of the additional instances that we have kept aside for validation. The model will therefore typically be less accurate than if it had access to the additional (validation) instances.

[23] This needs a little elaboration. Computational costs continue to reduce while the computational capabilities of environments available to researchers increase in both power and availability. As the cloud computing concept builds up steam, such environments may well become ubiquitous. However, creative projects have been available for some time to allow enterprising souls to build their own supercomputers, even from Sony Playstation PS3s!!! See http://blogs.zdnet.com/storage/?p=184, http://blogs.zdnet.com/storage/?p=220, and http://www.wired.com/techbiz/it/news/2007/10/ps3_supercomputer for more information.

How do we find the best estimator when we have small samples? For example, in many phase I studies, the number of patients is very small.[24] As we've indicated above, both bias and variance play a part in the accuracy and precision, or more importantly the inaccuracy and imprecision, of the error rate estimate. Since cross-validation techniques are unbiased but tend to have large variances for small samples, and this effect tends to dominate in small samples, we can use some *bootstrap* techniques to help us out.

One of the significant differences between the *bootstrapping* method and those we have discussed so far is that we *replace* each selected instance into the overall dataset so that it is equally likely to be selected a subsequent time. As one might guess, this methodology is referred to as *sampling with replacement*. There are many that have yielded good results for classification problems, and we shall consider one of the more commonly used methods: the .632 bootstrap.

We generate a training dataset consisting of n instances sampled *with replacement* from a sample of size n, selecting one instance from our dataset, placing a copy in our training dataset, and returning the instance back into our original dataset. Consider, for example, a dataset containing 100 instances. We randomly select one instance from the initial 100, place a copy in our training set, and return the original to the dataset. We continue this process until we have the same number of instances in our training dataset as we had in the original dataset. Instances in our original dataset that were not selected for our training dataset form the validation dataset. The error rate on the validation dataset is the bootstrap estimator.

As we can see, by replacing each instance back into our original dataset, there is a good possibility that an instance will be selected for inclusion in our training dataset more than once. Actually, if we try this process a number of times, it turns out that the average or expected fraction of nonrepeated cases in the training group is .632, that is, 63.2% of the original dataset will end up in our training dataset, and the expected fraction of such cases in the validation dataset is .368 (or 36.8%). Where do we get these percentages from?

If we are interested in generating a training dataset of n instances, from an original dataset of n instances, each instance has a probability of $\frac{1}{n}$ of being selected, and $\left(1 - \frac{1}{n}\right)$ of not being selected. Since we are doing this n times, to get a training dataset of n instances, the total probability of any specific instance not being selected is $\left(1 - \frac{1}{n}\right)^n$. The number e is defined as $e = \lim_{n \to \infty} \left(1 - \frac{1}{n}\right)^n$, from which we can deduce a value for $e^{-1} = \lim_{n \to \infty} \left(1 - \frac{1}{n}\right)^n$. We can therefore see that as n gets larger, our probability $\left(1 - \frac{1}{n}\right)^n$ tends to the value for e^{-1}, and $e^{-1} = 0.368$.

We typically repeat the sampling procedure over some number of iterations, k. In each iteration, we will use our current validation dataset to generate an accuracy

---

[24] We will take the traditional measure of "small" as being a sample of less than 30 cases.

measure for the model based on the current bootstrap training dataset. We can then generate an overall accuracy measure as shown below:

$$Accuracy(M) = \sum_{i=1}^{k} \left(0.632 \times Accuracy(M_i)_{validation\_dataset} \right.$$

$$\left. + 0.368 \times Accuracy(M_i)_{training\_dataset} \right)$$

where our notation $Accuracy(M_i)_{validation\_dataset}$ is a measure of the accuracy of the model M obtained using the bootstrap sample from the ith iteration when it is applied to the validation dataset used for that ith iteration.[25] Similarly, $Accuracy(M_i)_{training\_dataset}$ is a measure of the model's accuracy, obtained from the ith iteration when applied to the original instance dataset.

An advantage of the bootstrap method is that it works very well with small sample sizes. The .632 bootstrap method is a low variance estimator, which is typical of bootstrap methods in general.[26] Since, on average, such classifiers will be trained on only 63.2% of the instances available for training, these methods tend to be biased pessimistically for moderately sized datasets, as is the case with the e0 method. But the e0 method provides good results when the true error rate is high. The .632 bootstrap is biased optimistically as the sample size grows, but it provides good results when the true error rate is relatively low.

9.11.4   Improving Classifier/Predictor Accuracy

There are several generalized approaches we can take to improving the accuracy of classifiers and predictors, most of which use a combination of methods in order to improve the accuracy. Such approaches are therefore called *ensemble methods*[27]. Two widely used methods are *bagging* and *boosting*. In essence, ensemble methods take some number of individual learned models, $M_1, ..., M_k$, and use these models with the goal of developing an improved model, M_+.

Bagging can be illustrated by using a simple analogy: if you have a problem with your car that you want to have diagnosed, you might elect to ask not one mechanic, but several. If one particular diagnosis of the problem occurs most often, you can take this diagnosis as your best diagnosis – the majority vote principle; one mechanic, one (equally weighted) vote. If we now consider classifiers,[28] we use

---

[25] Recall that the validation dataset comprises those instances not selected for training.

[26] Another method, the e0 estimator, is similar.

[27] Also referred to as "perturb and combine," or "committee of experts" methods.

[28] Or predictors.

bootstrap aggregation (a.k.a. bagging) where we sample a training set, D_i, of instances (with replacement) from our original training dataset. We then build our classifier model, M_i, as we have described above. Once we have our set of classifiers, we can try to classify an as yet unseen instance I, with each classifier (model) returning its classification for this instance. The aggregate model, M_+, will simply count the various classifications and assign the class with the most votes to I.

The accuracy of the bagging model comes from the fact that the aggregate model M_+ reduces the variances of the individual classifiers. For predictors, there is a proof that a bagged predictor is more accurate than a single predictor (Breiman 1996 #139).

Boosting is similar to bagging except that we now assign *weights* to the values returned by each classifier/predictor. Returning to our car analogy, there may be a couple of mechanics we trust, some we don't know, and some we are ambivalent toward. The ones we trust will naturally provide us with diagnoses we count more highly.

9.12   Conclusion

Where we began was in defining our objective with classification, for categorical data, and prediction, for real-valued data: to be able to accept a before-unseen instance and accurately position it within our universe. In the simplest case, this is to place it in one of two categories of input. Thus, the problem is very easy to define.

As the complexity of our objectives increase, and the complexity of our data – both in how we want to partition the data and in the dimensionality – this simple problem takes on manifest complexity, with a broad range of tools being available for us to use.

One challenge we have to overcome is the issue of accuracy. While this is an issue whether our data is categorical or continuous, it holds an order of magnitude higher complexity in the continuous space since the difference between two instances that are at the boundary between two regions may be very small indeed. Unfortunately, and commonly, the computational cost and complexity similarly increases: increases at a rate that may be too costly for our project's objectives.

In one sense, this is often the greatest challenge when building classification/ prediction models for data mining: being able to determine the stopping point. As the size of our dataset increases, the "empty space" between our clusters shrinks and we have to be careful not to try and paint with too broad a brush, in which case multiple clusters can end up being seen as one. However, the converse is also true, and we need to be careful that we're not trying to paint a wall with too small a brush.

As is always the case, there is a trade-off, and the challenge is to find it. What can we safely ignore? Can we exclude instance attributes from our analysis? What can we simplify? Can we transform some of our attributes into a binary representation? Can we combine some of them into one without loss of significant information?

For clustering and prediction, as we have seen, similarity (or dissimilarity) is an important concept: but how similar is similar? We use some form of distance measure to help us determine this. But once again, the challenge manifests itself: when does a distance measure become significant (i.e., they are dissimilar and should be partitioned into different clusters) and when is it insignificant (i.e., they are similar and are in the same cluster)?

Tools available in most analytical environments provide an easy way of trying out a couple of different approaches to see how they fit. Intuition can be as valuable a tool as well, especially in the early stages. Often, if something doesn't seem to look right, it isn't. For example, using a simple clustering algorithm such as k-means, a ubiquitous piece of functionality, will allow you to quickly try out models with different numbers of clusters and see what the results look like.

Finally, remember that we will typically have some set of data for which we already know the results. Try your models against those datasets and their known results. What is valuable for other techniques, such as neural networks, is true here also: validation sets with known results can be a very powerful tool in the arsenal, allowing you to quickly see how accurate your model is.

Readers arriving at this point may be a little disappointed that our example applications were somewhat "classic" in nature and that more up-to-date applications such as systems biology and pharmacology, next-generation sequencing data analysis, eQTL, functional module identification, and the like were not described. We elected to defer discussion of these until later in the text, under Systems Biology.

References

Baladandayuthapani V et al (2008) Bayesian hierarchical spatially correlated functional data analysis with application to colon carcinogenesis. Biometrics 64:64–73

Berger JO (1993) Statistical decision theory and Bayesian analysis, Springer series in statistics. Springer, New York

Bishop CM (1995) Neural networks for pattern recognition. Clarendon Press/Oxford University Press, Oxford/New York

Breiman L (1996) Bagging predictors. Mach Learn 24:123–140

Cheeseman P (1988) AutoClass: a Bayesian classification system. In: Fifth international conference on machine learning. Morgan Kauffman, Ann Arbor, pp 54–64

Cheeseman P (1990) On finding the most probable model. In: Shrager J, Langley P (eds) Computational models of scientific discovery and theory formation. Morgan Kauffman, Palo Alto, pp 73–96

Cheeseman P, Stutz J (1996) Bayesian classification (AutoClass): theory and results. In: Advances in knowledge discovery and data mining. American Association for Artificial Intelligence, Menlo Park, pp 153–180

Dalgaard P (2002) Introductory statistics with R. In: Statistics and computing. Springer, New York

Duda RO, Hart PE, Stork DG (2001) Pattern classification. Wiley, New York

Efron B, Tibshirani R (1997) Improvements on cross-validation: the .632+ Bootstrap method. J Am Stat Assoc 92:548–560

Engelman JA et al (2007) MET amplification leads to Gefitinib resistance in lung cancer by activating ERBB3 signaling. Science 316:1039–1043

Fisher DH (1987) Knowledge acquisition via incremental conceptual clustering. Mach Learn 2:139–172

Fraley C, Raftery AE (1998) How many clusters? which clustering method? Answers via model-based cluster analysis. Comput J 41:578–588

Geiger D, Paz A, Pearl J (1990) Learning causal trees from dependence information, AAAI 1990. MIT Press, Boston, pp 770–776

Han X (2006) Inferring species phylogenies: a microarray approach. In: Computational intelligence and bioinformatics: international conference on intelligent computing, ICIC 2006, Kunming, China. Springer, Berlin/Heidelberg, pp 485–493

Hanson R, Stutz J, Cheeseman P (1991) Bayesian classification theory. NASA Ames Research Center, Moffett Field

Haughton D, Legrand P, Woolford S (2009) Review of three latent class cluster analysis packages: Latent Gold, poLCA, and MCLUST. Am Stat 63:81–91

Hoffman R et al (2002) Prostate-specific antigen testing accuracy in community practice. BMC Fam Pract 3:19

Holte RC (1993) Very simple classification rules perform well on most commonly used datasets. Mach Learn 11:63–91

Hori K, Furumoto S, Kubota K (2008) Tumor blood flow interruption after radiotherapy strongly inhibits tumor regrowth. Cancer Sci 99:1485–1491

Jain RK (1988) Determinants of tumor blood flow: a review. Cancer Res 48:2641–2658

Kohavi R (1995) A study of cross-validation and bootstrap for accuracy estimation and model selection. In: International joint conference on artificial intelligence 1995. Morgan Kaufmann, San Francisco, pp 1137–1143

Lu H, Setiono R, Liu H (1996) Effective data mining using neural networks. IEEE Trans Knowl Data Eng 8:957–961

MacKay DJC (1992) The evidence framework applied to classification networks. Neural Comput 4:720–736

MacQueen J (1967) Some methods for classification and analysis of multivariate observations. In: Cam LML, Neyman J (eds) Fifth Berkeley symposium on mathematical statistics and probability. University of California Press, Berkeley, pp 281–297

Medvedovic M, Sivaganesan S (2002) Bayesian infinite mixture model based clustering of gene expression profiles. Bioinformatics 18:1194–1206

Medvedovic M, Yeung KY, Bumgarner RE (2004) Bayesian mixture model based clustering of replicated microarray data. Bioinformatics 20:1222–1232

Ng SK et al (2006) A Mixture model with random-effects components for clustering correlated gene-expression profiles. Bioinformatics 22:1745–1752

Oken MM et al (2005) Baseline chest radiograph for lung cancer detection in the randomized prostate, lung, colorectal and ovarian cancer screening trial. J Natl Cancer Inst 97:1832–1839

Picard RR, Cook RD (1984) Cross-validation of regression models. J Am Stat Assoc 79:575–583

Prentice AM, Jebb SA (2001) Beyond body mass index. Obes Rev 2:141–147

Qin ZS (2006) Clustering microarray gene expression data using weighted Chinese restaurant process. Bioinformatics 22:1988–1997

Sing T et al (2005) ROCR: visualizing classifier performance in R. Bioinformatics 21:3940–3941

Tadesse MG, Sha N, Vannucci M (2005) Bayesian variable selection in clustering high-dimensional data. J Am Stat Assoc 100:602–617

Wang JT-L et al (1994) Combinatorial pattern discovery for scientific data: some preliminary results. In: Proceedings of the 1994 ACM SIGMOD international conference on management of data. ACM, Minneapolis, pp 115–125

Wang JTL et al (2000) Application of neural networks to biological data mining: a case study in protein sequence classification. In: Proceedings of the sixth ACM SIGKDD international conference on knowledge discovery and data mining. ACM, Boston, pp 305–309

Wu CH, McLarty JW (2000) Neural networks and genome informatics, vol 1, Methods in computational biology and biochemistry. Elsevier, Amsterdam/New York

Xiang Z, Qin ZS, He Y (2007) CRCView: a web server for analyzing and visualizing microarray gene expression data using model-based clustering. Bioinformatics 23:1843–1845

Yeung KY et al (2001) Model-based clustering and data transformations for gene expression data. Bioinformatics 17:977–987

Zheng F et al (2009) Computational neural network analysis of the affinity of N-n-alkylnicotinium salts for the α4β2* nicotinic acetylcholine receptor. J Enzyme Inhib Med Chem 24:157–168

Chapter 10
Informatics

Abstract Bioinformatics, chemoinformatics, and immunoinformatics are just three of the associated focus areas for informatics within the life sciences, but as a discipline, informatics is much broader which includes human-computer interaction, information sciences, and information technology, in addition to specific subject matter, such as life sciences. In this chapter, we are trying to provide an overview to how informatics and data mining intersect, using some example areas such as genomic and proteomic data and its sources, how data in different formats is integrated, and how annotations are incorporated into our analyses. In addition, we touch on some of the more common tools and databases, along with some of the ontologies such as the gene ontology that we've discussed earlier in this text. Microarray data, the use of regular expressions with restriction enzymes, and DNA analysis in the form of alignment are examined in more depth.

10.1 Introduction

A tremendous amount of data mining research is occurring at the confluence of machine learning, statistics, genomics, proteomics, computational biology, computer science, and other areas of artificial intelligence to name a few of the disciplines involved.

Systems biology has seen a tremendous boost from the advent of high-throughput technologies, which has resulted in a significant increase in the amount of biological data generated. More and more, we will depend upon generalized predictive models along with their capacity to integrate multiple information resources where the data is complex, distributed, and heterogeneous. The models we develop, however, are often associated with specific levels of the biological organization, and so we must also continue to improve our understanding of how to integrate such data.

As we have stated elsewhere in this book, generalization is the ability to make predictions about yet unseen data. But as we have also stated, we must be careful to

R. Sullivan, *Introduction to Data Mining for the Life Sciences*,
DOI 10.1007/978-1-59745-290-8_10, © Springer Science+Business Media, LLC 2012

ensure that the architecture, parameters, and training data do not lead to overfitting the model to the training data, leading to the situation where the model performs badly in its intended predictive function.

Earlier in this text, we introduced machine-learning techniques, how they are being used in many areas of the life sciences, and how the intersection with data mining provides a significant opportunity. In this chapter and subsequent chapters, we focus more specifically on how data mining in the informatics space can support our efforts.

Applying techniques from mathematics, computer science, and statistics to biological concepts allows us to analyze molecular data expressed as nucleotides, amino acids, DNA, RNA, peptides, and proteins. But by the very nature of this data, techniques must not only be able to process vast amounts of data but also to understand that data. Data mining, and the application of machine-learning techniques, has provided significant opportunity and value in this area. Applications include microarray analysis, genome, proteome, and chromosome database analysis, modeling of inhibition in metabolic networks, and pattern recognition in biomedical data, to name a few.

We need efficient techniques which can *elicit* knowledge from this vast breadth of data. Every day, the amount of this data generated increases, requiring us to develop evermore efficient methods for eliciting the knowledge (often) hidden in the data.

In this chapter, we're going to touch on some of the techniques and considerations more oriented toward providing value in mining data from the –omics disciplines. Genomics, proteomics, and the other subjects provide an intersection with bioinformatics, chemoinformatics, immunoinformatics, and related subjects. These subdisciplines continue to undergo significant refinement and expansion as the whole area of systems biology matures.

The nature of the data generated from these disciplines is usually provided to analysts in one of the restricted alphabets that we've already encountered and discussed. By their nature, the amount of data generated is often much larger than we would typically consider for an individual result. Whereas a CBC typically generates less than 20 data values, a microarray can generate tens of thousands of data points. If we multiply this by some "patient" population, the amount of data increases significantly. If this is repeated at several time points. . .well, you get the picture.

One technology that has radically altered the landscape in this arena has been microarray technology, a technology now readily available to researchers. We leave detailed discussion on this technology until later but highlight one facet of this technology: microarrays such as the Affymetrix GeneChip® Human X3P Array can now perform whole-genome expression profiling. Microarray technology has seen a wide and varied adoption since its inception. For example, Vrana et al. (2002 #391) illustrated a number of uses in toxicology. A quick search of PubMed[1] reveals a

---

[1] http://www.ncbi.nlm.nih.gov/pubmed?term=microarray%20uses&itool=QuerySuggestion

Table 10.1 Some common genomic data types and representations

Data type	Alphabet	Representation
DNA	{A, C, G, T}	String
mRNA	{A, C, G,U}	String
Protein	{A, R, N, D, C, E, Q, G, H, I, L, K, M, F, P, S, T, W, Y, V, B, Z, J, X}[a]	String
ESTs[b]	{A, C, G, U}	String

[a]The last four letters {B, Z, J, X} designate ambiguous amino acids
[b]Expressed sequence tags: partial mRNA sequences

valuable and illustrative list of research disciplines which currently gain value from this important technology.

DNA and RNA sequences constitute the classic molecular biology data type and are widely available via a growing number of publicly available databases. The sequencing activity to generate these sequences has become highly automated and is adding to our body of knowledge at a significant rate. Primary structures for proteins are similarly available and, from a data-mining perspective, differ in the *alphabet* that they use, as shown in Table 10.1.

These are by no means the only data types that are used. Structural data such as for macromolecules and metabolites is often represented as labeled 3-D graphs, interactions are often represented as graphs or Petri-nets, expression data may be delivered as vectors or matrices, and, of course, articles, abstracts, and the like are represented as natural language. To cover all of these types of data and their associated techniques is a significant task in its own right and, from the perspective of introducing data mining, may not be encountered as often as common sequence data. We will therefore limit our discussions in this book to mining sequence data of the form depicted in Table 10.1.[2]

10.1.1   Sources of Genomic and Proteomic Data

Sequencing systems are available from a wide variety of manufacturers and are in use by a substantial proportion of companies in the life sciences. Thus, more and more sequences are being generated in-house. However, much of the work being conducted in this area enhances the publicly available body of knowledge by submitting sequence data and annotations to the public repositories such as GenBank, Protein Data Bank, and the host of other repositories currently maintained. For this reason, much of the data-mining efforts in the genomic and proteomic space will require our incorporating data from these external repositories.

---

[2] We hope to expand upon this important area in a future publication.

Such sources of data provide their own challenges in that our internal data repository will almost invariably comprise not only a different technology set but also a different data representation for the sequence data we are dealing with (for example). We will consider some of these issues in the next section. The source(s) that will be used in your data-mining efforts may play a large part in where the most significant issues lie. Questions such as how many external sources do we need? How does the different data format used by each source play into the equation? Do we need to setup intermediary processes to first standardize and normalize the data before incorporating the data into our repository? How often does/will the data change? How do we determine whether or not these changes are significant? Although these questions are ones that we have discussed earlier in this book, they have specific issues in the genomic and proteomic spaces.

10.2   Data Integration

We have discussed data integration elsewhere in this book as it relates to the very general and, in some respects, to the very specific issues that arise from data mining. In today's scientific and data-mining environment, molecular biology resources are distributed across an interconnected network of related databases.[3] Maintaining the linkages and cross-references between these databases is a significant task and is often accomplished through a manual curation effort.

Such linkages, however, are a vitally important component of the overall data architecture, especially as it relates to more advanced mining and integration strategies. However, as Azuaje and Dopazo (2005 #20) stated, these introduce opportunities that are also challenges, including:

* Establishing the identity of common objects and concepts
* Integrating data described in different formats
* Resolving conflicts between different resources
* Synchronizing data stored in the different data repositories
* Presenting a unified view of the data

Data integration needs to resolve differences in syntax, semantics, and nomenclature since different resources describe data in different formats. This is a formidable challenge in its own right and is compounded when we consider the specialized tools and processes used to access data from specific sources.

Compounding this problem even more has been the development of high-throughput techniques to study the proteome and transcriptome, an issue we don't see going away any time soon. Since many equipment manufacturers use their own

---

[3] The website www.lsdm.org maintains a partial list of these databases.

standards and formats, we may conceivably be dealing with as many different formats of data as we have manufacturer's equipment within the enterprise.

To address this, several groups have come together to propose standards that have been successfully adopted by the industry as a whole. A good example of this can be seen in the area of microarrays. The *minimal information about a microarray experiment* (MIAME) defines the information that necessarily describes a microarray experiment. Out of these efforts has come the *microarray gene expression markup language* (MAGE-ML) format that has been used as an integration format by many groups.

10.2.1 Integrating Annotations for a Common Sequence

Annotations are often associated with specific parts, or regions, of a gene or protein sequence. We will often need to combine together all of the annotations defined in different data repositories. So long as the individual repositories are in agreement as to the sequence itself, and the coordinate system is compatible, we can reliably bring the individual annotations together. The *distributed annotation server* (DAS) protocol was developed to facilitate this. However, many repositories – including corporate repositories – will use their own system for defining the sequence and coordinates. This poses particular challenges since the annotations incorporate a significant amount of knowledge that we wish to elicit as part of our data-mining efforts.

10.2.2 Data in Different Formats

Some of the issues to do with data integration and formats for the data sources have different issues when looking at sequence data, trees, and graphs. These issues, in turn, are somewhat different to the issues associated with vector and matrix data that constitutes "expression" data (gene expression, protein expression, metabolite expression, etc.). However, some of the basic problems we discussed in Chaps. 2–5 also do not apply since many repositories of data, and many systems that conduct the experiment, have standardized on how they generate, store, or communicate the information.

With this in mind, the challenge is often how to store and process the data when it arrives into our mining environment. For example, if we look at the GenBank data for the human p53 protein mRNA, the entry is as shown in Fig. 10.1.

Thus, any information to be integrated from GenBank will need to be able to process the salient details out of the above file format. Consider the same accession (AF307851) but returning the data in FASTA format (Fig. 10.2).

As we can see, these two formats provide a very different layout and would need different tools to process them. If we need to extract information from public

```
LOCUS           AF307851                2521 bp    mRNA    linear   PRI 29-JAN-2001
DEFINITION      Homo sapiens p53 protein mRNA, complete cds.
ACCESSION       AF307851
VERSION         AF307851.1  GI:11066969
KEYWORDS        .
SOURCE          Homo sapiens (human)
  ORGANISM      Homo sapiens
                Eukaryota; Metazoa; Chordata; Craniata; Vertebrata; Euteleostomi;
                Mammalia; Eutheria; Euarchontoglires; Primates; Haplorrhini;
                Catarrhini; Hominidae; Homo.
REFERENCE       1  (bases 1 to 2521)
  AUTHORS       Chang,N.S., Pratt,N., Heath,J., Schultz,L., Sleve,D., Carey,G.B.
                and Zevotek,N.
  TITLE         Hyaluronidase induction of a WW domain-containing oxidoreductase
                that enhances tumor necrosis factor cytotoxicity
  JOURNAL       J. Biol. Chem. 276 (5), 3361-3370 (2001)
   PUBMED       11058590
REFERENCE       2  (bases 1 to 2521)
  AUTHORS       Chang,N.-S., Pratt,N. and Heath,J.
  TITLE         Direct Submission
  JOURNAL       Submitted (21-SEP-2000) Laboratory of Molecular Immunology, Guthrie
                Research Institute, 1 Guthrie Square, Sayre, PA 18840, USA
FEATURES             Location/Qualifiers
     source          1..2521
                     /organism="Homo sapiens"
                     /mol_type="mRNA"
                     /db_xref="dbEST:AI243172"
                     /db_xref="taxon:9606"
                     /clone="IMAGE:1847162"
     CDS             136..1317
                     /codon_start=1
                     /product="p53 protein"
                     /protein_id="AAG28785.1"
                     /db_xref="GI:11066970"
                     /translation="MEEPQSDPSVEPPLSQETFSDLWKLLPENNVLSPLPSQAMDDLM
                     LSPDDIEQWFTEDPGPDEAPRMPEAAPRVAPAPAAPTPAAPAPAPSWPLSSSVPSQKT
                     YQGSYGFRLGFLHSGTAKSVTCTYSPALNKMFCQLAKTCPVQLWVDSTPPPGTRVRAM
                     AIYKQSQHMTEVVRRCPHHERCSDSDGLAPPQHLIRVEGNLRVEYLDDRNTFRHSVVV
                     PYEPPEVGSDCTTIHYNYMCNSSCMGGMNRRPILTIITLEDSSGNLLGRNSFEVRVCA
                     CPGRDRRTEEENLRKKGEPHHELPPGSTKRALPNNTSSSPQPKKKPLDGEYFTLQIRG
                     RERFEMFRELNEALELKDAQAGKEPGGSRAHSSHLKSKKGQSTSRHKKLMFKTEGPDS
                     D"
ORIGIN
        1 ggcacgagcc accgtccagg gagcaggtag ctgctgggct ccggggacac tttgcgttcg
       61 ggctgggagc gtgctttcca cgacggtgac acgcttccct ggattggcag ccagactgcc
      121 ttccgggtca ctgccatgga ggagccgcag tcagatccta gcgtcgagcc ccctctgagt
      181 caggaaacat tttcagacct atggaaacta cttcctgaaa acaacgttct gtcccccttg
      241 ccgtcccaag caatggatga tttgatgctg tccccggacg atattgaaca atggttcact
      301 gaagacccag gtccagatga agctcccaga atgccagagg ctgctccccg cgtggcccct
      361 gcaccagcag ctcctacacc ggcggccccc tgcaccagcc cctcctggcc cctgtcatct
      421 tctgtccctt cccagaaaac ctaccagggc agctacggtt tccgtctggg cttcttgcat
      481 tctgggacag ccaagtctgt gacttgcaca tactcccctg ccctcaacaa gatgttttgc
      541 caactggcca agacctgccc tgtgcagctg tgggttgatt ccacacccc gcccggccac
      601 cgcgtccgcg ccatggccat ctacaagcag tacagccgtg ccgtggaggt tgtgaggcgc
      661 tgcccccacc atgagccgct ctcagatagc gatggtctgg ccccctcctca gcatcttatc
      721 cgagtggaag gaaatttgcg tgtggagtat ttggatgaca gaaacacttt tcgacatagt
      781 gtggtggtgc cctatgagcc gcctgaggtt ggctctgact gtaccaccat ccactacaac
      841 tacatgtgta acagttcctg catgggcggc atgaaccgga ggcccatcct caccatcatc
      901 acactggaag actccagtgg taatctactg ggacggaaca gctttgaggt gcgtgtttgt
      961 gcctgtcctg ggagagaccg gcgcacagag gaagagaatc tccgcaagaa agggggagcct
     1021 caccacgagc tgcccccagg gagcactaag cgagcactgc ccaacaacac cagctcctct
     1081 cccagccaa agaagaaacc actggatgga gaatatttca cccttcagat ccgtgggcgt
     1141 gagcgcttcg agatgttccg agagctgaat gaggccttga aactcaagga tgcccaggct
     1201 gggaaggagc caggggggag cagggctcac tccagccacc tgaagtccaa aaagggtcag
     1261 tctacctccc ggccataaaa actcatgttc aagacagaag ggcctgactc aggctgacat
     1321 tctccacttc ttgttcccca ctgacagcct cccaccccca tctctcccctc ccctgccatt
     1381 ttgggttttg ggtctttgaa ccttgcttg caataggtgt gcgtcagaag cacccaggac
     1441 ttccatttgc tttgtcccgg ggctccactg aacaagttgg cctgcactgg tgttttgttg
     1501 tggggaggag gatggggagt aggacatacc agcttagatt ttaaggtttt tactgtgagg
     1561 gatgtttggg agatgtaaga aatgttcttg cagttaaggg ttagtttaca atcagccaca
     1621 ttctaggtag gggcccactt caccgtacta accagggaag ctgtccctca ctgttgaatt
     1681 ttctctaact tcaaggccca tatctgtgaa atgctggcat ttgcacctac ctcacagagt
     1741 gcattgtgag ggttaataaa ataatgtaca tctggccttg aaaccacctt ttattacatg
     1801 gggtctagaa cttgacccc ttgagggtgc ttgttccctc tccctgttgg tcggtgggtt
     1861 ggtagtttct acagttgggc agctggttag gtagagggag ttgtcaagtc tctgctggcc
     1921 cagccaaacc ctgtctgacc acctcttggt gaaccttagt acctaaaagg aaatctcacc
     1981 ccatcccaca ccctgagaga tttcatctct tgtatatgat gatctggatc caccaaagact
     2041 tgttttatgc tcagggtcaa tttctttttt cttttttttt tttttttct ttttctttga
     2101 gactgggtct cgctttgttg cccaggctgg agtggagtgg cgtgatcttg gcttactgca
     2161 gcctttgcct ccccggctcg agcagtcctg cctcagcctc cggagtagct gggaccacag
     2221 gttcatgcca ccatggccag ccaacttttg catgttttgt agagatgggg tctcacactg
     2281 ttgcccaggc tggtctcaaa tcctgggctc caggcgatcc acctgtctca gcctcccaga
     2341 gtgctgggat tacaattgtg agccaccacg tccagctgga agggtcaaca tcttttacat
     2401 tctgcaagca catctgcatt ttcaccccac ccttcccctc cttctcccctt ttatatccc
     2461 attttatat cgatctctta ttttacaata aaactttgct gccaaaaaaa aaaaaaaaa
     2521 a
//
```

Fig. 10.1 GenBank format content

```
>gi|11066969|gb|AF307851.1|AF307851 Homo sapiens p53 protein mRNA, complete cds
GGCACGAGCCACCGTCCAGGGAGCAGGTAGCTGCTGGGCTCCGGGGACACTTTGCGTTCGGGCTGGGAGC
GTGCTTTCCACGACGGTGACACGCTTCCCTGGATTGGCAGCCAGACTGCCTTCCGGGTCACTGCCATGGA
GGAGCCGCAGTCAGATCCTAGCGTCGAGCCCCCTCTGAGTCAGGAAACATTTTCAGACCTATGGAAACTA
CTTCCTGAAAACAACGTTCTGTCCCCCTTGCCGTCCCAAGCAATGGATGATTTGATGCTGTCCCCGGACG
ATATTGAACAATGGTTCACTGAAGACCCAGGTCCAGATGAAGCTCCCAGAATGCCAGAGGCTGCTCCCCG
CGTGGCCCCTGCACCAGCAGCTCCTACACCGGCGGCCCCTGCACCAGCCCCCTCCTGGCCCCTGTCATCT
TCTGTCCCTTCCCAGAAAACCTACCAGGGCAGCTACGGTTTCCGTCTGGGCTTCTTGCATTCTGGGACAG
CCAAGTCTGTGACTTGCACGTACTCCCCTGCCCTCAACAAGATGTTTTGCCAACTGGCCAAGACCTGCCC
TGTGCAGCTGTGGGTTGATTCCACACCCCCGCCCGGCACCCGCGTCCGCGCCATGGCCATCTACAAGCAG
TCACAGCACATGACGGAGGTTGTGAGGCGCTGCCCCCACCATGAGCGCTGCTCAGATAGCGATGGTCTGG
CCCCTCCTCAGCATCTTATCCGAGTGGAAGGAAATTTGCGTGTGGAGTATTTGGATGACAGAAACACTTT
TCGACATAGTGTGGTGGTGCCCTATGAGCCGCCTGAGGTTGGCTCTGACTGTACCACCATCCACTACAAC
TACATGTGTAACAGTTCCTGCATGGGCGGCATGAACCGGAGGCCCATCCTCACCATCATCACACTGGAAG
ACTCCAGTGGTAATCTACTGGGACGGAACAGCTTTGAGGTGCGTGTTTGTGCCTGTCCTGGGAGAGACCG
GCGCACAGAGGAAGAGAATCTCCGCAAGAAAGGGGAGCCTCACCACGAGCTGCCCCCAGGGAGCACTAAG
CGAGCACTGCCCAACAACACCAGCTCCTCTCCCCAGCCAAAGAAGAAACCACTGGATGGAGAATATTTCA
CCCTTCAGATCCGTGGGCGTGAGCGCTTCGAGATGTTCCGAGAGCTGAATGAGGCCTTGGAACTCAAGGA
TGCCCAGGCTGGGAAGGAGCCAGGGGGGAGCAGGGGCTCACTCCAGCCACCTGAAGTCCAAAAAGGGTCAG
TCTACCTCCCGCCATAAAAAACTCATGTTCAAGACAGAAGGGCCTGACTCAGACTGACATTCTCCACTTC
TTGTTCCCCACTGACAGCCTCCCACCCCCATCTCTCCCTCCCCTGCCCATTTTGGGTTTTGGGTCTTTGAA
CCCTTGCTTGCAATAGGTGTGCGTCAGAAGCACCCAGGACTTCCATTTGCTTTGTCCCGGGGGCTCCACTG
AACAAGTTGGCCTGCACTGGTGTTTTGTTGTGGGGAGGAGGATGGGGAGTAGGACATACCAGCTTAGATT
TTAAGGTTTTTACTGTGAGGGATGTTTGGGAGATGTAAGAAATGTTCTTGCAGTTAAGGGTTAGTTTACA
ATCAGCCACATTCTAGGTAGGGGCCCACTTCACCGTACTAACCAGGGAAGCTGTCCCTCACTGTTGAATT
TTCTCTAACTTCAAGGCCCATATCTGTGAAATGCTGGCATTTGCACCTACCTCACAGAGTGCATTGTGAG
GGTTAATGAAATAATGTACATCTGGCCTTGAAACCACCTTTTATTACATGGGGTCTAGAACTTGACCCCC
TTGAGGGTGCTTGTTCCCTCTCCCTGTTGGTCGGTGGGTTGGTAGTTTCTACAGTTGGGCAGCTGGTTAG
GTAGAGGGAGTTGTCAAGTCTCTGCTGGCCCAGCCAAACCCTGTCTGACAACCTCTTGGTGAACCTTAGT
ACCTAAAAGGAAATCTCACCCCATCCCACACCCTGGAGGATTTCATCTCTTGTATATGATGATCTGGATC
CACCAAGACTTGTTTTATGCTCAGGGTCAATTTCTTTTTTCTTTTTTTTTTTTTTTCTTTTTCTTTGA
GACTGGGTCTCGCTTTGTTGCCCAGGCTGGAGTGGACGTGGCGTGATCTTGGCTTACTGCAGCCTTTGCCT
CCCCGGCTCGAGCAGTCCTGCCTCAGCCTCCGGAGTAGCTGGGACCACAGGTTCATGCCACCATGGCCAG
CCAACTTTTGCATGTTTTGTAGAGATGGGGTCTCACAGTGTTGCCCAGGCTGGTCTCAAACTCCTGGGCT
CAGGCGATCCACCTGTCTCAGCCTCCCAGAGTGCTGGGATTACAATTGTGAGCCACCACGTCCAGCTGGA
AGGGTCAACATCTTTTACATTCTGCAAGCACATCTGCATTTTCACCCCACCCTTCCCCTCCTTCTCCCTT
TTTATATCCCATTTTTTATATCGATCTCTTATTTTACAATAAAACTTTGCTGCCAAAAAAAAAAAAAAAAAA
A
```

Fig. 10.2 FASTA format content

sources that use different formats, this adds to the complication. Consideration of this should be borne in mind when extracting data from the public databases: many will now provide the ability for data to be extracted in more than one format. If we continue using GenBank as an example, we can get data in GenBank, FASTA, XML, or ASN.1 format.

There are several file formats that are relevant for any informatics data mining:

- GenBank[4]
- EMBL
- DDBJ
- FASTA
- SWISS-PROT
- Pfam
- PROSITE

---

[4] GenBank, EMBL, and DDBJ formats use a common, standardized format. This GenBank/EMBL/DDBJ format is what we refer to when using any of the three sources. All examples in this book work with any of the three sources.

This is not an exhaustive list by any means but simply lists some of the most common file formats encountered in practice. There are a number of resources that the reader can investigate for the details on each of the above formats, such as Markel and León (2003 #61), which provide a complete description of how to work with files from these sources. This being said, we will consider some of these further in this chapter.

The two examples above are different forms of the complete sequence held in GenBank for the mRNA for the p53 gene. If we were to want to update this sequence from an external database, for some reason, we can be reasonably confident that completely replacing the sequence and rerunning our models will work as expected. When dealing with sequence fragments, such as expressed sequence tags (ESTs), we have a larger number of fragments, coming from different sources, all of which require care to integrate. When conducting a manual analysis using a small number of sources, this may not be a significant concern. However, when the data warehouse is the enterprise-wide repository of data, coming from multiple sources, and for multiple projects, the issues are compounded.

10.3   Tools and Databases

The breadth, depth, and speed of change in the informatics space means that any significant data-mining effort will definitely require integrating data from outside of the organization. In fact, the majority of sequence data, for example, may well be from outside the organization. Aggregating this information together into a single coherent repository for analysis and mining is not a trivial step. As is the case with what we have termed "traditional" scientific data, the majority of the work will take place in getting the information into the "correct" format for your environment.

As we embark on this discussion, we should note the range of tools available to process data from these sources. The tools available from each individual database provide a significant amount of capability. Using GenBank again, the range of tools available to support analysis and data mining is shown in Table 10.2, and there are also application programming interfaces to allow direct access to data stored in the external repository from your own environment (Entrez programming utilities).

The array of tools in Table 10.2 may seem bewildering if you have not used them before; this is only a very small subset of the tools available: we've not included environments such as R, which has broad package-based support for handling genomic and proteomic sequences, Bioconductor, which has specialized packages for processing this type of data, or the more general environments such as SAS, Matlab, or the like which are now being augmented by capabilities to intelligently handle these types of data.

In the next section, we will discuss some of the environments and languages which can be used to develop your own tools. However, the number of tools available today, covering the breadth of the analytical space, means that the majority of analysis can be accomplished without the need to learn how to program.

Table 10.2 NCBI analysis tools

Tool	Description
Nucleotide sequence analysis	
BLAST	Compare gene and protein sequences against others in public databases. This tool has several different flavors such as PSI-BLAST, PHI-BLAST, and BLAST 2 as well as having specialized versions for human, microbial, malaria, and other genomes, as well as for vector contamination, immunoglobulins, and tentative human consensus sequences
Electronic PCR	Search a DNA sequence for sequence tagged sites (STSs) that have been used as landmarks in various types of genomic maps by comparing the query sequence against the NCBI unified database of STSs aggregated from various sources
Entrez gene	Retrieve and analyze Entrez Gene records. Each record contains a wide range of information for a given gene and organism and, if available, includes results of any analyses performed on the sequence data. The type of information presented, and the amount of information, depends on what is available for a particular gene and organism. Information can include a graphical summary of the genomic context, intron/exon structures, and flanking genes, as well as links to a graphic view of the mRNA sequence (showing biological features), and links to gene ontology and phenotypic information. Links to corresponding protein sequence data and conserved domains as well as links to related resources, such as mutation databases, are available
Model maker	View mRNAs, ESTs, and gene predictions that were used to build a gene model and edit the model by selecting or removing exons
ORF finder	Identifies all possible ORFs in a DNA sequence by locating the standard and alternative stop and start codons
SAGEmap	Perform statistical tests designed specifically for differential-type analyses of SAGE (serial analysis of gene expression) data
Spidey	Align one or more mRNA sequences to a single genomic sequence
Splign	Compute cDNA-to-genomic alignments based on a variation of the Needleman-Wunsch algorithm combined with BLAST for compartment detection and greater performance
VecScreen	Identify segments of a nucleic acid sequence that may be of vector, linker, or adapter origin prior to sequence analysis or submission
Viral genotyping tool	Identify the genotype (or subtype) of recombinant or nonrecombinant viral nucleotide sequences using BLAST to compare a query sequence to a set of reference sequences for known genotypes. Predefined reference genotypes exist for three major viral pathogens: human immunodeficiency virus 1 (HIV-1), hepatitis C virus (HCV), and hepatitis B virus (HBV), as well as for poliovirus
Protein sequence analysis and proteomics	
Blink	Displays the results of BLAST searches that have been done for every protein sequence in the Entrez Proteins data domain

(continued)

Table 10.2 (continued)

Tool	Description
CD search	Conserved domain database search with reverse position-specific BLAST
CDART	Displays the functional domains that make up the protein and lists proteins with similar domain architectures, given a protein sequence
Open mass spectrometry search algorithm	OMSSA allows researchers to submit the mass spectra of peptides and proteins for identification
TaxPlot	Three-way comparisons of genomes on the basis of the protein sequences they encode
Structures	
Cn3D	Web browser add-on that allows you to view three-dimensional structures from NCBI's Entrez retrieval service
VAST search	Structure-structure similarity search service that compares 3-D coordinates of a protein structure to those in the MMDB/PDB database
CD search	See above
Genome analysis	
Entrez genomes	Provides graphical overview of compete genomes and chromosomes with the ability to explore regions of interest in greater detail. Over 1,000 organisms have their complete genomes in this database, representing both completely sequenced organisms and those for which sequencing is in progress
COGs	Clusters of orthologous groups, delineated by comparing protein sequences from 43 complete genomes (30 major phylogenetic lineages), consisting of individual proteins or groups of paralogs from at least three lineages thus corresponds to an ancient conserved domain
Map viewer	Shows integrated views of chromosome maps for many organisms, including human and numerous other vertebrates, invertebrates, fungi, protozoa, and plants
SKY, M-FISH, and CGH database	Repository of publicly submitted data from spectral karyotyping (SKY), multiplex fluorescence in situ hybridization (M-FISH), and comparative genomic hybridization (CGH), permitting the simultaneous visualization of each human or mouse chromosome in a different color, facilitating the identification of chromosomal aberrations; CGH can be used to generate a map of DNA copy number changes in tumor genomes. Collaborative project with the National Cancer Institute
Gene expression	
Gene expression omnibus (GEO)	Tools to assist with visualizing and exploring GEO data. Datasets may be viewed as hierarchical cluster heat maps. Individual gene expression profiles showing significant differences between experimental subsets may be located using average subset rank value comparisons. Related gene expression profiles may be identified on the basis of sequence similarity, profile similarity, or homology. Indicators of dataset normalization quality are provided as distribution graphs and by flagging outliers

(continued)

Table 10.2 (continued)

Tool	Description
SAGEmap	See above
Cancer GenomeAnatomy Project (CGAP)	Goal: decipher the molecular anatomy of cancer cells. CGAP develops profiles of cancer cells by comparing gene expression in normal, precancerous, and malignant cells from a wide variety of tissues
UniGene DDD (digital differential display)	Compare computed gene expression profiles between selected cDNA libraries. Using a statistical test, genes whose expression levels differ significantly from one tissue to the next are identified and shown to the user

10.3.1 Programming Languages and Environments

Several data-mining *programming* environments exist that have libraries and add-ons that implement a wide variety of the methods we have described in this book. Such environments require a good understanding of a programming language such as Java, C++, or the like, and we will not expand our discussion of such environments here for a couple of reasons. First, since such environments are invariably built around a specific programming language, it is important to select one that your organization can support if you encounter problems; building some data-mining processes using Microsoft's .NET architecture, when your organization is primarily J2EE-based, may leave you little in the way of a support structure. Second, while any environment has a learning curve to it, programming languages can take a significant amount of time before you become proficient in the vagaries of the language: you can be spending more time on developing programming skills, which is not necessarily a bad thing, than you do on actually performing the analytical activities that are the goal of your endeavor. Consider whether there is a good return on the investment you would need to make in order to become proficient with such environments: there is often a diminishing return on the value that they bring to the non-IT professional, the primary reason for this being the learning curve.

That being said, one language has seen a particularly widespread adoption in the bioinformatics space: Perl. The language environment is available on a wide variety of operating system platforms and is available in many open-source variants as well as commercially developed products. A broad base of Perl packages are available that support bioinformatics and even the broader biological space.

Some good places for the interested reader to start are Tisdall (2001 #125, 2003 #430), Gibas and Jambeck (2001 #126), Bessant et al. (2009 #431), and Moorhouse and Barry (2004 #429), all of which provide a good combination of programming technique coverage and application. For two easy-to-read references on Perl itself, see Schwartz (2008 #432) and Wall et al. (2000 #433). For supporting packages, a good place to begin is the BioPerl home page at www.bioperl.org.

We've referred to the R platform throughout this text and used it to generate many of the examples. R is another platform that has a comprehensive built-in programming language, along with a broad base of packages that support many areas of data analysis. This general-purpose environment can be a valuable tool in the toolkit of any analyst and, although it has a learning curve, the benefits can be phenomenal. It is probably not too far a stretch – well maybe just a little – to say that there is probably an R package already available for your needs. If there isn't, you can probably use existing packages as a basis to add your own specific code onto in order to meet your needs. This can be obtained from www.r-project.org.

10.4   Standardization

In recent years, the concept of standardization has been extended beyond the focus of using standard names and the like to include standard vocabularies for other characteristics. This has a tremendous impact on our ability to mine the data. The *Gene Ontology* comprises a controlled vocabulary for annotating gene sequences and allows us to elicit patterns on a well-defined domain as well as the consistent presence of descriptive information. More recently, the advent of the *Open Biological Ontologies* (OBO) website[5] has facilitated access to many ontological vocabularies.

It can often be valuable to preprocess some of the data to ensure standardized names and concepts that are used across the complete dataset you are concerned with; this can greatly simplify your analysis and, as we discussed earlier, remove some of the errors that can creep in because of dissimilar terms due to data entry issues and the like. A good example of this can be seen when the data is originating with multiple investigators across countries, as is the case with global clinical trials.

This being said, consider the implications. At the very least, any new data has to be preprocessed in the same way. If not, the results from your analysis will be skewed or even completely unusable. Further, if your analytical code and process is going to be used by other people, either in parallel or after you move onto bigger and better things, they need to understand the implications, have the same processes available to them, and, most importantly, follow the same process. In this regard, analyses such as these should be documented as would any other scientific experiment: other people must be able to repeat your process and confirm your conclusions. Resuming the habit from college, of keeping a laboratory notebook, or beginning the habit is an important facet of your work and often a life saver in the event that something goes wrong.

We've discussed standardization earlier in this book and its importance to effective mining efforts. All of the same issues pertain to the informatics space and, once again, we simply refer the reader to that earlier discussion.

---

[5] http://obo.sourceforge.net

10.5 Microarrays

Consider the following quotation from Tu et al. (2002 #434):

> In the near future, it will be possible to profile the whole transcriptome of higher organisms, including Homo sapiens, with only a few DNA gene chips.

Why is this technology considered so important? Microarray technology will allow us to gain a global view of the genotypes that correspond to the various different cell phenotypes and has the potential to radically alter many areas of biomedical research and development, including advanced diagnostics, biological pathway and network analysis, and facilitating personalized medicine (Lockhart and Winzeler 2000 #436; Brown and Botstein 1999 #437).

DNA microarrays, or genomic microarrays, have revolutionized the way in which we measure gene expression levels since they allow us to measure many thousands of genes simultaneously. These have become a significant source for data mining due to the vast amount of data that even one microarray can generate. Practically, all of the cells in a given organism have the same genes, which can be expressed differently, at different times, and under different conditions. The various gene expression patterns that follow various biological programs according to characteristics such as genetic background, tissue type, developmental stage, and environment account for the large variety of both cell types and cell states.

Two strands of DNA *hybridize* if they are complementary to each other. As a principle, hybridization has been used for decades in the molecular biology discipline and underpins techniques such as Southern blotting, Northern blotting, and, more recently, microarrays.

DNA microarrays have given us the ability to obtain a global state of the cell for the first time by allowing us to investigate the cell's biological molecular state by simultaneously measuring the expression profile of tens of thousands of genes.[6]

We do not describe microarray technologies in detail in this book but refer the reader to texts such as Schena (2002 #1), Baldi (2002 #52), Kamberova and Shah (2002 #69), and Knudsen (2002 #49) for more information. Instead, we consider how the data produced from microarray experiments is analyzed and mined both independently of other types of data and in combination with other types of data.

Through the use of microarrays, we can create molecular datasets which represent systems of biological or clinical interest. We can use these expression profiles to uncover hidden taxonomies, improve molecular classification, and increase our understanding of an organism's normal state or an organism's state within the context of particular diseases. For example, Bair and Tibshirani (2003 #72) applied machine-learning techniques to microarray data and showed how cancer diagnosis can be improved.

---

[6] As of the time of writing, single-chip microarrays are commercially available that can measure the gene expression of more than 30,000 genes; enough to cover the human genome.

Application of machine-learning and statistical techniques to gene expression data has been used in areas ranging from prediction of posttreatment outcome to finding molecular markers for disease and tumor morphology to name a few areas of research, and is even beginning to be used in clinical trials (Shipp et al. 2002 #73).

Iacobas et al. (2002 #438) evaluated six different types of error that occur with this type of technology and proposed an approach to improving data accuracy by both changing the experimental process and introducing an analytical process.

Later in this book, we consider a real-world case study including microarray data along with other genomic and proteomic data as well as more traditional clinical data to show how some of this information can be brought together to significantly improve our ability to understand the interrelationships between what have often been traditionally separate subdisciplines.

10.5.1   Challenges and Opportunities

In other disciplines, a data-mining dataset is typically characterized by a large number of instances with a relatively small number of attributes. Since each attribute may invite dimensional analysis, the smaller the number of attributes, the "better." Microarray datasets, however, are often characterized by a small number of instances – fewer than 100 usually – with thousands of attributes since each attribute corresponds to a particular gene. We use the notation of Simon (2003 #74) to represent this: $p \gg n$, where p is the number of attributes (features) and n is the number of instances (cases).

This ratio of attributes to instances increases the likelihood of false positives being generated due to chance when building predictive models and also in finding differentially expressed genes. Thus, the methods we use to validate the model and assess the likelihood of our results being for valid reasons rather than through chance must be particularly robust.

Analytical methods used with microarray data typically fall into three categories:

- Classification
  We are interested in classifying diseases and predicting outcomes based on the gene expression patterns. This can extend to identifying the most appropriate treatment for a particular genetic signature.
- Clustering
  We are interested in identifying new biological classifications or refining the current ones.
- Gene Selection
  We are interested in finding the genes most strongly related to a particular class through the process of attribute selection.

Noise is unfortunately an inherent component of microarrays. As seen in Tu et al. (2002 #434), noise from the sample preparation stage is relatively small, whereas hybridization noise appears to correlate with expression levels. Replicating experiments that bifurcate at different stages of the assay allowed the noise to be separated out. The data is noisy: changes in transcript values come from both differences between different cell types and tissues (biological variations) and from experimental noise.

What is interesting in Tu et al. (2002 #434) is that they concluded that most of the noise originates in the hybridization step and proposed a data analysis method which takes such noise characteristics into account, and developing a tool for evaluating the statistical significance of gene expression changes across experiments. Techniques aimed at improving the signal-to-noise ratio is an important area of concern for researchers.

10.5.2 Classification

As noted above, the $p \gg n$ ratio between the (relatively) small number of instances (cases) and the large number of attributes (features) can lead to results that have more to do with random chance than with patterns in the underlying data. Simon (2003 #74) had identified some of the more common issues that arise in this domain:

- Feature selection
- Prediction model
- Fitting the predictive model to the training data
- Estimating prediction accuracy

Software such as Bioconductor (www.bioconductor.org) and packages for the R project (www.r-project.org) provide tools and models that can be used to analyze microarray data. Bair and Tibshirani (2003 #72) presented a method, the "nearest shrunken centroid," that they applied to identifying clinically relevant differences in cancer patients and also to dealing with noise that is unfortunately inherent in microarrays.

10.5.3 Gene Selection

In many cases, little is currently known about the normal biological variation expected in a given tissue or biological state. Further, the biological state is often defined only along phenotypic lines. These factors complicate our attempts to find invariant or differential molecular behavior that is relevant to any given biological problem.

Researchers are looking at ways of approaching this challenge, such as Nadimpally and Jaki (2003 #75), who have analyzed genes which show normal variance across genetically identical mice. The resulting set can be used to identify false positives in differential gene expression studies as well as identifying interesting facts about the processes underlying natural variance.

10.6   Finding Motifs

A *motif* is a short segment of DNA or protein that is of particular interest to us, and one of the most common activities is to look for motifs in one or more larger sequences. The motifs may be regulatory elements of DNA, protein fragments that are known to be conserved across species, or for any other purpose of interest.

Typically, these motifs are not one specific sequence; instead, they may have several variants, such as would be the case if there are positions in which it does not matter which base or residue is present. Such motifs may also have varying lengths to make the problem a little more challenging.[7]

10.6.1   Regular Expressions

Regular expressions are a representation used in many programming languages as a mechanism for identifying a potentially variable string of characters. Not only can we use these tools for searching and comparison but also as a mechanism for noting the targets of our searches. Many of the environments and languages we would use for data mining contain built-in regular expression engines for us to use.

Let's begin with an example. Suppose we are interested in seeing where the sequence GAATTC, which happens to be a cleavage site for the restriction enzyme EcoRI, occurs in a larger sequence, such as the sequence shown in Fig. 10.3.

If we do a simple search for our restriction enzyme sequence, we will see that there are three instances in this sequence fragment, informing us that EcoRI can separate the DNA at any or all of these points. If we look at Table 10.3, we can see that cleavage by EcoRI will result in the cleavage site being split into

```
5'---G        AATTC---3'

3'---CCTTA        G---5'
```

with additional residues being inserted between the cleaved portions. As we shall see, regular expressions provide us with a representation to identify the "after" sequence as well as the "before."

A regular expression (or regex, or regexp) is essentially a search pattern that we are interested in. It could be a specific sequence of characters, such as our cleavage site example above, or it could contain *wildcard* characters which stand for other elements. As a simple, nonscientific example, searching a document for the word "gray" might miss the British spelling of "grey." We can use regular expressions to search for both using the concept of a character class – contained within square

---

[7] For these reasons, the computational tool of *regular expressions* is often used to represent motifs.

Fig. 10.3 Partial DNA sequence for *C. elegans* chromosome I (See http://www.sanger.ac.uk/ Projects/C_elegans/Genomic_Sequence.shtm for the complete genome)

Table 10.3 Restriction enzymes (Roberts 1980 #428), N = {A,C,G,T}, W = {A,T}

Enzyme	Source	Recognition sequence	Cut
EcoRI	Escherichia coli	5'GAATTC	5'---G AATTC---3'
		3'CTTAAG	3'---CCTTA G---5'
EcoRII	Escherichia coli	5'CCWGG	5'--- CCWGG---3'
		3'GGWCC	3'---GGWWCC ---5'
BamHI	Bacillus amyloliquefaciens	5'GGATCC	5'---G GATCC---3'
		3'CCTAGG	3'---CCTAG G ---5'
HindIII	Haemophilus influenzae	5'AAGCTT	5'---A AGCTT---3'
		3'TTCGAA	3'---TTCGA A---5'
TaqI	Thermus aquaticus	5'TCGA	5'---T CGA---3'
		3'AGCT	3'---AGC T---5'
NotI	Nocardia otitidis	5'GCGGCCGC	5'---GC GGCCGC---3'
		3'CGCCGGCG	3'---CGCCGG CG---5'
Hinf	Haemophilus influenzae	5'GANTC	5'---G ANTC---3'
		3'CTNAG	3'---CTNA G---5'
Sau3A	Staphylococcus aureus	5'GATC	5'--- GATC---3'
		3'CTAG	3'---CTAG ---5'
PovII	Proteus vulgaris	5'CAGCTG	5'---CAG CTG---3'
		3'GTCGAC	3'---GTC GAC---5'
SmaI	Serratia marcescens	5'CCCGGG	5'---CCC GGG---3'
		3'GGGCCC	3'---GGG CCC---5'
HaeIII	Haemophilus aegyptus	5'GGCC	5'---GG CC---3'
		3'CCGG	3'---CC GG---5'
HgaI	Haemophilus gallinarum	5'GACGCN{5}	5'---NN NN---3'
		3'N{10}CTGCG	3'---NN NN---5'
AluI	Arthrobacter luteus	5'AGCT	5'---AG CT---3'
		3'TCGA	3'---TC GA---5'
EcoRV	Escherichia coli	5'GATATC	5'---GAT ATC---3'
		3'CTATAG	3'---CTA TAG---5'
EcoP15I	Escherichia coli	5'CAGCAGN{25}NN	5'--- CAGCAGN{25}NN---3'
		3'GTCGTCN{25}NN	3'--- GTCGTCN{25}NN---5'
KpnI	Klebsiella pneumoniae	5'GGTACC	5'---GGTAC C---3'
		3'CCATGG	3'---C CATGG---5'
PstI	Providencia stuartii	5'CTGCAG	5'---CTGCA G---3'
		3'GACGTC	3'---G ACGTC---5'
SacI	Streptomyces achromogenes	5'GAGCTC	5'---GAGCT C---3'
		3'CTCGAG	3'---C TCGAG---5'
SalI	Streptomyces albus	5'GTCGAC	5'---G TCGAC---3'
		3'CAGCTG	3'---CAGCT G---5'
ScaI	Streptomyces caespitosus	5'AGTACT	5'---AGT ACT---3'
		3'TCATGA	3'---TCA TGA---5'
SpeI	Sphaerotilus natans	5'ACTAGT	5'---A CTAGT---3'
		3'TGATCA	3'---TGATC A---5'

(continued)

Table 10.3 (continued)

Enzyme	Source	Recognition sequence	Cut
SphI	Streptomyces phaeochromogenes	5'GCATGC 3'CGTACG	5'---G CATGC---3' 3'---CGTAC G---5'
StuI	Streptomyces tubercidicus	5'AGGCCT 3'TCCGGA	5'---AGG CCT---3' 3'---TCC GGA---5'
XbaI	Xanthomonas badrii	5'TCTAGA 3'AGATCT	5'---T CTAGA---3' 3'---AGATC T---5'

Table 10.4 Simple regular expression rules

Concept	Description	Example
Character class	Identifying alternate options	CC[AT]GG matches to CCAGG or to CCTGG
Anything	Matching to (almost) any character	GA.TC
Optional	Make the preceding token optional	CCG?TATA matches to CCGTATA or to CCTATA
0, 1, or many	Match 0, 1, or many times	GACGC[N]* will match to GACGC, GACGCN, GACGCNN, etc.
1 or many (aka "at least once")[a]	Match 1 or more times	GACGC[N]+ will match to GACGCN, GACGCNN, etc.

[a]When to use "*" and when to use "+" can be subtle

brackets – to cover both cases: "gr[ae]y." This can be particularly useful where any residue might be applicable, such as is often represented by "N" in a sequence.[8]

We won't go into too much more details on regular expressions, which we have discussed earlier in this text, but satisfy ourselves with identifying a few of the capabilities, shown in Table 10.4.

With this knowledge, we can now consider evaluating a gene sequence in which DNA has been inserted via the mechanism of action of the EcoRI restriction enzyme. We know that after cleavage, the GAATTC sequence is split into G and AATTC, on one of the strands. If additional residues have been included, we can use regular expressions to search our extended sequence using something such as G [ACGT]*AATTC.[9] But there's an obvious problem with this in that the pattern will match to the first "G" residue it finds and extend the match until it finds the first "AATTC" sequence. Returning to the sequence in Fig. 10.3, this search pattern will match the sequence highlighted in blue below, obviously not what we want.

---

[8] An interesting fact is that there is almost always more than one way of representing the same search pattern. For example, if we consider the cleavage site for Hinf, we could use "GA[ACGT] TC" or GA.TC. In the latter case, however, this will match (pretty much) any character, so if a nongenomic alphabet character was included, this would still match. Be aware of this as/when you use regular expressions.

[9] Similarly, on the complementary strand, we could search for CCTTA[ACGT]*G.

```
gcctaagcctaagcctaagcctaagcctaagcctaagcctaagcctaagcctaagcctaagcctaagcctaagcctaagcctaagcctaagcctaagcct
aagcctaagcctaagcctaagcctaagcctaagcctaagcctaagcctaagcctaagcctaagcctaagcctaagcctaagcctaagcctaagcctaagc
ctaagcctaagcctaagcctaagcctaagcctaagcctaagcctaagcctaagcctaagcctaagcctaagcctaagcctaagcctaagcctaagcctaa
gcctaagcctaagcctaagcctaagcctaagcctaagcctaagcctaagcctaagcctaagcctaagcctaagcctaagcctaagcctaagcctaagcct
aagcctaagcctaagcctaagcctaagcctaaaaaattgagataagaaaacattttacttttcaaaattgttttcatgctaaattcaaaacgtttttt
tttagtgaagcttctagatatttggcgggtacctctaattttgcctgcctgccaacctatatgctcctgtgtttaggcctaatactaagcctaagcctaa
gcctaatactaagcctaagcctaagactaagcctaatactaagcctaagcctaagactaagcctaagactaagcctaagactaagcctaatactaagcct
aagcctaagactaagcctaagcctaatactaagcctaagcctaagactaagcctaagcctaatactaagcctaagcctaagactaagcctaagactaagcctaaga
ctaagcctaatactaagcctaagcctaagactaagcctaagcctaaaagaatatggtagctacagaaacggtagtacactcttctgaaaatacaaaaat
ttgcaattttatagctagggcactttttgtctgcccaaatataggcaaccaaaaataattgccaagttttttaatgatttgttgcatattgaaaaaaaca
tttttcgggtttttttgaaatgaatatcgtagctacagaaacggttgtgcactcatctgaaagtttgttttttcttgttttcttgcactttgtgcagaattc
```

How we overcome this depends on several factors, but a simple mechanism is to look at some sequence prior to the one we are most interested in and to incorporate that into the search pattern. For example, we could use the string "TTTGTGCA" as a prefix to "GAATTC" and use something such as "TTTGTGCAG[ACGT]*AATTC" for our search pattern.

This brief discussion provides another example of a theme running through the whole subject of data analysis, which is an important facet of data mining. Although we are most interested in the hidden patterns within our data, it's important to have a good understanding of the data we are analyzing, especially as it relates to sequence data: with a large amount of data, searching for a very specific pattern may generate a substantial number of false positives which will naturally skew our results. Conversely, selecting a prefix (or suffix) to reduce these false positives can easily result in sequences being ignored. Why did we select "TTTGTGCA" as a prefix in our above example? In this instance, we quickly reviewed our data, performed a couple of searches to ensure that this prefix wouldn't skew our results, and as a result, incorporated this into our experiment. (This is a good reason why we recommend maintaining a laboratory-style notebook for these experiments. We'll touch on this in the last chapter of this text.)

Although we've used gene sequences for our examples, everything also pertains to protein sequences and the like. For example, the *C. elegans* protein database[10] is a good source to use if this is your area of study, comprising over 10,000,000 residues and over 24,000 protein sequences. This and other such databases (e.g., PDB) contain vast amounts of data that you can incorporate into your mining activities.[11]

---

[10] http://www.sanger.ac.uk/Projects/C_elegans/WORMBASE/current/wormpep.shtml

[11] A piece of information which may only be of interest to a small number of readers is that almost all of these external sources provide a mechanism for downloading them into your environment, which will often make analytical activities a little easier. Of course, the effort, space, subsequent processes necessary to maintain these databases may not make it attractive to your organization. Be nice to your local database administrator!!!

10.7 Analyzing DNA

When looking at sequence data, we are often interested in answering questions such as

? What percentage of bases are the same, on average, between two (or more) DNA sequences?
? What is the average percentage of positions that are the same between pairs of DNA sequences in a sequence set?
? What can we say about the sequences under study and how they change over time?

Some of these questions would more appropriately fit under the subject of "data analysis" rather than "data mining," although they can all leverage techniques we've discussed. For example, Leng and Muller (2006 #439) considered temporal gene expression profiles and how classification techniques can provide low error rate classifications.

Much of the analysis of sequence data revolves around alignment and phylogeny that we now briefly introduce.

10.7.1 Pairwise Sequence Alignment

Probably the most fundamental task we undertake when analyzing sequence data is to ask if two sequences are alike. We do this by aligning the sequences as best as we can and then ask if this alignment occurred by chance or because the sequences are related to each other. This simple task contains some not so simple issues. Consider two sequences.

ACCTAGGCTGCGCAATTA, and
CCTAGGCTGGCAATTATA.

Initially, we might say that they are very unalike, although on reflection we can see some obvious similarities. In fact, if we shift the second one base pair to the right, we get a very close match between a subset of the nucleotides:

ACCTAGGCTGCGCAATTA__
_CCTAGGCTG_GCAATTATA

Notice that we also inserted a "space" into the middle to give us a match on a second subset of the nucleotides. This exemplifies one of the fundamental problems of sequence alignment: *what type(s) of alignment should we consider?*

Returning to our original sequences, we can see that if we simply left them as they were, the match was very poor. If we didn't insert the "space" into the middle of the second sequence above, we would have got a better match – because we matched on nine nucleotides in the pair – but not as good as when we inserted the "space." This exemplifies the second issue: *how do we assign a score to each alignment that will allow us to compare how "good" the various alignment options are?* Closely associated with this question is, of course, the question of *how do we find good scoring alignments?* Finally, also related, we need to consider the question *how do we evaluate alignment scores and determine how significant they are?*

Whatever approach we use, we can see that we have some fundamental approaches we can use. In comparing two sequences that we believe are alike, we naturally assume that they had a common ancestor, which means that any differences would have come about because of selection or mutation. A *substitution* would have swapped one *or more* nucleotide for another. Alternatively, one or more nucleotides may have been *inserted* into or *deleted* from one of the sequences to form a *gap*. It would therefore be natural to consider a score that includes some measure relating to the number of nucleotides that match, as well as some score to account for the gaps and substitutions. Bases which match, and bases where a substitution has taken place that is conservative by some measure of conservativeness, may apply a positive value to our score, whereas a gap or nonconservative substitution may apply a negative value to our score. Why? We assume that any bases which match would be more likely to have occurred if the sequences are related than they would be chance, and similarly for what we are calling conservative substitutions. Thus, they would tend to add weight to the sequences being related. Gaps and the like, however, would tend to be as likely to occur randomly, and so we decrease our score using these values.

There is a not so subtle assumption in the above discussion: that differences at different places in the sequences occurred independently of each other. That is, a gap of any length is a single mutation. For DNA, this is reasonable. For proteins, a little less so since residue interaction is important for protein structure. For RNA, however, this is not a reasonable assumption. We return to this issue later, but for the moment, allow the assumption to play out.

With our assumptions so far, we can now begin to build our model.

Assume that our two sequences S, T have lengths l_S, l_T, respectively. S, T will consist of a set of *symbols* (or *letters*) over some alphabet. For DNA, the *alphabet* will be $\{A, C, G, T\}$; for RNA, it is $\{A, C, G, U\}$; and for proteins, the alphabet will be $\{A, R, N, D, C, E, Q, G, H, I, L, K, M, F, P, S, T, W, Y, V, B, Z, J, X\}$, for example. By generalizing to symbols and alphabets, we can build models where components will be applicable irrespective of our underlying data. Symbols from the alphabet are typically denoted by the lowercase letters $a, b, \ldots$ (see Durbin (1998 #128), for example).

Our objective is to give a numeric score to a pair of aligned sequences where that numeric value – its score – is a measure that the sequences are related as opposed to a random chance. How do we do this? We will begin with the simplest case: that of two sequences of equal length, with no gaps, and build up to the more general case.

In the random case, we assume that any letter of the alphabet under consideration occurs independently with some frequency. For the alphabet $\{A, C, G, T\}$, the respective frequencies would be f_A, f_C, f_G, f_T, respectively. Since we have stated independence, the probability for the two sequences would simply be the product of the probabilities for the individual symbols[12]:

$$P(S, T|\text{Random}) = \prod_i f_{S_i} \prod_i f_{T_i}$$

In the above equation, f_{S_i} is the relative frequency for the symbol at position i in S. Similarly for f_{T_i} in T.

The same is not true in the case where we have achieved some level of match because of a common ancestor. In this case, any pair of symbols at position i have been independently derived from an (unknown) nucleotide (in the case of DNA) in their common ancestor. Thus, the probability for any given pair is the joint probability $p_{S_i T_i}$, which will give the equivalent equation

$$P(S, T|\text{Match}) = \prod_i p_{S_i T_i}.$$

We also need to incorporate substitution matrices into our analytical activities. We brought those into our discussion earlier in this text where certain bases may be substituted for others over evolutionary time. Durbin (1998 #128) described the process producing the log likelihood ratio of a residue pair (a,b) occurring as an aligned pair versus an unaligned pair as being

$s(a, b) = \log(\frac{p_{ab}}{q_a q_b})$, where q_a, q_b are the frequencies for residues a and b, and p_{ab} is the joint probability of the aligned pairs of residues occurring. Well-published matrices, such as the BLOSUM50 matrix, are readily available and should be incorporated into our alignment efforts.

A further factor we need to consider is what happens where a residue has either been inserted into one sequence, or eliminated from the other; a gap. Typically, we would incorporate a *gap penalty* into our algorithm. We would want

AAGTTGCCCGATATA
AACTTGCCCGATATT

to have a higher score than

AAGTTGCCCGATATA
AACTTGC_CGATATT

where the gap has been highlighted by the underscore.

---

[12] The reader is referred back to Chap. 8 and Appendix A for further explanation of the equations in this section.

Typically, the gap, of length g, $\gamma(g)$ is calculated using a linear or affine scoring mechanism. In the former case, a single value – a "gap opening" penalty – is used to give us a simple value:

$$\gamma(g) = -gd$$

If we use a common value of $d = 8$, we see that a gap of length 1 will result in a penalty of -8, whereas a gap of length 10 will result in a penalty of -80. This raises an interesting question as to whether it is realistic to say that a ten-residue gap should really have ten times the (negative) cost that a one-residue gap has. This is where the affine case can be useful. In this case, we use a second value – the "gap extension" penalty:

$$\gamma(g) = -d - (g - 1)e$$

Using $d = 12$ and $e = 2$, a one-residue gap would result in a penalty of 8; a ten-residue gap would result in a penalty of 30.

We've taken a liberty with the numbers for illustrative purposes. In reality, the values for d and e are actually calculated using base 2 of a probability. The exact values would be $d = (8 \log 2)/2$ in the linear case and $d = (12 \log 2)/2$ and $e = (2 \log 2)/2$ in the affine case.

As we look at the overall problem of alignment, we need to consider the *level* of alignment that we are most interested in – local or global – and how that choice affects the matching algorithms that we discussed above. Global alignment and local alignment have different algorithms and purposes.

In the global alignment case, we are interested in the optimal alignment between two sequences, allowing gaps. The standard algorithm for this is the Needelman-Wunsch algorithm (Needleman and Wunsch 1970 #440).[13] Essentially, the approach is to build up longer and longer optimal alignments using previous iterations that generated optimal alignments for smaller subsequences. A matrix is used to score the various subsequences.

Consider two sequences $X = x_1 x_2 \ldots x_n$ and $Y = y_1 y_2 \ldots y_m$ that we want to align. We develop a matrix $F(n, m)$ and store the optimal alignment between the segments $x_1 x_2 \ldots x_i$ and $y_1 y_2 \ldots y_j$ in $F(i, j)$. $F(i, j)$ can be built recursively. We begin by setting $F(0, 0) = 0$ and then proceed to fill in the matrix from the top left $(F(0, 0))$ to bottom right $(F(n, m))$. For any cell $F(i, j)$, its value can be calculated if $F(i - 1, j - 1)$, $F(i - 1, j)$, and $F(i, j - 1)$ are known.

Consider our location $F(i, j)$, which means that we are looking at adding the residues x_i and y_j into the alignment we have built so far. One of the three situations will occur:

- x_i could align to y_j.
  If this is the case, $F(i, j) = F(i - 1, j - 1) + s(x_i, y_j)$, where $s(x_i, y_j)$ is as described earlier.

---

[13] A more efficient implementation was described by Gotoh (1982 #441).

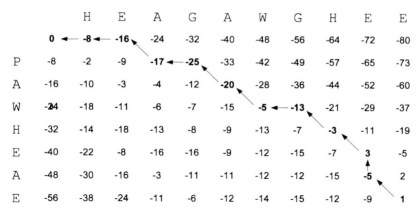

Fig. 10.4   Alignment dynamic programming matrix

- x_i could align to a gap.
  If this is the case, $F(i,j) = F(i-1,j) - d$.
- y_i could align to a gap.
  If this is the case, $F(i,j) = F(i,j-1) - d$.

The largest of these values is the best score up to (i,j):

$$F(i,j) = \max \begin{cases} F(i-1,j-1) + s(x_i, y_j), \\ F(i-1,j) - d, \\ F(i,j-1) - d. \end{cases}$$

The three situations can be visualized using the following examples:

```
A G T H x_i        H A G T H x_i        G T H x_i _
I G V T y_j        G V T y_j _ _        R G V T y_j
```

In the first case, the two residues we are interested in correspond to each other in their positional values. In the second, x_i aligns to a gap. In the third, y_j aligns to a gap.

Once the matrix has been completed, we can trace our path from the bottom right to the top left by tracking the cell from which that value was derived, that is, whether the value was derived from x_i aligning with y_j, x_i aligning with a gap, or y_j aligning with a gap.

A complete step-by-step example can be found in Durbin (1998 #128)[14] for the interested reader, using the sequences HEAGAWGHEE and PAWHEAE, which generates the dynamic matrix shown in Fig. 10.4.

By following the values highlighted in bold text, we have the alignment HEAGAWGHE-E and --P-AW-HEAE.

---

[14] This example appears on page 21 and includes a detailed discussion of the steps involved.

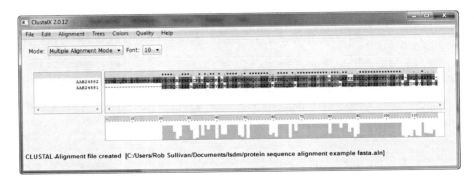

Fig. 10.5 Alignment using ClustalX

Many tools are available that automatically provide alignment according to the alignment matrix and algorithm you want to use. For example, aligning two human zinc-finger sequences, GenBank accession numbers AAB24881 and AAB24882:

```
AAB24881:  YECNQCGKAFAQHSSLKCHYRTHIGEKPYECNQCGKAFSKHSHLQCHK

           RTHTGEKPYECNQCGKAFSQHGLLQRHKRTHTGEKPYMNVINMVKPLH

           NS

AAB24882:  TYHMCQFHCRYVNNHSGEKLYECNERSKAFSCPSHLQCHKRRQIGEKT

           HEHNQCGKAFPTPSHLQYHERTHTGEKPYECHQCGQAFKKCSLLQRHK

           RTHTGEKPYECNQCGKAFAQ
```

using the ClustalX package, we obtain the following alignment, also shown in Fig. 10.5:

```
AAB24881  -------------------YECNQCGKAFAQHSSLKCHYRTHIGEKP

AAB24882  TYHMCQFHCRYVNNHSGEKLYECNERSKAFSCPSHLQCHKRRQIGEKT

AAB24881  YECNQCGKAFSKHSHLQCHKRTHTGEKPYECNQCGKAFKKCSLLQRHK

AAB24882  HEHNQCGKAFPTPSHLQYHERTHTGEKPYECHQCGQAFSQHGLLQRHK

AAB24881  RTHTGEKPYMNVINMVKPLHNS

AAB24882  RTHTGEKPYE-CNQCGKAFAQ-
```

Global alignment, the process of aligning across the complete sequence set, typically uses the Needleman-Wunsch algorithm. For cases where we are more interested in looking for the best alignment between two subsequences – local alignment – the Smith-Waterman algorithm is more commonly used.

One of the two major differences is in our alignment function where we have a fourth option: of allowing $F(i,j)$ to take a value of 0 if all other options have a value that is less than zero.

$$F(i,j) = \max \begin{cases} 0, \\ F(i-1,j-1) + s(x_i, y_j), \\ F(i-1,j) - d, \\ F(i,j-1) - d. \end{cases}$$

This zero value option has the effect of starting a new alignment.

Also, our alignment can now end anywhere in our matrix and not just the top left-hand corner. We leave it for the interested reader to investigate, but taking the two sequences from Durbin (1998 #128), HEAGAWGHEE and PAWHEAE, and using the Smith-Waterman algorithm will actually return an optimal local alignment of AWGHE against AW-HE.[15]

10.7.2 Multiple Alignment

In the previous section, we discussed the process for aligning two sequences. Once we move beyond two sequences, we are into a more complex problem since we now want to optimally align three, four, five, or some larger number of sequences. Inference and experience have traditionally been the primary tools for biologists in this regard, using their subject matter expertise to consider highly conserved residues, how structure affects sequence fragments, and what they would expect to see in terms of patterns of residue insertions and deletions. Tools and methods to help with this tedious activity have been greatly welcomed.

In our discussion on pairwise sequence alignment, one of our objectives was to make sure that the end-result provided us with the best sequence alignment of the various possibilities. Recall that we would consider gaps – residues that may or may not be inserted or deleted – when we developed our proposed alignment. We can generalize this to the multiple alignment case where one of our objectives will obviously be to obtain the best alignment we can across the set of sequences. Thus, our scoring scheme must be structured in such a way as to give better alignments and better scores. The challenge is to ensure that subject matter expertise is incorporated into the scoring matrices to provide these higher scores that we strive toward.

We'll use the term *homologous* as a key foundation for considering what it means to perform multiple alignment, and this term is used for both evolutionary similarity and for structural similarity. In the ideal sense, this would mean that

---

[15] See Durbin (1998 #128), pp. 22–23.

subsequences that we can align across a number of larger sequences would be seen as occupying similar positions in the underlying three-dimensional structures and would also diverge from a common ancestor.

A good example of this is the immunoglobulin superfamily. The work of Harpaz and Chothia (1994 #442) provided an insight into how such similarities for this superfamily have been conserved over time and how these highly similar motifs can be found across species.[16]

Intuitively, there is always a single correct evolutionary alignment that would be independent of any structural variation(s) that occurs. However, the challenge is that this evolutionary history is not available to us through an independent methodology and so must be inferred from the sequence data itself: from the alignment. This provides two challenges. The first is that a small sequence variation at the genomic level can have a significant impact at the protein level. Using an example from Tramontano (2005 #10), consider the implications of the insertion of a single nucleotide in human insulin and the effect of the change on protein sequence (Table 10.5).

As the above sequences show, a single nucleotide variation can be catastrophic on the translated sequence.

When we take a set of sequences and try to align them, our success will be very dependent on how related the sequences are to each other. However, from a data-mining perspective, we're not so much interested in aligning a set of sequences that are known to be similar, or suspected to be similar, but to find a set of sequences from a much larger base that *might* be similar to each other. As the work of Harpaz and Chothia (1994 #442) illustrated, typically, there will be small sets of key residues that can be unambiguously aligned for sequences in a family, irrespective of how the sequences in the family may have diverged. The key here (sic) is to define the key residues in the set of sequences we are analyzing.

Given this context, aligning such motifs correctly requires us to be careful about our scoring matrix. Specific factors to consider that differ from our pairwise alignment matrices include a need to incorporate *position-specific* scoring to account for areas that are more conserved than other areas and the *phylogenetic* interrelationship that occurs because sequences are related through a phylogenetic tree. We'll return to this in the next section.

An important factor to consider is that the vast majority of scoring algorithms will assume that the individual parts of an alignment – the individual columns – are statistically independent of each other, meaning that the overall score has a component such as $\sum s(r_i)$, where r_i is the residue at column i and s is the scoring algorithm itself.[i] We know that there is a second component to our scoring mechanism: a function accounting for any gaps that are introduced into the alignment. The typical gap scoring function is an affine scoring function where the cost of

---

[16] Much research has been performed on the globin family as it has been shown to be highly conserved across species. This family has been widely used computationally for this reason. However, to date, this family of proteins has been the exception rather than the rule.

Table 10.5 Single nucleotide insertion in human insulin

```
atg gcc ctg tgg atg cgc ctc ctg ccc ctg ctg gcg ctg ctg gcc
 M   A   L   W   M   R   L   L   P   L   L   A   L   L   A
ctc tgg gga cct gac cca gcc gca gcc ttt gtg aac caa cac ctg
 L   W   G   P   D   P   A   A   A   F   V   N   Q   H   L
tgc ggc tca cac ctg gtg gaa gct ctc tac cta gtg tgc ggg gaa
 C   G   S   H   L   V   E   A   L   Y   L   V   C   G   E
cga ggc ttc ttc tac aca ccc aag acc cgc cgg gag gca gag gac
 R   G   F   F   Y   T   P   K   T   R   R   E   A   E   D
ctg cag gtg ggg cag gtg gag ctg ggc ggg ggc cct ggt gca ggc
 L   Q   V   G   Q   V   E   L   G   G   G   P   G   A   G
agc ctg cag ccc ttg gcc ctg gag ggg tcc ctg cag aag cgt ggc
 S   L   Q   P   L   A   L   E   G   S   L   Q   K   R   G
att gtg gaa caa tgc tgt acc agc atc tgc tcc ctc tac cag ctg
 I   V   E   Q   C   C   T   S   I   C   S   L   Y   Q   L
gag aac tac tgc aac tag
 E   N   Y   C   N   -


atg gcc ctg tgg atg cgc ctc ctg ccc ctg ctg gcg ctg ctg gcc
 M   A   L   W   M   R   L   L   P   L   L   A   L   L   A
ctc tgg gga cct gac cca gcc gca gAc ctt tgt gaa cca aca cct
 L   W   G   P   D   P   A   A   D   L   C   E   P   T   P
gtg cgg ctc aca cct ggt gga agc tct cta cct agt gtg cgg gga
 V   R   L   T   P   G   G   S   S   L   P   S   V   R   G
acg agg ctt ctt cta cac acc caa gac ccg ccg gga ggc aga gga
 T   R   L   L   L   H   T   Q   D   P   P   G   G   R   G
cct gca ggt ggg gca ggt gga gct ggg cgg ggg ccc tgg tgc agg
 P   A   G   G   A   G   G   A   G   R   G   P   W   C   R
cag cct gca gcc ctt ggc cct gga ggg gtc cct gca gaa gcg tgg
 Q   P   A   A   L   G   P   G   G   V   P   A   E   A   W
cat tgt gga aca atg ctg tac cag cat ctg ctc cct cta cca gct
 H   C   G   T   M   L   Y   Q   H   L   L   P   L   P   A
gga gaa cta ctg caa cta g
 G   E   L   L   Q   L  ...
```

introducing a gap into the alignment has a cost that is higher than the cost associated with extending an existing gap.

The most common method of scoring is using a *sum of pairs* function, which uses a substitution scoring matrix such as PAN or BLOSUM to score the columns. Recalling our earlier discussion, the score $s(a, b)$ is used to provide a probability of a and b occurring as an aligned pair as opposed to an unaligned pair. $s(a, -)$ and $s(-, a)$ account for gap costs, and $s(-, -)$ is typically given a zero value. The substitution scores are now typically derived as log-odds scores for pairwise comparisons as opposed to a simple summation. That is, to use $\log(p_{abc}/p_a p_b p_c)$ rather than $\log(p_{ab}/p_a p_b) + \log(p_{bc}/p_b p_c) + \log(p_{ac}/p_a p_c)$.

There are some issues with the sum or pairs (SP) scoring algorithm that the interested reader may find more information about in Altschul et al. (1989 #443).

| Entries for the BLOSUM50 matrix at a scale of ln(2)/3.0. | | | | | | | | | | | | | | | | | | | | | | | | |
	A	R	N	D	C	Q	E	G	H	I	L	K	M	F	P	S	T	W	Y	V	B	J	Z	X	*
A	5	-2	-1	-2	-1	-1	-1	0	-2	-1	-2	-1	-1	-3	-1	1	0	-3	-2	0	-2	-2	-1	-1	-5
R	-2	7	-1	-2	-4	1	0	-3	0	-4	-3	3	-2	-3	-3	-1	-1	-3	-1	-3	-1	-3	0	-1	-5
N	-1	-1	7	2	-2	0	0	0	1	-3	-4	0	-2	-4	-2	1	0	-4	-2	-3	5	-4	0	-1	-5
D	-2	-2	2	8	-4	0	2	-1	-1	-4	-4	-1	-4	-5	-1	0	-1	-5	-3	-4	6	-4	1	-1	-5
C	-1	-4	-2	-4	13	-3	-3	-3	-3	-2	-2	-3	-2	-2	-4	-1	-1	-5	-3	-1	-3	-2	-3	-1	-5
Q	-1	1	0	0	-3	7	2	-2	1	-3	-2	2	0	-4	-1	0	-1	-1	-1	-3	0	-3	4	-1	-5
E	-1	0	0	2	-3	2	6	-3	0	-4	-3	1	-2	-3	-1	-1	-1	-3	-2	-3	1	-3	5	-1	-5
G	0	-3	0	-1	-3	-2	-3	8	-2	-4	-4	-2	-3	-4	-2	0	-2	-3	-3	-4	-1	-4	-2	-1	-5
H	-2	0	1	-1	-3	1	0	-2	10	-4	-3	0	-1	-1	-2	-1	-2	-3	2	-4	0	-3	0	-1	-5
I	-1	-4	-3	-4	-2	-3	-4	-4	-4	5	2	-3	2	0	-3	-3	-1	-3	-1	4	-4	4	-3	-1	-5
L	-2	-3	-4	-4	-2	-2	-3	-4	-3	2	5	-3	3	1	-4	-3	-1	-2	-1	1	-4	4	-3	-1	-5
K	-1	3	0	-1	-3	2	1	-2	0	-3	-3	6	-2	-4	-1	0	-1	-3	-2	-3	0	-3	1	-1	-5
M	-1	-2	-2	-4	-2	0	-2	-3	-1	2	3	-2	7	0	-3	-2	-1	-1	0	1	-3	2	-1	-1	-5
F	-3	-3	-4	-5	-2	-4	-3	-4	-1	0	1	-4	0	8	-4	-3	-2	1	4	-1	-4	1	-4	-1	-5
P	-1	-3	-2	-1	-4	-1	-1	-2	-2	-3	-4	-1	-3	-4	10	-1	-1	-4	-3	-3	-2	-3	-1	-1	-5
S	1	-1	1	0	-1	0	-1	0	-1	-3	-3	0	-2	-3	-1	5	2	-4	-2	-2	0	-3	0	-1	-5
T	0	-1	0	-1	-1	-1	-1	-2	-2	-1	-1	-1	-1	-2	-1	2	5	-3	-2	0	0	-1	-1	-1	-5
W	-3	-3	-4	-5	-5	-1	-3	-3	-3	-3	-2	-3	-1	1	-4	-4	-3	15	2	-3	-5	-2	-2	-1	-5
Y	-2	-1	-2	-3	-3	-1	-2	-3	2	-1	-1	-2	0	4	-3	-2	-2	2	8	-1	-3	-1	-2	-1	-5
V	0	-3	-3	-4	-1	-3	-3	-4	-4	4	1	-3	1	-1	-3	-2	0	-3	-1	5	-3	2	-3	-1	-5
B	-2	-1	5	6	-3	0	1	-1	0	-4	-4	0	-3	-4	-2	0	0	-5	-3	-3	6	-4	1	-1	-5
J	-2	-3	-4	-4	-2	-3	-3	-4	-3	4	4	-3	2	1	-3	-3	-1	-2	-1	2	-4	4	-3	-1	-5
Z	-1	0	0	1	-3	4	5	-2	0	-3	-3	1	-1	-4	-1	0	-1	-2	-2	-3	1	-3	5	-1	-5
X	-1	-1	-1	-1	-2	-1	-1	-1	-1	-1	-1	-1	-1	-1	-2	-1	-1	-1	-1	-1	-1	-1	-1	-1	-5
*	-5	-5	-5	-5	-5	-5	-5	-5	-5	-5	-5	-5	-5	-5	-5	-5	-5	-5	-5	-5	-5	-5	-5	-5	1

Fig. 10.6 BLOSUM50 scoring matrix

Let's take a look at a couple of examples to illustrate our discussion. We'll use the BLOSUM50 matrix[17] to obtain our scoring values. The matrix is shown in Fig. 10.6.

Consider a set of n sequences that we are about to align. If each of these sequences has a particular amino acid at a particular position i, say the amino acid proline (P), then from our table above, we get a score of 10. The sum of pairs (SP) score would then be $10 \times n(n-1)/2$, where $n(n-1)/2$ is the number of symbol pairs in the column. If, however, one of these sequences had a different amino acid in position i, say the amino acid lysine (K), and the other $(n-1)$ sequences had proline, we would have a different score. Our scoring matrix tells us that the P-K score is -1 instead of 10 for the P-P pair. Since there are $(n-1)$ pairs affected, the difference would be $11(n-1)$, from which we can determine that the score for a column where there is one difference (K) will be worse than the case where they are all the same (P) by a factor of

$$\frac{11(n-1)}{10n(n-1)/2} = \frac{11}{5n},$$

which is counterintuitive since one would reasonably expect the relative difference between the scores to increase with evidence of conservation, not decrease, as the inverse dependence on n indicates.

The most common approach to multiple alignments is *progressive alignment*, which constructs our multiple alignments by constructing successive pairwise alignments. The algorithms work by initially selecting two sequences and aligning them according to standard pairwise alignment methods. The resulting alignment is

---

[17] The matrix we are using, included in the text, was taken from http://www.ncbi.nlm.nih.gov/IEB/ToolBox/C_DOC/lxr/source/data/BLOSUM50

then fixed, and a third sequence is aligned to the first alignment. This is then continued for all remaining sequences until all sequences in our set have been aligned.

A simple Google search will turn up several different strategies by different authors, including Feng and Doolittle (1987 #444) and Waterman and Perlwitz (1984 #445), some of earliest introducers of progressive alignment, along with authors such as Thompson et al. (1994 #446) who developed one of the most widely used multiple alignment programs, CLUSTAL W.

Mining sequence data poses its own unique challenges in addition to those encountered with other types of data. Similarities between sequences definitely account for a large part of the analytical effort, but are certainly not the whole.

10.7.3   Trees

This is probably the most common, and well-known, representation used in phylogeny. We discussed trees and tree-building techniques comprehensively earlier in the book but now return to it within the context of informatics.

Alignment of two or more sequences is intended to optimally align the base pairs to show their evolutionary relationship and make the assumption that a larger number of substitutions between a set of (closely) related sequences are less plausible than a small smaller number of changes.

This provides an intuitive correlation with using trees as a visual tool for representing these relationships: more closely related sequences should be on branches that are closer to each other on a tree than those which are less closely related to each other.

Scientific study of organisms at the molecular level suggests that life on earth had a common ancestor. Therefore, all life is related, and the relationship is its phylogeny. A phylogenetic tree can be developed for the hierarchy of life, displaying relationships as branches of that tree. Up until the 1960s, morphological characteristics were typically used to develop the phylogenies through inference. Since that time, molecular sequences have become more and more widely used as a means to develop these phylogenies.

This does make the assumption that the genetic sequences that we are considering have been passed on, over millennia, from the common ancestor. However, this needs to be considered carefully since speciation is not the only means by which sequences can be passed on and changed; gene duplication can also occur, which means that a tree built up using just sequences will not always reflect the species' phylogeny.

Developing trees from sequence data typically requires that we define a distance measure between sequences. If we have n sequences, then we'll have $n(n - 1)$ distance measures in our set, with the measure d_{ij} denoting the distance between the ith and jth sequences in our set. In our discussions on distance elsewhere, we've seen numerous ways of defining the measure, and the same is true here.

```
Start() {
        Create a cluster C_i for each sequence i.
        Create a leaf node of tree T for each sequence at height = 0.
}
Iterate() {
        Identify clusters i, j where d_ij has its minimal value. If more than one exists,
                select one at random.
        Create new cluster C_k = C_i ∪ C_j and generate distance measures d_kl ∀l.
        Create a node of T for k at height d_kl / 2 with daughter nodes i and j.
        Add k to the cluster set and remove i and j.
}
Stop() {
        If the number of clusters = 2 (i, j); create a node of T (the root) at height d_kl / 2.
}
```

Fig. 10.7 UPGMA algorithm

One approach we could take is to measure the number of residue differences between two aligned sequences as a fraction of the whole. A challenge with this comes into play when we consider what random substitutions will do to this fraction when two sequences are unrelated to each other: this fraction will be close to the value that we would expect to see by chance. Since this is a fractional value, we'd like the distance measure to become as large as possible as the fraction tends to this value. As an example, the Jukes-Cantor model uses $d_{ij} = -\frac{3}{4}\log(1 - 4f/3)$, where f represents the fraction of sites where the residue differs for two sequences.

A widely used method for generating trees uses the unweighted pair-group method using arithmetic averages (UPGMA) procedure that is essentially used to create a new node on the tree by combining two clusters (Fig. 10.7).

But the most widely used algorithm is the *parsimony* algorithm. This defines the tree that can explain the sequences based on the *minimal number of substitutions* across all sequences (Fig. 10.8).

Some of the progressive alignment algorithms we touched on in the last chapter use the concept of a *guide tree* to help direct the clustering process, and we now introduce some of the concepts related to using trees in the informatics space, specifically, how these can be applied to alignment, and how they may be applied to your data-mining efforts.

Often, trees as applied to alignment and informatics consider *binary* trees, where each edge (or branch) that splits will do so into two daughter edges. This simplification is not terribly problematic as any *n*-ary branching pattern can be approximated by a binary pattern in which some of the edge lengths are very short (Fig. 10.9).

```
Start() {
        Set k=2*count(sequences)-1 //number of the root node
}
Iterate { // Compute Sₖ(a)
```

$$\text{if } k \text{ is a leaf node then if } a = x_u^k \text{ then } S_k(a) = 0 \text{ else } S_k(a) = \infty$$

$$\text{else } \{$$

$$\text{Compute } S_i(a), S_j(a) \text{ for daughter nodes } i, j$$

$$S_k(a) = \min_b (S_i(b) + S(a,b)) + \min_b (S_j(b) + S(a,b))$$

```
                }
}
Stop() {
```

$$treeCost = \min_a S_{2n-1}(a)$$

```
}
```

Fig. 10.8 (Weighted) parsimony algorithm

Fig. 10.9 Comparing n-ary tree and binary tree fragments

An important concept for many phylogenetic methods is to determine a set of distances $d_{i,j}$ for each pair i, j of sequences in our dataset. Consider the example dataset for *Drosophila Adh* sequences available with the Mega[18] software package shown in Fig. 10.10.

As the above figure shows, there is more than one way of defining distance. One approach often considered is to look at the fraction f of locations within aligned sequences where the residues at that location differ. For example, at position m in our sequences i, j, we would consider x_i^u and x_j^u. A challenge with this simple definition, however, is that in the case of two unrelated sequences, the natural random substitutions that occur will cause the value of f to approach the value expected by chance: our preference would be to have the value of f get very large as it tends to this value. The Jukes-Cantor model, the second distance measure in our above figure, for example, has a distance value $d_{ij} \rightarrow \infty$ when 75% of the residues differ: $d_{ij} = -\frac{3}{4} \log\left(1 - \frac{4f}{3}\right)$.

---

[18] Tamura et al. (2007 #447).

534 10 Informatics

M4: Pairwise Distances (C:\Program Files (x86)\MEGA 4\Examples\Drosophila_Adh.meg)

File Display Average Caption Help

	1	2	3	4	5	6	7	8	9	10	11
1. D. melanogaster											
2. D. pseudoobscura	0.138										
3. S. lebanonensis	0.199	0.199									
4. S. albovittata	0.248	0.240	0.256								
5. D. crassifemur	0.238	0.241	0.259	0.092							
6. D. mulleri	0.211	0.197	0.211	0.213	0.214						
7. D. affinidisjuncta	0.245	0.235	0.244	0.180	0.182	0.177					
8. D. heteroneura	0.245	0.232	0.247	0.176	0.192	0.177	0.037				
9. D. mimica	0.234	0.227	0.239	0.167	0.185	0.177	0.060	0.052			
10. D. adiastola	0.252	0.243	0.245	0.178	0.190	0.180	0.060	0.059	0.056		
11. D. nigra	0.251	0.227	0.234	0.173	0.182	0.180	0.091	0.083	0.075	0.091	

(D. melanogaster-D. melanogaster) / Nucleotide: p-distance

M4: Pairwise Distances (C:\Program Files (x86)\MEGA 4\Examples\Drosophila_Adh.meg)

File Display Average Caption Help

	1	2	3	4	5	6	7	8	9	10	11
1. D. melanogaster											
2. D. pseudoobscura	0.152										
3. S. lebanonensis	0.232	0.232									
4. S. albovittata	0.301	0.289	0.313								
5. D. crassifemur	0.286	0.291	0.317	0.098							
6. D. mulleri	0.248	0.228	0.248	0.250	0.252						
7. D. affinidisjuncta	0.297	0.282	0.295	0.206	0.209	0.202					
8. D. heteroneura	0.297	0.278	0.299	0.200	0.221	0.202	0.038				
9. D. mimica	0.280	0.270	0.288	0.188	0.212	0.202	0.063	0.054			
10. D. adiastola	0.307	0.293	0.297	0.204	0.219	0.206	0.063	0.062	0.059		
11. D. nigra	0.305	0.270	0.280	0.197	0.209	0.206	0.097	0.088	0.079	0.097	

(D. melanogaster-D. melanogaster) / Nucleotide: Jukes-Cantor

Fig. 10.10 Sequence distance computations using p-distance and Jukes-Cantor models

Clustering algorithms such as UPGMA described above can be used to generate trees. Consider a set of six sequences, whose distances are represented in two dimensions, as shown in Fig. 10.11a.

There is a potential pitfall with some such algorithms in that the edge lengths of the tree can be viewed according to a *molecular clock*, that is, that divergence occurs at a constant rate and that sum of the lengths down any path of the tree are the same. This can provide a challenge if our core data is not well-behaved in this way: the algorithm can reconstruct a tree that is not correct. The *ultrametric condition* is a test that can be used to determine whether or not the tree construction is likely to be correct. We simply mention these concepts here, but do not expand upon them as most analysis will most likely be performed using some phylogenetic package, using the built-in algorithms. Such packages have these validation algorithms built-in.

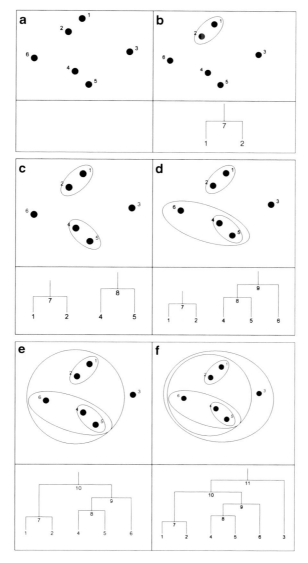

Fig. 10.11 Generation of a tree from a clustering algorithm. (**a**) Distances between six sequences, artificially represented in 2-D. (**b**) Sequences 1 and 2 represent the two closest sequences; a new branch node 7 is identified. (**c**). The next two nearest sequences, represented by 4 and 5 are clustered, generating a new branch node 8. (**d**) Continuing, sequence 6 is clustered with sequences 4 and 5, generating branch node 9. (**e**) The clustering algorithm now clusters our current sequence set together, generating branch node 10. (**f**) Finally, our algorithm incorporates sequence 3, generating branch node 11

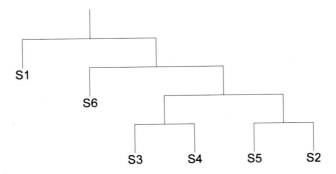

Fig. 10.12 MEGA v4 generation of tree using maximum parsimony

Probably the most widely applied method for building trees is the *parsimony* algorithm which attempts to explain the interrelationship between our set of sequences with the minimum number of substitutions.

Consider the following set of sequences:

S1	AAGATGC
S2	AAAATCG
S3	CGCGTAA
S4	CGGGTAT
S5	AGACTGG
S6	AAGATTA

We can see that there are some similarities between the sequences and could look to build trees and count the number of substitutions needed to move between the nodes, summing over the whole tree. For example, we could build a tree fragment for S1, S2, and S6, using (say) S2 as the root of this subtree, with S1 and S6 as daughter nodes, and count the number of substitutions that were necessary for each branch, as shown below.

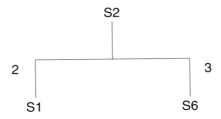

Our objective, using parsimony, is to keep the number of substitutions over the whole tree as small as possible. This fragment requires five substitutions. What would happen if we looked at the complete tree? Figure 10.12 shows the tree generated by MEGA (v4) for our sequence data using maximum parsimony. Figure 10.13 shows the tree generated using Jukes-Cantor and UPGMA.

Figure 10.14 depicts two versions of the parsimony algorithm: the traditional algorithm of Fitch and American Chemical Society (1971 #481) and the weighted parsimony algorithm according to Sankoff and Cedergren (1983 #482).

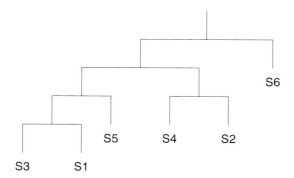

Fig. 10.13 Phylogenetic tree produced by Geneious using Jukes-Cantor distance model and UPGMA tree build method

a	b

init:
  k=2n-1; C=0; // k = number of root
                node
loop:
 	
  if k is leaf node then
    $R_k = x_u^k$
  else   { //k not leaf node
    Compute R_i, R_j
    for daughter nodes i,j of k;
    $R_k = R_i \cap R_j$
    if R_k is empty {
      $R_k = R_i \cap R_j$;
      C=C+1
    }
  }
stop:
  C = minimum cost of tree
	Init:
	  k=2n-1;
	
	loop:
	  compute $S_k(a) \forall a$ as follows:
	  if k is leaf node then
	    $S_k(a) = 0$ for $a = x_u^k$; $S_k(a) = \infty$ otherwise
	  else {
	    Compute $S_i(a).S_j(a) \forall a$
	    at daughter nodes i,j;
	    $S_k(a) = \min_b(S_i(b) + S(a.b)) + \min_b(S_j(b) + S(a.b))$
	
	  }
	stop:
	  $\min_a S_{2n-1}(a) =$ minimum cost of tree

The traditional parsimony algorithm	Weighted parsimony variant
{Fitch, 1971 #481}	{Sankoff, 1983 #482}

Fig. 10.14 Parsimony and weighted parsimony algorithms

In the weighted parsimony algorithm, each substitution of a by b incurs a cost, designated by $S(a,b)$, and our objective is to minimize this cost. It should also be noted that the two algorithms become identical if we designate costs of $S(a,a) = 0$ $\forall a$ and $S(a,b) = 1$ $\forall a \neq b$.

Phylogenetic activities and approaches such as *frequent structure mining* (FSM) have a goal of identifying patterns which occur in structural data such as that represented by trees and graphs. Shasha et al. (2004 #483), for example, presented a technique for discovering patterns in rooted, unordered trees. This type of technique has proven to be of great interest to both the informatics discipline and the data-mining community. Han (2006 #484), for example, proposed a novel microarray approach to attack the incongruence between gene trees and species. They first selected 28 genes from a set of statistically significant housekeeping genes from the *S. cerevisiae* cell cycle time series microarray data, used BLAST and synteny criteria to identify homologs and orthologs of the selected genes among the genomes of other species, and then applied the phylogenomic mining method for the aligned genes to infer the species phylogeny. In Wilson et al. (2009 #485), SUPERFAMILY (http://supfam.org) is described; this valuable resource provides structural, functional, and evolutionary information for proteins from all completely sequenced genomes and large sequence collections. Protein domain assignments for over 900 genomes are included in the database. HMMs are used to provide structural annotation, and the database, models, and associated scripts are available for download from the ftp site. Zaki (2005 #486) presented TREEMINER, an algorithm to discover all frequent subtrees in a forest, using a new data structure called scope-list and contrasted it with a pattern matching tree-mining algorithm (PATTERNMATCHER) and with TREEMINERD, which counts only distinct occurrences of a pattern. Shan (2006 #487) analyzed 36 single genes of six plants, which inferred 18 unique trees using maximum parsimony. As noted above, this incongruence is an important issue, and how to reconstruct the congruent tree still is one of the most challenges in molecular phylogenetics. Addressing this problem, { } attempted a genome-wide EST data-mining approach using EST data of 144 shared genes of six green plants from GenBank. Jiawei (2006 #488) presented a method based on the 3-D graphical representation of gene sequences to analyze the phylogenetic relationships of different genomes.

The above discussion represents only a small number of areas of active research, melding together some of the core topics of informatics and applying data-mining techniques to uncover those patterns using phylogenetic techniques. The interested reader may find Chen et al. (2008 #489) and Zhang and Wang (2006 #519) useful launching points.

10.8   Conclusion

We've left out quite a bit, as any reader with some background in this subject will recognize. For example, Markov chains and hidden Markov models (HMMs) are an important tool used in many areas, which have found particular use in sequence alignment. These techniques can be used to search pairs and groups of sequences and have also been very effectively used for processing sequence families. A full discourse of these techniques is beyond the introductory nature of this book, and we refer the interested reader to sources such as Hughey and Krogh (1996 #427).

Techniques such as alignment and phylogeny have an intuitive application within the data-mining domain since they naturally lead us to ask the question "where else do these motifs/trees/structures also exist?" Taking a particular protein sequence, for example, and comparing it with a typically much larger base of sequences – from your

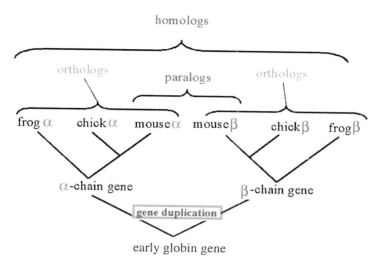

Fig. 10.15 Logs

own private library or from the public domain – can often uncover surprising results. However, the motif you use, too short or too generic, has to be carefully considered and any valid information is obviously lost in the noise of too many results.

Probabilistic models have been discussed at various points in this text, and they are also exceedingly relevant to the informatics space, although we did not expand upon them in this chapter primarily because of space but also because, although such models are available to represent phylogenetic methods, such interpretations are not always presented in such a way. Using probabilistic models for phylogenetic analysis has been a particular area where such models have been leveraged. For the interested reader, Durbin (1998 #128) had a particularly good exposition on this topic.

As we conclude this chapter, one point we want to stress here is that sequence similarity is **not** the same as homology! *Homologs* are sequences derived from a common ancestor. *Orthologs* are similar sequences in two different organisms which have arisen due to a speciation event. In this latter case, the functionality is retained. *Paralogs* are similar sequences within a single organism that have arisen due to a gene duplication event. *Xenologs* are similar sequences that have arisen out of horizontal transfer events (e.g., symbiosis or viruses). Figure 10.15[19] shows the interplay between these different types of similarity. Be careful that you don't infer too much from your analysis.

There is so much more that we could have included in this exciting and fast-moving domain. High-density oligonucleotide arrays, for example, have become a common technology to use in order to capture genome-wide expression levels, and the ubiquitous implementation is the Affymetrix GeneChip. This technology has been the source of a tremendous uptick in processing expression

---

[19] www.ncbi.nlm.nih.gov/Education/BLASTinfo/Orthology.html

levels, and, with the availability of standardized arrays and array sets for *E. coli*, *Drosophila*, mouse, rat, and human, it allows researchers to generate large levels of data from experiments that can be used to gain great insight into expression levels. Another valuable technology, SELDI-TOF[20] mass spectrometry protein data, is widely used for profiling protein markers from tissue, serum, or other bodily fluids and compared with other patients (or conditions) so that the sets of differentially expressed proteins can be analyzed to determine the biological processes and pathways that are involved in the different outcomes or the different phenotypes that we are studying. This is a particularly important technology used to identify biomarkers.

Both of these examples provide large amounts of data from experiments and are fertile ground for mining opportunities. But such technologies also involve important preprocessing and analysis approaches. The interested reader is recommended to Gentleman (2005 #51) for interesting insights and applications within the R and Bioconductor open-source tools.

Every day, new insight is gained into the genome, the proteome, biochemical pathways, and the myriad other disciplines that generate vast amounts of data that can be the source for data mining. In turn, these mining efforts can result in tremendous insight of their own accord. As an example, data mining, MALDI-TOF mass spectrometry, and the PROTEUS platform (www.icar.cnr.it/proteus) were used to analyze inherited breast cancer characteristics and classify patients based upon their proteome profiles[21].

We conclude each chapter by saying that there is much that we have left out, more than we have included in most cases, and this is a challenge with any introductory text but is particularly true within the informatics space. The sheer amount of data that is generated from, say, an oligonucleotide array is significant enough that analysis techniques and, in particular, data-mining techniques will increase in their value as a tool for the researcher looking for those hidden patterns in the data that might just provide a breakthrough for their research.

References

Altschul SF, Carroll RJ, Lipman DJ (1989) Weights for data related by a tree. J Mol Biol 207:647–653

Azuaje F, Dopazo J (2005) Data analysis and visualization in genomics and proteomics. John Wiley, Chichester/Hoboken

---

[20] Surface-enhanced laser desorption/ionization time-of-flight mass spectrometry. Another widely used variant of spectrometry is the MALDI-TOF or matrix-assisted laser desorption/ionization time-of-flight mass spectrometry.

[21] See http://oxford2005.healthgrid.org/documents/slides_pdf/Session_A/ Mazza_HealthGrid2005.pdf for more information.

Bair E, Tibshirani R (2003) Machine learning methods applied to DNA microarray data can improve the diagnosis of cancer. ACM SIGKDD Explor Newsl 5:48–55

Baldi P (2002) DNA microarrays and gene expression: from experiments to data analysis and modeling. Cambridge University Press, Cambridge

Bessant C, Shadforth I, Oakley D (2009) Building bioinformatics solutions: with Perl, R, and mySQL. Oxford University Press, Oxford

Brown PO, Botstein D (1999) Exploring the new world of the genome with DNA microarrays. Nat Genet 21:33–37

Chen D et al (2008) PhyloFinder: an intelligent search engine for phylogenetic tree databases. BMC Evol Biol 8:90

Durbin R (1998) Biological sequence analysis: probabilistic models of proteins and nucleic acids. Cambridge University Press, Cambridge/New York

Feng D-F, Doolittle RF (1987) Progressive sequence alignment as a prerequisite to correct phylogenetic trees. J Mol Evol 25:351–360

Fitch RM, American Chemical Society (1971) Polymer colloids: proceedings. Plenum Press, New York

Gentleman RC (2005) Bioinformatics and computational biology solutions using R and Bioconductor, Statistics for biology and health. Springer, New York

Gibas C, Jambeck P (2001) Developing bioinformatics computer skills. O'Reilly, Beijing/Cambridge

Gotoh O (1982) An improved algorithm for matching biological sequences. J Mol Biol 162:705–708

Han X (2006) Inferring species phylogenies: a microarray approach. In: Computational intelligence and bioinformatics: international conference on intelligent computing, ICIC 2006, Kunming, China. Springer, Berlin/Heidelberg, pp 485–493

Harpaz Y, Chothia C (1994) Many of the immunoglobulin superfamily domains in cell adhesion molecules and surface receptors belong to a new structural set which is close to that containing variable domains. J Mol Biol 238:528–539

Hughey R, Krogh A (1996) Hidden Markov models for sequence analysis: extension and analysis of the basic method. Comput Appl Biosci 12:95–107

Iacobas AD et al (2002) Improved procedures to mine data obtained from spotted cDNA arrays. J Biomol Tech 13:5–19

Jiawei L (2006) A novel method for constructing phylogenetic tree based on 3D graphical representation. International conference on computational intelligence for modelling, control and automation, 2006 and international conference on intelligent agents, web technologies and internet commerce, Sydney, NSW. In: Xizhen Z (ed). pp 244–244

Kamberova GL, Shah SK (2002) DNA array image analysis: nuts & bolts. DNA Press, Eagleville

Knudsen S (2002) A biologist's guide to analysis of DNA microarray data. Wiley-Interscience, New York

Leng X, Muller H-G (2006) Classification using functional data analysis for temporal gene expression data. Bioinformatics 22:68–76

Lockhart D, Winzeler E (2000) Genomics, gene expression and DNA arrays. Nature 405:827–836

Markel S, León D (2003) Sequence analysis in a nutshell: a guide to common tools and databases. O'Reilly, Sebastopol/Farnham

Moorhouse M, Barry P (2004) Bioinformatics, biocomputing and Perl: an introduction to bioinformatics computing skills and practice. Wiley, Chichester/Hoboken

Nadimpally V, Jaki MJ (2003) A novel approach to determine normal variation in gene expression data. ACM SIGKDD Explor Newsl 5:6–15

Needleman S, Wunsch C (1970) A general method applicable to the search for similarities in the amino acid sequence of two proteins. J Mol Biol 48:443–453

Roberts RJ (1980) Restriction and modification enzymes and their recognition sequences. Nucleic Acids Res 8:r63–r80

Sankoff D, Cedergren RJ (1983) Simultaneous comparison of three or more sequences related by a tree. In: Sankoff D, Kruskal JB (eds) Time warps, string edits, and macromolecules: the theory and practice of sequence comparison. Addison-Wesley, Reading, pp 253–263

Schena M (2002) Microarray analysis. Wiley, Hoboken

Schwartz R (2008) Biological modeling and simulation: a survey of practical models, algorithms, and numerical methods. MIT Press, Cambridge

Shan Y (2006) Genome-wide EST data mining approaches to resolving incongruence of molecular phylogenies. Quantitative Biology/Genomics, arXiv:13

Shasha D, Wang JTL, Zhang S (2004) Unordered tree mining with applications to phylogeny. In: Proceedings of the 20th international conference on data engineering. IEEE Computer Society, Boston, pp 708

Shipp MA et al (2002) Diffuse large B-cell lymphoma outcome prediction by gene-expression profiling and supervised machine learning. Nat Med 8:68–74

Simon R (2003) Supervised analysis when the number of candidate features (p) greatly exceeds the number of cases (n). ACM SIGKDD Explor Newsl 5:31–37

Tamura K, Dudley J, Nei M, Kumar S (2007) MEGA4: Molecular Evolutionary Genetics Analysis (MEGA) software version 4.0. Mol Biol Evol 24:1596–1599

Thompson JD, Higgins DG, Gibson TJ (1994) CLUSTAL W: improving the sensitivity of progressive multiple sequence alignment through sequence weighting, position-specific gap penalties and weight matrix choice. Nucleic Acids Res 22:4673–4680

Tisdall JD (2001) Beginning Perl for bioinformatics. O'Reilly, Beijing/Sebastopol

Tisdall JD (2003) Mastering Perl for bioinformatics. O'Reilly, Beijing/Farnham

Tramontano A (2005) The ten most wanted solutions in protein bioinformatics. Chapman & Hall/CRC, Boca Raton

Tu Y, Stolovitzky G, Klein U (2002) Quantitative noise analysis for gene expression microarray experiments. Proc Natl Acad Sci USA 99:14031–14036

Vrana KE, Freeman WM, Aschner M (2002) Use of microarray technologies in toxicology research. Neurotoxicity 24:321–332

Wall L, Christiansen T, Orwant J (2000) Programming Perl. O'Reilly, Beijing/Cambridge

Waterman MS, Perlwitz MD (1984) Line geometries for sequence comparisons. Bull Math Biol 46:567–577

Wilson D et al (2009) SUPERFAMILY – sophisticated comparative genomics, data mining, visualization and phylogeny. Nucleic Acids Res 37:D380–D386

Zaki MJ (2005) Efficiently mining frequent trees in a forest: algorithms and applications. IEEE Trans Knowl Data Eng 17:1021–1035

Zhang S, Wang JTL (2006) Mining frequent agreement subtrees in phylogenetic databases. In: Ghosh J et al (eds) Sixth SIAM international conference on data mining. SIAM, Bethesda, pp 222–233

Chapter 11
Systems Biology

Abstract Since the turn of the twenty-first century, a trend called "Systems Biology" has seen its genesis and involves bringing together a wide range of disciplines from traditional biosciences, computer science, and other nontraditional(?) areas to look at whether or not models can allow us to identify emergent behaviors of systems – the whole being more than the sum of the parts – and as an alternative to more reductionist areas of study. In this chapter, we briefly touch on some of the context and makeup of systems biology and hope to offer some insight into this exciting focus of research and how it may help us with more discoveries in the life sciences.

11.1 What Is This Systems Biology of Which You Speak?

Systems biology is a term which has been used, especially since 2000, as an aggregate title collecting together a number of trends in bioscience research. Bringing together capabilities and knowledge from many different perspectives, this trend has stated goals such as to model and discover emergent properties of systems. One could say that one of the understandings of systems biology is that the behavior of the whole is greater than what would be expected from the sum of its parts, which implies a goal of being able to predict the behavior of the whole organism based on what can be elicited from the "components" making up that organism.

With this context in mind, orienting our thoughts toward the data aspect of this challenge, we can see that one objective is to take disparate pieces of data, align (sic) them to each other in some sense, and see if we are able to make predictions based upon that amalgam of data. If this premise has merit, then it becomes obvious that we need to be able to deal with this vast amount of data being generated from different experimental techniques and different original research purposes in such a way as to make the whole meaningful, allowing us to draw conclusions. Thankfully, data-mining research has led to improved methods for mining patterns that exist in

R. Sullivan, *Introduction to Data Mining for the Life Sciences*,
DOI 10.1007/978-1-59745-290-8_11, © Springer Science+Business Media, LLC 2012

ever-increasing data repositories: classification methods for clustering, outlier analysis, visualization, and spatial/temporal methods have been just some of the areas of progress. As an example, the GOALIE algorithm (Antoniotti et al. 2005 #956) attempts to build dynamic temporal models of biological processes.

In other places within this text, we've described how different techniques can be applied to different types of data. With several techniques, the volume of data forces us to use aggregation methods to effectively elicit the information we are trying to obtain. A major difference in the systems biology arena is the magnitude of the data we are dealing with. High-throughput techniques, including screening, microarrays, (microscopy) images, and the like generate significant amounts of data, analysis of which, using inference methods, can allow us to reconstruct the underlying networks that exist as part of the overall biological processes. Techniques need to be able to deal with these vast amounts of data out of the box, so to speak.

New high-throughput sequencing technologies open challenge for data-mining applications. Since 2004, massively parallel DNA sequencing technologies (MPS) have exploded onto the scene and offer dramatically higher throughput with drastically lower per-base costs than was previously possible. Application of this generation of sequencing technologies and next-generation sequencing (NGS) technologies will allow for sequencing 1,000 human genomes, characterizing thousands of transcriptomes and associated microbial diversities within a few years with unprecedented depth and resolution. Tens of millions of sequencing tags can now be obtained at a cost similar to what tens of thousands used to cost.

MPS has recently been applied to profile protein-DNA interactions, cytosine methylation, genetic variation, genomic rearrangements, transcriptomes, and biodiversity studies, to name a few. Platforms such as the Roche (454) GS FLX sequencer, Illumina genome analyzer, and the Applied Biosystems SOLiD sequencer are able to produce millions of short-length sequence reads, producing outputs suitable for genome resequencing, the whole transcriptome acquisition, microRNA discovery, methylation inference, ChIPSeq experiments, and SNP discovery, as well as outputs useful for whole genome sequencing, assessing of structural rearrangements, DNA copy number alterations, as well as for SNP discovery.

Such large amounts of data require robust data-mining methods that can be used to analyze data for a large set of species: for instance, more than 200 bacterial species populate the human body and, more ideally, should be sequenced and studied as a whole.

Obviously, the challenge is that the required methods need to leverage small training sets and/or unsupervised learning methods, have good computational complexity, and work on the fly with a substantial flow of data.

But the challenge we face is that no single experimental technique allows us to record all of the interactions which occur within these biological processes at the same time. Instead, such data needs to be integrated together. But significant amounts of data are already available in thousands of publications. Using a combination of analysis of the literature using text-mining techniques and gene ontology

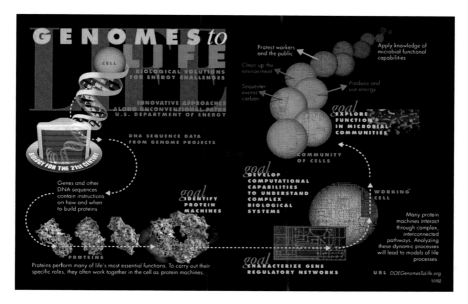

Fig. 11.1   An application of systems biology (http://genomicscience.energy.gov/)

can provide additional annotations as well as allowing us to reconstruct the associated networks.

Public databases provide another fertile source for data elements. Many databases provide navigation facilities that allow us to use visualization techniques and provide a mechanism that we can leverage for further exploration.

Hopefully, this cursory tour through *some* of the areas of application of data mining to systems biology gives a sense of the landscape of challenge and just how vast is the discipline that we refer to by systems biology. But, as we shall hopefully present, it is also a rapidly changing space.

At the same time, data integration, standardization, and normalization; leveraging of techniques across a broad spectrum of scientific disciplines – some nontraditional techniques such as those available in the computational linguistics community; and traditional data-mining techniques can provide further insight into the data at our disposal, extending and expanding our ability to further our understanding of the complexities of life; see Fig. 11.1 for an example.

So what is it? Let's take a few of the definitions available on the Internet:

• The study of the interactions between the components of *biological systems*, and how these interactions give rise to the function and behavior of that system (Wikipedia)
• The study of an organism, viewed as an *integrated* and *interacting network* of genes, proteins, and biochemical reactions which give rise to life (Institute for Systems Biology)

We can intuitively see how data mining becomes a core research tool in systems biology and almost an imperative to understanding that data. Machine-learning tools have become fundamental tools in extracting knowledge from biological data, as well as in automating tasks. Biological structures and processes are described by extremely large numbers of features, and complex interactions exist between these features. By leveraging machine-learning techniques, we can explore datasets in ways that were previously challenging, error-prone, or impossible due to their size and complexity. Gene prediction and annotation and text mining are two particular areas.

As we can see, massive amounts of biological data require interpretation, which, in turn, calls for formal modeling and computational methods to be used in order to effectively interpret and understand the dynamical and functional characteristics (physiology) of the organism(s) or disease progression under study.

So with this context, let's flesh out where and how systems biology and data mining come together, and probably the place to begin is with the data itself.

Postgenome, high-throughput techniques such as genome sequencing, global expression profiling (of coding genes and microRNA), protein expression, and protein-protein interactions, each result in large amounts of –omics data being generated. Managing, analyzing, and interpreting this data is inherently challenging and data mining plays a major role in each of these efforts. As we increase our use of these and other techniques, such as investigating posttranslational modifications, and apply them to the challenge of understanding the underlying complex diseases, such as cancers, as a step in the overall objective to develop therapies, we need techniques to effectively deal with the large volumes of data. But unfortunately, that's not the whole of it: We also need to deal with the higher than desired signal-to-noise ratio that high-throughput techniques often generate. Add to this the availability of many sources of this –omics data such as from the Human Genome Project, gene expression data that has been made available from microarray experiments, protein interaction database, to name but a few. However, there is another important source of data that has become important, especially in the systems biology realm: already published research via sources such as PubMed. Text mining has become an important area of research with the objective of uncovering knowledge hidden in the literature published to date. However, a challenge lies in the fact that such repositories were originally developed using discrete technological platforms and that the data therein is often presented to the user in heterogeneous, unstructured forms that require further processing before the data can be used.

Bringing these various sources together means we have an opportunity to apply mathematical and computational techniques that allow us to study both the structure of biological systems and the dynamics between components of said systems.

Genes are not independent from each other; they regulate each other and act collectively, which can be observed using microarray experiments. Interest is shifting from the classical static analysis to temporal, genome-wide expression profiling, which benefit greatly from microarray technology. Techniques such as clustering, PCA, multidimensional scaling, and network inference provide a toolset that allows us to investigate the interrelationships among genes that constitute gene regulatory networks.

From the systems science perspective, many important properties inherent in any complex system emerge from how the individual (system) components interact with each other. This is a key objective of systems biology: to discover emergent properties and functions that do not appear when individual components are studied, but are instead driven by the interactions among all the components (or component groups). As described in Peng and Zhang (2007 #957),

A general framework of systems biology can be described by three main steps:

1. *Identifying elements/components of the system;*
2. *Describing the system using connective networks, in which nodes represent the system components and edges represent interactions between nodes. The network describes the functional relationship among the system components, and the interactions ultimately determine an organism's behavior and functions;*
3. *Gaining insights into emergent properties of biological systems by means of analyzing structural properties and dynamics of the network.*

From this we can see a couple of differences between systems biology and more traditional molecular biology (Kell 2006 #989):

1. A concentration (in systems biology) on the dynamics of molecular interactions, not on the molecules themselves
2. An interplay between modeling, underlying theory, experimentation, and technology

Since the discipline of systems biology is such a dynamic area, we will try and provide a sense of some of the areas currently being explored, but even less so than previous chapters, this chapter will not provide a comprehensive overview by any means. The reader who is interested in a much broader and deeper exposition of systems biology is directed to texts such as Rigoutsos and Stephanopoulos (2007 #523) (2 volume) or Klipp et al. (2005 #987).

11.2 Biological Networks

One facet of systems biology that we have only touched upon in previous chapters is the importance of biological networks: we have presented very few techniques that process graphs and trees, yet this is a very fertile area of research within systems biology, as the framework above indicates. Constructing and enhancing biological networks, analyzing the constructed networks, and using the networks to interpret the dynamics and functions of interacting genes and proteins provide a robust framework for researchers.

Much research leverages network modeling as a fundamental approach, which naturally leads us to graph-theoretic principles, which we will describe later. For interested readers, Furber (2010 #988) presented a human aging network model,

Thomas et al. (2009 #990) described a network model for genetic association studies of nicotine addiction and treatment, and Shu et al. (2007 #991) showed the use of Probabilistic Boolean Network (PBN), a widely used technique, to model genetic regulatory networks. Street et al. (2011 #993) presents a systems biology model of the regulatory network in *Populus* leaves that reveals interacting regulators and conserved regulation.

As presented in Hucka et al. (2003 #992), the Systems Biology Markup Language (SBML) provides a free, open, XML-based format for representing biochemical reaction networks. In Schulz et al. (2006 #995), the SBMLmerge tool is described: a tool that aids the user in combining models of biological subsystems to larger biochemical networks. The Systems Biology Workbench, Sauro et al. (2003 #999), is an open-source framework of modules for quantitative systems biology, including simulators, model editors, and analysis tools, for modeling, analysis, visualization, and general data manipulation. CellDesigner, Funahashi et al. (2003 #998), is a structured diagram editor for drawing gene regulatory and biochemical networks. Cytoscape, Smoot et al. (2011 #1000) and Cline et al. (2007 #1001), is an open-source bioinformatics software platform for visualizing molecular interaction networks and biological pathways and integrating these networks with annotations, gene expression profiles, and other state data. BioTapestry (Longabaugh et al. 2005 #1002 and Longabaugh et al. 2009 #1003), is an interactive tool for building, visualizing, and simulating genetic regulatory networks. Bioconductor (Gentleman et al. 2004 #89), provides a broad base of tools that support manipulation and analysis of microarray data, among other things. This subset of software is by no means an exhaustive list, and as researchers mature their toolsets, more and more software is becoming available to help mine and model biological data.

As we look at systems biology, its goals to some extent rely on our capability to predict the reality of the target of our study from our models. Methods related to formal methods of dynamics systems area, such as Monte Carlo stochastic simulation or ordinary differential equations, partial differential equations, and the like, provide us with the ability to develop

- Algebraic models to support research into areas such as metabolic fluxes and stoichiometry
- Ordinary differential equation (ODE) models to allow us to study areas such as microbial growth and compartment models
- Partial differential equation (PDE) models to allow more realistic representations of diffusion and diffusion–reaction systems
- Stochastic models that support cell variability in gene expression studies, to name only a few.

Protein networks, signaling networks, and metabolic networks have classically been studied *statically*, without taking into account any time-dependent (metamorphic) changes in the network topology and functionality. But such systems are dynamic in nature, evolving over time as well as having diverse regulatory patterns, when considered over the various stages of the systems' development. Models and algorithms are more and more considering such dynamic aspects, incorporating the capability to deal with the multiple time scales that exist within the system: from the slowest (evolutionary time) to the fastest (cellular development), as appropriate to the system under study.

Petri Nets (PNs) are an important tool in modeling biological networks, as we described earlier in this text and as can be seen from Chaouiya (2007 #902), for example. The PNK and PNK2e Petri Net Kernel environments (see Appendix B) provide tools and algorithms for graphically manipulating PNs.

Modeling genetic networks requires tools and techniques that incorporate the ability to define rule-based dependencies between genes, since such dependencies may incorporate important biological information, but must also allow us to study the dynamics of the global network as well as the effects on the network of individual genes. A natural challenge that this identifies is the uncertainty, sample size, and noise that come into play, as well as how we can quantify the relative influence and sensitivity of genes as they interact with other genes within the network, allowing us to focus on individual genes or on groups of genes. Probabilistic Boolean Networks (PBNs) are a valuable tool for modeling gene regulatory networks. For practical approximation, gene regulatory networks have been treated with a Boolean formalism, which enormously simplifies the task. If our focus is to study the regulatory behavior of the network without worrying about its specific quantitative characteristics, PBNs can be used to qualitatively capture typical genetic behavior.

PBNs share the rule-based properties of Boolean networks but provide a more robust foundation in the event of uncertainty, which exists only because the model defines only a portion of the physical system, and so the function defining the next state of the variable is likely to be only partially accurate. We won't go any further into the rationale for using PBNs over Boolean networks, but instead refer the interested reader to Shmulevich et al. (2002 #1007) for further details. In addition to the rule-based properties, the dynamics of PBNs can be studied in the context of Markov chains.

To better understand cellular function, as has been said above, genes need to be studied in the holistic context as opposed to in isolation because the expressions and activities of these genes are similarly within the context or dependencies of other genes. Historically, there have been many approaches taken to model gene regulatory networks, including linear models (van Someren et al. 2000 #1008), Bayesian networks (Friedman et al. 2000 #1009), neural networks (Weaver et al. 1999 #1010), differential models (Mestl et al. 1995 #1011), and stochastic models (Smolen et al. 2000 #1012; Hasty et al. 2001 #1013). PBNs provide a rule-based uncertainty model for understanding gene regulatory networks, a natural extension of the Boolean model introduced by Kauffman (1969 #1015) in 1969. Therein, gene expression is quantized to two states – on and off – with the expression level (or state) being functionally related to the expression levels (states) of other genes using logical rules (see Yuh et al. 1998 #1016). The time trajectory of these expression levels (or states) can be modeled as functions of time (see Dougherty et al. 1999 #1014). As shown by Huang (1999 #1017), many biological questions can be realistically answered using

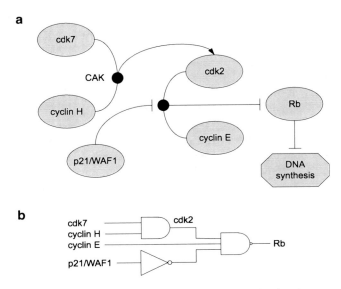

Fig. 11.2 (a) Cell cycle regulation example (*arrows* represent activation, *bars* represent inhibition). (b) Logic diagram representing the activity of the Rb protein in terms of four inputs (cdk7, cyclin H, cyclin E, and p21) (Shmulevich et al. 2002 #1007). The gate with inputs cdk7 and cyclin H is an AND gate; the gate with input p21/WAF1 is a NOT gate, and the gate with output Rb is a NAND (negative AND) gate

the simple Boolean formalism. Extending this model using PBNs allows us to incorporate the noise and uncertainty of the complicated network interplay of higher-order eukaryotes, to study large datasets, and to study the dynamic behavior of the networks. This allows us to model biologically meaningful phenomena. Huang (1999 #1017) also showed how this approach can be used to identify drug targets by inferring genetic models from expression data.

As an illustration, consider the example in Fig. 11.2 from Shmulevich et al. (2002 #1007). This represents the pathway relationships in (a) and the activity of Rb in terms of the variables in a logical fashion in (b).

From this we can define a Boolean network $G(V, F)$ as a set of nodes $V = \{x_1, ..., x_n\}$ and a list of Boolean functions $F = \{f_1, ..., f_n\}$, where a particular Boolean function with k input nodes, $f_i(x_{i1}, ..., x_{ik})$ is assigned to node x_i. There are various characteristics of this function that we refer the reader to Shmulevich et al. (2002 #1007) for further explanation and instead mention that the Boolean function set F represents the rules of regulatory interactions between the genes: a given gene transforms its inputs (that represent the regulatory factors that bind to it) to an output that is a representation of the expression state of the gene.

In the PBN case, for each node x_i, the set of functions is denoted $F_i = \left\{ f_j^{(i)} \right\}_{j=1,...,l(i)}$, where $f_j^{(i)}$ is a possible function determining the value of gene x_i and $l(i)$ is the number of possible functions for that gene. The functions are also

Table 11.1 Gene-function truth table

$x_1x_2x_3$	$f_1^{(1)}$	$f_2^{(1)}$	$f_1^{(2)}$	$f_1^{(3)}$	$f_2^{(3)}$
000	0	0	0	0	0
001	1	1	1	0	0
010	1	1	1	0	0
011	1	0	0	1	0
100	0	0	1	0	0
101	1	1	1	1	0
110	1	1	0	1	0
111	1	1	1	1	1
$c_j^{(i)}$	0.6	0.4	1	0.5	0.5

referred to as *predictors*, and we can say that the probability of that predictor is

$$c_j^{(i)} = P\left(f^{(i)} = f_j^{(i)}\right) = \sum_{k:f_{k_i}^{(i)}} P(\mathbf{f} = \mathbf{f}_k), \text{ where } \mathbf{f} = \left(f^{(1)}, ..., f^{(n)}\right) \text{ and } \sum_{j=1}^{l(i)} c_j^{(i)} = 1.$$

Using this as our basis, we define the matrix K to contain ordered rows where each row corresponds to a possible network configuration (see Shmulevich et al. 2002 #1007) such that row m corresponds to a network m, and the $(i,j)^{th}$ entry specifies that predictor $f_j^{(i)}$ should be used for gene x_i. From this we can determine the probability of network i being selected as $P_i = P(Network\ i\ selected) = \prod_{j=1}^n c_{K_{ij}}^{(j)}$.

Using Example 1 from Shmulevich et al. (2002 #1007), where we have three genes $V = (x_1, x_2, x_3)$, $F = (F_1, F_2, F_3)$, with $F_1 = \left\{f_1^{(1)}, f_2^{(1)}\right\}$, $F_2 = \left\{f_1^{(2)}\right\}$, and $F_3\left\{f_1^{(3)}, f_2^{(3)}\right\}$. The functions are given by the following truth table (Table 11.1).

This allows us to derive $K = \begin{bmatrix} 1 & 1 & 1 \\ 1 & 1 & 2 \\ 2 & 1 & 1 \\ 2 & 1 & 2 \end{bmatrix}$, where the second row means that

predictors $f_1^{(1)}, f_1^2, f_2^{(3)}$ will be used. From this, the state transition matrix A can be defined:

$$A = \begin{bmatrix} 1 & 0 & 0 & 0 & 0 & 0 & 0 & 0 \\ 0 & 0 & 0 & 0 & 0 & 0 & 1 & 0 \\ 0 & 0 & 0 & 0 & 0 & 0 & 1 & 0 \\ P_4 & P_3 & 0 & 0 & P_2 & P_1 & 0 & 0 \\ 0 & 0 & 1 & 0 & 0 & 0 & 0 & 0 \\ 0 & 0 & 0 & 0 & 0 & 0 & P_2+P_4 & P_1+P_3 \\ 0 & 0 & 0 & 0 & P_2+P_4 & P_1+P_3 & 0 & 0 \\ 0 & 0 & 0 & 0 & 0 & 0 & 0 & 1 \end{bmatrix}$$

Consider computing the transition probability $P\{(1,1,0) \to (1,0,0)\}$. This corresponds to $A_{7,5}$.[1] This requires that we use the truth table row for $(x_1, x_2, x_3) = (1,1,0)$ and then look for possible combinations of the predictors for each of the three genes that give us values $(1,0,0)$, which, we can see from visual inspection are either $\left(f_1^{(1)}, f_1^{(2)}, f_2^{(3)}\right)$ or $\left(f_2^{(1)}, f_1^{(2)}, f_2^{(3)}\right)$.

Experimental noise exists within this class of techniques, just as it does elsewhere, and novel approaches to addressing this issue continue to be developed. For example, Mitrofanova (2009 #1004) described a method tested in yeast two-hybrid (Y2H) networks, which are often used to provide primary data for protein complexes. This algorithm measures the connectivity between proteins by focusing on edge-disjoint paths, not by edge paths, the contention being that these reflect pathway evolution more appropriately within a single species network.

As the growth of models and algorithms within systems biology continues to expand, interesting approaches to validating and exercising those models continue apace. For example, the Dialogue for Reverse-Engineering Assessments and Methods (DREAM) initiative, see Prill et al. (2010 #1005) for a description of *DREAM3*, is a community effort to catalyze discussion about the design, application, and assessment of systems biology models through annual reverse-engineering challenges.

An interesting paper by Kell (2007 #994) described a potential goal for systems biology: the *digital human*, through the use of multiscale, distributed biochemical network models.

To provide an example of how much systems biological techniques are permeating the landscape, as of the time of writing, the Virginia Bioinformatics Institute at Virginia Tech is offering undergraduates the opportunity to gain experience in areas including the mathematical modeling of mammalian iron metabolism and the use of mathematical algorithms and software for modeling and simulation in systems biology. This is not isolated and shows how these important areas of network modeling, associated algorithms, and software tools to support the modeling effort are included in an ever-growing discipline for researchers at all levels.

Systems biology is an evolving discipline, the boundaries of which are being explored, expanded, and redefined, as is the case with any new discipline. Some of the exciting areas of research look to develop methods for:

- Reverse-engineering transcription regulatory networks from transcriptome data
- Identifying functional modules in integrated regulatory and protein interaction networks
- Understanding how physical interaction networks mediate the condition-dependent response to external stimuli
- Modeling the evolution of network modules after whole genome duplications

---

[1] Indexing of A starts with 1.

But these are only a very few of the challenging and exciting areas of research that fall under the title of systems biology. To provide a specific example, as we can see from our subset of areas of research above, networks manifest themselves in many areas. An example of this can be seen in research out of the University of Colorado that culminated in the development of the PathMiner algorithm.

Let us illustrate with a concrete example of data mining for network understanding. In 2004, a team from the University of Colorado developed an algorithm, PathMiner, based on heuristic search, to extract, or infer, biotransformation rules from the Kyoto Encyclopedia of Genes and Genomes (KEGG), a web-accessible database of pathways, genes, and gene expressions. Using KEGG, the team inferred 110 biotransformation rules about what happens when certain compounds interact. They used these rules, as well as mathematical algorithms, to predict how detoxification pathways would metabolize ethyl and furfuryl alcohol. The model's prediction is correlated with known patterns of alcohol metabolism.

11.3 How Much Biology Do We Need?

This book is about data mining and, more specifically, an introduction to data mining in the life sciences. Just as is the case with any area of specialty, we need to understand various fundamental concepts to get the most out of it. By now, anyone who has suffered through the previous chapters will have a good idea of how much we've glossed over or just simply left out. This chapter will be no different. In fact, this chapter will contain even more exclusions and glossing over simply because things are changing so rapidly.

That being said, there are a few nuggets that we believe will help to put some of the areas of study we describe below into context and so we include them here. We're naturally going to leave out much more than we include and for any reader that believes we should have included X and excluded Y, you are probably correct.

11.3.1 Biological Processes As Ordered Sequences of Events

It has been known for a long time that various biological processes consist of an ordered sequence of events. A good example of this that we are taught in high school is cell division, but on a more gross scale, metabolism and development are also good examples. This has led to very active research into developing temporal models of biological sequences and the relationships between them.

11.4   But, We Do Need Some Graph Theory

Do I Need to Read This section?

This is a lengthy section, containing a lot of basic definitions, and so is a little more boring to read through. We placed this inline in the text rather than as an appendix, as we did with the basic statistics, because we felt that fewer people would have had a graph theory course as part of their academic training. . .unless you were a math major. Since many software products for pathway analysis use graph theory concepts, it's worth reading through.

There are many excellent books that we recommend to the reader, including Diestel (2010 #958), Balakrishnan and Ranganathan (2000 #959), or Bollobás (1998 #960) among others, but we include a brief primer in this section that will make some of the subsequent discussion (hopefully) more meaningful.

Graph theory's creation is normally credited to Leonard Euler and one of the most famous problems concerns the Königsberg bridge problem which asked whether it was possible to take a walk through the town in such a way as to cross over every bridge once, and only once. See Fig. 11.3.

Another, abstract representation of this, with the land masses labeled can be seen in Fig. 11.4a, with yet a third representation – a more traditional graph – shown in Fig. 11.4b, which also has the distances labeled.

A graph then is a representation of a set of points and the way they are joined up. More formally, the points are called **vertices** or **nodes**, and the lines between them are called **edges**. The **degree** of a vertex is the number of edges that have that vertex as an endpoint. In Fig. 11.4, the degree of the node labeled B is 5; the degree of the node labeled A is 3.

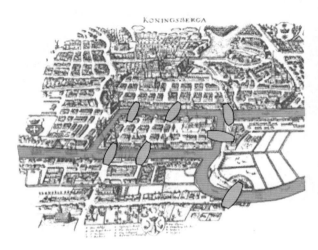

Fig. 11.3 Königsberg at the time of Euler with the bridges highlighted (Image from Wikipedia and used under the Creative Commons license)

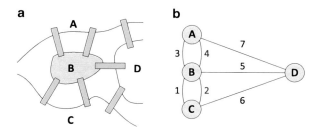

Fig. 11.4 Königsberg bridge problem

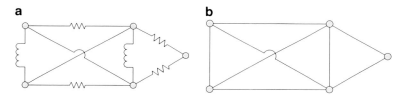

Fig. 11.5 An electrical network graph representation

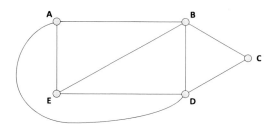

Fig. 11.6 Isomorphic representation

Consider the example shown in Fig. 11.5. Both (a) and (b) are equivalent representations of the electrical network, from our perspective, and highlight that there is no connection between the two diagonal lines.

We can redraw Fig. 11.5b to avoid any crosses, as shown below.

In Fig. 11.6, we have labeled the nodes and drawn the line connecting A and D outside of the others and, disregarding any metrical properties, Figs. 11.5b and 11.6 are regarded as essentially the same graph and we say that the two graphs are **isomorphic** if there is a one-to-one correspondence between their vertices (nodes) such that two vertices (nodes) are joined by an edge in one graph if and only if the corresponding vertices are joined by an edge in the other. Just to show this further, Fig. 11.7 is isomorphic to Fig. 11.5b and Fig. 11.6.

Fig. 11.7 Another
isomorphic graph

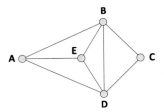

Fig. 11.8 Multiple edges and
loops

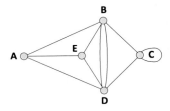

Graphs can be used to represent many things. For example, Fig. 11.7 could represent football games between teams, where each edge might correspond to a game being played by the two teams represented by the nodes. In this example, team E has played a game with each of teams A, B, and D, but has yet to play a game with team C.

Alternatively, Fig. 11.7 may represent roads that exist between the various locations. Such a representation may be useful in mapping traffic loads. Some nodes may need additional roads, called **multiple edges**, such as shown in Fig. 11.8 between B and D.

We could also represent other constructs, such as, say, a parking lot, by a **loop**, as shown above. Graphs typically contain loops and multiple edges. Where a graph does not contain these constructs, we call it a **simple graph**.

We'll use the road analogy one more time: what if all the roads (edges) are one-way streets? Then we have a **directed graph** or **digraph** and will typically use some notational device such as an arrow head symbol, as illustrated in Fig. 11.9.

Formalizing this further, a graph G is defined as the pair $(V(G), E(G))$, where $V(G)$ is a nonempty finite set of elements called **vertices** or **nodes** and $E(G)$ is a finite family[2] of unordered pairs of (not necessarily distinct) elements of $V(G)$ called **edges**. $V(G)$ is often referred to as the **vertex-set** and $E(G)$ referred to as the **edge-family**. If we use Fig. 11.9 as an example, $V(G)$ is {A, B, C, D, E}, and $E(G)$ is the family consisting of the edges {A, B}, {A, E}, {A, D}, {B, E}, {B, D}, {B, D}, {E, D}, {B, C}, {D, C}, and {C, C}.[3] An edge of the form {a, b} is said to **join** the vertices a and b and is usually abbreviated ab.

---

[2] The use of the term "family" will allow for the case where there are multiple edges.

[3] Typically, nodes are labeled with lower case letters, which we will do from here on out.

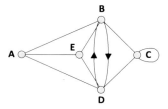

Fig. 11.9 Directed graph (digraph)

We did take a slight liberty with the example we used in the previous chapter. Recall that we said that a graph where the edges were "one-way" were called diagraphs, or directed graphs, as is the case with Fig. 11.9. A **digraph** D is defined by the pair $(V(D), A(D))$, where $V(D)$ is as defined above and $A(D)$ is a finite family of *ordered* pairs of elements of $V(D)$ called **arcs** or **di-edges**. An arc {v, w} or *vw* is said to be an **arc from v to w**. To be correct in our example, we would need to write {a, b}, {a, e}, {a, d}, {b, e}, **{d, b}, {b, d}**, {e, d}, {b, c}, {d, c}, and {c, c}, where the ordering is determined by the arrow.

Two vertices *v* and *w* of a graph *G* are said to be **adjacent** if there is an edge joining them; *v* and *w* are then said to be **incident** to the edge. Hence, two distinct edges of *G* are **adjacent** if they have at least one vertex in common. The **degree** or **valency** of a vertex *v* of *G* is the number of edges incident to *v* and is written **d(v)** or $\rho(v)$. When calculating $\rho(v)$ we will use the convention that a loop constitutes 2 to the degree of *v*. $d(v) = 0$ means that *v* is an **isolated vertex**; if $d(v) = 1$ then *v* is a **terminal vertex** or **endpoint**.

We're almost done with the terminology. We're just going to introduce a couple more terms, but begin with something that Euler knew over 200 years ago, the *handshaking lemma*. In essence, if we add up the degrees of all the nodes of a graph, the result will be an even number,[4] since each edge contributes exactly two to the sum. So why is it called the handshaking lemma? It implies that if several people shake hands, the total number of hands must be even, because two hands are involved in each shake. If this is true, then we have the corollary that the number of nodes where the degree of is odd must be even.

Two graphs G_1 and G_2 are said to be **isomorphic** if there is a one-one correspondence between the nodes of G_1 and the nodes of G_2 with the property that the number of edges joining any two nodes of G_1 is equal to the number of edges joining the corresponding nodes of G_2. The two graphs shown in Fig. 11.10 are isomorphic under the correspondence $u \leftrightarrow l, v \leftrightarrow m, w \leftrightarrow n, x \leftrightarrow p, y \leftrightarrow q, z \leftrightarrow r$.

A **subgraph** of a graph *G* is simply a graph all of whose vertices belong to $V(G)$ and all of whose edges belong to $E(G)$. Figure 11.11 is therefore a subgraph of Fig. 11.9, but not of either graph in Fig. 11.10.

---

[4] Actually, it will be twice the number of edges.

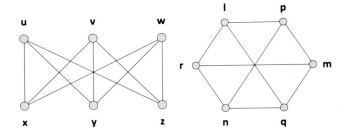

Fig. 11.10 Isomorphic graphs

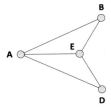

Fig. 11.11 A subgraph

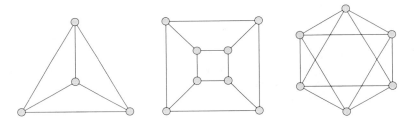

Fig. 11.12 Platonic graphs

   Given the definitions from above, we can now quickly see that we could have a graph where $E(G)$ is empty but where $V(G)$ is nonempty and we'll call this not very interesting graph a **null graph**, often denoted as N_n, where n is then number of nodes of the graph. If a simple graph has each pair of distinct vertices adjacent, it is called a **complete graph** and is usually denoted by K_n, where n indicates the number of vertices. K_n has exactly $\frac{1}{2}n(n-1)$ edges. (Check it!) If the degree of every vertex is the same, the graph is called a **regular graph**, or is **regular to degree r**.

   The so-called **Platonic graphs** are regular graphs formed by the nodes and edges of the Platonic solids, some of which are shown in Fig. 11.12. The tetrahedral graph is K_4.

Fig. 11.13 Bipartite graphs (simple, complete, and star)

Nodes on graphs can sometimes naturally be partitioned into two disjoint sets V_1 and V_2 in such a way that every edge of G joins a vertex in V_1 with a vertex in V_2, as exemplified in Fig. 11.13.

Such graphs are called **bipartite graphs** and often denoted $G(V_1, V_2)$ if we want to highlight the two sets. If it is true that every vertex of V_1 is joined to every vertex of V_2, then we call it a **complete bipartite graph** and denote it by $K_{r,s}$, where r denotes the number of vertices in V_1 and s denotes the number of vertices in V_2. A complete bipartite graph of the form $K_{1,s}$ is called a **star graph**. Note that any graph of the form $K_{r,s}$ has $r + s$ nodes and rs edges.

Ok, enough with the definitions, let's quickly breeze through some of the simple math associated with graphs and then get back to how they are used in data mining.

If we have two graphs, $G_1 = (V(G_1), E(G_1))$ and $G_2 = (V(G_2), E(G_2))$, where $V(G_1)$ and $V(G_2)$ are disjoint, then the union $G_1 \cup G_2$ is the graph with the vertex-set $V(G_1) \cup V(G_2)$ and the edge-family $E(G_1) \cup E(G_2)$. The sum $G_1 + G_2$ of G_1 and G_2 is obtained by taking the union of G_1 and G_2 and drawing an edge from each vertex in G_1 to each vertex in G_2.

Consider some edge e in our graph G. We may have the need to remove an edge from a graph, as we shall, for example, see in step 5 of our discussion on the work done by Gupta et al. (2009 #961) below, where we prune the graph. In such a case, we denote the graph resulting by deleting the edge e by $G - e$; in the more general case where we delete a set of edged F from G, we denote the resulting graph by G-F. Similarly, if we delete a vertex v from the graph, the resulting graph G-v is the graph where v and all edges incident to v have been eliminated. Analogously to the edge-family case, the graph G-S is the graph resulting from eliminating the set of nodes S and all incident edges from G. The notation $G \backslash e$ identifies the graph resulting from taking an edge e and contracting it so that its ends become a single node. If e joins nodes v and w, then $G \backslash e$ is the graph where distinct nodes v and w become a single node vw (say). Figure 11.14 shows the four cases we have just discussed.

So far, our discussion of graphs has had a common underlying assumption: that graphs are in one-piece, or **connected**. More formally, a graph G is considered connected if it cannot be expressed as the union of two graphs H and I, say. If it can be so expressed, we consider it to be **disconnected**. Any disconnected graph G can be expressed as the union of a finite set of graphs, where each such graph is referred to as a **component** of G.

This last definition can be very important in analyzing pathways as we may have multiple graphs in our dataset where components are known, but there is no known,

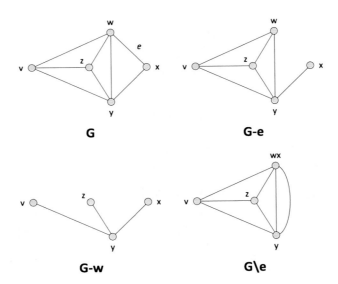

Fig. 11.14 Graph reduction

experimentally supported connection between them: Can our data-mining activities help us to identify *real* edges connecting such components?

A **circuit** is a connected graph which is regular of degree 2 and is denoted by C_n, where n is the number of vertices in the graph. If we have a **null graph**, a graph with no edges, or with no nodes (and hence no edges), denoted as N_n, with $n = 1$ and a circuit graph where $n > 2$, the graph resulting from summing the two is called a **wheel**.

Most areas of mathematics have the concept of a **complement**, and graph theory is no different. If G is a simple graph and its vertex-set is $V(G)$, then the complement, $\bar{G}$ also has $V(G)$ as its vertex-set but where vertexes adjacent in $\bar{G}$ are only adjacent if and only if they were *not* adjacent in G.[5]

We're very close to being done with the definitions, so stick with us. Now that we have these basic definitions, we can discuss the concepts of paths and circuits which will allow you to begin to see how this becomes practical for systems biology.

Pathways naturally lead us to looking at traversing graphs via an **edge-sequence** which, given a graph G is a finite sequence of edges, typically written as $v_0 v_1, v_1 v_2, \ldots, v_{n-1} v_n$ or $v_0 \to v_1 \to v_2 \to \ldots \to v_{n-1} \to v_n$. Recalling our earlier definitions, two consecutive edges in our sequence are either adjacent or identical, although this property in and of itself does not make for an edge-sequence

---

[5] We've already made this painful, so we're not going to say more about this other than if G has n nodes, then $\bar{G}$ can be constructed by removing all the edges of G from K_n and that the complement of a complete graph is the null graph and vice versa.

(consider a star graph). v_0 is the initial node (or initial vertex) and v_m is the final node and the number of edges in the edge-sequence is called its **length**. For example, the edge-sequence $u \rightarrow v \rightarrow w \rightarrow w \rightarrow x \rightarrow y \rightarrow y \rightarrow z \rightarrow w$ has length 8. If every edge in our edge-sequence is distinct, the edge-sequence is called a **trail**. If, in addition, the nodes are unique, with the possible exception of the initial node and the final node (i.e., $v_0 = v_n$), the trail is called a **path** and if $v_0 = v_n$ then the path or trail is **closed**. A closed path containing at least one edge is called a **circuit**.[6]

Readers will be happy to know that we're going to stop with the graph theory background now and move on. We'll pause while you celebrate. . .ok, back to the content.

Graph theory has seen applicability in many areas as a tool to solve practical problems, and that's certainly the case within systems biology, as we'll see below. However, it's also been used in myriad other areas, and we'll list some areas here for any reader interested in reading further. We mentioned Euler and the bridges of Königsberg, but Cayley's work in chemical molecule enumeration, Kirchhoff's work in electrical networks, but can also be seen in such diverse subjects as linguistics, operational research, geography, sociology, crystallography, and, of course, systems biology. Many people are familiar with the widely known "traveling salesman problem" and the "shortest path problem," which are two example problems to which that graph theory has been applied to and which are simple enough that they can be easily followed by persons with no background in graph theory. But they also provide a good insight into how graph theory can be applied, and interested readers can easily find good descriptions from a simple web search.

11.4.1   Data Mining by Navigation

We'll now describe some real data-mining research, published in Gupta et al. (2009 #961).[7] This approach proposes to use a navigational method for data mining by collecting data elements from diverse sources and associate them together without deriving any rules of association. One of the major challenges, as we've already

---

[6] We could have made this note earlier, but this is a good place to say that nomenclature in graph theory has been somewhat arbitrary, with different authors using different terminology. We've used the notation from Wilson (2010 #974) which has been our source for much of this section. However, other terminology abounds, for example, walk, route, chain, cycle, and the like. In most cases, the differences are intuitive, but that's why we went into such detail with the basic definitions; you should be able to figure out the mapping to your experience or the text(s) you are using. (At least, that's our excuse.)

[7] For interested readers, this work uses three primary data sources and applications: Gene Expression Omnibus (GEO, http://www.ncbi.nlm.nih.gov/geo/), Promoter Analysis Pipeline (PAP, http://cbmi.wustl.edu/html/PAP.html), and PathSys (http://biologicalnetworks.net/), which can provide value in many different mining domains and are well-worth exploring.

described, is the different format of source data. Gene transcription and signaling networks are often represented as graphs, to introduce yet another form of data.

Many applications of data mining that aggregate data from different sources and then attempt to uncover associations between the data through generalized association use techniques such as the chi-squared test as a measure of the significance of the association, but this only works where the data are of the same general form. As more and more data becomes available in different forms, we need to ask ourselves how we can process them together and obtain meaningful results. But it tends to go further because the semantic interpretation of many of the fundamental elements we deal with may be different when viewed through different lenses. Take the gene, for example, it may be viewed as a sequence in one (research) application, or a node on an interaction graph in another.

In this research, a graph of interacting genes (with transcription factors) is developed using PathSys, where connecting edges are labeled with a "relative importance" value, obtained from other research, to provide a more complete picture of gene interaction. Genes are nodes on the graph, along with their transcription factors (TFs) to allow us to see more clearly which genes are coexpressed with other genes and thus highlight which genes co-occur. Using GEO and PAP data, the graph can now be pruned to allow us to arrive at the final subgraph showing, in this research, which genes (and their associated transcription factors) co-occur and contribute significantly to hypertension (Fig. 11.15).

Figure 11.16 shows the final pruned graph created via PathSys for the above research.

11.4.2   So. . .How Are We Going to Cram All This into a Single Chapter?

Obviously, we can't and we're not. As we've stated for other domains, systems biology is large enough to be a book in its own right, or even several books. Instead, what we'll do in this chapter is take just a couple of problems, describe them from a systems biology perspective, and then introduce how data mining can be used at various points in the process to provide insight.

It's probably not overstating it by much to say that systems biology deals with vast amounts of data on a day-to-day basis. But going a step further, systems biology also deals with complex interactions between the data elements at a level beyond what is seen in many other disciplines. Pathways[8] are a good example of this.

---

[8] We're putting the (sic) in a footnote: we purposely used a generalized noun here as biochemical pathways are springing up everywhere.

Step 1: Correlation	For each gene obtained experimentally, GEO is searched to identify experiments where genes are co-expressed. For each pair of co-expressed genes X_i and Y_i, their expression values are used and the Pearson correlation coefficient is computed. A threshold of 0.7 for the Pearson correlation coefficient was used as the cut off for consideration.
Step 2: Extraction of TFs	Highly co-expressed pairs identified in step 1 were analyzed within PAP to find possible TFs. In this research, only those TFs with a 95% likelihood, and in the top 25 TFS, were considered.
Step 3: Identification of Protein-Protein Interaction	PathSys was used, together with the genes from step 1 and TFs from step 2 to build protein interaction maps with genes and TFs comprising nodes of the graphs.
Step 4: Second Correlation Phase	TF nodes and their regulators are used against the GEO database to study co-expression, repeating step 1
Step 5: Graph Pruning	Graphs identified in step 3 are pruned using the results from this step and extra nodes and edges deleted. Each remaining co-expression edge (gene-to-gene, TF-to-TF) is now labeled with its co-expression value.

Fig. 11.15 Development process to generate a pruned graph

11.5   Gene Ontology and Microarray Databases

We've highlighted the importance of initiatives such as the Gene Ontology (GO), along with microarray databases as one of the primary sources of data being generated and processed within systems biology, and to quote Peng and Zhang (2007 #957),

> Two [of the] most important genomic data resources for systems biology are the gene ontology (GO) and the publicly available microarray databases such as the Stanford Microarray Database (SMD) and the NCBI Expression Omnibus.

So we should provide a little more explanation on these important resources before we proceed.

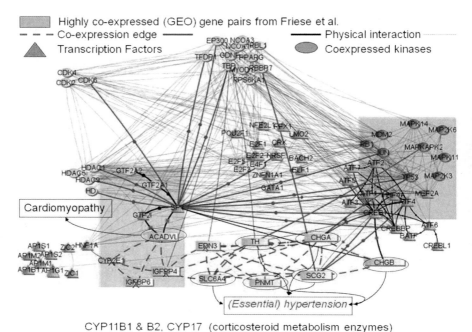

Fig. 11.16 PathSys interaction graph

11.5.1 Gene Ontology (GO)

The Gene Ontology (GO) project aims to standardize the representation of gene and gene product attributes across species and databases by providing a *controlled vocabulary* of terms describing gene product characteristics and gene product annotation data, as well as a set of supporting tools.

The ontology of defined terms, representing gene product properties, covers three domains:

- *Cellular component*, the parts of a cell or its extracellular environment but which is a part of some larger object. Examples are anatomical structures (such as rough endoplasmic reticulum (RER) or nucleus) or a gene product group (such as a ribosome or proteasome)
- *Molecular function*, the elemental activities of a gene product at the molecular level, such as binding or catalysis
- *Biological process*, operations or sets of molecular events with a defined beginning and end, pertinent to the functioning of integrated living units: cells, tissues,

organs, and organisms. For example, signal transduction and cellular physiological processes[9]

A biological process is a series of events accomplished by one or more ordered assemblies of molecular functions. Examples of broad biological process terms are cellular physiological process or signal transduction. Examples of more specific terms are pyrimidine metabolic process or alpha-glucoside transport. It can be difficult to distinguish between a biological process and a molecular function, but the general rule is that a process must have more than one distinct steps.

Using the example from the gene ontology web site (http://www.geneontology.org/GO.doc.shtml),

the gene product cytochrome c can be described by the molecular function term oxidore-ductase activity, the biological process terms oxidative phosphorylation and induction of cell death, and the cellular component terms mitochondrial matrix and mitochondrial inner membrane.

The ontology is structured as a directed acyclic graph[10] and designed to be species-neutral, including terms applicable to prokaryotes and eukaryotes, single and multicellular organisms.

11.5.2   Microarray Databases

Microarray databases, repositories for gene expression data, store the measurement data, manage a searchable index, and make the data available to other applications for analysis and interpretation.

While there are many available, and growing all the time, some of the most commonly used and important databases include the Stanford Microarray Database (SMD), the NCBI Expression Omnibus, and ArrayExpress archive (see Appendix B).

These repositories allow you to obtain valuable gene expression data, sometimes curated, but sometimes not, but typically MIAME compliant.

11.6   Text Mining

Even restricting a web search to only Google Scholar, for example, will typically return tens, hundreds, thousands, or more links for even the most restrictive terms. Yeah, we know that this is a gross generalization, but try it and see. In most cases, the numbers of results that get returned are surprisingly large.

---

[9] The Gene Ontology does not try to represent the dynamics or dependencies that would be required to fully describe a pathway; a biological process, as currently defined for GO, is not equivalent to a pathway.

[10] See, all that graph stuff is becoming useful.

What is probably the most interesting and daunting part of research is how to efficiently elicit the knowledge within the returned information set. Why? In most cases, they are documents rather than datasets. Most research papers today adhere to a relatively common format, but extracting the knowledge still requires reading and creative processing. It is this latter challenge that has been fertile ground for data mining under the text-mining discipline.

Intuitively, text mining is an understandable concept: We wish to leverage our data-mining tools and automatically process documents available from publicly published sources, as well as from our internal research repositories. But a working definition that we like is

> Text-mining in molecular biology [is] defined as the automatic extraction of information about genes, proteins, and their functional relationships from text documents.
>   Krallinger and Valencia (2005 #962) (Text-Mining and Information-Retrieval Services for Molecular Biology)

In parallel with the growth of data generation methods – the high-throughput methods we have mentioned several times – there has been an associated growth of the scientific literature in which experimental results are communicated, often in the form of free text that is easy on the humans, but more challenging for the machines. Because of this, there has been a growing interest in designing and building systems that can efficiently retrieve and classify documents obtained as a result of complex user queries, as well as to subsequently analyze the literature to elicit specific information and associations, such as protein functions or protein interactions.

One challenge is that because of the nature of scientific publications – complex and concise – generic mining tools are often inadequate for the task; mining tools adapted to the needs of analyzing biological texts, however, are now becoming available.

A simple search using a search engine such as Google or Bing will return a vast number of references, as we've already mentioned, with the links referencing a broad range of documents: generic documents such as press releases and news articles, as well as specific, scientific articles from sources such as PubMed. Even separating the wheat from the chaff can be an arduous task.

An area of artificial intelligence research, natural language programming (NLP) may be useful in helping with much of this challenge since its basic methodology, and underlying tools, are oriented toward extracting relevant functional information *into a structured form* from unstructured data. Combining document retrieval with NLP could provide an interesting set of techniques to also help us in various aspects of research.

How do we identify the (complete) set of relevant documents from a larger collection? The two basic strategies for this are either query-based or document-based searches. In the former, we use keywords along with Boolean operators, and we are pretty sure that every reader has done this through a search engine such as Google or Bing. In the scientific space, Entrez is a widely used document retrieval tool that supports the keyword/Boolean operator search methodology as well as having the ability to return all abstracts similar to a given document. Google Scholar provides a similar capability, returning documents based on which documents are connected via citations or web links. Other tools such as Crossref Search and the Nature Publishing Group search engine provide similar capabilities in more specific document domains (i.e., their own subset of documents).

In addition to the data generated directly from high-throughput techniques and more traditional experimental techniques, literature text mining is playing an increasingly important role in systems biology. With the vast amount of research conducted and published to date, eliciting the knowledge embedded in the literature and incorporating the extracted information into our knowledge base provides an unprecedented opportunity. Algorithms and tools for systematically mining experimental data and constructing structured knowledge bases from such data have been published in recent years. Biological text mining to recognize gene or protein entities within the literature and the ability to extract related information such as protein-protein interactions, protein modifications, and associated cell types, biological pathways, or phenotypes, to name a few, provide a wonderful opportunity to augment our data repositories and identify new patterns between these constructs.

But how can we effectively manage and understand this data? This is where biological ontologies, the formal representation of biological concepts or entities using controlled vocabularies and defining relations between concepts or entities, such as in Gene Ontology and Protein Ontology, provide a rigorous structure and offer a mechanism for more easily integrating heterogeneous data, enabling easier analysis and more intelligent data query and reasoning. An example can be seen in the text mining and ontology work of http://pir.georgetown.edu/staff/huz/hulab.html, the Cancer Bioinformatics and Systems Biology, Hu Laboratory at Georgetown.

Bringing these concepts together, we can apply data-mining techniques to biological data generated in the laboratory and optionally published to publicly available databases in several ways:

- Experimental high-throughput data (e.g., as from screening, microscopy images, or microarrays) against which we can leverage inferential methods to try and reconstruct networks.
- Analyze publications and bring together disparate data for which, at present, no unique experiment is available that can identify all interactions at the same time. The vast number of scientific publications containing biological facts available today provides fertile ground for analysis, when coupled with gene ontology and can advance genome annotation or network reconstruction.
- Apply visualization techniques to the many public relational, biological databases now available to enhance access and navigation, making possible user-friendly visual exploration a reality.

It is fair to say that in any complex system, many important properties of that system emerge when we investigate the interactions between the systems' components.

This fact has been recognized in many disciplines and has been recognized as an important and fertile area of study for systems biologists – focusing on discovering emergent properties and functions not evident from the individual components of the system, or even in component groups, but which are driven instead by the interactions between the components or component groups.

This concept allows us to develop a generic framework for systems biology which can be summarized as:

- Identify components of the system.
- Describe the system through connected graphs or networks with nodes representing system components and edges representing interactions between the nodes. This graph or network now provides the model for the organism's behavior and functions.
- Analyze the structural and dynamical properties of the network as a means of gaining insight into emergent properties of the underlying biological systems.

In our above discussion, we haven't really defined text mining in the systems biology discipline. For the sake of this text, we define it as the *automatic extraction of information about genes, proteins, and the functional relationships between them, from textual sources.*

A textual source is any machine-readable source where the content is text-based as opposed to image-based. While this would include eliciting information from tables, we exclude eliciting information from images.

We can think about the overall process as being segmented into the following phases:

- Efficiently retrieve documents in response to complex queries (information retrieval).
- Classify the documents appropriately.
- Analyze literature elements within documents to extract associations (e.g., protein-protein interactions).

Within this context, systems have to be able to handle large collections of biological texts efficiently, but also recognize that the complex (and concise) nature of scientific documents means that frameworks developed for generic documents will not work for specialized documents. However, generic documents (e.g., news documents) can sometimes have information that we would also like to include in our collection.

We're going to go out on a limb here and say that efficiently retrieving documents in response to complex queries has been solved – a la Google – but anyone who has performed a manual inquiry will know that the returned documents do not necessarily correlate to the specific of the query. We're likely to encounter a lot of noise and some level of duplication.

The act of searching can be thought of in two contexts: returning a list of entities relevant to a query *comprising keywords* and returning a list of entities relevant to a query comprising a single *document.*[11]

---

[11] For our purposes, we assume a single document as opposed to a group of documents.

The former is likely familiar to every reader, whereby a set of keywords are entered into a search engine and the engine returns the set of documents that contain combinations of those keywords. Typically, the engine will contain logic to eliminate so-called "stop words," such as "if," "and," "but," etc., that will have very high frequencies of occurrence. Such engines will also be capable of using Boolean connectives (and, or, not) to allow for more flexibility. However, the challenge is that a query such as

> molecular biology and text mining

would likely be converted to something of the form

> molecular and biology and text and mining

which would likely return documents where the words "molecular," "biology," "text," and "mining" occur anywhere in that document, rather than the more likely desire of returning those documents containing the phrases "molecular biology" and "text mining."

While we can use some traditional procedural techniques to help us out, the breadth and depth of the data available in documents and (web) pages, from different projects, mean that natural language processing (NLP) techniques may not only be valuable, but necessary.

In the second form of search we mentioned above, the purpose is to go beyond simply a set of keywords and instead to provide a *query document* that would return other documents that are similar in nature.

Thus, information retrieval, classification, and natural language processing may become more and more important as we look to elicit data, information, and knowledge in the form of new facts and interpretations from the documents available to us.

Much has been written, developed, and implemented in the area of information retrieval. In fact, this is the foundation for many multibillion dollar companies, such as Google. Their PageRank algorithm, Brin and Page (1998 #1022), provides a returned list of documents deemed appropriate, and ranked appropriately, in response to a user query.

Search engines, such as Google, are a generic resource. Search engines, such as Entrez and Google Scholar, provide a more specialized service. But even with these capabilities, there is typically an iterative process to hone the query, which makes them time consuming to use. Just as an example, as of the time of writing, PubMed has over 21,000,000 citations. Anyone care to guess how many billions of pages Google indexes?

Consider a protein: how would we refer to it in a search? It's unlikely that we would use an accession identifier, such as from SwissProt, because not every target document would be guaranteed to include it. Maybe we use the name or the symbol. For example, we might use POR1, porin, or *Saccharomyces cerevisiae* gene POR1, or even POR-1. Alternatively, we might use an available synonym, such as OMP2. Just using this simple example is illustrative: we have many alternative ways of simply identifying a single biological entity.

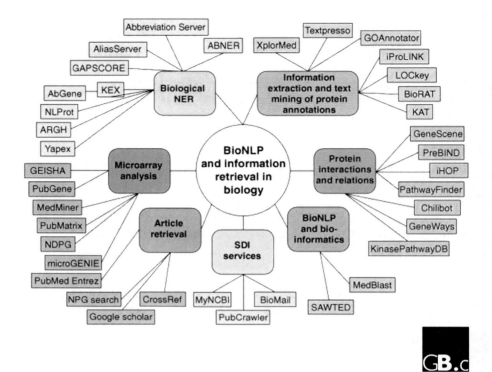

Fig. 11.17 Text-mining applications for biology (Krallinger and Valencia 2005 #962)

Named entity recognition (NER) is a technique that is used to identify biological entities in free text.[12]

We can see that these are two very different approaches. In the former case, we try and identify biological entities through variants of the naming conventions we see in various databases. In the latter, we try and analyze the syntactic structure (and, in some cases, the semantic structure) to try and elicit the entities. Unfortunately, neither is the panacea that we hope for. Tools such as GAPSCORE (Chang et al. 2004 #1024), NLProt (Mika and Rost 2004 #1025), Yapex (Franzen et al. 2002 #1026), AbGene (Tanabe and Wilbur 2002 #1027), ABNER (Settles 2004 #1028), KEX (Fukuda et al. 1998 #1029), and AliasServer (Iragne et al. 2004 #1030) provide intermediaries to bridge the gap between these techniques.

This is just one step in the process of text mining, an area of complexity, but of tremendous value. As can be seen from Fig. 11.17 (from Krallinger and Valencia 2005 #962), which is just a subset of the text-mining applications – as available in 2005 – this continues to be a fertile area of research.

---

[12] This is a more general technique, but we focus on our context here.

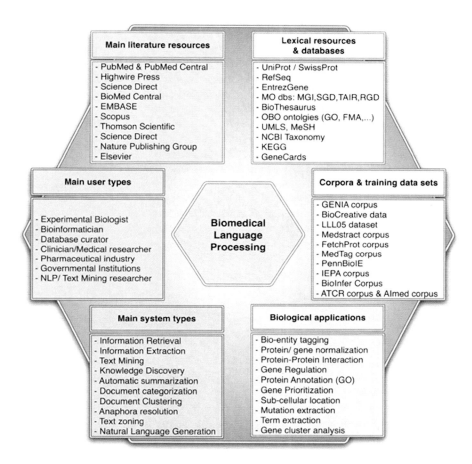

Main literature resources
- PubMed & PubMed Central
- Highwire Press
- Science Direct
- BioMed Central
- EMBASE
- Scopus
- Thomson Scientific
- Science Direct
- Nature Publishing Group
- Elsevier

Lexical resources & databases
- UniProt / SwissProt
- RefSeq
- EntrezGene
- MO dbs: MGI,SGD,TAIR,RGD
- BioThesaurus
- OBO ontolgies (GO, FMA,...)
- UMLS, MeSH
- NCBI Taxonomy
- KEGG
- GeneCards

Main user types
- Experimental Biologist
- Bioinformatician
- Database curator
- Clinician/Medical researcher
- Pharmaceutical industry
- Governmental Institutions
- NLP/ Text Mining researcher

Biomedical Language Processing

Corpora & training data sets
- GENIA corpus
- BioCreative data
- LLL05 dataset
- Medstract corpus
- FetchProt corpus
- MedTag corpus
- PennBioIE
- IEPA corpus
- BioInfer Corpus
- ATCR corpus & Almed corpus

Main system types
- Information Retrieval
- Information Extraction
- Text Mining
- Knowledge Discovery
- Automatic summarization
- Document categorization
- Document Clustering
- Anaphora resolution
- Text zoning
- Natural Language Generation

Biological applications
- Bio-entity tagging
- Protein/ gene normalization
- Protein-Protein Interaction
- Gene Regulation
- Protein Annotation (GO)
- Gene Prioritization
- Sub-cellular location
- Mutation extraction
- Term extraction
- Gene cluster analysis

Fig. 11.18 Aspects relevant to the development of biomedical literature processing systems (Krallinger et al. 2008 #1023)

If we can do it effectively, text mining has a huge potential for enabling and extending our knowledge. But as Krallinger et al. (2008 #1023) show (Fig. 11.18), this is not a trivial matter.

This particularly fruitful area of research is changing rapidly, and the interested reader is recommended to regularly execute a search for publications advancing text mining. As a launching point, some publications from the recent past, as of the time of writing this text, include Altman et al. (2008 #980), Faro et al. (2011 #978), Ananiadou et al. (2006 #982), and Krallinger and Valencia (2005 #962).

11.7 Some Core Problems and Techniques

In this section, we're going to provide some background to some of the problems we encounter.

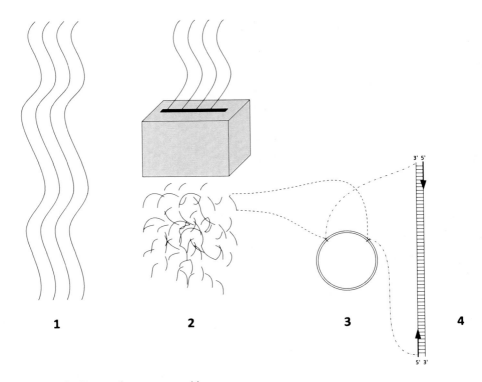

Fig. 11.19   Shotgun fragment assembly

11.7.1   *Shotgun Fragment Assembly*

The overall goal of this approach is to reconstruct a DNA target sequence as completely and as accurately as possible from a set of randomly selected substrings. In practice, these *fragments* (substrings) are sequenced from larger substrings called *clones*, and then inserted into *cloning vectors*, and finally sequenced from both ends of the clone.

Step 2, Fig. 11.19, is carefully crafted so that the clones produced have lengths that are at least one order of magnitude less than the target sequence, but also so that their lengths are normally distributed.

Let's do some mathematics to set us up for our analysis. We'll use the notation from Rigoutsos and Stephanopoulos (2007 #523).

Our ultimate target sequence, T, is a string of characters $t_1t_2t_3...t_n$ over a particular alphabet – in our case {A, C, G, T} – of length n. We define a fragment f_i to be a string of characters $f_{i1}f_{i2}f_{i3}...f_{il_i}$ over the same alphabet as T and with length l_i. Since we are ultimately interested in where, in T, f_i came from, we define a tuple (b_i, e_i) to be the interval of T from which f_i was derived.

Table 11.2 Confusion matrix

Reality data	$(b_i, e_i) \cap (b_j, e_j)$	$(b_i, e_i) \,\overline{\cap}\,(b_j, e_j)$
$(b_i, e_i) \cap (b_j, e_j)$	Correct (true positive)	False negative (type II)
$(b_i, e_i) \,\overline{\cap}\,(b_j, e_j)$	False positive (type I)	Correct (true negative)

We're going to be processing many fragments f in order to recreate T and one of our fundamental activities is going to determine whether some set of these fragments overlap or not. In fact, this is the core challenge in the problem: do two fragments overlap or not? Thus, in order to answer this question, we need to determine whether they really share a subsequence *of T* or not. If we can determine that they do, then we can say they overlap. In order to ascertain this, we need to compare each pair of fragments, f_i, f_j. If such a pair of fragments does share a common subsequence of T, then the tuples (b_i, e_i) and (b_j, e_j) will intersect.

We can use our type I and type II error definitions to show this (Table 11.2).

To complement this implementation of our concept, *sensitivity* is the ratio of true positive overlaps to the sum of true positive and false negative overlaps; *specificity* is the ratio of true positive overlaps to the sum of true positive and false positive overlaps. Obviously, our objective would be to have sensitivity and specificity as close to 1 as possible.

Given this context, we can immediately see some opportunities for problems to occur. For example, let's consider the fragments f. If we consider overlaps to be of one character (base pair) only, the number of false positives becomes enormous, so we obviously wouldn't use an overlap length of 1 for our analysis. What about 2? We could assume that two-character overlaps are likely to appear by chance in T. Thus, we have to choose our minimum length for f to be long enough to avoid those overlaps that could occur randomly in T. Conversely, a subsequence may be sufficiently long as to be unlikely to appear by chance but which actually occurs two or more times in T.[13]

To address these issues, we can develop probability models. In the former case, this is easily done by computing probabilities of short sequences being encountered by chance. Exact matches in overlaps can use the probability directly; inexact matches can be estimated. In the latter case, we first ask whether sequencing error is consistent with the number of differences between the two overlap sequences and use a probability model (and threshold) as our metric for determining this.

We have an analogous problem when it comes to false negatives. We may, in fact, have real overlap sequences which are short and which are likely to occur by chance in our target sequence T. From our discussion above, any such sequence will be discarded.

With today's sequences, these problems have become lesser challenges than in previous decades. We now deal with target sequences in the hundreds of thousands

---

[13] This latter case indicates that some biological event occurred that caused a subsequence of T to be conserved and duplicated within the overall sequence at a sufficiently high rate of fidelity.

of base pairs and above rather than the relatively short (<50 kbp) common in the 1970s and 1980s. Sequencing costs are lower, as are sequencing error rates, for which a 5–10% error rate was not uncommon. If we use a relatively long overlap bound – 15 base pairs is not an unusual length to use – then the overlaps tend to be true overlaps, even if there are differences between them (<15%).

Now let's return to reconstructing T.

If we assume that almost all long overlaps are true overlaps, and that the longer the overlap, the more likely it is to be a true overlap, then if T is reconstructed by merging overlapping fragments, then longer overlaps are preferred to shorter overlaps. In turn, a merged sequence that involves a smaller number of fragments (a shorter merged sequence) is preferred to one that uses a larger number of merged fragments because the shorter merged sequence must use longer overlaps. This problem, called the *shortest common superstring* (SCS) problem, assumes that there is no experimental error, sequencing or otherwise.[14] The challenge of this is that SCS has been proven to be NP-complete,[15] meaning that no algorithm of polynomial order[16] can exist. This is where heuristics are important.

The SCS algorithm has a very real and valuable application in the life sciences. The standard approach to large-scale sequencing ("shotgun" sequencing) is to sequence clones of many copies of the target molecule, break them randomly into small fragments, sequence those fragments, since it is relatively easy to sequence small fragments of DNA, and then propose that the shortest superstring is the correct sequence; whether or not the SCS is the most likely sequence, this approach works well in practice.

More formally, let $S = \{s_1, ..., s_m\}$ be a set of text strings from some alphabet Σ, then the output is the shortest possible string T such that each s_i is a substring of T.

The greedy algorithm (or heuristic) is typically used to solve this problem. In this approach, we repeatedly merge the two strings *with the largest overlap* until there is only one string left.

Consider the following set of strings, taken from Crochemore et al. (2010 #985):

$$s_1 = abaab$$
$$s_2 = baba$$
$$s_3 = aabbb$$
$$s_4 = bbab$$

---

[14] See Gusfield (1997 #19, p. 425) for more explanation and analysis on this problem.

[15] We don't prove it here, but SCS can be shown to be NP-complete by constructing an instance of SCS from a dedicated Hamiltonian path, which is well known to be NP-complete, and thus, so is SCS.

[16] Here, order refers to the "big O" notation. Polynomial order, $O(n^c)$, $c>1$, means that as the size of our problem increases, the complexity or performance increases in polynomial time. If a polynomial order solution cannot be found, the performance becomes even worse.

Table 11.3 Overlap table

	s_1	s_2	s_3	s_4
s_1	–	(1,1)	(0,3)	(0,2)
s_2	(1,1)	–	(1,1)	(0,1)
s_3	(3,0)	(1,1)	–	(2,0)
s_4	(2,0)	(1,0)	(0,2)	–

The greedy heuristic would result in the string $S = bbabaabbb$ as the result since

$$bb\,abaab\,bb$$
$$b\,baba\,abbb$$
$$bbab\,aabbb$$

Let's look at the first step in this process. The heuristic instructs us to look for the two strings that have the largest overlap. From Table 11.3, we can see that s_1 and s_3 have the largest overlap.

This gives us an SCS for these two strings of $ab(aab)bb$. We can continue to add s_4 in, by combining to give $bb(ab)aabbb$, and finally s_2 to give us our SCS for $S = \{s_1, s_2, s_3, s_4\}$.

For more information on a parallel implementation, see Crochemore et al. (2010 #985) and Liu (2005 #984); for a more complete, general discussion, see Gusfield (1997 #19), and for an approach using deposition and reduction, see Ning and Leong (2006 #986).

11.7.2   The BioCreAtIvE Initiative

The BioCreAtIvE (Critical Assessment of Information Extraction systems in Biology) challenge evaluation consists of a community-wide effort for evaluating text mining and information extraction systems applied to the biological domain. (BioCreAtIvE #975, Hirschman et al. 2005 #976)

As the number of groups working in the text-mining area, within the biological disciplines, increased, the lack of common standards and shared evaluation criteria meant that comparison among the different approaches in use was at the very least a challenging activity.

... various groups were addressing different problems, often using private datasets, and as a result, it was impossible to determine how good the existing systems were, whether they would scale to real applications, and what performance could be expected.

Thus, comparison of methods and assessment of progress is a core objective of the BioCreAtIvE initiative and within this context, extraction of biologically relevant – and useful – information from literature has been its focus through two activities:

- Detection of biologically significant entities – names, such as gene and protein names – and associating them with existing database entries
- Detection of entity-fact associations such as protein/functional term associations

2003/2004 saw the first BioCreAtIvE challenge evaluation, with BioCreAtIvE II occurring in 2006/2007, with BioCreAtIvE II.5 in 2009, and BioCreAtIvE III occurring in September 2010.

11.8   Data Mining in Systems Biology

As we hope we've shown in this text, and with the external references, data-mining research has produced many efficient and scalable methods for eliciting the interesting patterns and knowledge that reside in the large data repositories being developed by research groups throughout the world: from efficient classification methods to clustering, outlier analysis, frequent, sequential, and structured pattern analysis methods, to visualization and spatial/temporal data analysis tools.

Within the context of systems biology, such efficient algorithms, data structures, visualization methodologies, and communication metaphors allow us to use simulations to model ever more complex biological systems. Many of these techniques are used in concert to produce meaningful results, enabling our knowledge and understanding of such biological systems to improve over time. As an example, in 2004, a team from the University of Colorado developed an algorithm, PathMiner (McShan et al. 2003 #996), based on heuristic search, to extract, or infer, biotransformation rules from the Kyoto Encyclopedia of Genes and Genomes (KEGG), a web-accessible database of pathways, genes, and gene expressions. Using KEGG, the team inferred 110 biotransformation rules about what happens when certain compounds interact. They used these rules, as well as mathematical algorithms, to predict how detoxification pathways would metabolize ethyl and furfuryl alcohol. The model's prediction is correlated with known patterns of alcohol metabolism.

Searching the web shows that data mining tools that can help us in our analytical efforts exist today. Using the Web of Science database, with sets of keywords covering both the field of data mining and the field of systems biology, such as the following, resulted in more than 5,300 papers between 1994 and 2009, with a particularly noticeable growth after 2002:

- "Pathway," "regulatory network," "protein interaction," "regulatory network," "systems biology," or "biological network" (systems biology)
- "Large database," "amount of data," "high throughput," "knowledge discovery," "mining," "knowledge extraction," "information extraction," or "representation" (for data mining)

In particular, for this latter time period, the words "systems biology," "networks," and "gene ontology" emerge in the top ten most used keywords, and almost half of publications have been published since 2008.

11.8.1 Network Analysis

Different data-mining techniques are applied to network analysis and include some approaches not traditional to the knowledge discovery field.

Where the network structure is known, visualization and network inference approaches are generally used to improve our understanding of the structure and regularities of the network. A complex systems approach (social networks and network motifs) is typical and largely used for graphical analysis, as in signal transduction networks. Large-scale graphical visualization (spectral, Boolean, and sparse representation) has been used recently to elicit identification clues in such areas as the dense graph components that exist, such as in protein hubs, or when analyzing transcription factors. More recently, simpler approaches, such as decision trees, have been studied for visual drug delivery.

In all cases, the approaches used are aimed at extracting functional parts of the network and its topological and statistical properties.

If a network structure is not known, there are several methods that capture knowledge from high-throughput data, such as clustering, ontologies, and the like, many of which we've discussed throughout this text.

Combining more traditional statistical analysis methods, along with artificial intelligence techniques, have allowed researchers to reconstruct networks. Such techniques include probabilistic Bayesian inference, artificial neural networks, clustering, and logistic regression.

11.9 Novel Initiatives

We're going to wrap up this section with a shout-out for a couple of novel initiatives being pursued.

11.9.1 Data Mining Promises to Dig Up New Drugs

A robot scientist that can make informed guesses about how effective different chemical compounds will be at fighting different diseases could revolutionize the pharmaceutical industry by developing more effective treatments more cheaply and quickly than current methods.

The robot, known as Eve, uses advanced artificial intelligence combined with innovative data mining and knowledge discovery techniques to analyze the results of pharmacological experiments it conducts itself.

By relating the chemical structure of different compounds to their pharmacological activity, Eve is able to learn which chemical compounds should be tested next, bringing a degree of predictability to drug screening procedures that, until now, have tended to be a bit hit and miss.

"Over time, Eve will learn to pick out the chemical compounds that are likely to be most effective against a certain target by analyzing data from past experiments and comparing chemical structures to their pharmacological properties," explains Saso Dzeroski, a researcher at the Jozef Stefan Institute in Ljubljana who helped develop Eve's data mining capabilities.

"That should help scientists and pharmaceutical companies identify more effective compounds to treat different diseases, allowing them to find drug leads in a fraction of the time and at a fraction of the cost of current methods."

Eve could minimize the need for random testing of chemical compounds, Dzeroski says, noting that the robot scientist is the first computer system capable of originating its own experiments, physically performing them, interpreting the results and then repeating the cycle.[17]

11.9.2   Temporal Interactions Among Genes

In high school, we learned about processes such as cell division and how mitosis comprises interphase, comprised of G1, S, and G2, followed by mitosis, which is in turn comprised of prophase, metaphase, anaphase, telophase, and then followed by cytokinesis. As we expand our understanding of more and more biological processes, similar sequences are uncovered, along with an understanding of how these processes must be carefully synchronized in order for proper cell function to occur. Understanding how such events are coordinated over time is one of the complex problems within systems biology.

Ramakrishnan et al. (2010 #524) described a data-mining algorithm GOALIE (Gene Ontology based Algorithmic Logic and Invariant Extractor) with the objective of being able to reconstruct temporal models of cellular processes from gene expression data. One of the challenges when capturing such data is how we can use the data to understand higher-order processes such as cell division. While we can simultaneously capture temporal data about the activity of tens of thousands of genes, interpretation of the data requires that we think about our analysis tools differently. This is where an algorithm such as GOALIE comes into play.

A key goal of GOALIE is to be able to computationally integrate data from distinct stress experiments even when the experiments had been conducted independently.

(Naren Ramakrishnan, professor of computer science at Virginia Tech, lead author) GOALIE is part of a broader effort to combine data mining with modeling tools.

---

[17] http://cordis.europa.eu/ictresults/popup.cfm?section=news&tpl=article&ID=90390

(Bud Mishra, professor of computer science and mathematics with the Courant Institute of Mathematical Sciences at NYU, corresponding author)

GOALIE can not just mine patterns, but also extract entire formal models that can then be used for posing biological questions and reasoning about hypotheses.
(Mishra)

GOALIE incorporates techniques from mathematical optimization, computer science data mining, and computational biology to automatically mine the data, using unsupervised methods, in order to identify temporal relationships between groups of genes, allowing insight into time-based cellular behavior.

Specific strains of *S. cerevisiae* have been shown to have two robust biological cycles that occur simultaneously: the metabolic and cell division cycles. The yeast cell division cycle has been well studied, but its relationship to, interaction with, and coordination with the metabolic cycle has been less studied. GOALIE was able to identify the underlying temporal metabolic and cell cycle relationships in the datasets studied.

11.10   The Cloud

Warning: This section will be obsolete almost immediately!

Whether it is considered a computing architecture, hosting environment, or a provisioning environment, "the cloud" has entered the vernacular. Scientists, computer scientists, corporate IT departments, and business professionals are all investigating how the cloud can be incorporated into their strategies. This is especially true when talking to people from the Dark Side (aka sales people), where it is difficult to get through a discussion without the cloud being mentioned at least half a dozen times.

The capabilities of such environments, however, provide an interesting platform for some of the analysis methods we need to execute. The ability to obtain, on demand, a varying amount of processing capability and/or storage capability can enable us to perform analyses that may not have been possible in an environment where we have to purchase the requisite hardware and software.

Companies such as Amazon are offering services such as their *Elastic Compute Cloud* (EC2) service, which is probably one of the best-known environments, but is by no means the least, and interested readers are recommended to search and see what current vendors, and vendor services, are for this very dynamic business area.

But what is possibly more interesting for us is that we are starting to see customized environments being built on top of this infrastructure and then being made available. Two such examples are CloudNumbers[18] and SPotRun.[19] It is highly likely that more and more environments like this will exist, while others fall by the wayside, but it may provide a cost-effective environment for performing large-scale analyses if you don't already have access to such an environment.

---

[18] http://cloudnumbers.com/

[19] http://gaggle.systemsbiology.org/drupal/content/cspotrun

Conversely, leveraging such environments may be strategically advantageous, allowing you to invest in other components for your organization, rather than dedicated computing infrastructure.

11.11   Where to Next?

In the introduction to this chapter, we included a number of caveats due to the dynamic nature of systems biology, due to the dynamic expansion of scope as to what constitutes a component of systems biology, and because of the explosive research that's occurring in this arena.

What we've tried to do is include references for as much as we possibly can for each tool, technique, or concept that we highlight so that these references could be a launching point for interested readers to obtain further information, but also because it is highly likely that even newer research will reference these existing works, thus potentially providing a network foundation for newer works.

We have not provided a comprehensive treatise on systems biology, nor did we try to, because there are much more comprehensive texts that do a much better job than we can do. For example, Rigoutsos and Stephanopoulos (2007 #523) (2 volume) and Klipp et al. (2005 #987) are two such texts. In addition to texts, readers interested in courses can find a wealth of courses being offered around the world, as well as online.

But for some specific next (reading) steps, the interested reader may like Cho et al. (2006 #1031) for an overview of the application of systems biology to drug discovery, Street et al. (2011 #1032) for an exposition of reverse engineering of the regulatory network of *Populus* leaves from promoter information and expression levels, Yang et al. (2009 #1033) for a description of how data mining can be used to help drug target discovery, and Lincoln and Tiwari (2004 #1034) for a description of the modeling and analysis of dynamic and reactive biological systems involving both discrete and continuous behaviors.

11.12   Have We Left Anything Out? Boy, Have We Ever

In every chapter, we've left out more than we've included, but this is probably the chapter with the largest set of omissions. But, in our defense, if it is a defense, systems biology is changing so rapidly. That being said, we know we've left some things out. Some important things, like genome-wide association studies (GWAS), which is an approach that involves rapidly scanning markers across the complete sets of DNA, or genomes, of many people to find genetic variations associated with a particular disease. Just by this definition, we can see the application of data-mining techniques – many of which we **have** described – and their value.

But we had to stop somewhere, and if your area of research, your favorite technique, or models that you've used effectively are not included, please accept our apologies.

References

Altman R et al (2008) Text mining for biology – the way forward: opinions from leading scientists. Genome Biol 9:S7

Ananiadou S, Kell DB, Tsujii J-i (2006) Text mining and its potential applications in systems biology. Trends Biotechnol 24:571–579

Antoniotti M, Ramakrishnan N, Mishra B (2005) GOALIE, a common lisp application to discover "Kripke Models": redescribing biological processes from time-course data. In: Proceedings of the international Lisp conference, Stanford University, Stanford, 19–22 June 2005

Balakrishnan R, Ranganathan K (2000) A textbook of graph theory, Universitext. Springer, New York

Bollobás BI (1998) Modern graph theory, Graduate texts in mathematics. Springer, New York

Brin S, Page L (1998) The anatomy of a large-scale hypertextual Web search engine. Comput Networks ISDN Syst 30:107–117

Chang JT, Schütze H, Altman RB (2004) GAPSCORE: finding gene and protein names one word at a time. Bioinformatics 20:216–225

Chaouiya C (2007) Petri net modelling of biological networks. Brief Bioinform 8:210–219

Cho CR et al (2006) The application of systems biology to drug discovery. Curr Opin Chem Biol 10:294–302

Cline MS et al (2007) Integration of biological networks and gene expression data using Cytoscape. Nat Protoc 2:2366–2382

Crochemore M et al (2010) Algorithms for three versions of the shortest common superstring problem. In: 21st annual symposium on Combinatorial Pattern Matching (CPM2010). Springer, New York

Diestel R (2010) Graph theory. Springer, New York

Dougherty ER et al (1999) Nonlinear filters in genomic control. IEEE-EURASIP workshop on nonlinear signal and image processing, Antalya, pp 10–14

Faro A, Giordano D, Spampinato C (2011) Combining literature text mining with microarray data: advances for system biology modeling. Brief Bioinform

Franzen K et al (2002) Protein names and how to find them. Int J Med Inform 67:49–61

Friedman N et al (2000) Using Bayesian networks to analyze expression data. J Comput Biol 7:601–620

Fukuda K et al (1998) Toward information extraction: identifying protein names from biological papers. In: Pacific symposium on Biocomputing '98, Hawaii, pp 707–718

Funahashi A et al (2003) Cell designer: a process diagram editor for gene-regulatory and biochemical networks. Biosilico 1:159–162

Furber JD (2010) Systems biology of human aging – network model wall chart

Gentleman RC et al (2004) Bioconductor: open software development for computational biology and bioinformatics. Genome Biol 5:R80

Gupta A et al (2009) Data mining by navigation – an experience with systems biology. In: Chaudhury S et al (eds) Pattern recognition and machine intelligence. Springer, Berlin/Heidelberg, pp 158–164

Gusfield D (1997) Algorithms on strings, trees, and sequences: computer science and computational biology. Cambridge University Press, Cambridge/New York

Hasty J et al (2001) Computational studies of gene regulatory networks: in numero molecular biology. Nat Rev Genet 2:268–279

Hirschman L et al (2005) Overview of BioCreAtIvE: critical assessment of information extraction for biology. BMC Bioinformatics 6(Suppl 1):S1

Huang S (1999) Gene expression profiling, genetic networks, and cellular states: an integrating concept for tumorigenesis and drug discovery. J Mol Med 77:469–480

Hucka M et al (2003) The systems biology markup language (SBML): a medium for representation and exchange of biochemical network models. Bioinformatics 19:524–531

Iragne F et al (2004) AliasServer: a web server to handle multiple aliases used to refer to proteins. Bioinformatics 20:2331–2332

Kauffman SA (1969) Metabolic stability and epigenesis in randomly constructed genetic nets. J Theor Biol 22:437–467

Kell DB (2006) Metabolomics, modelling and machine learning in systems biology – towards an understanding of the languages of cells. FEBS J 273:873–894

Kell DB (2007) The virtual human: towards a global systems biology of multiscale, distributed biochemical network models. IUBMB Life 59:689–695

Klipp E et al (2005) Systems biology in practice: concepts, implementation and application. Wiley-VCH, Weinheim

Krallinger M, Valencia A (2005) Text-mining and information-retrieval services for molecular biology. Genome Biol 6:224

Krallinger M, Valencia A, Hirschman L (2008) Linking genes to literature: text mining, information extraction, and retrieval applications for biology. Genome Biol 9:S8

Lincoln P, Tiwari A (2004) Symbolic systems biology: hybrid modeling and analysis of biological networks. In: Bemporad A, Bicchi A, Buttazzo G (eds) Hybrid systems: computation and control HSCC, volume 2993 of LNCS. Springer, Berlin/Heidelberg/New York, pp 660–672

Liu, Y, Carbonell J et al (2005) Segmentation Conditional Random Fields (SCRFs): A New Approach for Protein Fold Recognition. Research in Computational Molecular Biology. S. Miyano, J. Mesirov, S. Kasif et al, Springer Berlin/Heidelberg. 3500: 408–422.

Longabaugh WJR, Davidson EH, Bolouri H (2005) Computational representation of developmental genetic regulatory networks. Dev Biol 283:1–16

Longabaugh WJR, Davidson EH, Bolouri H (2009) Visualization, documentation, analysis, and communication of large-scale gene regulatory networks. Biochimica et Biophysica Acta (BBA)-Gene Regul Mech 1789:363–374

McShan DC, Rao S, Shah I (2003) PathMiner: predicting metabolic pathways by heuristic search. Bioinformatics 19:1692–1698

Mestl T, Plahte E, Omholt SW (1995) A mathematical framework for describing and analysing gene regulatory networks. J Theor Biol 176:291–300

Mika S, Rost B (2004) NLProt: extracting protein names and sequences from papers. Nucleic Acids Res 32:W634–W637

Mitrofanova A (2009) Efficient systems biology algorithms for biological networks over multiple time-scales: from evolutionary to regulatory time. Doctoral dissertation, Department of Computer Science, Courant Institute of Mathematical Sciences, New York University

Ning K, Leong H (2006) Towards a better solution to the shortest common supersequence problem: the deposition and reduction algorithm. BMC Bioinformatics 7:S12

Peng Y, Zhang X (2007) Integrative data mining in systems biology: from text to network mining. Artif Intell Med 41:83–86

Prill RJ et al (2010) Towards a rigorous assessment of systems biology models: the DREAM3 challenges. PLoS One 5:e9202

Ramakrishnan N et al (2010) Reverse engineering dynamic temporal models of biological processes and their relationships. Proc Natl Acad Sci 107:12511–12516

Rigoutsos I, Stephanopoulos G (2007) Systems biology, Series in systems biology. Oxford University Press, Oxford/New York

Sauro HM et al (2003) Next generation simulation tools: the Systems Biology Workbench and BioSPICE integration. OMICS J Integrat Biol 7:355–372

Schulz M et al (2006) SBMLmerge, a system for combining biochemical network models. Genome Inform 17:62–71

Settles B (2004) Biomedical named entity recognition using conditional random fields and rich feature sets. In: Proceedings of the international joint workshop on natural language processing in biomedicine and its applications. Association for Computational Linguistics, Geneva, pp 104–107

Shmulevich I et al (2002) Probabilistic Boolean networks: a rule-based uncertainty model for gene regulatory networks. Bioinformatics 18:261–274

Shu et al (2007) Simulation study in Probabilistic Boolean Network models for genetic regulatory networks. Int J Data Min Bioinform 1:217–240

Smolen P, Baxter DA, Byrne JH (2000) Mathematical modeling of gene networks. Neuron 26:567–580

Smoot ME et al (2011) Cytoscape 2.8: new features for data integration and network visualization. Bioinformatics 27:431–432

Street N, Jansson S, Hvidsten T (2011) A systems biology model of the regulatory network in Populus leaves reveals interacting regulators and conserved regulation. BMC Plant Biol 11:13

Tanabe L, Wilbur WJ (2002) Tagging gene and protein names in biomedical text. Bioinformatics 18:1124–1132

Thomas PD et al (2009) A systems biology network model for genetic association studies of nicotine addiction and treatment. Pharmacogenet Genomics 19:538–551, 510.1097/FPC.1090b1013e32832e32832ced

van Someren EP, Wessels LFA, Reinders MJT (2000) Linear modeling of genetic networks from experimental data. In: Bourne PE et al (eds) Eighth international conference on intelligent systems for molecular biology. AAAI, La Jolla/San Diego, pp 355–366

Weaver DC, Workman CT, Stormo GD (1999) Modeling regulatory networks with weight matrices. Pac Symp Biocomput 4:112–123

Wilson RJ (2010) Introduction to graph theory. Longman, Harlow/New York

Yang Y, Adelstein SJ, Kassis AI (2009) Target discovery from data mining approaches. Drug Discov Today 14:147–154

Yuh C-H, Bolouri H, Davidson EH (1998) Genomic cis-regulatory logic: experimental and computational analysis of a sea urchin gene. Science 279:1896–1902

Chapter 12
Let's Call It a Day

Abstract What have we left out? Too much, as it happens, which is often the case with a broad subject such as data mining. What we'd like to leave you with is a pseudo-guide: try a few different approaches to your problem. Using multiple, different techniques can often uncover useful nuggets of information.

12.1 We've Covered a Lot, But Not Really

When we began this task, as is the case with many authors, from discussions we've had, what we thought we'd put in, what we thought we'd leave out, and what we thought would be the scope have changed dramatically from where we were when we started and where we now find ourselves.

Each chapter touches on a subject that is large enough for a book in its own right. Possibly, several books, and readers will hopefully use this as a launching pad to explore some of these subjects.

We've tried to cover the majority of techniques and concepts that are of interest to anyone starting data mining that haven't had much experience in the theory and techniques therein, but we would also be the first to agree that we've left much out. To include everything would have made this project go one for a lot longer and made it several thousand pages long. For any reader who does not see a particular model that they expected to see, or whom would wish for a longer exposition of some concept, accept our apologies.

One thing that we can say, and encourage any reader, who is so interested, is to investigate anything that stimulates you further: The Internet is a wonderful starting point, and there are a lot of very good resources to be had online. For hard-core bibliophiles, there is always Amazon.com as a source for books.

One important topic that we discussed at a high level, but omitted including at any level of detail, was experiment design. In the context of data analysis and data mining, excluding this topic is not necessarily significant because there would not necessarily be a need to design experiments as we commonly think of them.

R. Sullivan, *Introduction to Data Mining for the Life Sciences*,
DOI 10.1007/978-1-59745-290-8_12, © Springer Science+Business Media, LLC 2012

However, there may be occasions where we might want to create a simulation, using random data or hand-crafted data in order to study the accuracy of our models.

Like many subjects we touch on in this text, simulation is an active, expansive subject in its own right. Approaches will rightly diverge from a topic-independent discourse to a topic-dependent discussion very quickly.

For those readers interested in exploring modeling and simulation further, the following references are recommended starting points: Hoppensteadt and Peskin (2002 #286), Zeigler et al. (2000 #284), or Sokolowski and Banks (2009 #285). Velten (2009 #287) uses only open-source simulation environments such as Maxima. Schwartz (2008 #288) provides an important and valuable survey of the various approaches and models that are available to the biological scientist. The role of simulation in health care as a whole is becoming more and more important, especially as a valuable tool for expanding realistic scenarios into the educational process. Riley (2008 #289) provides a robust and readable introduction to how simulation and health care overlap. For readers interested in simulation in molecular modeling, they may find Schlick (2002 #39) or Leach (2001 #38) valuable.

Simulation environments abound. Commercially, some of the most well known include Simulink, Arena, and Simul8, but in addition, there are several open-source packages that offer specific simulation capabilities, including Maxima, Code_Saturne, Salome-Meca, CoSMoS, and DEVSJAVA. These are, of course, in addition to the simulation capabilities available within some of the tools we use in this text such as R and Weka. Many of these tools provide a wealth of capabilities once the initial learning curve has been surmounted, and readers are highly recommended to investigate this further to provide another tool in the arsenal for data mining.

We began this text with a somewhat "pure" definition of data mining: finding the hidden patterns lurking in our data. If we take this at face value, this would suggest our finding some means – that is, function – that trolls our data and highlights anything and everything that is a pattern. But, as we described at the very beginning of our discussion, the noise that this would generate would make this approach infeasible. While we have tried to provide a set of tools, techniques, and concepts to help, there are a lot more out there. Take simulation, for example. While beyond the scope of this text, we strongly encourage readers to use this as a stepping stone and continually broaden their exposure to anything that can help.

12.2   When Two Models Are Better Than One

To get to any of the three concourses in terminal C at Cincinnati airport, one has to travel underground. The underground tunnel has a train, with three stops – terminal/baggage claim, concourse A, concourse B/C – as well as moving walkways to allow passengers to walk to and from the concourses. Several years ago, before many of the security restrictions we now deal with, there were times when I'd cut it a little close in getting to the airport and then find myself rushing to get to the gate for my flight, which always seemed, by the way, to be the furthest gate away from wherever I was.

I always wondered whether waiting for the train, or walking as fast as my overweight, out-of-shape body could move, was the fastest. Every time I waited, my stress level went up; I always thought I'd be at my destination before the train even arrived. Every time I walked, I'd get to the gate panting and sweating – apologies to those people who sat next to me – and would wonder if I'd get there just as quickly if I'd waited. The interesting subjective view being that the alternate approach was *always* the better. But which really was?

So yes, I conducted an experiment. This was at a time when I traveled every week. Whenever I got there with enough time, I would alternately wait or walk and gather information. Of course, the conclusion was "it depends." If the train was at the opposite end of its track, walking was better; if it was on its way, waiting was better; if it had just left the station I was at, walking was the only option.

I had previously hypothesized that one or other method would always be the better, but in the end, it depended on the starting data, in this case, the position of the train. So what's the point?

In the above scenario, my choice or approach – my model – often depended on a piece of data I didn't always have: where the train was on its journey. Since I couldn't split myself in two, I would guess, and I always felt that I guessed wrong. In data mining, starting from such a tenuous position makes no sense whatsoever. Instead, we often approach a problem and utilize two, or maybe even more, models. Remember, different models have different strengths.

If you're looking to classify instances, try two different classification approaches. Sometimes, you can even get some interesting new information when comparing the results of your models.

12.3   The Most Widely Used Algorithms?

Wu et al. (2009 #243) identified the following algorithms as the most commonly used in data mining analyses as follows:

1. C4.5
2. *k*-Means
3. Support vector machines
4. Apriori
5. Expectation-maximization
6. PageRank
7. AdaBoost
8. *k*-Nearest neighbors
9. Naïve Bayes
10. Classification and regression trees

And readers may immediately notice a couple of algorithms missing from this book.

PageRank is probably an algorithm that we use every day, since it is the basis of the current search powerhouse – Google. But we elected to avoid including this in our book. Why? We considered that most people beginning their data-mining efforts would be working with datasets that are internal to their organization and likely to be stored as something other than Web pages.

As to AdaBoost (Freund and Schapire 1996 #207), short for *adaptive boosting*, as we mentioned earlier in this book, it can be used to boost the performance of many other machine-learning algorithms. The adaptive part comes into play in that subsequent classifiers are "tweaked" in order to favor instances that were misclassified by previous classifiers. Utilizing such an algorithm has various advantages for mining models that often run for protracted periods of time, and AdaBoost, being easy to program and tune – there is only one parameter – is particularly valuable. This is especially so when you consider that it can be combined with many classifiers, be they neural networks, nearest-neighbor classifiers, decision trees, or even simple rules, and can positively improve them all; it is worth including in your mining efforts. Once again, however, we felt that this algorithm would probably not be one of the common algorithms the reader would immediately reach for. In fact, as it applies to AdaBoost in particular, many data-mining environments that include multiple algorithms within their toolset will incorporate optimization techniques to provide an added boost to your analysis. Our feeling was, if you need to go further, you will likely involve several other specialists to help derive optimal algorithms and implementations.

12.4   Documenting Your Process

We've spent a lot of this text describing individual tools, techniques, and concepts that can be used to fulfill a wide variety of data-mining objectives. What we studiously avoided was any in-depth discussion on putting it all together. We touched on it in the early chapters, but when it came to the later detailed discussions on individual techniques and concepts, we didn't try to offer suggestions on how to combine techniques to provide a *solution* to any individual problem.

The primary reason for this is that we were trying to avoid corralling the thought process. After all, we want to elicit hidden patterns, the hidden information, and knowledge contained within the data. Further, each dataset is different. Each context is different. Each requires some amount of subject matter expertise – which may be the first step you undertake: to become familiar with that subject area – in order to accomplish your objectives. Hence, we intentionally shied away from recommending how you use the analytical lego™ bricks to build specific structures.

However, there is one facet of the process that we do want to recommend: consider your data analysis efforts to be similar to any scientific experiment.

They should be documented to the same degree as you would if this were a chemical reaction, a biological experiment, or any other scientific endeavor.

Once your analysis is complete, and your conclusions are presented, someone, somewhere, will need to be able to reproduce them. It is imperative that this be able to be completed and both your process and results be validated.

Let's take a simple example that we discussed when using regular expressions for analyzing sequence data in our informatics discussions. There we had a very small sequence dataset – only 1,100 base pairs – and we were interested in the EcoRI restriction enzyme cleavage site, where the GAATTC sequence is split into G and AATTC. Due to the nature of regular expressions, we had to consider a prefix for this sequence and selected "TTTGTGCA" for our illustrative purposes. If this was used in a real analysis, it would be imperative to document this along with our rationale for using that sequence as opposed to something else. For a start, anyone wishing to confirm our results would need to ensure they use the same such criteria since in the real world we would be dealing with much larger datasets, and allowing this value to change would almost certainly change the results. But secondly, this choice may actually affect the outcome. Yes, we **do** want it to affect the outcome inasmuch as it should exclude noise and erroneous results. However, we **don't** want it to affect the outcome by being the cause of erroneous results. It is quite possible that some subsequent analysis might identify our choice(s) as being problematic.

Notice that we didn't even approach the topic of documenting the complete analysis for publication or submission to a regulatory body; other very important reasons for ensuring that everything is documented.

Many people involved in data mining have a background in information technology. Some, the intended readers of this text, have a background in the life sciences. Whereas the latter are very attuned to documenting their processes, the former? Not so much. In fact, many points within the systems development process are often, unfortunately not documented. This is a widespread challenge in the IT space. However, it is vital that decisions made when implementing algorithms, when refining the code used, and when generating the output are known to all concerned. If you leverage the immense value that can be accrued from involving IT professionals in helping to develop the routines you need, just be sure to undertake a thorough review so that all of the variables and assumptions are well understood.

12.5   Where To From Here?

One of our major challenges when developing this text is what to put in and what to leave out: it's impossible to do justice to any of the subject areas we've touched on in this text since each discipline deserves its own book, and even then, we wouldn't cover everything.

They are all areas of very active research, with novel uses, methods, and conclusions being made every day.

1000 MB	=	1 GB						Gigabytes
		1000 GB	=	1 TB				Terabytes
				1000 TB	=	1 PB		Petabytes
						1000 PB	=	1 EB	Exabytes
							1000 EB	=	1 ZB	Zettabyte

Fig. 12.1 From megabyte to zettabyte

New types of data, larger volumes of data, new understandings of that data, and new applications of that data are being made every day by researchers around the world, giving us more insight into the vast amounts of data that are being generated.

This last characteristic – the amount of data generated – has been a common thread throughout this text: how do we manage the vast repository of data and make sense of it. Any reader actively involved in research as they read this only needs to think about the last 90 days and how much data has been generated by the experimentation in their lab. Now add to that the number of scientific papers written, the number of presentations given, and the resulting amount of data generated.

We made this reference earlier in this text, but it's interesting to repeat it here: a Cisco blogger predicts that we will enter the zettabyte era of data by 2015[1] (Fig. 12.1).

Just to put this into perspective, 1ZB would take 250,000,000 DVDs to store all the data, or contain 36,000 years of HD-TV, or be equivalent to streaming the entire Netflix™ catalog 3,177 times (as of June 2011).

The amount of data we seem to be generating doesn't look as though it's going to slow down. Using data mining to automatically elicit knowledge from this sea of data will become even more important, especially as we increase the types of data we want to look at to include videos and still images, for example.

References

Freund Y, Schapire RE (1996) Experiments with a new boosting algorithm. In: Machine learning: proceedings of the thirteenth international conference, San Francisco
Hoppensteadt FC, Peskin CS (2002) Modeling and simulation in medicine and the life sciences. Springer, New York

---

[1] http://blogs.cisco.com/news/the-dawn-of-the-zettabyte-era-infographic/

Leach AR (2001) Molecular modelling: principles and applications. Prentice Hall, Harlow/New York

Riley RH (2008) A manual of simulation in healthcare. Oxford University Press, New York

Schlick T (2002) Molecular modeling and simulation: an interdisciplinary guide, vol 21, Interdisciplinary applied mathematics. Springer, New York

Schwartz R (2008) Biological modeling and simulation: a survey of practical models, algorithms, and numerical methods. MIT Press, Cambridge

Sokolowski JA, Banks CM (2009) Principles of modeling and simulation: a multidisciplinary approach. John Wiley, Hoboken

Velten K (2009) Mathematical modeling and simulation: introduction for scientists and engineers. Wiley-VCH, Weinheim

Wu L-Y et al (2009) Conditional random pattern algorithm for LOH inference and segmentation. Bioinformatics 25:61–67

Zeigler BP, Kim TG, Praehofer H (2000) Theory of modeling and simulation: integrating discrete event and continuous complex dynamic systems. Academic, San Diego

Appendix A
Probability, Distribution Theory, and Statistical Inference

A.1 Definitions

We define an *event* as any set of possible outcomes of a random experiment. In turn, an *outcome* is the result of a single trial of a random experiment. A *random experiment* is an experiment that has an outcome that is not completely predictable, that is, we can repeat the experiment under the same conditions and potentially get a different result. The *sample space* (sometimes called *universe*) is the set of all possible outcomes for one trial of the random experiment and is often denoted by Ω.[1] The symbol ϕ denotes the set containing no outcomes, or the empty set.

Using the above definitions, we can now define the union, intersection, and complement of events. We use two events A and B:

The *union* of two events A and B is the set of outcomes that are in *either* A or B or both and is denoted by $A \cup B$.

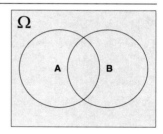

(continued)

---

[1] The letter U is also sometimes used for this and we may use either interchangeably.

R. Sullivan, *Introduction to Data Mining for the Life Sciences*,
DOI 10.1007/978-1-59745-290-8, © Springer Science+Business Media, LLC 2012

The *intersection* of two events A and B is the set of outcomes that are in both A and B simultaneously and is denoted by $A \cap B$.

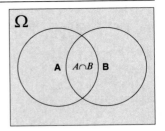

The *complement* of an event A is the set of outcomes that are not in A and is denoted by $\bar{A}$ or A'.

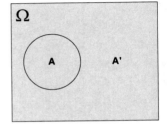

An event B is a *subset* of an event A if all of the outcomes of B are also outcomes of A.

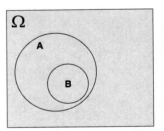

Two events A and B which have no outcomes in common are *mutually exclusive* or *disjoint*. In this case the occurrence of A, without loss of generality, precludes the occurrence of event B.

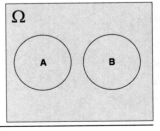

A.2   Axioms of Probability

A probability is a real number between 0 and 1 that is assigned to each of the events that an experiment generates, with higher values indicating that the event is more likely to occur. Assigning a value of 1 to an event means that the event is certain to occur while assigning a value of 0 means that the event can never occur. The following axioms must be satisfied for any consistent probability assignment:

1. $0 \leq P(A) \leq 1$ for any event A.
2. $P(\Omega) = 1$.
3. If A and B are mutually exclusive events, that is, $P(A \cap B) = \phi$, $P(A \cup B)$ $= P(A) + P(B)$. In the more general case, $P(A \cup B \cup C \cup ...) = P(A) + P(B)$ $+P(C) + \cdots$

We can now use these axioms to prove the following rules:

1. $P(\phi) = 0$.
   Since $\Omega \cup \phi = \Omega$ and $\Omega \cap \phi = \phi$, by axiom 3, $1 = 1 + P(\phi)$.
2. $P(\bar{A}) = 1 - P(A)$.
   Since $\Omega = A \cup \bar{A}$ and $A \cap \bar{A} = \phi$, by axiom 3, $1 = P(A) + P(\bar{A})$.
3. $P(A \cup B) = P(A) + P(B) - P(A \cap B)$.
   $A \cup B = A \cup (\bar{A} \cap B)$ which are disjoint. By axiom 3, $P(A \cup B) = P(A)$ $+P(\bar{A} \cap B)$. $B = (A \cap B) \cup (\bar{A} \cap B)$ which are disjoint. By axiom 3, $P(B)$ $= P(A \cap B) + P(\bar{A} \cap B)$. Substituting for $P(\bar{A} \cap B)$ in above gives $P(A \cup B)$ $= P(A) + P(B) - P(A \cap B)$.
   A visualization of this rule from the Venn diagram shows us that $P(A) + P(B)$ would actually include $P(A \cap B)$ twice, thus we subtract one from the sum.

A.3   Joint Probability

Consider a random experiment in which Ω includes two events A and B. We define the *joint probability* as the probability of both events occurring simultaneously.[2] The implication of this is that the set of outcomes occurs in both event A and event B, which, on the Venn diagram, is the quantity $A \cap B$. That is, the joint probability of the events A and B is $P(A \cap B)$. But what happens if the events are independent of each other? In this case, $P(A \cap B) = P(A) \times P(B)$.

We note here that independent events and disjoint events are not identical. In probability, two events are independent if they have no effect on each other: the occurrence of one has no impact on the occurrence, or lack thereof, of the other. Thus, independence is a property that arises from the probabilities assigned to the

---

[2] Actually, we really mean simultaneously on the same iteration or repetition of the random experiment.

events and their intersection. Disjoint, or mutually exclusive, events are events which have no outcomes in common: such events with non-zero probabilities cannot be independent since their intersection is the empty set, with $P(\phi) = 0$, which can never equal the product of the probabilities of the two events.

We call the probability of an event A, in the joint probability setting, its *marginal probability*, and this is calculated as $P(A \cap B) + P(A \cap \bar{B})$ using the axioms of probability. (The confirmation of this is left as an exercise for the reader.)

A.4   Conditional Probability

If we are told that event A has occurred, then we know that everything outside of $A(A')$ is no longer possible. We can consider the reduced universe $\Omega_r = A$ since we only need to consider outcomes within A. Consider a second event B. If we know that event A has occurred, will this affect the probability of our second event B occurring? That is, what is the *conditional probability* of B occurring given that A has occurred? The only part of the event B which will be relevant is that part which is also a part of A, that is, $A \cap B$. Given that we know that A has occurred, $P(\Omega_r) = 1$, by the second axiom or probability. Therefore, the probability of B given A, written $P(B|A)$, is the probability of $A \cap B$ multiplied by the scaling factor $\frac{1}{P(A)}$ due to our reduced universe Ω_r:

$$P(B|A) = \frac{P(A \cap B)}{P(A)} \tag{A.1}$$

Note that this equation tells us that $P(B|A) \propto P(A \cap B)$.

In the event that A and B are independent events, $P(B|A) = \frac{P(A \cap B)}{P(A)} = \frac{P(A) \times P(B)}{P(A)} = P(B)$, which states that knowledge about the event A does not affect the probability of the event B occurring when A and B are independent events.

Although it is tempting to consider $P(A|B)$ in the analogous way and write $P(A|B) = \frac{P(A \cap B)}{P(B)}$, we need to remember that B is an unobservable event. That is, when we calculate the conditional probability – the probability of B occurring *given that* A occurred – we are not observing either the occurrence or the nonoccurrence of B. Thus, the probability of A occurring will be dependent on which one of B or $\bar{B}$ has occurred: $P(A)$ is conditional on the occurrence of nonoccurrence of event B. Rewriting the conditional probability formula as

$$P(A \cap B) = P(B) \times P(A|B) \tag{A.2}$$

we get the rule known as the *multiplication rule for probability*. Although this may seem trivial, it provides us with a conditional probability rule for any observable event given an unobservable event and allows us to find the joint probability. Equation A.2 shows the relationship when B occurs and similarly,

$$P(A \cap \bar{B}) = P(\bar{B}) \times P(A|\bar{B})$$

covers the case when B does not occur.

A.5 Bayes' Theorem

Although we discuss Bayes' theorem at various points in the book, we include it here for completeness.

From its definition, the marginal probability of an event A is calculated by summing the probabilities of its disjoint parts: $P(A) = P(A \cap B) + P(A \cap \bar{B})$ and substituting this into Eq. A.1 gives

$$P(B|A) = \frac{P(A \cap B)}{P(A \cap B) + P(A \cap \bar{B})}$$

Using the multiplication rule, we can find the join probabilities and rewrite the equation to give Bayes' theorem for an event A:

$$P(B|A) = \frac{P(A|B) \times P(B)}{P(A|B) \times P(B) + P(A|\bar{B}) \times P(\bar{B})} \tag{A.3}$$

In A.3 and our definition for $P(A)$, we used B and $\bar{B}$ which comprised the universe – $\Omega = B \cup \bar{B}$. B and $\bar{B}$ are disjoint. We say that B and $\bar{B}$ partition the universe. This is the simplest case. Often we will have more than two events which partition the universe. Consider the case where we have n events such that $B_1 \cup B_2 \cup ... \cup B_n = \Omega$ and $B_i \cap B_j = \phi \ \forall i, j$, where $i = 1,...,n, j = 1,...,n, i \neq j$.

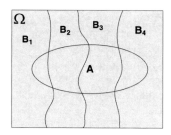

An observable event A will therefore be partitioned into n parts: $A = (A \cap B_1) \cup (A \cap B_2) \cup ... \cup (A \cap B_n)$ where $A \cap B_i$ and $A \cap B_j$ are disjoint because B_i and B_j are disjoint. Thus,

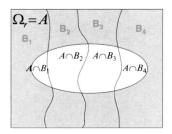

$$P(A) = \sum_{i=1}^{n} (A \cap B_i) \quad \text{(Law of Total Probability)}$$

Using the multiplication rule gives

$$P(A) = \sum_{i=1}^{n} P(A|B_i) \times P(B_i)$$

where each conditional probability is $P(B_i|A) = \frac{P(A \cap B_i)}{P(A)}$ and the multiplication rule is used to determine the joint probability of the numerator $P(A \cap B_i) = P(B_i) \times P(A|B_i)$ to give

$$P(B_i|A) = \frac{P(A|B_i) \times P(B_i)}{\sum_{i=1}^{n} P(A|B_i) \times P(B_i)}$$

A.6   Estimators

Consider a random sample from a distribution where we are tossing a thumb tack (or drawing pint) and where the random variable X takes a value of 1 if the tack lands on its head and 0 otherwise. Then in tossing the tack we are sampling from a distribution of X which has the probability distribution $p_0 = P(X_i = 0) = 1 - p$, $p_1 = P(X_i = 1) = p$, where p is the probability that the tack lands on its side.

We will not typically know the value of p, and so a problem we often face is to estimate the value of p using a random sample. In such cases, we know the distribution type, but it depends upon the values of one or more unknown parameters. In our example, the unknown parameter is p.

We therefore use a random sample to obtain *estimates* for the values of these parameters. In the general case, we have a random variable X whose distribution is of a known type, but which depends upon the value of some unknown parameter θ. We wish to obtain a numerical value for θ and use the procedure of obtaining a random sample from the distribution of X and then use the value of an appropriate statistic to estimate θ.

Thus, formally, an estimator for a parameter θ is a statistic (random variable) whose value is used to estimate θ. We typically use the notation $\hat{\theta}$ to denote an estimator for θ.

On occasions, it will be obvious what an estimator is for the unknown parameter. In our thumb tack example above, an obvious procedure would be to toss the tack n times, counting the number of times the tack lands on its side. If it lands on its side a total of a times, that is, the proportion of tosses which result in the tack landing on its size, then we could use

$$\hat{p} = \frac{a}{n}$$

as our estimator for p.

However, the choice is not always so clear. In fact, there may be several choices for an estimator. For example, a random variable with a probability distribution

$$f(x) = \tfrac{1}{\theta} e^{\frac{-x}{\theta}} \qquad \text{if } x \geq 0,$$
$$= 0 \qquad \text{otherwise}$$

could use either the sample mean or the sample standard deviation of a random sample of size n to estimate θ. An important question is which is the best estimator for θ.

If $\hat{\theta}$ is an estimator for θ, we obviously wish to know how good an estimator it is. An intuitive question to help us answer this is: How close is the estimated value to the real value? We use the mean to help us with this. Other terms for the mean of a random variable X with probability function p_x is defined as

$$E(X) = \sum_{i=1}^{n} x p_x$$

where the summation is over all possible values of X. The notation $E(X)$ is read as the expected value, or expectation.

If $E(\hat{\theta}) = \theta$, we say that $\hat{\theta}$ is an *unbiased estimator* for θ. If $E(\hat{\theta}) \neq \theta$, then we define the *bias* as given by

$$bias(\hat{\theta}) = E(\hat{\theta}) - \theta$$

and say that $\hat{\theta}$ is a *biased estimator* for θ.

If X is a random variable with mean μ and variance σ^2, then the sample mean $\bar{X}$ and the sample variance S^2 are unbiased estimators for μ and σ^2, respectively.

If we consider $S^2 = \frac{1}{n} \sum_{i=1}^{n} (X_i - \bar{X})^2$ as an estimator for σ^2, then $E(S^2) = \frac{n^{-1}(n-1)\sigma^2}{n}$ and so $bias(S^2) = -\frac{1}{n}\sigma^2$, which explains why $S^2 = \frac{1}{n-1} \sum_{i=1}^{n} (X_i - \bar{X})^2$ is usually used as the estimator of the population variance.

The variance of a random variable X is defined by $Var(X) = E[(X - \mu)^2]$ where $\mu = E(X)$ and the symbol σ^2 is reserved for the variance, with S^2 being used for the variance of a set of data. This is a measure of the dispersion of the probability distribution.

We say that an unbiased estimator $\hat{\theta}_1$ is a more efficient (better) estimator for θ than a second unbiased estimator $\hat{\theta}_2$ if $Var(\hat{\theta}_1)<Var\hat{\theta}_2)$ and the relative efficiency of θ_2 with respect to θ_1 is $Var(\hat{\theta}_1)/Var(\hat{\theta}_2)$.. This fraction is often expressed as a percentage by $[Var(\hat{\theta}_1)/Var(\hat{\theta}_2).] \times 100$. Thus, the relative efficiency is >1 (or 100%) if $\hat{\theta}_2$ is more efficient than θ_1 and less than 1 if θ_1 is more efficient than $\hat{\theta}_2$.

The criterion outlined above for comparing estimators can only be used when all the estimators under consideration are unbiased. However, under certain conditions, we may prefer to use a biased estimator. We illustrate this by returning to our thumb tack example above where we selected $\hat{p} = \frac{a}{n}$ as our estimator, which we will now denote by $\hat{p}_1$. Let us define a second estimator as follows:

$$\hat{p}_2 = \frac{a+1}{n+2}$$

We won't explain the origin of this estimator since we're using it for illustration purposes. Instead, we note that this does in fact occur as an estimator in certain more complex models.

$$E(\hat{p}_2) = \frac{E(a)+1}{n+2} = \frac{np+1}{n+2}$$

In order for $\hat{p}_2$ to be unbiased, $p = \frac{1}{2}$, otherwise it is biased. However, if n is large, the bias is small. Further, the value of $Var(\hat{p}_2)$ is also small, where n is large. Thus, the estimate is close to the true value of p. So how can we compare two such estimators? One common method is to use the *mean square error*.

The *mean square error* (MSE) of an estimator $\hat{\theta}$ for a parameter θ is defined as

$$MSE(\hat{\theta}) = E\left[\left(\hat{\theta} - \theta\right)^2\right]$$

As can be seen below, it is related to other quantities we have introduced above:

$$\begin{aligned}
MSE\left(\hat{\theta}\right) &= E\left[\left(\hat{\theta} - \theta\right)^2\right] \\
&= E\left[\hat{\theta}^2 - 2\hat{\theta}\theta + \theta^2\right] \\
&= E\left(\hat{\theta}^2\right) - 2\theta E\left(\hat{\theta}\right) + \theta^2 \\
&= E\left(\hat{\theta}^2\right) - \left[E\left(\hat{\theta}\right)\right]^2 + \left\{\left[E\left(\hat{\theta}\right)\right]^2 - 2\theta E\left(\hat{\theta}\right) + \theta^2\right\} \\
&= Var\left(\hat{\theta}\right) + \left[E\left(\hat{\theta}\right) - \theta\right]^2 \\
&= Var\left(\hat{\theta}\right) + \left[bias\left(\hat{\theta}\right)\right]^2
\end{aligned}$$

Thus, $MSE(\hat{\theta}) = Var(\hat{\theta}) + [bias(\hat{\theta})]^2$

Note also that if $\hat{\theta}$ is unbiased, then $MSE(\hat{\theta}) = Var(\hat{\theta})$. Therefore, we can think of the MSE as being a generalization of the variance that allows for bias.

An estimator $\hat{\theta}$, based on a sample of size n, for a parameter θ is said to be a *consistent estimator* for θ if,

$$E(\hat{\theta}) \rightarrow \theta \text{ and } Var(\hat{\theta}) \rightarrow 0 \text{ as } n \rightarrow \infty. \text{ Equivalently, } MSE(\hat{\theta}) \rightarrow 0.$$

This is an important consideration because when an estimator is consistent, it becomes increasingly likely that the estimate is close to the parameter's actual value as the sample size increases.

A.7 The Law of Large Numbers

The Law of Large Numbers states that for repeated, independent trials with the same probability p of success in each trial, the percentage of successes is increasingly likely to be close to the chance of success as the number of trials increases.

Formally, the chance that the percentage of successes differs from the probability p of success by more than a fixed positive amount, $e > 0$, tends to zero as the number of trials n tends to infinity, for every number $t > 0$.

Another way of thinking about this is to consider an experiment where the outcome is a random variable, and where the experiment is conducted repeatedly. The outcome for different repetitions is independent from any other. The law of large numbers says that as the number of independent repetitions increases, the average of the observed outcomes approaches the average of all possible outcomes.

This can be easily illustrated by using the example of a die being rolled. The average of all possible outcomes is the average value of the six numbers: $(1 + 2 + 3 + 4 + 5 + 6)/6 = 3.5$. Obviously, 3.5 is not a possible, observable outcome for any individual experiment since it is not on the face of a die. If the observed result we see for the ith experiment is denoted x_i, the average of the observed outcomes is

$$\frac{\sum_{i=1}^{n} x_i}{n}$$

If $x_1 = 3$, and $x_2 = 5$, then the average of the observed outcomes is $(3 + 5)/2 = 4$, if $x_3 = 1$, the average of the observed outcomes is $(3 + 5 + 1)/3 = 3$, and so on. We can make the value as close as we like to 3.5 by increasing the number of repetitions of the experiment.

Appendix B
Databases and Software Projects

A plethora of software products exist to support data mining efforts. These products include core technical infrastructure products such as the underlying database management systems and facilities within to support mining models, through general-purpose products to help with the various stages of the mining effort, on to those products which offer very specific, and complete support for specific subject areas such as microarray analysis. To include an exhaustive list of products is simply not feasible and would certainly be completely out of date by the time this book is published.

Instead, we have included a number of products and databases that we have found useful in our experiences and which, we believe, will continue to be available, developed, and supported. We include these software products and databases with the kind agreement of the respective various authors of the respective products and databases to illustrate the various mining techniques we describe.

All of the products or databases we use are listed here for easy reference by the reader. We have kept the information to a minimum, preferring to point the reader to the official web site or reference since the versions, licensing details, and scope of these products or databases may change drastically between the time of writing and when the reader accesses the software or data.

Wherever we have been granted permission, the actual version of the software/database used in this book can be located at www.lsdm.org/thirdparty.

The descriptions of the products and databases contained in this appendix are from the various vendors and not from the authors.

The nature of the Internet is such that URLs accurate at the time of writing may no longer be accessible. We have tried to provide enough context for a search in the event that the URL does not work.

B.1   Software Projects

B.1.1   Alyuda NeuroIntelligence

http://www.alyuda.com/neural-networks-software.htm
This is a neural networks software application designed to assist experts in solving real-world problems. NeuroIntelligence features only proven algorithms and techniques. It is fast and easy to use.

B.1.2   AmiGO

www.godatabase.org
This tool provides a mechanism for searching the gene ontology database, which comprises a controlled vocabulary of terms for biological concepts and for genes and gene products which have been annotated using the controlled vocabulary. For example, an inquiry using "protein kinase activity" returned 93 matches in the database.[3]

See also "The Gene Ontology."

B.1.3   AutoClass@IJM

http://ytat2.ijm.univ-paris-diderot.fr/AutoclassAtIJM.html
AutoClass@IJM is a freely available (to academia) computational resource with a web interface to AutoClass, a powerful unsupervised Bayesian classification system developed by the Ames Research Center at NASA AutoClass. End users upload their datasets through a web interface; computations are then queued into the cluster server. When the clustering is completed, an URL to the results is sent back to the user by e-mail.

B.1.4   Babelomics

http://babelomics.bioinfo.cipf.es/
An integrative platform for the analysis of transcriptomics, proteomics, and genomic data with advanced functional profiling, integrating primary (normalization, calls, etc.) and secondary (signatures, predictors, associations, TDTs, clustering,

---

[3] A sample run performed on May 5, 2007.

etc.) analysis tools within an environment that allows relating genomic data and/or interpreting them by means of different functional enrichment or gene set methods. This tool integrates primary (normalization, calls, etc.) and secondary (signatures, predictors, associations, TDTs, clustering, etc.) analysis tools within an environment that allows relating genomic data and/or interpreting them by means of different functional enrichment or gene set methods.

B.1.5   BioCarta

www.biocarta.com
This is an interactive, web-based resource for life scientists that includes information on gene function, proteomic pathways, ePosters, and research reagents.

B.1.6   Bioconductor

www.bioconductor.org
The Bioconductor project was started in 2001 with the overall objective of developing a set of tools for analyzing and understanding genomic data. Gentleman et al. (2001 #90) is the official FAQ for this project at www.bioconductor.org/docs/faq and the reader is referred to this page for more details on the project's goals and objectives.

The version of Bioconductor used in this book is version 1.9.

B.1.7   Biomedical Informatics Research Network (BIRN)

The Biomedical Informatics Research Network (BIRN) is a national initiative to advance biomedical research through data sharing and online collaboration. Funded by the National Center for Research Resources (NCRR), a component of the US National Institutes of Health (NIH), BIRN provides data-sharing infrastructure, software tools, strategies, and advisory services – all from a single source. http://www.birncommunity.org/

B.1.8   BioPAX

www.biopax.org
This is a data exchange format for biological pathway data.

B.1.9 BioTapestry

http://www.biotapestry.org/
BioTapestry is an interactive tool for building, visualizing, and simulating genetic regulatory networks.

B.1.10 BLAST

http://www.ncbi.nlm.nih.gov/BLAST

B.1.11 BLAT

http://genome.ucsc.edu/cgi-bin/hgBlat?command=start

B.1.12 BrainMaker

http://www.calsci.com/BrainIndex.html
This is a neural network software that lets you use your computer for business and marketing forecasting, stock, bond, commodity, and futures prediction, pattern recognition, medical diagnosis, sports handicapping...almost any activity where you need special insight.

B.1.13 Cambridge Structure Database (CSD)

The Cambridge Structural Database (CSD) records bibliographic, chemical, and crystallographic information for organic molecules and metal-organic compounds whose 3D structures have been determined using X-ray diffraction and neutron diffraction. Results are recorded for single crystal studies and powder diffraction studies, which yield 3D atomic coordinate data for at least all non-hydrogen atoms. In some cases, the Cambridge Crystallographic Data Centre (CCDC) is unable to obtain coordinates, and incomplete entries are archived to the CSD. Crystal structure data is included that arises from publications in the open literature or private deposits.
http://www.ccdc.cam.ac.uk/products/csd/

B.1.14 CDC National Center for Health Statistics

http://www.cdc.gov/nchs/datawh.htm

B.1.15 Clone\Gene ID Converter

http://idconverter.bioinfo.cnio.es/
This is a tool for converting gene, clone, or protein IDs to other IDs, which can be used for small queries or for tens of thousands of IDs (typically from a microarray experiment). Most of the conversions are pre-generated every time the databases are updated in order to get a fast answer for each query.

B.1.16 Clustal

http://www.clustal.org

B.1.17 Cognos

http://www-01.ibm.com/software/data/cognos/

B.1.18 COPASI: Biological Network Simulator

http://www.copasi.org/tiki-view_articles.php
COPASI is a software application for simulation and analysis of biochemical networks and their dynamics. COPASI is a stand-alone program that supports models in the SBML standard and can simulate their behavior using ODEs or Gillespie's stochastic simulation algorithm; arbitrary discrete events can be included in such simulations.

COPASI carries out several analyses of the network and its dynamics and has extensive support for parameter estimation and optimization. COPASI provides means to visualize data in customizable plots, histograms, and animations of network diagrams.

B.1.19 cMAP

cmap.nci.nih.gov

B.1.20 CompuCell3D

CompuCell is an open-source software modeling environment and PDE solver. It is largely used for cellular modeling (foams, tissues, etc.); however, efforts are being made to include fluid simulation capabilities. Created in collaboration between

groups at IU and Notre Dame, CompuCell provides an easy user interface for complex cellular modeling.
https://simtk.org/home/compucell3d
http://www.compucell3d.org/

B.1.21   Cytoscape

http://www.cytoscape.org/
Cytoscape is an open-source bioinformatics software platform for visualizing these molecular interaction networks and biological pathways and integrating these networks with annotations, gene expression profiles, and other data. Cytoscape was originally designed for biological research, now it is a general platform supporting complex network analysis and visualization. Its use of plug-ins to provide additional features supporting new file formats, profiling analysis, layouts, scripting, or database connectivity, to name but a few domains, allows this tool to be a more general-purpose tool.

B.1.22   Database for Annotation, Visualization, and Integrated Discovery (DAVID)

http://david.abcc.ncifcrf.gov/home.jsp
Database for Annotation, Visualization, and Integrated Discovery (DAVID) provides a comprehensive set of functional annotation tools for investigators to understand biological meaning behind large list of genes. Its functionality includes the ability to identify enriched biological themes, particularly GO terms, discover enriched functional-related gene groups, cluster redundant annotation terms, visualize genes on BioCarta and KEGG pathway maps, display related many-genes-to-many-terms on 2-D views, search for other functionally related genes not in the user-provided list, list interacting proteins, explore gene names in batch, link gene-disease associations, highlight protein functional domains and motifs, redirect the user to related literatures, and convert gene identifiers from one type to another.

B.1.23   EasyNN Plus

http://www.easynn.com/
This is a low-cost, intuitive software product for developing neural networks.

B.1.24 EMBOSS

http://www.hgmp.mrc.ac.uk/Software/EMBOSS

B.1.25 Entrez

www.ncbi.nlm.nih.gov/entrez

B.1.26 Evoker

Evoker is a graphical tool for visualizing genotype intensity data in order to assess genotype calls as part of quality control procedures for genome-wide association studies. It provides a solution to the computational and storage problems related to being able to work with the huge volumes of data generated by such projects by implementing a compact, binary format that allows rapid access to data, even with hundreds of thousands of observations.
http://www.sanger.ac.uk/resources/software/evoker/

B.1.27 Flapack

New software tools for graphical genotyping and haplotype visualization are required that can routinely handle the large data volumes generated by high throughput SNP and comparable genotyping technologies. Flapjack is a new visualization tool to facilitate analysis of these data types. Its visualizations are rendered in real time allowing for rapid navigation and comparisons between lines, markers, and chromosomes.

Based on the input of map, genotype, and trait data, Flapjack is able to provide a number of alternative graphical genotype views with individual alleles colored by state, frequency, or similarity to a given standard line. Flapjack supports a range of interactions with the data, including graphically moving lines or markers around the display, insertions or deletions of data, and sorting or clustering of lines by either genotype similarity to other lines or by trait scores. Any map-based information such as QTL positions can be aligned against graphical genotypes to identify associated haplotypes.

All results are saved in an XML-based project format and can also be exported as raw data or graphically as image files. We have devised efficient data storage structures that provide high-speed access to any subset of the data, resulting in fast visualization regardless of the size of the data.
http://bioinf.scri.ac.uk/flapjack/

B.1.28   GEO

www.ncbi.nlm.nih.gov/geo

B.1.29   Gene Ontology (GO)

The Gene Ontology (GO) is a bioinformatics initiative aimed at standardizing the representation of gene and gene product attributes (RNA or proteins resulting from the expression of a gene) across all species by developing a controlled vocabulary, annotating genes and gene products, assimilating and disseminating the annotations, and providing tools to access the data, such as the AmiGO browser. www.geneontology.org

B.1.30   g:Profiler

http://biit.cs.ut.ee/gprofiler/gconvert.cgi
This is a gene identifier tool that allows conversion of genes, proteins, microarray probes, standard names, and various database identifiers.

B.1.31   Graphviz

www.graphviz.org
This is an open-source graph visualization software.

B.1.32   HMMER

http://hmmer.wustl.edu

B.1.33   Java Data Mining (JDM) Toolkit

http://www.jcp.org/en/jsr/detail?id=247

B.1.34   ID Converter

http://biodb.jp/#ids
This is a tool for converting data IDs for biological molecules that are used in a database into other, corresponding data IDs that are used in other databases.

B.1.35   iModel

http://www.biocompsystems.com/products/imodel/

B.1.36   KnowledgeMiner

http://www.knowledgeminer.com/
KnowledgeMiner (yX) for Excel is a knowledge mining tool that works with data stored in Microsoft Excel for building predictive and descriptive models from this data autonomously and easily.

B.1.37   Libcurl

curl.haxx.se

B.1.38   MatchMiner

http://discover.nci.nih.gov/matchminer/MatchMinerLookup.jsp
This is a set of tools that enables the user to translate between disparate ids for the same gene using data from the UCSC, LocusLink, Unigene, OMIM, Affymetrix, and Jackson data sources to determine how different ids relate. Supported id types include gene symbols and names, IMAGE and FISH clones, GenBank accession numbers, and UniGene cluster ids.

B.1.39   MATLAB

http://www.mathworks.com/products/matlab/
MATLAB® probably needs no introduction to the majority of readers. It is a high-level technical computing language and interactive environment for algorithm development, data visualization, data analysis, and numeric computation. Using the MATLAB product, you can solve technical computing problems faster than with traditional programming languages, such as C, C++, and Fortran.

You can use MATLAB in a wide range of applications, including signal and image processing, communications, control design, test and measurement, financial modeling and analysis, and computational biology. Add-on toolboxes (collections of special-purpose MATLAB functions, available separately) extend the MATLAB environment to solve particular classes of problems in these application areas.

MATLAB provides a number of features for documenting and sharing your work. You can integrate your MATLAB code with other languages and applications, and distribute your MATLAB algorithms and applications.

Of more specific interest is the range of toolkits that are available within the MATLAB architecture to support specific needs.

Image Processing Toolkit

http://www.mathworks.com/products/image/#thd1
Image Processing Toolbox™ provides a comprehensive set of reference-standard algorithms and graphical tools for image processing, analysis, visualization, and algorithm development. You can perform image enhancement, image deblurring, feature detection, noise reduction, image segmentation, spatial transformations, and image registration.

B.1.40   MemBrain

http://www.membrain-nn.de/main_en.htm
MemBrain is a powerful graphical neural network editor and simulator for Microsoft Windows, supporting neural networks of arbitrary size and architecture.

B.1.41   Microarray Databases

Database	URL
Gene Expression Omnibus – NCBI	http://www.ncbi.nlm.nih.gov/geo/
Stanford Microarray database	http://smd.stanford.edu/
GeneNetwork system	http://www.genenetwork.org/
ArrayExpress at EBI	http://www.ebi.ac.uk/arrayexpress/
UNC Microarray database	https://genome.unc.edu/
Genevestigator database	https://www.genevestigator.com/
caArray at NCI	http://array.nci.nih.gov/caarray/
UPenn RAD database	http://www.cbil.upenn.edu/RAD
UNC modENCODE Microarray database	https://genome.unc.edu:8443/nimblegen
ArrayTrack	http://www.fda.gov/ScienceResearch/BioinformaticsTools/Arraytrack//
MUSC database	http://proteogenomics.musc.edu/ma/musc_madb.php?page=home&act=manage
UPSC-BASE	http://www.upscbase.db.umu.se/

B.1.42   Molecular Signatures Database (MSigDB)

http://www.broadinstitute.org/gsea/msigdb/index.jsp
This is a collection of annotated gene sets for use with GSEA software.

B.1.43   NAR

www3.oup.co.uk/nar/database/c

B.1.44   Neural Network Toolbox (MATLAB)

http://www.mathworks.com/products/neuralnet/
Neural Network Toolbox™ extends MATLAB® with tools for designing, implementing, visualizing, and simulating neural networks. Neural networks are invaluable for applications where formal analysis would be difficult or impossible, such as pattern recognition and nonlinear system identification and control. Neural Network Toolbox software provides comprehensive support for many proven network paradigms, as well as graphical user interfaces (GUIs) that enable you to design and manage your networks. The modular, open, and extensible design of the toolbox simplifies the creation of customized functions and networks.

B.1.45   NeuralWorks

http://www.neuralware.com/index.jsp
NeuralWorks Predict is an integrated, state-of-the-art tool for rapidly creating and deploying prediction and classification applications. Predict combines neural network technology with genetic algorithms, statistics, and fuzzy logic to automatically find optimal or near-optimal solutions for a wide range of problems. Predict incorporates years of modeling and analysis experience gained from working with customers faced with a wide variety of analysis and interpretation problems.

B.1.46   NeuroSolutions

http://www.nd.com/
This leading edge neural network development software combines a modular, icon-based network design interface with an implementation of advanced learning procedures, such as conjugate gradients and backpropagation through time.

B.1.47   NeuroXL

http://www.neuroxl.com/
NeuroXL Classifier is a fast, powerful, and easy-to-use neural network software tool for classifying data in Microsoft Excel. Designed to aid experts in real-world data mining and pattern recognition tasks, it hides the underlying complexity of neural network processes while providing graphs and statistics for the user to easily understand results. NeuroXL Classifier uses only proven algorithms and techniques, and integrates seamlessly with Microsoft Excel. OLSOFT Neural Network Library is the class to create, learn, and use Back Propagation neural networks and SOFM (Self-Organizing Feature Map). The library makes integration of neural networks' functionality into your own applications easy and seamless. It enables your programs to handle data analysis, classification, and forecasting needs.

B.1.48   Open Biological and Biomedical Ontologies (OBO Foundry)

This is a collaborative experiment involving developers of science-based ontologies who are establishing a set of principles for ontology development with the goal of creating a suite of orthogonal interoperable reference ontologies in the biomedical domain.
http://www.obofoundry.org/

B.1.49   Omegahat

www.omegahat.org

B.1.50   OMIM

www.ncbi.nlm.nih.gov/entrez

B.1.51   OpenDiseaseModels.Org

OpenDiseaseModels.org is an open-source disease/systems model development project. Analogous to open-source software development projects, the goal of this effort is to develop better, more useful models in a transparent and public collaborative forum.
http://www.opendiseasemodels.org/

B.1.52 Perl

http://strawberryperl.com/
http://www.activestate.com/activeperl/
Perl is a programming language that has seen a particularly widespread adoption in
the bioinformatics space. It is available on all the usual platforms.

B.1.53 PIPE

http://sourceforge.net/projects/pipe2/
It can create, model, and analyze Petri nets with a standards-compliant Petri net
tool. This is the active fork of the Platform Independent Petri net Editor project,
which originated at Imperial College London.

B.1.54 PNK

http://www2.informatik.hu-berlin.de/top/pnk/index.html
PNK provides an infrastructure for bringing ideas for analyzing, simulating, and
verifying Petri Nets.

B.1.55 PNK2e

http://page.mi.fu-berlin.de/trieglaf/PNK2e/index.html
This is a software environment for the modeling and simulation of biological
processes that uses Stochastic Petri Nets (SPNs), a graphical representation of
Markov Jump Processes.

B.1.56 Proper

Most databases employ the relational model for data storage. To use this data in a
propositional learner, a propositionalization step has to take place. Similarly, the
data has to be transformed to be amenable to a multi-instance learner. The Proper
Toolbox contains an extended version of RELAGGS, the Multi-Instance Learning
Kit MILK, and can also combine the multi-instance data with aggregated data from
RELAGGS. RELAGGS was extended to handle arbitrarily nested relations and to
work with both primary keys and indices. For MILK, the relational model is
flattened into a single table and this data is fed into a multi-instance learner.

REMILK finally combines the aggregated data produced by RELAGGS and the multi-instance data, flattened for MILK, into a single table that is once again the input for a multi-instance learner. Several well-known datasets are used for experiments which highlight the strengths and weaknesses of the different approaches. (Abstract from Reutemann et al. (2004 #848))
http://www.cs.waikato.ac.nz/ml/proper/

B.1.57   PseAAC

http://www.csbio.sjtu.edu.cn/bioinf/PseAAC/
This site allows you to generate pseudo amino acid compositions, according to Chou (2001 #520).

B.1.58   PubMed

www.ncbi.nlm.nih.gov/entrez

B.1.59   R

www.r-project.org
R is an open-source analytical environment that is not only comprehensive in its own right but is widely enhanced and extended through packages that have been developed. At the time of writing, several hundred add-on packages are available for R that cover a wide array of subjects and disciplines.

B.1.60 R Packages

We have used many R packages throughout this book and gratefully appreciate the skill and time that the various authors have spent developing these packages. In particular, we have used several packages extensively and highlight these herein.

These packages can all be accessed using the Comprehensive R Archive Network (CRAN) at http://cran.r-project.org.

B.1.60.1   odfWeave

The Sweave function combines R code and LATEX so that the output of the code is embedded in the processed document. The odfWeave package was created so that the functionality of Sweave can used to generate documents that the end{user can easily edit. The markup language used is the Open Document Format (ODF), which is an open, non{proprietary format that encompasses text documents, presentations and spreadsheets.

B.1.61   RapidMiner

http://rapid-i.com/content/view/181/190/
RapidMiner provides comprehensive data mining capabilities, including

- Data Integration, Analytical ETL, Data Analysis, and Reporting in one single suite
- Powerful but intuitive graphical user interface for the design of analysis processes
- Repositories for process, data, and metadata handling
- Only solution with metadata transformation: forget trial and error and inspect results already during design time
- Only solution which supports on-the-fly error recognition and quick fixes
- Complete and flexible: hundreds of data loading, data transformation, data modeling, and data visualization methods

RapidMiner Image Processing Extension

http://spl.utko.feec.vutbr.cz/en/component/content/article/21-zpracovani-medicinskych-signalu/46-image-processing-extension-for-rapidminer-5
This add-on package provides capabilities including

- Local image features extraction
- Segment feature extraction
- Global image feature extraction
- Extracting features from single/multiple image(s)
- Detect a template in image (rotation invariant)
- Point of interest detection
- Image comparison
- Image transforms
- Color mode transforms
- Noise reduction
- Image segmentation
- Object detection and object detector training (Haar-like features)

B.1.62   Reactome

www.reactome.org

B.1.63   Resourcerer

Pga.tigt.org/tigr-scripts/magic/r1.pl

B.1.64   RStudio

RStudio™ is a new integrated development environment (IDE) for R. RStudio combines an intuitive user interface with powerful coding tools to help you get the most out of R.
http://www.rstudio.org/

B.1.65   Systems Biology Graphical Notation (SBGN)

The Systems Biology Graphical Notation (SBGN) project is an effort to standardize the graphical notation used in maps of biochemical and cellular processes studied in systems biology.

Standardizing the visual representation is crucial for more efficient and accurate transmission of biological knowledge between different communities in research, education, publishing, and more. When biologists are as familiar with the notation as electronics engineers are familiar with the notation of circuit schematics, they can save the time and effort required to familiarize themselves with different notations, and instead spend more time thinking about the biology being depicted.
http://sbgn.org/

B.1.66   Systems Biology Markup Language (SBML)

http://sbml.org/
A free and open interchange format for computer models of biological processes. SBML is useful for models of metabolism, cell signaling, and more. It has been in development by an international community since the year 2000.

B.1.67   Systems Biology Workbench (SBW)

http://sys-bio.org/sbwWiki/doku.php?id=sysbio:sbw
This is an open-source framework connecting heterogeneous software applications. SBW is made up of two kinds of components:

- *Modules*: These are the applications that a user would use. We have a wide collection of model editing, model simulation, and model analysis tools.
- *Framework*: The software framework that allows developers to cross programming language boundaries and connect application modules to form new applications.

B.1.68   W3C

W3c.org

B.1.69   Weka

This is a machine learning toolkit that includes an implementation of an SVM classifier. Weka can be used both interactively through a graphical interface and as a software library. (The SVM implementation is called "SMO." It can be found in the Weka Explorer GUI, under the "functions" category.)
http://www.cs.waikato.ac.nz/ml/weka/

B.2   Data Sources

B.2.1   BioModels Database

This is a repository of peer-reviewed, published, computational models. These mathematical models are primarily from the field of systems biology, but more generally are of biological interest. This resource allows biologists to store, search, and retrieve published mathematical models. In addition, models in the database can be used to generate sub-models, can be simulated online, and can be converted between different representational formats. This resource also features programmatic access via web services.
http://www.ebi.ac.uk/biomodels-main/

B.2.2   DDBJ

http://www.ddbj.nig.ac.jp

B.2.3 EMBL

http://www.ebi.ac.uk/embl/index.html

B.2.4 GenBank

http://www.ncbi.nlm.nih.gov/GenBank

B.2.5 Pfam

http://pfam.wustl.edu

B.2.6 PROSITE

http://us.expasy.org/prosite

B.2.7 SWISS-PROT

http://us.expasy.org/sprot

B.3 Support Vector Machines

Support vector machines (SVMs) have seen a particular growth in the tools and software available to support this valuable supervised learning paradigm. We list a number of products available at the time of writing[4].

The Kernel-Machine Library (GNU) – C++ template library for support vector machines.

Lush – a Lisp-like interpreted/compiled language with C/C++/Fortran interfaces that has packages to interface to a number of different SVM implementations. Interfaces to LASVM, LIBSVM, mySVM, SVQP, SVQP2 (SVQP3 in future) are available. Leverage these against Lush's other interfaces to machine learning, hidden Markov models, numerical libraries (LAPACK, BLAS, GSL), and built-in vector/matrix/tensor engine.

---

[4] As available from the Wikipedia entry http://en.wikipedia.org/wiki/Support_vector_machine

SVMlight – a popular implementation of the SVM algorithm by Thorsten Joachims; it can be used to solve classification, regression, and ranking problems.

SVMProt – Protein Functional Family Prediction.

LIBSVM – A library for support vector machines, Chih-Chung Chang and Chih-Jen Lin.

YALE – a powerful machine learning toolbox containing wrappers for SVMLight, LibSVM, and MySVM in addition to many evaluation and preprocessing methods.

LS-SVMLab – MATLAB/C SVM toolbox; well-documented, many features.

Gist – implementation of the SVM algorithm with feature selection.

Weka – a machine learning toolkit that includes an implementation of an SVM classifier; Weka can be used both interactively through a graphical interface and as a software library. (The SVM implementation is called "SMO." It can be found in the Weka Explorer GUI, under the "functions" category.)

OSU SVM – MATLAB implementation based on LIBSVM.

Torch – C++ machine learning library with SVM.

Shogun – Large-Scale Machine Learning Toolbox that provides several SVM implementations (like libSVM, SVMlight) under a common framework and interfaces to Octave, MATLAB, Python, and R.

Spider – machine learning library for MATLAB.

kernlab – Kernel-based machine learning library for R.

e1071 – machine learning library for R.

SimpleSVM – SimpleSVM toolbox for MATLAB.

SVM and Kernel Methods MATLAB Toolbox

PCP – C program for supervised pattern classification; includes LIBSVM wrapper.

TinySVM – a small SVM implementation, written in C++.

pcSVM is an object-oriented SVM framework written in C++ and provides wrapping to Python classes. The site provides a stand-alone demo tool for experimenting with SVMs.

PyML – a Python machine learning package; includes: SVM, nearest neighbor classifiers, ridge regression, multi-class methods (one-against-one and one-against-rest), Feature selection (filter methods, RFE, multiplicative update), Model selection, Classifier testing (cross-validation, error rates, ROC curves, statistical test for comparing classifiers).

Algorithm::SVM – Perl bindings for the libsvm support vector machine library.

SVM Classification Applet – performs classification on any given dataset and gives 10-fold cross-validation error rate.

Appendix C
The Patient Dataset

C.1 Introduction

At various points in the book we refer to a patient dataset. We define this dataset in this appendix rather than in the main body of the book so as not to lose too much momentum in the book itself.

The patient dataset definition, together with some artificially created data, is available from the companion website along with some example code for various data mining techniques.

The datasets defined below are not intended to be viewed as complete, or even as necessarily valuable, but simply serve to provide us with a meaningful data environment with which to illustrate some of the data mining concepts we discuss within the book.

For the purposes of illustration of the data mining techniques, we have denormalized the patient dataset into two datasets – one for the patient, and one for the tests performed on specimens/isolates from those patients. A normalized version (to mimic a transactional environment) and a star-schema (to mimic a data warehouse environment) are available on the companion website.

C.2 Supporting Datasets

In addition to the dataset generated from our work, we would typically use a number of datasets that come from other sources. For example, in chapter two we use a body mass index dataset to allow us to calculate weight-related categories. Where so used, we indicate these in the main text.

C.3 Patient Dataset Definition

Key	Attribute	Format	Description
PK	Id	Integer	Unique key value for this record in the dataset. Every record will have a unique value
	Patient Label	String	Some identification for the patient. This may be their name, initials, or other "human-readable" attribute. Note that this is not an identifier in the pure sense, but is simply a text label
	MRN	String	Medical record number
	Patient Id	Integer	A unique identifier assigned to each patient. This is an integral value and may simply be used as a sequence, where the next available number is assigned to the next unique patient without any particular ordering
	Context Id	Integer	A unique identifier assigned to a particular context associated with this data. Contexts will typically be some project or study, or other high-level grouping for the data. In this book, the context is synonymous with a project
	Encounter Id	Integer	A unique identifier assigned to each encounter between a patient and a healthcare professional *within a specific context*. This italicized constraint is important since it is likely that this value will be a sequence within a project/study
	Age	Integer	The patient's age
	Weight	Double	The patient's weight. This is measured in kilograms
	Height	Double	The patient's height. This is measured in meters
	Gender	Character	The patient's gender. Allowed values are M(ale), F(emale), N(ot provided), and ' ' or NULL
	Smoker	Boolean	TRUE/FALSE values indicating whether the patient is a smoker or not
	Activity Factor	Integer	A scalar value from 0 to 10 indicating the level of activity/ exercise in the patient's daily life. 0 indicates immobility, whereas 10 indicates an extreme level of activity such as for professional athletes

C.4 Test Dataset Definition

Key	Attribute	Format	Description
PK	Id	Integer	Unique key value for this record in the dataset. Every record will have a unique value
FK	Patient Id	Integer	The patient id value from the patient dataset for the patient associated with this test result

(continued)

Key	Attribute	Format	Description
	Test Id	String	Some unique identifier for the test that is consistent within the data environment. For example, LDL-C might be a test id for measurement of LDL cholesterol. This can then be compared across instances
	Test Description	String	A description of the test
	Test Result Value String	String	The actual test result. This attribute will be populated based on the test result domain being a string or character value
	Test Result Value	Double	The actual test result. This attribute will be populated based on the test result domain being an integer or numeric value
	Test Result Domain	Integer	A value indicating the actual result value's domain. Values are S(tring), I(nteger), N(umeric), and C(haracter). This can be used to convert the values to their appropriate types
	Interpretation	String	The interpretive result, if any, associated with this test

Appendix D
The Clinical Trial and Data Mining

D.1 Introduction

Throughout our book we have referred to the clinical trial as an archetype for data mining. This is for some intuitive reasons along with some which may not be quite as intuitive to our readers.

It is definitely true to say that much of the data generated in the healthcare and life sciences arenas relate to the pharmaceutical product or medical device industries, and by our focus on these industries, we are certainly not intending to dismiss any of the other vitally important research and development disciplines that additionally form the foundation for the life sciences today. We instead have used the pharmaceutical development process since many more people outside of these disciplines have some knowledge of the pharmaceutical process due to its being front and center in the public psyche due to advertising, public information on the safety of drugs and devices, and other media outlets.

D.2 The Clinical Trial Process

D.2.1 Statistics of a Phase III Clinical Trial

We now present some of the basic statistics of a phase III clinical trial.

Number of patients (start of trial)	2,500
Number of visits per patient	12
Number of data attributes collected per patient per visit in bytes (characters)	4,000
Total	114.44 Mb

In the above list, the data is the **maximum** amount of data that might be captured. Thus there are several assumptions that typically do not occur in reality.

The most affective of which is the assumption that every patient is included in the trial from the beginning to the very end. This does not typically happen as patients drop out, are excluded, or, unfortunately, die before the trial ends. Since the largest driver of the data volume is obviously the number of patients involved in the trial, we will assume that only 25% of the patients initially enrolled see the trial through. This would result in 28.6 Mb of data.

References

Chou K-C (2001) Prediction of protein cellular attributes using pseudo amino acid composition. Proteins 43:246–255

Gentleman RC et al (2001) The Bioconductor FAQ

Reutemann P, Pfahringer B, Frank E (2004) A toolbox for learning from relational data with propositional and multi-instance learners. In: 17th Australian joint conference on Artificial Intelligence (AI2004). Springer, Berlin

Index

A

Accuracy, 5, 10, 12, 25, 42, 70, 80, 120, 133–135, 142, 192, 211, 217, 233, 240, 260, 278, 327, 332, 352, 364, 365, 370–373, 396, 407, 429, 458, 460, 467, 472, 474, 484, 489–497, 514, 515, 585

Aggregation, 21, 41, 110–113, 202, 209–211, 225, 379, 497, 544

Analytical entity, 193, 194

Apriori algorithm, 146, 148–150, 372, 447, 587

ARFF, 86, 333

Artificial neural networks, 396, 399–425, 577

Association, 4, 6, 8, 11, 14, 18, 25, 38, 42, 46, 69–73, 82, 86, 87, 105, 119, 121, 145–152, 161, 170–172, 183, 283–285, 289, 297, 339, 364, 365, 372, 397, 447, 548, 561, 562, 566, 568, 576, 580

Association analysis, 42, 46

Association rules, 69–73, 82, 145–152, 183, 364, 372, 447

Asymmetry, 75, 238, 272–273

Attribute, 4, 36, 87, 125, 192, 236, 304, 365, 459, 514, 564

B

Back-propagation, 396, 412–416, 423–425, 469, 477

Bayes factor, 312–315

Bayesian, 14, 29, 183, 186, 237, 240, 241, 303–360, 456, 457, 469, 471–477, 480, 549, 577

Bayesian belief networks, 337–340

Bayesian classification, 327–337, 469

Bayesian modeling, 471–477

Bayesian reasoning, 322–327

Bayes' theorem, 293, 304, 309–312, 317, 320, 327, 331, 339, 471

Bias, 10, 43–45, 47, 55, 129, 196, 222, 229, 239, 260, 269, 341, 351, 404, 411, 459, 495

Bias-variance decomposition, 55

Binary tree algorithm, 436–437

Binning, 211–215

Boolean logic, 440–448

Box plot, 154, 159–161, 272

Branching, 133–142, 144, 145, 532

Branching factor, 128

C

C4.5, 79, 138, 587

Causality, 8, 11

Characteristic, 24–26, 34, 36, 38, 42, 45, 48, 52, 57, 65, 70, 77, 81, 95, 102, 113, 133, 144, 145, 170, 216, 243, 261, 270, 286, 293, 294, 298, 325, 327, 351, 371, 375, 383, 386, 396, 399, 405, 424, 425, 431, 460, 472, 478, 482, 492, 512, 513, 515, 531, 540, 546, 549, 550, 564, 590

Characterization, 45, 351, 363

Classification, 4, 35, 87, 127, 241, 308, 364, 455–498, 513, 544, 587

Classification and regression trees, 129–145

Classification rules, 66–69, 72, 127–129, 371, 464, 465

Cluster analysis, 18, 47–48, 266, 364, 365, 396, 397, 446, 447

Clustering, 4, 14, 25, 73–74, 76, 77, 81, 119, 168, 169, 177, 187, 194, 211, 215, 371–373, 383, 396, 397, 426–431, 436, 446, 448, 456, 458–460, 473, 476, 477,

481, 483, 485, 486, 498, 514, 532, 533, 535, 544, 546, 576, 577
Concept, 2, 33–82, 85, 132, 194, 236, 304, 364, 456, 502, 553, 585
Concept hierarchy, 38, 52–55, 205, 206, 215, 227
Conditional random field (CRF), 351–355
Confidence, 13, 26, 42, 70, 75, 114, 145–148, 176, 238, 250, 259, 260, 278–282, 293, 341, 372, 394, 492
Confidence intervals (CI), 259, 260, 278–282, 293
Contingency tables, 127, 277, 278
Correlation, 2, 3, 6, 8, 11, 18, 24, 33, 35, 44, 45, 55, 75, 145, 161, 169, 186, 194, 219, 221, 224, 238, 241, 242, 259–265, 283, 284, 289, 295, 296, 314, 321, 322, 329, 396, 460, 480, 486–488, 531, 563
Co-training, 373, 374, 377–381, 387
Coverage, 4, 42, 70, 145, 208, 209, 260, 372, 467, 511
Cross-validation, 132, 143–144, 382, 493, 494

D

Data architecture, 2, 4, 12, 13, 29, 82, 85–122, 193
Database for Annotation, Visualization, and Integrated Discovery (DAVID), 208, 209, 297
Databases, 2–4, 11, 12, 14, 16, 24, 26, 29, 30, 34, 53, 85, 86, 94, 96, 98, 99, 103–105, 110, 111, 116–118, 148, 171, 176, 181, 197, 202–204, 206–208, 218, 222, 228, 266, 290, 294, 295, 297, 315, 327, 328, 349, 352, 378–380, 433, 447, 458, 502–504, 507–512, 520, 538, 545, 546, 553, 563–565, 567, 570, 576
Data curation, 111, 115, 504
Data format, 13, 22–23, 172, 198, 504
Data integration, 102–106, 504–508, 545
Data mart, 29, 110–112, 228
Data mining
  ethics, 10–12
  process, 15, 19, 24, 43
  results, 23, 24, 125–189
Data modeling, 85–122, 203
Data plot, 154–158
Data preparation, 19, 21–23, 93, 194–195, 459–460
Data reduction, 194, 212, 214, 215, 224–227

Data warehouse, 3, 4, 17, 29, 37, 53, 110–113, 115–116, 126, 191, 192, 207, 228, 230, 508
DAVID. *See* Database for Annotation, Visualization, and Integrated Discovery (DAVID)
Decision tables, 125, 127–129
Decision trees, 23, 38, 44, 63–68, 79–81, 127–129, 215, 327, 332, 371, 448, 457, 463–466, 469, 588
Denormalization, 40, 201–206
Dependent entity, 87, 88
Diffusion map, 426–431
Dimensionality, 49–51, 74, 80, 114, 211, 217, 394, 426, 480, 481, 497
Discretization, 62, 193, 194, 212, 215, 227
Discrimination, 45
Distance, 48, 76–79, 154, 162, 198, 199, 216, 272, 340, 369, 382, 383, 385, 389–391, 416, 417, 422, 423, 426, 446, 447, 459, 470, 480, 484, 486–488, 498, 531–535, 537, 554
Dynamical systems, 202, 546–548, 567, 580

E

Enrichment analysis, 294–297
Entity, 46, 86–92, 95, 102–103, 105–109, 120, 180, 181, 184, 193, 194, 196, 218, 374, 379, 380, 569, 570, 576
Entrez, 99, 176, 208, 508–510, 566, 569
Entropy, 75, 134, 137–138, 140, 145, 238, 269, 270, 351, 467
Error, 10, 36, 86, 138, 211, 239, 333, 367, 461, 512, 546
Expectation-maximization (EM) algorithm 119, 223, 346, 373–377, 382, 448, 587
External consistency, 195, 197, 206
Extract, 5, 17, 22, 91, 100, 120, 126, 132, 137, 204, 206–209, 217, 264, 363, 365, 378, 384, 466, 479, 505, 553, 567, 568, 576, 579

F

False discover rate (FDR), 296–300
Feature selection, 51, 79–81, 364, 515
Feed-forward network, 400, 411–413, 477
Frequency polygon, 154
Functional networks, 404, 411, 568
Fuzzy logic, 394, 440–448

G

Gaussian mixture, 375–377
Gene expression analysis, 394–398, 430
Gene identifier cross-referencing,
    208–209
Gene ontology (GO), 95–96, 116–118,
    152, 176, 294, 509, 512, 544,
    563–565, 567, 577, 578
Generalization, 4, 37, 43–45, 52, 81, 82,
    87–89, 226–227, 390, 393, 423, 469,
    493, 501, 565
Gene selection, 397, 514, 515
Genome-wide association studies (GWAS),
    171, 172, 297, 580
Genomic data, 169, 170, 503, 563
Genotype visualization, 171–172
Gini, 75, 134–140, 142, 145, 238,
    269–272
Graph theory, 130, 339, 554–563

H

Heat map, 166–170, 510
Heterogeneity, 75, 86, 104, 105, 238,
    269–270, 363
Hidden Markov models (HMM), 49,
    342–356, 358, 359, 374, 377, 387,
    480, 538
Histogram, 153–154, 268, 277, 296,
    298, 354
Hypothesis testing, 239–265, 300

I

Independent entity, 87, 88
Information gain, 134, 137–139
Input representation, 39–40
Instance, 10, 37, 87, 126, 193, 246, 304, 364,
    457, 514, 544, 587
Integrating annotations, 505
Interestingness, 26–28
Internal consistency, 192, 195–197
Interpretive data, 93

K

Kernels, 50, 368, 383–386, 388, 391–394,
    417, 426, 428, 431, 549
K-means, 49, 74, 375, 448, 477, 481–486,
    498, 587
K-nearest neighbor (k-NN), 198, 446, 457,
    470, 587
Kurtosis, 75, 238, 273–274

L

Learning algorithm, 49, 50, 73, 183, 382, 383,
    385, 388, 391, 399, 405, 407, 408, 425,
    448, 481, 588
Least squares, 74, 76, 286–290, 461
Linear model, 55, 74–75, 81, 130, 157, 161,
    282, 286, 463, 549
Linear regression, 74, 212, 283–290, 460–463,
    477, 488

M

Many-to-many relationship, 87, 88
Marginal probability, 309, 310, 471, 477
Maximum a posteriori (MAP) estimation, 235,
    293–294, 374
Maximum likelihood estimation (MLE), 75,
    76, 290–294, 374, 376
Measures of central tendency, 266–276
Metadata, 105, 215–217
MIAME. *See* Minimal information about a
    microarray experiment (MIAME)
Microarray databases, 563–565
Microarrays, 8, 9, 33, 121, 122, 171, 393,
    395–397, 447, 457, 502, 505, 513–515,
    537, 538, 544, 546, 548, 567
Minimal information about a microarray
    experiment (MIAME), 505, 565
Minimum confidence threshold, 146
Minimum support threshold, 146, 148
Mining by navigation, 561–562
Missing data, 21, 40–41, 55, 58, 62, 82, 94,
    104, 194, 199, 217–219, 222, 223,
    228, 231, 232, 366, 367, 460, 474
Missing values, 22, 40, 41, 62, 66, 128, 129,
    199, 217–223, 267, 374, 467
Model, 2, 34, 85, 126, 192, 236, 305, 364,
    456, 501, 543, 585, 586
Modeling, 13, 19, 22, 23, 29, 51, 56–58, 66,
    85–122, 126, 203, 216, 217, 230, 233,
    237, 241, 282, 314, 322, 326, 347, 352,
    355, 377, 438–440, 457, 461, 471–477,
    502, 546–549, 552, 578, 580, 586
Monte Carlo strategies, 56–60
Motifs, 57, 94, 295, 297, 373, 387, 431–436,
    480, 516–520, 528, 539, 577
Multiple sequence alignment, 99, 343

N

Naïve Bayes, 80, 304, 587
Naïve Bayes classifier, 183, 304, 309, 311,
    312, 332–337

Nearest neighbor, 81, 382, 383, 469–470, 588
Neighbors, 76–79, 99, 188, 434, 470
Network analysis, 176, 513, 577
Network (graph)-based analysis, 431
Network motif, 431–436, 577
Network visualization, 172–175
Neural networks, 3, 46, 49, 241, 327, 332,
    364, 370, 391, 392, 394, 396, 404,
    411, 424, 436, 456, 457, 460, 474,
    477–481, 492, 498, 549, 577, 588
Noisy data, 12, 211–215
Normal form (NF), 90, 91, 120, 201, 208
Normalization, 6, 49, 50, 90, 91, 121, 194, 196,
    198, 200–201, 204, 406, 426, 510, 545
Null hypothesis, 75, 164, 238, 241–245, 250,
    254, 256, 259, 263

O

Odds ratio, 312–315
One-to-many relationship, 87, 88, 203, 207
Ontologies, 95, 96, 105, 116, 152, 512, 564,
    565, 567, 577
Operational data store (ODS), 110–113
Outlier, 4, 21, 22, 38, 48–49, 154, 163,
    211, 239, 258, 268, 462, 488, 493,
    510, 544, 576
Over-fitting, 12, 26, 27, 51–52, 81, 134, 142,
    218, 290, 371, 393, 394, 458, 466,
    469, 474, 476, 502
Over-training, 50, 368

P

Pairwise sequence alignment, 521–527
Parameter estimation, 340–341
Partial ordering, 53
Patterns, 2, 34, 102, 126, 194, 236, 324, 364,
    457, 502, 543, 586
Perceptron, 391, 407–409, 411–412, 423,
    424, 477
Petri nets (PNs), 437–440, 503, 549
Probabilistic Boolean networks (PBN),
    548–550
Phylogenetic trees, 174, 188, 531, 537
Phylogenetic tree visualization, 177–178
Position map, 170–171
Posterior distribution, 304, 340
Prediction, 3, 4, 18, 27, 28, 34, 46–47, 52, 57,
    127, 132, 144, 170, 240, 322, 335,
    352–354, 356, 365, 372, 386–389,
    395–397, 416, 422, 455–498, 501, 509,
    514, 515, 543, 546, 553, 576

Principal component analysis, 51, 56, 80, 159,
    169, 170, 194, 224, 225, 426, 477, 546
Prior distribution, 304, 324, 475
Prior probability, 305, 306, 308, 311, 312, 319,
    324–326, 340, 471, 472, 477
Protein, 28, 33, 93, 172, 207, 290, 313, 386,
    478, 502, 544
Protein identifier cross-referencing, 208–209
Proteomic data, 8, 503–504, 514
P-value, 200, 243–245, 255, 261–265, 296–299

Q

Qualitative and quantitative data, 90–93

R

1R, 16, 41, 60–63, 82, 237, 304, 465–469
Radial basis function (RBFs), 50, 393, 416, 417
Random walk, 426–431
Receiver operator characteristic (ROC), 386,
    486, 492
Reducing (the) dimensionality, 80, 481
Regression, 27, 35, 74, 129–145, 156, 157, 161,
    166, 183, 186, 211, 212, 216, 238, 239,
    241, 259, 283–287, 289, 290, 364, 389,
    393, 407, 447, 457, 460, 577, 587
Regression analysis, 27, 46, 141, 282–290,
    456–458
Regular expressions, 480, 516–520, 589
Regulatory networks, 431, 547–549, 552,
    576, 580
Reinforcement learning, 425
Relational data model, 85, 94
Relevance, 80–82, 216, 242, 300, 473
Relevance analysis, 47, 194, 459

S

Sampling error, 239
Scatterplot, 154, 157, 161–162, 283–289
Self-organizing map (SOM), 49, 418, 419,
    422, 423
Semi-supervised learning (SSL), 373–383
Sequence data, 28, 34, 93–95, 207, 215, 319,
    386, 430, 492, 503–505, 508, 509, 520,
    521, 528, 531, 536, 589
Shortest common substring (SCS), 574, 575
Similarity, 14, 47, 48, 73, 76, 77, 94, 99, 173,
    368–369, 381–388, 392, 393, 426, 428,
    459, 464, 470, 478, 479, 486–488, 498,
    510, 527, 539
Singular value decomposition (SVD), 51

Skewness, 75, 238, 258, 274
Spectral clustering, 426–431
Standardization, 6, 194, 198, 222, 512, 545
Star schema, 86, 109, 193
Statistical inference, 10, 237, 239–265,
    269, 471
Statistical significance, 44, 242, 260, 300, 515
Structural risk minimization (SRM), 393–395
Subtype, 87–89, 354, 373, 397, 458, 509
Supertype, 88, 89
Supervised learning, 37, 216, 363–366, 368,
    370–372, 389, 395, 399, 407–423, 425,
    448, 473
Support, 2, 12, 13, 17, 19–21, 25, 29, 30, 38,
    42, 70, 82, 86, 103, 110, 121, 126,
    145–147, 162, 172, 175–177, 195, 196,
    207, 228, 239, 251, 262, 268, 297, 320,
    335, 351, 372, 378, 388, 390, 426, 429,
    430, 434, 443, 444, 456, 471, 477, 479,
    502, 508, 511, 512, 548, 552, 566
Support vector machines (SVMs), 46, 369,
    384, 387–398, 456, 457, 469, 492, 587
Systems biology, 7, 97, 152, 153, 184, 498,
    501, 502, 543–581
Systems biology graphical notation (SBGN),
    183–185
Systems biology markup language (SBML),
    176, 178–182, 186, 548

T
Temporal models, 544, 578
Text mining, 4, 97, 119, 120, 217, 377, 544,
    546, 565–571, 575

Time dimension, 112–113, 230
Tools, 2, 56, 95, 126, 207, 236, 323, 374, 456,
    504, 546, 586
Total ordering, 53, 54
Training, 23, 35, 91, 129, 260, 312, 364, 457,
    502, 544
Training data, 35–37, 39, 43, 52, 282, 329,
    333–335, 337, 345, 346, 353, 371,
    373, 393, 413, 457, 467, 469, 480,
    494, 502, 515
Transactional data model, 110–112
Transform and load, 17, 206–209
Transformation, 22, 82, 103, 104, 110, 126,
    181, 191, 194, 198–200, 207, 274,
    380, 412
Tree pruning, 133, 142
Twoing rule, 134, 137

U
Unsupervised learning, 37, 49, 50, 73,
    363–366, 368, 372–373, 396, 399,
    406, 407, 418, 423, 458, 459, 473,
    477, 481, 544

V
Validation, 14, 23, 24, 29, 52, 69, 111,
    132, 143, 216, 327, 371, 458, 460,
    465, 468, 469, 478, 490, 494–496,
    498, 534
Variation, 55, 75, 116, 170–172, 231, 238,
    289, 296, 355, 396, 493, 509, 515,
    528, 544, 580

Printed by Publishers' Graphics LLC
MO20120514